Frommer's®
™

W9-DAY-877

POSTCARDS

FROM

VANCOUVER
& VICTORIA

Only 15 minutes from Vancouver, the narrow, shaky Capilano Bridge spans the canyon floor, shrouded in mist from a waterfall below. See chapter 6. © Andrea Pistolesi Photography.

Nestled amid snowcapped mountains and lush forest, Vancouver offers big-city life in a wilderness setting. See chapter 6. © Wolfgang Kaehler Photography.

Watching the sunset over English Bay and False Creek while sipping a beer on a cafe patio is a great way to end the day. See chapter 9. © Catherine Karnow Photography.

Created out of a depleted limestone quarry, Butchart Gardens is one of the most beautiful—and tranquil—sights in Victoria. See chapter 13. © Wolfgang Kaehler Photography.

One of North America's largest and best, the Vancouver Aquarium houses more than 8,000 marine species—including beluga whales—most in meticulously re-created settings. See chapter 6. © Peter Timmerans/Tony Stone Images.

If you want to see orcas in the wild though, your best bet is a whale-watching tour from Victoria. See chapter 13. © Chris Huss/The Wildlife Collection.

Hints of Vancouver's turn-of-the-century boomtown days still linger within its post-modern landscape. See chapter 6 for architectural highlights. © Wolfgang Kaehler Photography.

At huge dim-sum palaces in Chinatown, carts of the little delicacies are rolled right to your table. Go with a large group and share. See chapter 5 for reviews of our favorite Chinatown restaurants. © Catherine Karnow Photography.

Stanley Park is North America's largest urban park. Rollerblade, bike, or jog its 5¹/₂-mile Seawall Walk and take in stunning views of the North Coast mountains and sandy beaches. See chapter 6. © Wolfgang Kaehler Photography.

Watch old pros pass down their Native American carving skills to a younger generation of artisans in Victoria's Thunderbird Park. See chapter 14. © Tim Thompson Photography.

Designed by 25-year-old Francis Rattenbury, and built between 1893 and 1898 at a cost of nearly C$1,000,000, the Parliament buildings in Victoria are an architectural gem. See chapter 13. © Robert Holmes Photography.

Victorian high tea is both a meal and a ritual—and nowhere is the experience as steeped in luxury and tradition as in the Empress Hotel. See chapter 12. © Dave Bartruff Photography.

One of the premier ski resorts in North America, the Whistler/Blackcomb complex boast:
more vertical runs, more lifts, and more and varied terrain than any other resort in North
America . . . and if you want to get away from it all, British Columbia's wilderness is alway:
within easy reach of the city at Garibaldi Park. See chapter 17. Above, © Stefan Schulhof
Tony Stone Images. Below, © Philip & Karen Smith/Tony Stone Images.

When should I travel to get the best airfare?
Where do I go for answers to my travel questions?
What's the best and easiest way to plan and book my trip?

frommers.travelocity.com

Frommer's, the travel guide leader, has teamed up with **Travelocity.com**, the leader in online travel, to bring you an in-depth, easy-to-use resource designed to help you plan and book your trip online.

At **frommers.travelocity.com**, you'll find free online updates about your destination from the experts at Frommer's plus the outstanding travel planning and purchasing features of Travelocity.com. Travelocity.com provides reservations capabilities for 95 percent of all airline seats sold, more than 47,000 hotels, and over 50 car rental companies. In addition, Travelocity.com offers more than 2,000 exciting vacation and cruise packages. Travelocity.com puts you in complete control of your travel planning with these and other great features:

>   **Expert travel guidance from Frommer's** - over 150 writers reporting from around the world!
>
>   **Best Fare Finder** - an interactive calendar tells you when to travel to get the best airfare
>
>   **Fare Watcher** - we'll track airfare changes to your favorite destinations
>
>   **Dream Maps** - a mapping feature that suggests travel opportunities based on your budget
>
>   **Shop Safe Guarantee** - 24 hours a day / 7 days a week live customer service, and more!

Whether traveling on a tight budget, looking for a quick weekend getaway, or planning the trip of a lifetime, Frommer's guides and Travelocity.com will make your travel dreams a reality. You've bought the book, now book the trip!

Vancouver
& Victoria
2001

by Shawn Blore &
Alexandra de Vries

HUNGRY MINDS, INC.
New York, NY • Cleveland, OH • Indianapolis, IN
Chicago, IL • Foster City, CA • San Francisco, CA

ABOUT THE AUTHORS

A native of California and resident by turns of Ottawa, Amsterdam, Moscow, and (for nearly the past decade) Vancouver, **Shawn Blore** is a newspaper journalist, award-winning magazine writer, and author of the best-selling *Vancouver: Secrets of the City*. He is also a coauthor of *Frommer's Canada*.

Alexandra de Vries took her first intercontinental flight at 6 weeks and developed a taste for travel early on. A resident by turns of Amsterdam and Rio de Janeiro, she has reported on Brazilian culture for Dutch publications, Dutch culture for Brazilian publications, and now (as a resident of Vancouver) West Coast culture and places for Frommer's readers. She also finds time to manage communications for various large B.C. nonprofit organizations.

Published by:

HUNGRY MINDS, INC.

909 Third Avenue
New York, NY 10022
www.frommers.com

ISBN 0-7645-6192-8
ISSN 1045-9316

Editors: Ron Boudreau, Nicole Daro, Justin Lapatine
Production Editor: Cara Buitron
Photo Editor: Richard Fox
Design by Michele Laseau
Cartographer: John Decamillis
Production by Hungry Minds Indianapolis Production Department

SPECIAL SALES

For general information on Hungry Minds' products and services please contact our Consumer Care department; within the U.S. at 800-762-2974, outside the U.S. at 317-572-3993 or fax 317-572-4002. For sales inquiries and reseller information, including discounts, bulk sales, customized editions, and premium sales, please contact our Customer Care department at 800-434-3422.

Manufactured in the United States of America

5   4   3   2   1

Contents

v

13   Exploring Victoria   228

14   Victoria Strolls   246

15   Victoria Shopping   257

16   Victoria After Dark   264

17   Side Trips: The Best of British Columbia   272

Appendix: History 101   316

Index   321

List of Maps

AN INVITATION TO THE READER

In researching this book, we discovered many wonderful places—hotels, restaurants, shops, and more. We're sure you'll find others. Please tell us about them, so we can share the information with your fellow travelers in upcoming editions. If you were disappointed with a recommendation, we'd love to know that too. Please write to:

Frommer's Vancouver & Victoria 2001
Hungry Minds, Inc.
909 Third Avenue
New York, NY 10022

AN ADDITIONAL NOTE

Please be advised that travel information is subject to change at any time—and this is especially true of prices. We therefore suggest that you write or call ahead for confirmation when making your travel plans. The authors, editors, and publisher cannot be held responsible for the experiences of readers while traveling. Your safety is important to us, however, so we encourage you to stay alert and be aware of your surroundings. Keep a close eye on cameras, purses, and wallets, all favorite targets of thieves and pickpockets.

WHAT THE SYMBOLS MEAN

✪ Frommer's Favorites

Our favorite places and experiences—outstanding for quality, value, or both.

The following abbreviations are used for credit cards:

AE	American Express	DISC	Discover
CB	Carte Blanche	MC	MasterCard
DC	Diners Club	V	Visa

FIND FROMMER'S ONLINE

www.frommers.com offers up-to-the-minute listings on almost 200 cities around the globe—including the latest bargains and candid, personal articles updated daily by Arthur Frommer himself. No other Web site offers such comprehensive and timely coverage of the world of travel.

The Best of Vancouver & Victoria

Vancouverites aren't much given to introspection—too much time spent outdoors—so it's perhaps a bit unfair to expect it of visitors. But if you really want to understand **Vancouver,** stand at the edge of the Inner Harbour (the prow of the Canada Place pavilion makes a good vantage point) and look up: past the floatplanes taking off over Stanley Park, around the container terminals, over the tony waterfront high-rises, and then up the steep green slopes of the North Shore mountains to the twin snowy peaks of the Lions. What you've seen—90% of it anyway—is the result of a collaboration, unique in history, between God and the Canadian Pacific Railway (CPR).

It was the Almighty—or Nature (depending on your point of view)—who raised the Coast Range and then sent a glacier slicing along its foot, simultaneously carving out a deep trench and piling up a tall moraine of rock and sand. When the ice retreated, water from the Pacific flowed in and the moraine became a peninsula, flanked on one side by a deep natural harbor and on the other by a river of glacial meltwater.

Some 10,000 years later, a CPR surveyor came by; took in the peninsula, the harbor, and the river; and decided he'd found the perfect spot for the railway's new Pacific terminus. He kept it quiet, as smart railwaymen tended to do, until the company had bought up most of the land around town. Then the railway moved in, set up shop, and the city of Vancouver was born.

The resulting boom was pretty small. Though the port did a good business shipping out grain and sawmills, and salmon canneries sprang up around town, the city was simply too far from the rest of North America for any serious manufacturing. Vancouver became a town of sailors, lumberjacks, and fishermen. Cheap draught was a staple; gambling and whoring were the major service industries. And so it remained until the 1980s, when the city decided to have a world's fair: Expo '86. The resulting summer-long celebration was a stunning success. The world came to visit, including many from the newly emerging tiger economies of Hong Kong, Taiwan, and Malaysia. The visitors looked at the mountains, the ocean, and the price of local real estate, and they were amazed. Many moved here.

New neighborhoods were born. On the Fraser River delta, the bedroom community of Richmond became a city, with a population more than half Chinese. In older neighborhoods, prices went ballistic, doubling and tripling overnight. And on the railyard-turned-Expo site,

The Raven & the First Men

According to a native legend, life on earth began when the raven flew down from the heavens thousands of years ago. The earth was covered in snow. He stole the sun from the gods and made rivers, oceans, thick green forests, and many animals. Then he found a clamshell on a sandy beach. He opened it and coaxed its inhabitants, five men, out of their dark prison into the land he created, promising them peace, harmony, and prosperity. Later on, he showed them where to find women.

40 new high-rise condominium towers began to rise. Unlike previous immigrants, these newcomers didn't worry about finding work; they made their own. Financial services, software, international education, engineering, and architectural consulting business came into being. A film industry sprang up. Vancouver became a postmodern town of Jags, Beemers, cell phones, and shining residential towers.

The newcomers brought a love of dining out. The steak house and the ubiquitous "Chinese and Canadian" diner gave way to a thousand little places offering sushi and Szechuan, tapas and bami, and, inevitably, fusion.

Working indoors, Vancouverites fell in love with the outside: mountain biking, windsurfing, kayaking, rock climbing, parasailing, snowboarding, and back-country skiing. When all these had been done, they began experimenting with new sports, and strange summer-winter combinations were born: skiing-kayaking, mountain biking-snowboarding, and snowshoeing-paragliding.

Splints and scrapes aside, folks seemed happy with the new state of affairs. And the rest of the world seemed to agree. *Outside* magazine voted it one of the 10 best cities in the world to live in. It's one of the 10 best to visit, according to *Condé Nast Traveler*. The World Council of Cities ranked it second only to Geneva for quality of life. Heady stuff, particularly for a spot that less than 20 years ago was routinely derided as the world's biggest mill town.

Eighty-some kilometers (50 miles) across the Strait of Georgia on Vancouver Island, little of this tumult was noticed in the dreamy city of **Victoria.** Set in an Arcadian parkland of oak and fir by the edge of a natural harbor, Victoria had spent the better part of the 20th century in a reverie, looking back to its glorious past as an outpost of England during the glory days of empire.

A busy trading post and booming colonial city in the 19th century, Victoria began to fade soon after Vancouver was established in the 1880s. When its economy finally crashed early in the century, shocked Victorians realized they were looking at a future with nothing much to live on but some fabulous Tudor and Victorian architecture, a beautiful natural setting, and a carefully cultivated sense of Englishness. So they decided to market that. Victoria would become a tourist town, a little bit of England on the North American continent. So successful was the sales job, Victorians soon began to believe it themselves. They began growing elaborate rose gardens, which flourished in the mild Pacific climate, and they cultivated a taste for afternoon tea with jam and scones.

For decades this continued. True, Victorians were flexible enough to accommodate some changes. Early on, it was discovered that not many shared a taste for English cooking, so Victoria restaurants branched out into seafood, and ethnic and fusion. And lately, as visitors have shown more interest in exploring the natural world, Victoria has quietly added whale-watching and mountain-biking trips to its traditional London-style double-decker bus tours. The result, at the dawn of the new millennium, is that Victoria is the only city in the world where you can zoom out on a Zodiac in the morning to see a pod of killer whales, and make it back in time for a lovely afternoon tea.

1 Frommer's Favorite Vancouver Experiences

- **Watching the Fireworks Explode over English Bay.** Every August during the Symphony of Fire, three international fireworks companies compete by launching their best displays over English Bay. As many as 500,000 spectators cram the beaches around English Bay, while those with boats sail out to watch from the water. See chapter 2.
- **Enjoying the F-F-F Festivals.** The Folk, the Fringe, and the Film, to be precise. The Folk Fest brings folk and world-beat musicians to a waterfront stage in Jericho Park. The setting's gorgeous, the music's great, and the crowd is something else. Far more urban is the Fringe, a festival of new and original plays that takes place in the artsy Commercial Drive area. The plays are wonderfully inventive. Better yet, they're short and cheap so you can see a lot of them. In October, the films of the world come to Vancouver. Serious filmies buy a pass and see all 500 flicks (or as many as they can before their eyeballs fall out). See chapter 2.
- **Exploring Chinatown.** Fishmongers call out their wares before a shop filled with crabs, eels, geoducks, and bullfrogs, while farther down the street elderly Chinese women haggle over produce while their husbands hunt for deer antler or dried seahorse at a traditional Chinese apothecary. And when you're tired of looking and listening, head inside to any one of a dozen restaurants to sample succulent Cantonese cooking. See chapters 5 and 7.
- **Strolling the Stanley Park Seawall.** Or jogging, running, blading, biking, skating, riding—whatever your favorite mode of transport is, use it, but by all means get out there. See chapter 6.
- **Visiting the Vancouver Aquarium.** It's a Jacques Cousteau special, live and right there in front of you. The Vancouver Aquarium does an extremely good job showing whole ecosystems. Fittingly enough, the aquarium has an excellent display on the Pacific Northwest, plus sea otters (cuter than they have any right to be), beluga whales, sea lions, and an orca. See chapter 6.
- **Kayaking on Indian Arm.** Vancouver is one of the few cities on the edge of a great wilderness, and one of the best ways to get there, quickly, is kayaking on the gorgeous Indian Arm. Rent a kayak or go with a company—they may even serve you a gourmet meal of barbecued salmon. See chapter 6.
- **Strolling the Beach.** It doesn't matter which beach, there's one for every taste. Wreck Beach below UBC is for nudists, Spanish Banks is for dog walkers, Jericho Beach is for volleyballers, Kits Beach is for serious suntanning, and English Bay Beach is for serious people-watching. See chapter 6.
- **Picnicking at the Lighthouse.** Everyone has their favorite picnic spot—one of the beaches or up on the mountains. Mine is Lighthouse Park on the North Shore. Not only do you get to look back over at Vancouver, but also the walk down to the rocky waterline runs through a pristine old-growth rain forest. See chapter 6.
- **Hiking the North Shore.** The forests of the North Shore are at the edge of a great wilderness and only 20 minutes from the city. Step into a world of muted light and soaring cathedral-like spaces beneath the tree canopy. Great North Shore trails include the very busy Grouse Grind, Cypress Falls Park, and the hike from Grouse back to Goat Mountain. (Whatever you do, go prepared. People die

Southern British Columbia

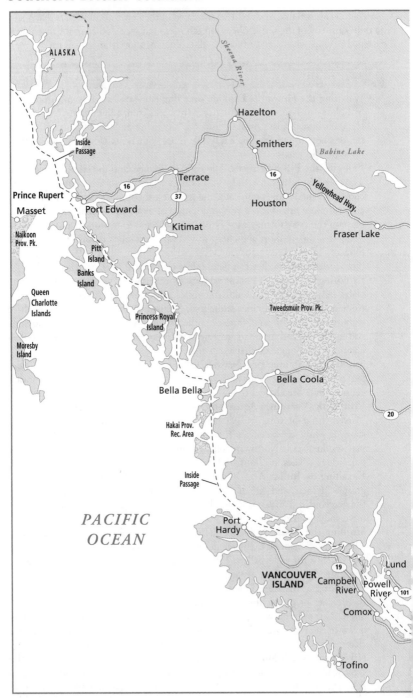

ALASKA

Skeena River

Hazelton

Smithers

Babine Lake

Inside
Passage

Terrace

16

Prince Rupert

Masset

Port Edward

37

16

Yellowhead Hwy.

Houston

Naikoon
Prov. Pk.

Kitimat

Fraser Lake

Pitt
Island

Banks
Island

Queen
Charlotte
Islands

Princess Royal
Island

Tweedsmuir Prov. Pk.

Moresby
Island

Bella Coola

Bella Bella

20

Hakai Prov.
Rec. Area

Inside
Passage

*PACIFIC
OCEAN*

Port
Hardy

Lund

19

**VANCOUVER
ISLAND**

Campbell
River

Powell
River

101

Comox

Tofino

4

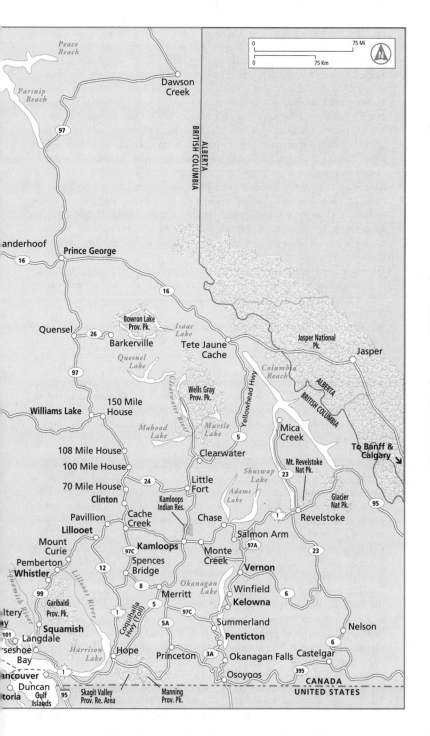

5

on those trails every year, cold and lost. A good local guidebook can give you more details on trails and tell you what you need to bring.) See chapter 6.

- **Exploring UBC's Museum of Anthropology.** The building—by native son Arthur Erickson—would be worth a visit in itself, but this is also one of the best places in the world to see and learn about West Coast native art and culture. See chapter 6.
- **Visiting the Library.** I'm serious. Vancouver's new main library building isn't so much a book depository as an urban gathering place. Outside, you'll find a permanent crowd of folks hanging out, playing music, or handing out political pamphlets. Inside is a huge glass atrium with little patio tables and several coffee bars, where folks sit and chat for hours. Sometimes they even go and look at books. See chapter 6.
- **Mountain Biking the Endowment Lands.** One of the best places to give this sport a try is on the trails running through the forest by the University of British Columbia. (The area's officially called Pacific Spirit Park, but everyone calls it the Endowment Lands.) On the east side of town, the trails on Burnaby Mountain are equally good, though steep enough to qualify as intermediate terrain. See chapter 6.
- **Having a Latte on Granville Island.** Down on False Creek, this former industrial site was long ago converted to an indoor public market and home for artists and artisans. Grab a latte at the public market and sit outside by the wharf and people- or boat-watch. See chapter 6.
- **Wandering the West End.** Encompassing the über-shopping strip known as Robson Street, as well as cafe-lined Denman and a forest of high-rise apartments, the West End is the urban heart of Vancouver. Enjoy the lush street trees, the range of architecture, and the neat little surprises on every side street. See chapter 7.
- **Watching the Sunset from a Waterside Patio.** Why else live in a city with such stunning views? There are good waterside patios on most establishments on False Creek, English Bay, and Coal Harbour. For something different, head to the North Shore, where you don't get to see mountains, but you do get to see the city. See chapter 9.

2 Frommer's Favorite Victoria Experiences

- **Savoring Afternoon Tea.** Yes, it's expensive and incredibly touristy, but it's also a complicated and ritual-laden art form. Besides, it's good. The Empress and the Butchart Gardens dining room are both good. Not quite as formal but also good is Point Ellice house. See chapter 12.
- **Catching the Fireworks at Butchart Gardens.** The best fireworks have something of the best of flowers, just as the best flowers have all the fire of explosives. Saturday nights in the summertime at Butchart Gardens, you get both. See chapter 13.
- **Touring the Royal BC Museum.** One of the best small museums in the world, the Royal BC does exactly what a good regional museum should do, explain the region. It just does it so much better than most. See chapter 13.
- **Watching Orcas.** Of all the species of orcas (killer whales), those on the B.C. coast are the only ones that live in large and complicated extended families. This makes Victoria a particularly good spot to whale-watch, because the orcas travel in large, easy-to-find pods. There's something magical about being out on the water and seeing a pod of 15 animals surface just a few hundred meters away. See chapter 13.
- **Touring by Miniferry.** Catch a Victoria Harbour Ferry and take a 45-minute tour around the harbor past the floating neighborhood of West Bay or up the gorge, where tidal waterfalls reverse direction with the changing tide. Moonlight

tours depart every evening at sunset. See chapter 10 under Getting Around and Chapter 13 under Specialty Tours.

- **Climbing Mount Douglas.** Actually, you don't even have to climb. Just drive up and walk around. The whole of the Saanich Peninsula lies at your feet. See chapter 13.
- **Beachcombing.** This is the world's cheapest fun activity. Just find a beach, preferably a rocky one, and turn stuff over or poke through the tide pools and see what turns up. Of course, what you find depends on where you look. The best beaches are out along Highway 14, starting with East Sooke Regional Park, and moving out to French Beach, China Beach, Mystic Beach, and, the very best of all, Botanical Beach Park, some 60 kilometers (37 miles) away by Port Renfrew. Remember to put the rocks back once you've had a peek. See chapter 13.
- **Strolling the Inner Harbour.** Watch the boats and aquatic wildlife come and go while walking along a paved pathway that winds past manicured flower gardens. The best stretch runs south from the Inner Harbour near the Government Buildings, past Undersea World, the Royal London Wax Museum, and the Seattle ferry dock. See chapter 14.
- **Biking the Dallas Road to Willows Bay.** Okay, I'm a view junkie, but where else can you find a bike path by an ocean with high mountain peaks for a backdrop? See chapter 14.

3 Frommer's Favorite Experiences Beyond Vancouver & Victoria

- **Skiing at Whistler and Blackcomb Resorts.** Why ski anywhere else? The best resorts in North America merged for a total of more than 200 runs on two adjoining mountains. Full-day lift passes are only about C$59 (US$40) for adults. See chapter 17.
- **Looking for Bald Eagles in Squamish.** The bald eagle is the national symbol of the United States, but in winter when the salmon are running, you can see more eagles in Squamish than just about anywhere else in the world. See chapter 17.
- **Watching for Whales and Storms in Pacific Rim National Park.** Few sights in nature match observing whales in the wild, except perhaps a winter storm on Vancouver Island's west coast. Here you can see both in abundance. See chapter 17.
- **Exploring B.C.'s Backcountry by Train or Horseback.** Exploring the B.C. backcountry—an incredibly beautiful land of alpine lakes, snowcapped peaks, grasslands, canyons, and high plateaus—could take the whole of a lifetime. But to get a taste of it, hop on board one of BC Rail's exploratory day trips. Those with time to see more can alight from the railcar and set off to explore on horseback. See chapter 17.

4 Two Trips of a Lifetime

British Columbia is really one of the most pristine, most spectacular, most naturally beautiful places on earth. What follows are two trips that can't be replicated anywhere else on the planet. Longer descriptions are given in chapter 17.

- **Sailing the Great Bear Rain Forest.** There are next to no roads in this area of mountains, fjords, bays, channels, rivers, and inlets—the geography's too intense. Thanks to that isolation, this is also one of the last places in the world where grizzly bears are still found in large numbers, not to mention salmon, large trees, killer whales, otters, and porpoises. But to get there, you'll need a boat. And if you're going to take a boat, why not take a 100-year-old, 100-foot-long, fully rigged sailing schooner?

• **Horse Trekking the Chilcotin Plateau.** The high plateau country of the B.C. interior has some of the most impressive scenery around. Soaring peaks rise above deep valleys, with mountain meadows alive with flowers that bloom for just a few weeks in high summer. Explore the territory on horseback and save your feet.

5 Best Vancouver Hotel Bets

For a full description of all the Vancouver accommodations, see chapter 4.

• **Best Historic Hotel: The Hotel Vancouver,** 900 W. Georgia St. (☎ **800/ 866-5577** or 604/684-3131), was built by the Canadian-Pacific Railway on the site of two previous hotels. It opened in 1929 as Vancouver's grandest hotel. The chateau-style exterior, the lobby, and even the rooms—now thoroughly restored—are built in a style and on a scale reminiscent of the great European railway hotels.

• **Best for Business Travelers:** The majority of guests at the **Metropolitan Hotel Vancouver,** 645 Howe St. (☎ **800/667-2300** or 604/687-1122), are repeat customers, thanks to the Business Class rooms. Each has a cordless phone, a halogen desk lamp, an office chair, and even a stapler, paper clips, and other small essentials. Printers, fax machines, laptops, and cellular phones are available through the business center (which has workstations, secretarial services, and document-binding equipment).

• **Best for a Romantic Getaway:** In the downtown area, there's the **Wedgewood Hotel,** 845 Hornby St. (☎ **800/663-0666** or 604/689-7777), an opulent, intimate, European-style hotel. Private balconies are accented with small flower beds and overlook Robson Square.

• **Best Trendy Hotel:** The **Sylvia Hotel,** 1154 Gilford St. (☎ **604/681-9321**), is the hottest place for hip 30-somethings. With a down-at-the-heels Beat Generation atmosphere, it's like Los Angeles's Chateau Marmont or New York's Gramercy Park Hotel. And it has a perfect view of English Bay. Wealthier travelers can find their crowd at the posh **Sheraton Wall Centre Vancouver,** 1088 Burrard St. (☎ **800/325-3535** or 604/331-1000).

• **Best for Families:** The **Four Seasons,** 791 W. Georgia St. (☎ **800/332-3442** in the U.S., or 604/689-9333), provides kids with milk and cookies in the evening, along with children's menus and terry robes. **The Quality Hotel Downtown/The Inn at False Creek,** 1335 Howe St. (☎ **800/663-8474** or 604/682-0229), offers families spacious accommodations and kitchens at reasonable prices. Some suites even have glassed-in play areas.

• **Best Moderately Priced Hotel:** In the heart of the West End and a 2-minute walk from Stanley Park, the **Buchan Hotel,** 1906 Haro St. (☎ **604/685-5354**), gives you great value for your money.

• **Best Inexpensive Hotel:** With all the facilities of a convention center plus cheap comfortable rooms, the **University of British Columbia Conference Centre,** 5961 Student Union Blvd. (☎ **604/822-1000**), is the best inexpensive choice in the city.

• **Best B&B:** Built in 1905 by two Vancouver photographers, the **West End Guest House,** 1362 Haro St. (☎ **604/681-2889**), is filled with their work as well as an impressive collection of Victorian antiques. Fresh-baked brownies or cookies accompany evening turndown service, and the staff is thoroughly professional.

- **Best Alternative Accommodation: The Rosellen Suites,** 102–2030 Barclay St. (☎ **888/317-6648** or 604/689-4807), has spacious furnished apartments with fully equipped kitchens, dining areas, and living rooms for the same price as many standard hotel rooms.
- **Best Service:** The **Crowne Plaza Hotel Georgia,** 801 W. Georgia St. (☎ **800/663-1111** or 604/682-5566), always had outstanding service. Now, thanks to a complete renovation, it has the luxury to match.
- **Best Location:** Everyone's definition of a great location is different, but the **Westin Bayshore,** 1601 Bayshore Dr. (☎ **800/228-3000** or 604/682-3377), offers something for everyone: Steps from Stanley Park and Denman Street, the Westin boasts a waterfront location with access to the seawall only 10 blocks from downtown. And the view of the North Shore mountains is great.
- **Best Views:** So many Vancouver hotels have outstanding views that it's difficult to choose just one. Still, there's something special about the upper floors of the **Pan-Pacific Hotel,** 300–999 Canada Place (☎ **800/937-1515** in the U.S. or 604/662-8111). The harborside rooms have unimpeded views of Coal Harbour, Stanley Park and the Lions Gate Bridge, and the North Shore's mountains.
- **Best Health Club:** For luxury, the indoor/outdoor pool, fitness center, weight and exercise room, aerobics classes, whirlpool, and saunas at the **Four Seasons,** 791 W. Georgia St. (☎ **800/332-3442** in the U.S. or 604/689-9333), are without a doubt the best in town. For a serious workout, the fitness center at the **Coast Plaza at Stanley Park,** 1763 Comox St. (☎ **800/663-1144** or 604/688-7711), has even more extensive facilities.
- **Best Hotel Pool:** The outdoor pool at the **Westin Grand Hotel,** 433 Robson St. (☎ **888/680-9393** or 604/602-1999), overlooks the Vancouver Public Library and Robson Street and offers a lovely deck to soak up those precious summer rays.
- **Best for Sports Fans:** The **Georgian Court Hotel,** 773 Beatty St. (☎ **800/663-1155** or 604/682-5555), is as close to the action as you can get with a bed in the room. B.C. Place Stadium is right across the street, and GM Place is just a few blocks away.

6 Best Victoria Hotel Bets

For a full description of all the Victoria accommodations, see chapter 11.

- **Best Historic Hotel:** Architect Francis Rattenbury's masterpiece, **The Empress,** 721 Government St. (☎ **800/866-5577** or 250/384-8111), has charmed princes (and their princesses), potentates, movie moguls, and the likes of you and me since 1908.
- **Best for Business Travelers:** With its central location, large desks and data ports, secretarial services, elegant lobby, small meeting rooms, dining rooms, and understated luxury at a reasonable price, **The Magnolia,** 623 Courtney St. (☎ **877/624-6654** or 250/381-0999), is Victoria's best spot for business.
- **Best Place to Pretend You Died and Went to Bel Air: The Aerie,** 600 Ebedora Lane, Malahat (☎ **250/743-7115**), a red-tiled mansion high atop Mount Malahat, features hand-carved king-size beds, massive wood-burning fireplaces, chandeliered Jacuzzis, and faux marble finish by the gross ton.
- **Best Hotel Lobby:** The two-story plate glass demi-lune in the lobby of the **Ocean Pointe Resort,** 45 Songhees Rd. (☎ **800/667-4677** or 250/360-2999), provides the best vantage in Victoria for watching the lights on the Legislature switch on. There are also comfy chairs and fireplaces to sit and warm by.

- **Best for Families:** The **Royal Scot Suite Hotel,** 425 Quebec St. (☎ 800/663-7515 or 250/388-5463), is a converted apartment building with spacious suites that'll make your family feel at home. They come with fully equipped kitchens, VCRs, and a video arcade and playroom in the basement.
- **Best B&B:** With rooms double the size of those in other B&Bs and every possible need taken care of, the friendly innkeepers at **A Haterleigh Heritage Inn,** 243 Kingston St. (☎ 250/384-9995), do themselves proud.
- **Best Small Hotel:** The tastefully indulgent **Abigail's Hotel,** 906 McClure St. (☎ 800/561-6565 or 250/388-5363), has sumptuous sleeping chambers and warm, welcoming hosts.
- **Best Moderately Priced Hotel:** On the edge of the Inner Harbour, the **Admiral Motel,** 257 Belleville St. (☎ 888/823-6472 or ☎/fax 250/388-6267), provides friendly service, free bikes, and the most reasonably priced harbor view around.
- **Best Inexpensive Hotel:** The **Victoria International Youth Hostel,** 516 Yates St. (☎ 250/385-4511), is a cheery but slightly Spartan IYHA accommodation with lockers, bike storage, and dining facilities. The atmosphere is friendly, and the hostel is right in the heart of the old town.
- **Best-Dressed B&B:** The owners of **Andersen House Bed & Breakfast,** 301 Kingston St. (☎ 250/388-4565), dress their venerable 1891 Queen Anne home in the latest decor, from raku sculptures to large cubist-inspired oil paintings and carved-wood African masks. Their taste is impeccable—the old gal looks great.
- **Best Alternative Accommodation: The Boathouse,** 746 Sea Dr. (☎ 250/652-9370), is a real (converted) boathouse, with a private dock and a rowing dinghy. Built in a secluded cove, the one-room cottage is a perfect spot for those seeking privacy.
- **Best Location:** Not only is **Swan's Suite Hotel,** 506 Pandora Ave. (☎ 800/668-7926 or 250/361-3310), in the heart of the old town and just a block from the harbor, it's also right above Swan's Pub, one of the most pleasant restaurant/brew-pubs in the entire city.
- **Best Small and Intensely Alcoholic City Masquerading as a Hotel:** Built before liquor regulations were imposed, **The Strathcona Hotel,** 919 Douglas St. (☎ 800/663-7476 or 250/383-7137), boasts four pubs, two beach volleyball courts, an upstairs sundeck, a downstairs nightclub, and 1,000-plus seats, stools, booths, and patio chairs where folks can sit and drink. It also has a few rooms.
- **Best Spa:** The **Ocean Pointe Resort,** 45 Songhees Rd. (☎ 800/667-4677 or 250/360-2999), houses the best spa in the Pacific Northwest. Complete skin and body treatments, aesthetics, and aromatherapy treatments pamper the body and spirit. The OPR also has the best hotel pool.
- **Best Fitness Center:** The fitness center at the **Clarion Hotel Grand Pacific,** 450 Quebec St. (☎ 800/228-5151 or 250/386-0450), offers aerobics classes, a 25-meter ozonated indoor pool, a separate kids' pool, and weight room; a sauna, whirlpool, and massage therapist help ease the pain from all that exercise.
- **Best Views:** With stunning panoramic harbor views in an elegant Japanese-influenced decor, the **Laurel Point Inn,** 680 Montreal St. (☎ 800/663-7667 or 250/386-8721), is the place for view junkies. Check out the vista from your private terrace or from the Jacuzzi, overlooking your private terrace.
- **Best Oceanside Inn:** In the little town of Sooke, just west of Victoria, the **Sooke Harbour House,** 1528 Whiffen Spit Rd. (☎ 250/642-3421), offers quiet West Coast elegance and an exceptional restaurant.

7 Best Vancouver Dining Bets

For a full description of all the Vancouver restaurants, see chapter 5.

- **Best Spot for a Romantic Dinner: Il Giardino di Umberto,** 1382 Hornby St. (☎ **604/669-2422**), has a lovely courtyard patio and warm Tuscan atmosphere.
- **Best Spot for a Celebration: Lumière,** 2551 W. Broadway (☎ **604/739-8185**), is expensive but worth it to be pampered by chef Rob Feenie.
- **Best View:** On the top floor of the tallest building in Vancouver, towering 42 floors above the city, **Cloud 9,** 1400 Robson St. (☎ **604/662-8328**), has 360° views that go on forever.
- **Best Wine List: Raincity Grill,** 1193 Denman St. (☎ **604/685-7337**), has a huge wine list that's focused on the Pacific Northwest and sold by the glass at a reasonable markup by a knowledgeable staff. Go on a tour of the region, glass by glass by glass.
- **Best Value:** Get gourmet-quality Indian cuisine in a West Broadway strip mall at **Sami's,** 986 W. Broadway (☎ **604/736-8330**). The well-known chef prepares amazing Indian cuisine with a hint of fusion; none of the main courses costs more than C$12 (US$8) or so.
- **Best for Kids: Romano's Macaroni Grill at the Mansion,** 1523 Davie St. (☎ **604/689-4334**). A huge kids' menu, high chairs, and a great old mansion to explore—kids will love it.
- **Best Chinese Cuisine:** Bustling and busy, always serving fresh food and a large selection of all your favorites and many lesser-known dishes, the **Pink Pearl,** 1132 E. Hastings St. (☎ **604/253-4316**), is a Vancouver institution.
- **Best French Cuisine:** From its early days, **Lumière,** 2551 W. Broadway (☎ **604/739-8185**), has been in the running for best restaurant in Vancouver. In 1999 and 2000, it won. You won't be disappointed.
- **Best Bistro:** Cozy and unpretentious, **Bukowski's,** 1447 Commercial Dr. (☎ **604/253-4770**), serves up great food and a chance to brush up on your Beat poetry.
- **Best Service: The Five Sails,** 999 Canada Place Way, in the Pan-Pacific Hotel (☎ **604/891-2892**), could also have won for best view, but that would've been too easy. We made them work for it, and they came through with flying colors. Service is knowledgeable, seamless, and very friendly.
- **Best Steak: Gotham Steakhouse and Cocktail Bar,** 615 Seymour St. (☎ **604/605-8282**), serves USDA prime, grilled to perfection. Need we say more?
- **Best Seafood:** The creativity of the chef, the quality of the ingredients, and the freshness of the seafood all combine to make **C,** 1600 Howe St. (☎ **604/681-1164**), the best seafood restaurant in Vancouver.
- **Best Tapas: La Bodega,** 1277 Howe St. (☎ **604/684-8815** or 604/684-8814), was serving tapas when chefs at all the new tapas upstarts were saving their nickels for a night at McDonald's. La Bodega still does it best.
- **Best West Coast Cuisine:** Chef Michael Noble's sure touch has made **Diva at the Met,** 645 Howe St. (☎ **604/602-7788**), the place to discover West Coast cooking.
- **Best Desserts:** Lemon tarts, berry pies, fruit and custard Danishes, butter croissants—if all this is making you hungry, you'll be a pushover for the fabulous sweet treats at **Patisserie Lebeau,** 1660 Cypress St. (☎ **604/731-3528**).
- **Best Late-Night Dining:** Housed in a renovated heritage building, **The Brickhouse Bistro,** 730 Main St. (☎ **604/689-8645**), has plenty of character and

great food. It's open well past midnight, when many of Vancouver's restaurants have already gone to sleep. Nightcaps can be had downstairs in the bar.

- **Best Martinis:** At **Delilah's**, 1789 Comox St. (☎ **604/687-3424**), a two-page menu includes such lovelies as a Black Widow, a Boston Tea Partini, and the Edsel (soaked in lemon), all served in the wonderfully decadent lounge.
- **Best Outdoor Dining:** Situated right next to the West Vancouver seawall, **The Beach House at Dundarave Pier,** 150 25th St., West Vancouver (☎ **604/922-1414**), has a lovely patio overlooking English Bay, Stanley Park, and the lights of Vancouver.
- **Best People-Watching:** In the heart of the Robson shopping area, **Joe Fortes Seafood House,** 777 Thurlow St. (☎ **604/669-1940**), is a favorite after-work gathering place for the young, rich, and beautiful—and those who wish to live as if they are.
- **Best Vegetarian: Annapurna,** 1812 W. Fourth Ave. (☎ **604/736-5959**). Fabulous, flavorful food, cozy little room, and the most reasonable wines in town. Who says you have to sacrifice when you're a veggie eater?

8 Best Victoria Dining Bets

For a full description of all the Victoria restaurants, see chapter 12.

- **Best Spot for a Romantic Dinner: Cafe Brio,** 944 Fort St. (☎ **250/383-0009**), delivers sumptuous food in an intimate room. Or was that intimate food in a sumptuous room? Anyway, it's good.
- **Best Spot for a Business Lunch: The Marina Restaurant,** 1327 Beach Dr. (☎ **250/598-8555**), in Oak Bay, is casual but elegant, with white linens, sufficient space between tables, comfortable seating, and an inspiring view. Plus there's ample parking—a rarity in Victoria.
- **Best Decor:** With better art than most museums, **Swan's Pub,** 506 Pandora Ave. (☎ **250/361-3310**), wins out for best decor.
- **Best View: Sooke Harbour House,** 1528 Whiffen Spit Rd., Sooke (☎ **250/642-3421**), has a lovely dining room, with views of the strait as well as the surrounding gardens. Try to reserve a window seat.
- **Best Fish-and-Chips: Barb's Place,** 310 St. Lawrence St. (☎ **250/384-6515**), on Fisherman's Wharf, sells 'em freshly fried and wrapped in newspaper. Is there any other way to eat them?
- **Best Wine List:** Not just your average wine list. At **Camille's,** 45 Bastion Sq. (☎ **250/381-3433**), it includes entertaining comments, as well as plenty of suggestions for that special occasion.
- **Best Value: Swan's Pub,** 506 Pandora Ave. (☎ **250/361-3310**), has original art, great food all day, and samples of home-brewed beer, all for an excellent price.
- **Best for Kids: Millos,** 716 Burdett Ave. (☎ **250/382-4422**), treats youngsters to a night on the town, with a kids' menu, children-loving waiters, and exciting Greek dishes such as stuffed grape leaves and lemon soup.
- **Best Chinese Cuisine: Don Mee Restaurant,** 538 Fisgard St. (☎ **250/383-1032**), offers the finest Hong Kong–style dining experience in Chinatown.
- **Best French Cuisine: Deep Cove Chalet,** 11190 Chalet Rd., near Sidney (☎ **250/656-3541**), often on the list of best restaurants in British Columbia, is French cooking at its finest. Located a 30-minute drive from Victoria, it's well worth the trip.
- **Best Over-the-Top:** The chef at **The Aerie,** 600 Ebedora Lane, Malahat (☎ **250/743-7115**), creates remarkable classic French dishes. You can savor a

cassoulet of smoked duck and venison sausage with a vintage Château Margaux Pavilion Rouge under a 24-carat gold-leaf ceiling next to an open-hearth fireplace in a mountaintop dining room.

- **Best Italian Cuisine:** All you have to do is ask around for Victoria's best Italian restaurant, and people will point you to **Il Terrazzo Ristorante,** 555 Johnson St., off Waddington Alley (☎ **250/361-0028**). Excellent northern Italian cooking and points for the lovely patio.
- **Best Seafood:** You may think that the food would have a hard time competing with the view from **The Blue Crab Bar and Grill,** 146 Kingston St., in the Coast Hotel (☎ **250/480-1999**), but you'd be wrong. The young and creative chef serves up the freshest seafood, the presentation is beautiful, and the dishes are outstanding.
- **Best West Coast Cuisine: Sooke Harbour House,** 1528 Whiffen Spit Rd. (☎ **250/642-3421**), serves the best gifts from the sea and its own garden, like red sturgeon in a raspberry, sweet cicely, and sake-butter sauce with glazed beets, maple-roasted celeriac, and wild rice Parmesan. It's a favorite spot among some of Vancouver's most successful restaurateurs.
- **Best Local Crowd: The Herald Street Caffe,** 546 Herald St. (☎ **250/381-1441**), showcases the best that West Coast cuisine has to offer. Young hip locals flock to the excellent Sunday brunch at this casual bistro.
- **Best Burgers and Beer: Six Mile Pub,** 494 Island Hwy., View Royal (☎ **250/478-3121**), offers 10 house brews, juicy burgers (even veggie burgers), and loads of British pub–style atmosphere.
- **Best Late-Night Dining: Pagliacci's,** 1011 Broad St. (☎ **250/386-1662**), is *the* Victoria late-night dining spot. Noisy and crowded, this is the place to be seen while you devour a plate of spaghetti Bolognese or a piping-hot sausage and mushroom pizza.
- **Best Outdoor Dining:** The best views of Victoria are from across the water, so head over to the patio of **Spinnaker's Brew Pub,** 308 Catherine St. (☎ **250/386-2739**), overlooking the Inner Harbour.
- **Best People-Watching:** At the great little **Süze Lounge and Restaurant,** 515 Yates St. (☎ **250/383-2829**), you'll find lots of buzz and a young crowd that's there to see and be seen.
- **Best Afternoon or High Tea: The Empress,** 721 Government St. (☎ **250/384-8111**). If you're doing this high tea thing only once, you may as well do it right, and there's no better place than in Victoria's crown jewel of a hotel.
- **Best Fast Food: Sam's Deli,** 805 Government St. (☎ **250/382-8424**), makes a great stop for a quick soup or sandwich. If you don't want to waste precious sightseeing time, order your food to go and head down to the waterfront.

2

Planning Your Trip: The Basics

Whether you're coming to Vancouver and Victoria for business or shopping, dining or dancing, beach walking or backwoods trekking, or all of the above at once, here are some tips to help you plan your trip.

1 Visitor Information & Entry Requirements

VISITOR INFORMATION

You can get Canadian tourism information at consulate offices in most major American cities. The provincial and municipal Canadian tourism boards are also great sources of travel information. Contact **Super Natural British Columbia–Tourism B.C.,** mailing address Box 9830 Stn. Prov. Government, Victoria, B.C. V8W 9W5 (☎ **800/HELLO-BC [435-5622]** or 604/435-5622; www.hellobc.com; www.snbc-res.com for reservations), for information about travel and accommodations throughout the province.

Tourism Vancouver's Vancouver Tourist Info Centre, 200 Burrard St., Vancouver, B.C. V6C 3L6 (☎ **604/683-2000;** www. tourismvancouver.com); and **Tourism Victoria,** 812 Wharf St., Victoria (☎ **250/953-2033;** for hotel bookings only 800/663-3883 and 250/953-2022; www.tourismvictoria.bc.ca), can help you with everything from booking accommodations to making suggestions for what to see and do.

If you're planning to spend time outside the cities, you may also wish to call or write the **Vancouver Coast and Mountains Tourism Region,** 204–1755 W. Broadway, Vancouver, B.C. V6J 4S5 (☎ **604/ 739-9011**). For travel information on Vancouver Island and the Gulf Islands, see the **Tourism Association of Vancouver Island,** 203-335 Wesley St., Nanaimo, B.C. V9R 2T5 (☎ **250/754-3500;** www. islands.bc.ca).

For cultural information, check out the Web site for *Vancouver Magazine* at www.vanmag.com.

ENTRY REQUIREMENTS

If you're driving from Seattle, you'll clear Customs at the Peace Arch crossing (open 24 hours) in Blaine, Washington. You'll pass through **Canadian Customs** (☎ **800/461-9999** or 204/983-3500) to enter Canada, and **U.S. Customs** (☎ **360/332-5771**) on your departure. Duty-free shops are located in Blaine at the last exit before the border

Travel Information Online:
The Best of What's Around

- **Tourism BC:** www.hellobc.com
- **Super Natural British Columbia:** www.snbc-res.com or www.iias. com/travel/
- **Nature and wildlife information:** www.travel.bc.ca
- **Tourism Vancouver:** www.tourismvancouver.com
- **Vancouver and area travel information:** www.lotusland.bc.ca
- **Discover Vancouver:** www.discovervancouver.com/
- **Tourism Victoria:** www.tourismvictoria.bc.ca
- **Vancouver Island and Gulf Islands:** www.islands.bc.ca
- **Gulf Islands:** www.gulfislands.net
- **Whistler & Blackcomb Resorts:** www.whistler.net/

Government or Public Services:

- **City of Vancouver:** www.city.vancouver.bc.ca/
- **City of Victoria:** www.city.victoria.bc.ca
- **Weather (Environment Canada):** www.weatheroffice.com/
- **BC Transit:** http://transitbc.com/ or www.translink.bc.ca (Vancouver region)
- **BC Ferries:** www.bcferries.com

Entertainment/Culture:

- *Vancouver Magazine:* www.vanmag.com/
- **In Vancouver!:** www.vancouver-bc.com/
- **Entertainment info:** www.vancouvertoday.com
- **Vancouver Internet:** http://207.194.94.111/van/ or http://vancouver. foundlocally.com

going into Canada. On the Canadian side, the shops are a little more difficult to find. They're on the right, just after the speed limit drops to 35 kilometers per hour (22 m.p.h.).

If you fly directly into Vancouver International Airport from another country, you'll clear Customs in the new International Terminal. Once you get through passport control, you and your luggage will go through Customs before you leave the terminal. (Even if you don't have anything to declare, Customs officials randomly select a few passengers and search their luggage.)

DOCUMENTS FOR U.S. CITIZENS

Citizens or permanent U.S. residents don't require visas to enter Canada. American citizens need to show proof of citizenship and residence; a passport or birth certificate plus a driver's license is sufficient. Naturalized citizens should carry their naturalization certificates.

Permanent U.S. residents who are not U.S. citizens should carry their passports and Resident Alien Card (U.S. form I-151 or I-551). Foreign students and other noncitizen U.S. residents should carry their passports or a Temporary Resident Card (form 1688) or Employment Authorization Card (1688A or 1688B); a visitor's visa; I-94 Arrival-Departure Record; a current I-20 copy of IAP-66 indicating student status; proof of sufficient funds for a temporary stay; and evidence of return transportation. In either case, citizens of other countries traveling to Canada from the United States should check with the Canadian Consulate before departure to see if a visitor's visa is required.

If you're bringing children into Canada, you must have proof of legal guardianship. Lack of it can cause long delays at the border, because there have been cases of parents involved in custody cases abducting their children and attempting to flee to Canada (despite the fact that the Canadian and U.S. governments cooperate closely to resolve matters of this sort). If you're under 18 and not accompanied by a parent or guardian, you should bring a permission letter signed by your parent or legal guardian allowing you to travel to Canada.

DOCUMENTS FOR COMMONWEALTH CITIZENS

Citizens of Great Britain, Australia, and New Zealand don't require visas to enter Canada, but they do need to show proof of commonwealth citizenship (such as a passport) as well as evidence of funds sufficient for a temporary stay (credit cards work well here). Naturalized citizens should carry their naturalization certificates. Permanent residents of commonwealth nations should carry their passports and resident status cards. Foreign students and other residents should carry their passports or temporary resident cards or employment authorization cards; a visitor's visa; arrival-departure record; a current copy of student status; proof of sufficient funds for a temporary stay; and evidence of return transportation. Check with the Canadian Consulate before departure to see if you will also need a visitor's visa.

CUSTOMS REGULATIONS

Your personal baggage can include the following: boats, motors, snowmobiles, camping and sports equipment, appliances, TV sets, musical instruments, personal computers, cameras, and other items of a personal or household nature. If you are bringing excess luggage, be sure to carry a detailed inventory list that includes the acquisition date, serial number, and cost or replacement value of each item. It sounds tedious, but it can speed things up at the border. Customs will help you fill in the forms that allow you to temporarily bring in your effects. This list will also be used by U.S. Customs to check off what you bring out. You will be charged Customs duties for anything left in Canada.

Here are a few other things to keep in mind:

- If you bring more than US$10,000 in cash, you must file a transaction report with U.S. Customs.
- Never joke about carrying explosives, drugs, or other contraband unless you want to have your bags and person searched in detail, plus face arrest for conspiracy. Remember, Canada is a foreign country. The officials don't have to let you in.
- Some prescription medicines may be considered contraband across the border. If you're bringing any, it's best to check with your doctor and bring a copy of your prescription, or contact the **Canadian Customs Office** (☎ **800/461-9999** or 204/983-3500).
- If you're over 18, you're allowed to bring in 40 ounces of liquor and wine or 24, 12-ounce cans or bottles of beer and ale, and 50 cigars, 400 cigarettes, or 14 ounces of manufactured tobacco per person. Any excess is subject to duty.
- Gifts not exceeding C$60 (US$40) and not containing tobacco products, alcoholic beverages, or advertising material can be brought in duty-free. Meats, plants, and vegetables are subject to inspection on entry. There are

restrictions, so contact the Canadian Consulate for more details if you want to bring produce.

- If you plan to bring your dog or cat, you must provide proof of rabies inoculation during the preceding 36-month period. Other types of animals need special clearance and health certification. (Many birds, for instance, require 8 weeks in quarantine.)
- If you need more information concerning items you wish to bring in and out of the country, contact the **Canadian Customs Office** (☎ **800/461-9999** or 204/983-3500).

2 Money

CURRENCY

The Canadian currency system is decimal and resembles both British and U.S. denominations. Canadian monetary units are dollars and cents, with dollars coming in different colors, just like British currency. The standard denominations are C$5 (US$3.35), C$10 (US$7), C$20 (US$13), C$50 (US$34), and C$100 (US$67). The "loonie" (so named because of the loon on one side) is the C$1 (US65¢) coin that replaced the C$1 bill. A C$2 (US$1.35) coin, called the "toonie" because it's worth two loonies, has replaced the C$2 bill.

Banks and other financial institutions offer a standard rate of exchange based on the daily world monetary rate. The best exchange rates can be had by withdrawing funds from bank ATMs. Hotels will also gladly exchange your notes, but they usually give a slightly lower exchange rate. Almost all stores and restaurants accept American currency, and most will exchange amounts in excess of your dinner check or purchase. However, these establishments are allowed to set their own exchange percentages, and generally offer the worst rates of all.

The exchange rate between Canadian and U.S. dollars should always be kept in mind. The *figures* charged in hotels and restaurants in Vancouver and Victoria are often incrementally higher than in comparable U.S. cities; the *cost* is typically about one-third less. Canada, at the moment, is a bargain.

The Canadian Dollar & the U.S. Dollar

The prices cited in this guide are given in both Canadian and U.S. dollars, with all dollar amounts over $5 rounded to the nearest dollar. Note that the Canadian dollar is worth 30% less than the U.S. dollar but buys nearly as much. As we go to press, C$1 is worth US67¢, which means that your C$100-a-night hotel room will cost only US$67 and your C$6 breakfast only US$4.

Here's a table of equivalents:

C$	U.S.$	U.S.$	C$
1	0.67	1	1.49
5	3.35	5	7.46
10	6.70	10	14.93
20	13.40	20	29.85
50	33.50	50	74.62
80	53.60	80	119.40
100	67.00	100	149.25

TRAVELER'S CHECKS

Traveler's checks in Canadian funds are the safest way to carry money and are universally accepted by banks (which may charge a small fee to cash them), larger stores, and hotels. If you are carrying American Express or Thomas Cook traveler's checks, you can cash them at the local offices of those companies free of charge.

ATM NETWORKS

The 24-hour PLUS and Cirrus ATM systems are available in both Vancouver and Victoria. The systems convert Canadian withdrawals to your account's currency within 24 hours, so don't panic if you call your bank and hear a one-to-one balance immediately after conducting a transaction. Cirrus network cards work at ATMs at the **Bank of Montreal** (☎ **604/665-2703**), **CIBC** (☎ **800/465-2422** or 204/983-3500), **Hong Kong Bank of Canada** (☎ **604/685-1000**), **Royal Bank** (☎ **800/769-2511**), and **Toronto Dominion** (☎ **800/983-2265**), and at all other ATMs that display the Cirrus logo. None of these ATM systems provides your current balance. You must have a four-digit PIN to access Canadian ATMs.

CREDIT & DEBIT CARDS

Major U.S. credit cards are widely accepted in British Columbia, especially American Express, MasterCard, and Visa. British debit cards like Barclay's Visa debit card are also accepted. Diners Club, Carte Blanche, Discover, JCB, and EnRoute are taken by some establishments, but not as many. The amount spent in Canadian dollars will automatically be converted by your issuing company to your currency when you're billed—generally at rates that are better than you'd receive for cash at a currency exchange.

3 When to Go

Tree experts say that a rain forest species like the Western Red Cedar needs at least 30 inches of precipitation a year. Vancouver gets about 47 inches a year, a cause for no small celebration amongst the local cedar population. Homo sapiens simply learn to adjust.

For example, most of that precipitation arrives in the wintertime, when with a 30-minute drive to the mountains you can trade the rain for snow. Skiing and snowboarding are popular and are practiced from mid-December until the mountain snowpack melts away in June. Except in Whistler, hotels in the winter are quiet. Restaurants are uncluttered. This is also when Vancouver's cultural scene is at its most active.

Around mid-February, the winds begin to slacken—the sun shines a bit more, and the blossoms on the cherry trees begin to poke their heads out, timid at first, but gaining more confidence with each day until by the beginning of March there's a riot of pink on every street. The sun comes out, and stays out. From then until the rains close in again in mid-October is prime visiting time for sun junkies. Of course, that's also when most other visitors arrive.

WEATHER

Both Vancouver and Victoria enjoy moderately warm, sunny summers and mild, rainy winters. Above the 49th parallel, you get more sun per summer day than you do down south. There are 16 hours of daylight in mid-June, which means more hours at the beach, shopping, or in the mountains than in other parts of North America. Only 10% of the annual rainfall occurs during the summer months. Victoria gets half as much rain as Vancouver, thanks to the sheltering Olympic Peninsula to the south and its own southeasterly position on huge Vancouver Island. The average annual rainfall in Vancouver is 46 inches; in Victoria, it's just 23 inches.

Daily Mean Temperature & Total Precipitation for Vancouver, B.C.

	Jan	Feb	Mar	Apr	May	Jun	Jul	Aug	Sept	Oct	Nov	Dec
Temp(F)	38.0	41.2	44.6	39.6	46.2	62.4	66.4	66.6	60.6	42.0	48.0	39.0
Prec.(in)	5.9	4.9	4.3	3.0	2.4	1.8	1.4	1.5	2.5	4.5	6.7	7.0

HOLIDAYS

The official British Columbian public holidays are as follows: New Year's Day (January 1); Good Friday, Easter, Easter Monday (April 13 to 16, 2001); Victoria Day (May 21, 2001); Canada Day (July 1); B.C. Day (August 6, 2001); Labour Day (September 3, 2001); Thanksgiving (October 8, 2001); Remembrance Day (November 11); Christmas (December 25); and Boxing Day (December 26).

Vancouver & Victoria Calendar of Events

Festivals held in Vancouver and Victoria draw millions of visitors each year. Things may seem a little quiet in the winter and early spring, but that's because most residents simply head for the ski slopes. Resorts such as **Whistler and Blackcomb** (☎ **604/932-2394**) have events happening nearly every weekend. If no contact number or location is given for any of the events listed below, **Tourism Vancouver** (☎ **604/683-2000**) should be able to provide further details.

VANCOUVER EVENTS

January

- **Polar Bear Swim,** English Bay Beach. Thousands of hardy citizens show up in elaborate costumes to take a dip in the icy waters of English Bay. January 1.
- ✪ **Annual Bald Eagle Count,** Brackendale. Bald eagles gather en masse every winter near Brackendale to feed on salmon. In January 1994, volunteers counted a world-record 3,700 eagles. The count starts at the **Brackendale Art Gallery** (☎ **604/898-3333**). Second Sunday in January. Meet at 9am at the Art Gallery for a guided tour.

February

- **Chinese New Year,** Chinatowns in Vancouver, Richmond, and Victoria. This is when the Chinese traditionally pay their debts and forgive old grievances to start the new lunar year with a clean slate. These Chinese communities launch a 2-week celebration, ringing in the new year with firecrackers, dancing dragon parades, and other festivities. Late January or early February.

March

- ✪ **Internional Wine Festival,** Vancouver. This is a major wine-tasting event featuringat the latest international vintages. Each winery sets up a booth where you may try as many varieties as you like. Cheese and pâté are laid out on strategically placed tables. Late March or early April.

April

- **Baisakhi Day Parade,** Vancouver. The Sikh Indian New Year is celebrated with a colorful parade around Ross Street near Marine Drive and ends with a vegetarian feast at the temple. Contact **Khalsa Diwan Gurudwara Temple** (☎ **604/324-2010**) for more information. Mid-April.
- **Vancouver Sun Run,** Vancouver. This is Canada's biggest 10K race, featuring over 40,000 runners, joggers, and walkers who race through 10 scenic kilometers (6.2 miles). The run starts and finishes at B.C. Place Stadium. Late April.

May

- **Vancouver International Marathon,** Vancouver. Runners from all over the world gather to compete in a run through the streets. For information, call ☎ **604/872-2928.** First Sunday in May (May 6, 2001).
- **New Play Festival,** Vancouver. Emerging playwrights show off their latest works at Granville Island. Call ☎ **604/685-6228** for more information. Mid-May.
- **Cloverdale Rodeo,** Cloverdale, Surrey. Professional cowboys from all over North America compete in roping, bull and bronco riding, barrel racing, and many other events. There are pony rides for kids, great food, and a country-fair atmosphere. For information call ☎ **604/576-9461.** May long weekend (May 18 to 21, 2001).

June

- **International Children's Festival,** Vancouver. Activities, plays, music, and crafts for children are featured at this annual event held in Vanier Park on False Creek. For information, call ☎ **604/708-5655.** Late May or early June (May 28 to June 3, 2001).
- **SlugFest,** Richmond Nature Park, 1185 Westminster Hwy. (☎ **604/273-7015**). Kids compete to find the biggest slug in the park. There are slug races as well as awards for the fastest, slowest, and ugliest slugs. Usually first weekend in June.
- **VanDusen Flower and Garden Show,** Vancouver. Presented at the **VanDusen Botanical Garden,** 5251 Oak St., at 37th Street (☎ **604/878-9274**), this is Vancouver's premier flora gala. Early June.
- **National Aboriginal Day Community Celebration,** Vancouver. This event offers the public an opportunity to learn about Canada's First Nations cultures. Many events take place at the **Vancouver Aboriginal Friendship Centre,** 1607 E. Hastings at Commercial Street (☎ **604/251-4844**). June 24.
- ✪ **Alcan Dragon Boat Festival,** Vancouver. Traditional dragon-boat racing is a part of the city's cultural scene. Watch the races from False Creek's north shore, where more than 150 local and international teams compete. Four stages of music, dance, and Chinese acrobatics are presented at the **Plaza of Nations** (☎ **604/688-2382**). Third week in June.
- ✪ **DuMaurier International Jazz Festival,** Vancouver. More than 800 international jazz and blues players perform at 25 venues ranging from the Orpheum Theatre to the Roundhouse. Includes a large number of free performances. Call the **Jazz Hotline** (☎ **604/872-5200**) or visit www.jazzvancouver.com for more information. Late June/early July.
- ✪ **Bard on the Beach Shakespeare Festival,** Vanier Park. The best backdrop for Shakespeare you will ever see! The Bard's plays are performed in a tent overlooking English Bay. Plays are different every summer. Mid-June to

late September, Tuesday through Sunday. Call the box office (☎ 604/739-0559 during the performance season, check www.bardonthebeach.org, or phone 604/737-0625 October through April.

- **Festival d'ete francophone de Vancouver,** various venues, includes street festival. A 4-day festival celebrating francophone music from around the world. Performers often include well-known Québec artists. Call ☎ 604/736-9806 for information. Mid-June.

July

✪ **Canada Day,** Vancouver. Canada Place Pier (☎ 604/775-8687; www.canadaplace.ca) hosts an all-day celebration that begins with the induction of new Canadian citizens. Music and dance are performed outdoors throughout the day. There's a 21-gun salute at noon, precision aerobatics teams perform overhead during the afternoon, and a nighttime fireworks display on the harbor tops off the festivities. Other locations that host Canada Day events include Granville Island and Grouse Mountain. July 1.

- **Steveston Salmon Festival,** Steveston. A parade, salmon barbecue, special crafts exhibits, and other forms of entertainment take place in this heritage fishing village at the Gulf of Georgia Cannery National Historic Site (☎ 604/664-9009). July 1.

- **Ecomarine Kayak Marathon,** Vancouver. Competitors race sea kayaks in the Georgia Strait's open waters. The **Ecomarine Kayak Centre** (☎ 604/689-7575), at Jericho Beach, hosts the race and can provide details. Early July.

- **Harrison Festival of the Arts** (☎ 604/681-2771; www.harrisonfestival.com) at Harrison Hot Springs, lower mainland. This arts festival in the Fraser River valley, just east of Vancouver, attracts an array of performing artists from around the world. Early July.

- **Dancing on the Edge,** Vancouver. Canadian and international dance groups perform modern and classic works at the **Firehall Arts Centre** and other venues. Call (☎ 604/689-0691) for more information. Early to mid-July.

- **Vancouver Folk Music Festival,** Vancouver. International folk music is played outdoors at Jericho Beach Park. Contact the **Vancouver Folk Music Society** (☎ 604/602-9798; www.thefestival.bc.ca). Second or third weekend in July.

✪ **Illuminares,** Trout Lake Park. Evening lantern procession circling Trout Lake is a phantasmagoric experience. Drums, costumes, fire-breathing apparitions, and lots of elaborate handcrafted lanterns—floating lanterns, kids' lanterns, 10-foot-high four-person lanterns. Various performances start at dusk. For info call ☎ 604/879-8611. End of July, always on Saturday.

- **Powell Street Festival,** Vancouver. An annual festival of Japanese culture includes music, dance, food, and more. Contact the Powell Street Festival Society (☎ 604/739-9388) for more information. Last weekend of July or first weekend of August.

August

- **Vancouver Pride Parade,** Vancouver. Sponsored by the Vancouver Pride Society, this colorful gay- and lesbian-pride parade covers a route along Denman and Davie streets, beginning at noon. Celebrations at many local gay and lesbian nightclubs take place the same weekend. For more information, visit the Pride Society's Web site (www.vanpride.bc.ca) or call the Pride Society (☎ **604/687-0955**). First Sunday in August (B.C. Day long weekend).

✪ **Benson & Hedges Symphony of Fire,** Vancouver. Three international fireworks companies compete for a coveted title by launching their best displays accompanied by music over English Bay Beach. Don't miss the big finale on the fourth evening, which attracts as many as 500,000 spectators to the West End. (*Note:* Because of the crowds, the West End's streets and Kits Point are closed to vehicles each night.) Other prime viewing locations include Kitsilano Beach and Jericho Beach. End of July through first week in August.

• **International Comedy Festival,** Vancouver. Comedians from all over Canada and the United States perform at a variety of venues around town. Contact the Festival office at ☎ **604/683-0883** or www.comedyfest. com for more information. Last week of July, first week in August.

• **Chilliwack Exhibition and Rodeo,** Chilliwack. Not far from Vancouver, this cowboy rodeo has been an annual event for over 125 years. Call ☎ **604/792-2861** for more information. Second weekend of August.

✪ **Abbottsford International Air Show,** Abbottsford. Barnstorming stuntmen and precision military pilots fly everything from Sopwith Camels to VTOLs and Stealth Bombers. This is one of the biggest air shows in the world. Call ☎ **604/852-8511** for more information. The second weekend in August (Aug 10 to 12, 2001).

• **Greater Vancouver Open (Air Canada Championship),** Surrey. This PGA tour event attracts professional golfers and golf fans from around the world to the Northview Golf Country Club, 6857–168 St., Surrey. Call ☎ **604/575-0324** for details. Late August.

• **Pacific National Exhibition,** Vancouver. The years 2001 or 2002 may be the final ones for the 10th-largest North American country-style fair, as the city council has voted to convert the grounds to green space. Offerings include one of North America's best all-wooden roller coasters, many other rides, big-name entertainment, and a demolition derby. Special events include livestock demonstrations, logger sports competitions, fashion shows, and a midway. Contact the Pacific National Exhibition (☎ **604/253-2311;** www.pne.bc.ca) for more details. Mid-August to Labour Day.

• **Wooden Boat Festival,** Granville Island. Free event and a must for wooden-boat aficionados. Call ☎ **604/688-9622.** Last Weekend of August (Aug 23 to 26, 2001).

September

• **Molson Indy,** Vancouver. The CART Indy Series holds its biggest annual event in the streets of Yaletown and False Creek, attracting more than 500,000 spectators. Contact **Molson Indy** (☎ **604/684-4639;** www.molsonindy.com) for information or tickets. Labour Day.

✪ **The Fringe—Vancouver's Theatre Festival,** Vancouver. The best place to catch new theater. Centered around Granville Island and with venues around the Commercial Drive area (the Havana and the Cultch) and Yaletown's Roundhouse, the Fringe Festival features more than 500 innovative and original shows performed by over 100 groups from across Canada and around the world. All plays cost under C$12 (US$8). Call ☎ **604/257-0350** or see www.vancouverfringe.com for more info. September 6 to 16, 2001.

- **The North Shore Heritage Weekend,** North and West Vancouver (☎ **604/987-5618**). A full weekend of walking and boat tours, craft and historic displays, a vintage-car exhibition, and afternoon teas at various locations on the North Shore, from Deep Cove to Horseshoe Bay. Third weekend in September.
- **Mid-Autumn Moon Festival,** Dr. Sun Yat-sen Garden. This outdoor Chinese celebration includes a lantern festival, storytelling, music, and, of course, moon cakes. For more info call the Garden at ☎ **604/662-3207.** Early to mid-September, according to the lunar cycle (15th day of the 8th month of the Chinese calendar).

October

✪ **Vancouver International Film Festival,** Vancouver. This highly respected film festival features 250 new works, revivals, and retrospectives, representing filmmakers from 40 countries. Asian films are particularly well represented. Attendance reaches more than 110,000 viewers, not including the stars and celebrities who appear annually. Contact the Vancouver International Film Festival (☎ **604/685-0260;** www.viff.org) for details. Late September and first 2 weeks of October.

- **Cranberry Harvest Festival,** Richmond Nature Park, 1185 Westminster Hwy. (☎ **604/273-7015**). Cranberries are indigenous to British Columbia's bogs, and the Richmond Nature Park has one of the few remaining wild patches. The Saturday of Thanksgiving weekend, early October.
- **Vancouver International Writers Festival,** Vancouver. Public readings conducted by Canadian and international authors as well as writers' workshops take place on Granville Island and at other locations in the lower mainland. Call ☎ **604/681-6330** for details. Mid-October.
- **Vancouver Snow Show,** B.C. Place Stadium (☎ **604/878-0754;** www.skiandboardshow.com). If you ski, Canada's largest annual ski show, sale, and swap is a must. Sporting-goods stores unload the previous year's inventory, and people consign their own skis to raise money for the Vancouver Ski Foundation's youth programs. Late October.
- **Parade of Lost Souls,** Grandview Park. A bizarre and intriguing procession takes place around Commercial Drive to honor the dead and chase away bad luck. For more information, call ☎ **604/879-8611.** Last Saturday of October.

November

- **Remembrance Day.** Celebrated throughout Canada, this day commemorates Canadian soldiers who gave their lives in war. Vintage military aircraft fly over Stanley Park and Canada Place, and at noon a 21-gun salute is fired from Deadman's Island. November 11.
- **Christmas Craft and Gift Market,** Van Dusen Botanical Garden. Popular craft and gift market in a beautiful garden setting. For info, call ☎ **604/878-9274.** November and December.

December

- **Christmas Carol Ship Parade,** Vancouver Harbour. Harbour cruise ships decorated with colorful Christmas lights sail around English Bay, while onboard guests sip cider and sing their way through the canon of Christmas carols. Throughout December.
- **Festival of Lights,** VanDusen Botanical Garden. Throughout December, the garden is transformed into a magical holiday land with seasonal

displays and over 20,000 lights illuminating the garden. Call ☎ **604/878-9274** for info. December.

- **First Night,** Vancouver. The city's New Year's Eve performing-arts festival and alcohol-free party. Vancouver closes the downtown streets for revelers. Events and venues change from year to year. Contact **Tourism Vancouver** at ☎ **604/683-2000** for more information. There's also a party in Victoria. December 31.

VICTORIA & SOUTHERN VANCOUVER ISLAND EVENTS

January

- ✪ **Annual Bald Eagle Count,** Goldstream Provincial Park. When the salmon swim up Goldstream Provincial Park's spawning streams, the tourists aren't the only ones who come to watch. More than 3,000 bald eagles take up residence to feed on the salmon. The salmon run starts in October and the eagles arrive shortly thereafter. The eagle count usually takes place in mid- to late January when the numbers peak. Throughout December and January, the park offers educational programs, displays, and guest speakers. Call ☎ **250/478-9414** for exact dates and events.
- **Robert Burns's Birthday.** January 25 is the birthday of the great Scottish poet. Celebrations around Victoria and Vancouver include Scottish dancing, piping, and feasts of haggis. Appropriate to the day, most events take place in Victoria's pubs. January 25.

February

- **Chinese New Year,** Chinatown, Victoria. See "Vancouver Events," above. Late January or early February.
- **Trumpeter Swan Festival,** Comox Valley. A weeklong festival celebrates these magnificent white birds that gather in the Comox Valley. Check with the tourist office (☎ **250/754-3500**) for exact dates.
- ✪ **Flower Count,** Victoria (☎ **250/383-7191**). So many flowers bloom in Victoria and the surrounding area that the city holds an annual flower count. The third week in February is a great time to see the city as it comes alive in vibrant color.

March

- **Pacific Rim Whale Festival,** Tofino, Ucluelet, and Pacific Rim National Park. Every spring, more than 20,000 gray whales migrate past this coastline, attracting visitors from all over the world to Vancouver Island's west coast beaches. In celebration of the gray whale, orca, humpback, and other whales in the area, the event features live crab races, storytelling, parades, art shows, Whales in the Park guided whale-spotting hikes, and whale-watching boat excursions. Call ☎ **250/726-4641** for more information (www.ucluelet.com/ucoc). Mid-March to early April.

April

- **Annual Brant Wildlife Festival,** Qualicum Beach (☎ **250/752-9171;** www.island.net/~bfest/). This is a 3-day celebration of the annual black brant migration to the area (20,000 birds). A true feast for birders are the guided walks through old-growth forest and salt- and freshwater marshes that are home to hundreds of bird species. Art, photography, and carving exhibitions as well as birding competitions highlight the event. April 6 to 8, 2001.
- **TerrifVic Dixieland Jazz Party,** Victoria (☎ **250/953-2011**). The city hosts bands from the United States, Europe, and Latin America that

perform swing, Dixieland, honky-tonk, fusion, and improv before dedicated audiences at venues all over Victoria. April 18 to 22, 2001.

May

- **Harbour Festival,** Victoria. This 10-day festival takes place in the downtown district and features heritage walks, entertainment, music, and more. For information call ☎ **250/953-2033.** Last week of May.
- **Swiftsure Weekend.** International sailing races make quite a spectacular sight on the waters around Victoria. For information call ☎ **250/953-2033.** End of May.

June

- **Jazz Fest International,** Victoria (☎ **250/388-4423**). Jazz, swing, bebop, fusion, and improv artists from around the world perform at various venues around Victoria during this 10-day festival. June 22 to July 1, 2001.
- ✪ **Folkfest,** Victoria (☎ **250/388-4728**). Free 8-day world-beat music festival takes place at the end of June or early July, with daily performances from 11:30am to 11:30pm. Main venues are the Inner Harbour and Market Square in downtown Victoria.

July

- **Canada Day,** Victoria. The provincial capital celebrates this national holiday with events centered on the Inner Harbour, including music, food, and fireworks. Every city on Vancouver Island has similar festivities, though not as grand as those in Victoria itself. July 1.
- **Bathtub Race,** Nanaimo. Competitors design and attempt to sail or row all sorts of bathtub craft. Contact the **Nanaimo Tourism Association** (☎ **800/663-7337**) for more information. End of July.

August

- **First Peoples Festival,** Victoria (☎ **250/384-3211** or 250/953-3557). This free event highlights the culture and heritage of the Pacific Northwest First Nations peoples, featuring dances, performances, carving demonstrations, and heritage displays at the Royal British Columbia Museum. First weekend in August.
- **Victoria Shakespeare Festival,** Victoria (☎ **250/360-0234**). Performances of the Bard's works take place around the Inner Harbour from the second week in July to the third week in August.
- **Canadian International Dragon Boat Festival,** Victoria. Traditional dragon-boat races take place in the Inner Harbour, where 120 local and international teams compete. Mid-August.

September

- **Malahat Challenge (Vintage Car Rally),** Nanaimo. Competitors race from Victoria to Nanaimo in an amazing array of classic chassis. To entertain both racers and spectators, an end-of-summer jazz festival occurs at the finish line in Nanaimo. For information, call ☎ **250/754-8141** or the Nanaimo Tourism Association at ☎ **800/663-7337.** Early September.

October

- **Royal Victorian Marathon,** Victoria (☎ **250/382-8181** or 250/382-0042). This annual race attracts runners from around the world. The air is fresh, the temperature is usually just cool enough, and the course consists of gentle ups and downs. Early October (Canadian Thanksgiving weekend).

November

- **The Great Canadian Beer Festival,** Victoria. Featuring samples from the province's best microbreweries, this event is held during the second week in November at the **Victoria Conference Centre,** 720 Douglas St. (☎ 250/952-0360).
- **Remembrance Day.** See "Vancouver Events," above. November 11.

December

- **Merrython Fun Run,** Victoria (☎ 250/370-7129). An annual event for nearly 20 years, this 10-kilometer (6.2-mile) race loops through downtown Victoria. Mid-December.
- **First Night.** See "Vancouver Events" above. Call **Tourism Victoria** at ☎ 250/953-2033 for more details. December 31.

4 Insurance & Safety

INSURANCE

American travelers should review their health insurance coverage for travel outside the United States. If you are not adequately covered, take advantage of one of the many health and accident plans that charge a daily rate for the term of your trip. They include the ones offered by Thomas Cook, the American Automobile Association (AAA), and Mutual of Omaha. Generally, plans cost about US$3 per day for up to 90 days.

Auto insurance is compulsory in British Columbia. Basic coverage consists of "no-fault" accident and C$200,000 (US$134,000) third-party legal liability coverage. If you plan to drive in Canada, check with your insurance company to make sure that your policy meets this requirement. Always carry your insurance card, your vehicle registration, and your driver's license in case you have an accident.

AAA also offers low-cost travel and auto insurance for its members. If you are a member and don't have adequate insurance, take advantage of this benefit. Canada has health care comparable in quality to that of the United States, but it is also comparably priced, and even for emergency services, insurance or other payment information will be required. **Wallach & Company,** 107 W. Federal St., P.O. Box 480, Middleburg, VA 20118 (☎ 800/237-6615; www.wallach.com), offers a comprehensive travel policy that includes trip-cancellation coverage and emergency assistance in the event of illness, accident, or loss.

SAFETY

Even though southwestern British Columbia has never had a major shake, it is situated in an earthquake zone and has experienced many minor tremors. Check the exit and emergency information in your hotel's guest-services book. It will advise you where to go and how to exit after the shaking has stopped. The front pages of the Vancouver Yellow Pages also offer a quick course in emergency procedures. If you feel a tremor, get under a table or into a doorway.

5 Tips for Travelers with Special Needs

FOR TRAVELERS WITH DISABILITIES

According to *We're Accessible,* a newsletter for travelers with disabilities, Vancouver is "the most accessible city in the world." There are more than 14,000 sidewalk wheelchair ramps, and motorized wheelchairs are a common sight in the downtown area. The stairs along Robson Square have built-in ramps. Most major attractions and venues have ramps or level walkways for easy access. Many Vancouver hotels have at least partial wheelchair accessibility, if not rooms built completely to suit. Most SkyTrain stations and the SeaBus are wheelchair accessible, and most bus routes are lift equipped. For more information about accessible public transportation, contact **Translink** (☎ **604/521-0400;** www.translink.bc.ca; or phone the department of accessible transit at 604/540-3400) and ask for its brochure, *Rider's Guide to Accessible Transit.*

Many downtown hotels are also equipping rooms with visual smoke alarms and other facilities for hearing-impaired guests. You'll also notice that downtown crosswalks have beeping alert signs to guide visually impaired pedestrians.

Victoria is, for the most part, similarly accessible. Nearly all Victoria hotels have rooms equipped to accommodate travelers with special needs, and downtown sidewalks are equipped with ramps, though very few intersections have beeping crosswalk signals for the visually impaired. The **Victoria Regional Transit System** (☎ 250/382-6161) publishes the *Rider's Guide,* which includes complete information on which bus routes are equipped with lifts and/or low floors. The most notable spot in Victoria that isn't readily wheelchair accessible is the promenade along the water's edge in the Inner Harbour, which has only one rather challenging ramp near the Pacific Undersea Gardens.

FOR GAY & LESBIAN TRAVELERS

What San Francisco is to the United States, Vancouver is to Canada—the laid-back town on the coast with a large, thriving gay community. Much of the social activity centers in the West End—particularly Denman and Davie streets—where many gay singles and couples live. The best way to find out what's going on is to pick up a copy of the biweekly gay and lesbian tabloid, *Xtra! West,* which is available throughout the West End. To obtain a copy ahead of time, contact *Xtra! West,* 501–1033 Davie St., Vancouver, B.C. V6E 1M7 (☎ 604/684-9696). Also check out the **Vancouver Pride Society** Web site (www.vanpride.bc.ca) for upcoming special events, including the annual Vancouver Pride Parade. Otherwise, here are some suggestions: Book a room at the West End Guest House or the Sylvia Hotel (see chapter 4) and head over to the numerous West End and downtown clubs, such as the Odyssey and the Lava Lounge; or have coffee at Delaney's on Denman Street or at the Edge on Davie Street.

FOR SENIORS

Older travelers often qualify for discounts at hotels and attractions and on public transit throughout Vancouver and Victoria. Make a habit of asking. You'll be pleasantly surprised at the number of discounts for which you're eligible. Discount transit passes for persons over 65 (with proof of age) may be purchased at shops in Vancouver and Victoria that display a FAREDEALER sign (Safeway, 7-Eleven, and most newsstands). To locate a **FareDealer vendor,** contact BC Transit (☎ **604/521-0400**). If you or your mate is over 50 and you are not already a member of the **American Association of Retired Persons (AARP),** 3200 E. Carson, Lakewood, CA 90712 (☎ **800/424-3410**), consider joining. The AARP card is valuable for additional restaurant and travel bargains throughout North America.

FOR FAMILIES

Vancouver and Victoria are two of the most child-friendly, cosmopolitan cities around. Where else would you find a Kids Market that's filled with children's stores and is located next to a free water park that's equipped with water guns and changing rooms? In addition to the standard attractions and sights, you'll find a lot of adventurous, outdoor, and free stuff that both you and your kids will enjoy (see "Especially for Kids" in chapters 6 and 13). You can try entertaining restaurants that aren't cafeteria-style or fast-food establishments, but are decidedly kid-friendly (see "Family-Friendly Restaurants" in chapters 5 and 12).

Some hotels even offer milk and cookies to kids for evening snacks, plus special menus and child-size terry robes (see "Family-Friendly Hotels" in chapters 4 and 11).

FOR STUDENTS

This is definitely a student-oriented area. The University of British Columbia (UBC) in the Point Grey area, Burnaby's Simon Fraser University, and a number of smaller schools contribute to the enormous student population. Student travelers have a lot of free and inexpensive entertainment options, both day and night. The nightlife is active, centering around Yaletown, Granville Street, the West End, and Kitsilano. Pick up a copy of *The Georgia Straight* to find out what's happening. Many attractions and theaters offer discounts if you have your student ID with you. While many establishments will accept a school ID, the surest way to obtain student discounts is with an International Student Identity Card (ISIC), which is available to any full-time high-school or college student from the **Council on International Educational Exchange (CIEE),** 205 E. 42nd St., New York, NY 10017 (☎ **212/822-2700**), or from your local campus student society. The CIEE has offices in major U.S. cities. To find the location nearest you, call ☎ **800/438-2643** or check the Web site www.ciee.org.

In Victoria, the University of Victoria (referred to locally as "U. Vic.") has a sprawling campus just east of downtown. The student population accounts for most, if not all, of Victoria's nightlife. Student discounts abound. Pick up a copy of Victoria's weekly paper, *Monday Magazine* (which comes out on Thursdays), for current nightclub listings.

6 Getting to Vancouver

BY PLANE

THE MAJOR AIRLINES The Open Skies agreement between the United States and Canada has made flying to Vancouver easier than ever. Daily direct flights between major U.S. cities and Vancouver are offered by **Air Canada** (☎ 888/247-2262 or 800/661-3936), **Canadian Airlines** (☎ 800/363-7530) (though Air Canada and Canadian Airlines are in the process of merging, for the time being they maintain separate facilities, including telephone lines), **United Airlines** (☎ 800/241-6522), **American Airlines** (☎ 800/433-7300), **Continental** (☎ 800/231-0856), and **Northwest Airlines** (☎ 800/447-4747). Direct flights on major carriers serve Phoenix, Dallas, New York, Houston, Minneapolis, Reno, San Francisco, and many other cities.

FINDING THE BEST AIRFARE The best advice we can give you on shopping for an airfare bargain is to call travel agencies or the major airlines 30 or more days before your departure. That's when you'll find the best discounted seats on flights. Most airlines offer restricted ticketing on these deals. You cannot change dates without paying extra, and the tickets are usually nonrefundable.

See "Planning Your Trip: An Online Directory," following this chapter, for more information on finding travel bargains on the Internet.

Non-U.S. and non-Canadian travelers can take advantage of the **Visit USA** air passes offered by **Continental** (☎ 800/231-0856) and similar coupons from **Air Canada** (☎ 800/776-3000). These tickets must be purchased out-side North America in conjunction with an international fare. For roughly an additional US$439, you can get three flight coupons that allow you to fly any-where on the continent (price varies seasonally). You can buy up to a maxi-mum of nine coupons for US$769. Low-season discounts are also available. **Canadian Airlines** (☎ 800/426-7000) offers a similar deal to every destina-tion on its flight schedule, including Hawaii.

BY TRAIN

VIA Rail Canada, 1150 Station St. (☎ 800/561-8630; www.viarail.ca), con-nects with Amtrak at Winnipeg, Manitoba. From there, you travel on a spec-tacular route that runs between Calgary and Vancouver. Lake Louise's beautiful alpine scenery is just part of this enjoyable journey. **Amtrak** (☎ 800/872-7245; www.amtrak.com) has regular service from Seattle and also has a direct route from San Diego to Vancouver. It stops at all major U.S. West Coast cities, and takes a little under 2 days to complete the entire journey. Fares are US$190. Substantial seasonal discounts are available. Non-U.S. and non-Canadian travelers can buy a 15- to 30-day **USA Railpass** for US$440 to US$550 at peak season. The pass can be used for rail connections to Vancouver.

    BC Rail, 1311 W. First St., North Vancouver (☎ 604/631-3500; www.bcrail.com), also connects Vancouver to other cities throughout the province, including Whistler. The trip to Whistler is 2½ hours each way, and the fare includes breakfast or dinner. A one-way ticket costs C$33 (US$22) for adults, C$29 (US$19) for seniors, and C$19 (US$13) for children 2 to 12. Children under 2 are free.

BY BUS

Greyhound Bus Lines (☎ 604/482-8747) and **Pacific Coach Lines** (☎ 604/662-8074) also have their terminals at the Pacific Central Station, 1150 Station St., Greyhound Canada's **Canada Pass** offers 15 or 30 days of unlimited travel for C$405 to C$480 (US$271 to US$322). Pacific Coach Lines provides service between Vancouver and Victoria. The cost is C$26 (US$17) one-way per adult and includes the ferry; daily departures are between 5:45am and 7:45pm. Pacific Coach Lines will also pick up passengers from most downtown hotels. Call ☎ 604/662-8074 to reserve. **Quick Coach Lines** (☎ 604/940-4428) connects Vancouver to the Seattle-Tacoma International Airport. The bus leaves from Vancouver's Sandman Inn, 180 W. Georgia St., can pick up passengers from most major hotels, and stops at the Vancouver International Airport. The 4½-hour ride costs C$39 (US$26) one-way or C$70 (US$47) round-trip.

BY CAR

You'll probably be driving into Vancouver along one of two routes. **U.S. Interstate 5** from Seattle becomes **Highway 99** when you cross the border at the Peace Arch. The 210-kilometer (130-mile) drive takes about 2½ hours. You'll drive through the cities of White Rock, Delta, and Richmond, pass under the Fraser River through the George Massey Tunnel, and cross the Oak Street Bridge. The highway ends there and becomes Oak Street, a very busy urban thoroughfare. Turn left onto 70th Avenue. (A small sign suspended above the left lane at the intersection of Oak Street and 70th Avenue reads CITY CENTRE.) Six blocks later, turn right onto Granville Street. This street heads directly into downtown Vancouver on the Granville Street Bridge.

Trans-Canada Highway 1 is a limited-access freeway running all the way to Vancouver's eastern boundary, where it crosses the Second Narrows bridge to North Vancouver. When coming on Highway 1 from the east, exit at Cassiar Street and turn left at the first light onto Hastings Street (Hwy. 7A), which is adjacent to Exhibition Park. Follow Hastings Street 6.4 kilometers (4 miles) into downtown. When coming to Vancouver from Whistler or parts north, take Exit 13 (the sign says TAYLOR WAY, BRIDGE TO VANCOUVER) and cross the Lions Gate Bridge into Vancouver's West End.

BY SHIP & FERRY

The **Canada Place** cruise-ship terminal at the base of Burrard Street (☎ **604/ 665-9085**) is a city landmark. Topped by five eye-catching white Teflon sails, Canada Place Pier juts out into the Burrard Inlet and is at the edge of the downtown financial district. **Princess Cruises, Holland America, Royal Caribbean, Crystal Cruises, Norwegian Cruise Lines, World Explorer Majesty Cruise Line, Hanseatic, Seabourn,** and **Carnival** cruise lines dock at Canada Place and the nearby Ballantyne Pier to board passengers headed for Alaska via British Columbia's Inside Passage. They carry approximately 700,000 passengers annually on their nearly 300 Vancouver-Alaska cruises. Public-transit buses and taxis greet new arrivals, but you can also easily walk to many major hotels, including the Pan-Pacific, Waterfront Centre, and Hotel Vancouver. (If you're considering an Alaska cruise, late May and all of June generally offer the best weather, the most daylight, and the best sightseeing opportunities.)

BC Ferries (☎ **888/223-3779** or 250/386-3431; www.bcferries.bc.ca) has three Victoria-Vancouver routes. Its large ferries offer onboard facilities such as restaurants, snack bars, gift shops, business-center desks with modem connections, and comfortable indoor lounges. The one-way fare is C$9 (US$6) for adults, C$4.50 (US$3) for children 5 to 11, and C$32 (US$21) per car. Children under 5 are free. In the summer it is advisable to reserve a space when traveling with a vehicle, especially on long weekends and to and from the Gulf Islands. Call BC Ferries reservations at ☎ **888/724-5223.**

The most direct route between the cities is the **Tsawwassen–Swartz Bay ferry,** which operates daily between 7am and 9pm. Ferries run every 2 hours. Check for extra sailings on holidays or peak travel season. The actual crossing takes 95 minutes. However, schedule an extra 2 to 3 hours for travel to and from both ferry terminals, including waiting time at the docks. Driving distance from Tsawwassen to Vancouver is about 12 miles. Take Highway 17 from Tsawwassen until it merges with Highway 99 just before the George Massey Tunnel, then follow the driving directions to Vancouver given in "By Car" above. If you prefer to travel by public transit, BC Transit has regular bus service to both terminals. From Swartz Bay, there's regular bus service to Victoria.

The **Mid-Island Express** operates between Tsawwassen and Duke Point, just south of Nanaimo. The two-hour crossing runs eight times daily between 5:15am and 10:45pm.

The **Horseshoe Bay–Nanaimo ferry** has eight daily sailings, leaving Horseshoe Bay near West Vancouver and arriving 95 minutes later in Nanaimo. From there, passengers bound for Victoria board the E&N Railiner (see "By Train" under "Getting to Victoria," below) or drive south to Victoria via the Island Highway (Hwy. 1).

To reach Vancouver from Horseshoe Bay, take the Trans-Canada Highway (Highways 1 and 99) east and then take Exit 13 (Taylor Way) to the Lions Gate Bridge and downtown Vancouver's West End.

BY PACKAGE TOUR
Air Canada (☎ 888/247-2262) offers a number of fly/drive packages. And **SNV International,** 402–1045 Howe St., Vancouver (☎ 604/683-5101), specializes in vacation packages to Vancouver and Victoria.

7 Getting to Victoria

BY PLANE
THE MAJOR AIRLINES Air Canada (☎ 888/247-2262 or 800/661-3936), **Canadian Airlines** (☎ 800/363-7530), and **Horizon Air** (☎ 800/547-9308) offer direct connections from Seattle, Vancouver, Portland, Calgary, Edmonton, Saskatoon, Winnipeg, and Toronto.

Provincial commuter airlines, including floatplanes that land in Victoria's Inner Harbour, and helicopters, service the city as well. They include **Air BC** (can be reached through Air Canada at ☎ 888/247-2262 or 604/688-5515); **Harbour Air Sea Planes** (☎ 604/688-1277); **Pacific Spirit Air** (☎ 800/665-2359), which also serves the south and north Gulf Islands from Vancouver Airport; **Kenmore Air** (☎ 800/543-9595); and **Helijet Airways** (☎ 250/382-6222 in Victoria, or 604/273-1414 in Vancouver).

BY TRAIN
Travelers on the Horseshoe Bay–Nanaimo ferry can board a train that winds down the Cowichan River Valley through Goldstream Provincial Park into Victoria. The VIA Rail's **E&N Railiner** leaves from Nanaimo at 3:37pm Monday to Saturday and arrives in Victoria at 6pm. On Sunday, it departs Nanaimo at 7:07pm and arrives in Victoria at 9:40pm. The Victoria **E&N Station,** 450 Pandora Ave. (☎ 800/561-8630 in Canada), is near the Johnson Street Bridge. The one-way fare from Nanaimo to Victoria is C$20 (US$13) for adults, C$18 (US$12) for seniors, C$12 (US$8) for students, and C$10 (US$7) for children. Seven-day advance-purchase discounts and other specials are available.

BY BUS
Pacific Coach Lines (☎ 800/661-1725 in Canada, or 604/662-8074) operates bus service between Vancouver and Victoria. The 4-hour trip from the Vancouver bus terminal (Pacific Central Station, 1150 Terminal Ave.) to the Victoria Depot (710 Douglas St.) includes passage on the Tsawwassen–Swartz Bay ferry and costs C$26 (US$17) one-way per adult. Departures are daily between 5:45am and 7:45pm.

BY SHIP & FERRY
See "By Ship & Ferry" under "Getting to Vancouver," above, for information about BC Ferries service between Victoria and Vancouver.

BC Ferries also provides year-round service on 24 routes throughout the province, including the Gulf Islands and the Inside Passage. Most vessels have a restaurant, snack bar, gift shop, play area, game arcade, and executive center.

Three ferry services offer daily, year-round connections between Port Angeles, Bellingham, or Seattle, Washington, and Victoria. **Black Ball Transport** (☎ 250/386-2202 in Victoria, or 360/457-4491 in Port Angeles) operates between Port Angeles and Victoria. One-way fares are C$11 (US$7) for adults, C$44 (US$29) for a car and driver (rates are based on U.S.-dollar fare). The crossing takes 1½ hours and there are four in the summer (mid-June through September), and usually two sailings a day throughout the rest of the year.

Clipper Navigation, 1000A Wharf St., Victoria (☎ **800/288-2535** in North America, or 250/382-8100 in Victoria), operates the *Victoria Clipper,* a high-speed catamaran that runs between Seattle and Victoria with some sailings stopping in the San Juan Islands. The *Victoria Clipper* is a passenger-only service; sailing time is approximately 3 hours with daily sailings. One-way adult fares are US$55 to US$69, round-trip US$91 to US$115.

From June through October, Victoria San Juan Cruises' MV *Victoria Star* (☎ **800/443-4552** in North America, or 360/738-8099) departs the Fairhaven Terminal in Bellingham, Washington at 9am and arrives in Victoria at noon. It departs Victoria at 5pm, arriving in Bellingham at 8pm. One-way fares are US$42 one-way or US$89 round-trip for an adult, and include a free salmon dinner on the return Victoria-Bellingham run. No meal is included with the trip from Bellingham to Victoria, but there is a snack bar with coffee service onboard.

BY PACKAGE TOUR

See "By Package Tour" under "Getting to Vancouver," above.

Planning Your Trip: An Online Directory

by Lynne Bairstow

Lynne Bairstow is the editorial director of *e-com* magazine.

Day by day, the Internet becomes more integrated into our lives—including the way we plan and book our travel. The Internet not only provides a wealth of destination information, but also gives you the chance to compare experiences with fellow travelers, ask experts for advice, seek out discounted fares once accessible only to travel industry insiders, and stay in touch via e-mail while you're away. The instant communication and storehouse of information has revolutionized the way travel is researched, reserved, and realized.

This Online Directory will help you take better advantage of the travel-planning information available online; it's best used along with this book. Section 1 lists general Internet resources that can make any trip easier, such as sites for finding the best prices on airline tickets. In Section 2 you'll find some top online guides for Vancouver and Victoria.

Keep in mind this isn't a comprehensive list but a discriminating selection to get you started. Unlike some Web-site rankings, which are based on payment, these listings recognize sites based on their content value and ease of use, and they aren't paid for. Finally, remember that this is a press-time snapshot of leading Web sites—some undoubtedly will have evolved, changed, or moved by the time you read this.

1 Top Travel-Planning Web Sites

WHY BOOK ONLINE?

Online agencies have come a long way over the past few years. They now provide tips for finding the best fare and give suggested dates or times to travel that yield the lowest price if your plans are flexible. Other sites even allow you to establish the price you're willing to pay, and they check the airlines' willingness to accept it. However, in some cases, these sites may not always yield the best price. Unlike a travel agent, for example, they may not have access to charter flights offered by wholesalers.

Online booking sites aren't the only places to reserve airline tickets. All major airlines have their own Web sites and often offer incentives—bonus frequent-flyer miles or Net-only discounts, for example—when you buy online or buy an E-ticket.

The best of the travel-planning sites are now highly personalized; they store your seating preferences, meal preferences, tentative itineraries, and credit-card information, allowing you to quickly plan trips or check agendas.

What You'll Find at the Frommer's Site

We highly recommend **Arthur Frommer's Budget Travel Online (www.frommers.com)** as an excellent travel-planning resource. Of course, we're a little biased, but you'll find indispensable travel tips, reviews, monthly vacation giveaways, and online booking. Among the site's most popular features are the regular "Ask the Expert" bulletin boards, which feature one of the Frommer's authors answering your questions in online postings.

Subscribe to Arthur Frommer's Daily Newsletter (**www.frommers. com/newsletters**) to receive the latest travel bargains and inside travel secrets in your e-mailbox every day. You'll read daily headlines and articles from the dean of travel himself, highlighting last-minute deals on airfares, accommodations, cruises, and package vacations. You'll also find great travel advice by checking the Tip of the Day or Hot Spot of the Month.

Search the Destinations archive (**www.frommers.com/destinations**) of more than 200 domestic and international destinations for great places to stay, tips for traveling there, and what to do while you're there. Once you've researched your trip, the online reservation system (**www.frommers.com/booktravelnow**) takes you to Frommer's favorite sites for booking your vacation at affordable prices.

In many cases, booking your trip online can be better than working with a travel agent. It gives you the widest variety of choices, control, and the 24-hour convenience of planning your trip when you choose. All you need is some time—and often a little patience—and you're likely to find that the fun of online travel research will greatly enhance your trip.

WHO SHOULD BOOK ONLINE?

Online booking is best for travelers who want to know as much as possible about their options, those who have flexibility in their travel dates and are looking for the best price, and bargain hunters driven by a good value who are open-minded about where they travel.

One of the biggest successes in online travel for both passengers and airlines is the offer of last-minute specials, such as American Airlines' weekend deals or other Internet-only fares you must purchase online. Another advantage is that you can cash in on incentives for booking online, such as rebates or bonus frequent-flyer miles.

Business and other frequent travelers also have found numerous benefits in online booking. Advances in mobile technology enable them to check flight status, change plans, or get specific directions from handheld computing devices, mobile phones, and pagers. Some sites will even e-mail or page passengers if their flights are delayed.

Online booking is increasingly able to accommodate complex itineraries, even for international travel. The pace of evolution on the Net is rapid, so you'll probably find additional features and advancements by the time you visit these sites. What the future holds for online travelers is ever-increasing personalization, customization, and reaching out to you.

TRAVEL-PLANNING & BOOKING SITES

Below are listings for sites for planning and booking travel. The sites offer domestic and international flight, hotel, and rental-car bookings, plus news, destination information, and deals on cruises and vacation packages. Free (one-time) registration is required for booking.

✪ Travelocity (incorporates Preview Travel). www.travelocity.com; www.previewtravel.com; www.frommers.travelocity.com
Travelocity is Frommer's online travel planning/booking partner. Travelocity uses the SABRE system to offer reservations and tickets for more than 400 airlines, plus reservations and purchase capabilities for more than 45,000 hotels and 50 car-rental companies. An exclusive feature of the SABRE system is its **Low Fare Search Engine,** which automatically searches for the three lowest-priced itineraries based on a traveler's criteria. Last-minute deals and consolidator fares are included in the search. If you book with Travelocity, you can select specific seats for your flights with online seat maps and also view diagrams of the most popular commercial aircraft. Its hotel finder provides street-level location maps and photos of selected hotels. With the **Fare Watcher** e-mail feature, you can select up to five routes and receive e-mail notices when the fare changes by $25 or more.

Travelocity's **Destination Guide** includes updated information on some 260 destinations worldwide—supplied by Frommer's.

Note to AOL Users: You can book flights, hotels, rental cars, and cruises on AOL at Keyword: Travel. The booking software is provided by Travelocity/Preview Travel and is similar to the Internet site. Use the AOL "Travelers Advantage" program to earn a 5% rebate on flights, hotel rooms, and car rentals.

Expedia. expedia.com
Expedia is Travelocity's major competitor. It offers several ways of obtaining the best possible fares: **Flight Price Matcher** service allows your preferred airline to match an available fare with a competitor; a comprehensive **Fare Compare** area shows the differences in fare categories and airlines; and **Fare Calendar** helps you plan your trip around the best possible fares. Its main limitation is that like many online databases, Expedia focuses on the major airlines and hotel chains, so don't expect to find too many budget airlines or one-of-a-kind B&Bs here.

TRIP.com. www.trip.com
TRIP.com began as a site geared toward business travelers, but its innovative features and highly personalized approach have broadened its appeal to leisure

Staying Secure

More people still look online than book online, partly due to fear of putting their credit-card numbers out on the Net. Secure encryption and increasing experience buying online have removed this fear for most travelers. In some cases, however, it's simply easier to buy from a local travel agent who can deliver your tickets to your door (especially if your travel is last minute or you have special requests). You can find a flight online and book it by calling a toll-free number or contacting your travel agent, although this is somewhat less efficient. To be sure you're in secure mode when you book online, look for a little icon of a key (in Netscape) or a padlock (in Internet Explorer) at the bottom of your Web browser.

travelers as well. It is the leading travel site for those using mobile devices to access Internet travel information.

TRIP.com includes a trip-planning function that provides the average and lowest fare for the route requested, in addition to the current available fare. An on-site "newsstand" features breaking news on airfare sales and other travel specials. Among its most popular features are Flight TRACKER and intelliTRIP. **Flight TRACKER** allows users to track any commercial flight en route to its destination anywhere in the United States, while accessing real-time FAA-based flight-monitoring data. **intelliTRIP** is a travel search tool that allows users to identify the best airline, hotel, and rental-car rates in less than 90 seconds.

In addition, the site offers e-mail notification of flight delays, plus city resource guides, currency converters, and a weekly e-mail newsletter of fare updates, travel tips, and traveler forums.

Yahoo! Travel. www.travel.yahoo.com
Yahoo! is currently the most popular of the Internet information portals, and its travel site is a comprehensive mix of online booking, daily travel news, and destination information. The **Best Fares** area offers what it promises, plus provides feedback on refining your search if you have flexibility in travel dates or times. There is also an active section of Message Boards for discussions on travel in general and specific destinations.

SPECIALTY TRAVEL SITES

Although the sites listed above provide the most comprehensive services, some travelers have specialized needs that are best met by a site catering specifically to them.

For adventure travelers, **iExplore (www.iexplore.com)** is a great source for information and booking adventure and experiential travel, as well as related services and products. The site combines secure Internet booking functions with hands-on expertise and 24-hour live customer support by seasoned adventure travelers, for those interested in trips off the beaten path. The company is a supporting member of the Ecotourism Society and is committed to environmentally responsible travel worldwide.

Another excellent site for adventure travelers is **Away.com (www.away.com),** which features unique vacations for challenging the body, mind, and spirit. Trips may include cycling in the Loire Valley, taking an African safari, or assisting in the excavation of a Mayan ruin. For those without the time for such an extended exotic trip, offbeat weekend getaways are also available. Services include a customer-service center staffed with experts to answer calls and e-mails, plus a network of over 1,000 prescreened tour operators. Trips are categorized by cultural, adventure, and green travel. Away.com also offers a Daily Escape e-mail newsletter.

GORP (Great Outdoor Recreation Pages; www.gorp.com) has been a standard for adventure travelers since outdoors enthusiasts Diane and Bill Greer founded it in 1995. Tapping their own experiences, they created this Web site, which offers unique travel destinations and encourages active participation by fellow GORP visitors through the sophisticated menu of online forums, contests, and discussions.

For travelers who prefer more unique accommodations, **InnSite (www.innsite.com)** offers listings for inns and B&Bs in all U.S. states and dozens of countries around the globe. Find an inn at your destination, look at images of the rooms, check prices and availability, then send an e-mail to the innkeeper if you have further questions. This is an extensive directory of bed-and-breakfast inns, but includes listings only if the proprietors submitted one. (*Note:* It's free to get an inn listed.) The descriptions are written by the innkeepers, and many listings link to the inn's own Web sites, where you can find more information and images.

Another good resource for mostly one-of-a-kind places in the United States and abroad is **Places to Stay (www.placestostay.com),** which focuses on resort accommodations.

"Have Kids, Still Travel!" is the motto of the **Family Travel Forum (www. familytravelforum.com),** a site dedicated to the ideals, promotion, and support of travel with children. FTF is supported by memberships, which are available in flexible prices from a $2.95 monthly fee to a heftier annual fee for more comprehensive services. Because no advertising is accepted, FTF provides its members with honest, unbiased information, informed advice, and practical tips designed to make traveling with children a healthier, safer, hassle-free experience, not to mention a better value.

FINDING LODGINGS ONLINE

Though the online booking services listed above offer hotel booking, it can be best to use a site devoted primarily to lodging because you may find properties that aren't listed on more general online travel agencies. Some lodging sites specialize in a particular type of accommodation, such as B&Bs, which you won't find on the more mainstream booking services. Other services, such as TravelWeb, offer weekend deals on major chain properties, which cater to business travelers and have more empty rooms on weekends.

All Hotels on the Web. www.all-hotels.com

Of course, this site doesn't include *all* the hotels on the Web, but it does have tens of thousands of listings throughout the world. Bear in mind that each hotel listed has paid a small fee ($25 and up) for placement, so it's not an objective list, but more like a book of online brochures.

Also see **Hotels and Travel on the Net (www.hotelstravel.com),** which claims to offer discount booking on more than 100,000 hotels and other lodgings in more than 120 countries.

HotelDiscount!com. www.180096hotel.com

HotelDiscount!com books blocks of rooms in advance, so sometimes it has rooms—at discount rates—at hotels that are "sold out." Select a city, enter your dates, and you'll get a list of the best prices for a selection of hotels. Beware, though, that HotelDiscount! occasionally fails to make your reservation at the hotel—it's best to confirm with the hotel to make sure your room is booked.

InnSite. www.innsite.com

Find an inn at your destination, check prices and availability, and then send an e-mail to the innkeeper if you have further questions. This isn't a comprehensive directory of B&Bs, but it's a place to start, and includes listings only if the proprietor submitted one. (*Note:* It's free to get an inn listed.) The descriptions are written by the innkeepers and many listings link to the inn's own Web sites, where you can find more information and images.

Also see: bedandbreakfast.com.

Local Hotels. www.localhotels.com

This site is a listing of local hotel directories throughout the world. From the home page, click on "United States" to get a listing of hotel directories by state.

Online Directory

Places to Stay. www.placestostay.com

Mostly one-of-a-kind places in the United States (and abroad), with a focus on resort accommodations. This isn't a comprehensive directory, but it can give you a sense of what's available at different destinations.

Quikbook. www.quikbook.com

At last look, Quikbook listed hotels for 27 major U.S. cities. It offers some good rates on these properties, such as rooms for under $200 at Manhattan's Omni, where the rack rate (top price) is as high as $389. Lists of amenities and expandable images of the hotel, room, and lobby round out Quikbook's listings. But remember to do some comparison shopping before you buy—Quikbook offers discounts, but they don't necessarily have the cheapest rates.

✪ TravelWeb. www.travelweb.com

TravelWeb lists tens of thousands of hotels worldwide, focusing on chains such as Westin, Hyatt, and Hilton, and you can book almost 90% of them online. TravelWeb's Click-It Weekends, updated each Monday, offers weekend deals at many leading hotel chains.

2 Top Web Sites for Vancouver & Victoria

Information updated by Shawn Blore

FOR VANCOUVER
CITY GUIDES

City Choices. www.citychoices.com

This new kid on the Internet block aims to do it all: with links and reviews of accommodations, attractions, shopping, dining, and traveler's tips. Also included are well-written feature articles on the cultural aspects of the city, including explorations of Vancouver's multicultural scene, and insider reports on the romantic side of the city.

Discover Vancouver. www.discovervancouver.com

A fun, colorful site with great local flavor; it provides links to various tourist sites and lists entertainment information.

In Vancouver. www.vancouver-bc.com

The most useful section of this site is called "things to do," which lists upcoming events and is updated regularly. You can see what's coming up while you're in Vancouver or, if you have some flexibility, you can plan your trip around events you'd like to attend. Click on "tourism" for city maps and information on guided tours. You'll also find some lodging and dining advice. This site also provides links to information on Victoria, Vancouver Island, Whistler, and the Gulf Islands.

✪ Tourism Vancouver. www.tourism-vancouver.org

The official tourism source for Vancouver and environs offers a wealth of valuable information on lodging, entertainment, dining, and shopping. Most useful are the updates about what's going on as well as the special offers, such as seasonal deals on hotel rooms. You'll find a special section for kids' activities and another called "Free or Almost Free" for great things to do without stretching your budget. If you don't know where to start, click on "Attractions" and check the Top 10 list. Perhaps the best aspect of this site is its extensive and up-to-date entertainment and special events listings, including top picks for each week.

Online Directory

Vancouver Magazine. www.vanmag.com
This online edition of Vancouver's lively city mag often has articles on new restaurants, intriguing shops (and which ones are having sales), and the hottest tickets in town.

Vancouver Sun. www.vancouversun.com
If you'd like to take the pulse of this dynamic city, have a look at one of its leading newspapers. You'll find current events, sports, culture, and more.

Vancouver Today. www.vancouvertoday.com
Want to be more than an average tourist? Read up on local news headlines, sports commentary, and your horoscope before heading out. This site has the most thorough events calendar, with detailed daily listings.

Vancouverwow.com. www.vancouverwow.com
This Yahoo!-style directory has links to sites for Vancouver's leading attractions, hotels, restaurants, stores, and much more. Not everything here is for the traveler, but it's easy to pick and choose what's interesting to you. The arts, entertainment, and movies listings are excellent.

LEADING ATTRACTIONS

Not all of Vancouver's top attractions have their own Web sites, but some do, and these sites can be quite helpful. If an attraction isn't listed below, check one of the general guides above.

Capilano Suspension Bridge. www.capbridge.com
What's so exciting about crossing an old suspension bridge? Well, you won't fully know until you're standing 60 meters (200 ft.) above the kayakers and salmon in the river below. With a stunning view to match the exhilaration of traversing this gorge, this one is hard to top.

Granville Island Public Market. www.granvilleisland.bc.ca
Here you'll find everything you want to know about the market: open hours, special events, merchants directory, specialty-shop listings, and theater and gallery information.

Museum of Anthropology. www.moa.ubc.ca
Curated by the University of British Columbia, the MOA is a window into the world of Native peoples of the Northwest. Check the site for ongoing and upcoming exhibits, museum hours, and special events.

Pacific Space Centre. www.pacific-space-centre.bc.ca
Don't be surprised if you're pressed into service as soon as you get to this site. When I visited, a virtual comet was heading straight toward Earth and I was urgently needed to help deflect it. Once you save the planet, you can enjoy virtual voyages, check show times for the planetarium, and get basic visitor information.

Science World British Columbia. www.scienceworld.bc.ca
"Create a cyclone. Crawl through a beaver lodge. Dance on a giant keyboard. Blow square bubbles. Light up a plasma ball." These are just some of the attractions you'll find at Science World, activities that are almost as fun for adults as they are for kids. Of course, you can't quite pull off these feats online, but you can get a sense of what's possible at the center. Also see what's playing at the OMNIMAX theater.

Vancouver Aquarium Marine Science Centre. www.vanaqua.org
Learn about current displays at the aquarium and take a peek at the sea creatures that inhabit it. You can print an online coupon for a discount at the museum or take a virtual tour by clicking on "Site Map."

Online Directory

Vancouver Art Gallery. www.vanartgallery.bc.ca
Take a virtual stroll through current exhibitions or have a look at what's in the permanent gallery. Upcoming exhibits are listed if you're planning a visit a few months hence.

Vancouver Maritime Museum. www.vmm.bc.ca
This is a can't-miss attraction for maritime enthusiasts, and the Web site is a terrific way to get a head-start on planning your visit. Learn about the exhibits, from the Children's Maritime Centre to the beguiling Treasures, or man the oars and map the coast.

Whistler Resort Guide. www.whistler.net
If you have any questions about Whistler's splendor and grandeur, click on "Gallery" for aerial views of this massive resort. If you're sold, you can create a personalized package and reserve it online. Of course, you'll also find loads of info about the resort and its activities.

RESTAURANTS

Flavour Finder. www.flavourfinder.com
Great resource for looking up restaurants in all of British Columbia, although the majority listed are in the Vancouver area. Select by name, cuisine, or city.

✪ Zagat.com. Vancouver. zagat.com
Because the Web address for the Vancouver section is so long, simply go to Zagat.com and select "Vancouver" from the pull-down menu. This outstanding site lists favorite restaurants selected by fellow diners and sorted by cuisine type, decor, service, and neighborhood.

NIGHTLIFE

Vancouver Nightlife. www.vancouver-nightlife.com
Get the latest information on local nightlife, including comprehensive concert listings. Clicking on any of the pubs or clubs connects you to www.clubvibes.com, which features comprehensive listings of the fast-changing club scene. While on the Net, you can print VIP club passes that—with luck and some goodwill from the bouncer—allow you to get in free or skip the line entirely. Or you may just find yourself in a lineup with all the other VIPs, which is still better than the long lineup everyone else is in.

FOR GAYS & LESBIANS

Gay Vancouver. www.gayvancouver.com
Entertainment, cultural happenings, local contacts, support groups—here you'll find everything in fact for the gay, lesbian, bisexual, or transgendered traveler.

LOCAL SKI MOUNTAINS

All three local mountains offer decent skiing, especially if you're a beginner or don't have a full day to go up to Whistler. In summer, the trails are open for hiking, mountain biking, and sightseeing. Check below for seasonal information, events, snow conditions, lift-ticket prices, and rental info.

Grouse Mountain. www.grousemtn.com

Mount Seymour. www.mountseymour.com

Cypress Bowl. www.cypressbowl.com

Online Directory

TOP SITES

Butchart Gardens. **www.butchartgardens.com**
This site offers a virtual peek at the gardens and provides information on upcoming events and suggested times to visit. You'll also find a botanical calendar, historical information, and descriptions of restaurants and other facilities.

City of Victoria. **www.city.victoria.bc.ca**
The official city government site for Victoria has lots of municipal information tourists probably don't need (you're really not too worried about paying those parking tickets, right?). However, the tourism section is worth visiting, with tours of the "City of Gardens." Other useful links include the various ferry schedules (including the U.S. ferries), accommodation listings, and day-trip suggestions.

Greater Victoria. **www.tourismvictoria.com**
Here you'll find lots of background information to the sights and attractions of the Victoria area. You'll also find links to walking tours and kids activities, as well as a live cam view of the Inner Harbour.

Monday Magazine. **www.monday.com**
If you want to know what's happening after dark in Victoria, *Monday* magazine's the place to check.

Public Transit. **www.bctransit.com**
An excellent stop for visitors, this site lists all the city's top spots (attractions, museums and galleries, parks and beaches, sports and recreation) and shows how to reach them on public transit, including route maps and schedules. Curiously, though the same company is also in charge of Vancouver's public transit, the Vancouver site (also accessible here) is not nearly as user-friendly.

Royal British Columbia Museum. **rbcm1.rbcm.gov.bc.ca/index.html**
Showcasing the human and natural history of British Columbia, this site offers a preview of what you'll find at the museum. Learn about the exhibits and get the lowdown on visiting in person.

Tourvic.com. **www.tourvic.com**
Though this isn't the best-designed site I've ever seen, it's a decent resource for finding events and entertainment in Victoria. Click on the Calendar of Events for a night-by-night guide of what's on.

✪ **Victoria BC.** **victoriabc.com**
The extensive site has lots of information on all sorts of lodging options (B&Bs, RV parks, vacation rentals), dining, shopping, outdoor activities, attractions, and events. For the full selection of options, see victoriabc.com/sitepage.html. If you're looking for the perfect Web site for planning a trip to Victoria, this is the one.

Victoria Tombstone Tales. **www.oldcem.bc.ca**
A visit to a cemetery is a fascinating way to get a true sense of a place. This online tour of Ross Bay Cemetery offers a unique view into the history of Victoria Island. The lantern-light tours of Victoria's Old Burying Ground are extremely popular.

Other Sites of Interest

Camping. www.camping.bc.ca
If you're interested in camping anywhere in British Columbia, this is the site to check. It contains a wealth of information on all of British Columbia's provincial campgrounds, including details on the area, the amenities offered, and the rates. The "camping tips" page answers all your questions, including those on road conditions and suitability of sites for travelers with disabilities.

Provincial Parks of BC. www.elp.gov.bc.ca/bcparks
On this government site you'll find a detailed description of each provincial park in British Columbia, including information on the flora and fauna, amenities offered, and how to get there.

Sunshine Coast, BC, Canada. www.BigPacific.com
The isolated stretch of coastline just north of Vancouver is known as the Sunshine Coast. Whether that's an apt name is hard to say, but you can learn more about the coast, find out what to do and where to stay (including some quaint B&Bs), and sample some of the outdoor activities listed here.

Tourism Association of Vancouver Island. www.islands.bc.ca
Here's a great place to get free maps and travel brochures ahead of time. Also good accommodations information.

Vancouver Island. www.vancouverislandabound.com
This vacation planner for Vancouver Island provides tons of outdoors and sports information. Whether you want to go scuba diving, whale watching, kayaking, fishing, hiking, windsurfing, or caving, you can find it on this site.

Getting to Know Vancouver

3

Losing yourself wandering around a fascinating new neighborhood is part of the joy of traveling. While that's certainly possible on a metaphorical level in Vancouver, getting physically lost is truly difficult—all you have to do to find your bearings is look up. The mountains are always in sight, and they're always north. If you're facing towards them, east is to your right, west is to your left, and the back of your head is pointing south. That one tip should keep you pointed in the right direction no matter where your exploration of the city takes you. The rest of this chapter offers more detailed information on how to find your way around town.

1 Orientation

ARRIVING

BY PLANE **Vancouver International Airport** is 13 kilometers (8 miles) south of downtown Vancouver on uninhabited Sea Island, bordered on three sides by Richmond and the Fraser River delta. The International Terminal features an extensive collection of First Nations sculptures and paintings set amid grand expanses of glass under soaring ceilings. Turn around and look up or take the up escalator on your right just before you leave the International Terminal to catch a glimpse of Bill Reid's huge jade canoe sculpture, *The Spirit of Haida Gwaii.*

Airport services include restaurants, cocktail lounges, bookstores, newsstands, florists, duty-free shops, food specialty shops, ATMs, currency exchanges, a post office, a barber shop, and hotel reservation telephones. **Tourist Information Kiosks** on Level 2 of the Main and International arrival terminals (☎ **604/303-3601**) are open daily from 8am to 11:30pm.

Parking is available at the airport for both loading passengers and long-term stays (☎ **604/276-6106** for all airport services inquiries). **Courtesy buses** to the airport hotels are available, and a **shuttle bus** links the Main and International terminals to the South Terminal, where smaller and private aircraft are docked.

The airport is easily accessible via three bridges. Travelers heading into Vancouver take the Arthur Laing Bridge, which leads directly to Granville Street, the most direct route to downtown.

There is an international departure surcharge of C$15 (US$10) per person for international air travelers outside of North America, C$10

(US$7) for passengers traveling within North America (including Hawaii and Mexico), and C$5 (US$3.35) for passengers departing on flights within British Columbia or the Yukon.

Leaving the Airport   The pale-green **YVR Airporter** (☎ 604/946-8866) provides **airport bus service** to downtown Vancouver's major hotels. It leaves from Level 2 of the Main Terminal every 15 minutes daily from 6:30am to 10:30pm, and every 30 minutes from 10:30pm until midnight, with a final run at 12:15am. The 30-minute ride to the downtown area whisks you through central Vancouver before taking the Granville Street Bridge into downtown Vancouver. The one-way fare is C$10 (US$7) for adults, C$8 (US$5) for seniors, and C$5 (US$3.35) for children; the round-trip fare is C$17 (US$11) for adults, C$16 (US$11) for seniors, and C$10 (US$7) for children. Bus service back to the airport leaves from selected downtown hotels every half hour between 5:35am and 10:55pm. Scheduled pickups serve the Bus Station, Four Seasons, Hotel Vancouver, Waterfront Centre Hotel, Georgian Court, Sutton Place, Landmark, and others. Ask the bus driver on the way in or ask your hotel concierge for the nearest pickup stop and time.

Getting to and from the airport with public transit is a pain. Buses are slow, and you have to transfer at least once to get downtown. Given that the YVR Airporter bus costs only C$10 (US$7), the hassle probably isn't worth the savings. If you insist, however, bus no. 100 stops at both terminals. At the Granville/West 71st Street stop, get off and transfer to bus no. 8 to downtown Vancouver. BC Transit fares are C$1.75 (US$1.15) during off-peak hours and C$2.50 (US$1.65) during weekdays until 6:30pm. But transfers are free in any direction within a 90-minute period.

The average **taxi** fare from the airport to a downtown Vancouver hotel is approximately C$25 (US$17) plus tip. Because the meter charges for time when the cab is stuck in traffic, and some hotels are closer to the airport than others, the fare can run up to C$40 (US$27). **AirLimo** (☎ 604/273-1331) offers flat-rate stretch-limousine service. AirLimo charges C$29 (US$19) per trip to the airport (not per person), plus tax and tip. The drivers accept all major credit cards.

Most major **car-rental firms** have airport counters and shuttles. Make advance reservations for fast check-in and guaranteed availability—especially if you want a four-wheel-drive vehicle or a convertible (see "Rentals," below).

BY TRAIN & BUS   The main **Vancouver railway station** is at 1150 Station St., near Main Street and Terminal Avenue just south of Chinatown. You can reach downtown Vancouver from there by cab for about C$7 (US$4.70). There are plenty of taxis at the station entrance. One block from the station is the SkyTrain's Main Street Station. Within minutes, you're downtown. The Granville and Waterfront stations are two and four stops away, respectively.

Greyhound Bus Lines and **Pacific Coach Lines** also have their terminals at the Pacific Central Station, 1150 Station St.

For information on arriving **by ferry,** see "Getting to Vancouver," in chapter 2.

VISITOR INFORMATION

TOURIST OFFICES & PUBLICATIONS   The **Vancouver Tourist Info Centre,** 200 Burrard St. (☎ 604/683-2000; www.tourismvancouver.com), is your single best travel information source about Vancouver and the North Shore. If you've ever been to London, you'll be happy to know that Tourism Vancouver is similar to the British Tourist Authority. That means you can buy bus passes and pick up maps, brochures, and travel guides. The staff is outgoing and can be very helpful if you need directions or recommendations. If you have trouble finding accommodations, the office has catalogues of registered hotels and B&Bs; the staff will even make reservations for you. The Info Centre is open from May to Labour Day daily from 8am to 6pm; the rest of the year, it's open Monday to Friday from 8:30am to 5pm, and Saturday from 9am to 5pm.

Tourism Richmond, George Massey Tunnel (☎ **604/271-8280**), has information about the Richmond and Delta area, including the heritage fishing village of Steveston. It's open daily from 9am to 7pm in July and August and daily from 10am to 4pm September through June. The office is located north of the George Massey Tunnel and is easily accessible when driving in from Delta. If you plan to see more of this beautiful province, **Super Natural British Columbia** (☎ **800/663-6000** or 604/663-6000) can help you.

Be sure to pick up a copy of the free weekly tabloid *The Georgia Straight* (☎ **604/730-7000**). It provides up-to-date schedules of concerts, lectures, art exhibits, plays, recitals, and other happenings. The *Straight* can be found all over the city in cafes, bookshops, and restaurants. Equally good—and with dollops more attitude—is the glossy city magazine *Vancouver* (☎ **604/877-7732**). "VanMag," as it's also known, is available on newsstands and on the Web at www.vanmag.com.

Coast: The Outdoor Recreation Magazine (☎ **604/876-4980**) publishes schedules of mountain biking, kayaking, skiing, hiking, and climbing events. Two free monthly tabloids, *BC Parent* (☎ **604/221-0366**) and *West Coast Families* (☎ **604/689-1331**), are geared for families with young children, listing many kid-friendly current events. Gay and lesbian travelers will want to pick up a copy of *Xtra! West* (☎ **604/684-9696**), a free biweekly tabloid available in shops and restaurants throughout the West End.

WEB SITES   See "Planning Your Trip: An Online Directory" following chapter 2.

CITY LAYOUT

With four different bodies of water lapping at its edges and mile after mile of shoreline, Vancouver's geography can seem a bit convoluted. That's part of the city's charm, of course, and visitors normally don't find it too hard to get their bearings. Think of the downtown peninsula as being like an upraised thumb on the mitten-shaped Vancouver mainland. Stanley Park, the West End, Yaletown, and Vancouver's business and financial center are all located on the "thumb," which is bordered to the west by English Bay, to the north by Burrard Inlet, and to the south by False Creek. The mainland part of the city—the mitten—is mostly residential, with a sprinkling of businesses along main arterial streets. Both mainland and peninsula are covered by a simple rectilinear street pattern.

MAIN ARTERIES & STREETS

On the downtown peninsula, there are four key east-west streets. **Robson Street** starts at B.C. Place Stadium on Beatty Street, flows through the West End's more touristed shopping district, and ends at Stanley Park's Lost Lagoon on Lagoon Drive. **Georgia Street**—far more efficient for drivers than the pedestrian-oriented Robson—runs from the Georgia Viaduct on the eastern edge of downtown, through Vancouver's commercial core; it then carries on through Stanley Park and over the Lions Gate Bridge to the North Shore. Three blocks north of Georgia is **Hastings Street,** which begins in the West End, runs east through downtown, and then skirts Gastown's southern border as it runs eastward to the Trans-Canada Highway. **Davie Street** starts at Pacific Boulevard near the Cambie Street Bridge, travels through Yaletown into the West End's more residential shopping district, and ends at English Bay Beach.

Greater Vancouver

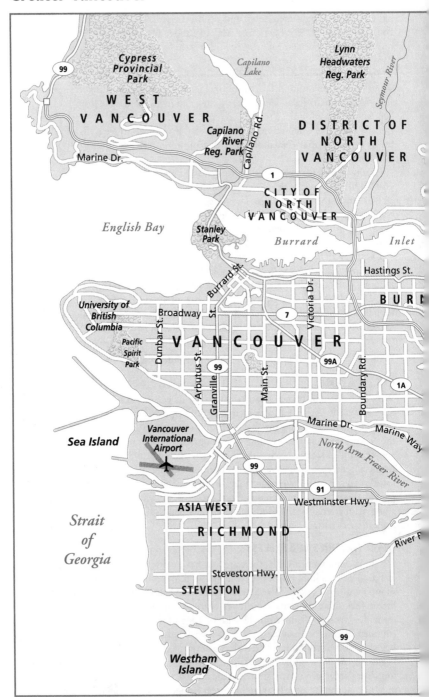

Cypress Provincial Park

Capilano Lake

Lynn Headwaters Reg. Park

Seymour River

99

WEST VANCOUVER

Capilano River Reg. Park

DISTRICT OF NORTH VANCOUVER

Capilano Rd.

Marine Dr.

1

CITY OF NORTH VANCOUVER

English Bay

Stanley Park

Burrard Inlet

Burrard St.

Hastings St.

BUR

University of British Columbia

Broadway

Victoria Dr.

7

Dunbar St.

VANCOUVER

Pacific Spirit Park

Arbutus St.

99

Granville St.

Main St.

99A

Boundary Rd.

1A

Marine Dr.

Marine Way

Sea Island

Vancouver International Airport

99

North Arm Fraser River

91

Westminster Hwy.

Strait of Georgia

ASIA WEST

RICHMOND

River F

Steveston Hwy.

STEVESTON

99

Westham Island

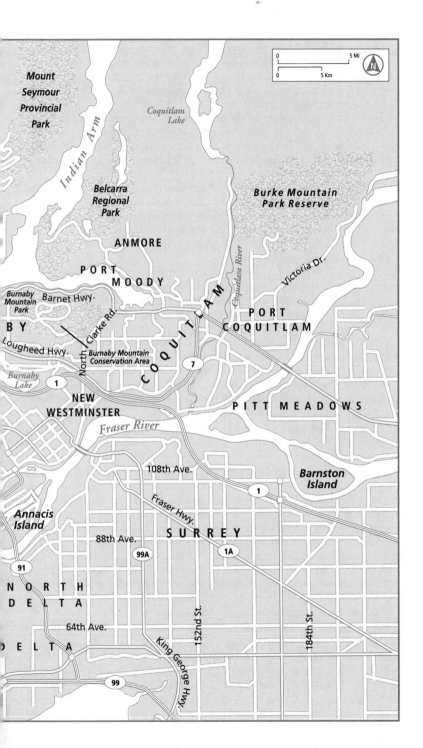

Three **north-south downtown streets** will get you everywhere you want to go in and out of downtown. Two blocks east of Stanley Park is **Denman Street,** which runs from W. Georgia Street at Coal Harbour to Beach Avenue at English Bay Beach. This main West End thoroughfare is where the locals dine out. It's also the shortest north-south route between the two ends of the Stanley Park Seawall.

Eight blocks east of Denman is **Burrard Street,** which starts near the Canada Place Pier and runs south through downtown, crosses the Burrard Street Bridge, and then forks. One branch, still **Burrard Street,** continues south and intersects **W. Fourth Avenue** and **Broadway Avenue** before ending at **W. 16th Avenue** on the borders of Shaughnessy. The other branch becomes **Cornwall Avenue,** which heads due west through Kitsilano, changing its name to **Point Grey Road** and then **N.W. Marine Drive** before entering the University of British Columbia campus.

Granville Street starts near the Waterfront Station on Burrard Inlet and runs the entire length of downtown, crosses the Granville Bridge to Vancouver's West Side, and carries on south across the breadth of the city before crossing the Arthur-Laing Bridge to **Vancouver International Airport.**

On the mainland portion of Vancouver, the city's east-west roads are successively numbered from First Avenue at the downtown bridges to 77th Avenue by the banks of the Fraser River. By far, the most important east-west route is **Broadway** (formerly Ninth Avenue), which starts a few blocks from the University of British Columbia (UBC) and extends across the length of the city to the border of neighboring Burnaby, where it becomes the Lougheed Highway. In Kitsilano, **W. Fourth Avenue** is also an important east-west shopping and commercial corridor. Intersecting with Broadway at various points are a number of important north-south commercial streets, each of which defines a particular neighborhood. The most significant of these streets are (from west to east) **Macdonald Street** in Kitsilano, **Granville Street, Cambie Street, Main Street,** and **Commercial Drive.**

FINDING AN ADDRESS   In many Vancouver addresses, the suite or room number precedes the building number. For instance, 100–1250 Robson St. is Suite 100 at 1250 Robson Street.

In downtown Vancouver, Chinatown's **Carrall Street** is the east-west axis from which streets are numbered and designated. Westward, numbers increase progressively to Stanley Park; eastward, numbers increase heading toward Commercial Drive. For example, 400 W. Pender would be about 4 blocks from Carrall Street heading toward downtown; 400 E. Pender would be 4 blocks on the opposite side of Carrall Street.

Similarly, the low numbers on north-south streets start on the Canada Place Pier side and increase southward in increments of 100 per block (the 600 block of Thurlow Street is 2 blocks from the 800 block) toward False Creek and Granville Island.

Off the peninsula the system works the same, but **Ontario Street** is the east-west axis. Also, all east-west roads are avenues (for example, Fourth Avenue), while streets (for example, Main Street) run exclusively north-south.

STREET MAPS   The Travel Info Centres (see "Visitor Information," above) and most hotels can provide you with detailed downtown maps. A good all-around metropolitan area map is the Rand McNally Vancouver city map, which is available for C$3 (US$2) at the Vancouver Airport Tourism Centre kiosk. If you're an auto-club member, the Canadian Automobile Association (CAA) map is also good. It's not for sale, but is free to both AAA and CAA members and is available at AAA offices across North America. **International Travel Maps and Books,** 552 Seymour St. (☎ **604/ 687-3320**), has the city's most extensive selection of Vancouver and British Columbia maps and specialty guide books.

Neighborhoods in Brief

What's West   The thing to keep in mind, when figuring out what's where in Vancouver, is that this is a city where property is king, and the word "west" has such positive connotations that folks have always gone to great lengths to associate it with their particular patch of real estate. Thus we have the **West End,** and the **West Side,** and **West Vancouver,** which improbably enough is located immediately beside **North Vancouver.** It can be a bit confusing for newcomers, but fortunately each west has its own distinct character. The West End is a high-rise residential neighborhood located on the downtown peninsula. The West Side is one whole half of Vancouver, from Ontario Street west to the University of British Columbia. (The more working-class **East Side** covers the mainland portion of the city, from Ontario Street east to Boundary Road.) Very tony West Vancouver is a city to itself on the far side of Burrard Inlet. Together with its more middle-class neighbor, North Vancouver, it forms an area called the **North Shore.**

Downtown   Vancouver's commercial and office core runs from Nelson Street north to the harbor, with Homer as the eastern edge, and a more ragged boundary running roughly along Burrard Street forming the western border. The truly prime office space is on or near Georgia Street. Howe Street, home of the (in)famous Vancouver Stock Exchange, is the local synonym for flashy and slightly disreputable wealth. Hotels stick mostly to the northern third of downtown, clustering especially thickly near the water's edge. Restaurants are sprinkled throughout. Walking is a good bet for transport downtown, day and night. Unlike many North American cities, there are lots of people living in and around Vancouver's central business district, so the area is always populated.

The West End   A fascinating neighborhood of high-rise condos mixed with old Edwardian homes, the West End has within its borders all the necessities of life: great cafes, good nightclubs, many and varied bookshops, and some of the best restaurants in the city. That so many can live so well in such a small area is partially due to the interesting and eclectic architecture, but mostly it's thanks to the beautiful surroundings—the Pacific Ocean laps against the West End on two sides, Burrard Inlet to the north and English Bay to the south, while Stanley Park occupies the western edge. Burrard Street forms the West End's eastern border.

Gastown   The oldest section of Vancouver, Gastown was named after Vancouver's first settler, riverboat skipper and saloon keeper Jack Deighton, nicknamed "Gassy" thanks to his long-winded habits of speech. It was rebuilt in brick after the 1886 fire wiped out the original wooden city. Gastown's cobblestone streets and late Victorian architecture make it well worth a visit, despite a rather heavy infestation of curio shops and souvenir stands. It lies to the east of downtown, in the six square blocks between Water and Hastings Streets, and Cambie and Columbia Streets.

Chinatown   Located south of Hastings Street, between Gore and Carrall to the east and west, and Keefer Street to the south, Vancouver's Chinatown is not large, but it is intense. Fishmongers stand calling out their wares in Cantonese before a shop filled with crabs, eels, geoducks, and bullfrogs. Elderly Chinese women haggle over produce, while their husbands hunt for deer antler or dried sea horse at a traditional Chinese apothecary. Inside any one of a dozen restaurants, meanwhile, entire extended families—father, mother, grandparents, grown children, and grandkids—sit at a single big round table, consuming a half-dozen plates of succulent Cantonese cooking.

Yaletown   Vancouver's former warehouse district—located below Granville Street and above Pacific Boulevard, from Davie Street over to Smithe Street—Yaletown has long since become an area of apartment lofts, nightclubs, restaurants, high-end furniture shops, and a fledgling multimedia biz. The conversion was less an organic occurrence than a calculated agreement between City Hall and area landowners. It took a long while to work (15 years), but the area is finally coming into its own.

False Creek North (Concorde Pacific)   Stretching along Pacific Boulevard on the north shore of False Creek, Concorde's 30-odd high-rise towers are bright, shiny, and brand-spanking new. Perhaps a bit too new—like a pair of runners that need to lose a little gloss before they'll really be comfortable. The area's worth visiting though, if only to admire one of the largest—and so far most successful—urban redevelopment projects on the continent.

Granville Island   Some 20 years ago, some clever lad in the federal government had the bright idea of redeveloping this former industrial site into something more people-oriented. The result would not be a park, though there are parks on the island. Nor would it be offices, though there are those too. In fact there's a bit of everything, including crafts shops, a boatyard, an art school, a public market, a pair of theaters, a hotel, and several pubs and restaurants. There's even a bit of heavy industry. The result is hard to describe, but well worth a visit. Just don't bring a car. There are 97,000 visitors every day, and only three parking spaces. Or that's what it feels like, anyway.

Kitsilano   Back in the '60s, Kitsilano was Canada's Haight-Ashbury, a slightly seedy enclave of coffeehouses, head shops, and lots of long-haired hippies. Its days as a counterculture hotbed have long since drifted away on a wave of fragrant smoke, but the area—known as Kits—remains one of Vancouver's most popular and sought-after neighborhoods. The attraction is the mixture of affordable apartments and 1920s Craftsman homes, together with funky shops, great restaurants, and pleasant walkable streets. And then, of course, there's Kits Beach, that bastion of bronzed skin and supple spandex. Less sought-after surrounding areas have recently taken to calling themselves "Upper Kits," making a precise definition of Kitsilano's borders problematic. Roughly speaking, Alma Street and Burrard Street form Kitsilano's east and west boundaries, with West 16th Avenue to the south and the ocean to the north.

Shaughnessy   Designed in the 1920s as an enclave for Vancouver's budding elite, Shaughnessy for the longest time refused even to admit that it was part of the city of Vancouver. Even today, traffic is carefully diverted away from the area, and it takes a concerted effort to see the stately homes and monstrous mansions, many of which are now featured in film shoots. To find the neighborhood, look on a map for the area of curvy and convoluted streets between Cypress and Oak Streets and 12th and 32nd Avenues. The center of opulence is the Crescent, an elliptical-shaped street to the southwest of Granville and 16th Avenue.

Richmond   Twenty years ago Richmond was mostly farmland, with a bit of sleepy suburb. Now it's Asia West, an agglomeration of shopping malls geared to the new—read: rich, educated, and successful—Chinese immigrant. The residential areas of the city are not worth visiting (unless tract homes are your thing), but malls like the Aberdeen Mall or the Yao Han Centre are something else. It's like getting into your car in Vancouver and getting out in Singapore.

Steveston   Steveston once existed for nothing but salmon. Located at the southwest corner of Richmond by the mouth of the Fraser River, Steveston was where the boats left to catch the migrating sockeye, returning with loads of fish to be cleaned and canned. In the huge processing plants covering its waterfront, thousands of workers gutted millions of fish. The catch has since declined, and the industry has automated, leaving Steveston a smaller and more pleasant place. The fixed-up waterfront is now an interesting place to stroll. There are public fish sales, a cannery museum, and charter trips up the river or out to the Fraser delta. Above all, there's a pleasant, laid-back, small-town atmosphere.

Commercial Drive   Every immigrant group that ever passed through the city left its mark on the "Drive." First came the Italians—who left quality espresso—then the Portuguese, the Hondurans and Guatemalans, the leftist alternative vegetarians, the artists, and finally the last wave of immigrants, the yuppies. The result is a peculiar but endearing mix: the Italian cafe next to the Marxist bookstore across from the vegetarian deli that has lately taken to selling really expensive yeast-free Tuscan bread.

Punjabi Market   India imported. For reasons still unknown, many of the businesses catering to Vancouver's sizable Punjabi population set up shop on a 4-block stretch of Main Street, from 48th up to 52nd Avenue. The area is best seen during business hours, when the fragrant scent of spices wafts from food stalls, while Hindi pop songs blare from hidden speakers. Young brides hunt through sari shops, or seek out suitable material in discount textile outlets. Shopping here is like sipping from the distilled essence of the Indian subcontinent.

The North Shore (North Vancouver & West Vancouver)   The most impressive thing about the North Shore is its mountain range. Huge, wild, and compellingly beautiful, the mountains are responsible for much of Vancouver's vaunted reputation for physical beauty. They are certainly worth a visit. But the two cities on the North Shore are not without their charms. West Vancouver has the distinction of being the richest city in Canada. That doesn't mean much to visitors, of course, but there are some worthwhile restaurants in the Dundarave area on the West Van waterfront. (Roughly speaking, West Vancouver is everything west of the Lions Gate Bridge.) Better from a visitor's point of view is North Vancouver. It's easily reached by public transit, and the Lonsdale Quay public market—where the SeaBus docks—makes a pleasant afternoon's outing.

2 Getting Around

BY PUBLIC TRANSPORTATION

The **Translink** (otherwise known as BC Transit; ☎ **604/521-0400**; www.translink. bc.ca) system includes electric buses, SeaBus catamaran ferries, and the magnetic-rail SkyTrain. It's an ecologically friendly, highly reliable, and inexpensive system that allows you to get everywhere, including the beaches and ski slopes. Regular service on the main routes runs from 5am to 2am, and less frequent "Owl" service operates on several downtown and suburban routes until 4:20am.

Schedules and routes are available at the Travel Info Centres, at many major hotels, online, and on buses. Pick up a copy of *Discover Vancouver on Transit* at one of the Travel Info Centres (see "Visitor Information," above). This publication gives transit routes for many city neighborhoods, landmarks, and attractions, including numerous Victoria sites.

FARES   Fares are the same for the buses, SeaBus, and SkyTrain. One-way, all-zone fares are C$1.75 (US$1.15) after 6:30pm on weekdays and all day on weekends and holidays. At other times, a one-zone fare costs C$1.75 (US$1.15) and covers the entire city of Vancouver. A two-zone fare—C$2.50 (US$1.65)—is required to travel to nearby suburbs such as Richmond or North Vancouver, while a three-zone fare—C$3.50 (US$2.35)—is required for travel to the far-off edge city of Surrey. Free transfers are available on boarding and are good for travel in any direction and for the SkyTrain and SeaBus, but they do have a 90-minute expiration. **DayPasses,** which are good on all public transit, are C$7 (US$4.70) for adults and C$5 (US$3.35) for seniors, students, and children. They can be used for unlimited travel on weekdays or weekends and holidays. Tickets and passes are available at Travel Info Centres, both SeaBus terminals, convenience stores, drugstores, credit unions, and other outlets displaying the "FareDealer" symbol.

BY SKYTRAIN The SkyTrain is a computerized, magnetic-rail train that services 20 stations along its 35-minute trip from downtown Vancouver east to Surrey through Burnaby and New Westminster.

BY SEABUS The SS *Beaver* and SS *Otter* catamaran ferries annually take more than 700,000 passengers, cyclists, and wheelchair riders on a scenic 12-minute commute between downtown's Waterfront Station and North Vancouver's Lonsdale Quay. On weekdays, a SeaBus leaves each stop every 15 minutes from 6:15am to 6:30pm, then every 30 minutes until 1am. SeaBuses depart on Saturdays every half hour from 6:30am to 12:30pm, then every 15 minutes until 7:15pm, then every half hour until 1am. On Sundays and holidays, runs depart every half hour from 8:30am to 11pm.

BY BUS There are some key routes to keep in mind if you're touring the city by bus: **no. 5** (Robson Street), **no. 22** (Kitsilano Beach to downtown), **no. 50** (Granville Island), **no. 35** or **135** (to the Stanley Park bus loop), **no. 240** (North Vancouver), **no. 250** (West Vancouver–Horseshoe Bay), and buses **no. 4** and **10** (UBC to Exhibition Park via Granville Street downtown). In the summer, the **Vancouver Parks Board** operates a bus route through Stanley Park (☎ **604/257-8400**).

BY TAXI

Cab fares start at C$2.30 (US$1.55) and increase at a rate of C$1.25 (US85¢) per kilometer, plus C30¢ (US20¢) per minute at stoplights. It's a little less than in most other major cities, but it still adds up pretty quickly. In the downtown area, you can expect to travel for less than C$6 (US$4) plus tip. The typical fare for the 13-kilometer (8-mile) drive from downtown to the airport is C$25 (US$17).

Taxis are easy to find in front of major hotels, but flagging one can be tricky. Most drivers are usually on radio calls. But thanks to built-in satellite positioning systems, if you call for a taxi, it usually arrives faster than if you go out and hail one. Call for a pickup from **Black Top** (☎ **604/731-1111**), **Yellow Cab** (☎ **604/681-1111**), or **MacLure's** (☎ **604/731-9211**). **AirLimo** (☎ **604/273-1331**) offers flat-rate stretch limousine service. AirLimo charges C$29 (US$19) per trip to the airport (not per person), plus tax and tip. The drivers accept all major credit cards.

BY CAR

Vancouver has nowhere near the near-permanent gridlock of northwest cities like Seattle, but neither are the roads exactly empty. Fortunately, if you're just sightseeing around town or heading up to Whistler (a car is unnecessary in Whistler), public transit and cabs should see you through. However, if you're planning to visit the North Shore mountains or pursue other out-of-town activities, then by all means rent a car or bring your own. Gas is sold by the liter, averaging around C65¢ (US45¢) per liter. This may seem inexpensive until you consider that a gallon of gas costs about C$2.70 (US$1.80). Also, speeds and distances are posted in kilometers.

RENTALS   Rates vary widely depending on demand and style of car. If you're over 25 and have a major credit card, you can rent a vehicle from **Avis,** 757 Hornby St. (☎ **800/879-2847** or 604/606-2847); **Budget,** 501 W. Georgia St. (☎ **800/ 472-3325,** 800/527-0700, or 604/668-7000); **Enterprise,** 585 Smithe St. (☎ **800/ 736-8222** or 604/688-5500); **Hertz Canada,** 1128 Seymour St. (☎ **800/263-0600** or 604/688-2411); **National/Tilden,** 1130 W. Georgia St. (☎ **800/387-4747** or 604/685-6111); or **Thrifty,** 1015 Burrard St. or 1400 Robson St. (☎ **800/847-4389** or 604/606-1666). These firms all have counters and shuttle service at the airport as well. To rent a recreational vehicle, contact **CC Canada Camper RV Rentals,** 4431 Vanguard Rd., Richmond (☎ **604/270-1833;** www.canada-camper.com). At **Exotic Motorcycle & Car Rentals,** 1820 Burrard St. (☎ **604/644-9128;** www.exoticcars. com), you can rent a Ferrari, Viper, Porsche, Hummer, Jaguar, Lotus, Volkswagen Beetle, or Corvette. A wide selection of Harley-Davidson motorcycles is also available; rental (C$239/US$160 per day) includes helmets, gloves, and leather jackets for two.

PARKING   All major downtown hotels have guest parking; rates vary from free to C$20 (US$13) per day. There's public parking at **Robson Square** (enter at Smithe and Howe Streets), the **Pacific Centre** (Howe and Dunsmuir Streets), and **The Bay** department store (Richards near Dunsmuir Street). You'll also find **parking lots** at Thurlow and Georgia Streets, Thurlow and Alberni Streets, and Robson and Seymour Streets.

Metered **street parking** isn't impossible to come by, but it may take a trip or three around the block to find a spot. Rules are posted on the street and are invariably strictly enforced. (Drivers are given about 2 minute's grace before their cars are towed away when the 3pm no-parking rule goes into effect on many major thoroughfares.) Unmetered parking on side streets is often subject to neighborhood residency requirements. Check the signs. If you park in such an area without the appropriate sticker on your windshield, eventually you'll get ticketed, then towed. If your car is towed away or if you need a towing service and aren't a member of AAA, call **Unitow** (☎ **604/ 251-1255**) or **Busters** (☎ **604/685-8181**).

SPECIAL DRIVING RULES   Canadian driving rules are similar to those in the United States. Stopping for pedestrians is required even outside crosswalks. Seat belts are required. Children under 5 must be in child restraints. Motorcyclists must wear helmets. It's legal to turn right at a red light after coming to a full stop unless posted otherwise. Unlike in the United States, however, daytime headlights are mandatory. Finally, the police have recently discovered the joys of automated ticketing: Photo radar is used extensively in Vancouver, and photo-monitored intersections are quickly coming into vogue. If you speed or go through a red light, you may get an expensive picture of your vacation from the RCMP. Fines start at C$100 (US$67).

AUTO CLUB   Members of the American Automobile Association (AAA) can get assistance from the **Canadian Automobile Association (CAA),** 999 W. Broadway, Vancouver (☎ **604/268-5600,** or for road service 604/293-2222).

BY BIKE

Vancouver is decidedly bicycle-friendly. There are plenty of places to rent a bike along Robson and Denman Streets near Stanley Park. (For specifics, see "Outdoor Activities" in chapter 6.) Bike routes are designated throughout the city. Paved paths crisscross through parks and along beaches (see chapter 6), and new routes are constantly being added. Helmets are mandatory and riding on sidewalks is illegal except on designated bike paths.

Cycling BC (☎ **604/737-3034;** www.cycling.bc.ca) accommodates cyclists on the SkyTrain and buses by providing "Bike & Ride" lockers at all "Park & Ride" parking lots. The department also dispenses loads of information about events, bike touring, and cycle insurance. Many downtown parking lots and garages also have no-fee bike racks.

You can take your bike on the SeaBus anytime at no extra charge. Bikes are not allowed in the George Massey Tunnel, but a tunnel shuttle operates four times daily from mid-May through September to transport you across the Fraser River. From May 1 to Victoria Day (the third weekend of May), the service operates on weekends only.

All the West Vancouver blue buses (including the bus to the Horseshoe Bay ferry terminal) can carry two bikes, first-come, first-served, free of charge. In Vancouver, only a limited number of suburban routes allow bikes on the bus; bus 351 to White Rock, bus 601 to South Delta, bus 404 to the airport, and the 99 Express to UBC.

BY FERRY

Crossing False Creek to Vanier Park or Granville Island on one of the blue miniferries is cheap and fun. The **Aquabus** docks at the foot of Howe Street. It takes you either to Granville Island's public market or east along False Creek to Science World and Stamps Landing. The **Granville Island Ferry** docks at Sunset Beach below the Burrard Street Bridge and the Aquatic Centre. It goes to Granville Island and Vanier Park. Ferries to Granville Island leave every 5 minutes from 7am to 10pm. Ferries to Vanier Park leave every 15 minutes from 10am to 8pm. One-way fares on all routes are $2 (US$1.35) for adults and C75¢ (US50¢) for seniors and children.

Fast Facts: Vancouver

American Express   666 Burrard St. (☎ **604/669-2813**). It's open Monday to Friday from 8am to 5:30pm, Saturday from 10am to 4pm.

Area Codes   The telephone area code for the lower mainland, including greater Vancouver and Whistler, is **604.** The area code for Vancouver Island, the Gulf Islands, and the interior of the province is **250.**

Baby-Sitters   Most major hotels can arrange baby-sitting service and have cribs available. If you need cribs, car seats, play pens, or other baby accessories, **Cribs and Carriages** (☎ **604/988-2742**) delivers them right to your hotel.

Business Hours   Vancouver **banks** are open Monday to Thursday from 10am to 5pm and Friday from 10am to 6pm. Some banks, like Canadian Trust, are also open on Saturday. **Stores** are generally open Monday to Saturday from 10am to 6pm. Last call at the city's **restaurant bars** and **cocktail lounges** is 2am.

Consulates   The **U.S. Consulate** is at 1095 W. Pender St. (☎ **604/ 685-4311**). The British Consulate is at 800–1111 Melville St. (☎ **604/ 683-4421**). The Australian Consulate is at 1225–888 Dunsmuir St. (☎ **604/ 684-1177**). Check the Yellow Pages for other countries.

Currency Exchange   Banks and ATMs have a better exchange rate than most foreign exchange bureaus (the latter charges transaction and service fees). See "Money," in chapter 2.

Dentist   Most major hotels have a dentist on call. **Vancouver Centre Dental Clinic,** Vancouver Centre Mall, 11–650 W. Georgia St. (☎ **604/682-1601**), is another option. You must make an appointment. The clinic is open Monday through Wednesday 8:30am to 6pm, Thursday 8:30am to 7pm, Friday 9am to 6pm, and Saturday 9am to 4pm.

Doctor   Hotels usually have a doctor on call. **Vancouver Medical Clinics,** Bentall Centre, 1055 Dunsmuir St. (☎ 604/683-8138), is a drop-in clinic open Monday to Friday 8am to 4:45pm. Another drop-in medical center, **Carepoint Medical Centre,** 1175 Denman St. (☎ 604/681-5338), is open daily from 9am to 9pm. See also "Emergencies" below.

Electricity   As in the United States, electric current is 110 volts AC (60 cycles).

Emergencies   Dial ☎ 911 for fire, police, ambulance, and poison control.

Hospitals   **St. Paul's Hospital,** 1081 Burrard St. (☎ 604/682-2344), is the closest facility to downtown and the West End. West Side Vancouver hospitals include **Vancouver General Hospital Health and Sciences Centre,** 855 W. 12th Ave. (☎ 604/875-4111), and **British Columbia's Children's Hospital,** 4480 Oak St. (☎ 604/875-2345). In North Vancouver, there's **Lions Gate Hospital,** 231 E. 15th St. (☎ 604/988-3131).

Hot Lines   Emergency numbers include **Crisis Centre** (☎ 604/872-3311); **Rape Crisis Centre** (☎ 604/255-6344); **Rape Relief** (☎ 604/872-8212); **Poison Control Centre** (☎ 604/682-5050); **Crime Stoppers** (☎ 604/669-8477); **SPCA** animal emergency (☎ 604/879-7343); **Vancouver Police** (☎ 604/717-3535); **Fire** (☎ 604/665-6000); and **Ambulance** (☎ 604/872-5151). See also "Emergencies" above.

Internet Access   Free Internet access is available at the Vancouver **public library** Central Branch, 350 W. Georgia St. (☎ 604/331-3600). **Dakoda's Internet Cafe,** 1602 Yew St. (☎ 604/731-5616), is a small pleasant cafe just across from Kits Beach. **Webster's Internet Cafe,** 340 Robson St. (☎ 604/915-9327), is just across from the main public library.

Laundry & Dry Cleaning   **Davie Laundromat,** 1061 Davie St. (☎ 604/682-2717), offers self-service, drop-off service, and dry cleaning. **Metropolitan Laundry & Suntanning,** 1725 Robson St. (☎ 604/689-9598), doesn't have dry-cleaning services, but you can have a cappuccino or work on your tan while you wait.

Liquor Laws   The legal drinking age in British Columbia is 19. Spirits are sold only in government liquor stores, but beer and wine can be purchased from specially licensed, privately owned stores and pubs. There are 22 LCBC (Liquor Control of British Columbia) stores scattered throughout Vancouver. Most are open Monday to Saturday from 10am to 6pm, but some are open to 11pm.

Lost Property   The **Vancouver Police** have a lost-property room (☎ 604/717-2726), open during office hours Monday to Saturday. If you think you may have lost something on public transportation, call **Translink** (BC Transit) during office hours at ☎ 604/682-7887.

Luggage Storage & Lockers   Most downtown hotels will gladly hold your luggage before or after your stay. Just ask at the front desk. Lockers are available at the main Vancouver railway station (which is also the main bus depot), **Pacific Central Station,** 1150 Station St., near Main Street and Terminal Avenue south of Chinatown (☎ 604/661-0328), for C$2 (US$1.35) per day.

Mail   Letters and postcards cost C50¢ (US35¢) to mail outside Canada, C45¢ (US30¢) within Canada, and C90¢ (US60¢) overseas. You can buy stamps and mail parcels at the main post office (see "Post Office," below) or at any of the many postal outlets operating inside drugstores and convenience stores. Look for a POSTAL SERVICES sign. You can mail items at any of the tall, red, rectangular mailboxes every few blocks on the street.

Maps   See "City Layout" earlier in this chapter.

Newspapers & Magazines   The two local papers are the *Vancouver Sun* (published Monday to Saturday) and *The Province* (published Sunday to Friday mornings). The free weekly entertainment paper *The Georgia Straight* comes out on Thursday. Other newsworthy papers are the national *Globe and Mail* or the *National Post,* the *Chinese Oriental Star,* the Southeast Asian *Indo-Canadian Voice,* and the *Jewish Western Daily. Where Vancouver,* a shopping and tourist guide, is usually provided in your hotel room or can be picked up from Tourism Vancouver. See "Visitor Information" earlier in this chapter for more information.

Pharmacies   Shopper's Drug Mart, 1125 Davie St. (☎ **604/685-6445**), is open 24 hours a day. Several Safeway supermarkets have late-night pharmacies, including the one at the corner of Robson and Denman Streets, which is open until midnight.

Police   For emergencies, dial ☎ **911.** Otherwise, the **Vancouver City Police** can be reached at ☎ **604/717-3535.**

Post Office   The **main post office** (☎ **604/662-5722**) is at West Georgia and Homer Streets (349 W. Georgia St.). It's open Monday to Friday from 8am to 5:30pm. Postal outlets are usually open Saturday and Sunday as well as later in the evening and can be found in souvenir stores, 7-11 stores, and drugstores displaying the red-and-white CANADA POST emblem.

Rest Rooms   Hotel lobbies are your best bet for downtown facilities. The shopping centers like Pacific Centre and Sinclair Centre, as well as the large department stores like the Bay, also have rest rooms.

Safety   Overall, Vancouver is a safe city; violent-crime rates are quite low. However, property crimes and crimes of opportunity (such as items being stolen from unlocked cars) do occur with troubling frequency, particularly downtown. Vancouver's Downtown East Side, between Gastown and Chinatown, is a troubled neighborhood and should be avoided at night.

Taxes   Hotel rooms are subject to a 10% tax. The provincial sales tax (PST) is 7% (excluding food, restaurant meals, and children's clothing). For specific questions, call the **B.C. Consumer Taxation Branch** (☎ **604/660-4500**).

Most goods and services are subject to a 7% federal goods and services tax (GST). You can get a refund on short-stay accommodations and all shopping purchases that total at least C$100 (US$67). (This refund doesn't apply to car rentals, parking, restaurant meals, room service, tobacco, or alcohol.) Hotels and the Info Centres can give you application forms. Save your receipts. For details on the GST, call ☎ **800/668-4748** in Canada or 902/432-5608 outside Canada (www.ccra-adrc.gc.ca/visitors).

Telephone   Phones in British Columbia are identical to U.S. phones. The country code is the same as the U.S. code (1). Local calls normally cost C25¢ (US15¢). Many hotels charge up to C$1 (US65¢) per local call and much more for long-distance calls. You can save considerably by using your calling card. You can also buy prepaid phone cards in various denominations at grocery and convenience stores. If you need a cellular phone, **Cell City,** 105–950 W. Broadway (☎ **604/656-2311**), rents them for C$19 (US$13) per day, plus C70¢ (US45¢) per minute, or C$39 (US$26) per week, plus C65¢ (US45¢) per minute.

Time Zone   Vancouver is in the Pacific time zone, as are Seattle and San Francisco. Daylight saving time applies from April through October.

Tipping   Tipping etiquette is the same as in the United States: 15% in restaurants, C$1 (US65¢) per bag for bellboys and porters, and C$1 (US65¢) per day for the hotel housekeeper. Taxi drivers get a sliding-scale tip—fares under C$4 (US$2.70) deserve a C$1 (US65¢) tip; for fares over C$5 (US$3.35), tip 15%.

Weather   Call ☎ **604/664-9010** or 604/664-9032 for weather updates; dial ☎ **604/666-3655** for marine forecasts. Each local ski resort has its own snow report line. Whistler/Blackcomb's is ☎ **604/687-7507.** Cypress Ski area's is ☎ **604/419-7669.**

4 Where to Stay in Vancouver

The past few years have seen a lot of activity in the Vancouver hotel business. Lots of new rooms have opened up, some in the high end, and a lot more in the moderate-to-budget range. Other hotels have undergone extensive renovations, and good-natured competition has flourished among all the city's hostelries. So no matter what your budget, there's no reason to settle for second best. Most of the hotels are in the downtown/Yaletown area, or else in the West End. Both neighborhoods are close to major sites and services. The West Side of Vancouver has a few hotels, plus many pleasant bed-and-breakfasts. Other good accommodations are found across Burrard Inlet on the North Shore.

Whichever area you choose, here are some tips for a more pleasant and possibly more affordable stay:

- Quoted prices don't include the 10% provincial accommodations tax or the 7% goods and services tax (GST). Non-Canadian residents can get a GST rebate on short-stay accommodations by filling out the Tax Refund Application (see "Taxes" under "Fast Facts: Vancouver" in chapter 3).
- The prices listed are the "rack rates"—the one listed on the door and given to the public. Always ask about discounts (senior citizen, corporate, military) or vacation packages, particularly in the October through April low season. A simple inquiry could save you up to 50%. In the summer high season, however, prices are much less flexible.
- Beware the incidentals. Though competition is making the practice less common, many establishments still tack on a $1 surcharge each time you make a local call. To avoid unpleasant surprises, ask beforehand what kind of surcharges exist. If presented with a sizable surcharge bill upon checkout, complain loudly. Local telephone fees have a way of magically evaporating.
- There are only a few small areas to avoid when booking a room. Granville Street offers location without the price, but, though the area has improved considerably, it's still the hangout for panhandling teenagers. Hotels on E. Hastings Street or E. Cordova Street are not worth the savings. These streets are in Vancouver's East Side skid row, which has some of Canada's highest property-crime rates.

Bed & Breakfast Registries

If you prefer to stay in a B&B, the following agencies specialize in matching guests to establishments that best suit their needs:

- **Beachside Bed & Breakfast Registry,** 4208 Evergreen Ave., West Vancouver, B.C. V7V 1H1 (☎ **800/563-3311** or 604/922-7773; www.beach.bc.ca; e-mail: info@beach.bc.ca). Rates average C$125 to C$200 (US$84 to US$134) double or C$250 to C$350 (US$168 to US$235) for a luxury room. Coordinators Gordon and Joan Gibbs arrange accommodations in Vancouver, the North Shore, Parksville, Whistler Mountain, and Victoria, to name just a few places. Joan is one of two B&B registry operators we found who personally inspects every one of the properties she represents. A wide range of accommodations is available, from popular romantic getaways and secluded retreats to cozy homes. Gordon and Joan have run the Beachside Bed & Breakfast for more than 12 years (see "The North Shore (North Vancouver & West Vancouver)," below).

- **Born Free Bed & Breakfast of BC,** 4390 Frances St., Burnaby, B.C. V5C ZR3 (☎ **800/488-1941** or 604/298-8815; www.vancouverbandb.bc.ca; e-mail: vancouverbandb@direct.ca). Norma McCurrach, president and founder of the B.C. Bed & Breakfast Association, regularly represents about 60 properties all across the province. If you provide her with your itinerary and budget for your trip, she will recommend and book all your B&B accommodations ahead of time. As a previous government inspector for B&B accommodations, Norma knows what they are all about and her registry covers budget travel as well as the most lavish and luxurious properties. Norma is usually available daily from 9am to 8pm.

- **Canada-West Accommodations Bed & Breakfast Registry,** P.O. Box 86607, North Vancouver, B.C. V7L 4L2 (☎ **800/561-3223** or 604/990-6730; www.b-b.com; e-mail: ellison@b-b.com). Ellison Massey covers all of British Columbia, including Vancouver, Victoria, Vancouver Island, Kelowna, and Whistler. Also, in Alberta, Ellison can arrange bookings for Jasper, Banff, Calgary, and Edmonton. Rates average C$85 to C$125 (US$57 to US$84) for a double. The registry has more than 100 B&B accommodations, and condos are available in Whistler. All serve a full breakfast, and most have a private guest bathroom.

- **Town and Country Bed & Breakfast,** P.O. Box 74542, 2803 W. Fourth Ave., Vancouver, B.C. V6K IK2 (☎/fax **604/731-5942;** www.townandcountrybedandbreakfast.com). Helen Burich arranges stays in Vancouver, Vancouver Island, and Victoria. Rates average C$75 to C$180 (US$50 to US$121) per night. This is British Columbia's oldest reservation service, representing dozens of host homes. Offerings range from modest houses to lovely heritage homes as well as a couple of cottages and self-contained suites. Helen is often available evenings and weekends.

RESERVATIONS   Reservations are highly recommended from June through September and over the holidays. If you arrive without a reservation or have trouble finding a room, call **Super Natural British Columbia's Discover British Columbia** hot line at ☎ **800/663-6000** or **Tourism Vancouver's** hot line at ☎ **604/683-2000.**

Specializing in last-minute bookings, either organization can make arrangements using its large daily listing of hotels, hostels, and B&Bs.

1 Downtown & Yaletown

All downtown hotels are within 5 to 10 minutes' walking distance of shops, restaurants, and attractions. Hotels in this area lean more toward luxurious than modest, a state of affairs reflected in their prices.

You can reach the downtown hotels by taking the **SkyTrain** to the **Granville** or **Burrard** stops, which are just a few blocks apart. The **Waterfront station** is close to the Pan-Pacific Hotel. The **Stadium station** is just a few blocks from the Georgian Court Hotel, Rosedale on Robson, and the YWCA. The **no. 1 or 5 bus** will take you to the West End hotels; the **no. 4 or 10 bus** will get you to hotels near False Creek.

VERY EXPENSIVE

✪ **Crowne Plaza Hotel Georgia.** 801 W. Georgia St., Vancouver, B.C. V6C 1P7. ☎ **800/663-1111** or 604/682-5566. Fax 604/642-5579. www.hotelgeorgia.bc.ca. E-mail: reservations@hotelgeorgia.bc.ca. 313 units. A/C TV TEL. May–Oct C$299–C$399 (US$200–US$267) double; Nov–Dec C$219–C$279 (US$147–US$187) double; Jan–Apr C$209–C$269 (US$140–US$180) double. Children under 16 stay free in parents' room. AE, CB, DC, DISC, MC, V. Parking C$18 (US$12).

Built in 1927, the Crowne Plaza Hotel Georgia has just recently undergone major renovations to restore it to its 1920s glory. The dark wood–paneled lobby is decorated with brass elevator doors, a black marble fireplace in the cozy sitting area, and original terrazzo tiles. Upstairs, the rooms have custom-designed art deco–style furniture. The rooms are comfortable with adequate workspace, modem access, coffee- and tea-making service, and two phone lines. The entire 12th floor consists of Club Level rooms, well worth the C$30 (US$20) surcharge. In addition to all the standard features, Club Level rooms have CD players, speakerphones, and robes. All Club Level guests also have access to the "Elvis Room" (Elvis stayed in this room when it used to be a suite, hence the blue suede lounge chairs). The rooms include complimentary breakfast, hors d'oeuvres, and drinks in the afternoon, a workstation with computer and office supplies, business publications, and meeting space.

Dining/Diversions: The Casablanca lounge, complete with leopard-skin wallpaper, is open for drinks, light lunches, and snacks. The As Time Goes By restaurant serves breakfast, lunch, dinner, and afternoon tea. Also housed in the hotel is the funky downstairs Chameleon Urban Lounge (see "Vancouver After Dark," chapter 9) and the street-level Georgia Street Bar and Grill.

Amenities: Concierge, 24-hour room service, dry cleaning, laundry service, newspaper delivery, express checkout, valet parking, free coffee, health club, business center, conference rooms, and beauty salon.

✪ **Four Seasons Hotel.** 791 W. Georgia St., Vancouver, B.C. V6C 2T4. ☎ **800/332-3442** in the U.S. or 604/689-9333. Fax 604/684-4555. www.fourseasons.com. 385 units. A/C MINI-BAR TV TEL. C$290–C$450 (US$194–US$302) double, C$340–C$500 (US$228–US$335) junior suite, C$375–C$570 (US$251–US$382) executive suite. Wheelchair-accessible units available. AE, DC, ER, MC, V. Parking C$20 (US$13). Pets are welcome.

This modern 28-story palace sits atop the Pacific Centre's 200 retail stores and is only a few blocks from the financial district. It's a particularly appealing location for both shoppers and business travelers. From the street, the hotel is so well hidden you could walk right past without noticing the enclosed driveway. Once inside, however, you are instantly immersed in understated luxury: wood paneling, Asian accessories, and sub-dued lighting. The guest rooms are tastefully appointed with French provincial furni-ture and marble bathrooms. The rooms aren't large, however, so for more space try a deluxe room on one of the building's corners, a deluxe "Four Seasons" room (they have a separately partitioned sitting area), or a spacious suite or junior suite.

Dining: Chartwell's serves an eclectic blend of continental, West Coast, and Asian dishes. The Garden Terrace and the Terrace Bar offer more casual dining.

Amenities: 24-hour room service, concierge, laundry and valet service, twice-daily housekeeping, limo service. Children get cookies and milk in the evening as well as special room-service menus and terry robes. There's an indoor/outdoor pool, weight and exercise room, whirlpool and saunas, sundeck, florist, and cigar store.

✪ **Hotel Vancouver.** 900 W. Georgia St., Vancouver, B.C. V6C 2W6. ☎ **800/866-5577** or 604/684-3131. Fax 604/662-1929. www.fairmont.com. E-mail: reserve@hvc.cphotels.ca. 556 units. A/C MINIBAR TV TEL. High-season rates C$259–C$489 (US$174–US$328) double, C$419–C$1,899 (US$281–US$1,272) suite. Low-season rates from C$179 (US$120) double, from C$339 (US$227) suite. AE, DC, DISC, MC, V. Parking C$19 (US$13). Small pets are wel-come for a C$25 (US$17) charge.

With a C$65-million renovation completed recently, the grande dame of Vancouver's hotels has been restored beyond her former glory. The Hotel Vancouver evokes a feel-ing of luxury and spaciousness. The bedrooms have marble bathrooms and mahogany furnishings and offer city, harbor, and mountain views. Most of the rooms have been specially equipped for business travelers: dedicated fax and modem lines, speaker-phones, coffeemakers, and desk supplies. The best rooms are on the Entrée Gold floors. Offering upgraded furniture, these rooms include a private concierge, check-in/out service, continental breakfast, free local calls, shoe-shine, and afternoon tea with hors d'oeuvres.

Dining: Serving West Coast cuisine, 900 West is one of Vancouver's best spots for fine dining. Griffins is the casual, brasserie-style restaurant. The Lobby Bar also serves a light menu.

Amenities: 24-hour room service; concierge; valet; laundry; indoor pool; wading pool; Jacuzzi; health club with weight room; sauna; tanning salon; day spa; shops, including Louis Vuitton, Bally, and Aquascutum.

✪ **Metropolitan Hotel Vancouver.** 645 Howe St., Vancouver, B.C. V6C 2Y9. ☎ **800/667-2300** or 604/687-1122. Fax 604/643-7267. www.metropolitan.com. For reservations: reservations@metropolitan.com. 197 units. A/C MINIBAR TV TEL. Apr–Oct C$229–C$385 (US$153–US$258) double; Nov–Mar C$209–C$335 (US$140–US$224) double; C$1,500 (US$1,005) suite. Business Class C$30 (US$20) extra per unit. Children under 18 stay free in parents' room. AE, DC, MC, V. Underground valet parking C$18 (US$12).

The luxurious Metropolitan is centrally situated between the financial district and downtown shopping areas, and caters to business travelers on weekdays. A very clever design has rendered the tiny lobby quite elegant—it's furnished with overstuffed arm-chairs and dominated by a huge, hand-carved, gilded Chinese screen. Most units in the 18-story hotel have small balconies. All rooms have stately dark-wood furnishings, queen-size beds, marble bathrooms, fluffy bathrobes, complimentary in-room coffee, and morning paper delivery. We recommend the studio suites, which are much roomier and only slightly more expensive. Each of the Business Class rooms and stu-dio suites has a fax machine, printer, modem hookup, cordless speakerphone, power strip, and other home-office amenities.

Dining/Diversions: Diva at the Met is one of Vancouver's finest restaurants, serv-ing innovative Pacific Northwest cuisine until 1am; the bar serves excellent martinis.

Downtown Vancouver Accommodations

Barclay House in the West End **10**

Best Western Downtown Vancouver **16**

Blue Horizon **23**

Buchan Hotel **3**

Canadian-Pacific Hotel Vancouver **30**

Coast Plaza at Stanley Park **4**

Days Inn Downtown **26**

Delta Vancouver Suite Hotel **27**

Empire Landmark Hotel & Conference Centre **7**

Executive Inn **14**

Four Seasons Hotel **33**

Georgian Court Hotel **37**

Granville Island Hotel **13**

Hostelling International Downtown **12**

Hotel Georgia **32**

Howard Johnson Hotel **18**

Hyatt Regency Vancouver **29**

Kingston Hotel **34**

Le Soleil (Sheraton Suites) **28**

Listel Vancouver **9**

Metropolitan Hotel Vancouver **31**

Pacific Palisades Hotel **24**

Pan-Pacific Hotel Vancouver **25**

Parkhill Hotel **11**

Quality Hotel Downtown/The Inn at False Creek **15**

Ramada Inn & Suites **17**

Rosedale on Robson Suite Hotel **36**

Rosellen Suites **2**

Sheraton Wall Centre Vancouver **19**

Sunset Inn Travel Apartments **6**

Sutton Place Hotel **22**

Sylvia Hotel **5**

Wedgewood Hotel **20**

West End Guest House **8**

Westin Bayshore **1**

Westin Grand **35**

YMCA **21**

YMCA Hotel/Residence **38**

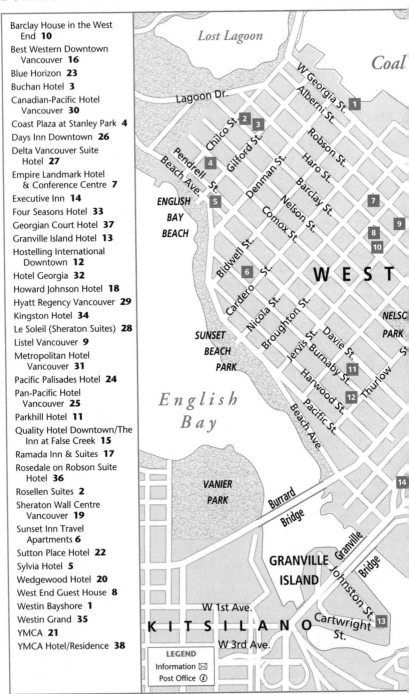

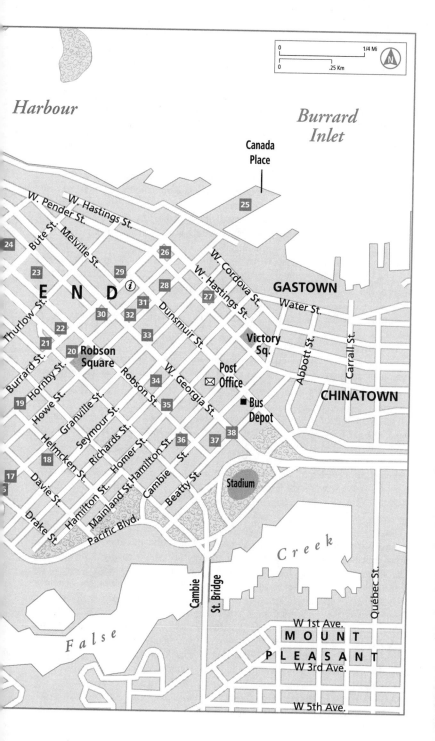

Harbour

Burrard
Inlet

Canada
Place

25

W. Hastings St.

W. Pender St.

Bute St.

Melville St.

24

23

E N D

30

31

32

33

Thurlow St.

22

21

20 Robson
Square

19

Burrard St.

Hornby St.

Howe St.

Granville St.

18

Helmcken St.

17

Davie St.

Drake St.

Hamilton St.

Seymour St.

Richards St.

Homer St.

Hamilton St.

Mainland St.

Robson St.

Dunsmuir St.

W. Cordova St.

W. Hastings St.

26

29

28

27

GASTOWN

Water St.

Victory
Sq.

Abbott St.

Carrall St.

CHINATOWN

Post
Office

Bus
Depot

34

35

W. Georgia St.

Cambie St.

Beatty St.

36

37 38

Stadium

Creek

Pacific Blvd.

Cambie
St. Bridge

False

W 1st Ave.

MOUNT

PLEASANT

W 3rd Ave.

W 5th Ave.

Québec St.

0   1/4 Mi
0   .25 Km

Amenities: Concierge, 24-hour room service, dry cleaning, newspaper delivery, baby-sitting, secretarial services, express checkout, valet parking, courtesy car or limo, free coffee, in-room movies. Facilities include business center, lap pool, health club, Jacuzzi, men's steam room, squash and racquetball courts, saunas, sundeck.

✪ **Pan-Pacific Hotel Vancouver.** 300–999 Canada Place, Vancouver, B.C. V6C 3B5. ☎ **800/937-1515** in the U.S. or 604/662-8111. Fax 604/685-8690. www.panpac.com. E-mail: reservations@panpacific-hotel.com. 504 units. A/C MINIBAR TV TEL. May–Oct C$465–C$545 (US$312–US$365) double; Nov–Apr C$380–C$430 (US$255–US$288) double; C$565–C$3,000 (US$379–US$2,010) suite year-round. AE, DC, DISC, JCB, MC, V. Parking C$21 (US$14).

Apart from Vancouver's natural surroundings, the city's most distinctive landmark is Canada Place Pier. Its five gleaming-white Teflon sails are reminiscent of a giant sailing vessel. Atop this busy complex is a spectacular 23-story hotel. (If you're taking an Alaskan cruise, this is the closest accommodation available.) An escalator lifts arriving guests to the third-floor lobby. The lobby lounge has a full menu, huge picture windows, and a fountain that flows from outside into an ornate channel that runs through the lobby. Upstairs, all of the guest rooms are modern, spacious, and comfortably furnished with soft colors, down duvets on king-size beds, and elegant marble bathrooms. Many of the rooms look out over the harbor and up to the mountains; they have some of the most spectacular views in town.

Dining: Whether you stay here or not, the Five Sails restaurant is worth a visit. It's one of the city's best. (See chapter 5.)

Amenities: 24-hour room service, concierge, valet, limo service. There's an outstanding health club, which guests can use for an additional C$10 (US$7). The outdoor pool and terrace overlook the cruise ships. Wheelchair-accessible rooms are available.

Sheraton Suites Le Soleil-Vancouver. 567 Hornby St., Vancouver, B.C. V6C 2E8. ☎ **604/632-3000.** Fax 604/632-3001. www.lesoleilhotelcom. 122 units. MINIBAR TV TEL. May 1–Oct 15 C$350 (US$235) double, C$400 (US$268) suite, C$600 (US$402) penthouse; Oct 16–Apr 30 $250 (US$168) double, C$300 (US$201) suite, C$500 (US$335) penthouse. AE, DC, ER, MC, V. Valet parking C$20 (US$13).

Stepping into Le Soleil is like entering a European luxury hotel. The uniformed doorman will welcome you into the lobby decorated with crystal chandeliers, Italian marble, plush carpeting, and gilded, vaulted ceilings. The opulence of the hotel can get a bit overwhelming in the narrow guest hallways, where a mix of prints and colors seems, at times, like too much of a good thing. In the suites (all units except 10 doubles are suites), however, the luxury comes off about right. Interiors are decorated in either crimson or gold color schemes, with maple-finished Biedermeier-style furniture. The sitting areas are comfortable; the sofas can convert into beds. As you would expect, all the little touches are there—the fruit plate upon check-in, the turndown service with Godiva chocolates. Rooms also include two-line speakerphones, data ports, cordless phones, in-room safes, and coffee- and tea-makers. Because the hotel is right downtown, nearly all suites feature skyline views—you get to look at surrounding buildings. However, for good views, not to mention ultimate luxury, you could try one of the Penthouse suites. The Versace-inspired bedroom-and-den Penthouse has a black Jacuzzi tub in the living room and 18-foot floor-to-ceiling windows.

Dining: The Oritalia restaurant serves up Italian-inspired West Coast fusion.

Amenities: 24-hour room service, concierge, twice-daily maid service, business center, health-club facilities available nearby.

The Sutton Place Hotel. 845 Burrard St., Vancouver, B.C. V6Z 2K6. ☎ **800/961-7555** or 604/682-5511. Fax 604/682-5513. www.suttonplace.com. E-mail: info@vcr.suttonplace.com. 397 units. A/C MINIBAR TV TEL. Nov–Apr C$189–C$299 (US$127–US$200) double, C$289–C$1,500 (US$194–US$1,005) suite; May–Oct C$269–C$439 (US$180–US$294) double, C$375–C$1,700 (US$251–US$1,139) suite. AE, CB, DC, DISC, ER, JCB, MC, V. Underground valet parking C$17 (US$11). Pets accepted C$150 (US$100), non-refundable, per stay.

Don't let the big pink hospital-like exterior fool you. Once you enter the lobby of this centrally located five-diamond hotel, it's pure luxury. The grand lobby is elegantly decorated with beige marble, fresh flowers, chandeliers, and European artwork. All standard rooms are tastefully decorated in a classic European style with a maroon and gold color scheme. In-room amenities include bathrobes, ice dispensers, minibars, umbrellas, newspapers, and desks with data ports and two phone lines. The one- or two-bedroom junior suites have a small parlor. In larger suites, double French doors separate the bedroom from the large sitting area.

Your four-legged furry friend will also receive five-diamond treatment at the Sutton Place: Your pet will be registered and photographed at the Sit & Stay check-in while all its pet-icular preferences are noted. For C$95 (US$64), you can purchase the VIP program which comes with gourmet dinner (T-bone or seared fresh tuna) and turn-down service with doggie treats.

Dining/Diversions: The Fleuri Restaurant serves three meals daily, Sunday jazz brunch, and a seafood buffet on Friday and Saturday evenings. It also features an extensive "chocoholic" dessert bar Thursday to Saturday evenings. La Promenade offers light snacks and live piano music. The dark wood–paneled Gerard Lounge has oversized armchairs, a fireplace, and light snacks.

Amenities: Concierge, 24-hour room service, dry cleaning, laundry service, newspaper delivery, in-room massage, twice-daily maid service, baby-sitting, secretarial services, express checkout, valet parking, courtesy car and limo, free coffee and refreshments, video rentals, bike rental, indoor heated pool, children's programs, health club, Jacuzzi, sauna, sundeck, business center, conference rooms, and tour desk.

EXPENSIVE

Delta Vancouver Suite Hotel. 550 W. Hastings St., Vancouver, B.C. V6B 1L6. ☎ **800/268-1133** or 604/689-8188. Fax 604/605-8881. www.deltahotels.com. E-mail: vancouversuite@deltahotels.com. 226 units. A/C MINIBAR TV TEL. Jan–Apr C$185–C$370 (US$124–US$248) double; May–Oct C$245–C$400 (US$164–US$268) double; Nov–Dec C$195–C$370 (US$131–US$248) double. Children under 18 stay free in parents' room. AE, CB, DC, JCB, MC, V. Valet parking C$15 (US$10).

The Delta Vancouver Suite Hotel considers itself a Manhattan-style hotel. The spacious and bright lobby is decorated with black marble, cherry-colored wood, and stone white walls. The indoor atrium extends up to the third floor and connects to Simon Fraser University's conference space in the adjacent building. Note that none of the suites have kitchen facilities. Each suite does have a living room and bedroom with either queen, king, or two double beds. The layout allows for a lot of natural light and, wherever possible, floor-to-ceiling windows. For more comfort, ask for a suite with a sofa, chair, and ottoman; some suites only come with two chairs. Designed for business travelers, the rooms provide a large workspace, with voice mail, two phone lines, and speakerphone. Internet access is available in the room for a maximum of C$10 (US$7) for 24 hours. The top three floors are reserved for Signature Club guests. The C$30 (US$20) premium upgrades you to a great view, down duvets, CD players, and access to the Signature Lounge with complimentary breakfast and afternoon cocktails.

Dining: Manhattan, located on the first floor, is becoming popular with the lunch crowd from the surrounding offices. It's open for breakfast, lunch, and dinner.

Amenities: Indoor pool, fitness center with sauna and whirlpool, full-service business center.

✪ **Georgian Court Hotel.** 773 Beatty St., Vancouver, B.C. V6B 2M4. ☎ **800/663-1155** or 604/682-5555. Fax 604/682-8830. www.georgiancourt.com. E-mail: info@georgiancourt. com. 180 units. A/C MINIBAR TV TEL. May 1–Oct 15 C$210–C$275 (US$141–US$184) double; Oct 16–Apr 30 C$125–C$215 (US$84–US$144) double. AE, CB, DC, MC, V. Parking C$8 (US$5).

This modern, 14-story brick hotel is extremely well located—it's a block or two from B.C. Place Stadium, G.M. Place Stadium, the Queen Elizabeth Theatre, the Playhouse, and the Vancouver Public Library, making it ideal for sports fans, trade-show attendees, and culture vultures. The guest rooms are large and attractively decorated with crown moldings and wooden baseboards. Especially welcome for business travelers, each room comes equipped with a writing desk, cordless phone, three phone lines, and voice mail.

Dining/Diversions: The William Tell Restaurant serves classic Swiss dishes prepared by 1995 Restaurateur of the Year Erwin Doebeli (see chapter 5). If you don't have tickets to a local game, you can always catch the action on one of 15 televisions in the Beatty St. Bar & Grill.

Amenities: Concierge, room service until 11pm, dry cleaning, laundry service, newspaper delivery, baby-sitting, secretarial services. A small health club is equipped with weights, LifeCycle, StairMaster, whirlpool, and sauna.

Hyatt Regency Vancouver. 655 Burrard St., Vancouver, B.C. V6C 2R7. ☎ **800/233-1234** or 604/683-1234. Fax 604/643-5812. www.hyatt.com. 644 units. A/C MINIBAR TV TEL. Apr 16–Oct 31 C$230–C$465 (US$154–US$312) double; Nov 1–Apr 15 C$119–C$320 (US$80–US$214) double. C$680–C$1,250 (US$456–US$838) suite. Regency Club rooms C$50 (US$34) extra. Weekend discounts available. AE, DC, DISC, ER, JCB, MC, V. Parking C$19 (US$13).

The Hyatt is an ultramodern white tower built over the huge Royal Centre Mall, which contains 60 specialty shops. The chandeliered atrium lobby reflects Vancouver's verdant outdoors, filled with trees and flower beds in marble planters. The very large guest rooms are tastefully decorated with understated yet comfortable furnishings. Corner rooms on the north and west sides have balconies with lovely views. Rooms on the Regency Club floors have a separate keyed elevator, concierge, continental breakfast, 5pm hors d'oeuvres service, and evening pastries, coffee, tea, and soda in a private lounge with a stereo and large-screen TV.

Dining/Diversions: Fish and Co. offers upscale seafood and continental cuisine at lunch and dinner and a Sunday brunch buffet. The Café serves casual breakfast and lunch. Peacocks Lounge offers an à la carte menu. The Gallery Bar serves a weekly lunch buffet and features big-screen sports.

Amenities: Room service, concierge, laundry, valet service, doctor and dentist on call, in-room coffeemaker, in-room iron and ironing board, heated outdoor pool, health club, saunas, access to squash and racquetball courts, business center, 26 meeting rooms.

✪ **The Sheraton Vancouver Wall Centre Hotel.** 1088 Burrard St., Vancouver, B.C. V6Z 2R9. ☎ **800/325-3535** or 604/331-1000. Fax 604/331-1001. www.sheratonvancouver. com. 735 units. A/C MINIBAR TV TEL. Oct 23–May 14 C$129–C$249 (US$86–US$167) double, C$179–C$399 (US$120–US$267) suite; May 15–Oct 22 C$199–C$399 (US$133–US$267) double, C$249–C$549 (US$167–US$368) suite. AE, DC, MC, V. Valet parking C$19 (US$13).

The Wall Centre is hard to miss. Look for the towering two-tone oval spire, the result of a strange compromise between city hall—which wanted the tower to have clear glass—and the developer, who preferred his glass opaque and black. Set together with two other sizable towers on one of the downtown area's highest points, the Wall Centre is development mogul Peter Wall's personal tribute to everything he's ever liked in the world's finest accommodations.

The opulent decor would not look out of place in a modern-art gallery, from the lobby's gold-leaf staircase, custom-designed furniture, and handblown glass chandeliers, to the half dozen peepholes on each guest room door. The guest rooms are elegantly appointed with blond wood furnishings, luxury bathrooms, heated floors, and king-size or double beds with down duvets and Egyptian cotton sheets. Every room has stunning floor-to-ceiling windows. In-room amenities include video checkout in five languages, in-room safes, and three two-line phones. For an additional C$25 to C$40 (US$17 to US$27) fee, you can upgrade to one of the 25th- or 26th-floor Crystal Club rooms, which brings added room amenities as well as access to the two-level Crystal Club lounge. Not only does the lounge serve complimentary breakfast and afternoon appetizers and drinks, it is also one of the nicest spaces to relax, with comfortable sitting areas and a north-facing (mountain view) terrace.

Dining/Diversions: Indigo features innovative West Coast cuisine in modern decor. Patio seating is also available. The hotel's bar, Cracked Ice, offers deep club chairs, an intimate atmosphere, and a lighter menu.

Amenities: Concierge, 24-hour room service, dry cleaning, laundry service, newspaper delivery, in-room massage service available, baby-sitting, secretarial services, express checkout, valet parking, courtesy car or limo, indoor heated pool, health club, Jacuzzi, sauna, business center, conference rooms, beauty salon.

✪ **Wedgewood Hotel.** 845 Hornby St., Vancouver, B.C. V6Z 1X1. ☎ **800/663-0666** or 604/ 689-7777. Fax 604/608-5349. www.wedgewoodhotel.com. E-mail: info@wedgewoodhotel. com. 89 units. A/C MINIBAR TV TEL. C$200–C$380 (US$134–US$255) double, C$480 (US$322) suite, C$680 (US$456) penthouse. AE, CB, DC, DISC, JCB, MC, V. Underground valet parking C$15 (US$10).

The romance, elegance, and opulence of this European-style hotel are personal touches created by owner and general manager Ileni Skalbania. In 1984 she acquired the failing 13-story Mayfair Hotel, and then completely gutted and rebuilt the interior, furnishing the public spaces with many pieces from her own art and antiques collection. The result is a four-diamond hotel with an eclectic decor that blends French Provincial, Italianate, and Edwardian styles. On weekdays, the hotel draws a corporate crowd. On weekends, it's transformed into a romantic getaway. All guest rooms have balconies with flower beds overlooking Robson Square. Terry robes, room-darkening drapes, a morning paper, and a box of chocolates are just a few of the hotel's special touches.

Dining/Diversions: Bacchus Restaurant, well known for its fine dining, recently hired chef Robert Sulatycky, who specializes in modern French cuisine. The Bacchus Lounge features live jazz Monday to Saturday nights (see chapter 9). The restaurant also serves breakfast, lunch, afternoon tea (Saturday and Sunday from 2 to 4pm), cocktails, and snacks.

Amenities: Concierge, 24-hour room service, dry cleaning, laundry service, newspaper delivery, in-room massage service available, twice-daily maid service, baby-sitting, secretarial services, express checkout, valet parking, health club, sauna, business center, conference rooms.

⚫ **The Westin Grand.** 433 Robson St., Vancouver, B.C. V6B 6L9. ☎ **888/680-9393** or 604/602-1999. Fax 604/647-2502. www.westingrandvancouver.com. E-mail: play@ westingrandvancouver.com. 207 suites. A/C MINIBAR TV TEL. May 16–Oct 14 C$199–C$349 (US$133–U$234) suite. Oct 15–May 15 C$149–C$299 (US$100–US$200) suite. Children under 17 stay free in parents' room. AE, DC, DISC, JCB, MC, V. Parking: C$15 (US$10) self, C$19 (US$13) valet.

Showbiz can be such a headache. The luxurious Westin Grand opened in April 1999, right next to Vancouver's new Broadway-style music hall, the Ford Centre for the Performing Arts. The location was considered a key selling feature—the building itself was shaped to look like a grand piano. Unfortunately, shortly after the Grand opened, Livent—the company producing the musicals—went bankrupt, leaving the Grand all alone. Fortunately, the fundamentals are still good. The Grand is also across from the public library (could have shaped the hotel like a great big book, eh guys?) and within easy walking distance of Yaletown, GM Place, and the Robson shopping area. The 207 spacious suites are brightened by lots of natural light and decorated in mahogany and elegant earth tones. Sitting rooms come with a kitchenette tucked away behind the blond wood cabinet doors (no stove, but a microwave, toaster, coffee/tea maker, mini-dishwasher, and all utensils). Bedrooms have either queen or king beds, and for the corporate traveler there are big work spaces, data ports, and lots of electrical plugs. Some 40 of the Guest Office suites also have speakerphones, cordless phones, and combo fax/laser printer/photocopiers. Rooms for travelers with disabilities include safety bars in the bathroom, handheld showers, and safety/emergency flashing lights.

Dining/Diversions: The Aria restaurant has received great reviews from local food critics and Club Voda offers live and canned music.

Amenities: 24-hour room service, outdoor pool, sundeck, Jacuzzi, health club, business center, meeting rooms, valet parking.

MODERATE

Best Western Downtown Vancouver. 718 Drake St., Vancouver, B.C. V6Z 2W6. ☎ **888/ 669-9888** or 604/660-9888. Fax 604/669-3440. www.bestwesterndowntown.com. E-mail: welcome2@bestwesterndowntown.com. 143 units. A/C TV TEL. C$139–C$209 (US$93–US$140) double, C$280–C$350 (US$188–US$235) penthouse. AE, DC, DISC, MC, V. Parking C$5 (US$3.35).

The 12-story Best Western is located on Granville and Drake, a 5-block walk from the theater area on Granville Street at the south end of downtown. Of the 143 rooms, 32 have full kitchens, available for an additional C$20 to C$25 (US$13 to US$17). The rooms are comfortable; the corner rooms are a bit smaller than the rest, but they do have more light. Some rooms have harbor views. This hotel is not overflowing with facilities, but the rooms are well furnished and the location is convenient. If you need a workspace, ask for a corporate room, which includes a full-size desk and activities table. All rooms have voice-mail phones and data ports. In addition, there's a rooftop exercise room, game area, Ping-Pong table, VCR and movies, sauna, Jacuzzi, and sundeck. Complimentary deluxe continental breakfast is served in the breakfast lounge in the lobby.

Days Inn Downtown. 921 W. Pender St., Vancouver, B.C. V6C 1M2. ☎ **800/329-7466** or 604/681-4335. Fax 604/681-7808. www.daysinnvancouver.com. E-mail: welcome2@ daysin-van.com. 85 units. TV TEL. May–Oct C$149–C$189 (US$100–US$127) double, C$209 (US$140) suite; Nov–Apr C$105–C$125 (US$70–US$84) double, C$155 (US$104) suite. AE, CB, DC, DISC, JCB, MC, V. Valet parking C$10 (US$7).

Situated in a heritage building dating back to 1910, Days Inn Downtown provides a central location for exploring Vancouver. The building is well maintained—all the

⊕ Family-Friendly Hotels

Vancouver hotels offer a wide range of choices if you're bringing your kids, and you don't have to sacrifice service or quality. To add to their appeal, a lot of the downtown hotels offer baby-sitting.

Four Seasons Hotel *(see page 60)*   Kids get cookies and milk in the evening as well as special room-service menus and warm terry robes.

Westin Bayshore *(see page 73)*   Its Coal Harbour location makes this a great family hotel. Guests can walk to Stanley Park, the Vancouver Aquarium, the Nature House, and other park attractions without even crossing a street.

Quality Hotel Downtown/The Inn at False Creek *(see page 69)*   Family suites in this hotel are spacious and well designed. Some upper-floor suites even have glass-enclosed balconies. The full kitchen facilities, casual restaurant, and off-season "Adventure Passport" discounts also make this an excellent deal for families.

Rosellen Suites *(see page 75)*   This is the perfect place if you're looking for a homelike atmosphere in fully equipped apartment accommodations. It's conveniently located near grocery shopping and play areas. Stanley Park, the beaches, and Denman Street are only a block away.

rooms were refurbished in 1998, and the lobby underwent complete renovations in the summer of 1999. For travelers who don't need all the amenities of a large hotel, these rooms are comfortable and simply furnished. Each has a minifridge, ceiling fan, desk, data port, voice mail, and safe. Ten of the rooms have stand-up showers only. Rooms facing east stare directly at the concrete walls of the building next door, so ask for a water view or consider a harbor-facing suite. The Chelsea Restaurant serves three meals daily. The English-pub–style Bombay Bicycle Club lounge and the Bull and Bear Sports Lounge—featuring a large-screen TV—are popular spots with local businesspeople. Facilities include a coin laundry and refrigerators. The front desk will provide photocopying, faxing, and secretarial services for a nominal charge.

The Executive Inn. 1379 Howe St., Vancouver, B.C. V6Z 2R5. ☎ **800/570-3932** or 604/688-7678. Fax 604/688-7679. www.executiveinnhotels.com. 134 units. A/C TV TEL. May–Oct C$179 (US$120) standard double, C$199 (US$133) deluxe double, C$295 (US$198) 1-bedroom suite, C$395 (US$265) 2-bedroom suite; Nov–Apr C$119 (US$80) standard double, C$139 (US$93) deluxe double, C$255 (US$171) 1-bedroom suite, C$355 (US$238) 2-bedroom suite. AE, DC, MC, V. Parking C$6 (US$4).

Located at the on-ramp to the Granville Street Bridge, next to the Inn at False Creek, The Executive Inn lacks a bit of character. The hotel focuses mainly on business travelers. The rooms are well furnished, with lots of light, as many have floor-to-ceiling windows. Desks, data ports, safes, and sitting areas are standard in all rooms. For rooms with a view, ask for south or southwest facing rooms looking towards English Bay. The one- and two-bedroom suites are excellent, containing all the conveniences of an apartment: comfortable furniture, TV, VCR, stereo with CD player, dining area, full luxury kitchen, large storage space, in-suite laundry, Jacuzzi tub, desk, and separate bedroom. The hotel also has an in-house business center, fitness center, laundry, restaurant, and lounge.

✪ **Quality Hotel Downtown/The Inn at False Creek.** 1335 Howe St. (at Drake St.), Vancouver, B.C. V6Z 1R7. ☎ **800/663-8474** or 604/682-0229. Fax 604/662-7566. www. qualityhotelvancouver.com. E-mail: quality@qualityhotelvancouver.com. 157 units. A/C TV TEL. May 1–Oct 12 C$169 (US$113) double, C$189–C$209 (US$127–US$140) suite; Oct

13–Apr 30 C$99 (US$66) double, C$99–C$109 (US$66–US$73) suite. AE, CB, DC, DISC, ER, MC, V. Parking C$8 (US$5).

Strange to have a hotel with a Tex-Mex theme in Vancouver, but surprisingly, it works. The Inn at False Creek is a boutique hotel decorated with Mexican art, pottery, and rugs, all in a kind of Santa Fe style. Room decor consists of dark green, terra-cotta, and earth tones, and brick for a touch of authenticity. The spacious suites are great for families—15 have full kitchens and a number of others have glassed-in balconies, which double as enclosed play areas (the hotel staff keeps a supply of board games and puzzles behind the front desk). Rooms on the back side are preferable because the hotel is situated beside the Granville Bridge on-ramp. The traffic noise is minimized in the front, however, by double-pane windows and dark-out curtains. In the low season, the hotel's "City Passport" entitles guests to two-for-one discounts at numerous attractions, theaters, and restaurants.

On the lobby level, the Creekside Café serves decent basics at reasonable prices throughout the day; the Sports Lounge offers a relaxed atmosphere, friendly service, and a full bar. The hotel has laundry and valet services. There's an outdoor pool, plus you have complimentary use of the extensive fitness facilities at Fitness World, a block away.

Rosedale on Robson Suite Hotel. 838 Hamilton (at Robson St.), Vancouver, B.C. V6B 6A2. ☎ **800/661-8870** or 604/689-8033. www.rosedaleonrobson.com. E-mail: reserve@direct.ca. 275 units. A/C TV TEL. May–Sept C$205–C$285 (US$137–US$191) suite; Oct–Apr C$125–C$185 (US$84–US$124) suite. Additional adult C$20 (US$13). Kitchen utensils C$5 (US$3.35). AE, DC, ER, JCB, MC, V. Parking C$8 (US$5).

The Rosedale has a tower capped by a 15-foot-tall rose emblem and is located directly across the street from Library Square. Guests arrive through a covered driveway and are welcomed in a large marble lobby. The one- and two-bedroom suites feature separate living rooms, two TVs each, and full kitchenettes equipped with microwaves, stoves, ovens, sinks, and half-size refrigerators. Dishes and cooking utensils are available on request. The rooms are rather small, but ample bay windows and light wood furnishings create a feeling of spaciousness. Corner suites have more windows. Upper-floor suites have furnished terraces and great city views. Guests on executive floors get bathrobes, free local calls, a daily newspaper, nightly turndown service, in-room movies, Nintendo games, and modem and fax access lines. This end of Robson Street is a few minutes' stroll from most shops and restaurants, and the Pacific Centre Mall, Library Square, the Queen Elizabeth Theatre, and B.C. Place and General Motors Place stadiums are only a block or two away.

Rosie's is a New York-style deli (without the attitude, of course). It's a rarity in this city filled with West Coast and Pacific Northwest cuisine. There's also a lounge off the lobby. The hotel also has an indoor pool, a Jacuzzi, a sauna, a weight- and exercise-room, and a gift shop.

INEXPENSIVE

The Howard Johnson Hotel. 1176 Granville St., Vancouver, B.C. V6Z 1L8. ☎ **888/ 654-6336** 604/688-8701. Fax 604/688-8335. www.hojovancouver.com. E-mail: info@ hojovancouver.com. A/C TV TEL. May 1–Oct 15 C$129–C$149 (US$86–US$100) double, C$149–C$169 (US$100–US$113) suite; Oct 16–Apr 30 C$69–C$89 (US$46–US$60) double, C$99–C$119 (US$66–US$80) suite. Children under 17 stay free in parents' room. AE, MC, V. Parking C$6 (US$4).

Yet another sign of south Granville's rapid gentrification, this formerly down-at-the-heels hotel was bought, gutted, renovated, and reopened in 1998 with an eye to the budget-conscious traveler. Hallways are decorated with photographs of Vancouver's early days, while the rooms themselves are comfortably if simply furnished. Some rooms have mini-kitchenettes, and the suites provide sofa beds, convenient for those traveling with children. If you need a desk, fax machine, and e-mail and Internet access, book a home-office suite. A continental breakfast is included and served in the lounge on the mezzanine. The hotel also houses the Lava Lounge, a popular gay Vancouver nightspot.

The Kingston Hotel. 757 Richards St., Vancouver, B.C. V6B 3A6. ☎ **604/684-9024.** Fax 604/684-9917. www.kingstonhotelvancouver.com. 57 units, 9 with bathroom and TV TEL. C$55–C$105 (US$37–US$70) double. Extra person C$10 (US$7). Continental breakfast included. AE, MC, V. Parking C$10 (US$7) per day, half a block away.

An affordable downtown hotel is a rarity for Vancouver. If all you need is a clean and comfortable place to sleep and a cup of coffee and breakfast to start your day, then the Kingston is your place. Called a European-style hotel, it is indeed reminiscent of the small Parisian or Roman pensiones: no elevators, very small rooms, and only nine of the 57 rooms have private bathrooms and TVs. The rest have hand basins and the use of shared shower and toilets on each floor. However, you will not find a cheaper hotel so close to all the downtown action.

The Ramada Inn and Suites. 1221 Granville St., Vancouver, B.C. V6Z 1M6. ☎ **888/ 835-0078** or 604/685-1111. Fax 604/685-0707. www.ramadavancouver.com. E-mail: ramada@intergate.bc.ca. 133 units. TV TEL. May–June C$99–C$129 (US$66–US$86) double; July–Sept C$125–C$169 (US$84–US$113) double; Oct–Apr C$69–C$99 (US$46–US$66) double. Suites cost C$20–C$40 (US$13–US$27) more than a standard room. AE, MC, V. Valet parking C$10 (US$7). Pets are welcome.

The Ramada was recently converted from a rooming house into a tourist hotel. The bright lobby and the guest rooms are all decorated in an art deco theme. The rooms are pleasant, with dark wood furniture, everything very new. Small desks, TV, and a coffee/tea maker are standard in all. Suites feature a pull-out sofa bed, kitchenette, and small dining area, making them very attractive for families. The location is convenient for exploring downtown and Yaletown, as well as hopping over to Granville Island or Kitsilano. A restaurant and Irish pub are located downstairs.

YMCA. 955 Burrard St., Vancouver, B.C. V6Z 1Y2. ☎ **604/681-0221.** Fax 604/681-1630. www.ymca.vancouver.bc.ca. E-mail: vancouver.hotel@vanymca.org. 113 units, all with shared bathroom. May–Sept C$59 (US$40) double; Oct–Apr C$49 (US$33) double. Cot C$8 (US$5) extra. MC, V. Parking C$6 (US$4).

Male and female guests here are mostly a mixture of new arrivals, businesspeople with limited expense accounts, and budget-minded travelers seeking an alternative to youth hostels. The building is not nearly as new as the YWCA, but it's as conveniently located. Rooms are small, simply furnished, and spotless. Some include private TVs for C$2 (US$1.35) extra. The bathrooms are shared, as are the pay phones. Guests have use of the extensive facilities, including two swimming pools, LifeCycles, Nautilus and Universal equipment, a rooftop running track, racquetball courts, and a coin laundry. The restaurant, Jonathan T's, is open Monday to Saturday for breakfast and lunch. No alcoholic beverages are permitted in the building. The facility is not wheelchair accessible.

✪ **The YWCA Hotel/Residence.** 733 Beatty St., Vancouver, B.C. V6B 2M4. ☎ **800/ 663-1424** or 604/895-5830. Fax 604/681-2550. www.ywcahotel.com. E-mail: hotel@ywcavan. org. 155 units, 53 with bathroom. A/C TEL. C$68–C$88 (US$46–US$59) double with shared bathroom; C$74–C$112 (US$50–US$75) double with private bathroom. Weekly, monthly, group, and off-season discounts available. AE, DC, MC, V. Parking C$5 (US$3.35) per day.

Built in 1995, this attractive 12-story residence is next door to the Georgian Court Hotel. It's an excellent choice for male and female travelers as well as families with limited budgets. Bedrooms are simply furnished; some have TVs. There are quite a few reasonably priced restaurants nearby (but none in-house). All guest rooms do have mini-refrigerators, and three communal kitchens are available for guests' use. (There are a number of small grocery stores nearby, as well as a Save-On Foods Supermarket, a 10-minute walk west on Davie Street.) There are also three TV lounges, a coin laundry, and free access to the best gym in town at the nearby co-ed YWCA Fitness Centre.

2 The West End

About a 10-minute walk from the downtown area, the West End's hotels are nestled amid the tree-lined residential streets bordering Stanley Park, within close proximity to Robson Street's many shops, restaurants, and attractions, as well as the natural beauty of the park itself and the surrounding beaches. Though there are fewer hotels here than downtown, there's a wider variety of accommodations.

EXPENSIVE

Empire Landmark Hotel & Conference Centre. 1400 Robson St., Vancouver, B.C. V6G 1B9. ☎ **800/830-6144** or 604/687-0511. Fax 604/687-2801. www.asiastandard.com. E-mail: ehlsales@asiastandard.com. 357 units. A/C TV TEL. C$210–C$240 (US$141–US$161) double. AE, CB, DC, JCB, MC, V. Parking C$7 (US$4.70).

If you are looking for a room with a view, this is the place to be. The 42-story Landmark stands taller than all the surrounding buildings, near the peak of a small rise at the western end of Robson Street. Stanley Park, the beaches of English Bay, and Denman Street are all within walking distance. The rooms make the most of the location—all have balconies, and the higher you go the more you see. Thanks to a recent renovation, which brought in new carpets, wallpaper, beds, and lighting, the view of the room now matches the view from the room. Standard rooms are comfortable and bright, decorated in burgundy tones with dark-wood furnishings. Above the 33rd floor, the Emily Carr rooms—named for the B.C. artist whose art graces the walls—expand out to include a sitting area and wet bar.

Dining/Diversions: The Spice Gallery Cafe & Bar on the lobby level serves a fusion of Western and Asian cuisine in tapas-sized portions. For those who can't get enough of the vistas, take the elevator to the 42nd floor to the rotating Cloud 9 Lounge and Restaurant (see chapter 5).

Amenities: Concierge, limited-hour room service, dry cleaning, laundry service, baby-sitting, secretarial services, express checkout, health club, Jacuzzi, sauna, business center, conference rooms, self-service Laundromat, and car-rental desk.

Listel Vancouver. 1300 Robson St., Vancouver, B.C. V6E 1C5. ☎ **800/663-5491** or 604/684-8461. Fax 604/684-8326. www.listel-vancouver.com. 130 units. A/C MINIBAR TV TEL. May–Sept C$240–C$300 (US$161–US$201) double, C$260–C$320 (US$174–US$214) suite; Oct–Apr C$150–C$190 (US$101–US$127) double, C$170–C$210 (US$114–US$141) suite. AE, DC, DISC, ER, JCB, MC, V. Parking C$14 (US$9).

This hotel has always had a killer location—right at the western end of the Robson Street shopping strip. Recently, the owners have been putting a lot of effort—and money—into making the interior match the address. A recent renovation turned the lobby from a rather plain space to something modern and elegant, if still diminutive. Rooms now feature top-quality bedding and cherry-wood furnishings, including little window-banquettes on which to sit and read or relax. Particularly noteworthy are the

Gallery Rooms on the top two floors. Each of these rooms and suites is like a small art gallery, hung with original art works borrowed from the Buschlen Mowatt Gallery, one of the city's leading private art dealers. On a more practical note, these rooms feature upgraded amenities—including Aveda toiletries—and better views. The upper-floor rooms facing Robson Street, with glimpses of the harbor and the mountains beyond, are worth the price. (The others face the alley and nearby apartment buildings.) Soundproof windows eliminate traffic noise, which can be pretty loud on summer weekends.

Dining: With sidewalk tables and picture windows all around, O'Doul's restaurant is a good spot for people-watching. And despite the sports-bar name (and history), the restaurant has been slowly reinventing itself as a spot for fine dining. Breakfast, lunch, and dinner are served all day.

Amenities: Room service, concierge, valet, laundry, secretarial services, newspaper delivery, express checkout, exercise room, whirlpool, meeting and banquet space, two-line phones.

Pacific Palisades Hotel. 1277 Robson St., Vancouver, B.C. V6E 1C4. ☎ **800/663-1815** or 604/688-0461. Fax 604/688-4374. www.pacificpalisadeshotel.com. E-mail: reservations@ pacificpalisadeshotel.com. 233 units. A/C MINIBAR TV TEL. May 1–Oct 15 C$275 (US$184) double, C$325 (US$218) suite; Oct 16–Apr 30 C$200 (US$134) double, C$250 (US$168) suite. Full kitchens C$10 (US$7) extra. AE, DC, DISC, JCB, MC, V. Parking C$15 (US$10).

The Pacific Palisades is a luxury hotel in every aspect but price. Standing on the crest of Robson Street, it was converted from two luxury apartment towers in 1991. It's popular with visiting film and TV production companies who demand sterling service, privacy, spacious accommodations, and more-than-great value. The intimate lobby and side-street entrance are more discreet than grand. Accommodations come in studio suites (i.e., rooms) and one-bedroom suites. All are spacious and come equipped with sinks, microwave ovens, coffeemakers, and minibars. Most have panoramic views and private terraces. Thanks to a recent full renovation, decor is now an elegant new update on '50s Moderne, with blonde-wood tables, bright walls, and simple, comfortable couches, beds, and chairs. For business travelers, all rooms come equipped with writing desks, two phone lines, and voice mail. As of press time, a next-door restaurant has been promised but not yet delivered.

Amenities: 24-hour room service; concierge; twice-daily maid service; complimentary tea and coffee; laundry; business center; voice-mail message service; daily newspaper; in-room movies; complete fitness center with whirlpool, sauna, and indoor lap pool; bicycle rentals (mountain bikes available); meeting and banquet rooms.

✪ **Westin Bayshore Resort & Marina.** 1601 Bayshore Dr., Vancouver, B.C. V6G 2V4. ☎ **800/228-3000** or 604/682-3377. Fax 604/687-3102. www.westinbayshore.com. E-mail: bayshorereservations@westin.com. 510 units. A/C MINIBAR TV TEL. Mid-Apr to Oct C$289 (US$194) double, C$450–C$700 (US$302–US$469) suite; Nov to mid-Apr C$195 (US$131) double, C$370–C$420 (US$248–US$281) suite. Children under 19 stay free in parents' room. AE, CB, DC, ER, MC, V. Self-parking C$10 (US$7), Valet Parking C$15 (US$10).

Thanks to a C$50-million renovation, this venerable '60s resort hotel looks better than ever. The lobby has been completely redesigned to show off the surrounding park and mountains; achieving much the same thing are two new restaurants and a coffee bar, one of which has a huge outdoor deck overlooking the harbor. Perched on the water's edge overlooking Coal Harbour at Stanley Park's eastern entrance, the Bayshore is still just a short stroll along the seawall from the Canada Place Pier and downtown. Rooms in the original 1961 building have been completely refurbished with classic-looking decor. In the newer tower, the rooms are spacious and come with balconies and large windows. Both towers offer unobstructed views of the harbor's dazzling array of sailboats, fishing boats, and luxury yachts. (Many crafts are available for charter through the hotel's on-site charter service.) The hotel's Guest Office rooms include a fax/copier/printer, speakerphone, and other business amenities. Two floors of the hotel are wheelchair accessible.

Dining: Currents At Bayshore offers three meals daily. The Seawall Bar & Bistro is open for lunch and dinner. The coffee bar, Stanley Perks, is open for breakfast and lunch.

Amenities: 24-hour room service, concierge, laundry, business center, boat charters, bicycle and car rentals, free shuttle service to the downtown area, indoor and outdoor pools, a complete health club, nine retail shops, barber shop, beauty salon.

MODERATE

✪ **Barclay House in the West End.** 1351 Barclay St., Vancouver, B.C. V6E 1H6. ☎ **800/ 971-1351** or 604/605-1351. Fax 604/605-1382. www.barclayhouse.com. 5 units. TV/VCR TEL. C$145–C$225 (US$97–US$151) double. MC, V. Free parking.

Barclay House in the West End is located just one block from the heritage Barclay square, on one of the West End's quiet maple-lined streets. Open as a bed-and-breakfast since 1999, this beautiful house built in 1904 by Thomas Hunter, a local developer, can be a destination on its own. The elegant parlors and dining rooms are perfect for lounging on a rainy afternoon, sipping a glass of complimentary sherry before venturing out for dinner in the trendy West End. On a summer day, the front porch with its comfortable chairs makes for a great spot to read a book. All rooms are beautifully furnished in Victorian style, a number of the pieces are family heirlooms. The modern conveniences such as CD players, TV/VCRs, and luxurious bathrooms blend in perfectly. It is hard to pick a favorite room, but it would probably be the Penthouse suite with its skylights and claw-foot tub, or maybe the south room with a queen-size brass bed and an elegant sitting room overlooking the front of the house.

✪ **Blue Horizon.** 1225 Robson St., Vancouver, B.C. V6E 1C5. ☎ **800/663-1333** or 604/ 688-1411. Fax 604/688-4461. www.bluehorizon.com. E-mail: info@bluehorizon.com. 214 units. A/C MINIBAR TV TEL. C$159–C$199 (US$107–US$133) double; C$279 (US$187) suite. Children under 16 stay free in parents' room. Extra person C$15 (US$10). AE, DC, MC, V. Parking C$8 (US$5).

This unmistakable, blue-tiled, 1960s high-rise on Robson Street capitalizes on one of Vancouver's best assets—the view. The small lobby, designed by artist Pam Pavelek, features her tall glass sculpture *Water and Air,* a theme she has carried throughout the restaurant and lounge on the ground floor. Upstairs, the rooms are spacious—every room is a corner room, which maximizes light and window space. The best views are on the 15th floor and higher. All feature safes, voice mail, data ports, coffee/tea makers, ironing boards, sitting areas, and, of course, balconies. There is no concierge or room service, but all rooms have either a refrigerator or a minibar. The next-door bar, Shenanigan's, features sidewalk seating, darts, big-screen sports, a good selection of ales and beers, and a reasonably priced pub and pasta menu. The exercise area includes a lap pool, Jacuzzi, sauna, and exercise equipment.

✪ **Coast Plaza Suite Hotel at Stanley Park.** 1763 Comox St., Vancouver, B.C. V6G 1P6. ☎ **800/663-1144** or 604/688-7711. Fax 604/688-5934. www.coasthotels.com. E-mail: info@coastplazasuitehotel.com. 267 units. A/C MINIBAR TV TEL. C$129–C$199 (US$86– US$133) double, C$155–C$290 (US$104–US$194) suite. AE, DC, DISC, MC, V. Parking C$8 (US$5).

This 35-story hotel above the Denman Place Mall attracts a wide variety of guests, from business travelers and bus tours to film and TV actors. The guest rooms are large, each with in-room coffeemaker and balcony; many have commanding views of English Bay—the best seats in the city for the Symphony of Fire fireworks display in late July and early August. Most of the units are suites with fully equipped kitchens.

The Comox Street Long Bar & Grill is open from lunch through late dinner, serving simple bar fare. The Brasserie specializes in lamb chops, steaks, and some seafood.

There's an indoor pool, an outstanding full-service health club with squash courts and saunas, and a gift shop. Denman Place Mall's 30 shops and restaurants are accessible via the lobby.

Parkhill Hotel. 1160 Davie St., Vancouver, B.C. V6E 1N1. ☎ **800/663-1525** or 604/685-1311. Fax 604/681-0208. www.parkhillhotel.com. E-mail: prkhillres@aol.com. 192 units. A/C TV TEL. Apr 16–Oct 15 C$185–C$200 (US$124–US$134) double; Oct 16–Apr 15 C$89–C$135 (US$60–US$90) double with continental breakfast. AE, DC, ER, JCB, MC, V. Parking C$7 (US$4.70).

This modern 24-story hotel is the only accommodation of merit on Davie Street, one of the West End's residential, shopping, and dining strips. The dark-marble lobby is welcoming and tastefully decorated. The guest rooms are large and decorated in tranquil, pale tones. The small, private balconies offer fabulous views of either False Creek and Granville Island or English Bay and the Gulf Islands. All rooms are equipped with coffeemakers and hair dryers. The deluxe rooms on the upper floors (comprising the upper end of the rate range above) have in-room safes, terry robes, and upgraded amenities. The hotel has an indoor pool, sundeck, sauna, and large gift shop.

Byron's restaurant provides standard continental fare; Taiko's Japanese Noodle restaurant is very casual. The Lounge serves snacks and drinks, and for your caffeine fix, the hotel has a cappuccino bar.

✪ Rosellen Suites. 102–2030 Barclay St., Vancouver, B.C. V6G 1L5. ☎ **888/317-6648** or 604/689-4807. Fax 604/684-3327. www.rosellensuites.com. E-mail: info@rosellensuites.com. 30 apts. A/C TV TEL. May–Aug C$175 (US$117) 1-bedroom apt, C$200–C$280 (US$134–US$188) 2-bedroom apt, C$375 (US$251) penthouse; Sept–Apr C$110 (US$74) 1-bedroom apt, C$140–C$200 (US$94–US$134) 2-bedroom apt, C$300 (US$201) penthouse. Minimum 3-night stay. Extra person C$15 (US$10). Cots and cribs free. AE, CB, DC, DISC, JCB, MC, V. Limited parking in the rear of the building C$5 (US$3.35).

On a quiet residential street, this unpretentious low-rise apartment building is just a few hundred yards from Stanley Park and 2 blocks from loads of restaurants. Converted into an apartment hotel in the 1960s, the Rosellen has no lobby and the manager's office is open only from 9am to 5pm. Each guest receives a front door key and a personal phone number with voice mail. Modern and extremely comfortable, each suite features a spacious living room, separate dining area, and full-size kitchen with all necessary utensils. It's just like having an apartment in Vancouver. Autographed movie-star photos in the manager's office give you an idea of the luminaries who have stayed here. The penthouse is named after Katharine Hepburn, who has called this her favorite Vancouver hotel.

There's full maid service twice a week, coin laundry facilities, dry cleaning, free local calls, a business center, and access to the West End Community Centre's weight room.

Sunset Inn Travel Apartments. 1111 Burnaby St., Vancouver, B.C. V6E 1P4. ☎ **800/786-1997** or 604/688-2474. Fax 604/669-3340. www.sunsetinn.com. E-mail: sunsetinn@netcom.ca. 50 units. A/C TV TEL. C$88–C$158 (US$59–US$106) studio, C$98–C$168 (US$66–US$113) 1-bedroom suite. Weekly rates and other off-season discounts available. AE, DC, MC, V. Free parking.

Located on a quiet side street, this tall gray concrete structure looks like any other West End apartment building. It offers self-contained suites that are nicely furnished in strikingly contemporary if slightly mismatched colors. Each has a small private balcony. Kitchens are completely equipped with toaster, coffeemaker, can opener, and utensils. The living rooms are spacious, the beds comfortable, and the closets reasonably large. There are leather armchairs and settees as well as a dining table and chairs. There's also a small fitness room on the main floor.

✪ **West End Guest House.** 1362 Haro St., Vancouver, B.C. V6E 1G2. ☎ **604/681-2889.** Fax 604/688-8812. www.westendguesthouse.com. E-mail: wegh@idmail.net. 7 units. TV TEL. C$145–C$225 (US$97–US$151) double. Rates include full breakfast. AE, MC, V. Free valet parking.

Experience the West End the way it was. A beautiful heritage home built in 1906, the West End Guest House is a fine example of what the neighborhood looked like up until the early '50s, before the concrete towers and condos replaced the original Edwardian homes. Decorated with beautiful early-century antiques and an amazing collection of old photographs of Vancouver, this is a wonderful respite from the hustle and bustle of the West End. The seven guest rooms are beautifully furnished with antiques, ensuite bathrooms, and the ultimate in bed-time luxury: feather mattresses, down duvets, and pillows, robes, and your very own resident stuffed animal. Particularly indulgent is the Grand Queen Suite, an attic-level bedroom with skylights, brass bed, fireplace, sitting area, and claw-foot bathtub. Owner Evan Penner pampers his guests with a scrumptious breakfast and serves iced tea and sherry in the afternoon. Throughout the day, guests have access to the parlor, sundeck, porch kitchen stocked with home-baked munchies and refreshments, and bikes. If you ask nicely, Penner will crank up the gramophone.

INEXPENSIVE

✪ **Buchan Hotel.** 1906 Haro St., Vancouver, B.C. V6G 1H7. ☎ **604/685-5354.** Fax 604/685-5367. www.3bc.sympatico.ca/buchan/. E-mail: buchanhotel@telus.net. 60 units, 30 with bathroom. TV. May–Sept C$75–C$95 (US$50–US$64) double, C$125–C$145 (US$84–US$97) executive room; Oct–Apr C$45–C$70 (US$30–US$47) double, C$100–C$140 (US$67–US$94) executive room. Children under 12 stay free in parents' room. Weekly rates and off-season discounts available. AE, DC, MC, V. Street parking available.

Built in the 1930s, this charming three-story building overlooks a small park on a quiet tree-lined residential street. It's less than 2 blocks from Stanley Park and Denman Street and 10 minutes by foot from the business district. The rooms are small and the bathrooms smaller, but the rates are low and the staff is friendly. Rooms overlooking the park are brighter; the four front-corner executive rooms are the largest. The hotel also offers in-house bike and ski storage and a coin laundry. There are no exercise facilities, but the nearby West End Community Centre has weights, aerobics, sauna, and a pool, and charges a nominal visitor's fee. Smoking isn't permitted in the rooms.

Hostelling International Vancouver Downtown Hostel. 1114 Burnaby St. (at Thurlow St.), Vancouver, B.C. V6E 1P1. ☎ **888/203-4302** or 604/684-4565. Fax 604/684-4540. www.hihostels.bc.ca. E-mail: van-downtown@hihostels.bc.ca. 239 beds in 4-person units; some double and triple units. Beds C$20 (US$13) IYHA members, C$24 (US$16) nonmembers; doubles C$55 (US$37) members, C$64 (US$43) nonmembers; triples C$70 (US$47) members, C$86 (US$58) nonmembers. Annual adult membership C$27 (US$18). MC, V. Limited free parking.

Located in a converted nunnery, this new and modern hostel is an extremely convenient base of operations from which to explore downtown. The beach is a few blocks south; downtown is a 10-minute walk north. Most beds are in quad dorms, with a limited number of doubles and triples available. There are common cooking facilities, as well as a patio and game room. The hostel gets extremely busy in the summertime, so book ahead. Many organized activities and tours can be booked at the hostel. There's free shuttle service to the bus/train station and Jericho Beach. Open 24 hours.

✪ **Sylvia Hotel.** 1154 Gilford St., Vancouver, B.C. V6G 2P6. ☎ **604/681-9321.** Fax 604/82-3551. www.sylviahotel.com. 118 units. TV TEL. Apr–Sept C$75–C$125 (US$50–US$84) double; Oct–Mar C$75–C$100 (US$50–US$67) double. Children under 18 stay free in parents' room. AE, DC, MC, V. Parking C$7 (US$4.70).

Built in 1912, when the West End was relatively unpopulated, the Sylvia is on the shores of English Bay just a few blocks from Stanley Park. It's one of Vancouver's oldest hotels, and although it's only eight stories high, it was the tallest building in western Canada until World War II. In recent years, it has become deservedly trendy. The gray-stone, ivy-wreathed Sylvia resembles a mansion. The lobby sets the tone: It's small, restful, dark, and furnished with red carpets, ivory drapes, and overstuffed chairs. The same atmosphere prevails in the adjoining restaurant and crowded cocktail lounge (which was Vancouver's first when it opened in 1954). The restaurant emphasizes seafood and continental cuisine, and has the same fabulous view as the historic cocktail lounge.

In the guest rooms, furnishings from the 1950s through 1970s are appropriately mismatched. The views from the upper floors are unparalleled. The suites have fully equipped kitchens and are large enough for families. Sixteen rooms in the 12-year-old low-rise annex offer individual heating but have less atmosphere. Valet and room service are available in both sections. Make reservations a few months ahead for a summer stay.

3 The West Side

Right across False Creek from downtown and the West End is Vancouver's West Side. If your agenda includes a Granville Island shopping spree, exploration of the island's numerous artists' studios and galleries, or strolls through the sunken garden at Queen Elizabeth Park; or if you require close proximity to the airport without staying in an "airport hotel," you'll find both cozy B&Bs and hotels that'll meet your needs.

EXPENSIVE
✪ **Granville Island Hotel.** 1253 Johnston St., Vancouver, B.C. V6H 3R9. ☎ **800/663-1840** or 604/683-7373. Fax 604/683-3061. www.granvilleislandhotel.com. 54 units. A/C TV TEL. C$219 (US$147) double. Off-season discounts available. AE, CB, DC, JCB, V. Parking C$6 (US$4). Pets welcome.

This small, modern hotel—with a unique waterfront location on the east end of Granville Island—is surrounded by artists' studios and galleries on one side and pleasure boats on the other. It has a cozy lobby, attractively decorated with dark wood paneling and stone floors. The guest rooms have skylights and bathrooms with marble floors and oversize tubs. Some accommodations also have balconies. Pets are welcome free of charge.

Dining/Diversions: The Creek microbrewery restaurant and bar has a harborside patio and a large humidor stocked with Cuban and Dominican cigars.

Amenities: Concierge, dry cleaning, laundry service, newspaper delivery, in-room massage, baby-sitting, secretarial services, express checkout, free coffee. The rooftop health club offers fitness equipment, a sauna, and a Jacuzzi. The hotel staff arranges boat charters at the marina. Downtown and English Bay are a two-minute miniferry ride away.

MODERATE

The Cherub Inn. 2546 W. Sixth Ave., Vancouver, B.C. V6K 1W5. ☎ 604/733-3166. Fax 604/733-3106. www.cherubinn.com. E-mail: unwind@cherubinn.com. 5 units. May 1–Oct 15 C$139–C$180 (US$93–US$121); Oct 16–Apr 30 C$119–C$149 (US$80–US$100). MC, V. Free parking.

A beautifully restored and renovated character house from 1913, the Cherub Inn is a comfortable home away from home. In the heart of Kitsilano, you are only 2 blocks away from busy Fourth Avenue and Broadway, with great shopping and dining, and a 10-minute walk from the beach, the park, the outdoor swimming pool, museums, and Granville Island. All rooms are elegant and beautifully furnished with antiques and fine featherbeds and linen. For the romantically inclined, the Cherub room is a must: hand-carved walnut sleigh bed, cast-iron fireplace, skylight, and a large bathroom with an oversized bathtub and heated floors. On the ground floor, the Seraphim room is particularly attractive. Although smaller than some of the other rooms, its stained-glass bay windows, dark wood, and elegant furniture make it a little piece of paradise perfect for recovering from the stress of everyday life. For families or friends traveling together, the Amoretti suite on the ground floor provides you with a spacious one-bedroom suite with full kitchen, dining area, and a four-piece (separate shower and bath) bathroom, as well as a sizable toy chest and a VCR.

Kenya Court Guest House. 2230 Cornwall Ave., Vancouver, B.C. V6K 1B5. ☎ 604/738-7085. E-mail: htdwilliams@telus.net. 4 units. TV TEL. C$135–C$165 (US$90–US$111) double. Rates include full breakfast. Extra person C$50 (US$34). No smoking. No credit cards. Garage or street parking.

Every room in this three-story apartment building at Kitsilano Beach has an unob-structed waterfront view of Vanier Park, English Bay, downtown Vancouver, and the Coast Mountains. This architectural landmark is an ideal launching pad for strolls around Granville Island, Vanier Park, the Maritime Museum, the Vancouver Museum, and other Kitsilano sights. An outdoor pool, tennis courts, and jogging trails are nearby. Run by a retired doctor and his wife (Dr. and Mrs. Williams), the Kenya Court has the feel of a bed-and-breakfast. Each guest suite—with a living room, bath-room, separate bedroom, and full kitchen—is a large converted apartment that's been tastefully furnished. A full breakfast (including eggs and bacon) is served in a glass solarium up on the rooftop, where there's a spectacular view of English Bay.

Pillow 'n Porridge Guest Suites. 2859 Manitoba St., Vancouver, B.C. V5Y 3B3. ☎ 604/879-8977. Fax 604/879-8966. www.pillow.net. E-mail: suites@pillow.net. 7 suites. TV TEL. May 15–Sept C$115–C$255 (US$77–US$171) suite; Oct to May 14 C$85–C$195 (US$57–US$131) suite. 5-night minimum. Monthly rates available. 1 suite wheelchair accessible. No credit cards. Free parking.

Pillow 'n Porridge's one-, two-, and three-bedroom suites are in three side-by-side her-itage buildings. Each suite has a theme, from Mayan to West Coast to Corner Store. The antique-filled suites have working fireplaces and fully equipped kitchens stocked with the basics. All have dishwashers, and the two- and three-bedroom suites also have washers and dryers. Situated in the City Hall heritage district, the suites are within walking distance of fine dining, ethnic restaurants, retail shops, Granville Island, and Queen Elizabeth Park. The minimum stay varies depending upon availability.

INEXPENSIVE

Hostelling International Vancouver Jericho Beach Hostel. 1515 Discovery St., Vancouver, B.C. V6R 4K5. ☎ 888/203-4303 or 604/224-3208. Fax 604/224-4852. www. hihostels.bc.ca. E-mail: van-jericho@hihostels.bc.ca. 286 beds in 14 dorms; 10 private family rooms. C$18 (US$12) IYHA members, C$22 (US$15) nonmembers dorm rooms; C$47–C$53 (US$31–US$36) members, C$56–C$62 (US$38–US$42) nonmembers family rooms. Annual adult membership C$27 (US$18). MC, V. Not wheelchair accessible. Parking C$3 (US$2).

Located in an old military barracks, this hostel is surrounded by an expansive lawn right next to Jericho Beach. Individuals, families, and groups are welcome, but there are no facilities for children under 5 or pets. The 10 private rooms can accommodate up to six people. These particular accommodations go fast, so if you want one, call far in advance. The dormitory-style arrangements are well maintained and supervised. Linens are provided. Basic, inexpensive food is served in the cafe from April through October. During the rest of the year, food is available at the front desk. You have the option of cooking for yourself year-round in the hostel's kitchen. If you're looking for adventures, an on-premises program director operates tours and activities outside of the hostel.

Johnson Heritage House Bed & Breakfast. 2278 W. 34th Ave., Vancouver, B.C. V6M 1G6. ☎ **604/266-4175.** Fax 604/266-4175. www.johnsons-inn-vancouver.com. E-mail: fun@ johnsons-inn-vancouver.com. 4 units. C$115–C$180 (US$77–US$121) double. Rates include full breakfast. No credit cards. Free parking.

This charming white-shingled home, in Vancouver's quiet residential district of Kerrisdale, is within a 15-minute drive of the Vancouver airport and about a 10-minute drive from the University of British Columbia campus. Outside the house, the rock garden and sculpture catch your eye; inside, there are wooden carousel animals and other antiques. The cozy guest rooms are outfitted with an eclectic array of antique trunks, biplane propellers, and gramophones, and feature queen-size brass beds. A full breakfast is served in the spacious dining room that looks out onto the tree-shaded garden.

Maple House Bed and Breakfast. 1533 Maple St., Vancouver, B.C. V6J 3S2. ☎ **604/ 739-5833.** Fax 604/739-5877. www.maplehouse.com. E-mail: info@maplehouse.com. 5 units. June–Sept C$95–C$130 (US$64–US$87) double; Oct–May C$75–C$105 (US$50–US$70) double. No credit cards. Free parking.

This conveniently located Kitsilano B&B is 2 blocks from the beach, half a block from the buses to downtown, and 6 blocks from the trendy shopping and restaurant area on Fourth Avenue. Maple House is a simple and elegant home that dates back to the turn of the last century. The breakfast parlor overlooks the street and is decorated with a mix of antique and Japanese furniture, reflecting the tastes of hosts Brian and Fumi, the Canadian and Japanese owners. The house has a total of five rooms. Of the three on the second floor, one has a queen-size bed with private ensuite bathroom, while the other two have double beds and share a bathroom. On the third floor, the attic has two cozy twin rooms with a separate, shared bathroom one floor down. A full breakfast is included with your stay.

✪ **Penny Farthing Inn.** 2855 W. Sixth Ave., Vancouver, B.C. V6K 1X2. ☎ **604/ 739-9002.** Fax 604/739-9004. www.pennyfarthinginn.com. E-mail: farthing@uniserve.com. 4 units. May–Oct C$115 (US$77) double, C$170 (US$114) suite; Nov–Apr C$95 (US$64) double, C$145 (US$97) suite. Rates include full breakfast. No credit cards. Street parking.

Built in 1912, this landmark house on a quiet residential street is filled with antiques and stained glass. The guest rooms are decorated with pine furniture and distinctive touches like four-poster beds. "Abigail's Suite" is a favorite with honeymooners; it's bright and self-contained, featuring a terrific view, a sitting room with a TV/VCR and CD player, and a private bathroom with a skylight. Breakfast is served on the brick patio of an English-country–style garden filled with trees and fragrant flowers. You can watch the resident cats at play while you relax. Bikes are available for guest use, as are free videos. Smoking isn't permitted inside.

✪ **The University of British Columbia Conference Centre.** 5961 Student Union Blvd., Vancouver, B.C. V6T 2C9. ☎ **604/822-1000.** Fax 604/822-1001. www.conferences.ubc.ca. E-mail: reservation@housing.ubc.ca. About 1,900 units. Walter Gage Residence units available only May 10–Aug 26: C$34–C$52 (US$23–U$35) standard or premium single with shared bathroom; C$69–C$172 (US$46–US$115) studio, 1-, or 6-bedroom suites. Vanier Hostel: C$24 (US$16) single, C$48 (US$32) double, C$59 (US$40) studio suite with private bathroom. Located adjacent to the Gage Residence, the 47 Gage Court Suites are available year-round: May–Sept C$99–C$124 (US$66–US$83) suite; Oct–Apr C$81–C$91 (US$54–US$61) suite. AE, MC, V. Free parking May 4–Aug 26 at Walter Gage Residence, other areas C$5 (US$3.35) per day. Bus: 4, 10, or 99.

The University of British Columbia is in a gorgeous forested setting on the tip of Point Grey—a convenient location if you plan to spend a lot of time either in Kitsilano or at the university itself. It's also not bad if you have a car, but otherwise it's a good half-hour bus ride from downtown. With two residences and nearly 2,000 rooms, there's also plenty of variety. The 17-story Walter Gage Residence has new, comfortable studio, one-bedroom, and six-bedroom suites, as well as single rooms with shared bathrooms. Many are located on the upper floors with sweeping views of the city and ocean. All rooms are furnished with extra-long twin beds. All suites in the Gage Residence come equipped with private bathrooms, kitchenettes, TVs, and phones. Each studio suite has a twin bed; each one-bedroom suite features a queen bed; the six-bedroom Tower suites—a particularly good deal for families—each feature one double bed and five twin beds. Located next door, the year-round Gage Court suites have two twin beds in one bedroom and a queen-size Murphy bed in the sitting room. Housekeeping is provided daily in the Gage Residence, but only weekly in the more Spartan Vanier residence. Breakfast can be purchased in the campus cafeteria. There are plenty of on-campus facilities and services, including restaurants, a pub, tennis courts, and banking. Athletic facilities, including the campus gym and pool, are open to guests for about C$5 (US$3.35) per use per person. Nearby attractions include Spanish Banks, Wreck Beach, Pacific Spirit Park, Nitobe Memorial Gardens, the Museum of Anthropology, and the University Golf Course.

4 The North Shore (North Vancouver & West Vancouver)

The North Shore cities of North and West Vancouver are pleasant and lush and much less hurried than Vancouver. Staying here also offers easy access to the North Shore mountains and its attractions, including hiking trails, the Capilano Suspension Bridge, and the ski slopes on Mount Seymour, Grouse Mountain, and Cypress Bowl. Staying here is also often cheaper than in Vancouver. The disadvantage is that if you want to take your car into Vancouver, there are only two bridges, and during rush hours they're painfully slow. The SeaBus, however, is not only quick, but kind of scenic.

EXPENSIVE

Lonsdale Quay Hotel. 123 Carrie Cates Court, North Vancouver, B.C. V6M 3K7. ☎ **800/ 836-6111** or 604/986-6111. Fax 604/986-8782. www.lonsdalequayhotel.bc.ca. E-mail: sales@lonsdalequayhotel.bc.ca. 83 units. A/C MINIBAR TV TEL. High season C$150–C$225 (US$101–US$151) double or twin, C$350 (US$235) suite; low season C$140–C$165 (US$94–US$111) double or twin, C$250 (US$168) suite. Extra person C$25 (US$17). Senior discount available. AE, CB, DC, DISC, ER, MC, V. Parking C$7 (US$4.70), free on weekends and holidays. No smoking. SeaBus: Lonsdale Quay.

Directly across the Burrard Inlet from the Canada Place Pier, the Lonsdale Quay Hotel is at the water's edge above the Lonsdale Quay Market at the SeaBus terminal. An escalator rises from the midst of the market's food, crafts, and souvenir stalls to the front desk on the third floor. The rooms are simply furnished and tastefully decorated, without the grandeur or luxurious touches of comparably priced downtown hotels. Nevertheless, the hotel has unique and fabulous harbor and city views, and is only 15 minutes by bus or car from Grouse Mountain Ski Resort and Capilano Regional Park.

Dining: The Waterfront Bistro serves lunch, cocktails, and dinner. The relaxed Q Café serves three meals daily.

Amenities: Whirlpool, weight and exercise room, in-room coffeemakers and water coolers.

Park Royal Hotel. 540 Clyde Ave., West Vancouver, B.C. V7T 2J7. ☎ **877/926-5511** or 604/926-5511. Fax 604/926-6082. www.parkroyalhotel.com. 30 units. TV TEL. May–Sept C$159–C$189 (US$107–US$127) double, C$229 (US$153) suite; Oct–Apr C$99–C$129 (US$66–US$86) double, C$169 (US$113) suite. AE, DC, MC, V. Free parking. Cross the Lions Gate Bridge into West Vancouver, and take the first right onto Taylor Way. Turn right immediately at Clyde Ave. Bus: 250, 251, 252, 253.

Make reservations months in advance for this Tudor-style country inn with exposed beams, a stone fireplace, and a pub. The hotel sits on the bank of the Capilano River—a great place for salmon and steelhead fly-fishing. The comfortably sized rooms, furnished in the same Tudor decor, have nice touches like brass beds. The only tricky part of this hideaway is finding it. Once you do, it's a 1-minute drive to the Park Royal Mall, one of North America's largest shopping centers.

Dining/Diversions: The Tudor Room Restaurant offers three meals daily plus Sunday brunch; the Pub is a popular gathering spot for more genteel locals.

Amenities: Complimentary coffee or tea and a morning newspaper.

MODERATE

○ Beachside Bed & Breakfast. 4208 Evergreen Ave., West Vancouver, B.C. V7V 1H1. ☎ **800/563-3311** or 604/922-7773. www.beach.bc.ca. E-mail: info@beach.bc.ca. 3 units. C$150–C$250 (US$101–US$168) double. Extra person C$30 (US$20). Rates include full breakfast. MC, V. Free parking. Bus: 250, 251, 252, 253.

Bouquets of fresh flowers in every room are a signature touch at this beautiful, modern waterfront home located at the end of a quiet cul-de-sac. The all-glass southern exposure of this Spanish-style house affords a panoramic view of Vancouver. The private beach is just steps from the door. You can watch the waves from the patio or outdoor Jacuzzi, or just spend the afternoon fishing and sailing. Hosts Gordon and Joan Gibb know the area and will direct you to Stanley Park, hiking, skiing, and other highlights. (Gordon is a registered tour guide.)

INEXPENSIVE

Deep Cove Bed & Breakfast. 2590 Shelley Rd., North Vancouver, B.C. V7H 1V9. ☎ **604/929-3932.** Fax 604/929-9330. E-mail: deepcove@istar.ca. 2 units. TV. C$90 (US$60) double. Rates include breakfast. MC, V. Free parking. Bus: 210 from Vancouver to Phibbs Exchange in North Vancouver, transfer to bus 214. Driving: Hwy. 1, Exit 22 (Mt. Seymour Pkwy.), east on Mt. Seymour to Berkley, left on Berkley for a few blocks, right on Shelley Rd.

Only 20 minutes from downtown Vancouver, Diane and Wayne Moore's B&B provides the privacy of a large, secluded property and easy access to city attractions. The rooms—one with twin beds, one with a queen-size bed—are in a separate guest cottage, with private entrances. There's a red-cedar hot tub on the outside terrace between the cottage and the house; the cottage's guest lounge has a billiard table, wood-burning fireplace, TV, and VCR. Hearty breakfasts of French toast, omelets, freshly baked breads, and muffins topped with homemade jams and jellies or Quebec maple syrup are served in the morning room or on the patio. The Moores also accommodate special diets, and request that guests refrain from smoking in the rooms.

Mountainside Manor. 5909 Nancy Greene Way, North Vancouver, B.C. V7R 4W6. ☎ **604/990-9772.** Fax 604/985-8484. E-mail: mtnside@attglobal.net. 4 units. TV. May–Oct C$95–C$155 (US$64–US$104) double; Nov–Apr C$85–C$135 (US$57–US$90) double. Rates include breakfast. Off-season discounts available. DC, MC, V. Free parking.

This is the closest house to both the ski slopes on Grouse Mountain and the 42-kilometer-long (26 miles) Baden-Powell hiking trail. It's a spectacular, modern home nestled in a peaceful alpine setting. High above the city on a tree-covered ridge, the Mountainside Manor has a magnificent view of the Coast Mountains and the Burrard Inlet from the rooms and the outdoor hot tub. The Panorama Room—the largest of the rooms—has a queen-size bed, rosewood furniture, a Jacuzzi with a separate shower, and views of the mountains and the city. All rooms are stocked with fresh flowers and lots of amenities.

Where to Dine in Vancouver

Two thousand restaurants? Five thousand? Hard to say really, but Vancouverites do dine out more than residents of any other Canadian city. Outstanding meals are available in all price ranges and in many different cuisines—Caribbean, Chinese, Japanese, Greek, French, Italian, Spanish, Mongolian, Ethiopian, Vietnamese. Even better, over the past few years Vancouverites have come to expect top quality, and yet they absolutely refuse to pay the kind of top dollar restaurant goers pay in New York or San Francisco. Somehow, restaurateurs have managed to square this circle. For discerning diners from elsewhere, Vancouver is a steal.

The cuisine buzzwords here are tapas and West Coast. Justifiable pride in local produce, game, and seafood is combined with innovation and creativity. More and more restaurants are shifting to seasonal, even monthly, menus, giving their chefs greater freedom. As for tapas, it seems that diners in Vancouver have grown more sociable, ordering two or three small tapas plates and sharing them with their friends.

Once less than palatable, British Columbian wines have improved to the point that local vintners are now winning international acclaim. The big wine-producing areas are in the Okanagan Valley (in southern British Columbia's dry interior) or else on southern Vancouver Island. (If you have a few extra days, either area is definitely worth a visit.) In the hills surrounding Lake Okanagan and the Okanagan River, there are more than 30 wineries, including Mission Hill, Grey Monk, Summerhill, Quail's Gate, Cedar Creek, and Sumac Ridge. On the Island, Burrowing Owl and Venturi-Shultz are the vintners to watch. Fortunately, these wines have received far less publicity than they deserve, so some great bargains can still be had.

Because they're so numerous, Vancouver restaurants aren't hard to find. If you're staying in downtown Vancouver, you can walk to the West End and English Bay (west of downtown from Thurlow Street to Stanley Park), Gastown, or Chinatown. If you're willing to travel farther, you can venture to the West Side. Or if you'd like to head in the opposite direction, cross the Lions Gate Bridge and turn left, and you'll be in West Vancouver. For something fun and casual, head east to a bistro on Main Street or Commercial Drive.

There's no provincial tax on restaurant meals in British Columbia, but venues add the 7% federal goods and services tax (GST). Restaurant hours vary. Lunch is typically served from noon to 1 or 2pm; Vancouverites begin dining around 6:30pm, later in summer.

Reservations are recommended at most restaurants and are essential at popular places. Reservations may not be accepted at some inexpensive and moderately priced restaurants.

1 Restaurants by Cuisine

AMERICAN
Brothers Restaurant (p. 94)
Sophie's Cosmic Café (p. 103)
The Tempelton (p. 92)
The Tomahawk Restaurant (p. 106)

BISTRO
Avenue One Bistro (p. 107)
The Brickhouse Bistro (p. 104)
Bukowski's (p. 104)
The Locus Café (p. 104)

CANADIAN
Rooster's Quarters (p. 99)

CARIBBEAN
The Reef (p. 104)

CASUAL
Bin 941 Tapas Parlour (p. 91)
Bukowski's (p. 104)
Cactus Club Café (p. 97)
The Cat's Meow (p. 101)
Hamilton Street Bar and Grill (p. 91)
The Locus Café (p. 104)
Mark's Fiasco (p. 102)
The Reef (p. 104)

CHINESE/DIM SUM
Park Lock Seafood Restaurant (p. 94)
Pink Pearl (p. 94)
Shao Lin Noodle Restaurant (p. 103)
Sun Sui Wah (p. 103)
Sun Wong Kee (p. 105)

CONTINENTAL
Delilah's (p. 95)
The Teahouse Restaurant (p. 96)
William Tell Restaurant (p. 87)

DESSERTS
Death by Chocolate (p. 106)

FAMILY STYLE
Brothers Restaurant (p. 94)
Romano's Macaroni Grill at the Mansion (p. 97)
Sophie's Cosmic Café (p. 103)

FISH & CHIPS
Olympia Oyster & Fish Co. Ltd. (p. 92)

FRENCH
Bishop's (p. 99)
Café de Paris (p. 95)
Lumière (p. 99)
Pastis (p. 100)
The Smoking Dog (p. 100)

GREEK
Stephos (p. 99)

HUNGARIAN
Bandi's (p. 90)

INDIAN
Annapurna (p. 102)
Sami's (p. 97)
Vij's (p. 102)

ITALIAN
Amarcord (p. 87)
Il Giardino di Umberto (p. 90)
La Terrazza (p. 91)
Romano's Macaroni Grill at the Mansion (p. 97)

JAPANESE
Gyoza King (p. 98)
Tanpopo (p. 98)
Tojo's Restaurant (p. 100)

MEDITERRANEAN
Bacchus Ristorante (p. 90)
Cin Cin (p. 95)

PIZZA

Incendio (p. 94)

SEAFOOD

Aqua Riva (p. 87)
C (p. 85)
The Cannery (p. 92)
The Fish House in Stanley Park
(p. 96)
Joe Fortes Seafood House (p. 90)
The Salmon House on the Hill
(p. 105)
Sun Sui Wah (p. 103)

STEAK

Gotham Steakhouse and Cocktail Bar
(p. 87)
Mark's Fiasco (p. 102)

TAPAS

Bin 941Tapas Parlour (p. 91)
La Bodega (p. 92)

TEX-MEX/SOUTHWESTERN

Andales (p. 101)
Cactus Club Café (p. 97)
The Locus Café (p. 104)

THAI

Just One Thai Bistro (p. 98)

VEGETARIAN

Annapurna (p. 102)
The Naam Restaurant (p. 102)

VIETNAMESE

Phnom Penh Restaurant (p. 94)

VIEW

Aqua Riva (p. 87)
The Beach House at Dundarave Pier
(p. 105)
C (p. 85)
Cloud 9 (p. 86)
The Five Sails (p. 86)
Raincity Grill (p. 96)

WEST COAST (PACIFIC NORTHWEST)

Aqua Riva (p. 87)
Avenue One Bistro (p. 101)
The Beach House at Dundarave Pier
(p. 105)
C (p. 85)
Cloud 9 (p. 86)
The Crime Lab (p. 91)
Diva at the Met (p. 86)
The Five Sails (p. 86)
Hamilton Street Bar and Grill
(p. 91)
Liliget Feast House & Catering
(p. 96)
Raincity Grill (p. 96)
Raintree Restaurant at the Landing
(p. 93)
The Salmon House on the Hill
(p. 105)
Star Anise (p. 100)

2 Downtown & Yaletown

VERY EXPENSIVE

✪ ✪ **C.** 1600 Howe St. ☎ **604/681-1164.** Fax 604/605-8263. www.crestaurant.com. E-mail: info@crestaurant.com. Reservations recommended. Main courses C$21–C$32 (US$14–US$21). AE, DC, MC, V. Daily 11:30am–2:30pm and 5:30–11pm; Sun brunch 11am–2pm. Valet parking C$6 (US$4). Bus: 1, 2. SEAFOOD.

It's become almost habit to quietly backhand the conspicuous consumption of the '80s generation—what's forgotten is just how well they consumed. C brings it all back, in a room done up in brilliant shades of Miami white, with the food itself providing a little postindustrial commentary. Look for pale-green bread baskets made from cut sheets of heavy-gauge rubber, footrests upholstered with truck-tire retreads, and faux vinyl siding in the washrooms. Beyond the decor, however, C recreates the '80s through the sheer indulgent quality with which they serve fish. C's taster box—a kind of small wooden high-rise of appetizers—includes salmon gravlax cured in Saskatoonberry tea, artichoke carpaccio, abalone tempura, and grilled garlic squid. A variety of seafood main courses are available, but for the ultimate dining experience, let chef Robert Clark show off (he's dying to), and order the seven-course sampling menu. First up is a Maui ahi tuna sashimi, lightly dabbed with 50-year balsamic vinegar and presented on a piece of rough-cut marble. Artichoke carpaccio, pan-seared Dover sole, and spotted prawns with kumquat follow, as does a Nova Scotia lobster. Then comes the Alaskan scallop wrapped in octopus bacon. Wine pairings throughout are brought to you by Peter, a sommelier of exceptional knowledge. Savor the exquisite cuisine as you watch the sun go down over the marina.

✪ **Cloud 9.** 1400 Robson St. ☎ **604/662-8328.** Reservations recommended. Lunch main courses C$8–C$12 (US$5–US$8), dinner main courses C$20–C$40 (US$13–US$27), brunch C$22 (US$15). AE, DC, ER, MC, V. Daily 6:30–11am, 11:30am–2pm, and 5–10pm; Sun brunch 11:30am–2pm. Bus: 5. PACIFIC NORTHWEST.

Want the city laid out at your feet and delivered to your table? Take the elevator to the Landmark Hotel's 42nd floor. The view may be of English Bay, Stanley Park with the North Shore Mountains, or the towers of downtown. Yes, it's a revolving restaurant, but hang on just a minute before you think "tourist trap" and dive for the escape hatch. Things at Cloud 9 have been…ahem…evolving. The restaurant has been working hard on improving the menu, and the new chef is able to offer cuisine that almost equals the superlative views. Appetizers feature mostly seafood—the platter allows you to sample the smoked salmon, oysters, sushi, and pâté. For main courses, seafood plays an important role, but other high points include steak, lamb, chicken, and a few Asian dishes. The prices are slightly higher than in comparable restaurants, but consider that a fair premium for the million-dollar view.

If you decide not to stay for supper, the lounge has excellent—and reasonably priced—martinis. On weekends there's a small cover.

✪ **Diva at the Met.** 645 Howe St. ☎ **604/602-7788.** www.metropolitan.com. E-mail: reservations@divamet.com. Reservations recommended. Dinner main courses C$26–C$38 (US$17–US$25), lunch C$12–C$23 (US$8–US$15). AE, DC, DISC, JCB, MC, V. Daily 6:30am–11pm. Bus: 4, 7. WEST COAST.

Since opening a few years ago next to the newly revamped Metropolitan Hotel, Diva at the Met and its chef Michael Noble have made walking off with city restaurant awards a bit of a habit. Noble himself has represented Canada at the Bocuse d'Or competition in France. His dishes extol the virtues of fresh seasonal ingredients and a light approach to spices and seasonings. Starters include house-smoked salmon with Québec foie gras. For the main course, try halibut cheeks with black-olive tapenade. Diva's tasting menu is also very popular, and its weekend brunch is among the best in town.

✪ **The Five Sails.** 999 Canada Place Way, in the Pan-Pacific Hotel. ☎ **604/891-2892.** Reservations recommended. Main courses C$23–C$38 (US$15–US$25), tasting menu C$34–C$45 (US$23–US$30). AE, DC, ER, JCB, MC, V. Daily 6–10pm. SkyTrain: Waterfront. WEST COAST.

The Five Sails' view of Coal Harbour, the Lions Gate Bridge, and the Coast Mountains is as spectacular as the food. Where other city restaurants have scrambled over each other trying to bring ingredients and seasonings from the four corners of the world together on a single plate, the Five Sails has taken a steadier, more cautious approach. That's not to say they don't create winning combinations—witness the pan-seared halibut cheeks with cardamom-scented tomato fondue on a bed of saffroned potatoes, or the poached oyster glazed with a hollandaise sauce just lightly infused with chili. But equally indicative of the Five Sails approach are top-quality ingredients given just enough preparation to bring out their finest flavors. Think dry-aged Angus beef done to perfection, or fresh-caught Pacific salmon. The Five Sails' wine selection leans slightly towards hard-to-find Cascadian bottles. The decor is elegant, refined, and very simple, and the view is among the best in town.

✪ Gotham Steakhouse and Cocktail Bar. 615 Seymour St. ☎ **604/605-8282.** Fax 604/605-8285. www.gothamsteakhouse.com. Reservations recommended. Main courses C$27–C$42 (US$18–US$28). AE, MC, V. Mon–Fri 11:30am–2:30pm; daily 5–11pm (cocktail bar somewhat later). Bus: 4, 7. STEAK.

Vegetarians beware: Gotham means meat. Okay, potatoes and a bit of seafood, but that's it. The room is of ambitious proportions—a 40-foot high timber ceiling divided down the middle with a cocktail bar on one side, a dining room on the other, and a patio with fireplace balancing things out. Furnishings are aggressively masculine—thick leather, dark wood, plush velvet, acrylic paintings of women in half-laced corsets. The wine list is encyclopedic. And then there's the food. The deep-fried calamari appetizer was a light and tasty revelation. Jumbo shrimp were sumo-sized. And the steaks, these were incredible: a porterhouse cut the size of a catcher's mitt; a petit filet mignon as tall as half a bread loaf. The meat just melts away on your tongue. Veggie side dishes are eminently forgettable. Better to pass on them entirely and spend the money on another glass of French merlot. The service is impeccable.

William Tell Restaurant. 765 Beatty St., in the Georgian Court Hotel. ☎ **604/688-3504.** Reservations recommended at dinner. Lunch main courses C$8–C$15 (US$5–US$10), dinner main courses C$20–C$30 (US$13–US$20). AE, DC, ER, JCB, MC, V. Daily 7–11am; Mon–Fri 11:30am–2pm; Mon–Sat 5:30–9:30pm; Sun buffet 5:30–8pm. SkyTrain: Stadium. CONTINENTAL.

One of Vancouver's foremost restaurateurs, Erwin Doebeli, has maintained the William Tell as one of the city's premier places for 30 years. His traditional Swiss cuisine is a sharp contrast to the trendy dishes you'll find elsewhere downtown. The decor is refined and up-to-date. The breaded veal Schnitzel Holstein is crisp and tender; the cheese fondue is superb. A few lighter alternatives have crept onto the menu, but most dishes are loaded with cream and butter. And that's exactly what keeps people coming back. This is the place for a business lunch.

EXPENSIVE

Amarcord. 104-1168 Hamilton St. ☎ **604/681-6500.** Reservations recommended. Main courses C$13–C$19 (US$9–US$13). AE, DC, MC, V. Mon–Fri 11:30am–2pm; daily 5:30–10pm. Bus: 2. ITALIAN.

Traditional Italian cuisine doesn't get much respect these days, but that's just what Amarcord does, and so well that it's worth swearing off mango-corn chutney sauté and rediscovering the joys of freshly made pasta or risotto teamed with a lovingly prepared sauce. Think gnocchi with Italian sausage, fresh tomato and basil, or linguini with mussels, scallops, and tiger prawns. Wines hail from Tuscany and California. The atmosphere is formal without being fussy—a place you could bring your 9-year-old. Service is knowledgeable and very friendly.

Aqua Riva. 30-200 Granville St. ☎ **604/683-5599.** www.aquariva.com. Reservations recommended. Main courses C$19–C$24 (US$13–US$16). AE, MC, V. Daily 11:30am–10pm. Bus: 4, 7. SEAFOOD/PACIFIC NORTHWEST.

It's rare to find a place with both stunning views and top-quality cuisine, but Aqua Riva has both. Located at the foot of Granville Street, the restaurant commands stunning views of the North Shore Mountains and Burrard Inlet, allowing you to watch

Downtown Vancouver Dining

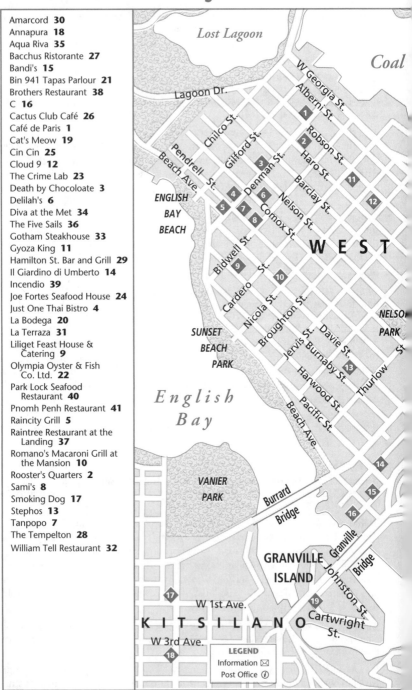

Lost Lagoon

Coal

ENGLISH BAY BEACH

SUNSET BEACH PARK

English Bay

VANIER PARK

WEST

NELSON PARK

GRANVILLE ISLAND

KITSILANO

W 1st Ave.

W 3rd Ave.

Cartwright St.

Burrard Bridge

LEGEND
Information ✉
Post Office ⓘ

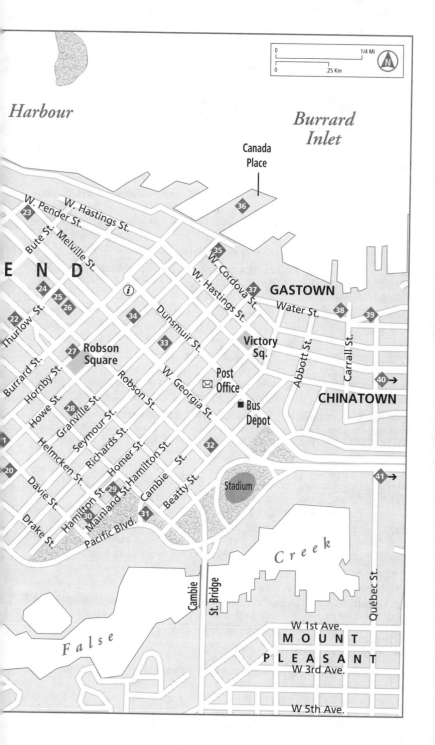

Harbour

Burrard
Inlet

Canada
Place

W. Hastings St.

W. Pender St.
23

Bute St.
Melville St.

E N D

24

25
26

Thurlow St.

22

Burrard St.

Hornby St.

Howe St.

27 Robson
Square

Robson St.

Dunsmuir St.

34

33

W. Georgia St.

W. Cordova St.
35

W. Hastings St.
37

GASTOWN

Water St.
38

39

Abbott St.

Carrall St.

Victory
Sq.

Post
Office

Bus
Depot

40 →

CHINATOWN

28

Granville St.

Seymour St.

Richards St.

Helmcken St.

1

20

Davie St.

Homer St.

Mainland St.

Hamilton St.

29

30

Cambie St.

Beatty St.

32

Stadium

41 →

31

Pacific Blvd.

Drake St.

Creek

False

Cambie

St. Bridge

Québec St.

W 1st Ave.
M O U N T
P L E A S A N T
W 3rd Ave.

W 5th Ave.

0   1/4 Mi
0   .25 Km

the tugs, freighters, and cruise ships while biting into wood-roasted ahi tuna steaks, pan-seared salmon, or spit-roasted chicken with lemon-herb seasonings. The lunchtime crowd buzzes with media people (the city's two major newspapers are located in the same building).

Bacchus Ristorante. 845 Hornby St., in the Wedgewood Hotel. ☎ **604/608-5319.** www. wedgewoodhotel.com. Reservations required for dinner. Main courses C$6–C$16 (US$4–US$11) breakfast; C$13–C$16 (US$9–US$11) lunch; C$18–C$35 (US$12–US$23) dinner. AE, DC, MC, V. Daily 6:30am–2:30pm and 6–10pm; lounge menu until 11pm, Sat lounge menu until midnight. Weekend tea 2–4pm, weekend brunch 11am–2pm. Live entertainment daily. MEDITERRANEAN.

Bacchus is the centerpiece of Eleni Skalbania's Wedgewood Hotel. With cherry-wood paneling, a carved limestone fireplace, white linens, and comfortable chairs, the decor is wonderfully romantic. Award-winning chef Robert Sulatycky has created an eclectic menu that includes such diverse dishes as Brill sole and spot prawns and saddle of spring rabbit with sage jus and pâté de truffle. For dessert, the apricot soufflé Rothschild and caramelized apple tart with cardamom ice cream are luscious.

Bandi's. 1427 Howe St. ☎ **604/685-3391.** Reservations recommended. Main courses C$17–C$23 (US$11–US$15). AE, MC, V. Tues–Fri 11:30am–2pm; Tues–Sun 5:30–11pm. Bus: 1, 2. HUNGARIAN.

Owner, proprietor, chef, and occasional maître d' Bandi Rinkhy serves up big, garlicky, paprika-laden country specialties in this pretty yellow dollhouse of a restaurant. The formula's been the same for years, but with a romantic house for a setting and old-world panache in the service, who needs innovation? Savor the sour cherry soup before moving on to the signature crispy duck with red cabbage. Other options include pan-fried trout, stuffed herring fillets, breaded mushrooms, and the inevitable goulash. Servings are very generous, so if you're headed here for dinner, skip lunch.

✪ **Il Giardino di Umberto.** 1382 Hornby St. ☎ **604/669-2422.** Fax 604/669-9723. www.umberto.com. E-mail: umberto@intergate.ca. Reservations required. Main courses C$14– C$33 (US$9–US$22). AE, DC, MC, V. Mon–Fri noon–2:30pm; daily 5:30–11pm. Bus: 1, 22. ITALIAN.

Restaurant magnate Umberto Menghi's empire includes Umberto al Porto Borgo Antico on Water Street and two locations in Whistler. Il Giardino has created its own niche. Decorated in tones of burnt sienna with exposed wood beams, this restaurant re-creates the ambiance of an Italian seaside villa, down to the enclosed garden terrace and a Tuscan menu emphasizing pasta and game. Entrees include osso bucco Milanese with saffron risotto, tortellini with portobello mushrooms in truffle oil, roasted reindeer loin with port peppercorn sauce, and pheasant breast stuffed with wild mushrooms. After sampling the cuisine, more than a few devoted foodies have run off to enroll in Umberto's Tuscan cooking school, set in one of the hill towns of Tuscany.

✪ **Joe Fortes Seafood House.** 777 Thurlow St. (at Robson). ☎ **604/669-1940.** www. joefortesseafoodrest.com. Reservations recommended. Main courses C$17–C$37 (US$11–US$25). AE, DC, DISC, ER, MC, V. Mon–Fri 11:30am–10:30pm, Sat–Sun 11am–10:30pm. Bus: 5. SEAFOOD.

Named after the burly Caribbean seaman and popular local hero who became English Bay's first lifeguard, Joe Fortes has been known for years as the place where the young and tanned would meet for mutual schmoozing and raw oysters.

Joe's staff still all look like extras on a "90210" episode, but lately, under the direction of chef Brian Faulk, Joe's has been making a serious play as a top spot on the city's list of best seafood fusion. And the oyster bar is still among the city's best. Joe's rooftop patio—equipped with its own bar and kitchen—makes an extremely pleasant retreat on sunny days, particularly if you've just come from the Robson Street shopping bustle.

La Terrazza. 1088 Cambie St. ☎ **604/899-4449.** Reservations recommended. Main courses C$16–C$30 (US$11–US$20). AE, DC, ER, MC, V. Mon–Thurs 5–11pm, Fri–Sat 5pm–midnight, Sun 5–10pm. Bus: 2. ITALIAN.

Located on the edge of Yaletown, La Terrazza's sleek, modern exterior contrasts sharply with the warm bustling dining room inside. Two of the three owners hail from Italy and the kitchen is in the capable hands of chef Gennaro Iorio, originally from Naples. You will not find fusion or complicated culinary acrobatics on his menu. On the contrary, many of his dishes stand out for their simplicity. The menu changes with the seasons, and a tasting menu with matching wines highlights a different culinary region of Italy every month. One of the more intriguing appetizers is the bocconcini cheese, wrapped in prosciutto and raddicchio, grilled and drizzled with strawberry vinaigrette. Main courses include various pasta dishes, but following the chef's recommendation, we tried the roasted guinea hen and duck breast with frangelico brandy. Fresh vegetables and risotto or polenta accompany the dishes. The wine list offers bottles from most continents. A number of these are available by the glass. Save room for dessert, particularly the white cheesecake baked in phyllo pastry topped with sour cherries and fruit coulis.

MODERATE

Bin 941 Tapas Parlour. 941 Davie St. ☎ **604/683-1246.** Reservations not accepted. Tapas C$3–C$10 (US$2–US$7). MC, V. Mon–Sat 5pm–2am, Sun 5pm–midnight. Bus: 4, 5, 8. TAPAS.

Still booming two years on, Bin 941 is the latest in trendy tapas dining. True, the music's too loud and the room's too small, but the food that alights on the bar or ever so tiny tables is quite delicious, and, like all tapas, a lot of fun to eat. Look especially for local seafood offerings like scallops and tiger prawns in bonito butter sauce. Sharing is unavoidable in this sliver of a bistro, so come prepared for socializing. So successful was the original model that a second Bin, dubbed Bin 942, has opened up at 1521 West Broadway.

The Crime Lab. 1280 W. Pender St. ☎ **604/732-7463.** Reservations accepted. Main courses C$15–C$16 (US$10–US$11). AE, DC, MC, V. Sun–Thurs 5:30pm–midnight, Fri–Sat 5:30pm–2am. Bus: 135. WEST COAST/FUSION.

Illuminated by the cheap glow of neon and with menus covered by lurid jacket drawings of 1930s pulp fiction, the Crime Lab is an eternity of fun. The martini list is inspired by figures from Vancouver's underworld. Tables are tight in this stiletto-thin establishment, but for a group of 8 to 12, it's tough to beat the triangular table set at the point of the Lab's long blade. And then, of course, there's the food. Like most Vancouver restaurants, the menu covers all possibilities, but seafood is the specialty. Appetizers are superb—crab cakes with mango ginger aioli; mussels steamed with a salsa of scallions, cilantro, and vinegar; or Earl Bay oysters with a vinaigrette of sake ginger and cucumber. And when it comes to main courses, the seafood paella provides proof of the kitchen's abilities. The wine list sticks close to home, and service is both friendly and knowledgeable.

Hamilton Street Bar and Grill. 1009 Hamilton St. ☎ **604/331-1511.** Reservations recommended. Main courses C$12–C$34 (US$8–US$23). AE, DC, JCB, MC, V. Mon–Thurs 5pm–midnight, Fri–Sat 5pm–1am, Sun 5–11pm. Bus: 2. PACIFIC NORTHWEST.

This fun and funky eatery in the heart of Vancouver's dot-com district offers a superior brand of comfort food. Grab a seat at the long bar or sink into a plush booth and try one of the many warm tapas dishes, like tiger prawns in garlic or chicken sate in peanut sauce, or one of the well-prepared burgers or steaks. Together with a craft-brewed beer and a warm and buzzing atmosphere, it's the perfect way to cap off a hectic day of seeing the sights or launching a Web startup.

○ **La Bodega.** 1277 Howe St. ☎ 604/684-8814. Reservations accepted. Main courses C$10–C$16 (US$7–US$11). AE, DC, JCB, MC, V. Mon–Fri 11:30am–midnight, Sat 5pm--midnight, Sun 5–11pm. Bus: 4, 7. TAPAS/SPANISH.

This warm, dark Spanish bar has a dozen or so tables and some great little romantic corners. Expect authentic Spanish tapas—garlic prawns, ceviche, marinated mushrooms, pan-fried squid, and good black olives. Specials on the blackboard regularly include *conejo* (rabbit with tomatoes and peppers), quail, and B.C. scallops. All of it comes with lots of crusty bread for soaking up the wonderful garlicky goo. La Bodega has a good selection of Portuguese and Spanish wines and the best sangria in town.

INEXPENSIVE

○ **Olympia Oyster & Fish Co. Ltd.** 820 Thurlow St. ☎ **604/685-0716.** Main courses C$6–C$10 (US$4–US$7). AE, MC, V. Mon–Thurs 10am–8pm, Fri 8:30am–8pm, Sat 10am–7pm, Sun 11am–7pm. Bus: 5. FISH & CHIPS.

In a brand-new spot just around the corner from its old Robson Street location, this tiny fish store and restaurant is still a neighborhood favorite. And it still produces Vancouver's best fish-and-chips. There are only a few tables and a window-seat counter, plus three sidewalk tables, weather permitting, but the fish is always fresh and flaky and can be grilled if you prefer. The seafood platter is enough for two. If the place is packed, ask for a takeout order and head 2 blocks east down Robson Street to Robson Square for a picnic. Or you can shop for smoked salmon or caviar which can be shipped home. Sip a ginger beer while you wait.

The Tempelton. 1087 Granville St. ☎ **604/685-4612.** Main courses C$3.50–C$9 (US$2.35–US$6). V. Sun–Mon 10am–10pm, Tues 10am–midnight, Wed–Thurs 10am–11pm, Fri–Sat 10am–1am. Bus: 4, 7, 8, 10. AMERICAN.

A diner, but not really a diner. More like a trendy retro commentary on the diner, except that this place has been in continuous operation since 1934. True, back then the green Hamilton Beach milk-shake makers were the height of modern and the serving staff likely didn't go in for nose and belly-button rings and tattoos. Don't show up with a hangover and expect greasy eggs and bacon. Instead, think jambalaya, chili, blackened chicken breast, or a portobello-mushroom vegetarian burger. (Okay, there are eggs and burgers too, but they almost always have little fusion-y touches.) Saturday brunch is 10% off if you arrive in your pajamas. Staff already have them on.

3 Gastown & Chinatown

EXPENSIVE

The Cannery. 2205 Commissioner St., near Victoria Dr. ☎ 604/254-9606. www.canneryseafood.com. E-mail: info@canneryseafood.com. Reservations recommended. Main courses C$17–C$27 (US$11–US$18). AE, DC, DISC, JCB, MC, V. Daily 11:30am–2:30pm; Sun–Fri 5:30–9:30pm, Sat 5:30–10pm. Closed Dec 24–26. Bus: 7 to Victoria Dr. From downtown, head east on Hastings St., turn left on Victoria Dr. (2 blocks past Commercial Dr.), then right on Commissioner St. SEAFOOD.

At least some of the pleasure of eating at The Cannery comes from simply finding the place. Hop over the railway tracks and thread your way past container terminals and

Dinner on the *Starlight Express*

BC Rail's Pacific Starlight Dinner Train departs from the North Vancouver train terminal, transporting passengers past West Vancouver's waterfront mansions, along Howe Sound's scenic shoreline, past Porteau Cove, and back. The elegant restored coaches recall a time when rail travel was as much about going as it was about getting somewhere. The cars are appointed with inlaid wood, brass, and all the other touches you'd expect in a first-class dining car from rail travel's golden age. Seating in the salon (C$84/US$56 per person, excluding taxes, tips, and alcohol) is slightly less expensive than seating in the glass-domed observation car (C$100/US$67 per person), but the spectacular 360° view of the sun setting over Howe Sound and the surrounding mountains is worth every cent. Bring your camera. But even more than the views, the fine service and outstanding West Coast cuisine make either choice worthwhile. Recent entree selections have included roasted British Columbia salmon, stuffed breast of guinea fowl, fillet of beef tenderloin, beef Wellington, and vegetable rotolo (a medley of roasted vegetables and pasta topped with sage-and-tomato sauce and ricotta cheese). For dessert, the white-chocolate soup is fast becoming the signature dish.

The train operates every Wednesday to Sunday evening from May 1 to November 1, departing from the BC Rail Station, 1311 W. First St., North Vancouver, at 6:15pm and returning at 9:45pm. The dress code stipulates "fine dining attire" but recommends that women shouldn't wear high heels. For information or reservations, call BC Rail Passenger Services (☎ **800/363-3733** or 604/984-5246).

fish packing plants until you're sure you're lost and then with a last turn the road opens onto a brightly lit parking lot and there it is—a great ex-warehouse of a building hanging out over the waters of Burrard Inlet. The building itself—its beam-laded warehouse interior, loaded with old nets and seafaring memorabilia—is another hefty portion of The Cannery's charm. As for the view, that's simply stunning, one of the best in Vancouver. So how about the food? Good, solid, traditional seafood, often alder-grilled, with ever-changing specials to complement the salmon and halibut basics. Chefs Frederic Couton and Jacques Wan have been getting more inventive of late, but when an institution's 27 years old and still going strong, no one's ever *too* keen to rock the boat. The wine list is stellar and the desserts are both wonderful and wonderfully inventive.

Raintree Restaurant at the Landing. 375 Water St. ☎ **604/688-5570.** Reservations recommended. Main courses C$16–C$27 (US$11–US$18). AE, DC, JCB, MC, V. Daily 11:30am–2:30pm and 5:30–10pm. Skytrain: Waterfront. WEST COAST.

Once the darling of food critics and fusion aficionados, the Raintree fell on (comparatively) hard times for a few years. But it's back with a new chef and a new focus on West Coast cuisine, local ingredients (including wild salmon), and vegetarian and vegan dishes. Located in a beautiful heritage building in Gastown, the dining room's exposed brick walls frame a fabulous panoramic harborside view of the North Shore. The service is attentive and professional, and the menu is filled with the creativity that made Raintree the city's first and best spot for West Coast cuisine. Try the kelp-crusted sea scallops, the broiled Pacific snapper, or the seared Washington duck breast with grilled pear and gooseberry compote.

MODERATE

Park Lock Seafood Restaurant. 544 Main St. (at E. Pender St.). ☎ **604/688-1581.** Reservations recommended. Main courses C$10–C$35 (US$7–US$23); dim sum dishes C$2.50–C$3.25 (US$1.65–US$2.15). AE, MC, V. Daily 8am–3pm; Tues–Sun 5–9:30pm. Bus: 19, 22. CHINESE/DIM SUM.

If you've never done dim sum, this traditional dining room in the very heart of China-town is the place to give it a try. From 10am to 3pm daily, waitresses wheel little carts loaded with Chinese delicacies past white-linen–covered tables. When you see some-thing you like, you grab it. The final bill is based upon how many little dishes are left on your table. Dishes include spring rolls, *hargow* and *shumai* (steamed shrimp, beef, or pork dumplings), prawns wrapped in fresh white noodles, small steamed buns, sticky rice cooked in banana leaves, curried squid, and lots more. Parties of four or more are best—that way you get to try each other's food.

✪ **Pink Pearl.** 1132 E. Hastings St. ☎ **604/253-4316.** www.pinkpearl.com. Main courses C$12–C$35 (US$8–US$23); dim sum C$2.95–C$6 (US$1.95–US$4). AE, DC, MC, V. Daily 9am–10pm. CHINESE/DIM SUM.

This is the city's best spot for dim sum. The sheer volume and bustle are astonishing. Dozens of waiters parade a cavalcade of little trolleys stacked high with baskets and steamers and bowls filled with dumplings, spring rolls, shrimp balls, chicken feet, and even more obscure and delightful offerings. At the tables, extended families of Chinese banter, joke, and feast. Towers of empty plates and bowls pile up in the middle, a trib-ute to the appetites of hungry brunchers, as well as the growing bill; fortunately, dim sum is still a steal, perhaps the best and most fun way to sample Cantonese cooking.

INEXPENSIVE

✪ **Brothers Restaurant.** 1 Water St. ☎ **604/683-9124.** Fax 604/683-9124. Reservations recommended. Main courses C$8–C$25 (US$5–US$17); children's courses C$2.95–C$4.95 (US$1.95–US$3.30). AE, DC, MC, V. Daily 11:30am–10pm. Bus: 1, 50. AMERICAN.

Decorated like a Franciscan monastery, complete with staff in friars' robes, Brothers has a warm ambiance especially appealing to families. Main dishes include chowder, pastas, burgers, and serious prime rib. Children get balloons and their own menu. A bistro lounge featuring sushi and an oyster bar caters primarily to a younger crowd.

✪ **Incendio.** 103 Columbia St. ☎ **604/688-8694.** E-mail: incendio@imag.net. Main courses C$7–C$12 (US$4.70–US$8). AE, MC, V. Mon–Fri 11:30am–3pm and 5–10pm; Sat–Sun 5–11pm. Bus: 1, 8. PIZZA.

If you're looking for something casual and local that won't be full of other people read-ing downtown maps, this little Gastown hideaway is sublime. The 22 pizza combina-tions are served on fresh, crispy crusts baked in an old wood-fired oven. Pastas are homemade, and you're encouraged to mix and match—try the mussels with spinach fettuccine, capers, and tomatoes in lime butter. The wine list is decent; the beer list is inspired. And now, there's a patio. Sunday night features all-you-can-eat pizza for C$8 (US$5).

Phnom Penh Restaurant. 244 E. Georgia St., near Main St. ☎ **604/682-5777.** Dishes C$4.50–C$11 (US$3–US$7). DC, MC. Wed–Mon 10am–9:30pm. Bus: 8, 19. CAMBODIAN/VIETNAMESE.

This family-run restaurant serves a mixture of Vietnamese and slightly spicier Cam-bodian cuisine. Phnom Penh is a perennial contender for, and occasional winner of, *Vancouver Magazine*'s award for the city's best Asian restaurant. The walls are adorned with artistic renderings of ancient Cambodia's capital, Angkor. Khmer dolls are sus-pended in glass cases, and the subdued lighting is a welcome departure from the harsh glare often found in inexpensive Chinatown restaurants. Try the outstanding hot-and-sour soup, loaded with prawns and lemongrass. The deep-fried garlic squid served with rice is also delicious. For dessert, the fruit-and-rice pudding is an exotic treat. There's a second location at 955 Broadway at Oak Street (☎ **604/734-8898**), open during the same hours.

4 The West End

EXPENSIVE

Café de Paris. 751 Denman St. (at Robson). ☎ **604/687-1418.** Reservations recommended. Main courses C$18–C$26 (US$12–US$17), fixed-price menu C$23 (US$15). AE, MC, V. Mon–Fri 11:30am–2pm, Sun 11am–2:30pm and 5–9pm; Mon–Sat 5:30–10pm. Bus: 5. FRENCH.

The bike-and-blade rental zone on lower Denman would seem an unlikely place to seek out Paris, but enter and there you are on the Left Bank. Edith Piaf's voice fills a cozy room of wood and brass, decorated with Rabelaisian oil paintings and a map of Haussmann's Paris. A big wood bar is stocked with an empire of fine French liquors and cognacs. The wine list never leaves the Fifth Republic (you expected otherwise?) and ranges from a C$24 house red to a C$1,500 (US$16 to US$1,000) bottle of Chateau Haut-Brion Bordeaux, 1985. Cuisine is ever so French (though the friendly service is anything but). Appetizers include Burgundy snails in garlic butter, braised rabbit in Dijon mustard sauce, and, of course, onion soup. The menu also includes classics such as tournedos, pepper steak, and roasted chicken. Whatever you do, make sure you save some room for dessert. Selections include frangelico-poached pears, fresh raspberry custard tart, and maraschino chocolate cake. Odds are, after a meal at Café de Paris, you'll leave a little heavier. I did. Do I care? *"Non, je ne regrette rien."*

Cin Cin. 1154 Robson St. ☎ **604/688-7338.** www.cincin.net. Reservations recommended. Main courses C$16–C$40 (US$11–US$27). AE, DC, MC, V. Mon–Fri 11:30am–2:30pm; daily 5–11pm. Bus: 5, 22. MEDITERRANEAN.

Cin Cin is known almost as well for who eats here as for what's eaten here. Celebrities, models, politicians, and tourists all frequent this second-story, villa-style bistro. The dining room is built around the open kitchen, which is built around a huge alderwood-fired oven. The heated terrace overlooking Robson Street is an equally nice dining and people-watching spot. Food? Dishes range from elegant pastas and pizzas—capellini alla pomodoro, penne puttanesca, and pizza Margherita—to more substantial dishes such as rosemary-marinated rack of lamb, sea bass crusted with porcini mushrooms, and smoked chicken breast. The wine list is extensive, as is the selection of wines by the glass.

✪ **Delilah's.** 1789 Comox St. ☎ **604/687-3424.** Reservations accepted for parties of 6 or more. Fixed-price menu C$21–C$34 (US$14–US$23). AE, DC, ER, MC, V. Daily 5:30pm–midnight. Bus: 5 to Denman St. CONTINENTAL.

Walk down the steps from the Denman Place Mall and you've entered Delilah's French bordello of a room—red velvet chaise longues, little private corner rooms, cherubim cavorting on the ceiling, and wall-mounted lamps with glass shades blown to look like orchids at their most outrageously sensuous. First order of business is a martini—Delilah's forte, and the fuel firing the laughter and conversation all around. The two-page martini list comes with everything from the basic Boston Tea Partini (Citron vodka and iced tea in a glass with sugared rim and lemon wedge) to the ultimate in Southern excess, the Miranda (pineapple, vodka, and fresh floating fruit). The staff are brisk and helpful and run to the Miranda side—flamboyant, friendly, and over the top. The menu is seafood heavy, which Delilah's does well, sticking to freshness and simple sauces such as the seared jumbo scallops with saffron risotto or grilled swordfish with a sun-dried cherry-cranberry compote. The chef gets a bit over his head with land-based fare, so go with the flow and order something from the sea.

The Fish House in Stanley Park. 8901 Stanley Park Dr. ☎ **604/681-7275.** www.fishhousestanleypark.com. Email: info@fishhousestanleypark.com. Reservations recommended. Main courses C$17–C$30 (US$11–US$20). AE, DC, DISC, JCB, MC, V. Mon–Sat 11:30am–10pm, Sun 11am–10pm. Bus: 1, 35, 135. SEAFOOD.

Reminiscent of a more genteel era, this white-clapboard clubhouse is surrounded by public tennis courts, bowling greens, and ancient cedar trees. Three rooms decorated in hunter green with dark wood and whitewashed accents complete the clubhouse atmosphere. The menu includes some innovative dishes, such as tender pan-seared Alaskan scallops with sweet chili glaze, lemongrass crusted prawn satay, and a smoked-salmon sampler. The oyster bar has at least a half dozen fresh varieties daily. The desserts are sumptuous. The restaurant and the bar draw a mix of golfers, strollers, and local execs.

Liliget Feast House & Catering. 1724 Davie St. ☎ **604/681-7044.** Reservations recommended. Main courses C$16–C$30 (US$11–US$20). Daily 5–10pm. AE, DC, ER, MC, V. Bus: 5. WEST COAST/FIRST NATIONS.

The nondescript entrance gives no hint of the unique restaurant located downstairs from an East Indian restaurant. The dining room is filled with natural cedar columns rising from the water-worn stone floor; the tables are sunken into stone platforms around a central cedar-and-stone walkway. Recorded song-stories about potlatch ceremonies play in the background. The food is traditional West Coast First Nations fare. Appetizers include grilled oysters, clam fritters, grilled prawns, breaded and fried smelt, salmon or venison soup, and bannock (delicious fried bread). Entrees like sweet alder-smoked salmon, lightly smoked duck breast, and grilled marinated venison steak are sumptuous. Local side dishes include fiddleheads, sea asparagus, and wild rice. Available in various sizes, the "Potlatch Platters" are an ideal way to sample a bit of everything. For people curious about modern First Nations culture, this is one experience that shouldn't be missed.

✪ **Raincity Grill.** 1193 Denman St. ☎ **604/685-7337.** www.raincitygrill.com. Reservations recommended. Main courses C$18–C$34 (US$12–US$23). AE, DC, ER, MC, V. Mon–Fri 11:30am–2:30pm, Sat–Sun 10:30am–2:30pm; daily 5–10:30pm. Bus: 1, 5. WEST COAST.

Raincity's room is long and low and hugs the shoreline, the better to let the evening sun pour in. With the location—by English Bay Beach—and the spacious patio, you wonder if the owner didn't have to kill for the spot. Then you realize he's paying off the view with volume—they do pack 'em in at Raincity, making dinner more of a social occasion than you may have wished. Ah, but the view. And the food. Raincity's forte is local ingredients, West Coast style. That means appetizers of barbecued quail with a sage and goat-cheese polenta, crispy jumbo spot prawns, or a salad of smoked steelhead. Entrees include grilled Fraser Valley free-range chicken and fresh-caught spring salmon. And then there's the award-winning wine list. It's huge and, in keeping with the restaurant's theme, it sticks pretty close to home. Better yet, most varieties are available by the glass.

✪ **The Teahouse Restaurant.** Ferguson Point, Stanley Park. ☎ **604/669-3281.** www.sequoiarestaurants.com. Reservations required. Lunch main courses C$11–C$17 (US$7–US$11), dinner main courses C$17–C$28 (US$11–US$19). AE, MC, V. Mon–Sat 11:30am–2:30pm, Sun brunch 10:30am–2:30pm; daily 5:30–10pm. Bus: 135 or 1. CONTINENTAL.

Nestled into secluded Ferguson Point on the far side of Stanley Park are the low main building and greenhouse that make up The Teahouse Restaurant. The original structure was built in 1928 as a troop barracks, but time and careful decorating have transformed it into something resembling an English hunter's cottage. Soft light and muted florals create what would be one of Vancouver's most romantic locations—if it weren't for the busloads of big-eyed tourists. Still, even with lots of company, the Teahouse is a special spot. Book a table on the terrace—at least a day in advance, longer on weekend evenings—and arrive in time to dine while the sun slowly sets behind Vancouver Island far across the Strait of Georgia. And surprisingly enough, the food is consistently high caliber. The menu covers all the bases—a tender, delicious roasted rack of lamb is the signature dish, though the breast of Barbary duck with squash cappelletti and tarragon jus is a strong contender—yet still manages to do some innovative West Coast dishes, especially with fresh-caught salmon. Desserts include baked Alaska for two and orange Grand Marnier crème brûlée. Monday to Saturday between 2:30 and 5pm, the tearoom and (weather permitting) the patio serve light snacks and refreshments.

MODERATE

✪ **Cactus Club Café.** 1136 Robson St. ☎ **604/687-3278.** (Also 1508 Broadway at Granville, and 15 other locations.) Main courses C$6–C$19 (US$4–US$13). AE, MC, V. Daily 11am–midnight (later in the summer). SOUTHWESTERN.

So it's not fine dining. That's not why you come. The crowd is young, the room is fun, the beer is cold, and the waitresses invariably beautiful. Dinner almost always starts at the bar, 'cause there's always a line and they don't take reservations. Hang out, have a beer and some calamari, hot wings, or potato skins. When you finally reach your table, the food is consistently good—sizzling fajitas, six variations of Caesar salad, slow-cooked Jamaican-style jerk chicken, and succulent barbecued ribs.

✪ **Romano's Macaroni Grill at the Mansion.** 1523 Davie St. ☎ **604/689-4334.** Reservations recommended. Main courses C$8–C$16 (US$5–US$11), children's courses C$3.95–C$6 (US$2.65–US$4). AE, DC, MC, V. Sun–Thurs 4–10pm, Fri–Sat 4–11pm. Bus: 5. FAMILY-STYLE ITALIAN.

Housed in a huge stone mansion built in the early 20th century by sugar baron B. T. Rogers, Romano's is fun and casual. Wood paneling, stained-glass windows, and chandeliers surround tables covered with red-and-white checked tablecloths. The menu is Southern Italian, and the pastas are definitely favorites. This isn't high-concept Italian; the food is simple, understandable, and consistently good. You're charged for the house wine based on how much you pour from the bottle. Your kids will love the children's menu, which features lasagna and meat loaf as well as tasty pizzas, and the permissive staff that bursts into opera at the slightest provocation.

✪ **Sami's.** 1795 Pendrell St. ☎ **604/915-7264.** Bus: 5. Also at 986 W. Broadway. ☎ **604/736-8330.** Bus: 10. Reservations not accepted. Main courses C$12 (US$8). DC, MC, V. Daily May–Oct 11:30am–2pm and 4–11pm, Nov–Apr 4–11pm. INDIAN.

Who says things don't get better with time? A year ago anyone wanting to try Sami Lalji's fabulous East-meets-West South Asian cooking had to make the trip out to a strip mall off West Broadway. True, the food was worth the journey, but so successful was this formula that Lalji decided to open a second Sami's downtown, just off Denman Street and a stroll-and-a-half from English Bay. Like the original, Sami's on Denman offers inventive and delicious dishes—try the Mumbai-blackened New York steak set atop spiked mashers with blueberry coriander jus—that won't put a large hole in your wallet. Service is efficient, if a tad too friendly.

Tanpopo. 1122 Denman St. ☎ **604/681-7777.** Reservations recommended. Main courses C$7–C$19 (US$4.70–US$13). AE, DC, MC, V. Daily 11:30am–10:30pm. Bus: 5. JAPANESE.

Occupying the second floor of a corner building on Denman Street, Tanpopo has a partial view of English Bay, a large patio, and a huge menu of hot and cold Japanese dishes. But the lines of people waiting 30 minutes or more for a table every night are here for the all-you-can-eat sushi. The unlimited fare includes the standards—makis, tuna and salmon sashimi, California and B.C. rolls—as well as cooked items such as tonkatsu, tempura, chicken kara-age, and broiled oysters. There are a couple of secrets to getting seated. Call ahead, but they take only an arbitrary percentage of reservations for dinner each day, or ask to sit at the sushi bar.

INEXPENSIVE

Gyoza King. 1508 Robson St. ☎ **604/669-8278.** Main courses C$6–C$13 (US$4–US$9). MC, V. Sat–Sun 11:30am–3pm; Mon–Sat 5:30pm–2am, Sun 5:30pm–midnight. Bus: 5. JAPANESE.

Gyoza King features an entire menu of *gyoza*—succulent Japanese dumplings filled with prawns, pork, vegetables, and other combinations—as well as Japanese noodles and staples like *katsu-don* (pork cutlet over rice) and *o-den* (a rich, hearty soup). This is the gathering spot for hordes of young Japanese visitors looking for cheap eats that still taste close to home cooking. Seating is divided among Western-style tables, the bar (where you can watch the chef in action), and the Japanese-style front table, which is reserved for larger groups if the restaurant is busy. The staff is very courteous and happy to explain the dishes if you're not familiar with Japanese cuisine.

Just One Thai Bistro. 1103 Denman St. ☎ **604/685-8989.** www.thaihouse.com. Main courses C$10–C$15 (US$7–US$10). AE, MC, V. Daily 11am–11pm. Bus: 5. THAI.

The rare four-headed golden Buddha at the entrance and the collection of smaller Buddhas set into wall recesses, combined with stone floors, palm trees, and fresh flowers, give this place the serenity of a temple and the exotic elegance of a Thai palace garden. The house specialty is Thai barbecue, the beef satay is outstanding, and the curries and stir-fries are equally good. If you have a cold, there's no better cure than a

---

ⓘ Family-Friendly Restaurants

Romano's Macaroni Grill at the Mansion *(see p. 97)*   The huge children's menu offers numerous dinner choices, and the friendly staff will even let kids wander up the inviting mansion staircase to explore the upper rooms.

Brothers Restaurant *(see p. 94)*   Kids get balloons along with a special menu at this Gastown establishment.

Mark's Fiasco *(see p. 102)*   Crayons on every paper-covered table and a friendly staff are coupled with excellent burgers and fries, pizzas, and pasta.

The Naam Restaurant *(see p. 102)*   The Naam offers highchairs, very easy-going service, a big patio for kids to run around on, and lots of good finger food.

Sophie's Cosmic Café *(see p. 103)*   Great finger food, crayons and coloring paper, and lots and lots of eye-candy to keep kids occupied.

Any Chinese Restaurant   Chinese families almost always dine en masse, so Chinese restaurants are used to accommodating children. And given the size of most menus, there's guaranteed to be something they'll like.

steaming bowl of *tom yum goong,* a hot-and-sour soup heaping with prawns, mushrooms, and lemongrass.

Rooster's Quarters. 836 Denman St. ☎ **604/689-8023.** Dishes C$8–C$14 (US$5–US$9). AE, MC, V. Daily 11am–11pm. Bus: 5. CANADIAN.

Rooster's Quarters offers the antidote to diet food. Succulent baby back ribs are served in a sweet-and-tangy, maple barbecue sauce, and the Québec-style barbecued chicken is crispy on the outside, tender and juicy on the inside. If those don't hit the spot, try the *poutine,* a Quebec dish of french fries covered with melted curd cheese and brown gravy. The decor is as casual as the menu and the atmosphere, with wallpaper images of garden scenes, potted plants, and shelves with over 300 rooster and chicken knick-knacks. It can get a little crowded, but just pick out a table and seat yourself if there is no line. That's what the regulars do.

✪ **Stephos.** 1124 Davie St. ☎ **604/683-2555.** Reservations accepted for parties of 5 or more. Main courses C$4.25–C$10 (US$2.85–US$7). AE, MC, V. Daily 11:30am–11:30pm. Bus: 5. GREEK.

There's a reason Stephos is packed every day for lunch and dinner: The cuisine is simple Greek fare at its finest and cheapest. Customers line up outside to wait up to 30 minutes for a seat amid Greek travel posters, potted ivy, and whitewashed walls. (The average wait is about 10 to 15 minutes.) But once you're inside, the staff will never rush you out the door. Generous portions of delicious marinated lamb, chicken, pork, or beef over rice pilaf; *tzatziki* (a garlicky yogurt dip); and heaping platters of calamari are just a few of the offerings. While success is too often the downfall of a neighborhood restaurant, Stephos recently doubled in size and completely renovated, without raising its prices or compromising its quality.

5 The West Side

VERY EXPENSIVE

✪ **Bishop's.** 2183 W. Fourth Ave. ☎ **604/738-2025.** www.bishops.net. Reservations required. Main courses C$27–C$34 (US$18–US$23). AE, MC, V. Mon–Sat 5:30–11pm, Sun 5:30–10pm. Closed Jan 1–15. Bus: 4, 7. FRENCH.

John Bishop doesn't behave like someone who owns what has been one of Vancouver's finest restaurants for the past decade. He personally greets you, escorts you to your table, and introduces you to an extensive list of fine wines and a menu he describes as "contemporary home cooking." The atmosphere is set by candlelight, white linen, and soft jazz playing in the background. The service is impeccable, and the food is even better. The menu changes three or four times a year. Recent dishes have included roast duck breast with sun-dried Okanagan Valley fruits and candied ginger glacé; steamed smoked black cod with new potatoes and horseradish sabayon; and marinated lamb with garlic mashed potatoes and a fresh mint, tomato, and balsamic vinegar reduction. If you plan on splurging one night, this is one of the best places to do it.

✪ **Lumière.** 2551 W. Broadway. ☎ **604/739-8185.** Reservations recommended. Tasting menu (8 courses) C$60–C$100 (US$40–US$67). AE, DC, MC, V. Tues–Sun 5:30–9:30pm. Bus: 9, 10. FRENCH/WEST COAST.

The success of this French-fusion dining experiment in the heart of Kitsilano has turned chef Rob Feenie into a very hot commodity. He now regularly jets off to New York to teach folks back east how to do it right. And how is that? Preparation and presentation are immaculately French, while ingredients are resolutely local, which makes for interesting surprises like fresh local ginger with the veal, or raspberries in the foie gras. Lumière's tasting menus are a series of 8 or 10 delightful plates that change with the season, perfectly matched to a local wine vintage (not included in the fixed price) and gorgeously presented. Diners simply choose one of the four tasting menus (including one vegetarian menu) and then sit back and let the pilots in Lumière's kitchen take them on a culinary journey they won't soon forget. If you can afford it, it's a voyage you shouldn't miss.

✪ **Tojo's Restaurant.** 777 W. Broadway. ☎ **604/872-8050.** Reservations required for sushi bar. Full dinners C$23–C$100 (US$15–US$67). AE, DC, MC, V. Mon–Sat 5–11pm. Closed Christmas week. Bus: 9. JAPANESE.

I had never met Hideki Tojo, or even tried his cooking, until one afternoon at Vancouver's first-ever sumo wrestling demonstration, when a diminutive man on the tatami mat next to me lifted up a bento box and proffered a tray of delicate sushi rolls. As two thunderous giants eyed each other in the ring, I picked out a piece with fresh salmon and popped it in my mouth. Incredible. A thousand pounds of screaming human flesh were smashing each other in the ring, but my attention was entirely captured by the exquisite flavors exploding in my mouth. Back in Tojo's modest sushi bar, the ever-changing menu offers such specialties as sea urchin on the half shell, herring roe, lobster claws, tuna, crab, and asparagus. I'd like to say I've since become a regular, but at the prices Tojo charges for his creations, regulars are either film stars or fully mortgaged for the next seven generations. Still, if you don't mind splurging and you want the very best, Tojo is your man.

EXPENSIVE

Pastis. 2153 W. Fourth Ave. ☎ **604/731-5020.** Reservations recommended. Main courses C$16–C$26 (US$11–US$17). AE, DC, MC, V. Mon–Sat 5:30–10:30pm, Sun 5:30–10pm. Bus: 4, 7. FRENCH.

For those seeking an elegant refuge on the city's west side, there's Pastis, a candlelit French outpost in the heart of Kitsilano. Appetizers include escargot with portobello mushrooms and goat cheese with oven-dried tomatoes, while mains include such delectables as sweetbreads and morels cooked *en cocotte* (in a puff pastry), roasted duck with field rhubarb, and pan-seared ahi tuna on celery hearts. The accompanying wine list is excellent, as is the service.

The Smoking Dog. 1889 W. First Ave. ☎ **604/732-8811.** Reservations accepted. Main courses C$22–C$30 (US$15–US$20). AE, ER, MC, V. Mon–Fri 11:30am–2:30pm; Mon–Sat 5:30–10:30pm. Bus: 2, 22. FRENCH.

To date, the little Kitsilano neighborhood of Yorkville Mews has remained a local secret, perhaps because those few tourists who do venture into this delightful one-block stretch are immediately confronted with a confusing variety of choices. Should one stop at one of the three cafes, the tapas bar, the sushi spot, the vegan cafe, or this traditional Parisian bistro, complete with patio umbrellas, obsequious waiters dressed in black, and a friendly bear of an owner who greets everyone at the door? Food-wise, the Dog is undoubtedly the best (and priciest) of the lot, featuring New York pepper steak, grilled halibut with Pernod sauce, and scallops with beurre blanc. If the weather allows, grab a spot on the heated patio and enjoy the bustling street life.

Star Anise. 1485 W. 12th Ave. ☎ **604/737-1485.** Reservations recommended. Main courses C$16–C$29 (US$11–US$19). AE, DC, ER, MC, V. Daily 11am–2pm and 5:30–midnight. Bus: 8, 10. PACIFIC NORTHWEST.

When the Star first opened back in 1993, Vancouver foodies were wowed by the kitchen's innovative combinations of Indian and Chinese flavors with traditional West

Coast ingredients such as salmon and scallops. Since then, however, the fusion boundaries have been pushed even farther elsewhere, so the fickle foodie crowd has largely moved on. Too bad. Quality at this intimate eatery on the edge of South Granville's gallery row has never faltered. Ingredients are fresh, presentation scrumptious, and the service welcoming and knowledgeable. The wine list leans heavily on French and Californian vintages, and the small number available by the glass are well chosen. The room is warm to the point of being cozy, and owners Justin Cote and Ellen Lalji recently brought in Toronto chef Robert Fortin to rekindle some of that early excitement. Look for new dishes like chilled curry-mango soup with mint yogurt; roast rabbit-leg confit with sweet-potato galette, mizuna leaves, and Saskatoonberry chutney; or marinated ahi tuna with baby bok choy and cilantro pomme purée. As for dessert, however, tradition reigns: cardamom crème brûlée is fine, but the real treat is chocolate tarte cooled with crème anglaise.

MODERATE

Andales. 3211 W. Broadway. ☎ **604/738-9782.** Reservations accepted. Main courses C$10–C$18 (US$7–US$12). AE, MC, V. Daily 11am–midnight. Bus: 9. MEXICAN/SPANISH.

Mexican food has had a hard time. In this part of the world it's gone from nonexistent to suddenly trendy to the equivalent of the '50s burger and fries. Nobody takes it seriously, not even the folks at Andales—they just do it well. The menu borrows a lot from Spain, so look for (and order) the sautéed squid with garlic and tortillas, chorizo con queso, or the 10-layer dip. All make a good beginning for fajitas, chimichangas, or paella. Better yet, order the Puntas a las Mexicanas, a kind of spicy beef stew. Your taste buds will thank you, even if your waistline won't. The decor leans towards bullfight posters and silly Mexican hats, but don't let that scare you off. Also at 1175 Davie St. (☎ **604/682-8820**).

Avenue One Bistro. 2209 W. First Ave. ☎ **604/734-1113.** Fax 604/421-0788. Main courses C$13–C$32 (US$9–US$21). MC, V. Daily 5:30–11:30pm; Sat–Sun 9:30am–3:30pm. Bus 2 or 22. BISTRO/WEST COAST FUSION.

If you're ever in the neighborhood of Kits Beach and find yourself hankering after something more than nachos and home brew, walk two blocks uphill on Yew Street and sit yourself down at this little gem of a bistro. In the summer, the small patio provides a quiet refuge from the traffic and crowds. The tapas menu has plenty of nibbling options. The seared ahi tuna with lime and ginger or the mango salad masala prawns don't skimp on flavor or spices and are perfect for sharing. The main menu offers a range of seafood choices (as well as a few nonseafood options) but the real stars here are the lobsters. A steaming lobster pot set up outside the main entrance will cook them just right. Real seafood gluttons shouldn't miss the seafood platter (C$32/US$21) of lobster, crab, scallops, and mussels. Wines are mostly British Columbian, Italian, or French with a decent selection by the glass. As a juiced-up alternative, the bar offers 24 different martinis.

The Cat's Meow. 1540 Old Bridge St. (Granville Island). ☎ **604/647-2287.** Main courses C$8–C$19 (US$5–US$13). AE, MC, V. Mon–Fri 11am–midnight, Sat 9am–1am, Sun 9am–10pm. Bus: 50. CASUAL.

Locals may be unfamiliar with the Cat's Meow, but if you tell them it's where Isadora's used to be, their eyes will light up. The long-running cooperative restaurant was sadly missed when it finally closed its doors. Fortunately, the Cat's Meow has done a good job filling the delightful room and patio by providing tasty and affordable sandwiches, burgers, pizzas, and pastas. Appetizers such as crab cakes and salmon canapés perfectly match a beer on a sunny day. The back patio overlooks the kids' water-play area, where they can frolic in the sprinklers and fountains. Later on in the evening kids and parents give way to a younger crowd.

Mark's Fiasco. 2468 Bayswater St. (at W. Broadway). ☎ **604/734-1325.** Reservations recommended. Main courses C$7–C$19 (US$4.70–US$13). AE, MC, V. Daily 11:45am–11pm (bar stays open later). Bus 9. STEAK.

Mark's is the casual pub of choice for the Kitsilano jock-boy crowd, with a brass bar, 15 microbrews on tap, and at least four channels of sports on strategically placed boob tubes. On the restaurant side, Mark's offers a well-rounded menu of pastas, pizzas, seafood, and meat dishes. Appetizers include steamed mussels, fried calamari, and a delicious baked spinach dip. With a burger and fries starting at C$7 (US$4.70), crayons on every paper-covered table, and a congenial staff, Mark's is also kid-friendly.

✪ **Vij's.** 1480 W. 11th Ave. ☎ **604/736-6664.** Fax 604/736-3701. Reservations not accepted. Main courses C$14–C$19 (US$9–US$13). AE, MC, V. Daily 5:30–10pm, later if busy. Bus: 8, 10. INDIAN.

Vij doesn't take reservations, but then he really doesn't have to: There's a line outside his door every single night. Patrons huddled under Vij's violet neon sign are treated to complimentary tea and *papadums.* For a few dollars more, an Indian Pale Ale (IPA) can be rustled up to help soothe the wait. Inside, the decor is as warm and subtle as the seasonings, which are all roasted and ground by hand, then used with studied delicacy. The menu changes monthly, though some of the more popular entrees remain constants. Recent offerings included coconut curried chicken and saffron rice, and marinated pork medallions with garlic-yogurt curry and *naan* (flat bread). Vegetarian selections abound, including curried vegetable rice pilaf with cilantro cream sauce, and Indian lentils with naan and *raita* (yogurt-mint sauce). The wine and beer list is short but carefully selected. And for teetotalers, Vij has developed a souped-up version of the traditional Indian chai, the chaiuccino.

INEXPENSIVE

✪ **Annapurna.** 1812 W. Fourth Ave. ☎ **604/736-5959.** Main courses C$10–C$11 (US$7–US$8). AE, MC, V. Daily 11:30am–10pm. Bus: 4, 7. INDIAN/VEGETARIAN.

Annapurna gets my vote as Vancouver's best vegetarian restaurant, and it's up there in the running for best Indian as well. A Kitsilano favorite, the restaurant's small dining room is hung with dozens of rice-paper lamps in whites, yellows, oranges, and reds that, when combined with the mirrors, bask the room in a soft, warm glow. The menu is all vegetarian, but with the amazing combinations of Indian spices, herbs, and local vegetables, the dishes are rich and satisfying. Appetizers include samosas, pakoras, and lentil dumplings soaked in tangy yogurt with chutney. A variety of breads, such as paratha, naans, and chapatis, are served piping hot. Entrees such as *aloo-ghobi* (potato curry with cauliflower, onions, and cilantro) or *navrattan korma* (seasonal vegetables simmered in poppy-seed paste, flavored with saffron, aniseed, and sliced almonds) can be prepared from mild to screaming hot. The wine list is small but very reasonably priced. With food, wine, and atmosphere this good, Annapurna lets you feel like you're splurging when you're not.

The Naam Restaurant. 2724 W. Fourth Ave. ☎ **604/738-7151.** www.thenaam.com. Reservations accepted on weekdays only. Main courses C$4.95–C$10 (US$3.30–US$7). AE, ER, MC, V. Daily 24 hours. Live music every night 7–10pm. Bus: 4, 22. VEGETARIAN.

Back in the sixties, when Kitsilano was Canada's hippie haven, the Naam was tie-dye central. Things have changed a tad since then, but Vancouver's oldest vegetarian and natural-food restaurant retains a pleasant granola feel. The decor is simple, earnest, and welcoming: well-worn wooden tables and chairs, plants, and an assortment of local art. The brazenly healthy fare ranges from open-face tofu melts, enchiladas, and burritos to tofu teriyaki, Thai noodles, and a variety of pita pizzas. The sesame spice fries are a Vancouver institution. And though the Naam is not yet vegan, they do cater to the anti-egg-and-cheese crowd with specialties like the macrobiotic Dragon Bowl of brown rice, tofu, peanut sauce, sprouts, and steamed vegetables. As with all Naam dishes, quality is excellent. The only real trick is to arrive well before you're actually hungry. Serving staff will invariably disappear on an extended search for personal fulfillment at some point during your meal.

Shao Lin Noodle Restaurant. 548 W. Broadway. ☎ **604/873-1816.** Main courses C$5–C$10 (US$3.35–US$7). No credit cards. Mon–Fri 11am–3pm, Sat–Sun 11:30am–3:30pm; daily 5–9:30pm. Bus: 9. CHINESE.

Why play with your food when you can eat here and watch the professionals do it? Traditional Chinese noodle shops are a rarity in North America, which is a shame because the experience is so much fun. Enclosed by glass, the noodle makers toss the pasta, stretch it over their heads, spin it around, and dramatically transform it into fine strands. All noodles are handmade and contain no MSG. (Unfortunately, the classic trick of cutting the noodle dough on top of their heads with a cleaver is banned in Canada. However, there is a picture of it on the wall.) Bowls of noodles are served with a vast selection of meat and vegetable combinations. Tea is poured from a 3-foot-long pot originally designed to allow male servants to maintain a polite distance from an 18th-century Chinese empress.

Sophie's Cosmic Café. 2095 W. Fourth Ave. ☎ 604/732-6810. Main courses C$4.85–C$16 (US$3.25–US$11). MC, V. Daily 8am–9:30pm. Bus: 4, 7. FAMILY-STYLE AMERICAN.

Sophie's is readily identifiable by the giant silver knife and fork bolted to the outside front walls. Inside, every available space has been crammed with toys and knickknacks from the 1950s and 1960s, creating an experience much akin to having lunch inside a McDonald's Happy Meal. For that very reason, children are inordinately fond of Sophie's. Crayons and coloring paper are always on-hand. The menu is simple: pastas, burgers and fries, great milk shakes, and a few classic Mexican dishes. The slightly spicy breakfast menu is hugely popular with Kitsilano locals. Lines can stretch to half an hour on post-hangover Sunday mornings, but the staff eases the wait with outdoor coffee.

6 The East Side

Many of these "east side" restaurants are on Main Street, which is on the borderlands between upscale west and working-class east. Main thus has some funky urban authenticity to go with its ever-increasing trendiness.

EXPENSIVE

Sun Sui Wah. 3888 Main St. ☎ **604/872-8822.** Also in Richmond: 102 Alderbridge Place, 4940 No. 3 Rd. ☎ **604/273-8208.** Reservations accepted. Main courses C$11–C$50 (US$7– US$34). AE, MC, V. Daily 10:30am–3pm and 5–10:30pm. Bus: 3. CHINESE/SEAFOOD.

One of the most elegant and sophisticated Chinese restaurants in town, the award-winning Sun Sui Wah is well known for its seafood. Fresh and varied, the catch of the day can include fresh crab, rock cod, geoduck, scallops, abalone, oyster, prawns, and more. Pick your own from the tank or order from the menu if you don't like to meet your food eye-to-eye before it's cooked. The staff is quite helpful for those unfamiliar with the cuisine. Dim sum is a treat, with the emphasis on seafood. Just point and choose. For land lovers and vegetarians, there are plenty of other choices, though they are missing out on one of the best seafood feasts in town.

MODERATE

✪ **The Brickhouse Bistro.** 730 Main St. ☎ **604/689-8645.** Reservations accepted. Main courses C$10–C$16 (US$7–US$11). MC, V. Tues–Thurs 5:30pm–1am, Fri–Sat 5:30pm–2:30am. Bus: 3. BISTRO.

There were once two partners who opened a bar in a slightly seedy section of town. It ought to do well, they reasoned, for there are many with money who have recently bought condos, and right now they have nowhere to drink. And do well it did. Encouraged, the partners refurbished the room right above their very successful bar, and opened up a bistro—a casual funky kind of place, all bricks and wood beams. They hired a chef capable of cooking up simple but superior food, dishes like New Zealand rib eye in Madeira jus and roast potatoes or specials of fresh fish. To lure customers, the partners kept their prices very low. A selection of B.C. wines was also available, at two-thirds the price charged by other bistros. Word of the cuisine and ambiance has spread far and wide enough to make dinner on a weekend a pleasant social affair, but the Brickhouse is still a tasty steal.

✪ **Bukowski's.** 1447 Commercial Dr. ☎ **604/253-4770.** Reservations accepted. Main courses C$8–C$15 (US$5–US$10). MC, V. Mon–Thurs 5pm–1am, Fri–Sat noon–1am, Sun noon–midnight. Live Jazz Mon–Tues. Bus: 20. BISTRO/WEST COAST FUSION.

The last and booziest of the American Beat poets gets what he always wanted, a bistro named in his honor. So what if he never made it to Vancouver, much less the Bohemian-and-becoming-more-so strip on Commercial Drive. The cuisine is not Polish, but instead a fusion-y kind of comfort food perfectly suited to casual dining. Think beef satay, charbroiled chicken on focaccia bread, catfish with black-bean salsa, or steak with peppercorn garlic jus. And beer. Or any one of several wines featured on a daily blackboard. Even more attractive than the food is the friendly, buzzing atmosphere, and a clientele slightly too rich to really be artists, but hip enough to dress the part. Service is wonderfully unhurried. Dawdle for hours if you will, reading the snippets of Sylvia Plath inscribed on your table.

The Locus Café. 4121 Main St. ☎ **604/708-4121.** Reservations not accepted. Main courses C$9–C$14 (US$6–US$9). AE, MC, V. Mon–Fri 11:30am–1am, Sat 11am–1am, Sun 11am–midnight. Bus: 3. SOUTHWEST/FUSION.

Even if you arrive on your lonesome, you'll have plenty of friends soon enough—the Locus is a cheek-by-jowl kind of place, filled to bursting with a friendly, funky crowd of arsty Mount Pleasant types. A big bar dominates the center of the room, overhung with "swamp-gothic" lacquer trees and surrounded by a tier of stools with booths and tiny tables farther out. Cuisine originated in the American Southwest but picked up an edge somewhere along the way—think roasted half-chicken with a cumin-coriander crust and sambuca citrus demi-glace. Keep an eye out for fish specials, such as grilled tomba tuna with a grapefruit and mango glaze. The pan-seared calamari makes a perfect appetizer. Bowen Island brewery provides the beer, so quality's high. Your only real problem is catching the eye of the hyper-busy bartender.

✪ **The Reef.** 4172 Main St. ☎ **604/874-JERK.** www.thereefrestaurant.com. Reservations accepted. Main courses C$9–C$15 (US$6–US$10). AE, MC, V. Sun–Wed 11am–midnight, Thurs–Sat 11am–1am. Bus: 3. CARRIBEAN.

The JERK in the phone number refers neither to a Steve Martin film nor to the guy two cubicles down from you at the office, but rather to a spicy marinade: bay leaves, scotch bonnets, allspice, garlic, soya, green onions, vinegar, and cloves. The result is piquant, scrumptious chicken. The Reef serves up a number of jerk dishes, including their signature quarter jerk chicken breast. Other dishes are equally delightful, including a tropical salad of fresh mango, red onions, and tomatoes; shrimp with coconut milk and lime juice; grilled blue marlin; and Trenton spiced ribs. Choose a glass of wine from the thoughtfully selected list and you have gourmet dining in a great room—cleverly decorated with chicken wire, bamboo, and original mixed media artwork—at a bargain price. Afternoons, the tiny patio is drenched in sunlight, while in the evenings a DJ spins the sounds of the Islands.

Sun Wong Kee. 4136 Main St. ☎ **604/879-7231.** Reservations accepted. Main courses C$9–C$15 (US$6–US$10). AE, MC, V. Wed–Mon 11am–3pm and 5pm–midnight. Bus: 3. CHINESE.

This is a great little place for tasty everyday Chinese cooking. The thick menu has all the usual suspects, but the real fun is the specials board above the door to the kitchen. It's there that you'll find fresh delectables such as live crab, lobster, and rock cod. As always with Chinese food, it's best to bring lots of folks so you can share many plates, but if you go for the spicy salt spareribs, make sure you get yours first. The spicy crab—said to be the best in the city—is another dish tough to share with competitive eaters. The room is a crab's leg up from the basic Chinese eatery—tablecloths are linen and some thought has gone into the decor. Not that any of Sun Wong Kee's many Chinese patrons seem to notice. Whole families, from Grandma down through four generations, sit around tables set for 14, intent on nothing but the food.

7 The North Shore

EXPENSIVE

✪ **The Beach House at Dundarave Pier.** 150 25th St., West Vancouver. ☎ **604/922-1414.** www.beachhousewestvan.com. Reservations recommended. Main courses C$12–C$16 (US$8–US$11) lunch; C$19–C$35 (US$13–US$23) dinner. AE, DC, ER, MC, V. Mon–Fri 11:30am–3pm, Sat–Sun brunch 11am–3pm; Sun–Thurs 5–10pm, Fri–Sat 5–11pm. Light appetizers served 3–5pm. Bus: 255 to Ambleside Pier. WEST COAST.

Set on a dramatic waterfront location, the House offers a panoramic view of English Bay. Those on the heated patio also get sunshine, but they miss out on the rich interior of this restored 1912 teahouse. The food is consistently good—innovative, but not so experimental that it leaves the staid West Van burghers gasping for breath. Appetizers include soft-shell crab with salt-and-fire jelly; grilled scallops with baby spinach, crispy onions, and red-pepper cream; and grilled portobello mushroom with Okanagan Valley goat cheese. Entrees have included garlic-crusted rack of lamb with honey balsamic glaze and baked striped sea bass with basil mousse and rock prawns. The wine list is award-winning.

✪ **The Salmon House on the Hill.** 2229 Folkstone Way, West Vancouver. ☎ **604/926-3212.** www.salmonhouse.com. Reservations recommended for dinner. Lunch main courses C$6–C$15 (US$4–US$10), dinner main courses C$16–C$30 (US$11–US$20). AE, DC, ER, MC, V. Mon–Sat 11:30am–2:30pm, Sun brunch 11am–2:30pm; Sun–Thurs 5–10pm, Fri–Sat 5–10:30pm. Bus: 251 to Queens St. WEST COAST/SEAFOOD.

High above West Vancouver, The Salmon House offers a spectacular view of the city and Burrard Inlet. The rough-hewn cedar walls are adorned with a growing collection of indigenous West Coast art; the colorful masks and figurative works by modern First Nations craftspeople relate the traditional myths and legends of the ancient culture. Chef Dan Atkinson's menu reflects his extensive research into local ingredients and

First Nations cuisine. An alderwood-fired grill dominates the kitchen, lending a delicious flavor to many of the dishes. To start, we recommend the Salmon House Sampler, featuring salmon, fresh salsas, chutneys, and relishes. Entrees include grilled British Columbia salmon with local prawns, fiddlehead ferns, and Fraser Valley blueberry salsa; Fraser Valley free-range chicken with roasted onion jus; and smoked West Coast black cod with wasabi cream and balsamic mustard-seed vinaigrette. Desserts bear little resemblance to early First Nations cuisine: mocha torte with pecan-toffee crust, turtle pie, blueberry tiramisu. The wine list earned an award of excellence from *Wine Spectator.*

INEXPENSIVE

The Tomahawk Restaurant. 1550 Philip Ave., North Vancouver. ☎ **604/988-2612.** Reservations not accepted. Main courses C$4.25–C$17 (US$2.85–US$11). MC, V. Sun–Thurs 8am–9pm, Fri–Sat 8am–10pm. Bus: 239 to Philip Ave. FAMILY-STYLE AMERICAN.

Just a typical American-style diner, but with one critical difference that makes it worth a visit. It's not that a teenaged Brian Adams used to work here. Nor is it simply longevity—the restaurant has been around since 1926. The Tomahawk's worth a visit 'cause it's wall-to-wall and roof-beam tall with Native knickknacks and gewgaws and some truly first-class First Nations art. It all started back in the 1930s when proprietor Chick Chamberlain began taking carvings from Burrard Band Natives in lieu of payment. Over the years the collection just kept growing. So how's the food? Good, in a burgers-and-fries kind of way. Portions are large, burgers are tasty, milk shakes come so thick the spoon stands up straight like a totem pole. If you're on the North Shore and wracked by hunger, the Tomahawk's worth a chop.

8 Coffee & Sweets

Death by Chocolate. Various locations, including 1001 Denman St., ☎ **604/899-CHOC,** and 1598 W. Broadway, ☎ **604/730-CHOC.** www.deathbychocolate.com. C$4.95–C$11 (US$3.30–US$7). AE, MC, V. Generally open until midnight; hours vary at each location.

If your idea of heaven includes rich desserts, then Death by Chocolate is the place to get dispatched. The large menu comes with photographs, but beware—objects on the page may appear smaller than they are; sharing is encouraged. Some of the tested favorites include: Simply Irresistible—a chocolate pudding with fudge center, covered in chocolate sauce; and Devil in Disguise—mocha fudge ice cream in Kahlúa chocolate sauce. Guilt-prone types can salve their consciences with a more wholesome, fruitier dessert like Sticky Bits—strawberries with chocolate sauce and whipped cream for dipping. Hell-bent ultra-chocoholics, on the other hand, should order up a Multitude of Sins—chocolate cake, chocolate mousse, chocolate crepes stuffed with fruit, chocolate sauce, and, well, you get the idea. To wash it all down, the restaurant serves a variety of coffees, teas, and hot chocolates, as well as alcoholic beverages.

Exploring Vancouver

6

A city perched on the edge of a great wilderness, Vancouver offers unmatched opportunities for exploring the outdoors. Paradoxically, within the city limits Vancouver is intensely urban. There are sidewalk cafes to match those in Paris, and shopping streets that rival London's. The forest of downtown residential high-rises looks somewhat like New York, while the buzz and movement of Chinatown reminds you of San Francisco or Canton. Comparisons with other places soon begin to pall, however, as you come to realize that Vancouver is entirely its own creation: a self-confident, sparklingly beautiful city, like no place else on earth.

Sightseeing Suggestions

If You Have 1 Day

See the sights while you eat your eggs. The breakfast spot with the best view is the **Cafe Pacifica** (☎ **604/895-2480**) in the lobby of the Pan-Pacific Hotel, where you can watch the morning rush of floatplanes dropping in. After breakfast, walk or ride or inline-skate the **Stanley Park Seawall.** While in Stanley Park, say hi to the sea otters in the **Vancouver Aquarium.** By now it's definitely lunchtime, so come back to the West End, drop off your skates or bike, and have lunch at one of the sidewalk cafes on **Denman.** Then wander through the **West End** (there's a good walking tour in chapter 7), maybe stop by the Vancouver Art Gallery or the public library. Wherever you wander, try and finish up around sunset at the foot of Denman Street on **English Bay Beach.** You won't be sorry. Have supper at one of the nearby restaurants specializing in West Coast cuisine. Then head up to **Robson Street** and watch the evening parade of beautiful people.

If You Have 2 Days

On day 2, grab a coffee and a croissant and head down to **Chinatown.** Explore the area for a bit—it's often most active in the early hours—then go for dim sum. Afterwards, drive or take the bus out to the **Museum of Anthropology** on the campus of UBC. The masks and carvings are worth the trip. While out at UBC, walk down the steep trail to **Wreck Beach** (bear in mind there are nudists at the bottom) or come back and explore the urban waterfront at **Granville Island.** Have dinner in **Kitsilano,** or across False Creek in **Yaletown.** Then go barhopping, or find a brew pub and try some of the local ales.

If You Have 3 Days

On day 3, get active—go **kayaking** on Indian Arm, **mountain biking** through the Endowment Lands, **hike** through Cypress Falls park, or take the **tram** up to Grouse Mountain. Take a picnic lunch along (if you've come by SeaBus, then Lonsdale Quay is a good spot for supplies) and eat outside. **Lighthouse Park** in West Vancouver is a particularly good picnic area. Come suppertime, eat at one of the North Shore restaurants with a view of the city—the **Salmon House** or the **Beach House** or the **Grouse Nest** up on Grouse Mountain.

If You Have 4 Days or More

On days 4 and 5, the thoroughly urban can retreat to the city and spend the next 2 days exploring neighborhoods like **Kitsilano,** the **Punjabi market,** and **Commercial Drive,** and touring your way through Vancouver's **art gallery, craft museum,** and **public library.** For **outdoors lovers,** make like a Nike ad, and just do it. Go to Whistler and go skiing. Go to Squamish and see the bald eagles. Hike up to Joffre Lake and touch the glacier. Do a horse trek in the high country. Or take your bike. Sail up into grizzly country. Kayak Clayoquot Sound.

1 The Top Attractions

DOWNTOWN & THE WEST END

B.C. Sports Hall of Fame and Museum. 777 Pacific Blvd. S. (B.C. Place Stadium, Gate A, Beatty and Robson Sts.). ☎ **604/687-5520.** Admission C$6 (US$4) adults, C$4 (US$2.70) seniors and students, free for children under 5. MC, V. Daily 10am–5pm. SkyTrain: Stadium. Bus: 15.

A great destination for sports-minded, active kids with endless energy, the museum's Participation Gallery features interactive running, climbing, throwing, riding, rowing, and racing competitions where they can pit themselves against video-simulated competitors. There are also a climbing wall, pitching cages, and stationary bikes. For parents, the Hall of Champions and Builders Hall document the achievements of British Columbia's most lauded athletes, including runners Terry Fox and Rick Hansen and the Vancouver Canucks hockey team, in both video and photographic displays.

The Canadian Craft Museum. 639 Hornby St. ☎ **604/687-8266.** E-mail: craftmus@ direct.ca. Admission C$5 (US$3.35) adults, C$3 (US$2) seniors and students, free for children under 12. Thurs evening 5–9pm admission is by donation. Mon–Wed and Fri–Sat 10am–5pm, Thurs 10am–9pm, Sun and holidays noon–5pm. Closed Tues Sept–May. SkyTrain: Granville. Bus: 3.

Hidden behind the Cathedral Place building at the edge of a beautiful outdoor courtyard, the Canadian Craft Museum presents a vast collection of Canadian and international crafts in glass, wood, metal, clay, and fiber. A top-quality small museum, it will appeal to anyone who devours interior design and architectural magazines. Recent shows have included an impressive display of carved Chinese signature seals and calligraphy, British Columbian artist Bill Reid's gold and silver jewelry, and furniture created by Canada's best industrial designers. You can also purchase some of the unique ceramics, sculptures, and crafts in the museum's gift store.

✪ **Vancouver Aquarium Marine Science Centre.** Stanley Park. ☎ **604/659-FISH.** www.vanaqua.org. Admission C$13 (US$9) adults, C$11 (US$7) seniors/students/youths 13–18, C$9 (US$6) children 4–12, free for children under 4, C$43 (US$29) family. June 23–Sept 4 daily 9:30am–7pm; Sept 5–June 22 daily 10am–5:30pm. Bus: 135; "Around the Park" shuttle bus June–Sept only. Parking C$5 (US$3.35) summer, C$3 (US$2) winter.

One of North America's largest and best, the Vancouver Aquarium houses more than 8,000 marine species, most in meticulously re-created environments.

In the icy-blue Arctic Canada exhibit, you can see beluga whales whistling and blowing water at unwary onlookers. Human-sized freshwater fish inhabit the Amazon Rain Forest gallery, while overhead an hourly rainstorm is unleashed in an atrium and exhibit that houses three-toed sloths, brilliant blue and green poison tree frogs, and piranhas. Regal angelfish glide through a re-creation of Indonesia's Bunaken National Park coral reef, and blacktip reef sharks menacingly scour the Tropical Gallery's waters. (Call for the shark and sea otter feeding times.) The Pacific Canada exhibit is dedicated to sea life indigenous to B.C. waters, including the Pacific salmon and the giant Pacific octopus.

On the Marine Mammal Deck, there are sea otters, Steller sea lions, beluga whales, and a Pacific white-sided dolphin. During regularly scheduled shows, the aquarium staff explain marine mammal behavior while working with these impressive creatures.

In addition to tours, the aquarium has a regular program of special events, including behind-the-scenes tours, sleepover programs for children and youths, and evening barbecues.

The **Clamshell Gift Shop** (☎ 604/659-3413) sells a great collection of marine-oriented mementos, crafts, souvenirs, and books. The aquarium's Upstream Café is open daily for lunch, snacks, and coffee.

Vancouver Art Gallery. 750 Hornby St. ☎ **604/662-4719** or 604/662-4700. www. vanartgallery.bc.ca. Admission C$10 (US$7) adults and seniors, C$6 (US$4) students and youths, free for children 12 and under, C$30 (US$20) family. Thurs 6–9pm by donation. Mon–Wed and Fri–Sun 10am–5:30pm, Thurs 10am–9pm. SkyTrain: Granville. Bus: 3.

Designed as a courthouse by British Columbia's leading early 20th-century architect Francis Rattenbury (the architect of Victoria's Empress Hotel and the Parliament buildings), and renovated into an art gallery by British Columbia's leading late 20th-century architect Arthur Erickson (see "Architectural Highlights," below), the VAG is an excellent stop for anyone who wants to see what sets Canadian and West Coast art apart from the rest of the world. There is an impressive collection of paintings by B.C. Native Emily Carr, as well as examples of a unique Canadian art style created during the 1920s by members of the "Group of Seven," who included Vancouver painter Fred Varley. The first Canadian artists to break free from the then-dominant European schools of painting, their bold and dramatic style was strongly influenced by the dramatic Canadian landscape. On the contemporary side, the VAG hosts rotating exhibits of sculpture, graphics, photography, and video art, some from B.C. artists, many from around the world. Geared to younger audiences, the Annex Gallery offers rotating presentations of visually exciting educational exhibits. Thanks to its selection of art books, crafts, multiples (original prints, jewelry, and objects produced and signed by artists), and toys (lots of toys), the Gift Shop is a favorite destination. The Gallery Café, overlooking the Sculpture Garden, is a great place to snack.

THE WEST SIDE

✪ **Museum of Anthropology.** 6393 NW Marine Dr. ☎ **604/822-3825.** www.moa. ubc.ca. Admission C$7 (US$4.70) adults, C$5 (US$3.35) seniors, C$4 (US$2.70) students and children 6–18, free for children under 6, C$20 (US$13) families. Free Tues after 5pm. May 20–Sept 30 Wed–Mon 10am–5pm, Tues 10am–9pm; Oct 1–May 19 Wed–Sun 11am–5pm, Tues 11am–9pm. Closed Dec 25–26. Bus: 4 or 10.

This isn't just any old museum. In 1976, architect Arthur Erickson (see "Architectural Highlights," below) re-created a classic Native post-and-beam structure out of

Downtown Vancouver Attractions

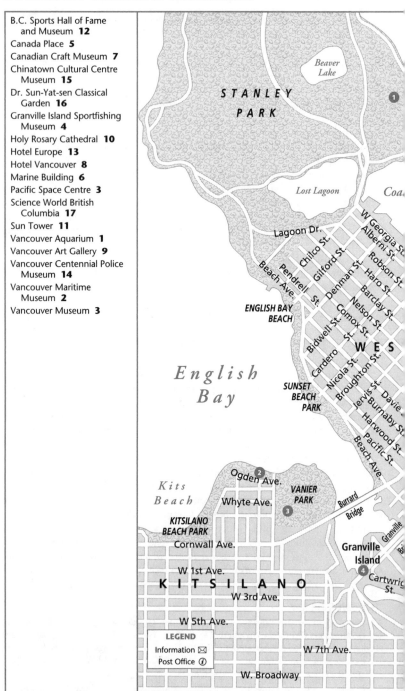

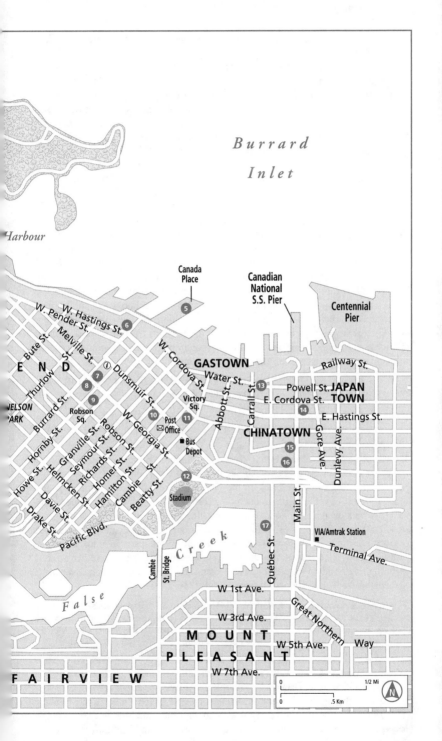

Burrard

Inlet

Harbour

Canada
Place

Canadian
National
S.S. Pier

Centennial
Pier

W. Hastings St.

W. Pender St.

Bute St.

Melville St.

Thurlow St.

Dunsmuir St.

GASTOWN

W. Cordova St.

Water St.

Railway St.

Powell St. JAPAN
E. Cordova St. TOWN

E. Hastings St.

E N D

NELSON
PARK

Burrard St.

Robson
Sq.

Hornby St.

Howe St.

Granville St.

Helmcken St.

Seymour St.

Richards St.

Robson St.

W. Georgia St.

Homer St.

Post
Office

Bus
Depot

Victory
Sq.

Abbott St.

Carrall St.

CHINATOWN

Gore Ave.

Dunlevy Ave.

Davie St.

Hamilton St.

Cambie St.

Beatty St.

Stadium

Drake St.

Pacific Blvd.

Main St.

VIA/Amtrak Station

Cambie

St. Bridge

Creek

Québec St.

Terminal Ave.

False

W 1st Ave.

W 3rd Ave.

Great Northern

MOUNT

W 5th Ave.

Way

PLEASANT

W 7th Ave.

FAIRVIEW

0   1/2 Mi

0   .5 Km

N

modern concrete and glass to house one of the world's finest collections of West Coast Native art.

You enter through doors that resemble a huge, carved bent-cedar box. Artifacts from potlatch ceremonies flank the ramp leading to the Great Hall's collection of totem poles. Haida artist Bill Reid's touchable cedar bear and sea-wolf sculptures sit at the Cross Roads, where source books rest on a reading-height display wall. Reid's masterpiece, *The Raven and the First Men,* is worth the price of admission all by itself. The huge carving in glowing yellow cedar depicts a Haida creation myth, in which Raven—the trickster—coaxes humanity out into the world from its birthplace in a clamshell. Some of Reid's fabulous creations in gold and silver are also on display. Intriguingly, curators have recently begun salting contemporary Native artworks in among the old masterpieces—a sign that West Coast artistic traditions are alive and well.

The Koerner Ceramics Gallery's European collection is unique to North America. The Masterpiece Gallery's argillite sculptures, beaded jewelry, and hand-carved ceremonial masks lead the way to the Visible Storage Galleries, where more than 15,000 artifacts are arranged by culture. You can open the glass-topped drawers to view small treasures and stroll past larger pieces housed in tall glass cases. (You can also read more detailed information about the items in conveniently placed reference catalogues.)

The gift shop sells contemporary Native artwork as well as books and publications. Don't forget to take a walk around the grounds behind the museum. Overlooking Point Grey are two longhouses built according to the Haida tribal style, resting on the traditional north-south axis. Ten hand-carved totem poles stand in attendance along with contemporary carvings on the longhouse facades.

Pacific Space Centre. 1100 Chestnut St., in Vanier Park. ☎ **604/738-STAR.** www. hrmacmillanspacecentre.com. Admission C$13 (US$9) adults, C$10 (US$7) seniors and youths 11–18, C$9 (US$6) children 5–10, C$5 (US$3.35) children under 5, C$40 (US$27) families (up to 5, maximum 2 adults). Additional family members C$8 (US$5) each. Additional Virtual Voyages experiences C$5 (US$3.35) each. Tues–Sun 10am–5pm, daily in July and Aug. Closed Dec 25. Bus: 22.

Housed in the same building as the Vancouver Museum, the space center and observatory has hands-on displays and exhibits that will delight both kids and astronomy, space, science, and computer buffs. In the Virtual Voyages Simulator, you can go on a voyage to Mars, or collide with an oncoming comet. In the interactive Cosmic Courtyard, you can look at an Apollo 17 manned-satellite engine, try your hand at designing a spacecraft, or maneuver a lunar robot. In the GroundStation Canada Theatre there are video presentations about Canada's contributions to the space program, and about space in general. The StarTheatre shows movies—many of them for children—on an overhead dome. And on selected nights, you can shoot the moon through a half-meter telescope for C$10 (US$7) per camera (☎ **604/736-2655**).

✪ **Science World British Columbia.** 1455 Quebec St. ☎ **604/443-7443.** www. scienceworld.bc.ca. Admission C$12 (US$8) adults; C$8 (US$5) seniors, students, and children; free for children under 4. Combination tickets available for OMNIMAX film. Mon–Fri 10am–5pm, Sat–Sun and holidays 10am–6pm. SkyTrain: Main Street–Science World.

Science World is impossible to miss. It's in the big blinking geodesic dome on the eastern end of False Creek. Inside, it's a hands-on scientific discovery center where you and your kids can light up a plasma ball, walk through a 1,700-square-foot maze, lose your shadow, walk through the interior of a camera, create a cyclone, blow square bubbles, watch a zucchini explode as it's charged with 80,000 volts, stand inside a beaver lodge, play in wrist-deep magnetic liquids, create music with a giant synthesizer, and watch mind-blowing three-dimensional slide and laser shows as well as other optical effects. In the OMNIMAX Theatre—a huge projecting screen equipped with Surround-Sound—you can take a death-defying flight through the Grand Canyon and perform other spine-tingling feats. Science World also hosts many spectacular traveling exhibitions, such as "Backyard Monsters," which featured giant robotic bugs. Call for presentation times and current productions. When it's time for a break, the cafeteria and a science-oriented gift shop offer refreshments and shopping.

✪ **Vancouver Maritime Museum.** 1905 Ogden Ave., in Vanier Park. ☎ **604/257-8300.** www.vmm.bc.ca. Admission C$7 (US$4.70) adults, C$4 (US$2.70) seniors and students, free for children under 6, C$16 (US$11) families. Daily 10am–5pm; closed Mon from Labour Day to Victoria Day (early Oct to late May). Bus: 22, then walk 4 blocks north on Cypress St. Boat: False Creek Ferries dock at Heritage Harbour.

This museum houses the 1920s RCMP Arctic patrol vessel *St. Roch*. That may not sound like much, but from the time Chris Columbus proved that the continent directly west of Europe was not Cathay, every European explorer's overriding quest was to find the Northwest Passage, the seagoing shortcut to the riches of the east. This little ship is the one that finally did it. The boat has been preserved in a large atrium, with most of its original stores and equipment still onboard. Tours of the *St. Roch* are particularly popular with children—they get to clamber around the boat poking and prodding stuff.

The other half of the museum holds intricate ship models (a few too many of these, unless you're a serious model buff), antique wood and brass fittings, maps, prints, and a number of permanent exhibits including "Pirates!," a treasure chest of an exhibit filled with pirate lore, artifacts, and a miniature ship where kids can dress up and play pirate for the day. The aft cabin of a schooner and the bridge of a modern tugboat lead the way to the Children's Maritime Discovery Centre, which houses computers, a wall of drawers filled with ship models and artifacts, and observation telescopes aimed at the ships moored in English Bay. You can maneuver an underwater robot in a large water tank. And kids can dress up in more naval costumes.

If the weather is pleasant, be sure to walk across the expansive front lawn at the edge of False Creek to Heritage Harbour, where the museum keeps a collection of beautiful vintage boats. It's also where you can catch the miniferry to Granville Island or the West End.

Vancouver Museum. 1100 Chestnut St. ☎ **604/736-4431.** www.vanmuseum.bc.ca. Admission C$8 (US$5) adults, C$6 (US$4) youths. Group rates available. Fri–Wed 10am–5pm, Thurs 10am–9pm. Closed Mon Sept–June. Bus: 22, then walk 3 blocks south on Cornwall Ave. Boat: Granville Island Ferry to Heritage Harbour.

Established in 1894, the Vancouver Museum is dedicated to amassing evidence of the city's history, from its days as a Native settlement and European outpost to the city's early 20th-century maturation into a modern urban center. The exhibits allow visitors to walk through the steerage deck of a 19th-century passenger ship, peek into a Hudson's Bay Company frontier trading post, or take a seat in an 1880s Canadian-Pacific Railway passenger car. Re-creations of Victorian and Edwardian rooms show how early Vancouverites decorated their homes. Rotating exhibits include a display of the museum's collection of neon signage from Vancouver's former glory days as the West Coast's glitziest neon-sign–filled metropolis during the 1940s and 1950s.

The museum's self-service vending-machine lunch area offers simple sandwiches and refreshments. The gift shop sells contemporary Native jewelry and crafts as well as publications and souvenirs.

GASTOWN & CHINATOWN

Chinese Cultural Centre Museum Archives. 555 Columbia St. ☎ **604/687-0729.** Free admission. Mon–Sat 11am–5pm. Bus: 4 or 7.

Recently opened, this small museum has rotating exhibits of photographs, documents, and other artifacts depicting the Chinese experience in Canada. Many of the exhibits are designed to help promote cultural understanding.

✪ **The Dr. Sun Yat-sen Classical Garden.** 578 Carrall St. ☎ **604/689-7133.** www. discovervancouver.com/sun. E-mail: sunyatsen@telus.net. C$8 (US$5) adults, C$6 (US$4) seniors, C$5 (US$3.35) children and students. Daily May 1–June 14 10am–6pm, June 15–Sept 30 9:30am–7pm, Oct 1–Apr 30 10am–4:30pm. Bus: 4, 7.

This small, tranquil oasis is concealed behind high, whitewashed walls. Gnarled limestone scholar rocks jut skyward amid clusters of pine, bamboo, and winter-blooming plum; dark reflecting pools are filled with turtles and *koi* (decorative carp); and a meandering tiled path connects the various spaces. The Classical Garden was built in the Suzhou province of northern China around 1492 and relocated to Vancouver just in time for Expo '86. It was packed in 950 crates, and 52 artisans took nearly 10 years to completely reassemble it, replant it, and stock it with turtles and ornamental carp. This serenely beautiful garden is the only one of its kind in the western hemisphere.

✪ **Vancouver Centennial Police Museum.** 240 E. Cordova St. ☎ **604/665-3346.** www.city.vancouver.bc.ca/police/museum. Admission C$5 (US$3.35) adults, C$3 (US$2) students and seniors, children under 6 free. Year-round Mon–Fri 9am–3pm; May 1–Aug 31 Sat 10am–3pm. Bus: 4 or 7.

A bizarre, macabre, and utterly delightful little museum, dedicated to memorializing some of the best crimes and crime-stoppers in the city's short but colorful history. Housed in the old Vancouver Coroner's Court—where actor Errol Flynn was autopsied after dropping dead in the arms of a 17-year-old girl—the museum features photos, text, and vintage equipment from files and evidence rooms of Vancouver's finest. The confiscated illegal-weapons display looks like the props department for the film *Road Warrior.* There's also a morgue with bits and pieces of damaged body parts on the wall, a simulated autopsy room, a forensics lab, and a police radio room. One display shows how the police solved the case of the milk-shake poisoner, involving a local radio celebrity who was feeding his wife milk shakes made from arsenic. On the lighter side, the museum also houses an immense collection of matchbox-sized toy police cars from around the world. And the Cop Shoppe carries caps, pins, T-shirts, and books.

NORTH VANCOUVER & WEST VANCOUVER

Capilano Suspension Bridge & Park. 3735 Capilano Rd., North Vancouver. ☎ **604/985-7474.** www.capbridge.com. Admission C$11 (US$7) adults, C$9 (US$6) seniors, C$7 (US$4.70) students, C$3.25 (US$2.15) children 6–12, free for children under 6. Winter discounts available. May–Sept daily 8:30am–dusk, Oct–Apr daily 9am–5pm. Closed Dec 25. Bus: 246 from downtown Vancouver, 236 from Lonsdale Quay SeaBus terminal.

Vancouver's first and oldest tourist trap (built in 1889), this attraction still works—mostly because there's still something inherently thrilling about standing on a narrow, shaky walkway, 69 meters (230 ft.) above the canyon floor, held up by nothing but a pair of miserable cables. Set in an 8-hectare (20-acre) park about 15 minutes from the city, the suspension bridge itself is a 135-meter-long (450-ft.) cedar-plank and steel-cable footbridge, which sways gently above the Capilano River. You can nervously cross above kayakers and salmon shooting the rapids far below, shrouded by mist from a 60-meter (200-ft.) waterfall.

The *Other* Suspension Bridge

Lynn Canyon Park, in North Vancouver between Grouse Mountain and Mount Seymour Provincial Park on Lynn Valley Road, offers a cheaper and possibly more impressive alternative to the Capilano Suspension Bridge. Originally built in 1912, the 68-meter (225-ft.) **Lynn Canyon Suspension Bridge** is only half as long as the Capilano (see "The Top Attractions," above), but it's an extra 3 meters (10 ft.) above the canyon floor. And it's been a free attraction for more than 75 years.

The park in which the bridge is located is a heavily wooded, 247-hectare (617-acre), century-old Douglas fir rain forest. It's also home to an **Ecology Centre,** 3663 Park Rd. (☎ 604/981-3103), which presents natural history films, tours, and displays. Staff members lead frequent walking tours. The center is open daily from 10am to 5pm.

Six kilometers (Four miles) up Lynn Valley Road is the **Lynn Headwaters Regional Park** (☎ 604/985-1690 for trail conditions). Until the mid-1980s, this was an inaccessible wilderness and bear habitat. The park and the bears are now managed by the Greater Vancouver Regional Parks Department, B.C. Parks, 1610 Mt. Seymour Rd., North Vancouver, B.C. V7G 2R0 (☎ 604/924-2200; www.env.gov.bc.ca), and there are 12 marked trails of various levels of difficulty that wind through beautiful forest scenery, the former site of a working mill (Cedar Mill), and a waterfall. To get there, take the SeaBus to Lonsdale Quay, then transfer to bus no. 229; or take the Trans-Canada Highway to the Lynn Valley Road exit (about a 20-min. drive from downtown).

In addition to the bridge, there's a **carving centre** where Native carvers show their skill, an exhibit explaining the region's natural history, a pair of restaurants, and—surprise—a gift shop. For those who want a less commercial experience, the nearby Lynn Canyon Suspension Bridge stands 3 meters (10 ft.) higher and is free of charge, but has no gift shops. (See the box, "The *Other* Suspension Bridge," below.)

Grouse Mountain Resort. 6400 Nancy Greene Way, North Vancouver. ☎ **604/984-0661.** www.grousemountain. SkyRide C$18 (US$12) adults, C$16 (US$11) seniors, C$12 (US$8) youths, C$7 (US$4.70) children 6–12, free for children under 6. SkyRide free with advance Grouse Nest restaurant reservation. Daily 10am–10pm. SeaBus: Lonsdale Quay, then transfer to bus no. 236.

Once a small local ski hill, Grouse has been slowly developing itself into a year-round mountain recreation park, offering impressive views and instantaneous access to the North Shore mountains. Located only a 20-minute drive from downtown, the SkyRide gondola transports you to the mountain's 1,110-meter (3,700-ft.) summit in about 10 minutes. (Hikers and cardio-fitness fiends can take a near vertical trail called the Grouse Grind. The best of them can do it in 28 minutes.) At the top, there's a bar, restaurant, large-screen theatre, ski and snowboard area, hiking and snowshoeing trails, skating pond, children's snow park, interpretive forest trails, logger sports show, helicopter tours, mountain bike trails, and Native feast house. Some of these are free with your SkyRide ticket—most aren't—and the view is one of the best around: the city and the entire lower mainland, from far up the Fraser Valley east across the Gulf of Georgia to Vancouver Island. The Himwus Feast House has gotten good reviews for its Native food and dance.

2 Architectural Highlights

Vancouver was leveled by fire in 1886 (the same year it was incorporated as a city), so most of its architecture is less than a century old. The city had a reputation as a boomtown from the start, attracting a number of famous architects who were eager to practice their art in new and less developed surroundings. The results range from the slightly absurd to the truly impressive. Serious architecture buffs should pick up a copy of *Exploring Vancouver: The Essential Architectural Guide,* by authors Kalman, Phillips, and Ward.

HISTORIC BUILDINGS & MONUMENTS

Vancouver's oldest surviving edifice is the **Hastings Sawmill Store Museum,** 1575 Alma St., Jericho Beach (☎ **604/734-1212**). Housed in an 1865 heritage structure that served as the city's first general store, it was moved here by barge in 1930 from its original Gastown location. Inside, you'll find Victorian period clothing, furnishings, hardware, toiletries, woven Native basketry, and historical photographs. Admission is by donation. The museum is open from mid-June to mid-September, Tuesday to Sunday from 11am to 4pm, and on weekends from mid-September to mid-June from 1 to 4pm. Take bus no. 4 or 7 to Alma Street.

The triangular **Hotel Europe,** 43 Powell St., was an architectural wonder when it opened in 1912. Designed by local architects Parr and Fee, the luxury hotel proudly stood as Vancouver's first steel-reinforced concrete structure and fireproof hotel—a concept so foreign that contractors had to be imported from Cincinnati. The design was an intentional imitation of New York's Flatiron Building (erected in 1903), and the lobby was famous for its marble and brass detailing. Subsequent renovations had stripped the building of only a few of its interesting features. Unfortunately, when Gastown fell into decline during and after the Great Depression, so did the hotel. The main entrance was blocked off to expand the lobby's beer parlor, and the original entrance balcony lamps were stolen. Recent renovations have saved the hotel and other historic buildings surrounding Maple Tree Square from the wrecking ball (see chapter 7). The hotel appeared in *Legends of the Fall,* among other movies.

Topped by a patina-green copper cupola and mansard windows, the **Sun Tower,** 100 W. Pender St. at Beatty Street, stands amid a somewhat desolate landscape that is slowly being redeveloped. Designed by W. T. Whiteway and erected in 1911, the 17-story hexagonal structure is crowned by a three-story beaux arts copper roof. The heritage building was constructed by Vancouver mayor L. D. Taylor, who ran his *Vancouver World* newspaper enterprise here from 1912 until 1915. The *Vancouver Sun* took over the building in 1937 and stayed until 1963.

At the outbreak of World War II, Point Grey residents watched artillery carriages rumble through the streets toward the headlands, followed by more weighty ordnance as the Point Grey Battery—complete with concrete gun emplacements and officers' quarters—was erected on the cliffs on the end of Point Grey. The installation was closed 9 years later and abandoned during the 1960s. In the 1970s, however, the site was reclaimed for the **UBC Museum of Anthropology.** In a particularly elegant touch, architect Arthur Erickson turned the foundation of a death-dealing gun-emplacement into the pedestal for his friend Bill Reid's master carving, *The Raven and the First Men,* which depicts the origins of life.

The art deco **Marine Building,** 355 Burrard St. at Thurlow Street, is a lovely office building; it was the British Commonwealth's tallest structure when it opened in 1930. Designed by McCarter and Nairne, the building was meant to emulate a rocky

Arthur Erickson

Vancouver's greatest architect, Arthur Erickson, is a puzzling contradiction. Avowedly modernist in principle, he nonetheless never hesitates to put form over function in order to satisfy his unique aesthetic sense. A firm believer in listening to what the landscape has to say, Erickson often turns a deaf ear to the needs of those who inhabit his buildings. Combine these features with exceptional eloquence, a driven personality, and flamboyant charm, and you get a lot of buildings, all of which look good on paper—and some that also work in real life. As this is his native town, Vancouver is blessed with a great deal of Erickson's work. Those with an interest can check out the **Museum of Anthropology** (1973), 6993 NW Marine Dr., UBC; the **Provincial Law Courts** (1973), 800 Smithe St.; **Simon Fraser University** (1963), Burnaby Mountain, Burnaby; the **MacMillan Bloedel Building** (1969), 1075 W. Georgia St; and the **Khalsa Diwan Society Sikh Temple** (1970), 8000 Ross St.

promontory rising from the sea. Its facade is detailed with terracotta, brass, stone, and marble bas-reliefs depicting the local aquatic environment. Its best features are in the lobby near the elevators. The vaulted ceiling is lit by sconces shaped like ships' prows, the center of the stone floor is inlaid with a giant zodiac, and the ornate brass elevator doors open to reveal even more ornate wood inlay inside.

John S. Archibald and John Schofield designed the Canadian-Pacific Railway's **Hotel Vancouver** (see chapter 4 for a review). Replacing a smaller hotel on the same site, the dignified French Renaissance structure took 10 years to complete. When it finally opened in 1929, it dominated Vancouver's skyline. Topped by a green-patina copper roof decorated with intricately carved stone gargoyles and a statue of the Roman god Hermes, the grand hotel's exterior walls are made of Haddington Island stone—the same stone used in Victoria's Parliament buildings. Sweeping marble staircases and a grand Edwardian lobby elegantly grace the interior.

Built in the shape of a ship with five soaring Teflon sails, **Canada Place Pier** is to Vancouver what the Opera House is to Sydney, Australia—a focal point on the downtown waterfront. Built in time for Expo '86, the pier houses Vancouver's largest convention center, a hotel, the Alaska cruise ship terminal, restaurants, and the CN IMAX Theatre.

Another Expo '86 structure is the giant sparkling silver sphere at the east end of False Creek—**Science World.** Originally erected as the Expo Centre, it's been expanded and renovated to house a wealth of entertaining and educational permanent and traveling exhibits for children and adults (see "The Top Attractions" above).

The **Vancouver Museum** (see "The Top Attractions" above) sits on a promontory near the Burrard Street Bridge. A little over a century ago, Vanier Park was the site of a Native village inhabited by the Coast Salish tribe. During World War II it became a military defense base, and in the 1960s it was dedicated as a park. The museum's roof resembles the unique cone-shaped, woven-cedar-bark hat worn by Coast Salish men. The crab-shaped metal fountain standing in front of the museum is possibly Vancouver's most photographed object.

Resembling the Roman Coliseum with its multiple tiers of arches (architect Moshe Safdie denies there was any intentional similarity), **Library Square** on Robson Street contains voluminous rooms of books, a coffee shop and small restaurant, a day-care center, and a seven-story reading atrium where visitors can comfortably take in the view. Many do. In fact, the atrium and the square outside have become two of Vancouver's favorite public gathering spots.

Behind sheltered walls in the heart of Chinatown lies the **Dr. Sun Yat-sen Classical Garden** (see "The Top Attractions," above), a painstakingly exact Ming Dynasty private courtyard garden.

CHURCHES & TEMPLES

Despite its reputation as one of North America's more secular cities, Vancouver has a wide variety of churches, synagogues, temples, and other houses of worship that serve its growing and ethnically diverse population. Vancouver has more than 60 Catholic churches as well as dozens of Protestant churches; Orthodox, Conservative, Reform, and Hasidic Jewish temples; and Sikh, Buddhist, and Islamic temples.

Holy Rosary Cathedral, 646 Richards St. (☎ 604/682-6774), is a Gothic Revival–style Roman Catholic cathedral built in 1899 to 1900. On Sunday mornings, the carillon bells call the congregation to worship.

Colorful late-morning Sikh wedding ceremonies frequently take place at the Arthur Erickson–designed **Khalsa Diwan Gurudwara Temple,** 8000 Ross St. (☎ 604/324-2010). You are welcome to observe a ceremony if you call for permission in advance.

The Byzantine iconography and architecture of **St. George's Greek Orthodox Cathedral,** 4500 Arbutus Street, at W. 31st Avenue (☎ 604/266-7148), constructed in 1930, are as classic as the Sunday services, which are conducted in Greek.

Golden porcelain roof tiles sweep upward to two glittering flying dragons high atop the International Buddhist Society's **Kuan-Yin Buddhist Temple,** 9160 Steveston Hwy., Richmond (☎ 604/274-2822). After ascending the bleached granite stairway, you are greeted by two marble lions as you enter the burnt-red doorway of the Main Gracious Hall. Inside, a treasury of Chinese sculpture, woodwork, painting, and embroidery is on display. The center courtyard contains a ceramic mural of the goddess Kuan-Yin resting in a bamboo grove and a magnificent bonsai collection. Visitors are welcome to participate in prayers on Saturday at 10:30am and in other religious and cultural events.

On your way to this beautiful temple, check out the **Buddha Supplies Centre,** 4158 Main St. (☎ 604/873-8169), where you can pick up incense or joss sticks and tiny paper replicas of earthly belongings like CD players, Mercedes vehicles, and cellular phones (they're burned to send the deceased off with ample luxuries).

COLLEGES & UNIVERSITIES

During the academic year, more than 32,000 students attend the **University of British Columbia (UBC),** one of Canada's largest universities. Many UBC attractions are open to the public, including the **Museum of Anthropology** (see "The Top Attractions," above); the **Botanical Garden** and **Nitobe Memorial Garden** (see "Parks & Gardens," below); **TRIUMF (Tri-University Meson Facility),** 4004 Wesbrook Mall (☎ 604/222-1047), where the world's largest subatomic cyclotron is housed; the **M. Y. Williams Geological Museum,** Geological Sciences Centre, Stores Road, Gate 6 (☎ 604/822-2449); and the **UBC Astronomical Observatory** and the **UBC Geophysical Observatory,** Main Mall, Gate 1 (☎ 604/822-6186). For campus tours, call ☎ 604/822-8687.

You can also use the university's sports facilities, including the **Aquatic Centre, Thunderbird Winter Sports Centre,** and nearby **tennis courts.** Miles of trails wind

You Paid What?

47,000 hotels, 700 airlines, 50 rental car companies. And a few million ways to save money.

Travelocity.com
A Sabre Company

Go Virtually Anywhere.

AOL Keyword: Travel

Will you have enough stories to tell your grandchildre

Yahoo! Travel

Do You
YAHOO!
?

through the **University Endowment Lands** and **Point Grey beaches,** overlooking the Strait of Georgia and English Bay (see "Outdoor Activities" below).

The **Belkin Art Gallery** (☎ 604/822-2759), **Frederic Wood Theatre** (☎ 604/822-2678), and **UBC School of Music** (☎ 604/822-5574) are venues that present student and professional work (see chapter 9 for details on the latter two). Also worth checking out is the **Chan Centre for the Performing Arts** (☎ 604/822-9197). For more information, contact the **Public Affairs Office,** 207–632B Memorial Rd. (☎ 604/822-3131). To get to UBC, take bus no. 4 or 10, or the 99 B-Line.

Sitting atop 360-meter (1,200-ft.) Burnaby Mountain, the **Simon Fraser University** campus has an expansive view of metropolitan Vancouver. Architect Arthur Erickson won immediate acclaim for his stunning design when the school opened in 1965. Though it has since won mixed reviews from the students, the SFU campus was for many years known and loved by "X-files" fans as none other than FBI headquarters.

The **Museum of Archaeology and Ethnology** (☎ 604/291-3325) exhibits historic Native works created by Inuit, Kwakiutl, and other provincial aboriginal bands, while contemporary work is shown at the **University Art Gallery** (☎ 604/291-4266). Admission to both is free. For more information about points of interest at Simon Fraser University, call ☎ 604/291-3210 or campus tours at ☎ 604/291-3397. Take bus no. 135, 144, or 145 to the campus.

3 Neighborhoods to Explore

The best way to get to know a city is to explore its different neighborhoods. Here's a quick guide on where to go and what to look for. For more in-depth explorations, turn to the neighborhood walking tours in chapter 7.

THE WEST END

This was Vancouver's first upscale neighborhood, settled in the 1890s by the city's budding class of merchant princes. By the 1930s, most of these formerly grand Edwardian homes had become rooming houses, and in the late '50s, as the Baby Boomers left home, the Edwardians came down and high-rise apartments went up. The resulting neighborhood owes more to Manhattan than to the sprawling cities of the west. All the necessities of life are contained within the West End's border: great cafes, good nightclubs, many and varied bookshops, and some of the best restaurants in the city. That's part of what makes it such a sought-after address, but it's also the little things, like the street trees, the mix of high-rise condos and old Edwardians, and the way that, in the midst of such an urban setting, you now and again stumble on a view of the ocean or the mountains.

GASTOWN

The oldest section of Vancouver, Gastown's charm shines through the souvenir shops and panhandlers. For one thing, it's the only section of the city that has the feel of an old Victorian town—the buildings stand shoulder to shoulder and cobblestones line the streets. The current Gastown was built from scratch just a few months after an 1886 fire wiped out the entire city. (There are photographs of proper-looking men in black coats selling real estate out of tents on the still-smoking ashes.) Also, rents in Gastown have stayed low so it's still the place to look for a new and experimental art gallery, or a young fashion designer setting up shop on a little back street, or even (until a few months ago) a "Legalize Marijuana" campaigner selling grow lights and cannabis seeds out of a storefront cafe.

Alcohol has always been a big part of Gastown's history. The neighborhood is named for a saloon keeper—Gassy Jack Deighton—who according to local legend, talked the local mill hands into building a saloon as Vancouver's first structure in return for all the whisky they could drink. Nowadays, Gastown is still liberally endowed with pubs and clubs—it's one of two or three areas where Vancouverites congregate when the sun goes down.

CHINATOWN

Chinatown's a kick, mostly because there's little that's overtly touristy about it. For the thousands of Cantonese-speaking Canadians who live in the surrounding neighborhoods, it's simply the place they go to shop. And for many others who have moved to more outlying neighborhoods, it's still one of the best places to come and eat. One of North America's more populous Chinatowns, the area was settled about the same time as the rest of Vancouver, by migrant laborers brought in to build the Canadian Pacific Railway. Many white settlers resented the Chinese labor, and periodically race riots broke out. At one point Vancouver's Chinatown was surrounded with Belfast-like security walls. By the '40s and '50s, however, the area was mostly threatened with neglect. In the '70s, there was a serious plan to tear the whole neighborhood down and put in a freeway. A huge protest stopped that, and now the area's future seems secure. For visitors, the fun is to simply wander, look, and taste.

YALETOWN

Vancouver's former warehouse district, Yaletown has long since been converted to an area of apartment lofts, nightclubs, restaurants, high-end furniture shops, and a fledgling multimedia biz. For visitors, it features some interesting cafes and patios, some high-end shops, and a kind of gritty urban feel that you won't find elsewhere in Vancouver.

FALSE CREEK NORTH (CONCORDE PACIFIC)

Stretching along Pacific Boulevard on the north shore of False Creek, Concorde's 30-odd high-rise towers are bright and shiny and brand-spanking new. Perhaps a bit too new—like a pair of sneakers that need to lose a little gloss before they'll really be comfortable. The area's worth visiting, though, if only to admire one of the largest—and so far most successful—urban redevelopment projects on the continent.

GRANVILLE ISLAND

Part crafts fair, part farmers market, part artist's workshop, part mall, and part heavy industrial site, Granville Island seems to have it all. Some 20 years ago the federal government decided to try its hand at a bit of urban renewal, so they took this piece of industrial waterfront and redeveloped it into…well, it's hard to describe. But everything you could name is there: theaters, pubs, restaurants, artists' studios, bookstores, crafts shops, an art school, a hotel, a cement plant, and lots and lots of people. One of the most enjoyable ways to experience the Granville Island atmosphere is to head down to the Granville Island Public Market, grab a latte (and perhaps a piece of cake or pie to boot), then wander outside to enjoy the view of the boats, the buskers, and the children endlessly chasing flocks of squawking seagulls.

KITSILANO

Hard to believe, but in the '60s Kitsilano was a neighborhood that had fallen on hard times. Nobody respectable wanted to live there—the 1920s homes had all been converted to cheap rooming houses—so the hippies moved in. The neighborhood became

Canada's Haight-Ashbury, with coffeehouses, head shops, and lots of incense and long hair. Once the boom generation stopped raging against the machine, they realized that Kitsilano—right next to the beach, but not quite downtown—was a groovy place to live, and a darn fine place to own property. Real estate began an upward trend that has never stopped, and Kits became thoroughly yuppiefied. Nowadays it's a fun place to wander. There are great bookstores and trendy furniture and housewares shops, lots of consignment clothing stores, snowboard shops, coffee everywhere, and lots of places to eat. Indeed, every third storefront is a restaurant. The best parts of Kitsilano are the stretch of W. Fourth Avenue between Burrard and Balsam Streets, and W. Broadway between Macdonald and Alma Streets.

SHAUGHNESSY

Shaughnessy's a terrible place to wander around, but it's a great place to drive. Designed in the 1920s as an enclave for Vancouver's budding elite, this is Vancouver's Westmount or Nob Hill. (Distances within the neighborhood are a little too great for a comfortable stroll.) Thanks to the stranglehold Shaughnessy exerts on local politics— every second mayor hails from this neighborhood—traffic flow is carefully diverted away from the area, and it takes a little bit of driving around to find your way in. It's an effort worth making, however, if only to see the stately homes and monstrous mansions, many of which are now featured in film shoots. To find the neighborhood, look on the map for the area of curvy and convoluted streets between Cypress and Oak Streets and 12th and 32nd Avenues. The center of opulence is the Crescent, an elliptical street to the southwest of Granville and 16th Avenue.

RICHMOND

Twenty years ago Richmond was mostly farmland, with a bit of sleepy suburb. Now it's Asia West, an agglomeration of shopping malls geared to the new—read: rich, educated, and successful—Chinese immigrant. The residential areas of the city are not worth visiting (unless tract homes are your thing), but malls like the Aberdeen Mall or the Yao Han Centre are something else. It's like getting into your car in Vancouver and getting out in Singapore.

STEVESTON

Steveston once existed for nothing but salmon. Located at the southwest corner of Richmond by the mouth of the Fraser River, Steveston was where the boats left to catch the migrating sockeye, and Steveston was where they brought the fish back to be cleaned and canned. Huge processing plants covered its waterfront, where thousand of workers gutted millions of fish. Much of that history is reprised in the **Gulf of Georgia Cannery National Historic Site,** near the wharf at Bayview Street and Fourth Avenue (☎ **604/664-9009**). Since the fishery was automated long ago, Steveston's waterfront has been fixed up into a pleasant place to stroll. There are public fish sales, charter trips up the river or out to the Fraser delta, and, above all, a pleasant, laid-back, small-town atmosphere.

COMMERCIAL DRIVE

Known as "The Drive" to Vancouverites, it's the 12-block section from Venables Street to E. Sixth Avenue. The Drive has a counterculture feel to it. There are posters for Cuba Libre! rallies, and bits of graffiti reading Smash Capitalism! But The Drive also has an immigrant feel to it. The first wave of Italians left cafes such as **Calabria,** 1745 Commercial Dr. (☎ **604/253-7017**) and **Caffe Amici,** 1344 Commercial Dr. (☎ **604/255-2611**). More recent waves of Portuguese, Hondurans, and Guatemalans have also left their mark. And lately, lesbians and vegans and artists have moved in—the kind of trendy moneyed folks who love to live in this kind of milieu. Shops and restaurants reflect the mix. Think Italian cafe next to the Marxist bookstore across from the vegan deli selling yeast-free Tuscan bread.

PUNJABI MARKET

India imported. Most of the businesses on this 4-block stretch of Main Street, from 48th up to 52nd Avenues, are run by and cater to Indo-Canadians, primarily Punjabis. The area is best seen during business hours, when the fragrant scent of spices wafts out from food stalls, while the sound of Hindi pop songs blares from hidden speakers. Young brides hunt through sari shops or seek out suitable material in discount textile outlets. **Memsaab Boutique,** 6647 Main St. (☎ **604/322-0250**), and **Frontier Cloth House,** 6695 Main St. (☎ **604/325-4424**), specialize in richly colored silk saris, shawls, fabrics, and costume jewelry. A good place to eat is **Nirvana,** 2313 Main St. (☎ **604/872-8779**), which offers a medley of Indian favorites.

4 Vancouver's Plazas & Parks

OUTDOOR PLAZAS

A waterfall serves as the centerpiece of the **Burrard Street Plaza,** between Alberni and Dunsmuir Streets in the heart of downtown Vancouver. You can rest here for a moment and ponder the Hotel Vancouver and Christ Church Cathedral or the bustle of nearby business traffic.

Designed by architect Arthur Erickson to be Vancouver's central plaza, **Robson Square**—between Hornby and Howe Streets from Robson to Smithe Streets—has never really worked. Though beautifully executed with shrubbery, cherry trees, sculptures, and a triple-tiered waterfall, the square suffers from a basic design flaw: it's sunk one story below street grade. Even though there are cafes and an outdoor skating rink, people just don't seem to like going down.

At the opposite end of things, **Library Square**—at the corner of Robson and Homer Streets—is immensely popular with locals, and has been since it was built just 4 years back. People sit on the Coliseum-like steps, bask in the sunshine, read, harangue passersby with half thought-out political ideas, and generally seem to enjoy themselves.

PARKS & GARDENS

The city's parks and gardens are filled with life and amusements. Scattered throughout Vancouver are publicly and privately maintained areas appealing to anyone seeking an hour or two of escape from urban life. You can encounter raccoon families in the West End, go downhill or cross-country skiing in West Vancouver, spot bald eagles and peregrine falcons in Richmond, or observe tai chi masters in Chinatown. For general information about Vancouver's parks, call ☎ **604/257-8400.**

✪ **Stanley Park** is a 400-hectare (1,000-acre) rain forest near the busy West End. It is named after the same Lord Stanley whose name is synonymous with professional hockey success—the Stanley Cup. The park is filled with towering western red cedar trees, placid lagoons, walking trails, manicured lawns, and flower gardens. It's surrounded by water except for a small portion of its eastern edge that connects it to the West End. Stanley Park houses the Vancouver Aquarium, a petting zoo, three restaurants, and a handful of snack bars, cricket greens, a swimming pool, a miniature railway, and a water park. It also boasts abundant wildlife, including beavers, coyotes,

Strange but True Facts About Lord Stanley's Park

- The 400-hectare (1,000-acre) peninsula now known as Stanley Park was originally set aside as a military reserve in 1859, to ward off a potential invasion by aggressive American troops.

- Lost Lagoon was named by the Native poet Pauline Johnson. Before the construction of the road that leads to the Lions Gate Bridge, the lagoon's water flowed out at low tide, and the lagoon disappeared.

- A large British sea cannon, known as the "Nine O'clock Gun," has sounded every evening for nearly 100 years except for a short period during World War II when it was conscripted into service. Originally, the gun was there to help ships in the harbor set their chronometers.

- All of Stanley Park's squirrels are direct descendants of the 16 squirrels presented in 1909 as a gift from a visiting New York City mayor.

- Hallelujah Point is named after the Salvation Army revivals that used to take place there every Sunday around the turn of the 20th century. Reportedly, the cries of "Hallelujah" could be heard all the way across the water in downtown.

- Of the more than 700,000 passengers who board Stanley Park's miniature railroad each year, roughly half are adults.

bald eagles, raccoons, trumpeter swans, brant geese, ducks, and skunks, as well as pristine natural settings and amazing marine views. This is where Vancouverites go to run, skate, bike, walk, or just sit. As North America's largest urban park, it is 20% larger than New York's Central Park (which is only 354 hectares/886 acres) and considerably safer. Take bus no. 23, 35, or 135 to the Stanley Park loop at the base of West Georgia Street.

In Chinatown, the **Dr. Sun Yat-sen Classical Garden** (see "The Top Attractions," above) is a small, tranquil oasis in the heart of the city. On the West Side, **Queen Elizabeth Park**—at Cambie Street and West 33rd Avenue—sits atop a 150-meter-high (500 ft.) extinct volcano and is the highest urban vantage point south of downtown, offering panoramic views in all directions. It's Vancouver's most popular location for wedding-photo sessions, with well-manicured gardens and a profusion of colorful flora. There are areas for lawn bowling, tennis, pitch-and-putt golf, and picnicking. The **Bloedel Conservatory** (☎ **604/257-8570**) stands next to the park's huge sunken garden, an amazing reclamation of an abandoned rock quarry. A 42-meter-high (140 ft.) domed structure with a commanding 360° view, the conservatory houses a tropical rain forest with more than 100 plant species as well as free-flying tropical birds. Admission for the conservatory is C$3.50 (US$2.35) for adults and C$2 (US$1.35) for seniors and children. Take bus no. 15 to reach the park.

VanDusen Botanical Garden, 5251 Oak St. at 37th Avenue (☎ **604/878-9274**), is nearby. Formerly the Shaughnessy Golf Course, the 22-hectare (55-acre) formal garden features rolling lawns, lakes, Elizabethan hedge mazes, and marble sculptures. The **Sino-Himalayan Garden** is just one of its international displays. Admission is C$6 (US$3.75) for adults; C$2.75 (US$1.85) for seniors, students, and children; and C$11 (US$7) for families. Off-season admission is usually less expensive. The garden opens at 10am, and closing hours vary between 6 and 9pm, depending on the time of year. Take bus no. 17.

The University of British Columbia campus incorporates a number of parks and gardens. Established nearly a century ago, the **UBC Botanical Garden,** 6250 Stadium Rd., Gate 8 (☎ 604/822-9666), has 28 hectares (70 acres) of formal alpine, herb, and exotic plantings. Nearby is the **Nitobe Memorial Garden,** 6565 NW Marine Dr., Gate 4 (☎ 604/822-6038), a traditional Japanese garden. From early March to mid-October, both gardens are open daily from 10am to 6pm. Admission to the Botanical Garden is C$4.50 (US$3) for adults, C$1.75 (US$1.15) for seniors, C$2.25 (US$1.50) for students, C$1.75 (US$1.15) for children 6 to 12, and children under 6 are free. Admission for Nitobe Memorial Garden is C$2.50 (US$1.65) for adults and C$1.75 (US$1.15) for seniors, students, and children 7 to 18 years old. A dual pass for both gardens is C$6 (US$4), for adults only. From October 5 to March 6, the Botanical Garden is open daily during daylight hours, while the Nitobe Memorial Garden is open Monday to Friday from approximately 10am to 2:30pm.

Out near UBC, **Pacific Spirit Park** (usually called the *Endowment Lands*) comprises 754 hectares (1,885 acres) of temperate rain forest, marshes, and beaches and includes nearly 35 kilometers (22 miles) of trails suitable for hiking, riding, mountain biking, and beachcombing.

Across the Lions Gate Bridge, there are six provincial parks that delight outdoor enthusiasts year-round. The publicly maintained **Capilano River Regional Park,** 4500 Capilano Rd. (☎ 604/666-1790), surrounds the Capilano Suspension Bridge & Park (see "The Top Attractions," above). Hikers can follow the river for 7 kilometers (4½ miles) down the well-maintained **Capilano trails** to the Burrard Inlet and the Lions Gate Bridge, or about a mile upstream to **Cleveland Dam,** which serves as the launching point for white-water kayakers and canoeists.

The **Capilano Salmon Hatchery,** on Capilano Road (☎ 604/666-1790), is on the river's east bank about a half a kilometer (quarter mile) below the Cleveland Dam. Approximately two million Coho and Chinook salmon are hatched annually in glass-fronted tanks connected to the river by a series of channels. You can observe the hatching fry (baby fish) before they depart for open waters, as well as the mature salmon that return to the Capilano River to spawn. Admission is free, and the hatchery is open daily from 8am to 7pm (until 4pm in the winter). Drive across the Lions Gate Bridge and follow the signs to North Vancouver and the Capilano Suspension Bridge. Or take the SeaBus to Lonsdale Quay and transfer to bus no. 236; the trip takes less than 45 minutes.

Eight kilometers (5 miles) west of the Lions Gate Bridge on Marine Drive West, West Vancouver, is **Lighthouse Park.** This 74-hectare (185-acre) rugged-terrain forest has 13 kilometers (8 miles) of groomed trails and—because it has never been clear-cut—some of the largest and oldest trees in the Vancouver area. One of the paths leads to the 18-meter (60-ft.) **Point Atkinson Lighthouse,** on a rocky bluff overlooking the Strait of Georgia and a panoramic view of Vancouver. It's an easy trip on bus no. 250. For information about other West Vancouver parks, call ☎ 604/925-7200 weekdays.

Driving up-up-up the mountain from **Lighthouse Park** will eventually get you to the top of **Cypress Provincial Park.** Stop halfway at the scenic viewpoint for a sweeping vista of the Vancouver skyline, the harbor, the Gulf Islands, and Washington State's Mount Baker, which looms above the eastern horizon. The park is 12 kilometers (7½ miles) north of Cypress Bowl Road and the Highway 99 junction in West Vancouver. Cypress Provincial Park has an intricate network of trails maintained for hiking during the summer and autumn, and for downhill and cross-country skiing during the winter.

Stanley Park

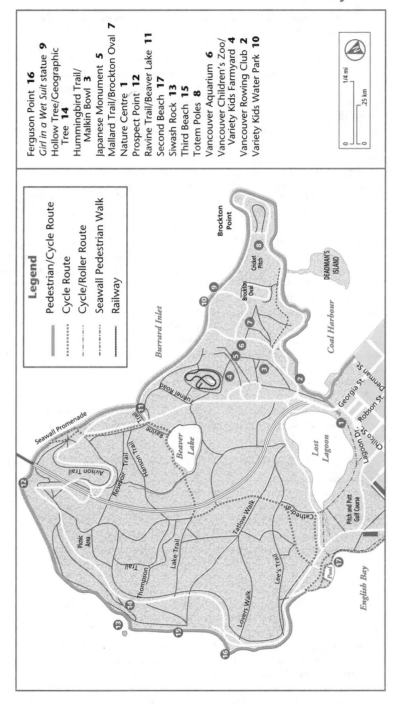

Legend

Pedestrian/Cycle Route
Cycle Route
Cycle/Roller Route
Seawall Pedestrian Walk
Railway

Ferguson Point **16**
Girl in a Wet Suit statue **9**
Hollow Tree/Geographic Tree **14**
Hummingbird Trail/ Malkin Bowl **3**
Japanese Monument **5**
Mallard Trail/Brockton Oval **7**
Nature Centre **1**
Prospect Point **12**
Ravine Trail/Beaver Lake **11**
Second Beach **17**
Siwash Rock **13**
Third Beach **15**
Totem Poles **8**
Vancouver Aquarium **6**
Vancouver Children's Zoo/ Variety Kids Farmyard **4**
Vancouver Rowing Club **2**
Variety Kids Water Park **10**

Rising 1,430 meters (4,767 ft.) above Indian Arm, **Mount Seymour Provincial Park,** 1700 Mt. Seymour Rd., North Vancouver (☎ 604/986-2261 or 604/872-6616), offers another view of the area's Coast Mountains range. The road to this park roams through stands of Douglas fir, red cedar, and hemlock. Higher than Grouse Mountain, Mount Seymour has a spectacular view of Washington State's Mount Baker on clear days. It has challenging hiking trails that go straight to the summit, where you can see Indian Arm, Vancouver's bustling commercial port, the city skyline, the Strait of Georgia, and Vancouver Island. The trails are open all summer for hiking; during the winter, the paths are maintained for skiing, snowboarding, and snowshoeing. A cafeteria and gift shop are open year-round. Mount Seymour is open daily from 7am to 10pm.

The Fraser River delta is south of Vancouver. Thousands of migratory birds following the Pacific flyway rest and feed in this area, especially at the 340-hectare (850-acre) **George C. Reifel Bird Sanctuary,** 5191 Robertson Rd., Westham Island (☎ 604/946-6980), which was created by a former bootlegger and wetland-bird lover. Many other waterfowl species have made this a permanent habitat. More than 263 species have been spotted, including a Temminck's stint, a spotted redshank, bald eagles, Siberian (trumpeter) swans, peregrine falcons, blue herons, owls, and coots. The **Snow Goose Festival,** celebrating the annual arrival of the huge, snowy white flocks, is held here during the first weekend of November. The snow geese stay in the area until mid-December. (High tide, when the birds are less concealed by the marsh grasses, is the best time to visit.) An observation tower, 3 kilometers (2 miles) of paths, free birdseed, and picnic tables make this wetland reserve an ideal outing spot from October through April, when the birds are wintering in abundance. The sanctuary is wheelchair accessible and open daily from 9am to 4pm. Admission is C$4 (US$2.70) for adults and C$2 (US$1.35) for seniors and children.

The **Richmond Nature Park,** 1185 Westminster Hwy. (☎ 604/273-7015), was established to preserve the Lulu Island wetlands bog. It features a Nature House with educational displays and a boardwalk-encircled duck pond. On Sunday afternoons, knowledgeable guides give free tours and acquaint visitors with this unique environment. Admission is by donation.

5 Spectacular Views

The busy harbor at the **Port of Vancouver** can be seen from a variety of vantage points, each revealing a different aspect. You can look down at the harbor from the **VanTerm** public viewing area, at the foot of Clark Drive, or from **The Cannery** restaurant's picture windows, which face the harbor (see chapter 5).

Lonsdale Quay has a great view of Vancouver's skyline from the north. Get in the middle of the action by taking the 15-minute **SeaBus** commute across the Burrard Inlet or by taking the **MPV *Constitution,*** a historic stern-wheeler (see "Organized Tours" below), across the harbor.

Canada Place Pier, at the north end of Burrard Street, has a dockside view of landing and departing floatplanes and of commercial ferries and Alaska-bound cruise ships.

Vancouver's skyline can be seen from many vantage points and angles. The most popular (and most touristed) is high atop the space needle observation deck at the **Lookout!, Harbour Centre Tower,** 555 W. Hastings St. (☎ 604/689-0421). It's a great place for first-time visitors who want a panorama of the city. The glass-encased Skylift whisks you up 166 meters (553 ft.) to the rooftop deck in less than a minute.

The 360° view is remarkable. (Yes, that is Mt. Baker looming above the southeastern horizon.) Angled viewing windows, powerful telescopes, and descriptive point markers enhance the viewing experience, as do the bright and relentlessly chipper "ambassadors" who staff the Lookout. A panoramic multiprojector historical presentation is shown regularly throughout the day. And the **Harbour Centre Mall** in the lower concourse contains 50 specialty shops and an international food fair. Skylift admission is C$9 (US$6) for adults, C$8 (US$5) for seniors, C$6 (US$4) for students, and C$25 (US$17) for families. It's open daily in summer from 8:30am to 10:30pm and in winter from 9am to 9pm.

The **sunsets** over **English Bay Beach** are stupendous (see "Beaches" below). Freighters moored in the bay stand silhouetted against the broad, blazing sky while great blue herons fly overhead or perch pensively in the shallows. If you're lucky, you can turn toward the city and catch a peek of a sun-shower rainbow. Afterward, **Milestone's** and **Benny's Bagels** on Denman and Davie Streets offer lighter fare, and **Raincity Grill** and the **cocktail lounge at the Sylvia Hotel** (see chapter 4) are perfect retreats for dinner or cocktails.

One of Vancouver's best **evening views** is from **Cloud 9** (☎ **604/662-8328**) at the Landmark, 1400 Robson St. (see chapter 5). From this revolving restaurant and lounge, you can see the twinkling lights of the Lions Gate Bridge and the North Shore mountaintops, which are illuminated for night skiing during winter and spring.

From North Vancouver, the city's skyline is best seen from **Grouse Mountain** (see "The Top Attractions" above), **Mount Seymour,** or the access road leading to Cypress Bowl in **Cypress Provincial Park** (see "Parks & Gardens" above). Halfway up the drive, there's a scenic overlook on the right-hand side. From these vantage points, the city spreads out like a giant postcard, day or night.

6 Little-Known Vancouver

LITERARY LANDMARKS

The down-and-out North Shore home of *Under the Volcano* author Malcolm Lowry is concealed in a North Vancouver thicket that was the site of a shantytown during the 1940s. The **Malcolm Lowry Walk** is a well-marked, easy trail located in Cates Park, a small wooded point at the mouth of the Indian Arm fjord. To get there from Vancouver, take the Trans-Canada Highway (Hwy. 1) across the Second Narrows Bridge. Exit onto the Dollarton Highway. Drive east for about 6 kilometers (4 miles). The highway runs along the park's northern border. Follow the signs to the parking area, then get ready to walk back in time to the Beat Generation. If you prefer to travel via public transit, take bus no. 212 to Cates Park.

The ashes and memorial of Native princess-poet **Pauline Johnson** overlook Stanley Park's Third Beach near the Hollow Tree—even though she specifically asked that no monument be erected after her death. Her local claim to fame was that she named Lost Lagoon. She is internationally known for *Legends of Vancouver,* her 1911 compilation of Native folktales.

Vancouver's monumental central library is anything but square. The new $100-million ❂ **Library Square** resembles a terracotta version of Rome's Coliseum. Cozy reading tables are positioned in front of floor-to-ceiling windows throughout the seven-story complex. It's a popular spot to do research or just sit and daydream.

The library has Internet access, a computer lab, and more than one million books, but that's just the beginning. The complex also houses 10 stores and coffee bars, Book-Mark (the library shop), and a day-care center. The central library, 350 W. Georgia St.

(☎ **604/331-3601**), is open Monday to Thursday from 10am to 8pm, Friday and Saturday from 10am to 5pm, and Sunday from October through June from 1 to 5pm.

Throughout the year, you can attend prose and poetry readings at **Bukowski's,** 1447 Commercial Dr. (☎ **604/214-1348**); **Women in Print,** 3566 W. Fourth St. (☎ **604/732-4128**); **Cafe Deux Soleils,** 2096 Commercial Dr. (☎ **604/254-1195**); and **Black Sheep Books,** 2742 W. Fourth Ave. (☎ **604/732-5087**), as well as branches of **Chapters** (☎ **604/682-4066**). Schedules change constantly, so call ahead for current information or check the free weekly *Georgia Straight.*

HAUNTED PLACES & SCANDAL SITES

The 1906 **Vancouver Art Gallery** (see above) has a ghost among its collections. The gallery was formerly the provincial courthouse, and "Charlie," as the ghost is known, lives in the catacombs where the holding cells were located. He's said to be the spirit of an immigration officer named William Charles Hopkinson, who was murdered there in 1914.

An architect haunts his own building at 207 Hastings St. The **Dominion Bank Building** was designed in 1910 by J. S. Helyer, who stumbled on the treads of his prized trapezoidal wrought-iron staircase and fell to his death shortly before construction was completed.

Deadman's Island, at the edge of Stanley Park, is now a Canadian naval base. During the late 1800s, it was used as a quarantine area for smallpox victims. Before that, the island served as a burial ground for the Native tribe that lived in the area for hundreds, if not thousands, of years. Today the island is haunted by a ghost who makes his presence known with a little mischief now and then (he's credited with slamming doors, making rooms inexplicably chilly, and even making small objects vanish and mysteriously reappear days later). The road through Stanley Park that passes by Deadman's Island was constructed in 1886 over a cemetery. The last burial had taken place on the grounds only 2 years earlier.

The **Hotel Vancouver,** 900 W. Georgia St., houses a spectral "Lady in Red," who has been sighted from time to time drifting noiselessly along the corridors of the hotel's 14th floor (actually the 13th floor).

7 Especially for Kids

Pick up copies of the free monthly newspapers *BC Parent,* 4479 W. 10th Ave., Vancouver, B.C. V6R 4P2 (☎ **604/221-0366**); and *West Coast Families,* 8–1551 Johnston St., Vancouver, B.C. V6H 3R9 (☎ **604/689-1331**). *West Coast Families'* centerfold "Fun in the City" and event calendar list everything currently going on, including **CN IMAX** (see chapter 9) shows at Canada Place Pier, **OMNIMAX** (☎ **604/443-7443**) shows at Science World British Columbia, and free children's programs. Both publications are available at Granville Island's Kids Only Market and at neighborhood community centers throughout the city.

Stanley Park offers a number of attractions for children. Stanley Park's Children's Farm (☎ **604/257-8530**) has peacocks, rabbits, calves, donkeys, and Shetland ponies (see "Parks & Gardens" above). Next to the petting zoo is Stanley Park's Miniature Railway (☎ **604/257-8531**). The diminutive steam locomotive with passenger cars runs on a circuit through the woods, carrying nearly as many passengers annually as all of the Alaska-bound cruise ships combined. During the holidays, the railway is strung with festive lights. The zoo and railway are open daily from April through September, plus Christmas week and on weekends from October through March. Admission for the petting zoo is C$2.50 (US$1.65) for anyone over 12 and C$1.75

(US$1.15) for kids 6 to 12 (admission is free for kids under 6 accompanied by a paying adult). Admission for the railway is C$6 (US$4) for anyone over 12 and C$3.95 (US$2.65) for kids 6 to 12 (admission is free for kids under 6 accompanied by a paying adult).

Also in Stanley Park, the ✪ **Vancouver Aquarium** has sea otters, sea lions, whales, and numerous other marine creatures, as well as many exhibits geared towards children (see "The Top Attractions" above). Across Burrard Inlet on the North Shore, **Maplewood Farm,** 405 Seymour River Place, North Vancouver (☎ **604/929-5610**), has more than 200 barnyard animals (cows, horses, ponies, pigs, sheep, donkeys, ducks, chickens, and more) living on its 2-hectare (5-acre) farm, which is open daily year-round. A few working farms once operated in the area but were put out of business by competition from the huge agricultural concerns in Fraser River valley. The parks department rescued this one and converted it into an attraction. The ticket booth (a former breeding kennel) sells birdseed for feeding the ducks and other fowl, as well as guidebooks. The farm also offers pony rides. Special events include the summertime Sheep Fair, the mid-September Farm Fair, 101 Pumpkins Day in late October, and the Country Christmas weekend. The farm is open Tuesday to Sunday from 10am to 4pm, and on designated holiday Mondays during the same hours. Admission is C$1.75 (US$1.15) for adults, C$1.25 (US85¢) for seniors and children, and C$6 (US$4) for families. Take bus no. 210 and transfer to the no. 211 or 212.

Three-quarters of an hour east of the city, the **Greater Vancouver Zoological Centre,** 5048–264th St., Aldergrove (☎ **604/856-6825**), is a lush 48-hectare (120-acre) farm filled with lions, tigers, jaguars, ostriches, elephants, buffalo, elk, antelope, zebras, giraffes, a rhino, hippos, and camels. In all, 124 species roam free or in spacious paddocks on the grounds. Located 48 kilometers (30 miles) from Vancouver, the wildlife reserve also has food service and a playground. It's open daily from 9am until dusk. Admission is C$11 (US$7) for adults, C$8 (US$5) for seniors and children 3 to 15, and free for children under 3 with an adult.

Right in town, **Science World** is a hands-on kids' museum where budding scientists can get their hands into everything (see "The Top Attractions" above). At the **Vancouver Maritime Museum,** kids can dress up like a pirate or a naval captain for a day, or board the RCMP ice-breaker *St. Roch* (see "The Top Attractions" above).

The **Burnaby Village Museum,** 6501 Deer Lake Ave., Burnaby (☎ **604/293-6501**), is a 3.5-hectare (9-acre) re-creation of the Victorian era. You can walk along boardwalk streets among costumed townspeople, watch a blacksmith pound horseshoes, shop in a general store, ride a vintage carousel, peek into an authentic one-room schoolhouse, and visit a vintage ice-cream parlor that's been at the same location since the turn of the 20th century. At Christmastime the whole village is aglow in Christmas lights and Victorian decorations. Admission is C$7 (US$4.70) for adults; C$4.35 (US$2.90) for seniors, travelers with disabilities, and students; C$4.55 (US$3.05) for youths 13 to 18; C$3.75 (US$2.50) for children 6 to 12; and free for children under 6. It's open daily from 11am to 4:30pm. From the Metrotown Skystation take bus no. 110 to Deer Lake.

The **Fort Langley National Historic Site,** 23433 Mavis Ave., Fort Langley (☎ **604/513-4777**), is the birthplace of British Columbia. In 1827, the Hudson's Bay Company established this settlement to supply its provincial posts. Costumed craftspeople demonstrate blacksmithing, coppering, and woodworking skills, bringing this landmark back to life. It's open daily from 10am to 5pm, March 1 to October 31. From November 1 to February 28 pre-booked groups only; please call ahead. Admission is C$4 (US$2.70) for adults, C$3 (US$2) for seniors, C$2 (US$1.35) for children 6 to 16, and free for children under 6. Take the SkyTrain to Surrey Central Station; transfer to bus no. 501.

Athletic kids can work up a sweat at the Participation Gallery in the **B.C. Sports Hall of Fame and Museum** (see "The Top Attractions," above). They can run, jump, climb, race, throw fastballs, and attempt to beat world records. At **Granville Island's Water Park and Adventure Playground,** 1496 Cartwright St., kids can really let loose with movable water guns and sprinklers. They can also have fun on the water slides or in the wading pool. The facilities are open during the summer daily (weather permitting) from 10am to 6pm. Admission is free; changing facilities are nearby at the False Creek Community Centre (☎ **604/257-8195**).

Open during summer, **Splashdown Park,** 4799 Nu Lelum Way, Tsawwassen (☎ **604/943-2251**), is a 3-minute drive from the Tsawwassen ferry terminal, just south of Vancouver. With 13 enormous water slides, a giant hot tub, a pool, a picnic area, inner tubes, and volleyball and basketball courts, it's a great escape for kids of all ages. During summer it's open daily from 10am to 8pm, weather permitting. Admission is C$19 (US$13) for anyone over 48 inches tall, C$13 (US$9) for anyone under 48 inches tall, and C$11 (US$7) for people entering the park but not going on the water slides.

Rainy days are no problem at the **Playdium at Metrotown,** 4700 Kingsway, Burnaby (☎ **604/433-7529**), where a huge variety of electronic diversions awaits kids and adults. It's open Sunday to Thursday from 10am to midnight, Friday and Saturday from 10am to 2am. Cost depends on the number of games you play. From 4pm to midnight you can purchase 3 hours of play time for C$22 (US$15).

For a more traditional family experience, go to **Playland Family Fun Park,** Exhibition Park, East Hastings and Cassiar Streets (☎ **604/255-5161**). Admission for unlimited rides is C$21 (US$14) for those 4 feet and taller, and C$10 (US$7) for those under 4 feet tall for limited rides. Admission for an adult with a paying child under 12 is C$10 (US$7). Relive your childhood at this amusement park by riding on the ornate carousel and wooden roller coaster and playing miniature golf. There's also a Nintendo Pavilion, Electric City Arcade, and petting zoo. The park is open weekends and holidays from late April to mid-June and Labour Day to Thanksgiving from 11am to 7pm; mid-June to Labour Day daily from 11am to 9pm. Take bus no. 14 or 16.

The prospect of walking high above the rushing waters is the main draw at the **Capilano Suspension Bridge** (see "The Top Attractions," above) and the **Lynn Canyon Suspension Bridge** (see the box "The *Other* Suspension Bridge," above). In winter, **Mount Seymour Provincial Park** (see "Skiing & Snowboarding" below) and **Grouse Mountain** (☎ **604/984-0661**) offer ski programs for kids and adults.

Granville Island's **Kids Only Market,** 1496 Cartwright St. (☎ **604/689-8447**), is open daily from 10am to 6pm. Playrooms and 21 shops filled with toys, books, records, clothes, and food are all child-oriented. Kids will also love taking the Aquabus or Granville Island Ferry (see "By Ferry" in chapter 3) to get there.

Only a 45-minute drive north of Vancouver, the **B.C. Museum of Mining,** Highway 99, Britannia Beach (☎ **604/688-8735**), is impossible to miss. Located at the head of Howe Sound, it's marked by a 235-ton truck parked in front. It offers guided tours of the old copper mine, live demonstrations of mining techniques, even a gold-panning area where anyone can try straining gravel for the precious metal for C$3.50 (US$2.35). It's open daily from 10am to 4:30pm; call ahead for tour schedule. Closed from Thanksgiving (early October) until early May. Admission is C$10 (US$7) for adults and C$8 (US$5) for students and seniors; free for children under 5; family rate C$34 (US$23).

8 Organized Tours

If you don't have the time to arrange your own sightseeing tour, let the experts take you around Vancouver. They will escort you in a bus, trolley, double-decker bus, seaplane, helicopter, boat, ferry, taxi, vintage car, or horse-driven carriage.

BUS TOURS

Gray Line of Vancouver, 255 E. First Ave. (☎ 604/879-3363), offers a wide array of tour options. The "Deluxe Grand City Tour" is a 3½-hour excursion through Stanley Park, Gastown, Chinatown, Canada Place, Queen Elizabeth Park, Robson Street, Shaughnessy, and English Bay Beach. Offered year-round, it costs C$44 (US$29) for adults, C$42 (US$28) for seniors, and C$31 (US$21) for children. Departing at 9:15am and 2pm, the bus picks you up from downtown hotels approximately 30 minutes before departure. The daily "Mountains and Sea Tour" takes you up to Grouse Mountain and the Capilano Suspension Bridge. Departing daily at 2pm, it costs C$71 (US$48) for adults, C$65 (US$44) for seniors, and C$46 (US$31) for children, including admission and the skytram. Other offerings include day, overnight, and multinight package tours of Vancouver, Victoria, and Whistler, plus helicopter tours and dinner cruises.

Vancouver Trolley Company, 4012 Myrtle St., Burnaby (☎ 604/451-5581; www.vancouvertrolley.com), operates gas-powered trolleys along a route through downtown, Chinatown, the West End, and Stanley Park. Between 9am and 6pm in summer (4:30pm in winter), passengers can get on and off at any of the 16 stops, explore, and catch another scheduled trolley. Onboard, drivers provide detailed tour commentary. Tickets are C$22 (US$15) for adults and C$10 (US$7) for children 4 to 12.

West Coast City and Nature Sightseeing, 4012 Myrtle St., Burnaby (☎ 604/451-1600), offers seven different minicoach tours, including a Native Culture Tour for C$45 (US$30) for adults and C$27 (US$18) for children, which includes a stop at the Stanley Park totem poles and a visit to the Museum of Anthropology at UBC; Grouse Mountain/Capilano Suspension Bridge for C$65 (US$44) for adults and C$42 (US$28) for children; and Whistler/Shannon Falls for C$62 (US$42) for adults and C$38 (US$25) for children; as well as Vancouver City/Capilano Suspension Bridge with a new price: C$48 (US$32) for adults, C$45 (US$30) for seniors, students, and youth (13 to 18), C$29 (US$19.50) children 4 to 12. Children under 4 are free. Minicoaches pick up passengers from downtown hotels, cruise ships, the airport, and the bus/railway station; phone for departure times. Charters and private tours are also available.

RAIL TOURS

On the **Pacific Starlight Dinner Train** (☎ 800/363-3733), a gourmet meal is served in the dome or salon car onboard a vintage locomotive as it travels from North Vancouver to Porteau Cove along the edge of Howe Sound. It costs C$84 (US$56) for adults and C$64 (US$43) per child for the salon car. For the dome car the cost is C$100 (US$67), with no discount for children. The dinner train runs from May to late September, Wednesday to Sunday; in October, weekends only. Call ahead for days of operation.

A 1939 Hudson steam engine chugs up through Howe Sound from North Vancouver to Squamish. The **Royal Hudson Steam Train** (☎ 604/984-5246) departs North Vancouver at 10am daily, returning at 4pm, and costs C$48 (US$32) for adults, C$41 (US$27) for seniors and youths, and C$13 (US$9) for children.

BOAT TOURS

Harbour Cruises, Harbour Ferries, no. 1, north foot of Denman Street (☎ **604/ 688-7246;** www.boatcruises.com), will take you on a 3-hour Sunset Dinner Cruise, including a catered gourmet meal and onboard entertainment; cost for adults/ seniors/youths is C$60 (US$40); for children 2 to 11, $50 (US$34). The cruise leaves at 7pm, May through October. The 4-hour Indian Arm Luncheon Cruise includes a salmon lunch, with departure at 11am. Cost for adults and seniors is C$45 (US$30), $40 (US$27) for children. A senior special of $40 (US$27) applies on Monday and Tuesday.

The company also conducts a 75-minute narrated Harbour Tour aboard the **MPV Constitution,** an authentic 19th-century stern-wheeler with a smokestack. Tours depart at 11:30am, 1pm, and 2:30pm daily from mid-May to mid-September, once a day at 2pm in April and October. Fares are C$18 (US$12) for adults, C$15 (US$10) for seniors and youths (12 to 17), C$6 (US$4) for children 5 to 11, and free for children under 5. Boat/train day trips depart Wednesday to Sunday and holiday Mondays from May through September at 9am aboard the **MV Britannia,** with a run up Howe Sound, and passengers return on the **Royal Hudson Steam Train** at about 4:40pm. Prices, including lunch, are C$75 (US$50) for adults, C$70 (US$47) for seniors and youths 12 to 17, and C$30 (US$20) for 5- to 11-year-olds.

From June through September, **Paddlewheeler River Adventures,** New Westminster Quay, New Westminster (☎ **604/525-4465**), operates Fraser River tours from New Westminster aboard the 19th-century vessel SS *Native.* The company offers a 3-hour lunch cruise on Tuesday, Wednesday, and Friday. Ticket prices, which include a luncheon buffet, are C$36 (US$24) for adults, C$32 (US$21) for seniors and students, C$12 (US$8) for children 6 to 12, and children under 6 are free. On Thursday and Saturday at 9:30am, there's a 7-hour Show Boat river cruise to historic Fort Langley (see "Especially for Kids" above) along the Fraser River. The fare is C$90 (US$60) for adults, C$80 (US$54) for seniors and students, and C$40 (US$27) for children 6 to 12, including breakfast, lunch, live entertainment, and a visit to Fort Langley. Ask about one-way cruises to Fort Langley. English High Tea is served Tuesday and Friday, with staff dressed the part. Tea cruises depart at 3pm. Adult fare is C$36 (US$24), seniors and students C$32 (US$21). You can also book sunset dinner cruises, theme cruises, and event cruises year-round, including Christmas Carol and Santa cruises in December.

Experience one of the world's largest commercial ports on **Burrard Water Taxi,** 2255 Commissioner St. (☎ **604/293-1160**). There are no scheduled tour times, so call ahead to book. The guides offer a fascinating insider's view of the busy harbor. The water taxis are available for tours at a rate of C$145 (US$97) per hour for 12 people. When the boats aren't escorting visitors around the harbor, they're shuttling the captains and crews of the freighters anchored in the Burrard Inlet to and from their vessels.

AIR TOURS

Baxter Aviation, Barbary Coast Marina, P.O. Box 1110, Nanaimo, B.C. V9R 6E7 (☎ **800/661-5599** or 604/683-6525; www.baxterair.com), operates 11 daily float-plane flights from downtown Vancouver. The 30-minute "Vancouver Scenic" tour flies over Stanley Park and the Coast Mountains; the 5-hour "Whistler Mountain Resort" tour includes a 3-hour stopover. Fares range from C$76 (US$51) per person for 30 minutes to C$359 (US$241) per person for 5 hours, with a variety of midrange tours in between. Other packages offer flights to Victoria, Johnstone Strait, glacial lakes, and prime fly-in fishing and whale-watching spots.

Harbour Air (☎ 604/688-1277; www.harbour-air.com) is on Coal Harbour just steps west of the Canada Place Pier. Look for the seaplanes arriving and departing. Thirty-minute seaplane flights over downtown Vancouver, Stanley Park, and the North Shore are C$76 (US$51) for adults, C$38 (US$25) for children under 12, and free for infants under 2. Many longer tours to alpine lakes and glaciers and nearby islands, as well as regularly scheduled flights to Victoria and Prince Rupert, are also available.

Helijet Charters, 5911 D Airport Rd. S., Richmond (☎ 800/987-4354 or 604/270-1484; www.helijet.com), offers a variety of daily tours that depart from the Vancouver Harbour Heliport near Canada Place Pier. The "West Coast Spectacular" is a 20-minute tour of the city, Stanley Park, and North Shore mountains for C$110 (US$74) per person. For a bird's-eye view of the city, the 30-minute "Greater Vancouver Scenic Tour" costs C$155 (US$104) per person; and the "North Shore Discovery" tour lasts 45 minutes and costs C$215 (US$144) per person. Tours that depart from the Grouse Mountain summit take 10 to 15 minutes and cost C$50 to C$90 (US$34 to US$60) per person. The "Fly, Dine, and Drive" package takes you by helicopter from downtown Vancouver to the top of Grouse Mountain for dinner, returning to the city by limousine; it costs C$250 (US$168) per person for a party of two. Custom mountaintop heli-picnics, heli-golfing packages, and special trips can also be arranged.

SPECIALTY TOURS

Early Motion Tours, 1–1380 Thurlow St. (☎ 604/687-5088), offers private sightseeing tours around Vancouver aboard a restored 1930 Model A Ford Phaeton convertible that holds up to four passengers plus the driver. Reservations are required. Limousine rates apply, C$100 (US$67) per hour for up to four people, and include a souvenir Polaroid of you in the car. There is a 1-hour minimum. The office is open daily from 7:30am to 8pm.

AAA Horse & Carriage Ltd., Stanley Park (☎ 604/681-5115), carries on a century-old tradition of horse-drawn carriage rides through Stanley Park. Tours depart every 30 minutes between May and October from the lower aquarium parking lot on Park Drive across from the Vancouver Rowing Club near the park entrance. Tours last an hour and cover portions of the park that even most locals have never seen. Rates are C$17 (US$11) for adults, C$16 (US$11) for seniors and students, C$11 (US$7) for children 6 to 12, and children under 6 are free.

X Tour (☎ 604/609-2770) offers guided tours of *X-Files* shooting locations around Vancouver, along with other sights guaranteed to delight an *X-Files* fan. Costs are from C$59 (US$40).

WALKING TOURS

Walkabout Historic Vancouver (☎ 604/720-0006) offers 2-hour walking tours through Vancouver historic sites, complete with guide dressed as a 19th-century schoolmarm. Tours depart daily at 9am, noon, and 3pm June through September, by request during other months. The cost is C$18 (US$12) per person. Walking tours of Chinatown are available from the **Chinese Cultural Centre** (☎ 604/687-7993) for C$5 (US$3.35) adults, C$4 (US$2.70) seniors, and C$3 (US$2) students and children. July through September, tours depart daily at 11am and 1:30pm; during other times, please phone ahead to book a tour. The Vancouver Tourism Info Centre at 200 Burrard St. (see also chapter 3) has a number of brochures on self-guided tours throughout the city.

9 Outdoor Activities

Just about every imaginable sport has a world-class outlet within the Vancouver city limits. Downhill and cross-country skiing, snowshoeing, sea kayaking, fly fishing, diving, hiking, paragliding, and mountain biking are just a few of the options. Activities that can be practiced close by include rock climbing, river rafting, and heli-skiing. If you don't find your favorite sport listed here, take a look at chapter 17.

Pick up a copy of *Coast: The Outdoor Recreation Magazine* (☎ 604/876-4980), which is published every other month. Available at many outfitters and recreational-equipment outlets, it lists snow conditions, bike trails, climbing spots, competitions, and organized events, as well as where to get bike tune-ups, where to find equipment rentals, and what to look for when purchasing sports equipment.

An excellent resource for outdoor enthusiasts is **Mountain Equipment Co-op,** 130 W. Broadway (☎ 604/872-7858). The MEC's retail store has a knowledgeable staff, and the Co-op also publishes an annual mail-order catalogue.

BEACHES

Only 10% of Vancouver's annual rainfall occurs during June, July, and August; 60 days of summer sunshine is not uncommon. In addition to being a great place for viewing sunsets, **English Bay Beach,** at the end of Davie Street off Denman Street and Beach Avenue, has an interesting history. It was Joe Fortes's front yard for more than 35 years. Fortes was a legendary Caribbean-born lifeguard and bartender who made English Bay Beach his home. The bathhouse dates to the turn of the 20th century, and a huge playground slide is mounted on a raft just off the beach every summer.

South of English Bay Beach, near the Burrard Street Bridge and the Vancouver Aquatic Centre, is **Sunset Beach.** Running along False Creek, it's actually a picturesque strip of sandy beaches filled with hulking sections of driftwood that serve as windbreaks and provide a little privacy for sunbathers and picnickers. There's a snack bar, a soccer field, and a long, gently sloping grassy hill for people who prefer lawn to sand.

On **Stanley Park's** western rim, **Second Beach** is a quick stroll north from English Bay Beach. A playground, a snack bar, and an immense heated freshwater pool—C$3.80 (US$2.55) for adults, C$2 (US$1.35) for seniors, C$2.55 (US$1.70) for youths 13 to 18, and C$8 (US$5) for families—make this a convenient spot for families. Farther along the seawall lies secluded **Third Beach,** which is due north of Stanley Park Drive. Locals tote along grills and coolers to this spot, a popular place for summer-evening barbecues and sunset watching. The hollow tree, Geographic Tree, and Siwash Rock are neighboring points of interest.

Kitsilano Beach, along Arbutus Drive near Ogden Street, is affectionately called Kits Beach. It's an easy walk from the Maritime Museum and the False Creek ferry dock. A heated saltwater swimming pool is open throughout the summer. Admission is the same as for Second Beach Pool, above. The summertime amateur theater, **Kitsilano Showboat,** attracts a local crowd looking for evening fun.

Farther west on the other side of Pioneer Park is **Jericho Beach** (Alma Street off Point Grey Road). This is another local after-work and weekend social spot. **Locarno Beach,** off Discovery Street and NW Marine Drive, and **Spanish Banks,** NW Marine Drive, wrap around the northern point of the UBC campus and University Hill. (Be forewarned that beachside rest rooms and concessions on the promontory end abruptly at Locarno Beach.) Below UBC's Museum of Anthropology is **Point Grey Beach,** a restored harbor defense site. The next beach is **Wreck Beach**—Canada's largest nude beach. You get down to Wreck Beach by taking the very steep Trail 6 on the UBC campus near Gate 6 down to the water's edge. Extremely popular with locals, Wreck Beach is also the city's most pristine and least-developed sandy stretch. The Wreck Beach Preservation Society maintains it. It's bordered on three sides by towering trees.

At the northern foot of the Lions Gate Bridge, **Ambleside Park** is a popular North Shore spot. The quarter-mile beach faces the Burrard Inlet.

BICYCLING & MOUNTAIN BIKING

The most popular cycling path in the city runs along the Seawall around the perimeter of Stanley Park. Offering stunning views of the city, the Burrard Inlet, and English Bay, this pathway is extremely popular with cyclists, in-line skaters, and pedestrians alike. Other marked cycle lanes traverse the rest of the city, among them the crosstown Off-Broadway route, the Adanac route, and the Ontario route. Runners and cyclists have separate lanes on developed park and beach paths. Some West End hotels offer guests bike storage and rentals. One of the city's most scenic cycle paths has been extended and now runs all the way from Canada Place Pier to Pacific Spirit Park. It connects Canada Place, Stanley Park and the Seawall Promenade, English Bay and Sunset beaches, and Granville Island to Vanier Park, Kitsilano and Jericho beaches, and Pacific Spirit Park. Cycling maps are available at most bicycle retailers and rental outlets.

Local mountain bikers love the cross-country ski trails on **Hollyburn Mountain** in Cypress Provincial Park. The Secret Trail Society started building trails 4 years ago along **Grouse Mountain's** backside, and they are now considered some of the lower mainland's best. Mount Seymour's very steep **Good Samaritan Trail** connects to the Baden-Powell Trail and the Bridle Path near Mount Seymour Road. The route is recommended only for world-class mountain bikers—the types who pour Gatorade on their Wheaties. Closer to downtown, both **Pacific Spirit Park** and **Burnaby Mountain** offer excellent beginner and intermediate off-road trails.

Hourly rentals run around C$3.75 (US$2.50) for a one-speed "Cruiser" to C$10 (US$7) for a top-of-the-line mountain bike, C$15 to C$40 (US$10 to US$27) for a day, helmets and locks included. Bikes and child trailers are available by the hour or day at **Spokes Bicycle Rentals & Espresso Bar,** 1798 W. Georgia St. (☎ 604/688-5141). **Alley Cat Rentals,** 1779 Robson St., in the alley (☎ 604/684-5117), is a popular shop that rents city or mountain bikes, child trailers, child seats, locks, helmets, and in-line skates (protective gear included). **Bayshore Bicycle and Rollerblade Rentals,** 745 Denman St. (☎ 604/688-2453), rents 21-speed mountain bikes, bike carriers, tandems, city bikes, in-line skates and kids' bikes. **Cycling B.C.,** 1367 W. Broadway (☎ 604/737-3034; www.cycling.bc.ca), is a nonprofit bicycling advocacy group.

BOATING

You can rent 15- to 17-foot power boats for as little as a few hours or up to several weeks at **Stanley Park Boat Rentals Ltd.,** Coal Harbour Marina (☎ 604/682-6257). **Granville Island Boat Rentals, Ltd.,** 1696 Duranleau St., Granville Island (☎ 604/682-6287), offers hourly, daily, and weekly rentals of 15- to 19-foot speedboats and also offers sportfishing, cruising, and sightseeing charters. **Jerry's Boat Rentals,** Granville Island (☎ 604/644-3256), is just steps away and offers similar deals. Rates on all the above begin at around C$30 (US$20) per hour and C$135 (US$90) per day for a sport boat that holds four. **Delta Charters,** 3500 Cessna Dr., Richmond (☎ 800/661-7762 or 604/273-4211), has weekly and monthly rates for 32- to 58-foot powered boat craft. Prices begin around C$1,400 (US$938) per week for a boat that sleeps four (which isn't a bad deal when you consider that you won't need a hotel room).

CANOEING & KAYAKING

Both placid, urban False Creek and the incredibly beautiful 30-kilometer (19-mile) North Vancouver fjord known as Indian Arm have launching points that can be reached by car or bus. Rentals range from C$10 (US$7) per hour to C$40 (US$27) per day for single kayaks and about C$50 (US$34) per day for canoe rentals. Customized tours range from C$70 to C$110 (US$47 to US$74) per person.

Adventure Fitness, 1510 Duranleau St., Granville Island (☎ **604/687-1528**), rents canoes and kayaks, offers lessons, and has a cool showroom filled with outdoor gear. **Ecomarine Ocean Kayak Centre,** 1668 Duranleau St., Granville Island (☎ **604/689-7575**), has 2-hour, daily, and weekly kayak rentals. The company also has an office at the **Jericho Sailing Centre,** 1300 Discovery St., at Jericho Beach (☎ **604/222-3565**). In North Vancouver, **Deep Cove Canoe and Kayak Rentals** (at the foot of Gallant Street), Deep Cove (☎ **604/929-2268**), is an easy starting point for anyone planning an Indian Arm run. It offers hourly and daily rentals of canoes and kayaks as well as lessons and customized tours.

Lotus Land Tours, 2005–1251 Cardero St. (☎ **800/528-3531** or 604/ 684-4922), runs guided kayak tours on Indian Arm. Tours come complete with transportation to and from Vancouver, a barbecue salmon lunch, and incredible scenery. Operator Peter Loppe uses very wide stable kayaks, perfect for first-time paddlers. One-day tours cost C$135 (US$90).

DIVING

People do it. Some even rave about it. And the marine life and wrecks and drift dives can indeed be amazing. The problem is, prime diving season is winter, when the rivers aren't blowing silt into the ocean and the suspended critters that make the water cloudy have sensibly opted not to breed. So if you can handle diving in 6°C (43°F) water, when the air temperature is around the same, by all means go. Most local divers use dry suits.

Cates Park in Deep Cove, Whytecliff Park and Porteau Cove near Horseshoe Bay, and Lighthouse Park are nearby dive spots. **Rowand's Reef Scuba Shop Ltd.,** 1512 Duranleau St., Granville Island (☎ **604/669-3483**), offers instruction, equipment rental, and charters. The **Diving Locker,** 2745 W. Fourth Ave. (☎ **604/736-2681**), rents equipment and offers courses and lots of free advice. Rentals cost around C$50 (US$34) per day or C$60 (US$40) with a second tank included; hiring a dive master to accompany you costs approximately C$60 (US$40) per dive. The Sunday Safari to the Sunshine Coast, including equipment, transportation, and two dives costs C$100 (US$67).

Join the **Underwater Archaeological Society of British Columbia,** Vancouver Maritime Museum, 1905 Ogden St., Vancouver, B.C. V6J 1A3 (☎ **604/980-0354**), before you arrive in Vancouver. Membership is C$40 (US$27) per year, C$20 (US$13) for students and seniors. Then you can volunteer for the society's sponsored shipwreck excavations in the good name of marine heritage preservation and conservation.

ECOTOURS

Lotus Land Tours, 2005–1251 Cardero St. (☎ **800/528-3531** or 604/684-4922), runs guided kayak tours on Indian Arm (see "Canoeing & Kayaking," above). **Rockwood Adventures,** 1330 Fulton Ave. (☎ **604/926-7705**), has guided walks of the North Shore rain forest, complete with a trained naturalist and a gourmet lunch.

Tours cover Capilano Canyon, Bowen Island, or Lighthouse Park, and cost C$49 (US$33) for a half day, including snack and drink, or C$105 (US$70) for a full day, including transportation, guide, and lunch.

FISHING

Five species of salmon, rainbow and Dolly Varden trout, steelhead, and even sturgeon abound in the local waters. To fish, you need a nonresident saltwater or freshwater license. Tackle shops sell licenses, have information on current restrictions, and often carry the BC Tidal Waters Sport Fishing Guide and BC Sport Fishing Regulations Synopsis for Non-tidal Waters. Independent anglers should also pick up a copy of the BC Fishing Directory and Atlas. **Hanson's Fishing Outfitters,** 102–580 Hornby St. (☎ **604/684-8988** or 684-8998), and **Granville Island Boat Rentals,** 1696 Duranleau St. (☎ **604/682-6287**), are outstanding outfitters. Licenses for freshwater fishing are C$16 (US$11) for 1 day or C$32 (US$21) for 8 days. Saltwater fishing licenses cost C$8 (US$5) for 1 day, C$20 (US$13) for 3 days, and C$39 (US$26) for 5 days.

Bonnie Lee Fishing Charters Ltd., on the dock at the entrance to Granville Island (mailing address: 744 W. King Edward Ave., Vancouver, B.C. V5Z 2C8; ☎ **604/ 290-7447**), is another reputable outfitter. **Corcovado Yacht Charters Ltd.,** 1696 Duranleau St., Granville Island (☎ **604/669-7907**), has competitive rates.

The *Vancouver Sun* prints a daily **fishing report** in the B section that details which fish are in season and where they can be found. You can pick up equipment at **Corcovado Saltwater Tackle Shop** (see Corcovado Yacht Charters Ltd., above) or **Ruddick's Fly Shop,** 1654 Duranleau St. (☎ **604/681-3747**). If you go to Granville Island, be sure to stop by the **Granville Island Sport Fishing Museum,** 1502 Duranleau (☎ **604/683-1939**).

Fly-fishing in national and provincial parks requires special permits, which you can get at any park site for a nominal fee. Permits are valid at all Canadian parks.

GOLF

This is a year-round Vancouver sport. With five public 18-hole courses and half a dozen pitch-and-putt courses in the city and dozens more nearby, no golfer is far from his or her love. The public **University Golf Club,** 5185 University Blvd. (☎ **604/ 224-1818**), is a great 6,560-yard, par-71 course with a clubhouse, pro shop, locker rooms, bar and grill, and sports lounge. Or call **A-1 Last Minute Golf Hotline** (☎ **800/684-6344** or 604/878-1833) for substantial discounts and short-notice tee times at more than 30 Vancouver-area courses. There's no membership fee.

Leading private clubs are situated on the North Shore and in Vancouver. Check with your club at home to see if you have reciprocal visiting memberships with one of the following: **Capilano Golf and Country Club,** 420 Southborough Dr., West Vancouver (☎ **604/922-9331**); **Marine Drive Golf Club,** W. 57th Avenue and S.W. Marine Drive (☎ **604/261-8111**); **Seymour Golf and Country Club,** 3723 Mt. Seymour Pkwy., North Vancouver (☎ **604/929-2611**); **Point Grey Golf and Country Club,** 3350 SW Marine Dr. (☎ **604/266-7171**); and **Shaughnessy Golf and Country Club,** 4300 SW Marine Dr. (☎ **604/266-4141**). Greens fees range from C$42 to C$72 (US$28 to US$48).

HIKING

Great trails for hikers of all levels run through Vancouver's dramatic environs. Good trail maps are available from the **Greater Vancouver Regional Parks District** (☎ **604/432-6350**) and from **International Travel Maps and Books,** 552 Seymour

St. (☎ **604/687-3320**), which also stocks guidebooks and topographical maps. Or pick up a local trail guide at any bookstore.

Just a few yards from the entrance to Grouse Mountain Resort is one entry to the world-famous **Baden-Powell Trail,** a 42-kilometer (26-mile) span of thick forest, rocky bluffs, and snow-fed streams racing through ravines. It starts at Cates Park on the Dollarton Highway and stretches west to Horseshoe Bay. Even if you only want to cover the stretch from Grouse Mountain to Mount Seymour, start early and be ready for some steep ascents. The timer guide at the trailhead marker has been annotated by hikers who've found it takes longer to do the loop than is indicated. Give yourself a full day for this hike.

If you're looking for a challenge without the time commitment, hike the aptly named **Grouse Grind** from the bottom of Grouse Mountain to the top, then buy a one-way ticket down on the Grouse Mountain SkyRide gondola. The one-way fare (down) is C$5 (US$3.35) per person.

If you're looking for a bit more scenery with a bit less effort, take the Grouse Mountain SkyRide up to the **Grouse chalet** and start your hike at an altitude of 1,100 meters (3,700 feet). The trail north to Goat Mountain is well marked and should take approx. 6 hours round trip, though you may want to build in some extra time to linger on the top of Goat and take in the spectacular 360° views of Vancouver, Vancouver Island, and the snow-capped peaks of the Coast Mountains.

Lynn Canyon Park, Lynn Headwaters Regional Park, Capilano River Regional Park, Mount Seymour Provincial Park, Pacific Spirit Park, and **Cypress Provincial Park** (see "Parks & Gardens" above) have good, easy to challenging trails that wind up through stands of Douglas fir and cedar and contain a few serious switchbacks. Pay attention to the trail warnings posted at the parks; some have bear habitats. And always remember to sign in with the park service at the start of your chosen trail. Golden Ears in Golden Ears Provincial Park, and The Lions, in West Vancouver, are for seriously fit hikers.

ICE-SKATING

Robson Square has free skating on a covered ice rink directly under Robson Street between Howe and Hornby Streets. It's open from November to early April. Rentals are available in the adjacent concourse. The **West End Community Centre,** 870 Denman St. (☎ **604/257-8333**), also rents skates at its enclosed rink, which is open from October through March. The enormous Burnaby 8 Rinks **Ice Sports Centre,** 6501 Sprott, Burnaby (☎ **604/291-0626**), is the Vancouver Canucks' official practice facility. It has eight rinks, is open year-round, and offers lessons and rentals.

IN-LINE SKATING

You'll find locals rolling along beach paths, streets, park paths, and promenades. If you didn't bring a pair of blades, go to **Alley Cat Rentals** (see "Bicycling & Mountain Biking," above), the preferred local outfitter because it has earlier and later shop hours than its competitors. Or try **Bayshore Bicycle and Rollerblade Rentals,** 745 Denman St. (☎ **604/688-2453**). Rentals generally run C$5 (US$3.35) per hour, or C$19 (US$13) for 8 hours.

JOGGING

You'll find fellow runners traversing the **Stanley Park Seawall, Lost Lagoon,** and **Beaver Lake.** If you're a dawn or dusk runner, take note that this is one of the world's safer city parks. However, if you're alone, don't tempt fate—stick to open and lighted areas. If you feel like doing a little racing, competitions take place throughout the year; ask at any runners' outfitters, such as **Forerunners,** 3504 W. Fourth Ave. (☎ **604/732-4535**), or **Running Room,** 679 Denman St. (corner of Georgia; ☎ **604/684-9771**).

PARAGLIDING

Summertime paragliding may be the ultimate flying experience. Most of the areas in British Columbia where it's offered are outside Vancouver: **Parawest Paragliding,** in Whistler (☎ **604/932-7052**), even has paramotoring. In North Vancouver, **First Flight Paragliding School** (☎ **604/988-1111**) offers tandem flights from the peak of Grouse Mountain. A tandem flight with instructor costs C$150 (US$101) for two hours (the flight takes approximately 20 minutes). Summer only.

SAILING

Navigating sailboats in the unfamiliar surrounding straits is unsound unless you enroll in a local sailing course before attempting it. Knowing the tides, currents, and channels is essential. Multiday instruction packages sometimes include guided Gulf Island cruises.

If all you want is to get out for a day, you can charter a 3-hour yacht cruise with one of the following outfitters. **Cooper Boating Centre,** 1620 Duranleau St. (☎ **604/687-4110;** www.cooperboating.com), offers cruises, boat rentals, and sail-instruction packages on 20- to 43-foot boats. **Sea Wing Sailing School and Yacht Charters,** 1815 Mast Tower Rd. (☎ **604/669-0840**), offers all of the above and also hosts a sailing club. Prices for skippered cruises start at C$49 (US$33) per person for a half-day tour. Boat rentals start at C$69 (US$46) for a half-day rental in the off-season and go as high as C$600 (US$402) for a full-day rental in the peak season, depending on the size of the boat.

SKIING & SNOWBOARDING

Top-notch skiing lies outside the city at the Whistler and Blackcomb Resorts, 112 kilometers (70 miles) north of Vancouver (see chapter 17). However, if you have only a day or two in Vancouver, you don't even have to leave the city to get in a few runs. It seldom snows in the city's downtown and central areas, but Vancouverites can ski before work and after dinner at the three ski resorts in the North Shore mountains.

Grouse Mountain Resort, 6400 Nancy Greene Way, North Vancouver (☎ **604/984-0661;** snow report 604/986-6262; www.grousemountain.com), is about three kilometers (2 miles) from the Lions Gate Bridge, overlooking the Burrard Inlet and Vancouver's skyline (see "The Top Attractions" above). Four chairs, two beginner tows, and two T-bars take you to 22 alpine runs. The resort has night skiing, special events, instruction, and a spectacular view, as well as a 90-meter (300-ft.) half pipe for snowboarders.

Though the area is small, all skill levels are covered, with two beginner trails, three blue trails, and five black-diamond runs, including Coffin and Inferno, which follow the east slopes down from 1,230 meters to 750 meters (4,100 to 2,500 ft.).

Rental packages and a full range of facilities are available. Lift tickets good for all-day skiing are C$29 (US$19) for adults, C$16 (US$11) for seniors, C$22 (US$15) for youths, and C$16 (US$11) for children under 12.

Mount Seymour Provincial Park, 1700 Mt. Seymour Rd., North Vancouver (☎ **604/986-2261;** snow report 604/986-3999; www.mountseymour.com), has the area's highest base elevation; it's accessible via four chairs and a tow. Lift tickets on weekdays are C$19 (US$13) all day for adults and youths 12 to 19, C$15 (US$10) for seniors, and C$9 (US$6) for children 6 to 11; on weekends C$26 (US$17) all day for adults, C$15 (US$10) for seniors, C$21 (US$14) for youths 12 to 19, C$12 (US$8) children 6 to 11. Nighttime skiing is C$19 (US$13) for adults, C$17 (US$11) for seniors, C$17 (US$11) for youths 12 to 19, and C$9 (US$6) for children 6 to 11. In addition to day and night skiing, the facility offers snowboarding, snowshoeing, and tobogganing along its 22 runs. There are 26 kilometers (16 miles) of cross-country trails. The resort specializes in teaching first-timers. Camps for children and teenagers, and adult clinics, are available throughout the winter.

Mount Seymour has one of Western Canada's largest equipment rental shops, which will keep your measurements on file for return visits. Shuttle service is available during ski season from various locations on the North Shore, including the Lonsdale Quay SeaBus. For more information call ☎ **604/986-2261.**

Cypress Bowl, 1610 Mt. Seymour Rd. (☎ **604/926-5612;** snow report 604/926-6007; www.cypressbowl.com), has the area's longest vertical drop (525m/1,750 ft.), challenging ski and snowboard runs, and 16 kilometers (10 miles) of track-set cross-country ski trails (including 5km/3 miles set aside for night skiing). Full-day lift tickets are C$35 (US$23) for adults, with reduced rates for youths, seniors, and children. Cross-country full-day passes are C$12 (US$8) for adults, with reduced rates for youths, seniors, and children. Snowshoe trail tickets are available for C$5 (US$3.35). Discounts for half-day, nighttime, and multiday tickets are available. **Cypress Mountain Sports,** 510 and 518 Park Royal S., West Vancouver (☎ **604/ 878-9229**), offers shuttle service to and from the ski area. Round-trip tickets are C$9 (US$6).

Cypress Mountain Sports stocks a complete selection of downhill, cross-country (including backcountry, skating, racing, and touring), and snowboarding equipment and accessories. The rental and repair department, staffed by avid skiers, offers a broad selection of equipment. Rental and repair prices are quite reasonable. The store also offers guided hikes in summer and snowshoe treks in winter.

SWIMMING & WATERSPORTS

Vancouver's midsummer saltwater temperature rarely exceeds 65°F (18°C). Some swimmers opt for fresh- and saltwater pools at city beaches (see "Beaches," above). Others take to the water at public aquatic centers.

The **Vancouver Aquatic Centre,** 1050 Beach Ave. at the foot of Thurlow Street (☎ **604/665-3424**), has a heated, 50-meter Olympic pool, saunas, whirlpools, weight rooms, diving tanks, locker rooms, showers, child care, and a tot pool. Adult admission is C$3.85 (US$2.55). The new, coed **YWCA Fitness Centre,** 535 Hornby St. (☎ **604/895-5777**), in the heart of downtown, has a six-lane, 25-meter ozonated (much milder than chlorinated) pool, steam room, whirlpool, conditioning gym, and aerobic studios. A day pass is C$12 (US$8) for adults. UBC's **Aquatic Centre** (☎ **604/822-4521** for the pool schedule, or 604/822-4522), located next door to the Student Union Building, has designated hours when facilities are open for public use. Adult admission is C$3.75 (US$2.50); youths and students, C$2.75 (US$1.85); seniors, C$2 (US$1.35).

TENNIS

The city maintains 180 outdoor hard courts that have a 1-hour limit and accommodate patrons on a first-come, first-served basis from 8am until dusk. Local courtesy dictates that if people are waiting, you surrender the court on the hour. (Heavy usage times are evenings and weekends.) With the exception of the Beach Avenue courts, which charge a nominal fee, all city courts are free.

Stanley Park has four courts near Lost Lagoon and 17 courts near the Beach Avenue entrance, next to the Fish House Restaurant. **Queen Elizabeth Park's** 18 courts service the central Vancouver area, and **Kitsilano Beach Park's** 10 courts service the beach area between Vanier Park and the UBC campus.

You can play at night at the **Langara Campus** of Vancouver Community College, on West 49th Avenue between Main and Cambie Streets. The **UBC Coast Club,** on Thunderbird Boulevard (☎ **604/822-2505**), has 10 outdoor and four indoor courts. Indoor courts are C$10 (US$7) per hour, plus C$3 (US$2) per person; outdoor courts are C$3 (US$2) per person.

Bayshore Bicycle and Rollerblade Rentals, 745 Denman St. (☎ **604/688-2453**) rents tennis rackets for C$10 (US$7) per day.

WHITEWATER RAFTING

Located just a 2½-hour drive from Vancouver on the wild Nahatlatch river, **Reo Rafting** (☎ **800/736-7238**; www.reorafting.com) offers some of the best guided whitewater trips in the province, at a very reasonable price. One-day packages—including breakfast, lunch, all your gear, and four to five hours on the river—start at C$99 (US$66). Multiday trips and group packages are also available.

WILDLIFE WATCHING

Where else do you find brant geese flying overhead on a major downtown thoroughfare and nesting on office buildings? Even in the city, nature hasn't lost the battle to civilization. Vancouver is an internationally famous stop for naturalists, ecotourists, and thousands of migratory birds, so bring your cameras, binoculars, and spotting books! Orcas, salmon, bald eagles, herons, beavers, and numerous rare, indigenous marine and waterfowl species live in the metropolitan area.

During the winter, thousands of bald eagles line the banks of the **Squamish, Cheakamus,** and **Mamquam** Rivers to feed on spawning salmon (see chapter 17). The official January 1994 eagle count in Brackendale (a small community near Squamish) recorded 3,700—the largest number ever seen in North America.

The annual summer salmon runs attract more than bald eagles. Tourists also flock to coastal streams and rivers to watch the waters turn red with leaping coho and sockeye. The salmon are plentiful at the **Capilano Salmon Hatchery** (see "Parks & Gardens," above) and **Goldstream Provincial Park** (see chapter 13), and numerous other freshwaters.

Along the Fraser River delta, more than 250 bird species migrate to or perennially inhabit the **George C. Reifel Sanctuary's** wetland reserve. Nearby, **Richmond Nature Park** has educational displays for young and first-time birders, plus a boardwalk-encircled duck pond (see "Parks & Gardens," above).

Stanley Park and **Pacific Spirit Park** are both home to heron rookeries. You can see these large birds nesting just outside the Vancouver Aquarium. Ravens, dozens of species of waterfowl, raccoons, skunks, beavers, and even coyotes are also full-time residents.

WINDSURFING

Windsurfing is not allowed at the mouth of False Creek near Granville Island, but you can bring a board to Jericho and English Bay Beaches or rent one there. Equipment sales, rentals (including wet suits), and instruction can be found at **Windsure Windsurfing School,** 1300 Discovery St., at Jericho Beach (☎ **604/224-0615**). Rentals start at C$17 (US$11) per hour.

10 Spectator Sports

Spectators and participants will find plenty of activities in Vancouver. You can get schedule information on all major events at Tourism Vancouver's **Travel Info Centre,** 200 Burrard St. (☎ **604/683-2000**). You can also get information and purchase tickets from Ticketmaster at the **Vancouver Ticket Centre,** 1304 Hornby St. (☎ **604/ 280-3311**), which has 40 outlets in the greater Vancouver area. (Like every other Ticketmaster, they do charge a fee.) Popular events like Grizzlies and Canucks games and the Vancouver Indy can sell out weeks or months in advance, so it's a good idea to book ahead.

AUTO RACING

In early September, the CART Indy Series mounts its biggest annual event, the Labour Day **Molson Indy,** 765 Pacific Blvd. (☎ **604/684-4639** for information, 604/280-4639 for tickets). General admission starts at C$10 (US$7), depending on the race day. A 3-day general admission ticket costs C$50 (US$34). The race roars through Vancouver's streets around B.C. Place Stadium and the north and south shores of False Creek, attracting more than 350,000 spectators.

BASKETBALL

True, at the moment, the **Vancouver Grizzlies** are absolute bottom of the pond, setting records for games lost and points against. But ya gotta hope. There are new draft picks coming in all the time. Besides, you can always watch the visiting teams. The Grizzlies play at **General Motors Place Stadium,** 800 Griffith Way (☎ **604/ 899-7469;** event hot line 604/899-7444), where they take on the rest of the NBA. Tickets run from C$13 to C$89 (US$9 to US$60), with decent seats in the C$40 (US$27) range.

BIKE RACING

There are many small races on- and off-road throughout the year. Pick up a copy of *Coast: The Outdoor Recreation Magazine* (☎ 604/876-4980) at local outfitters for a race calendar. Or head to Whistler during the summer, when there's a race event practically every weekend. There's generally no admission charge for spectators.

FOOTBALL

The Canadian Football League's **B.C. Lions** (☎ 604/930-5466) play their home and Grey Cup championship games (in good seasons) in the 60,000-seat **B.C. Place Stadium,** 777 Pacific Blvd. S. (at Beatty and Robson Streets). Canadian football differs from its American cousin: It's a three-down offense game on a field that's 10 yards longer and wider. Some of the plays you see will have NFL fans leaping out of their seats in surprise. Tickets run C$25 to C$47 (US$17 to US$31).

HOCKEY

The National Hockey League's **Vancouver Canucks** play at **General Motors Place** (otherwise know as the Garage), 800 Griffith Way (☎ 604/899-4600; event hot line 604/899-7444), which they now share with the Vancouver Grizzlies of the NBA (see "Basketball," above). Tickets are C$26 to C$95 (US$17 to US$64).

HORSE RACING

Thoroughbreds run at **Hastings Park Racecourse,** Exhibition Park, East Hastings and Cassiar Streets (☎ 604/254-1631; www.hastingspark.com), from mid-April through October. On Wednesday and Friday, post time is 6:30pm. On weekends and holidays, post time at the elegant track is 1:30pm. There is a decent restaurant, so you can make a full evening or afternoon of dining and racing. Place a wager or two.

LACROSSE

Canada's official national summertime sport, lacrosse was adopted from a traditional Native ball game that was played between neighboring villages across miles of rugged terrain. The sport is now played indoors by the **Western Lacrosse Association** at **Queens Park** in New Westminster (home of the champion Salmonbellies, who got their odd name in the 1890s when rival fans taunted them for representing a fish-canning community), **Cam Neeley Arena** in Maple Ridge, **Burnaby Lake Arena,** and the **North Vancouver Rec Centre.** The season runs from May through September. Contact the **B.C. Lacrosse Association** (☎ **604/421-9755**) for schedules and ticket information.

RUGBY

Another British sport, rugby is played through the fall and winter. The **Vancouver Rugby Union** (☎ **604/988-7660**) and the **B.C. Rugby Union** (☎ **604/737-3065**) schedule games at playing fields around Vancouver.

RUNNING

The **Sun Run** in April and the **Vancouver International Marathon** in May attract many runners from around the world and even more spectators. Contact the **Pacific Roadrunners** (☎ **604/988-8899**), the **Vancouver International Marathon Society,** 127–555 W. 12th Ave. (☎ **604/872-2928**), or the **Vancouver Sun Run,** 655 Burrard St. (☎ **604/689-9441**), for information.

SOCCER

The American Professional Soccer League's **Vancouver Whitecaps** (☎ **604/930-5466**) play at Swangard Stadium (☎ **604/435-7121**) in Burnaby. Admission is normally C$15 to C$25 (US$10 to US$17).

7

Vancouver Strolls

Down below's Stanley Park. On the side of the trees there's a beach. You can't see it [points over to left]. Steveston's over there. [points to left] Coast Guard station. There's the Yacht Club, and beyond it, the docks. Then over on the other side of the inlet, there's Grouse Mountain. It's about 4,000 feet high. There's a restaurant on top of it. Nice restaurant.

— from the screenplay for *Playback*, by Raymond Chandler

Chandler's detective Philip Marlow was one of Hollywood's most enduringly popular creations, but studio executives so hated his set-in-Vancouver screenplay that it never made it into celluloid. Too bad. Chandler's geography in the above excerpt was a bit off, but there's no doubt he had the right idea. The best way to get to know Vancouver is to wear out some of the ol' shoe leather, to get out and snoop around a little. The tours below provide some clues on where to begin.

Walking Tour 1—Downtown & the West End

Start: The Hotel Vancouver.
Finish: The Canadian Craft Museum.
Time: 2 to 3 hours, not including museum and shopping and eating stops.
Best Times: Daytime, particularly during the week when the Law Courts building is open.
Worst Times: Too late in the evening when the shops and offices have closed.

An appropriate place to begin this tour is:

1. **The Hotel Vancouver,** 900 W. Georgia St. (☎ **604/684-3131**). The hotel is owned by the Canadian Pacific Railway (CPR), just as the city itself was for many, many years. In return for agreeing in 1885 to make Vancouver its western terminus, the CPR was given 2,400 hectares (6,000 acres) of prime downtown real estate—nearly the whole of downtown. The Hotel Vancouver is built in the CPR's signature chateau style, complete with verdigris-green copper roof. It's worth stepping inside for a moment to experience the Gatsbyesque ambiance of the lobby.

Leaving by the Burrard Street exit, turn left. The International Style building at 750 Burrard St. used to be home to the Vancouver Public Library, but was recently taken over by Vancouver

Walking Tour 1—Downtown & the West End

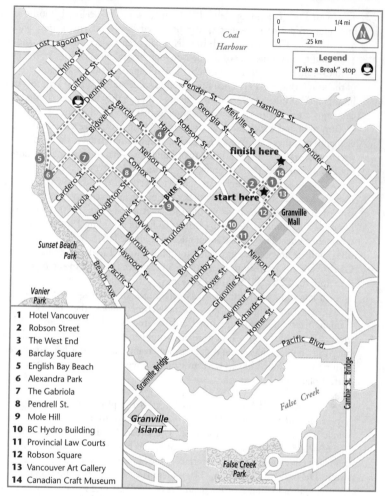

0   1/4 mi
0   .25 km

Legend
"Take a Break" stop

Coal Harbour

finish here ★

start here ★

Granville Mall

Sunset Beach Park

Vanier Park

Granville Island

False Creek

False Creek Park

1   Hotel Vancouver
2   Robson Street
3   The West End
4   Barclay Square
5   English Bay Beach
6   Alexandra Park
7   The Gabriola
8   Pendrell St.
9   Mole Hill
10   BC Hydro Building
11   Provincial Law Courts
12   Robson Square
13   Vancouver Art Gallery
14   Canadian Craft Museum

Television (VTV). The library, somewhat symbolically, moved east to a brand-new edifice built to look like an ancient Roman ruin. When you reach the corner, turn right, cross Burrard Street, and you're on:

2. **Robson Street.** The shops on this corner get more foot traffic than any other in Canada. Things were different back it the '50s, when so many German delis and restaurants opened up that for a time the street was nicknamed "Robsonstrasse." Beginning in the 1980s, these older stores were replaced with high-end clothiers, and new restaurants and gift shops with signs in Japanese. Whether you're into shopping or not, Robson Street is still a great place to walk and gawk and people-watch. When that palls, grab an ice cream or an espresso, pull up a patio table, and listen to the babble of Cantonese, Russian, Japanese, and other tongues.

Two blocks farther down Robson at Bute Street, turn left and walk 1 block south through a minipark to Barclay Street and you're in:

3. The West End. Beginning about 1959, this down-at-its-heels neighborhood of once-grand Edwardian houses was transformed by the advent of the concrete high-rise. By 1970, most of the Edwardians had been replaced by towers, and the West End had become one of the densest—and simultaneously one of the most livable—inner cities on the continent. The minipark at Bute and Barclay is one of the things that makes the neighborhood so successful: Traffic is kept to a minimum on West End streets, so that residents—though they live in the city center—can enjoy a neighborhood almost as quiet as that of a small town.

Turn right and walk west down Barclay Street and you'll see some of the other elements that make the West End such a sought-after enclave: the gardens and street trees, and the range and variety of buildings—including even a few surviving Edwardians, like the Arts and Crafts house at 1351 Barclay, or the set of two houses at the corner of Barclay and Nicola Streets, otherwise known as:

4. Barclay Square. This beautifully preserved bit of 19th-century Vancouver consists of Barclay Manor, built in the Queen Anne style in 1890, and Roedde House, a rare domestic design by British Columbia's leading 19th-century institutional architect Francis Rattenbury. Roedde House (1415 Barclay St.; ☎ 604/684-7040) is now a museum, open for guided tours Tuesday to Friday at 2pm; C$4 (US$2.70) admission. Every third Sunday, tea is served in the parlor from 2 to 4pm for C$5 (US$3.35) per person.

Turn left and walk south down Nicola Street for 1 block—past Fire Station No. 6—then turn right and go west on Nelson 1 block, then left again onto Cardero Street, passing by the tiny Cardero Grocery at 1078 Cardero St. All the grocery needs of the West End were once supplied by little corner stores like this one. You could even go in and grab an ice cream, but a better bet would be to turn right and walk 2 blocks west on Comox Street to reach Denman Street, the perfect place to:

☕ **TAKE A BREAK**   If Robson Street is the place Vancouverites go for hyperactive shopping sprees, Denman is where they go to sit back, sip a latte, and watch their fellow citizens stroll past. The **Bread Garden,** 1040 Denman St. (☎ 604/685-2996), is a fine spot for coffee and baked goods, particularly if you can nab a table on their outdoor terrace. One block down on the west side of the street, **Delany's on Denman,** 1105 Denman St. (☎ 604/662-3344), is a favorite man-watching spot for members of the West End's sizable gay community. Heteros are more than welcome too, of course, and the pies and cakes at this little cafe are to die for. Two blocks farther downhill and you're at:

5. English Bay Beach. The place to be when the sun is setting, or on one of those crystal-clear days when the mountains of Vancouver Island can be seen looming in the distance—or any day at all really, so long as the sun is shining. Every January 1, shivering Vancouverites in fancy costumes surround the bathhouse at the very foot of Denman Street (entrance at beach level) to take part in the annual Polar Bear Swim. Walk southeastwards a little bit on Beach Avenue and you come to a tiny green space with a band shell known as:

6. Alexandra Park. Back around the turn of the 20th century, a big Bahamian immigrant named Joe Fortes used to make his home in a cottage near this spot, that is, when he wasn't down on the beach teaching local kids to swim. In recognition of his many years of free service, the city finally appointed Fortes its first lifeguard. Later, a marble water fountain was erected in his memory by the Beach Avenue entrance to the park.

On the far side of the park, head up Bidwell Street 1 block to Davie Street, cross the street, turn right, walk 2 blocks farther on Davie Street, and on your left you'll see:

7. **The Gabriola,** 1531 Davie St. This was the finest mansion in the West End when it was built in 1900 for sugar magnate B. T. Rogers. Its name comes from the rough sandstone cladding, quarried on Gabriola Island in the Strait of Georgia. Unfortunately for Rogers, the Shaughnessy neighborhood soon opened up across False Creek and the West End just wasn't a place a millionaire could afford to be seen anymore. By 1925 the mansion had been sold off and subdivided into apartments. Since 1975 it's been a restaurant of one sort or another—currently the Macaroni Grill. The wrought-iron tables in the garden are particularly fine spots to sit out on summer days.

Cut through the garden, then turn left on Nicola Street and walk up through the Nicola Street minipark, then turn right on:

8. **Pendrell Street,** a typical West End street, with a few interesting bits of architecture. At the corner of Broughton Street is the Thomas Fee house (1119 Broughton St.), where one of the city's leading turn-of-the-century developer-architects made his home. Note how the modern addition has been blended with the old Edwardian structure. Farther along, at the southeast corner of Pendrell and Jervis Streets, is St. Paul's Episcopal Church, a 1905 Gothic Revival church built entirely of wood, an act of faith that has so far been rewarded. One block farther along at 1254 Pendrell is the Pendrellis—a piece of architecture so unbelievably awful, one gets a perverse delight just looking at it. Built as a seniors home at the height of the '70s craze for concrete, the multistory tower is one great concrete block, with nary a window in sight.

At Bute Street, turn left and walk 1 block north to Comox Street, and you're at:

9. **Mole Hill.** These 11 preserved Edwardian homes provide a rare view of what the West End would have looked like in, say, 1925. That they exist at all is more or less a fluke. The city bought the buildings in the 1970s but continued renting them out, thinking one day to tear them down for a park. By the 1990s, however, heritage had become all-important. The residents of the houses waged a sophisticated political campaign, renaming the area Mole Hill and bringing in nationally known architectural experts to plead the case for preservation. The city soon gave in.

Cut across the park to Nelson Street and continue down Nelson Street past Thurlow Street to Burrard Street, where you get your first view of:

10. **The BC Hydro Building,** 970 Burrard St. Built in 1958 by architect Ned Pratt, it was one of the first modernist structures erected in Canada, and has since become a beloved Vancouver landmark, thanks in no small part to its elegant shape and the attention to detail at every scale. Note how the windows, the doors, even the tiles in the lobby and forecourt echo the six-sided lozenge shape of the original structure. In the mid-90s, the building was converted to condominiums and rechristened The Electra.

From here, continue on Nelson Street, crossing Burrard Street and Hornby Street to:

11. **The Provincial Law Courts.** Internationally recognized architect Arthur Erickson (see Erickson sidebar in chapter 6) has had an undeniable impact on his native city of Vancouver. His 1973 Law Courts complex covers three full city blocks, including the Erickson-renovated Vancouver Art Gallery at its north end. Linking the two is Robson Square, which Erickson—and everyone else—envisioned as the city's main civic plaza. As with so many Erickson designs, alas, this one has elements of brilliance—the boldness of the vision itself, the cathedral-like space of the courthouse atrium—but was marred by Erickson's fetish for raw concrete and by his unconscious disdain for the mere human beings forced to make use of his creations.

As an example of the latter, note the unmarked concrete stairway—the one that looks like a parking garage exit—at the corner of Nelson and Hornby Streets. Unpromising as it seems, this is actually the entranceway to a very pleasant elevated pedestrian concourse, and one of three possible pathways we can take. The second and best route—available only during business hours—is to enter the courthouse and walk through the glorious glass-covered atrium. This is a truly inspired space, so it's worth timing your visit to when the doors are open. The fallback route, should the courthouse be locked and the stairway impossible to find, is to turn left and proceed down Hornby Street between the double row of street trees, cross over Smithe Street and carry on to about halfway down the block, then cut right into the courtyard by the Motor Vehicle office (look for the giant orange paper clip sculpture). Whichever way you go, 2 blocks north of this point you'll end up at:

12. Robson Square. Though it's best if you come down the zigzagging steps from the Law Courts concourse (hidden behind the waterfalls are the offices of the Crown Attorney—the Canadian equivalent of a district attorney), Robson Square is still somewhat underwhelming. Its basic problem is that it's sunk 6 meters (20 ft.) below street grade, and psychologically, most folks have an aversion to basements and cellars. So although there's a pleasant cafe in the square, and an outdoor ice rink in the wintertime, Robson square lacks the throngs of people that should attend a real civic plaza. On the other hand, the steps of the old courthouse on the far side of Robson are a great gathering place, the perfect spot to see jugglers and buskers, pick up a game of outdoor speed chess, or listen to an activist haranguing the world at large about the topic du jour.

To the left of the steps (and directly across from Robson Square) is the:

13. Vancouver Art Gallery, 750 Hornby St. Designed as a courthouse by Francis Rattenbury, and renovated into an art gallery by Arthur Erickson, the Vancouver Art Gallery (see "The Top Attractions" in chapter 6) is home to a tremendous collection of works by West Coast painter Emily Carr, as well as rotating exhibits ranging from Native masks to the video installations of Stan Douglas. Film buffs may remember the entrance steps and inside lobby from the movie *The Accused*.

To continue, go round the gallery by the left-hand side and proceed down Hornby Street. Note the fountain on the Art Gallery's front lawn. It was installed by a very unpopular provincial government as a way—according to some—of forever blocking protesters from gathering on the gallery lawn. Cross Georgia Street and have a glance inside the Hong Kong Bank building (885 W. Georgia St.) at the massive pendulum designed by artist Alan Storey. The lobby doubles as an art gallery and frequently features interesting exhibits. Cross to the west side of Hornby, and carry on about halfway down the block, then turn to your left and walk up the short flight of stairs to a small outdoor courtyard. On the north side is the:

14. Canadian Craft Museum, 639 Hornby St. A reprise of the much larger Cathedral Place, which it faces across the courtyard, the Canadian Craft Museum (see "The Top Attractions" in chapter 6) is the quintessential postmodern structure, with small art deco parts melded onto a basically Gothic edifice. Some of the panels on its front were salvaged from the Georgia Medical-Dental building, a much loved skyscraper that used to stand on this site. The courtyard has the feel of a formal French garden. Sit on the wooden benches and enjoy the peacefulness, or walk to the end of the square and explore the Craft Museum.

Walking Tour 2—Gastown & Chinatown

Chinatown and Gastown are two of Vancouver's most fascinating neighborhoods. Gastown has history and great old-fashioned architecture. Chinatown has all that plus the buzz of modern-day Cantonese commerce. One small travel advisory, however: The two neighborhoods border on Vancouver's Downtown Eastside—otherwise known as skid road—an area of taverns and cheap rooming hotels that is troubled by alcoholism and drug use. While there is very little actual danger for outsiders, there is a good chance of here and there stumbling across a scary-looking down-and-outer, particularly around Pigeon Park at the corner of Carrall and Hastings Streets. The tour route has been designed to avoid these areas.

Start: Canada Place.

Finish: Maple Tree Square.

Time: 2 to 4 hours, not including shopping, eating, and sightseeing stops.

Best Times: Any day during business hours, but Chinatown is particularly active in the mornings. If you arrive before noon, you can indulge in dim sum at many of the restaurants.

Worst Times: Chinatown's dead after 6pm, except on weekends in the summer, when they close a few streets to traffic and hold a traditional Asian Night market from 6:30 to 11pm.

Begin the tour at:

1. **Canada Place,** 999 Canada Place. With its five tall Teflon sails and bowsprit jutting out into Burrard Inlet, Canada Place is supposed to look like a great sailing ship. Some folks see it, some don't. Inside it's a hotel, cruise ship terminal, and convention center. Around the outside there's a promenade with plaques at regular intervals explaining the sights or providing historical tidbits. To follow the promenade, start by the fountain with the flags of Canada's provinces and territories just above it and head north out along the walkway. (*Note:* A planned expansion of the cruise ship terminal may make it impossible to reach the end of the pier, at least while construction is ongoing. If so, proceed directly to point 2.) At the far end of the pier—the prow—a pair of bronze lions point up and out towards a pair of peaks on the North Shore also called the Lions (supposedly for their resemblance to the Landseer Lions in Trafalgar Square, but mostly because the local morality squad wanted to eliminate forever the name given the peaks by the rough-minded early settlers—Sheila's Paps). Turn and look back over the railway tracks. The line of low-rise older buildings just beyond the railway tracks is Gastown.

   To continue the tour, walk back towards shore along the promenade, drop down the steps, turn left, and curve along the sidewalk until you pass the Aqua Riva restaurant. Then turn left and go up the steps and walk along an elevated pathway until you see a large wooden abstract sculpture. You're now in:

2. **Granville Square,** 200 Granville St. Had some forward-looking politicians and developers had their way, all of Gastown and Chinatown would have been

replaced by towers and plazas like the one you see here at 200 Granville. The plans had been drawn up and the bulldozers were set to move around 1970 when a coalition of hippies, heritage lovers, and Chinatown merchants took to the barricades in revolt. This building was the only one ever built, and the plan was abandoned soon afterwards.

At the east side of the plaza is a set of stairs leading down into:

3. **Waterfront Station,** 601 W. Cordova St. Though this beaux-arts edifice was converted to the SeaBus terminal in the 1970s (SkyTrain was added in 1986), this building still shows its origins as the CPR's Vancouver passenger-rail terminal. Look up high on the walls and you can see oil paintings depicting scenes you might see as you take the train across Canada—much easier then than now. On the main floor there's a Starbucks and some tourist shops.

Leave by the front doors, turn left, and wander east onto the cobblestones of Water Street, Gastown's main thoroughfare. **The Landing,** at 375 Water St., is home to some high-end retail stores and offices, including the office of the **BC Film Commission** (☎ **604/660-2732;** www.bcfilmcommission.com), where you can pick up a list of the film and TV productions being shot in the city. There's also a truly fine brew pub on the basement floor called **Steamworks** (☎ **604/689-2739**). Like most of Gastown's buildings, the Landing was built in the boom years between the Great Fire of 1886 and World War I. Klondike gold fueled much of the construction. As you walk along, note the **Magasin Building** at 322 Water St. Each of the column capitals bears the bronze head of a Gastown notable, among them Ray Saunders, the man who designed the:

4. **Steam Clock.** A quirky kind of timepiece, the Steam Clock gives a breathy rendition of the Westminster Chimes every 15 minutes. It draws its power from the city's underground steam-heat system. A plaque on the base of the clock explains the mechanics of it all.

Carry on down, past **Hills Indian Crafts** (165 Water St.), where Bill Clinton picked up a little bear statuette as a gift for you-know-who. Cross to the south side of the street at Abbot Street and continue on Water Street until you come to the Gaoler's Mews building (12 Water St.). Duck in through the passageway and:

☕ TAKE A BREAK   The name Gaoler's Mews refers to Vancouver's very first jail, which was built on this site. When that burned to the ground in the 1886 fire, the jail was replaced by a fire hall. The current structure was built as a parking garage but was renovated in the 1970s into a remarkably pleasant complex joined to a common courtyard/atrium. **The Black Cat Coffee** has fine coffee, while the **Paprika Cottage Restaurant** offers more substantial fare. For excellent beer and superior food, however, try the **Irish Heather,** 217 Carrall St. (☎ **604/688-9779**), accessible either via its back solarium—facing onto the mews—or by going out through the far passageway onto Carrall Street. You have to come this way eventually in order to reach:

5. **Maple Tree Square.** A historic spot, Maple Tree Square is where Vancouver first began. The statue by the maple tree (not the original one, but a replacement tree planted in more or less the same spot) is of Gassy Jack Deighton, a riverboat captain and innkeeper who erected Vancouver's first significant structure—a saloon—in 1867. Deighton got the nickname Gassy thanks to his propensity for jawing on at length (gassing, as it was known) about whatever topic happened to spring to mind. In 1870, when the town was officially incorporated as Granville, it was home to exactly six businesses: a hotel, two stores, and three saloons. Most folks called it Gastown, after Jack.

Walking Tour 2—Gastown & Chinatown

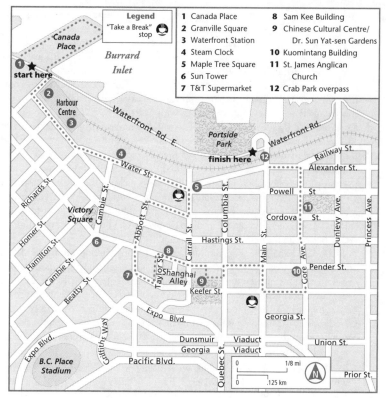

Legend

"Take a Break" stop

1 Canada Place
2 Granville Square
3 Waterfront Station
4 Steam Clock
5 Maple Tree Square
6 Sun Tower
7 T&T Supermarket
8 Sam Kee Building
9 Chinese Cultural Centre/ Dr. Sun Yat-sen Gardens
10 Kuomintang Building
11 St. James Anglican Church
12 Crab Park overpass

Just a half block south of the statue is a little laneway with the rather foreboding name of Blood Alley. So far as I can ascertain, nothing too nefarious ever happened here; the name appears to have been invented to appeal to tourists. Strangely, however, there's nothing much to see in this sanguine spot.

Continue south on Carrall Street to W. Cordova, turn right and walk 1 block west until you reach Abbot Street. Turn left and walk 2 blocks south down Abbot, crossing W. Hastings Street and stopping at W. Pender Street, where you get a great view of the:

6. **Sun Tower,** 500 Beatty St. It was the tallest building in the British Empire when it was built in 1911 to house the publishing empire of one Louis D. Taylor, publisher of *Vancouver World.* Not only was the building big, it was also slightly scandalous, thanks to the nine half-nude caryatids who gracefully support the cornice halfway up the building. Unfortunately, the girls couldn't bear the debt load with quite the same aplomb; three years later Louis D. was forced to sell.

Cross Pender Street and continue on Abbot Street, rounding the curve of the building on your right-hand side until you come to the entrance of the:

7. **T&T Supermarket,** 179 Keefer Place. So you've seen supermarkets? Unless your hometown is Hong Kong or Singapore, you haven't seen one like this. Just have a gander at the seafood display inside the doors: king crab, scallops, three different kinds of oysters, lobster, geoduck, all alive, some pinching mad. Farther in is a host of wondrous products for sale, including strange Asian fruits like rambutan, lychee, and the pungent durian. Browse at will, maybe pick up something

you don't recognize, and have an impromptu picnic in nearby Andy Livingstone Park.

Outside, walk 1 block east on Keefer Street to Taylor Street. The park is to your right, but to continue the tour turn left. Walk 1 block back up to Pender Street, then turn right and walk 1 more block. You're in Chinatown, an area distinguished architecturally by tall narrow buildings with recessed balconies, commercially by a profusion of vegetable and apothecary shops, and culturally by the sheer exuberance of immigrant life. First stop is the:

8. **Sam Kee Building,** 8 W. Pender St. The world's thinnest office building—4 feet 11 inches deep—was Sam Kee's way of thumbing his nose at both the city and his greedy next-door neighbor. In 1912 the city expropriated most of Kee's land in order to widen Pender Street, but refused to compensate him for the tiny left-over strip. Kee's neighbor, meanwhile, hoped to pick up the leftover sliver dirt cheap. The building was Kee's response. Huge bay windows helped maximize the available space, as did the extension of the basement well out underneath the sidewalk (note the glass blocks in the pavement). The building is now home to Jack Chow insurance.

Just behind the Sam Kee Building is the forlorn-looking **Shanghai Alley,** which just 40 years ago was jam-packed with stores, restaurants, a pawnshop, a theater, rooming houses, and a public bath. More interesting is the **Chinese Freemason's building,** just across the street at 1 W. Pender. The building could be a metaphor for the Chinese experience in Canada. On predominantly Anglo Carrall Street, the building is the picture of Victorian conformity. On the Pender Street side, on the other hand, the structure is exuberantly Chinese.

One block farther east on Pender Street is the:

9. **Chinese Cultural Centre/Dr. Sun Yat-sen Gardens.** A modern building with an impressive traditional gate, the cultural center provides services and programs for the neighborhood's thousands of Chinese-speaking residents. Through the smaller inner gate, the Dr. Sun Yat-sen Classical Chinese Garden (see "Parks & Gardens" in chapter 6) is well worth a visit. The only full-size classical Chinese garden outside China, it was modeled after a Ming Period (1368 to 1644) scholar's retreat in the Chinese city of Suzhou.

Exit the gardens by the gate on the right-hand (east) side, then turn left and you'll find the **Chinese Cultural Centre Museum and Archives** at 555 Columbia St. From here, go back up to Pender and turn right and continue going east, peeking in here and there to explore apothecaries like **Vitality Enterprises** at 126 E. Pender. At Main Street, turn right and walk south 1 block to Keefer Street and:

⚫ **TAKE A BREAK**   Though it's Canada's largest Chinese restaurant, **Floata Seafood Restaurant,** 400–180 Keefer St. (☎ **604/602-0368**), isn't easy to find. In classic Hong Kong restaurant style, it's on the third floor of a bright red shopping plaza/parking garage. Time your arrival for midmorning dim sum (a kind of moving Chinese smorgasbord).

To continue the tour, keep strolling east on Keefer Street. You'll pass grill shops displaying roasted ducks, and bakeries like the **Garden Bakery and Tea House,** 249 E. Pender St. (☎ **604/682-1608**), where the display counters are filled with freshly made *bao* (buns filled with sweetened pork or black beans). The **New Chong Lung Seafood and Meat Market** at the corner of Gore and Keefer

Streets is also worth a look. The market stocks geoduck, salmon, and that local favorite, bullfrog. All (except the frogs) are available for shipping anywhere in the world.

Turn left and walk 1 block north up Gore to the corner of Pender Street to find the:

10. **Kuomintang Building,** 296 E. Pender St. Though often a mystery to outsiders, politics was and remains an important part of life in Chinatown. Vancouver was long a stronghold of the Chinese Nationalist Party or Kuomintang (KMT). The party's founder, Dr. Sun Yat-sen, stayed in Vancouver for a time raising funds. In 1920, the party erected this building to serve as its Western Canadian headquarters. When the rival Chinese Communist party emerged victorious from the Chinese civil war in 1949, KMT leader Chiang Kai-shek retreated to Taiwan. Note the Taiwanese flags on the roof.

Carry on down Gore 2 more blocks and you come to:

11. **St. James Anglican Church,** 303 E. Cordova St. Architect Adrian Gilbert Scott had designed a cathedral in Cairo before getting this commission, and it shows. Step inside to experience a hushed and beautiful gloom. One block east on Pender, the **Vancouver Police Museum** in the former Coroner's Court (240 E. Cordova) is well worth a visit. Among other displays, the museum has the autopsy pictures of Errol Flynn, who died in Vancouver in 1959 in the arms of his 17-year-old personal assistant.

Back on Gore Street, walk north, passing by Sunrise market (cheapest veggies in town) to Alexander Street. Turn left and walk 1 block west on Alexander to the:

12. **Crab Park overpass.** City Hall calls it Portside Park, and that's how it appears on the map, but to everyone else it's Crab Park. It was created after long and vigorous lobbying by eastside activists, who reasoned that poor downtown residents had as much right to beach access as anyone else. The park itself is pleasant enough, though perhaps not worth the trouble of walking all the way up and over the overpass. What is worthwhile, however, is walking halfway up to where two stone Chinese lions stand guard. From here, you can look back at Canada Place—where the tour started—or at the container port and fish plant to your right.

To bring the tour to an end, return back to Alexander Street and walk 2 blocks west back to Maple Tree Square (point 5).

Walking Tour 3—Kitsilano, Granville Island & Yaletown

Start: The Caper's Building, 2285 W. Fourth Ave. (at Vine), in Kitsilano (accessible via bus no. 4 and no. 7).
Finish: Vancouver Public Library Central Branch at Homer and Georgia Streets.
Time: 2 to 4 hours, not including shopping, eating, and sightseeing stops.
Best Times: Any day during business hours.
Worst Times: After 6pm, when Granville Island's shops have closed.

This tour takes you through three of Vancouver's most interesting neighborhoods: the former hippie enclave of Kitsilano, the industrial park turned public market called Granville Island, and the funky former warehouse district of Yaletown. The tour also includes a stroll along the beach.

We begin at:

1. **The Capers Building,** 2285 W. Fourth Ave. Back in the 1960s, Kitsilano was Canada's hippie-central, a Haight-Ashbury–like enclave of head shops, communes, and coffeehouses. At one point in the early 1970s, Vancouver's oh-so-square mayor, Tom Campbell, proposed rounding up all the tie-dyed long-hairs and shipping them off to a central detention center. Fortunately, that was never done, and as the years passed the hippies' waistlines and wallets got thicker, run-down communes and boarding houses were renovated or replaced with new apartments and condos, and the shops came to reflect Kitsilano's new affluence, though still with a touch of counterculture. The retail/office/apartment building at 2285 W. Fourth Ave. was built according to an innovative energy-efficient design and now serves as the home of the environmentally focused **David Suzuki Foundation,** an excellent bookstore called **Duthie's,** and **Capers,** an organic supermarket. The small outdoor patio is a great place to grab a coffee and people-watch. Further east on Fourth Avenue there are several good retro-clothing shops, a travel bookstore, a number of furniture and interiors boutiques, several bakeries, and numerous other spots in which to grab a bite.

To continue the tour from here, walk north (downhill) 4 blocks on Yew Street to:

2. **Starbucks,** 1500 Yew St. Okay, so it's not exactly a tourist attraction. It's included in the tour because it makes a fine alternative starting place. Bus no. 22 from out front of Starbucks will take you to downtown (south side of street) and bring you from downtown (north side). Also, the surrounding enclave of patio-mad bistros and restaurants is interesting in its own right. Most of the clientele have sauntered over from nearby Kits Beach, making tank tops and Tevas the fashion norm. The **Urban Well,** 1516 Yew St. (☎ 604/737-7770), is a particularly popular post-beach rehydration station. **Malone's Restaurant**—across from Starbucks—makes its home in a former gas station.

Crossing north over Point Grey Road leads you onto:

3. **Kits Beach.** Vancouver is blessed with beaches. They stretch almost unbroken from here to the University of British Columbia, 10 kilometers (6 miles) west on the tip of the Point Grey peninsula, and each has its own distinct personality. Below UBC, Wreck Beach is a semi-wild strand for nudists and nature lovers. Beaches in between cater to dogs, picnicking families, and lone hikers. Kits Beach is the home of the spandex and testosterone set. Hard-bodied males and females parade up and down, scoping out each other's pecs. The action on the volleyball courts is fast and furious. For the less than physically perfect, the logs lined up on the beach make it a fine place to lay out a blanket and laze the day away. Small children can often be found playing on the nearby swings, while older kids favor the life-guarded swimming area or the world's largest outdoor saltwater swimming pool. On a clear day, the views of the mountains are tremendous.

Walk down the beach and around the corner on the paved pathway to the:

4. **Totem Pole.** Carved by the exceptional Kwakiutl carver Mungo Martin (who also did many of the poles displayed in the Museum of Anthropology and in Stanley Park), the 10 figures on this 30-meter-tall (100 ft.) pole each represent an ancestor of the 10 Kwakiutl clans. An identical pole was presented to Queen Elizabeth in 1958 to mark B.C.'s centenary. It now stands in Windsor Great Park.

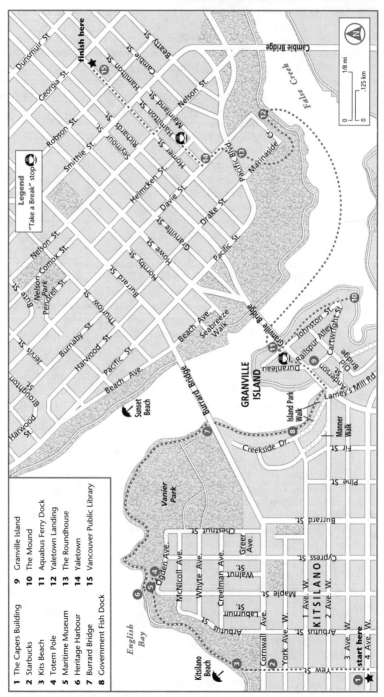

Legend
● "Take a Break" stop

1 The Capers Building
2 Starbucks
3 Kits Beach
4 Totem Pole
5 Maritime Museum
6 Heritage Harbour
7 Burrard Bridge
8 Government Fish Dock
9 Granville Island
10 The Mound
11 Aquabus Ferry Dock
12 Yaletown Landing
13 The Roundhouse
14 Yaletown
15 Vancouver Public Library

Turn north (towards the mountains) and walk down the steps to the:

5. **Maritime Museum,** 1905 Ogden Ave. Ever since it was realized that Columbus had found a new continent instead of Cathay, every European explorer's overriding quest was to find the Northwest Passage, the seagoing shortcut to the riches of the east. The little ship housed inside the **Maritime Museum** (☎ **604/ 257-8300**) is the one that finally did it. Tours of the RCMP vessel, the *St. Roch,* are available at regular intervals through the day (see "The Top Attractions" in chapter 6). Out back of the museum, the junk on the lawn by the north side all comes from various ships wrecked on the B.C. coast.

Proceed down the crushed-stone pathway to:

6. **Heritage Harbour.** Many older wooden boats find shelter here, including the seiner BCP45 shown on the back of the old Canadian $5 bill. Those interested in a shortcut can pick up a ferry (False Creek Ferries, ☎ **604/684-7781**) at this point and float down to Granville Island (stop 9). On weekdays and off-season the ferries run less frequently. Hours and fares are posted on the sign at the end of the dock. Walkers should proceed east (towards the city) along the shoreline. In summer, squadrons of brilliantly colored kites—some with wingspans topping 30 feet—dip and soar in the air above Vanier Park. To your right stands artist Chung Hung's massive twisted iron sculpture, *Gate to the Northwest Passage.* Just beyond that, the conical building is the **Vancouver Museum,** 1100 Chestnut St. (☎ **604/736-4431**) and **Pacific Space Centre** (☎ **604/738-STAR**). The low building next to that is the **Vancouver Archives,** 1150 Chestnut (☎ **604/ 736-8561**), home to some truly fascinating panoramic photographs of Vancouver back in the early days. Carry on along the pathway around the point, passing the Coast Guard station on your right, and you're walking underneath the:

7. **Burrard Bridge.** In 1927, the city fathers commissioned noted urban planner Harland Bartholomew to provide some guidance on how to expand their rather raw seaport city. One of Bartholomew's first injunctions: Build Beautiful Bridges! The Burrard Bridge is the result, an elegant steel span with two castles guarding the approaches at either end. Motorists often wonder what's inside the now inaccessible rooms atop the decorated castle keeps. The answer: not much. Maintenance bric-a-brac mostly, together with the remains of an elevator that was never installed. Cross beneath the bridge and continue along the pedestrian path. You'll have to go up the steps to walk above the fenced-off docks (or go around the back for wheelchair access) before coming down on the other side at the:

8. **Government Fish Dock.** Want to buy fresh from the boat? This is the place to do it. Fresh salmon in season (summer and early fall), prawns, scallops, and other shellfish much of the rest of the year. Sales take place every day in high season, and on weekend mornings the rest of the year. Hours and availability, of course, depend on the catch. From here, amble on down the seaside walkway past the gaggle of Canada geese (in the spring there are usually also downy Canada goslings) to:

9. **Granville Island.** Okay, so it's not really an island. But it is a fascinating collection of shops and restaurants, theaters, a hotel, artist workshops, housing, and still-functioning heavy industry—one of the few successful examples of 1970s urban renewal. The **Granville Island Information Centre,** 1592 Johnston St. (☎ **604/666-5784**), near the Public Market, has excellent free maps, but they're not really necessary—the place is so compact, the best thing to do is simply wander and explore.

To continue the tour, bear left down Duranleau Street. Shops in this section specialize in marine tours of all kinds, which makes it a good place to look for a fishing charter or kayak tours. The **Net Loft** building on the far side of the street is a great spot for pottery, glasswork, paper products, and ladies' hats, both classic and funky. It's also home to **Blackberry Books,** 1663 Duranleau (☎ 604/685-6188). Just past the Net Loft is **Triangle Square,** an open space where street buskers often perform. Cut through the square, cross the street, and:

TAKE A BREAK   You name it, so long as it's edible, the **Granville Island Public Market** probably has it, from chocolate to fresh salmon to fresh bread to marinated mushrooms to strawberries picked this morning out in the Fraser Valley. Those with an immediate hunger gravitate to the far side of the market, where **A La Mode** (☎ 604/685-8335) sells lattes and rhubarb-strawberry pie that'll have you trading in your mother for whoever does their baking. The most fun way to feed yourself, however, is to roam the market stalls for picnic supplies—artichoke hearts, Danish cheese, cold smoked salmon, Indian candy, pepper pâté, fresh baked bread—then head outside for an alfresco feast at one of the tables on the dock overlooking False Creek. The views are great, the fresh air invigorating, and, if you've brought small children along, it's the perfect place to play that endlessly fascinating (to kids) game of Catch the Seagull.

When your hunger pangs have eased, continue east on the water's edge—note the Aquabus ferry dock, to which we'll be returning later—and follow the path around the Arts Club pub, underneath the Granville Street Bridge and then to your right, away from the water, and go through what is, perhaps, the perfect little outdoor courtyard. You emerge on the far side next to a carving shed where First Nations artists can be seen working on a canoe or totem pole. Turn right and proceed down Johnston Street. This is the more industrial section of the island, and gravel and cement trucks are not uncommon. About halfway down the street is **Emily Carr College,** a high-caliber school of photography and art. Student projects are often on display in the lobby gallery. At the far end of Johnston Street is the **Creek Lounge,** 1253 Johnston St. (☎ 604/685-7070), a pub blessed with good beer and a geographically advantaged patio (it's on the edge of False Creek). Alternatively, just to the right, you can climb the low circular hill known as:

10. The Mound. Gaze out over False Creek. The blinking geodesic dome at the far end of the creek is **Science World** (see "The Top Attractions" in chapter 6). In the same direction but closer is a small marina and restaurant complex, situated on Leg-in-Boot Square. The name refers to an incident late in the 19th century when a human leg, boot and all, washed up on what was then a highly industrial shoreline. Police posted the leg up in a public place for a week or so in hopes that someone would come forward to identify it (or maybe claim it?), but no one ever did.

Descend from The Mound and retrace your steps (or wind your way back through some of the side streets) to the:

11. Aquabus Ferry Dock. From here Aquabus harbor ferries (☎ 604/689-5858) arrive and depart to a variety of places including Leg-in-Boot Square and Science World down the Creek. Our destination is on the far side of False Creek at the:

12. Yaletown Landing (at the foot of Davie Street). The small forest of high-rises ringing the north shore of False Creek are the creation of one company—Concorde Pacific, owned by Hong Kong billionaire Li Ka Shing. Formerly a railway switching yard, the area was transformed for the Expo '86 World's Fair. When the fair came to an end, the provincial government sold the land to Li Ka Shing for a song on the understanding he would build condominiums. And did he ever. The towers have been rising at the rate of three or four a year ever since.

At the landing site, note the large art piece, *Street Light,* designed by Bernie Miller and Alan Tregebov and installed in 1997. The large panels, each of which depicts a seminal event in False Creek's history, have been arranged so that on the anniversary of that event the sun will shine directly through the panel, casting a shadowed image on the street. From here, turn to the left and walk along the waterfront to David Lam Park, turn right, and follow the path to:

13. The Roundhouse, named because that's exactly what this brick and timber frame building was, back when this land was the CPR's switching yard. The structure has since been converted into a community center. It's worth ducking inside, whether to experience this wonderful space, make use of the public washrooms, or have a look at the locomotive that pulled the first passenger train ever to chug into Vancouver, way back in 1887.

Leave the Roundhouse by the front entrance on Pacific Boulevard, then cross the street and walk up Davie Street 1 block to Mainland Street. You're now in:

14. Yaletown. Vancouver's former warehouse district, Yaletown was originally where roughneck miners from Yale (up the Fraser Valley) came to drink and brawl. The city considered leveling the area in the 1970s until someone noticed that the former loading docks would make fine terraces, and the low brick buildings themselves could be renovated into offices and condos. Though it's taken 20 years for the neighborhood to really catch on, the result is a funky upscale district of furniture shops, restaurants, multimedia companies, and "New York–style" lofts. Note the metal canopies over the loading docks on many buildings—they used to keep shipping goods dry, now they do the same for tourists and latte-sipping Web programmers. Turn right and walk up Mainland to Helmcken Street and:

☕ TAKE A BREAK Helmcken Street between Mainland and Hamilton Streets has something for every taste. For coffee and pastry lovers there's a **Bread Garden** at Hamilton and Helmcken. Heartier appetites can grab pub grub at **Milestones** on the opposite corner. For those who prefer their barley and yeast in liquid form, there's the **Yaletown Brewing Company** at 1111 Mainland St. Remember, if it's raining at 11:30am on a Thursday, all pints of brewed-on-the-premises beer are C$3.75 (US$2.50) for the rest of the day.

From here, continue on Mainland or Hamilton 1 block up to Nelson Street, then turn left and go up 2 blocks to Homer Street. Turn right and walk up 3 blocks to the:

15. Vancouver Public Library, 350 W. Georgia St. (☎ **604/331-3600**). Designed by noted architect Moshe Safdie to look like the ruin of a Roman coliseum, the library was enormously controversial when it first went up. Architectural critics pooh-poohed it as derivative and ignorant of West Coast architectural traditions. But when the public got a look at the building, it was love at first sight. The steps out front have become a popular public gathering place, the lofty atrium inside a favored hang-out spot and "study-date" locale for visiting language-school students and teens with protective parents. Go and have a look for yourself. Grab a coffee. Browse the books. Enjoy.

From here, a short walk west along Georgia Street will take you to the Granville Street bus mall, where there are public buses running to any and all destinations.

Vancouver Shopping

8

Blessed with a climate that seems semitropical in comparison to the rest of Canada, Vancouverites never really developed a taste for indoor malls. Instead, the typical Vancouverite shops on the street—parking the car or, better yet, leaving it at home—and browses from one window to the next, always on the lookout for something new. Below are a few suggestions on where to start exploring.

1 The Shopping Scene

ROBSON STREET   It's been said that the corner of Robson and Burrard gets more foot traffic than any other corner in Canada. Urban myth? Who knows. Anyway, it's a busy, colorful parade of humanity, many from Asia (hence the sushi bars and shops with Japanese signs), most with money. Look for high-end fashions, with a focus on clothes for the younger set.

SOUTH GRANVILLE   The 10-block stretch of Granville Street—from Sixth Avenue up to 16th Avenue—is where Vancouver's old-money enclave of Shaughnessy comes to shop. Classic and expensive men's and women's clothiers, and houseware and furniture boutiques predominate. This area is also the heart of Vancouver's gallery row.

WATER STREET   Though a little too heavy on the knickknack shops (it's the wrought-iron lamp stands that bring them out), Water Street and Gastown are by no means just a tacky tourist enclave. Look for antique and cutting-edge furniture, galleries of First Nations art, and funky basement retro shops.

MAIN STREET   Antiques, and lots of 'em. From about 19th up to 27th, Main Street is chock-a-block with antique shops. Rather than outbid each other, the stores have evolved so that each covers a particular niche, from art deco to country kitchen to fine Second Empire. It's a fun place to browse, and if your eyes start to glaze over at the thought of yet another divan, the area also has cafes, bookshops, and clothing stores.

GRANVILLE ISLAND   A rehabilitated industrial site beneath the Granville Street Bridge, the Public Market is paradoxically one of the best places to pick up salmon and other seafood. It's also a great place to browse for crafts and gifts. Particularly interesting is Kid's Market, a kind of mini-mall for children, complete with Lilliputian entrance-way, toy and crafts and book stores, and play areas and services for the not-yet-10 demographic.

ASIA WEST   If you've never been to Hong Kong, or are just itching to get back, this new commercial area on Richmond's No. 3 Road between Capstan and Alderbridge is the place to shop. Stores in four new malls—the Yaohan Centre, President Plaza, Aberdeen Centre, and Parker Place—cater to Vancouver's newly arrived Asian community by bringing in goods direct from Asia. If the prices seem a bit high, a simple inquiry is often enough to bring them plummeting down as much as 80%.

PUNJABI MARKET   India imported. The 4 blocks of Main Street on either side of 49th Avenue contain the whole of the subcontinent, shrunk down to a manageable parcel. Look for fragrant spice stalls and sari shops and textile outlets selling luxurious fabrics—at bargain-basement prices.

2 Shopping A to Z

ANTIQUES

Bakers Dozen Antiques. 3520 Main St. ☎ **604/879-3348.**

This charming shop specializes in antique toys, model ships and boats, folk art, and unusual 19th- and early 20th-century furniture.

Mihrab. 2229 Granville St. ☎ **604/879-6105.**

Part museum, part subcontinental yard sale, Mihrab specializes in one-of-a-kind Indian antiques for the house and garden. Think intricately carved teak archways, or tiny jewel-like door pulls, all selected by partners Lou Johnson and Kerry Lane on frequent trips to the subcontinent.

Potter's Gallery. Westin Bayshore Hotel, 1601 W. Georgia St. ☎ **604/685-3919.**

Established in 1924, this store sells Chinese and Japanese art as well as Kurf Sutton's fine porcelain flowers.

Three Centuries Shop. 321 Water St. ☎ **604/685-8808.** www.threecenturiesshop.com.

French and English decorative arts, especially from the art deco and art nouveau periods, are featured at this store, three doors down from the Gastown Steam Clock.

Uno Langmann Limited. 2117 Granville St. ☎ **604/736-8825.** www.langmann.com.

Catering to upscale shoppers, Uno Langmann specializes in European and North American paintings, furniture, silver, and objets d'art from the 18th through early 20th centuries. Open Wednesday to Saturday from 10am to 5pm.

Vancouver Antique Centre. 422 Richards St. ☎ **604/669-7444.**

Housed in a heritage commercial building, this maze contains 14 separate shops on two levels, specializing in everything from china, glass, and jewelry, to military objects, sports, toys, retro, '50s and '60s collectibles, home furnishings, and watches. There are even more shops in the neighboring buildings.

BOOKS

Blackberry Books. 1663 Duranleau St. ☎ **604/685-4113** or 604/685-6188.

Books about art, architecture, and fine cuisine are the specialties of this Granville Island store, which also has a wide variety of more general categories. New titles are displayed with staff reviews posted beside them.

Chapters. 788 Robson St. ☎ **604/682-4066.**

There was grumbling amongst the literati when this big-box baddie came to town a couple years back. Since then Chapters seems to have won folks over with the sheer quality of its book-buying experience—stores are pleasant and well planned, with little nooks and comfy benches; coffee is often available on the ground floor. And though it pains a local booster like myself to say it, Chapters' book selection is—gasp—every bit as good as homegrown favorite Duthie's. There is another location at 2505 Granville St. (☎ **604/731-7822**).

✪ **Duthie Books.** 2239 W. Fourth Ave., Kitsilano. ☎ **604/732-5344.**

Since 1957, this locally owned chain has been synonymous with good books in Vancouver. Though its recent financial troubles and retrenchment have left Duthie's with just one store, it remains a particularly good place to find local authors, in addition to an excellent inventory of Canadian and international titles. Staff are knowledgeable, and the shop offers custom services such as special, by-mail, and out-of-print ordering.

Granville Book Company. 850 Granville St. ☎ **877/838-BOOK** or 604/687-2213. www.granvillebooks.com.

Located in the heart of Vancouver's entertainment district, this bookstore has a great selection and staff with a true love for books. The generous open hours (till midnight daily and 1am on Fridays and Saturdays) make this a great spot for browsing after dinner or before a movie.

✪ **International Travel Maps and Books.** 552 Seymour St. ☎ **604/687-3320.** www.itmb.com.

Best selection of travel books, maps, charts, and globes in town. The selection of special-interest British Columbia guides is impressive, with topics ranging from back-country skiing and minimum-impact hiking to off-road four-wheeling. This is the hiker's best source for detailed topographic charts of the entire province. One of the city's secret bargains is the bin of free outdated provincial maps near the door that often includes maps of the parks around Whistler (outside Vancouver, the province changes slowly enough that they're still accurate).

Kidsbooks. 3083 W. Broadway. ☎ **604/738-5335.**

Largest and most interesting selection of children's literature in the city; also has an amazing collection of puppets, and regular readings. Also at 3040 Edgemont Blvd., North Vancouver (☎ **604/986-6190**).

Little Sister's Book & Art Emporium. 1238 Davie St. ☎ **604/669-1753.**

What makes one book literature and another pornography? Canada Customs officers used to routinely duck this difficult question by simply seizing whole shipments of Little Sister's books. They stopped only after the Supreme Court ruled that—whatever the answer to the question—it wasn't for Customs to decide. To see for yourself, come down and browse this West End bookstore's large selection of lesbian, gay, bisexual, and transgender books, videos, and magazines, as well as its huge adult novelties department.

CHINA, SILVER & CRYSTAL

One local artisan, **Martha Sturdy,** has a shop downtown, across the street from the Hotel Vancouver. There's also a great array of sophisticated international china and crystal in the downtown stores. On Granville Island you can observe potters, silversmiths, and glassblowers as they work their magic.

Gallery of BC Ceramics. 1359 Cartwright St. ☎ **604/669-5645.** www.bcpotters.com.

This Granville Island gallery loft is owned and operated by the Potters Guild of British Columbia. It presents a lively, juried collection of more than 70 sculptural and functional ceramic works. The gallery also carries a full range of books for ceramics enthusiasts. Closed on Mondays.

✪ **Martha Sturdy Originals.** 3039 Granville St. ☎ **604/737-0037.**

Designer Martha Sturdy—once best known for her collectible, usable, handblown glassware trimmed in gold leaf—is now creating a critically acclaimed line of cast-resin housewares, as well as limited-edition couches and chairs. Expensive but, if you've got the dough, well worth it.

CHINESE GOODS

T&T Supermarket. 181 Keefer St. ☎ **604/899-8836.**

Racks and racks of goods you won't find at home (unless your home is China), but the real entertainment is the seafood bins and the produce section, where strange and ungainly comestibles lurk: fire-dragon fruit, lily root, and enoki mushrooms.

Ten Ren Tea & Ginseng Co. 550 Main St. ☎ **604/684-1566.**

Whether you prefer the pungent aroma of Chinese black or the exotic fragrance of chrysanthemum, jasmine, or ginger flower, you must try the numerous varieties of drinking and medicinal teas in this Chinatown shop. It also carries Korean, American, and Siberian ginseng for a lot less than you might pay elsewhere.

Tung Fong Hung Foods Co. 536 Main St. ☎ **604/688-0883.** www.tung-fong-hung.com.

If you've never been to a Chinese herbalist, this is the one to try: jars, bins, and boxes full of such things as dried sea horse, thinly sliced deer antler, and bird's nest. It's lots of fun to explore and potentially good for what ails ya. Chinese remedies can have side effects, however, so before ingesting anything unfamiliar, it's usually wise to consult the on-site herbalist.

CIGARS & TOBACCO

What did Bill bring back for Monica from Vancouver? A cigar, of course, and you can too. (Sorry, I couldn't resist.) Just remember, if they're Cuban, you'll have to light up on this side of the border.

✪ **La Casa del Habano.** 980 Robson St. ☎ **604/609-0511.**

Directly across from Planet Hollywood on Robson Street, Casa del Habano has Vancouver's largest walk-in humidor. Cigars range in price from a few dollars to over a hundred. Better customers are occasionally invited to relax in the private smoking room. Members have small locker/humidors where they can store their purchases along with a bottle of fine cognac or single-malt scotch.

Vancouver Cigar Company. 1093 Hamilton St. ☎ **604/685-0445.** www.vancouvercigar.com.

The selection here is reputed to be the city's most extensive, featuring brands such as Cohiba, Monte Cristo, Macanudo, Hoyo De Monterrey, Romeo y Julieta, Partagas, Ashton, and A. Fuente. The shop also carries a complete line of accessories.

DEPARTMENT STORES

The Bay (Hudson's Bay Company). 674 Granville St. ☎ **604/681-6211.**

From the establishment of its early trading posts during the 1670s to its modern coast-to-coast chain, the Bay has built its reputation on quality goods. You can still buy a Hudson's Bay woolen "point" blanket (the colorful stripes originally represented how many beaver pelts each blanket was worth in trade), but you'll also find

Tommy Hilfiger, Polo, DKNY, and more. The store doesn't accept pelts anymore, but it does take all major credit cards.

Hills of Kerrisdale. 2125 W. 41st Ave. ☎ **604/266-9177.**

This neighborhood department store in central Vancouver is a city landmark. Carrying full lines of quality men's, women's, and children's clothes, as well as furnishings and sporting goods, it's a destination for locals because the prices are often lower than those in the downtown core.

DISCOUNT SHOPPING

The strip of West Fourth Avenue between Cypress and Yew Streets has recently emerged as consignment-clothing central. New shops open regularly.

In-Again Clothing. 1962 W. Fourth Ave. ☎ **604/738-2782.**

Good variety of seasonal consignment clothing. The selection keeps up with fashion trends. Don't forget to look at the collection of purses, scarves, and belts.

Second Suit for Men & Women. 2036 W. Fourth Ave. ☎ **604/732-0338.**

This resale- and sample-clothing store has the best in men's and women's fashions, including Hugo Boss, Armani, Donna Karan, Nautica, Calvin Klein, and Alfred Sung. The inventory changes rapidly.

Upstairs on 4th. 2144 W. Fourth Ave. ☎ **604/732-3924.**

This upstairs shop is jam-packed with men's and women's secondhand clothing, some of it quality, all of it cheap, cheap, cheap. It takes a bit of browsing, but if you find something good in here, guaranteed it'll be a steal.

    And elsewhere in the city is…

Wear Else? Clearance Centre. 78 E. Second Ave. ☎ **604/879-6162.**

Carrying the same items as its retail shops, this outlet store offers savings of 30% to 80% on Tommy Hilfiger, Jones New York, and other designer collections.

FASHIONS
FOR CHILDREN

Isola Bella. 5692 Yew St. ☎ **604/266-8808.**

This store imports an exclusive collection of rather expensive, high-fashion newborn and children's clothing from designers like Babar, Babymini, Milou, Petit Bateau, and Paul Smith.

✪ **Please Mum.** 2951 W. Broadway. ☎ **604/732-4574.**

This Kitsilano store sells attractive Vancouver-made toddler's and children's cotton clothing.

FOR MEN & WOMEN

Vancouver has the Pacific Northwest's best collection of clothes from Paris, London, Milan, and Rome, in addition to a great assortment of locally made, cutting-edge fashions. International designer outlets include **Chanel Boutique,** 900 W. Hastings St. (☎ **604/682-0522**); **Salvatore Ferragamo,** 918 Robson St. (☎ **604/669-4495**); **Gianni Versace Boutique,** 757 W. Hastings St. (☎ **604/683-1131**); **Versace's Versus,** 1008 W. Georgia St. (☎ **604/688-8938**); **Polo/Ralph Lauren,** the Landing, 375 Water St. (☎ **604/682-7656**); and **Plaza Escada,** Sinclair Centre, 757 W. Hastings St. (☎ **604/688-8558**).

It seems that almost every week a new designer boutique opens in Yaletown, Kitsilano, or Kerrisdale.

✪ **Christine and Company.** 201–657 Marine Dr., West Vancouver. ☎ **604/922-0350.**

More than 20 years ago, Christine Morton started out selling delicate, antique, lacy sleepwear along with a few of her own lingerie creations. She then expanded to silky blouses and heirloom-quality trousseau lingerie. And she's now regarded as the city's hottest bridal-wear designer.

✪ **Dorothy Grant.** Sinclair Centre, 250–757 W. Hastings St. ☎ **604/681-0201.**

Designed to look like a Pacific Northwest longhouse, this shop is where First Nations designer Dorothy Grant exhibits her unique designs as well as her husband's (acclaimed artist Robert Davidson) collection of exquisitely detailed Haida motifs, which she appliqués on coats, leather vests, jackets, caps, and accessories. The clothes are gorgeous and collectible. She also carries contemporary Haida art and jewelry.

Dream 311. W. Cordova. ☎ **604/683-7326.**

Big-name designs can be found anywhere, but this little shop is one of the few places to show early collections—clothing and jewelry—of local designers.

Leone. Sinclair Centre, 757 W. Hastings St. ☎ **604/683-1133.**

Shop where the stars shop. Versace, Donna Karan, Byblos, Armani, and fabulous Italian and French accessories are sold in this very elegant building; valet parking provided.

Lulu Island Designs. Steveston Landing, 119–3800 Bayview St., Richmond. ☎ **604/275-0558.**

Inside this historic cannery, amid artifacts from Steveston's days as a 19th-century Japanese fishing village, you'll find high-quality embroidered and silk-screened shirts.

Roots Canada. 1001 Robson (corner of Burrard). ☎ **604/683-4305.**

For more than 20 years, this chain has featured sturdy, Canadian-made casual clothing. The flagship store on Robson is in the heart of the busiest shopping area of Vancouver. You'll find leather jackets, leather bags, footwear, outerwear, and athletic wear for the whole family. There are many other locations around town, including in the Pacific Centre, 701 W. Georgia St. (☎ **604/683-5465**).

Straiths. Hotel Vancouver, 900 W. Georgia St. ☎ **604/685-3301.**

If Valentino, Ungaro, Bally, and Testoni are your preferences, then visit this well-known shop, which features the best clothing and accessories from the world's leading designers, at designer prices (though if you're visiting from the States, you may discover that many items carry the same price tag, and the currency conversion becomes a 30% discount).

Swimco. 2166 W. Fourth Ave. ☎ **604/732-7946.** www.swimco.com.

Located near Kitsilano Beach, this store caters to swimmers and sunbathers. You will find a large variety of bikinis and bathing suits in the latest prints and colors for men, women, and children. Check out the latest in active beachwear, shorts, and tops.

Venus & Mars. 315 Cambie St. ☎ **604/687-1908.** www.venusandmars.nu.

This Gastown boutique features Vancouver designer Sanné Lambert's work, specializing in one-of-a-kind handmade gowns and velvet robes.

✪ **Zonda Nellis Design Ltd.** 2203 Granville St. ☎ **604/736-5668.**

Rich colors and intricate patterns highlight this Vancouver designer's imaginative hand-woven separates, pleated silks, sweaters, vests, and soft knits. Nellis has also introduced a new line of hand-painted silks and sumptuous, sheer hand-painted velvet evening wear.

VINTAGE CLOTHING

Deluxe Junk Co. 310 W. Cordova St. ☎ **604/685-4871.** www.deluxejunk.com.

The name fits—there's tons of junk. Amid the polyester jackets and worn-out dress shirts, however, are some truly great finds. Some real bargains have been known to pop up.

Legends Retro-Fashion. 4366 Main St. ☎ **604/875-0621.**

Specializing in unique retro clothing, Legends is well known among vintage purists for its cache of one-of-a-kind pieces. Most of the clothes, such as evening dresses, shoes, kid gloves, and other accessories, are in immaculate condition.

Tapestry Vintage Clothing. 321 Cambie St., Gastown. ☎ **604/687-1719.**

Consignment shop with an interesting collection of vintage women's clothing.

True Value Vintage Clothing. 710 Robson St. ☎ **604/685-5403.**

This underground shop has a collection of funky fashions from the 1930s through the 1990s, including tons of fake furs, leather jackets, denim, soccer jerseys, vintage bathing suits, formal wear, smoking jackets, sweaters, and accessories.

FIRST NATIONS ART

You'll find First Nations art all over the city. You don't have to purchase a pricey antique to acquire original Coast Salish or Haida work. As the experts at the **Museum of Anthropology** explain, if an item is crafted by any of the indigenous Pacific Northwest artisans, it's a real First Nations piece of art. The culture is ancient yet still very much alive. Pick up a copy of *Publication No. 10: A Guide to Buying Contemporary Northwest Coast Art* by Karen Duffel (available at the Museum of Anthropology), which details how to identify and care for these beautifully carved, worked, and woven pieces.

Even if you're not in the market, go gallery-hopping to see works by Haida artists **Bill Reid** (the province's best-known Native artist) and **Richard Davidson,** and by Kwakwaka'wakw artist and photographer **David Neel.**

Coastal Peoples Fine Arts Gallery. 1024 Mainland St. ☎ **604/685-9298.** www. coastalpeoples.com.

This Yaletown boutique offers an extensive collection of fine First Nations jewelry. The motifs—bear, salmon, whale, raven, and others—are drawn from local myths and translated into 14-karat or 18-karat gold and sterling-silver creations. Inuit sculptures and items made of glass or wood are also worth a look. Custom orders can be filled quickly or shipped worldwide.

✪ **Images for a Canadian Heritage.** 164 Water St. ☎ **604/685-7046.**

This store and the Inuit Gallery of Vancouver (see below) are government-licensed First Nations art galleries, featuring traditional and contemporary works such as native designs on glass totems and copper plates. With a collection worthy of a museum, this shop deserves a visit whether you're buying or not.

Inuit Gallery of Vancouver. 345 Water St. ☎ **604/688-7323.**

Home to one of Canada's foremost collections of Inuit and First Nations art. The prices are oriented toward serious buyers, but it's worth a visit.

✪ **Leona Lattimer Gallery.** 1590 W. Second Ave. ☎ **604/732-4556.**

This beautiful gallery presents museum-quality displays of Pacific Northwest First Nations art, including ceremonial masks, totem poles, limited-edition silk-screen prints, argillite sculptures, and expensive gold and silver jewelry. Prices start at a few dollars for an original print, and escalate quickly to the three-digits mark for most items.

Marion Scott Gallery. 481 Howe St. ☎ **604/685-1934.** www.marionscottgallery.com.

For more than 20 years, this gallery has been well regarded for its Inuit (Eskimo) and First Nations art collections.

FIRST NATIONS CRAFTS

Bold, traditional, and innovative geometric designs; intricate carvings; strong primary colors; and rich wood tones are just a few of the elements you'll find in First Nations works. Pacific Northwest tribes, including the Haida, Coast Salish, and Kwak-waka'wakw, create crafts, jewelry, and art that are collected throughout the world.

Authentic Cowichan Indian Knits. 424 W. Third St., North Vancouver. ☎ **604/988-4735.**

Freda Nahanee's cottage-industry shop on the North Vancouver Squamish Band Reserve carries thick Cowichan sweaters, carved-silver Kwakiutl jewelry, Squamish wood carvings, beaded-leather moccasins, and woven baskets. Call ahead for open hours.

Hill's Indian Crafts. 165 Water St. ☎ **604/685-4249.**

In a re-creation of a trading post interior, this shop sells moccasins, ceremonial masks, Cowichan sweaters, wood sculptures, totem poles (priced up to C$35,000/US$23,450), silk-screen prints, soapstone sculptures, and gold, silver, and argillite jewelry.

✪ **Khot-La-Cha Salish Handicrafts.** 270 Whonoak St., West Vancouver. ☎ **604/987-3339.**

Hand-tanned moose-hide crafts, wood carvings, Cowichan sweaters, porcupine-quill jewelry, and bone, silver, gold, and turquoise accessories are just a few of the selections at this Coast Salish crafts shop.

Museum of Anthropology. University of British Columbia, 6393 NW Marine Dr. ☎ **604/822-5087.**

Works by contemporary First Nations artisans as well as books about the culture and publications on identifying and caring for Pacific Northwest crafts.

FOOD

You'll find **salmon** everywhere in Vancouver. Many shops package whole, fresh salmon with ice packs for visitors to take home. Shops also carry delectable smoked salmon in travel-safe, vacuum-packed containers. Some offer decorative cedar gift boxes; most offer overnight air transport. Try other salmon treats such as salmon jerky and Indian candy (chunks of marinated smoked salmon), which are available at public markets such as Lonsdale Quay Market and Granville Island Public Market.

And even though salmon is the most popular item to buy in Vancouver, coffee flows like water—as does Belgian chocolate.

Cheena BC Limited. 667 Howe St. ☎ **604/684-5374.**

If fresh seafood is on your souvenir list, place your order in advance from this downtown shop. The staff will stow your catch (or selection) in a sturdy carton surrounded by ice packs and have it ready for pickup on the day of your departure. For something different and delicious, try the salmon jerky.

Chocolate Arts. 2037 W. Fourth Ave. ☎ **604/739-0475.**

The works at this West Fourth Avenue chocolatier are of such exquisite craftsmanship, they're sometimes a wrench to eat, occasionally also a hammer or nail—they make little chocolate toolboxes filled with tiny chocolate tools. Seasonal treats include pumpkin truffles around Halloween or eggnog truffles for Christmas. Look for the all-chocolate diorama in the window—it changes every month or so. Worth picking up for a gift are the native masks of thick dark chocolate.

House of Brussels Chocolates. Factory 208–750 Terminal Ave. ☎ **604/687-1524.**

Ever wonder whence cometh the little chocolate hedgehogs that have burrowed their way into every chocolate shop in town? These hazelnut-filled truffles were invented by none other than Brussels Chocolate, which was, alas, unable to secure a patent. They're still the best all-chocolate rodents for sale in the city, however, and if you make it down to the factory on Terminal Avenue, they're also the cheapest. Retail outlets are on Granville Island and in Cathedral Place.

The Lobsterman. 1807 Mast Tower Rd. ☎ **604/687-4531.** www.lobsterman.com.

Live lobsters, Dungeness crabs, oysters, mussels, clams, geoducks, and scallops are just a few of the varieties of seafood swimming in the saltwater tanks at this Granville Island fish store. The staff steams the food fresh on the spot, free. Salmon and other seafood can also be packed for air travel.

Murchie's Tea & Coffee. 970 Robson St. ☎ **604/669-0783.**

This Vancouver institution has been the city's main tea and coffee purveyor for more than a century. You'll find everything from Jamaican Blue Mountain and Kona coffees to Lapsang Souchong and Kemun teas. The knowledgeable staff will help you decide which flavors and blends fit your taste. There's also a fine selection of bone china and crystal serving ware as well as coffeemakers and teapots.

South China Seas Trading Company. Granville Island Public Market. ☎ **604/681-5402.**

The South Seas have always been a source of intrigue. This shop re-creates a bit of that wonder, with a remarkable collection of rare spices and hard-to-find sauces. Look for fresh kaffir lime leaves, Thai basil, young ginger, sweet Thai chili sauce, and occasional exotic produce like mangosteens and rambutans. Pick up recipes and ideas from the knowledgeable staff.

FURNITURE
Inform. 97 Water St. ☎ **604/682-3868.**

Contemporary designer furniture, including Ingo Maurer, Eurolang, and the designs of co-owner Neils Bentson. The guy riding his mountain bike around the display floor may well be Brian Adams, who stops by occasionally on the way to his recording studio down the street.

VINTAGE FURNITURE

Metropolitan Home. 450 W. Hastings St. ☎ **604/681-2313.**

Modernism is back—sleek lines and elegant simplicity. This showroom bursts with so much current and vintage 20th-century modernist furniture that it's almost a museum.

Panther Decor. 2924 W. Fourth Ave. ☎ **604/733-5665.**

Crammed with furniture, clothing, and housewares from the 1950s to the 1970s. Prices are very reasonable.

GALLERIES

On the first Thursday of every month, many galleries hold free openings from 5 to 8pm. Check the *Georgia Straight* or *Vancouver Magazine* for listings.

Buschlen Mowatt. 111–1445 W. Georgia St. ☎ **604/682-1234.**

The city's leading "establishment" gallery. Look for paintings, sculptures, and prints from well-known Canadian and international artists.

Dianne Farris Gallery. 1565 W. Seventh Ave. ☎ **604/737-2629.**

Contemporary painting and sculpture, from up-and-coming artists and those who already have arrived.

Monte Clark Gallery. 2339 Granville St. ☎ **604/730-5000.**

This cutting-edge gallery—in the otherwise slightly staid confines of south Granville's gallery row—is one of the best spots to look for that rising superstar without the rising prices.

GIFTS & SOUVENIRS

Buddha Supply Centre. 4158 Main St. ☎ **604/873-8169.**

Want money to burn? At Chinese funerals people burn joss—paper replicas of earthly belongings—to help make the afterlife for the deceased more comfortable. This shop has more than 500 combustible products to choose from, including $1-million notes (drawn on the bank of hell), luxury penthouse condos, and that all-important cell phone.

Cows Vancouver. 1301 Robson St. ☎ **604/682-2622.**

Everybody knows at least one cow memorabilia collector, right? T-shirts, tableware, accessories, children's clothes, and trinkets are just a few of the bovine items sold. The ice-cream parlor serves delicious handmade ice cream in freshly baked waffle cones.

Nikaido Gifts. 150–3580 Moncton St., Steveston. ☎ **604/275-0262.**

Wedding kimonos, antique Hina dolls, *yukata* (cotton dressing gowns), plates, dishes, origami, imported teas, and many other lovely Asian items fill this Steveston gift store.

The Ocean Floor. 1522 Duranleau St. ☎ **604/681-5014.**

If you want to bring home a few gifts from the sea, then select from this Granville Island shop's collection of seashells, ship models, lamps, chimes, coral, shell jewelry, stained glass, and marine brass.

JEWELRY

With influences ranging from European and Asian to First Nations, local jewelers offer a wide selection of baubles and bangles in all price ranges.

Forge & Form. 1334 Cartwright St. ☎ **604/684-6298.**

Master Granville Island metal designers Dietje Hagedoorn and Jürgen Schönheit specialize in customized gold and silver jewelry. Renowned for their gold and silver bow ties, they also create unique pieces like "tension set" rings, which hold a stone in place without a setting. Their studio is located just past the False Creek Community Centre.

Henry Birk & Sons Ltd. 698 W. Hastings St. ☎ **604/669-3333.**

Established in 1879, Birk's has a long tradition of designing and crafting beautiful jewelry and watches.

✪ **Karl Stittgen + Goldsmiths.** 2203 Granville St. ☎ **604/737-0029.**

Stittgen's gold pins, pendants, rings, and other accessories demonstrate his eye for clean, crisp design and fine craftsmanship. Each work is a miniature architectural wonder.

The Raven and the Bear. 1528 Duranleau St. ☎ **604/669-3990.**

If you've never seen West Coast native jewelry, it's worth making a trip. Deeply inscribed with stylized creatures from Northwest mythology, these rings, bangles, and earrings are unforgettable. (See also "First Nations Crafts.")

MALLS & SHOPPING CENTERS

So maybe it does rain a little in Vancouver in the winter. Locals have two techniques. Some don Gore-Tex outerwear, head out, and embrace the damp. Others go inside. Fortunately, there are numerous indoor shopping centers, some of which stretch for blocks underground. There are even a few downtown shopping centers in renovated landmark buildings that are worth strolling through solely for their architecture.

The Landing. 375 Water St. ☎ **604/687-1144.**

This 1905 Gastown heritage warehouse was renovated into an upscale complex of shops and offices. Inside are designer boutiques such as Polo/Ralph Lauren and Fleet Street, as well as a few good restaurants.

Pacific Centre Mall. 700 W. Georgia St. ☎ **604/688-7236.**

This 3-block complex contains 200 shops and services, including Godiva, Benetton, Crabtree & Evelyn, and Eddie Bauer.

Park Royal Shopping Centre. 2002 Park Royal S., West Vancouver. ☎ **604/925-9576.**

Park Royal consists of two malls that face each other on Marine Drive, just west of the Lions Gate Bridge. The Gap, Coast Mountain Sports, Cypress Mountain Sports, Future Shop, Marks & Spencer, Disney, Eaton's, the Bay, Eddie Bauer, and a public market are just a few of the 250 stores in the center. Next door are also cinemas, bowling lanes, a golf driving range, community and special events, and a food court.

Sinclair Centre. 757 W. Hastings St. ☎ **604/659-1009.** www.sinclaircentre.com.

The Sinclair Centre incorporates four Vancouver landmarks: the Post Office (1910), Winch Building (1911), Customs Examining Warehouse (1913), and Federal Building (1937). Now restored, they house elite shops like Armani, Leone, and Dorothy Grant, as well as smaller boutiques, art galleries, and a food court.

Vancouver Centre. 650 W. Georgia St. ☎ **604/688-5658.**

The Bay, restaurants, a food fair, and more than 115 specialty stores connect underground to the adjoining Pacific Centre Mall (see above).

MARKETS

There are **green markets** scattered throughout the city. You don't have to go grocery shopping to have fun at these enclosed atriums and multilevel spaces; you just need to enjoy sampling food, looking at crafts, tasting British Columbian wines, or simply watching people. There's also a huge **flea market** in an old warehouse by the railway tracks, with as great a mix of stuff as you could possibly imagine.

Chinatown Night Market. 200 Keefer St. and 200 E. Pender St. Phone the Vancouver Tourism Info Centre at ☎ **604/683-2000.**

Across Asia, prime shopping time comes only after the sun has gone down and the temperature has dropped to something bearable. Friday and Saturday nights from May through September, merchants in Chinatown bring the tradition to Canada by closing two separate blocks to traffic and covering them with booths and tables and food stalls offering all manner of things, useful and otherwise. Come down, grab a juicy satay skewer, sip the juice from a freshly cracked coconut, and see what's up.

✪ **Granville Island Public Market.** 1669 Johnston St. ☎ **604/666-5784.** www.granvilleisland.com.

This 50,000-square-foot public market features produce, meats, fish, wines, cheeses, arts and crafts, and lots of fast-food counters offering a little of everything. Open daily from 9am to 6pm. From mid-June through September, the Farmers' Truck Market operates Thursday from 9am to 6pm.

Lonsdale Quay Market. 123 Carrie Cates Court, North Vancouver. ☎ **604/985-6261.** www.lonsdalequay.com.

Located at the SeaBus terminal, this public market is filled with produce, meats, fish, specialty fashions, gift shops, food counters, coffee bars, a hotel, and Kids' Alley (a section dedicated to children's shops and a play area). The upper floor houses a variety of fashion stores, bookstores, and gift shops.

New Westminster Quay Public Market. 810 Quayside, New Westminster. ☎ **604/520-3881.**

A smaller version of Granville Island, it is located 25 minutes away by SkyTrain from downtown Vancouver. The market has a variety of gift shops, specialty stores, a food court, a delicatessen, and produce stands. Once finished browsing the market, make sure to have a gander at the neighboring Fraser River. A walkway extends along the river and allows great views of the waterfront, the busy boat traffic, and the occasional seal or sea lion.

Robson Public Market. 1610 Robson St. ☎ **604/682-2733.**

Located a few blocks from Stanley Park, this neighborhood market is housed in a modern glass atrium. You'll find produce sellers, two bakeries, a salmon shop, and one of the city's best butcher shops, R. B. Meats, which, in addition to fine steaks, lamb, and poultry, sells meat pies, South African–style dried meats, and other delicacies. The upstairs food court has French, Italian, Greek, Chinese, and Japanese restaurants. Open daily from 9am to 9pm.

Vancouver Flea Market. 703 Terminal Ave. ☎ **604/685-0666.**

Near the train/bus terminal, Vancouver's largest flea market boasts more than 350 stalls. Admittedly, most are stocked with cheap T-shirts, linens, used tools, and such, but it's still possible to discover some real finds. Go early or the savvy shoppers will have already cleaned out the real gems. Admission is C60¢ (US40¢) for adults, free for children under 12. Open Saturday, Sunday, and holidays from 9am to 5pm.

MUSIC

Crosstown Music. 518 W. Pender St. ☎ **604/683-8774.**

This small shop is filled with used rock, jazz, and blues CDs, tapes, and albums.

Sam the Record Man. 568 Seymour St. ☎ **604/684-3722.**

Four floors of tapes, CDs, and videos cover a full range of sounds. Many albums here aren't available in the States.

Virgin Megastore. 788 Burrard St. at Robson St. ☎ **604/669-2289.**

With over 150,000 titles housed in a three-story, 42,000-square-foot space, it's Canada's largest music and entertainment store.

Zulu Records. 1972 W. Fourth Ave. ☎ **604/738-3232.**

Located in Kitsilano, Zulu Records specializes in alternative music, local and import, new and used. You will also find a good selection of vinyl and magazines. Staff are happy to make recommendations and bring you up to speed on what's hot in the local music scene.

SHOES

A walking city has to have some great shoe outlets. Vancouver has an abundance of ornate cowboy boots, sturdy Doc Martens, funky clogs, weatherproof hiking shoes and boots, and fine Swiss and Italian footwear.

The Australian Boot Company. 1968 W. Fourth Ave. ☎ **604/738-2668.** www. australianboot.com.

These shoes may look a bit like Doc Martens, but the Australian shoemaker Blundstone has been making them that way for most of the century. The Australian Boot Company, 1½ blocks west of Burrard Street, carries a wide selection of Blundstone's and R. M. Williams's finest and most rugged footwear.

David Gordon. 822 Granville St. ☎ **604/685-3784.**

This is Vancouver's oldest Western boot, hat, and accessories store. But it's far from stodgy. Boots include an extensive selection of Tony Lama, Boulet, Durango, HH Brown, and Dan Post. You'll also find Vans, Doc Martens, and a lineup of other funky footwear that attracts skateboarders and club kids.

John Fluevog Boots & Shoes Ltd. 837 Granville St. ☎ **604/688-2828.**

This native Vancouverite has a growing international cult following of designers and models clamoring for his under-C$200 (US$134) creations. You'll find outrageous platforms and clogs, Angelic Sole work boots, and a few bizarre experiments for the daring footwear fetishist.

SPECIALTY

Lush. 1118 Denman St. ☎ **604/608-1810.**

Although it has the look of an old-fashioned deli store with big wheels of cheese, slabs of sweets, chocolate bars, dips, and sauces, take a bite and you'd be washing your mouth with soap; literally. All these beautiful, mouthwatering displays are indeed soaps, shampoos, skin treatments, massage oils, and bath bombs. Made from all natural ingredients, these deceptively real looking treats are the perfect pampering gift. Everything is sold by the gram. Various other Lush stores can be found around town, including 100-1025 Robson St. (☎ **604/687-5874**). Just follow your nose.

The Market Kitchen Store. 2–1666 Johnston (Net Loft, Granville Island). ☎ **604/681-7399.**

Everything you'd like to have on your kitchen counters or in your kitchen drawers—gourmet kitchen accessories, baking utensils, and gadgets. Anyone need a citrus zester?

Railway World. 150 Water St. ☎ **604/681-4811.**

Lovers of model trains, cars, and planes will be in seventh heaven in this small, jam-packed shop. There are some great Canadian model trains in N, HO, and O gauges, as well as collectors' books and magazines.

Spy-Central. 1463 Robson St. ☎ **604/642-0324.**

A haven for spies, paranoids, and the just plain snoopy, Spy-Central offers cell-phone scanners, miniature cameras, night-vision gear, and a good selection of useful books with titles such as *How to Get Anything on Anyone.* Clumsy shoppers take note: If you break it, they know your credit card number.

Three Dog Bakery. 2186 W. Fourth Ave. ☎ **604/737-3647.**

Beagle Bagels, Scottie Biscotti, or Gracie's Rollovers. Canines will have a hard time deciding on a favorite treat from this gone-to-the-dogs bakery. The store also has leashes, collars, greeting cards, and other dog paraphernalia.

SPORTING GOODS
Boardhead Central.

Not a shop, but a phenomenon. In the past few years, the corner of Fourth Avenue and Burrard Street has become the spot for high-quality snow/skate/surf board gear, and the spot to see top-level boarders and their groupies hanging out. **Pacific Boarder** is at 1793 W. Fourth Ave. (☎ **604/734-7245**). **Thriller** is at 1710 W. Fourth Ave. (☎ **604/736-5651**). **West Beach,** at 1766 W. Fourth Ave. (☎ **604/731-6449**), sometimes hosts pro-skate demos on the half-pipe at the back of the store.

Mountain Equipment Co-op. 130 W. Broadway. ☎ **604/872-7858.** www.mec.ca.

A true West Coast institution and an outdoors lover's dream come true, this block-long store houses the best selection of top-quality outdoor gear: rain gear, clothing, hiking shoes, climbing gear, backpacks, sleeping bags, tents, and more. Memorize the MEC label, you're sure to see it later—at the beach, the bar, the concert hall.

TOYS
The Games People. 157 Water St. ☎ **604/685-5825.**

The Games People carries a huge selection of board games, strategy games, role-playing games, puzzles, models, toys, hobby materials, and other amusements. It's difficult to walk past this store, whether you're an adult or a kid.

Kid's Market. 1496 Cartwright St. (on Granville Island). ☎ **604/689-8447.** www.kids-market.net.

Probably the only mall in North America dedicated to kids, the Kid's Market on Granville Island features a Lilliputian entranceway, toy and craft and book stores, play areas, and services for the younger set, including even a "fun hairdresser."

Kites on Clouds. The Courtyard, 131 Water St. ☎ **604/669-5677.**

This little Gastown shop has every type of kite. Prices range from C$10 to C$20 (US$7 to US$13) for nylon or Mylar dragon kites to just under C$200 (US$134) for more elaborate ghost clippers and nylon hang-glider kites.

WINE

British Columbia's **wines** are worth buying by the case, especially rich, honey-thick ice wines such as Jackson-Triggs gold-medal–winning 1994 Johannesburg Riesling Ice wine, and bold reds, such as the Quail's Gate 1994 Limited Release Pinot Noir. Five years of restructuring, reblending, and careful tending by French and German master vintners have won the province's vineyards world recognition.

When buying B.C. wine, look for the VQA (Vintner Quality Alliance) seal on the label; it's a guarantee that all grapes used are grown in British Columbia and meet European standards for growing and processing.

Summerhill, Cedar Creek, Mission Hill, and **Okanagan Vineyards** are just a few of the more than 50 local estates producing hearty cabernet sauvignons, honey-rich ice wines, and oaky merlots. These wines can be found at any government-owned **LCB** liquor store, such as the one at 1716 Robson St. (☎ **604/660-4576;** or call 604/660-9463 for the nearest location), and at some privately owned wine stores.

Marquis Wine Cellars. 1034 Davie St. ☎ **604/684-0445** or 604/685-2246. www.marquis-wines.com.

The owner and staff of this West End wine shop are dedicated to educating their patrons about wines. They conduct evening wine tastings, featuring selections from their special purchases. They also publish monthly newsletters. In addition to carrying a full range of British Columbian wines, the shop also has a large international selection.

The Okanagan Estate Wine Cellar. The Bay, 674 Granville St. ☎ **604/681-6211.**

This department store annex, located in the Vancouver Centre mall concourse's Market Square, offers a great selection of British Columbian wines by the bottle and the case.

9

Vancouver After Dark

Vancouver is a fly-by-the-seat-of-the-pants kind of town. There's so much to see and do—and the outdoors always beckons—that Vancouverites wait till the day or the hour before a show to plunk their cash down on the barrel. It drives promoters crazy. Not that they stop promoting. Indeed, for a city its size—or twice its size—Vancouver is blessed with entertainment options, from cutting-edge theater companies to a well-respected opera and symphony to folk and jazz festivals that draw people from up and down the coast. And then there are the bars and pubs and clubs and cafes—lots of them—for every taste, budget, and fetish; you just have to get out there and see. Just keep in mind that most dance clubs and even bars downtown charge a cover and have a line on Fridays and Saturdays. There often doesn't seem to be a correlation between the number of people entering and the number of people exiting; you are at the mercy of the bouncers. Some techniques to beat the line: arrive unfashionably early (before 9pm), make friends with the bouncers or anyone who can get your name on the VIP list, be outrageously beautiful, or arrive in fancy wheels.

For an overview of Vancouver's nightlife, pick up a copy of the weekly tabloid, the *Georgia Straight*. It gives up-to-date music and entertainment schedules as well as information about what's going on in the city and surrounding areas. Or get a copy of *Xtra! West,* the free gay and lesbian biweekly tabloid, available in shops and restaurants throughout the West End. The Thursday edition of the *Vancouver Sun* contains the weekly entertainment section *Queue.* You can find the publications at bookstores, venues, and curbside boxes.

The monthly *Vancouver Magazine* is filled with listings and strong views about what's really hot in the city. On the Internet, you can check out Vancouver club listings, band profiles, and restaurant reviews at **www.vanmag.com.**

The **Vancouver Cultural Alliance Arts Hotline,** 100–938 Howe St. (☎ **604/684-2787** or 604/681-3535; www.allianceforarts.com), is a great information source for all performing arts, music, theater, literary events, art films, and dance, including where and how to get tickets. The office is open Monday to Friday from 9am to 5pm.

Ticketmaster (Vancouver Ticket Centre), 1304 Hornby St. (☎ **604/ 280-3311;** www.ticketmaster.ca), has 40 outlets in the greater Vancouver area, and the same monopoly on venues as in most Canadian cities, along with the same steep service charges. With a credit card, tickets can be purchased over the phone and picked up at the venue.

Three major Vancouver theaters regularly host touring performances. The **Orpheum Theatre,** 801 Granville St. (☎ **604/665-3050;** www.city.vancouver. bc.ca), is the refurbished home of the Vancouver Symphony Orchestra. It's an elegant 1927 theater that originally hosted the Chicago-based Orpheum vaudeville circuit. The theater's ornate interior is filled with crystal chandeliers, gilded arches, domes, and an original Wurlitzer organ. The theater also hosts pop, rock, and variety shows.

The **Queen Elizabeth Complex,** 600 Hamilton St., between Georgia and Dunsmuir Streets (☎ **604/665-3050;** www.city.vancouver.bc.ca), consists of the Queen Elizabeth Theatre and the Vancouver Playhouse. It hosts major national and touring musical and theater productions. It's also home to the Vancouver Opera and Ballet British Columbia. The 670-seat Vancouver Playhouse presents chamber-music performances and recitals.

Located in a converted turn-of-the-20th-century church, the **Vancouver East Cultural Centre** (the "Cultch" to locals), 1895 Venables St. (☎ **604/254-9578;** www. vecc.bc.ca), coordinates an impressive program that includes avant-garde theater productions, performances by international musical groups, festivals and cultural events, children's programs, and art exhibitions. Advance ticket sales are through Ticketmaster. See above for phone number.

On the campus of UBC, the **Chan Centre for the Performing Arts,** 6265 Crescent Rd. (☎ **604/822-2697**), showcases the work of the UBC music and acting students, and also hosts a winter concert series. Designed by local architectural luminary Bing Thom, the Chan Centre's crystal-clear acoustics are the best in town.

Generally bars and clubs are open until 2am every day but Sunday, when they close at midnight.

1 The Performing Arts

THEATER

Theater isn't only an indoor pastime here. There is an annual summertime Shakespeare series, **Bard on the Beach,** in Vanier Park (☎ **604/737-0625**). You can also bring a picnic dinner to Stanley Park and watch **Theatre Under the Stars** (see below), which features popular musicals and light comedies. For more original fare, don't miss ✪ **The Fringe—Vancouver's Theatre Festival** (☎ **604/257-0350;** www. vancouverfringe.com). Centered on Granville Island, the Fringe Festival features more than 500 innovative and original shows each September, all costing under C$12 (US$8).

✪ **Arts Club Theatre Company.** Granville Island Stage at the Arts Club Theatre, 1585 Johnston St., and The Stanley Theatre, 2750 Granville St. ☎ **604/687-1644.** www.artsclub. com. Tickets C$13–C$45 (US$9–US$30). Senior, student, and group discounts available. Box office 9am–7pm.

The 425-seat Granville Island Mainstage presents major dramas, comedies, and musicals, with post-performance entertainment in the Backstage Lounge. The Arts Club Revue Stage is an intimate, cabaret-style showcase for small productions, improvisation nights, and musical revues such as *The Cripple of Inishmaan* and *The Threepenny Opera.* The old art deco Stanley has recently undergone a glorious renovation and now plays host to longer running plays and musicals, such as *A Closer Walk with Patsy Cline.*

Firehall Arts Centre. 280 E. Cordova St. ☎ **604/689-0926.** www.firehall.org. Tickets C$8–C$18 (US$5–US$12). Senior and student discounts available. Box office Mon–Fri 9:30am–5pm, and 1 hr. before show time.

Housed in Vancouver's Firehouse No. 1, the Centre has for 20 years been home to the cutting-edge Firehall Theatre Company. Expect original, experimental, and challenging plays, such as last year's hit *Filthy Rich* by George F. Walker and Kudelka's *Janus/Janis*. The companies also present dance events, arts festivals, and concerts.

Frederic Wood Theatre. Gate 4, University of British Columbia. ☎ **604/822-2678.** Tickets C$15 (US$10) adults, C$9 (US$5) students. No performances in the summer. Box office Mon–Fri 10:30am–3pm. All shows start at 7:30pm.

Forget that "student production" thing you've got in your head. Students at UBC are actors in training, and their productions are extremely high-caliber. For the price, they're a steal. They present classic dramatic works to Broadway musicals to new plays by Canadian playwrights.

Theatre Under the Stars. Malkin Bowl, Stanley Park. ☎ **604/687-0174.** www.tuts.bc.ca. Tickets C$23 (US$15) adults, C$16 (US$11) seniors and children. Box office Mon–Sat 10am–5pm and 7–8pm (show time).

From mid-July to mid-August, old-time favorite musicals like *Annie Get Your Gun, West Side Story, South Pacific,* or *Grease* are performed outdoors by a mixed cast of amateur and professional actors. Bring a blanket (it gets cold once the sun sets) and a picnic dinner for a relaxing evening of summer entertainment.

Vancouver Little Theatre. Heritage Hall, 3102 Main St. (enter from the back alley). ☎ **604/876-4165.** Tickets usually C$7–C$12 (US$4.70–US$8). Senior and student discounts available. Box office opens 30 min. before show time.

Works by new Canadian playwrights and an international array of controversial dramatists are presented here by professional, local, and traveling companies.

Vancouver Playhouse. 600 Hamilton, between Georgia and Hamilton Sts. in the Queen Elizabeth complex. ☎ **604/665-3050.** Tickets usually C$8–C$16 (US$5–US$11). Senior and student discounts available. Box office opens 30 min. before show time.

Well into its third decade, the company at the Vancouver Playhouse presents a program of six plays each season, usually a mix of the internationally known, nationally recognized, and locally promising.

OPERA

Vancouver Opera. 500–845 Cambie St. ☎ **604/683-0222.** www.vanopera.bc.ca. Tickets usually C$36–C$96 (US$24–US$64). Box office Mon–Fri 9am–4pm.

In a kind of willful flirtation with death, the Vancouver Opera Company alternates between obscure or new (and Canadian!) works and older, more popular perennials, often sung by international stars such as Placido Domingo and Bryn Terfel. The formula seems to work, for the company is over 35 years old and still packing 'em in. The season runs from October through June, with performances normally in the Queen Elizabeth Theatre. English supertitles projected above the stage help audiences follow the dialogue of the lavish productions. In 2001, look for Wagner's *The Flying Dutchman* (Mar 24 to Mar 31) and Mozart's *Magic Flute* (Apr 28 to May 7).

CLASSICAL MUSIC

Fans of chamber music, baroque fugues, Russian romantic symphonies, and popular show tunes will find world-class concert performances in Vancouver.

University of British Columbia School of Music. Recital Hall, Gate 4, 6361 Memorial Rd. ☎ **604/822-5574.** www.music.ubc.ca. E-mail: concerts@interchange.ubc.ca. Tickets purchased at the door, C$4–C$24 (US$2.70–US$16) adults, C$4–C$14 (US$2.70–US$9) seniors and students. Many concerts are free. The Wed noon hr. series costs C$4 (US$2.70).

From September through November and during January and March, UBC presents eight faculty and guest-artist concerts. They feature piano, piano and violin, opera, or quartets, plus occasional performances by acts like the Count Basie Orchestra. If the concert is in the Chan Centre, go. There are few halls in the world with such beautiful acoustics.

✪ Vancouver Bach Choir. 805-235 Keith Rd., West Vancouver. ☎ **604/921-8012.** Tickets C$15–C$30 (US$10–US$20) depending on the performance. Tickets available through Ticketmaster.

Vancouver's international, award-winning amateur choir, a 150-voice ensemble, presents five major concerts a year at the Orpheum Theatre. Specializing in symphonic choral music, the Choir's sing-along performance of Handel's *Messiah* during the Christmas season is a favorite.

Vancouver Cantata Singers. 5115 Keith Rd., West Vancouver. ☎ **604/921-8588.** www.cantata.org. Tickets C$20 (US$13) adults, C$16 (US$11) seniors and students. Tickets through Ticketmaster or at the door.

This semiprofessional 40-person choir specializes in early music. The company performs works by Bach, Brahms, Monteverdi, Stravinsky, and Handel, as well as Eastern European choral music. The season normally includes three programs: in October, December, and March at various locations.

Vancouver Chamber Choir. 1254 W. Seventh Ave. ☎ **604/738-6822.** www.vancouverchamberchoir.com. E-mail: info@vancouverchamberchoir.com. Tickets C$15–C$35 (US$10–US$23) adults, C$13–C$25 (US$9–US$17) seniors and students. Tickets through Ticketmaster.

Western Canada's only professional choral ensemble presents an annual concert series at the Orpheum Theatre, the Chan Centre, and Ryerson United Church. Under conductor John Washburn, the choir has gained an international reputation.

Vancouver New Music. 207 W. Hastings St. ☎ **604/606-6440.** www.newmusic.org. Tickets C$20–C$35 (US$13–US$23) adults, C$16 (US$11) students.

This company presents seven annual concerts, featuring the works of contemporary and avant-garde composers as well as mixed-media performances that combine dance and film. Performances take place at the Vancouver East Cultural Centre between September and June. The society also hosts a biannual new-music festival, but the next one, alas, is not until June 2002.

Vancouver Symphony. 601 Smithe St. ☎ **604/876-3434** for ticket information. www.culturenet.ca/vso. Tickets C$22–C$60 (US$15–US$40) adults. Senior and student discounts available. Box office Mon–Fri 1–5pm and 6pm to show time day of performance.

At its home in the Orpheum Theatre during the fall, winter, and spring, Vancouver's extremely active orchestra presents the "Masterworks" series of great classical works; "Casual Classics," featuring light classics from a single area or composer and a casually dressed orchestra; "Tea & Trumpets," highlighting modern classics and ethnic works, hosted by the CBC's Otto Lowy; "Symphony Pops," selections of popular and show tunes; and "Kid's Koncerts," a series geared toward school-age children. The traveling summer concert series takes the orchestra from White Rock and Cloverdale on the U.S. border to the tops of Whistler and Blackcomb Mountains.

DANCE

For fans of modern and original dance, the time to be here is early July, when the **Dancing on the Edge Festival** (☎ 604/689-0691) presents 60 to 80 envelope-pushing original pieces over a 10-day period. For more information about other festivals and dance companies around the city, call the **Dance Centre** at ☎ 604/606-6400.

Ballet British Columbia. 1101 W. Broadway. ☎ **604/732-5003.** www.balletbc.com. Tickets C$18–C$52 (US$12–US$35) adults. Senior and student discounts available.

Just over 16 years old, this company strives to present innovative works, such as those by choreographers John Cranko and William Forsythe, along with more traditional fare, including productions by visiting companies such as American Ballet Theatre, the Royal Winnipeg Ballet, and the Moscow Classical Ballet. Performances are usually at the Queen Elizabeth Theatre at 600 Hamilton St.

2 Laughter & Music
COMEDY CLUBS
Vancouver TheatreSports League. Arts Club Stage, Granville Island. ☎ **604/738-7013.** www.vtsl.com. Shows Wed–Thurs 7:30pm, Fri–Sat 8, 10, and 11:45pm. Weekends C$15 (US$10) adults, C$11 (US$7) seniors and students; weeknights C$7 (US$4.70).

Part comedy, part theater, and partly a take-no-prisoner's test of an actor's ability to think on his or her feet, TheatreSports involves actors taking suggestions from the audience and spinning them into short skits or full plays, often with hilarious results. Since moving to the Arts Club Stage, Vancouver's TheatreSports leaguers have had to reign in their normally raunchy instincts for the more family-friendly audience— except, that is, for Friday and Saturday at 11:45pm, when the Red-Hot Improv show takes the audience into the R-rated realm.

Yuk Yuk's Komedy Kabaret. Plaza of Nations, 750 Pacific Blvd. ☎ **604/687-5233.** Cover C$5–C$10 (US$3.35–US$7). Shows Tues–Thurs 9pm, Fri–Sat 9 and 11pm.

A constantly changing lineup of leading Canadian and American stand-up comics play at Yuk Yuk's. Amateurs take the stage for Wednesday night open mike. In the 200-seat theater, it's hard to get a bad seat.

STRICTLY LIVE
Besides the listings below, every June the **du Maurier International Jazz Festival** (☎ 604/872-5200) takes over many venues and outdoor locations around town. The festival includes a number of free concerts. The **Vancouver Folk Festival** (☎ 604/ 602-9798) takes place outdoors in July on the beach at Jericho Park. The **Coastal Jazz and Blues Society,** 316 W. Sixth Ave. (☎ 604/872-5200), has information on current and upcoming events throughout the year.

The Commodore Ballroom. 868 Granville St. ☎ **604/739-7469.** www.commodoreballroom. com. Tickets C$5–C$50 (US$3.35–US$34).

Every town should have one, but sadly very few do: a huge old-time dance hall, complete with suspended hard-wood dance-floor that bounces gently up and down beneath your nimble or less-than-nimble toes. And though the room and floor date back to the jazz age, the lineup nowadays includes many of the best modern bands coming through town. Sightlines are excellent. Indeed, the Commodore's one of the best places I know to catch a midsized band—and thanks to a recent renovation, the room looks better than ever.

The Roxy. 932 Granville St. ☎ **604/684-7699.** www.roxyvan.com. Cover C$5–C$8 (US$3.35–US$5).

Live bands play every day of the week in this casual club, which also features show-off bartenders with Tom Cruise *Cocktail*-style moves. The house bands Joe's Garage and Dr. Strangelove keep the Roxy packed, and on weekends lines are long. Theme parties (often with vacation giveaways), Extreme Karaoke, Canadian content, '80's only, and comedy events add to the entertainment.

The Starfish Room. 1055 Homer St., near Helmcken St. ☎ **604/682-4171.** Cover C$3–C$30 (US$2–US$20), depending on the act.

The Room itself is a big echoing chamber with less-than-optimum sightlines, yet Starfish promoters consistently bring in some of the best talent on tour. Lineups include international recording stars as well as local artists, playing everything from jazz and blues to Celtic to lounge, funk, and, in rare fits of nostalgia, even punk. Jon Spencer Blues Explosion, the Paperboys, Kevin Kane, and Jeff Buckley are just a few of the acts that have played here recently. Tables can be a bit of a squeeze, especially when local groups like the Colorifics take the stage.

The WISE Club. 1882 Adanac St. ☎ **604/254-5858.** Cover depends on show; C$15 (US$10) for most bands.

Folk, folk, and more folk. In the far-off reaches of East Vancouver (okay, Commercial Drive area), the WISE Hall was unplugged long before MTV ever thought of reaching for the power cord. Bands are local and international, and the room's a lot of fun—like a church basement or community center—with alcohol.

Yale Hotel. 1300 Granville St. ☎ **604/681-9253.** www.theyale.com. Cover Thurs–Sat C$3–C$15 (US$2–US$10).

This century-old tavern on the far south end of Granville is Vancouver's one and only home of the blues. Visiting heavyweights have included Koko Taylor, Stevie Ray Vaughan, Junior Wells, and Jeff Healey. The pictures in the entryway are a who's who of the blues. When outside talent's not available, the Yale makes do with what's home-grown, including Long John Baldry and local bluesman Jim Byrne. Shows are Monday to Saturday at 9:30pm. On Saturday and Sunday there's an open-stage blues jam from 3 to 7pm.

ALMOST LIVE

Over the past few years, DJs have slowly replaced bands on the local music scene. Bars that exclusively book live music are nearly nonexistent; many places feature DJs only, and a few offer a mix.

Babalu. 654 Nelson St. (at Granville). ☎ **604/605-4343.** Cover C$3–C$7 (US$2–US$4.70).

Located about halfway down the Granville Street strip, this hopping little club offers R&B, swing, salsa, Latino, and jazz to a late 20's and 30's crowd. Midweek belongs to the house band, The Smoking Section, while on other nights there are visiting acts or DJs. A tiny dance floor means constant jostling, but no one in this good-natured crowd ever seems to mind. Open Thursday to Sunday.

Chameleon Urban Lounge. 801 W. Georgia St. (entrance on Howe St.). ☎ **604/669-0806.** www.chameleonlounge.com. Cover Mon–Thurs C$5 (US$3.35), Fri–Sat C$7 (US$4.70).

Under the landmark Hotel Georgia, the Chameleon feels like a scene out of a Fellini movie. Set in a high-ceilinged, plush basement lounge, it features live jazz, funk, and salsa most evenings, offers a full martini menu, and attracts a very urban crowd. No Doubt, Weezer, Jason Priestly, Christopher Walken, and many more celebs have dropped in for an evening.

Hot Jazz Society. 2120 Main St. ☎ **604/873-4131.** Cover C$10–C$12 (US$7–US$8) only for special acts, otherwise no cover.

Playing everything from Dixieland to swing, Latin to progressive, this club caters to dedicated fans of both jazz and dance. The dance floor is packed no matter who is playing. On Tuesday nights the Wow Big Band plays swing tunes and on Thursday nights dance lessons are included in the price of admission. Call for more details.

✪ **The Purple Onion.** 15 Water St. ☎ **604/602-9442.** www.purpleonion.com. Cover C$5–C$8 (US$3.35–US$5).

Some clubs do DJ to survive, some have bands; the Onion serves up both, all for the same cover. The Club room is dance floor pure and simple. At the moment, an '80s dance party is alternating nights with house. Down the hall and round a left turn is the Lounge, where the house band squeals out funky danceable jazz for a slightly older crowd three nights a week. There's karaoke on oh-so-dead Sunday. During the Jazz Festival, this place hops.

The Sugar Refinery. 1115 Granville St. ☎ **604/683-2004.** No cover.

This tiny hole up a darkened stairway on the unfashionable end of Granville Street is immensely popular. Try as I might, I don't get it. The room is cramped and narrow, the sightlines horrible. Bands are still able to find a spot and perform. When there's a DJ, the decidedly lo-fi sound system has all the resonance of your little brother working the family turntable. But people are voting with their feet, and I'm outnumbered.

3 Bars, Pubs & Other Watering Holes

Visitors to Vancouver need to know that when it comes to liquor regulations, our city is a bizarre and Byzantine place. For historical and political reasons too difficult to get into, bars and pubs are still seen by officialdom as a Bad Thing, so new pub licenses are impossible to come by. What are available are restaurant licenses and, as Vancouverites love a drink as much as anyone, there are many restaurants that look suspiciously like pubs. The trick is that patrons in a restaurant can drink only if they eat or—here's the Kafkaesque kicker—have the intention of eating. So if a waitress in a place that looks for all the world like a pub asks if you'll be eating, take the appetizer menu, smile, and say "Yes." As long as the menu's on the table, odds are the establishment's liquor license is safe. Occasionally, after a few pints you'll be asked to buy some fries or wings or even a large chocolate chip cookie in order to satisfy the letter of the law. Take it in stride, or take off for a new pub (er, restaurant); just please, don't take offense—remember, it's our bureaucrats, not us.

RESTAURANTS MASQUERADING AS BARS

The Alibi Room. 157 Alexander St. ☎ **604/623-3383.** www.alibiroom.com.

Higher-end trendy restaurant/bar brought to you at least in part by "X-Files" Gillian Anderson, the Alibi Room offers upstairs diners modern cuisine and a chance to flip through shelves full of old film scripts. Monthly script readings provide a venue for ever hopeful wanna-be screenwriters. Downstairs there's a DJ. Located on the eastern edge of Gastown.

✪ **The Atlantic Trap and Gill.** 612 Davie St. ☎ **604/806-6393.**

Regulars in this sea shanty of a pub know the words to every song sung by the Irish and East Coast bands that appear onstage most every night. Guinness and Keith's are the brews of choice, and don't worry too much about ordering food. As the song goes: *"I'se the bye that orders the pint, I'se the bye that drinks her, keep your menus up in sight, and the government's none the wiser."* Or something like that.

Cellar Jazz Cafe. 3611 W. Broadway. ☎ **604/738-1959.**

Jazz has a loose definition on the West Coast. In this dark downstairs Kitsilano boîte, the often-as-not live sounds stretch to include funk, fusion, jazz, and occasionally even

Caffeine Nation

"I've never seen so much coffee in all my life. The whole town is on a caffeine jag," said Bette Midler, when she performed in Vancouver.

Though the population had been softened up to the idea by a generation of Italian immigrants, it must still be admitted that the recent fine-coffee explosion started in our sister city to the south. There are now more than 60 of the Seattle-based **Starbucks** shops in the city (including 11 that are unionized—gotta love B.C.) as well as Blenz, Roastmasters, and other chain cafes. Starbucks is what it is in all places at all times. The franchises facing each other on Robson and Thurlow are famed for the movie stars who drop in now and again and the regular crowd of bikers who sit sipping lattes on their hogs. The city's best java joint—fittingly enough—is **Vancouver's Best Coffee,** 2959 W. Fourth Ave. (☎ **604/739-2136**), on a slightly funky section of W. Fourth Avenue at Bayswater.

Nearly as good and far more politically correct is **Joe's Cafe,** 1150 Commercial Dr. (☎ **604/255-1046**), in the heart of the immigrant- and activist-laden Commercial Drive area. Lesbian-activists, Marxist intellectuals, Guatemalan immigrants, and little old men from Portugal all sit and sip their cappuccinos peacefully now, but such was not always the case. For a hilarious take on the clash between identity politics and immigrant values that came to be known as the Joe's Cafe Boycott, check out Bruce Serafin's essay "Cultural Workers and Moslem Hats," in the anthology *Vancouver: Representing the Post-Modern City.*

The city's best espresso is found in the **Epicurean Deli,** 1898 W. First Ave. (☎ **604/731-5370**), an Italian-run deli with six outdoor tables in a tiny but terribly trendy area of Kitsilano.

If you're looking for a fabulous view and a nice outdoor patio, try **Benny's Bagels,** 1780 Davie St. (☎ **604/685-7600**), overlooking English Bay Beach. More than just bagels, try the 1-pound cookies for serious snacking.

hip-hop. Local jazz aficionados swear by this place and almost begged us not to list their favorite hangout for fear of crowds.

DV8. 515 Davie St. ☎ **604/682-4388.** www.dv8lounge.com.

Even skate rats and snowboarders have to alight sometime, and this little Davie Street eatery is where the tribe comes to quaff pints and swap a brand of shoptalk incomprehensible to anyone born before Reagan took office. Bask in their youth. Enjoy the beer. DJs and live music weekly. Also check out the gallery space for monthly changing exhibits of innovative artwork.

✪ **The Jupiter Cafe.** 1216 Bute St. ☎ **604/609-6665.** www.jupitercafe.com.

Located just off busy Davie Street in the West End, the Jupiter Cafe combines a postapocalyptic industrial look with lounge chic. Black ceilings, exposed pipes, and roof struts mix surprisingly well with chandeliers, velvet curtains, and plush chairs. More importantly, the Jupiter is open late (till 4am some nights). True, it can be a challenge to flag down your waiter, but that gives you more time to scope out the crowd: gay and straight, funky and preppy, casual and dressed to kill. A huge outdoor patio provides a pleasant refuge from the street, but on colder nights it's the exclusive domain of die-hard smokers. The menu—burgers, pastas, and pizzas—is largely decorative.

Monsoon Restaurant. 2526 Main St. ☎ **604/879-4001.**

What this slim little bistro in the otherwise sleepy section of Main and Broadway does really well is beer and fusion-induced tapas, accompanied by a buzzing atmosphere generated by interesting and sometimes beautiful people.

✪ **Naked.** 432 Richards St. ☎ **604/609-2700.**

Naked is located up a marble staircase on the top floor of a former bank building down-town. The room is something out of Arabian Nights; rich warm light from candles and lanterns diffuses through billowing swaths of fabric hanging around low divans, couches, and foot-high tables. It's the perfect place to meet friends for cocktails—early or late—and share some food, served up in the kitchen of the downstairs Ballantynes Restaurant. Among the menu offerings are shiitake mushroom–and–bean-sprout salad rolls and smoked-salmon sushi. DJs spin acid and/or jazz and other down-tempo grooves, without drowning out all conversation. Open Thursday to Sunday.

Urban Well. 1516 Yew St. ☎ **604/737-7770.**

The tanned and taut from nearby Kits Beach drop into the Well as the sun goes down, and often don't emerge until the next day. Monday and Tuesday there's comedy, with DJs the rest of the week. Regulars line up on the patio counter to people-watch, while inside there's a tiny dance floor for demonstrating once again that you can get down in beach sandals.

✪ **The Whip Gallery Restaurant.** 209 E. Sixth Ave. ☎ **604/874-4687.**

The Whip's the one place in the city where the wall art and the clientele match. The folks sipping and munching look like they could—and probably did—produce the art hanging on the walls. Young and angry isn't the look here. Whip customers have some success under their belts and are mellowing into their 40s and 50s. Food is above aver-age, which is good, 'cause they occasionally do insist you order something. Jazz com-bos sometimes set up in the corner.

ACTUAL BARS

The Arts Club Backstage Lounge. 1585 Johnston St., Granville Island. ☎ **604/687-1354.**

The Arts Club Lounge has a fabulous location under the bridge by the water on the edge of False Creek. Crowd is a mix of tourists and art school students from neigh-boring Emily Carr college. Friday and Saturday there's a live band in the evenings. Most other times, if the sun's out, the waterfront patio is packed.

✪ **The Brickhouse Bar.** 730 Main St. ☎ **604/689-8645.**

Anthropologists and urban planners often speak of Gentrifiers—that tribe of mostly younger humanity who move into a down-at-heels neighborhood and by their pres-ence and earning ability transform "gritty" into "funky," and then as the even-more-upscale yuppies arrive, into just plain freaking expensive. Main Street is still in the funky stage, and an evening at the Brickhouse is your chance to watch the tribe at play. The warm and bustling bar has pool tables and comfy couches from which to watch artists and dot-commers and their upscale cousins vie for table time, bar space, and reproductive success. And if that palls, you can watch the fish in the wall-length trop-ical tanks. The tapas menu from the upstairs bistro is superb.

Fred's Uptown Tavern. 1006 Granville St. ☎ **604/605-4350.** www.fredstavern.com.

As the *Georgia Straight* recently noted, the best sign that Vancouver's bar scene is under-served is this: Fred's, a pleasant little downstairs tavern with neither band nor

DJ nor dance floor, charges a cover (usually about C$5/US$3.35). What's more, there's a line to get in. So what's the attraction? A TV for every sightline, a cadre of buxom serving staff supplying an endless stream of pints, and a crowd of early 20-somethings so intent on each other that it really doesn't matter where they meet.

✪ **The Irish Heather.** 217 Carrall St. ☎ **604/688-9779.**

A bright and pleasant Irish pub in the dark heart of Gastown, the Heather boasts numerous nooks and crannies, some of the best beer in town, and a menu that does a lot with the traditional Emerald Isle spud. The clientele is from all over the map, including artsy types from the local gallery scene, urban pioneers from the new Gas-town condos, and kids from Kitsilano looking for some safe but authentic grunge.

✪ **The Lennox Pub.** 800 Granville St. ☎ **604/408-0881.**

Part of the renewal of Granville Street, this new pub fills a big void in the neighbor-hood; it's a comfortable spot for a drink without having to deal with lines or ordering food. The beer list is extensive, containing such hard-to-find favorites as Belgian Kriek, Hoegaarden, and Leffe. There is a great selection of single-malt scotches. The pub has a turn-of-the-20th-century feel with lots of brass, wood paneling, and a long bar. The menu covers all the pub-food basics.

SPORTS BARS

The Shark Club Bar and Grill. 180 W. Georgia St. ☎ **604/687-4275.** C$5 (US$3.35) cover on the weekend after 9pm.

The city's premier sports bar, where men are men and dress the part—except on Hal-loween, when a squad of erstwhile jocks shows up dressed in white hot pants and fringed halter tops like Dallas Cowboys cheerleaders. Anyway, the Shark Club—in the Sandman Inn—features lots of wood and brass, TVs everywhere, and on weekend evenings, lots of young and beautiful women who don't look terribly interested in sports. Despite this—or because of it—weekend patrons often score.

BARS WITH VIEWS

If you're in Vancouver, odds are you're here for the views. Everybody else is. The entire population could go make more money living in a dull flat place like Toronto, but we stay 'cause we're addicted to the scenery. As long as that's your raison d'être, you may as well do it in style at one of the places below.

Cardero's Marine Pub. 1583 Coal Harbour Quay. ☎ **604/669-7666.**

On the water at the foot of Cardero Street, this Coal Harbour pub and restaurant offers an unmatched view of Stanley Park, the harbor, and the North Shore. Overhead heaters take away the chill when nights grow longer.

✪ **Cloud Nine.** 1400 Robson St. (42nd floor of the Empire Landmark Hotel). ☎ **604/ 662-8328.** Cover C$5 (US$3.35) Thurs–Sat.

View junkies will think they've died and gone to heaven. As this sleek hotel-top lounge rotates 6° a minute, your vantage point circles from volcanic Mount Baker to the Fraser estuary to English Bay around Stanley Park to the towers of downtown, the har-bor, and East Vancouver. And who knew paradise served such good martinis?

The Creek Restaurant and Brewery. 1253 Johnson St. ☎ **604/685-7070.**

Located in the Granville Island Hotel, this watering hole offers an unmatched view of False Creek and great brews to boot. The food's also pretty good. Atmosphere is laid-back hip. Inhabitants are mostly 30-somethings who've discovered there's no office fire so serious it can't be quenched with another round.

The Flying Beaver Bar. 4760 Inglis Rd. ☎ **604/273-0278.**

A unique West Coast tradition: Beaver and Cessna pilots pull up to the floating docks and step ashore to down a few in the floatplane pub. Located beneath the flyway of Vancouver International, the Beaver offers nonflyers great views of incoming jets, along with mountains, bush planes, river craft, and truly fine beer.

The Sylvia Lounge. 1154 Gilford St. ☎ **604/681-9321.** www.sylviahotel.com.

One of the city's oldest hotels and the West End's first "high-rise," the Sylvia—overlooking English Bay Beach—features a ground floor lounge beloved mostly for its view, location, and history. For a time in the 1950s, the Sylvia was the hippest cocktail bar in town. Fifty years later, it's a quiet, low-key room with reasonably priced drinks and a view out over the water. A great place to duck into either before or after a stroll along English Bay.

LOUNGES

Bacchus Lounge. 845 Hornby St. (in the Wedgewood Hotel). ☎ **604/608-5319.** www.wedgewoodhotel.com.

Step into Bacchus and bask in the low light cast by fireplace and tealights, its Turneresque wall paintings, and the irony-free evocation of piano bars of yore. Lounge has (or had) staged a hip, self-aware second coming, but for Bacchus it's still and forever the days of Ike and Mamie's first White House term. The piano man in the corner pounds out Neil Diamond, and the crowd of boomers and their children hum along.

Georgia Street Bar and Grill. 801 W. Georgia St. ☎ **604/602-0994.**

The Dr. Jekyll and Mr. Hyde of the downtown lounges, the GSB&G on weeknights has the quiet piano-plinking feel of a hotel bar (in, fact, it's attached to the Hotel Georgia). On weekends—or anytime during the summer Jazz Festival—a band squeezes into one corner, refugees from the downstairs Chameleon Lounge squeeze in another, and the suits, jeans, khakis, and Kangol caps shake it up on the tiny dance floor.

Gerard Lounge. 845 Burrard St. ☎ **604/682-5511.**

Upscale taken to the edge of hyperbole, the Gerard faithfully re-creates the atmosphere of an English club, including not just the rustic oil paintings and dead animals on the walls, but also the lesser sons of the local (Hollywood) nobility having a bit of a rip with the native girls. The Gerard is also known for its exotic cocktails and Tuesday Chocoholic's Buffet.

✪ Gotham Cocktail Bar. 615 Seymour St. ☎ **604/605-8282.**

A clear case of the law of unintended consequences: The lounge adjoining this new steak house was designed for a male clientele—thick leather benches and a room-long mural of sensuous women in Jazz Age clothes. Men certainly did show up—well-off suits in their 30s and 40s particularly—but they were soon a tiny minority midst the great gaggles of women, all seemingly sharing Ally McBeal's age, romantic aspirations, and hem length.

BREW PUBS

Sailor Hägar's Brew Pub. 235 W. First St., North Vancouver. ☎ **604/984-3087.**

Best brews on offer on the North Shore. The room itself is nothing to write home about—just a popular local pub, with students, firemen, and off-duty search and rescue personnel munching nachos, savoring Sailor Hägar's brews, and playing billiards.

☉ Steamworks Pub & Brewery. 375 Water St. ☎ **604/689-2739.**

Wending your way from room to room in this Gastown brewery is almost as much fun as drinking. Upstairs, by the doors, it's a London city pub where stockbrokers ogle every new female entrant. Farther in by the staircase, it's a refined old-world club, with wood paneling, leather chairs, and great glass windows overlooking the harbor. Down in the basement it's a Bavarian drinking hall—long lines of benches set up parallel to the enormous copper kettles support large groups of people intent on sucking back the brew in depth and at length. Fortunately, the beer's good. Choose from a dozen in-house beers.

Yaletown Brewing Company. 1111 Mainland St. ☎ **604/681-2739.**

Remember, if it's raining at 11:30am on a Thursday, all pints of brewed-on-the-premises beer are C$3.75 (US$2.50) for the rest of the day. The excellent beer is complemented by an extremely cozy room, a great summertime patio, and a good appetizer menu. Resist the urge to stay for supper, however. Snacks are the true forte. Sunday, all pizzas are half price.

4 Dance Clubs

Au Bar. 674 Seymour St. ☎ **604/648-2227.** Cover C$5–C$7 (US$3.35–US$4.70).

An address is unnecessary for Au Bar; the long Seymour Street corral of those not-quite-beautiful-enough for expedited entry immediately gives it away. Inside, this newest of downtown bars is packed with beautiful people milling from bar to dance floor to bar (there are two) and back again. Observing them is like watching a nature documentary on the Discovery Channel: doelike women prance and jiggle while predatory men roam in packs, flexing pecs and biceps. To maintain some form of natural order, black-clad bouncers scan the room like game wardens, searching the horizon for trouble in paradise.

The Legion. 2205 Commercial Dr. Cover $6 (US$4). For up-to-date info on Vancouver's swing scene, call the **Swing Hotline** at ☎ **604/377-1394.**

Swing's not dead, but the boom has definitely come and gone. Some of the more talented hep cats can still be found cuttin' a rug on Tuesday, Friday, and Saturday on the 3,400-square-foot dance floor upstairs in the Legion auditorium. Not sure about your moves? Dance lessons are included with the cover and are at 7:30pm on Tuesday nights for the Lindy Hop and 8:30pm on Friday and Saturday nights for East Coast Swing. The evening is all ages, so alcohol's out, but you can go downstairs and sign yourself into the Legion pub where the draught is very cheap.

☉ Luv-a-fair. 1275 Seymour St. ☎ **604/685-3288.** Cover C$2–C$6 (US$1.35–US$4).

Where the pale-skinned go to sweat: '80s early in the week, then Brit pop, alt-rock, house, and industrial mayhem as they head toward the weekend. Girls dance on the catwalk, guys—a cuter, less attitude-filled bunch than elsewhere, says my female companion—shake their stuff on the floorboards. Behind the chain-link fence in the upstairs mezzanine are the pool table and Foosball.

The Palladium Club. 1036 Richards St. ☎ **604/687-6794.** Cover varies, up to C$10 (US$7).

Dancing is the order of the evening at this industrial space with a dance floor the size of Texas and a ceiling soaring up so high you can hardly make out the duct work.

Late-Night Bites

The ✪ **Bread Garden,** 812 Bute St., south of Robson Street (☎ **604/ 688-3213**), is a spot (actually, one of nine Vancouver locations) where you can get breakfast, lunch, or dinner until 2am. The food—baked goods, salads, quiches, lasagna, frittatas, and desserts—is fresh and on the light side, and the prices are reasonable.

Look for the convertible car on the awning at **Doll & Penny's Café,** 1167 Davie St. (☎ **604/685-3417**). This hip restaurant has comfortable booths, service with attitude, low prices, and great burgers ranging from vegetarian to oversized beef. It's open Sunday to Thursday until midnight and Friday and Saturday until 3am. Friday nights mistress Simone puts on one of the best drag shows in town.

On the West Side, **Calhoun's,** 3035 W. Broadway (☎ **604/737-7062**), is a great barn of a place. Excellent coffee is available 24 hours a day, along with a behind-the-glass selection of ready-made lasagnas, salads, frittatas, and baked goods.

On the edge of the East Side, the **Grind & Gallery Coffee Bar,** 4124 Main St. (☎ **604/874-1588**), is always open and full, largely because it's the perfect place for those with an armload of books, a need to study, and money for only one cup of coffee. If you arrive without books, check out the ever-changing art displays on the walls, or pick up a mag from the extensive reading rack.

Monday, young 20-somethings dive into the '80s. Tuesday, Wednesday, and Saturday it's house. Sunday night the Goths come out to play. For the boogie-less, there's pool.

The Rage. 750 Pacific Blvd. (Plaza of Nations). ☎ **604/685-5585.** Cover Fri C$5 (US$3.35), Sat C$7 (US$4.70).

Tune in to radio station Z95 on the weekends after 8pm and you'll hear exactly what's going on in this airplane hangar of a dance club: five bars and speaker stacks loud enough to liquefy your brain make this the weekend house party to beat.

Richards on Richards. 1036 Richards St. ☎ **604/687-6794.** www.richardsonrichards. com. Cover Fri–Sat C$8 (US$5) for the club, concerts C$10–C$30 (US$7–US$20).

Dick's on Dicks has been packing 'em in longer than you'd care to know. What's the attraction? For years, the club was a notorious pickup spot. Things have mellowed a touch since then, but as the line of limos out front on busy nights attests, Dick's is still hot. Inside there are two floors, four bars, a laser light system, and lots of DJ'ed dance tunes. Occasional live acts have included the likes of Junior Wells, James Brown, and, just recently, 2 Live Crew and Jack Soul.

Sonar. 66 Water St. ☎ **604/683-6695.** www.sonar.bc.ca. Cover varies, C$5–C$10 (US$3.35–US$7) and up to C$20 (US$13) for special events.

Loud bass. Flashing lights. The endlessly thrumming rhythms of house. It's a combination that really works best with the aid of psychogenic substances with four-letter initials. Of course, the Sonar crowd of ravers-on-holiday already know that.

Stone Temple Cabaret. 1082 Granville St. ☎ **604/488-1333.** Cover C$5–C$20 (US$3.35–US$13).

Don't let the name fool ya, this is disco, pure and simple. A moderate-size dance floor in the front room features lights, smoke, booming bass, and a collegiate crowd swigging from beer bottles as they get down. The back room has plush banquettes and a balconied upstairs with pool tables. Open Tuesday to Sunday.

✪ **Voda Nightclub.** 783 Homer St. (in the Westin Grand Hotel). ☎ **604/684-3003.** Cover C$5 (US$3.35).

Voda has quickly made a name for itself, attracting folks young, old, and in-between, with the only real common denominator being cash. Intriguing interior boasts a mix of waterfalls, rocks, and raw concrete—like a beautiful piece of 1950s modernism. The small dance floor basks in the warm light from the hundreds of candles everywhere. Tuesday is Salsa night with the 15-piece salsa band performing Latin tunes. Thursdays are disco, with a mix of DJs and bands filling out the rest of the week.

Wett Bar. 1320 Richards St. ☎ **604/662-7707.** www.wettbar.com. Cover C$3–C$7 (US$2–US$4.70).

The '80s live on here, from the Artist once again known as Prince to spleen-shattering bass levels to squads of steroid-injected bouncers, complete with earphones, attitude, and, in the case of the Chief Beef, a full Kevlar vest and handcuffs. What's he guarding against? Judging by the clientele, willow-thin girls bopping timidly round their purses, desperately trying not to look uncool. Open Tuesday to Saturday.

5 Gay & Lesbian Bars

The near complete lack of persecution in laid-back Vancouver has had a curious effect on the city's gay scene—it's so attitude-free it's often hard to tell apart from the straight dance world, male go-go dancers and naked men in showers notwithstanding. Many clubs feature theme nights and dance parties, drag shows are ever-popular, and every year in early August, as Gay Pride nears, the scene goes into overdrive. The **Gay Lesbian Transgendered Bisexual Community Centre,** 2–1170 Bute St. (☎ 604/684-5307), has information on the current hot spots, but it's probably easier just to pick up a free copy of *Xtra West!,* available in most downtown cafes.

The Dufferin Pub. 900 Seymour St. ☎ **604/683-4251.** www.dufferinhotel.com.

Buff at the Duff is a city institution; other drag shows might be raunchier, but none have quite the style. Shows are Monday to Thursday. Friday and Sunday the go-go boys strut their stuff (and yes they do take it all off). The rest of the time—and before, during, and after many of the shows—the DJs keep you grooving.

Heritage House Hotel. 455 Abbott St. ☎ **604/685-7777.** Cover C$4–C$10 (US$2.70–US$7) some nights.

This aging beauty of a downtown hotel plays host to three separate gay bars. Downstairs, the lesbian **Lotus Cabaret** has a big bar, little alcoves for sitting, an adequate dance floor, and an upbeat atmosphere. The crowd is mixed, except for Friday when it's women only. **Charlie's Lounge** on the main floor is casual and elegant. Saturday night's "Charlie's Angels" is women only, sorry guys! The most endearing of the three is **Chuck's Pub.** More than slightly seedy, with comfortable wicker chairs and the cheapest draught in town, Chuck's is home on Friday evenings to Guys in Disguise, an amateur drag-queen revue. None of the acts is especially talented, but the patrons and performers all seem to know each other, and everyone sings along.

Homers. 1249 Howe St. ☎ **604/689-2444.**

Billed as a "neighborhood club," this casual pub has a relaxed atmosphere. There's no heavy cruising, but there are billiards tables, a great pub menu, inexpensive food and drinks, and the occasional surprised cruise ship passenger.

Lava Lounge. 1176 Granville St. ☎ **604/605-1154.** Cover C$2–C$10 (US$1.35–US$7).

Great things were expected when Howard Johnson's bought this sleazy hotel and closed the in-house club for renovations. It reopened with a different name, but the same decor, all the way down to the floor plants. That aside, and whatever your orientation, it's well worth coming here just to see the Lush. Thursday nights is the Electrolush Lounge night, when the show tunes on the turntable are matched to the clips from Busby Berkeley musicals flickering on the walls. The crowd is gay but not flamboyantly so. Indeed, the clientele could be confused with that of a jock bar were it not for the tall and striking drag queens swishing about and good-looking men dancing together. On non-Lush nights acts vary from live to DJ and from house to reggae to retro. Tables surround and overlook the dance floor.

Numbers Cabaret. 1098 Davie St. ☎ **604/685-4077.** Cover Fri–Sat C$3 (US$2).

A multilevel dance club and bar, Numbers has been around for 20 years and hasn't changed a bit. Extroverts hog the dance floor while admirers look on from the bar above. On the second floor, carpets, wood paneling, pool tables, darts, and a lower volume of music give it a neighborhood pub feel.

✪ **The Odyssey.** 1251 Howe St. ☎ **604/689-5256.** Cover Mon, Thurs, and Sun C$3 (US$2), Fri–Sat C$5 (US$3.35), Tues C$1 (US65¢), Wed no cover.

If this is what lay over the rainbow, I don't think anyone ever told Dorothy. Odyssey is the hottest and hippest gay/mixed dance bar in town (alley entrance is for men, women go in by the front door). The medium-sized dance space is packed. Up above, a mirrored catwalk is reserved for those who can keep the beat. Shows vary depending on the night. Monday it's Sissy Boy, Saturday it's Fallen Angel go-go dancers, Sunday it's the Feather Boa drag show. And on Thursday, it's Shower Power—yes, that is a pair of naked men in the shower above the dance floor. No, you're not in Kansas anymore.

The Royal Hotel. 1025 Granville St. ☎ **604/685-5335.**

This recently renovated gay bar has constantly changing theme nights. At the moment, Monday night is Divas Inc, a popular drag show. On Tuesday, the Empress of Vancouver hosts gay bingo. Thursday night's Libido's Lounge features Latin funk. Friday nights the Royal is packed with professionals and other nine-to-fivers kicking off the weekend.

6 Other Diversions

CINEMA

Thanks to the number of resident moviemakers (both studio and independent), Vancouver is increasingly becoming quite a film town. First-run theaters show the same Hollywood fare seen everywhere in the world (on Tues at a discount rate), but for those with something more adventurous in mind, there are lots of options.

Attendance at the ✪ **Vancouver International Film Festival** (☎ 604/685-0260; www.viff.org) reaches over 100,000, not including the stars and celebrities who regularly drop in. At this highly respected October event, over 250 new works are shown, representing filmmakers from 40 countries. Asian films are particularly well represented.

ART HOUSE & REPERTORY THEATERS

Since 1972, the **Pacific Cinematheque,** 1131 Howe St. (☎ 604/688-3456; www.cinematheque.bc.ca), has featured classic and contemporary films from around the world. Screenings are organized into themes, such as Jean Luc Godard's Early

Efforts, film noir, or the Hong Kong Action Flick: A Retrospective. Schedules are available in hipper cafes, record shops, and video stores around town. Admission is C$7 (US$4.70) for adults, C$5 (US$3.35) for seniors and students; double features cost C$1 (US65¢) extra. Annual membership, required to purchase tickets, is C$5 (US$3.35).

The alternative alternative theater, the **Blinding Light!,** 36 Powell St. (☎ 604/878-3366; www.blindinglight.com), is the Vancouver venue for all that is offbeat and experimental in film. Screenings to date have included new Vancouver shorts, bring-your-own-movie nights, experimental animation, and found-in-the-attic home movies and industrial films from the '50s and '60s. Admission is C$5 (US$3.35), with a C$3 (US$2) annual membership fee. There's also a yearly Vancouver Underground Film Festival.

SPECIALTY THEATERS

At the **CN IMAX,** Canada Place (☎ 604/682-IMAX), a gargantuan screen features large-format flicks about large and none-too-bright denizens of the animal kingdom (sharks, wolves, elephants, X-treme athletes).

A similar large screen at the **Alcan Omnimax,** Science World (☎ 604/443-7440), features flicks about empty, wide-open spaces: Antarctica, Alaska, Arkansas, etc.

Way off in the strip-mall lands of farthest Kingsway stands the **Raja,** 3215 Kingsway (☎ 604/436-1545), a modest single-screen movie house dedicated to bringing in the best flicks from the world's moviemaking capital, Bombay. For those unfamiliar with the Indian masala genre, expect raw violence mixed with big production numbers, a kind of *Mary Poppins* does *Die Hard*. Sometimes there are even English subtitles, though strictly speaking they're not really necessary. If Kingsway's too far off, there's another Raja on 639 Commercial Dr. (☎ 604/253-0402).

CASINOS

Well, it's not Vegas, and there's no alcohol and no floor shows, but on the other hand, you haven't really lived till you've sat down for some serious gambling with a room full of Far Eastern big shots trying to re-create the huge night they had in Happy Valley or Macau. (Once you have, you may not live much longer; in fact, the secondhand smoke inhalation may drop you on the spot.) Betting limits are in force, so you can't lose too much, and half of the proceeds go to charity, so it's all for a good cause.

Gateway Casino. 611 Main St. (3rd floor), in the heart of Chinatown. ☎ 604/688-9412.

Pai gow poker, blackjack, roulette, sic bo, mini bac, let it ride. Open from 10am to 4am daily. C$500 (US$335) maximum bet.

Great Canadian Casino—Downtown. 1133 W. Hastings St. ☎ 604/682-8145.

Blackjack, roulette, sic bo, red dog, and let it ride. Open daily from noon to 2am. There are others on the West Side at 709 W. Broadway (☎ 604/872-5543); in Richmond, at 8440 Bridgeport Rd. (☎ 604/273-1895); and in Surrey, at 13538 73rd Ave. (☎ 604/543-8388).

Royal Diamond Casino. 750 Pacific Blvd. (in the Plaza of Nations). ☎ 604/685-2340. www.rdc.com.

Blackjack, roulette, pai gow poker, and mini-baccarat. Free parking. Open daily from noon to 4am.

10 Getting to Know Victoria

I was in the Bengal Lounge, sinking in a leather fantasy of an armchair, when I first began to understand something of Victoria. Sipping on a cold drink, looking smugly at the pukka fans wafting back and forth on the ceiling and the light from the roaring fire ricocheting off the glass eyeballs of the Bengal tiger mounted above the mantelpiece, I found it easy for a moment to imagine I was Somerset Maugham— or better still, Stamford Raffles—that the year was 1845, and that The Empress was a grand colonial hotel, an outpost of Empire on the edge of a barbarous wasteland.

Except that the drink I was sipping was a fluorescent blue martini, the music wafting from an unseen sound system was 1960s jazz, and the coats piled up on a nearby armchair were made not of wool or oilskin but of Gore-Tex and fleece. These small tokens of reality aside, however, it was a seductive and compelling vision.

I asked my drinking companion—the editor of the local alternative paper—just who first came up with Victoria's "little patch of Empire" shtick.

"For a while at the turn of the century people here actually bought into it," he said. "They'd come out from England and, whatever their politics back home, here they'd morph into super-patriots, singing 'God Save the Queen' at the drop of a hat."

World War I largely put an end to that, he continued, but then in the 1920s Victoria was hit by another shock—the population began to drop as business shifted over to Vancouver. Local merchants panicked. And it was then that San Francisco–born George Warren of the Victoria Publicity Bureau put forward his proposal: Sell the Olde England angle.

Warren had never been to England and had no idea what it looked like. But to him, Victoria seemed English. To the city's merchants, Warren's scheme seemed like just the thing. And so it was. For three-plus generations it served the city well. While other places were leveling their downtowns in the name of progress, Victoria nurtured and preserved its heritage buildings, adding gardens and lavish city parks. Soon enough it possessed that rarest of commodities for a North American city, a gorgeous, walkable 19th-century city center.

True, the "this is Sussex" paradigm meant ignoring some details. Whales sometimes swam into the Inner Harbour. Snowcapped mountain peaks loomed just across the water from Ross Bay. Trees in the surrounding forests towered far higher than Big Ben.

Only in the past half-decade, in fact, has Victoria finally begun to make use of its stunning physical surroundings. Whale watching is now a major industry. Kayak tours are becoming ever more popular. Mountain bikes have taken to competing for road space with the bright-red double-decker buses. Still, ecotourism is in its infancy. Many of the tours and expeditions on offer have never been done before. Guides regard the territory with the same fresh eye as visitors.

But if making peace with where you are has made for better business, it has also brought its share of challenges, at least one of them existential. If Victoria is no longer a little bit o' Blimey, just what exactly is it? The best answer, surprisingly enough, comes from another journalist, the poet of the Empire himself, Rudyard Kipling.

"To realize Victoria," Kipling wrote after visiting the city around 1908, "you must take all that the eye admires most in Bournemouth, Torquay, the Isle of Wight, the Happy Valley at Hong Kong, the Doon, Sorrento and Camps Bay; add reminisces of the Thousand Islands, and arrange the whole round the Bay of Naples, with some Himalayas in the background. Real estate agents recommend it as a little piece of England—the Island on which it stands is about the size of Great Britain—but no England is set in any such seas or so fairly charged with the mystery of the large ocean beyond. The high, still twilights along the beaches are out of the old East, just under the curve of the world."

1 Orientation

Victoria is on the southeastern tip of Vancouver Island, across the Strait of Juan de Fuca from Washington State's snowcapped Olympic peninsula. It's 72 kilometers (45 miles) south of the 49th Parallel, the border between most of Canada and the contiguous United States.

Once you've arrived, head for the Inner Harbour. Lovingly restored vintage sailboats are berthed side by side with modern watercraft in the snug harbor, right in the heart of the city. A waterfront causeway runs along it in front of The Empress hotel, one of Victoria's most picturesque spots. Just a few blocks away are the Royal British Columbia Museum, Undersea World, the Crystal Gardens, Thunderbird Park's totem poles, downtown and Old Town's shopping streets and restaurants, and Beacon Hill Park.

ARRIVING

BY PLANE   The **Victoria International Airport** is near the Sidney ferry terminal, 26 kilometers (16 miles) north of Victoria off the Patricia Bay Highway (Highway 17). For airport information, call ☎ **250/953-7500.** Highway 17 heads south to Victoria, becoming Douglas Street as you enter downtown.

The **airport bus service,** operated by AKAL Airport (☎ **250/386-2526**), makes the trip into town in about half an hour. Buses leave every 30 minutes daily from 4:30am to midnight; the fare is C$13 (US$9) one-way or C$23 (US$15) round-trip. Drop-offs are made at most hotels and pickups can be arranged as well. A limited number of hotel courtesy buses also serve the airport. A cab ride into downtown Victoria costs about C$40 (US$27) plus tip. **Empress Cabs** and **Blue Bird Cabs** (see "Getting Around") make airport runs.

Several **car-rental firms** have desks at the airport. Though all accept people without reservations, during peak travel times they may sell out a few days in advance. They include **Avis** (☎ **250/656-6033**), **Hertz** (☎ **250/656-2312**), and **Tilden** (☎ **250/656-2541**).

BY TRAIN, BUS & FERRY   VIA Rail trains arrive at Victoria's **E&N Station,** 450 Pandora Ave., near the Johnson Street Bridge (☎ **800/561-8630** in Canada).

The **Victoria Bus Depot** is at 700 Douglas St., behind the Empress Hotel. **Pacific Coach Lines** (☎ **250/385-4411**) offers daily service to and from Vancouver. **Laid-law Coach Lines** (☎ **250/385-4411**) has daily scheduled runs to Nanaimo, Port Alberni, Campbell River, and Port Hardy.

For information on arriving by **ferry,** see "Getting to Victoria" in chapter 2.

VISITOR INFORMATION

TOURIST OFFICES & MAGAZINES   On the Inner Harbour's wharf, across from The Empress hotel, is the **Tourism Victoria Visitor Info Centre,** 812 Wharf St. (☎ **250/953-2033;** www.tourismvictoria.bc.ca or www.travel.victoria.bc.ca; e-mail: info@tourismvictoria.com). You can get there on bus 1, 27, or 28 to Douglas and Courtney Streets. If you didn't reserve a room before you arrived, you can go to this office or call its **reservations hot line** (☎ **800/663-3883** or 250/953-2033) for last-minute bookings at hotels, inns, and B&Bs. The staff will help you locate discounts. The center is open daily: September 1 to June 15 from 9am to 5pm and June 16 to August 31 from 8:30am to 8pm.

If you want to explore the rest of 456-kilometer-long (285-mile-long) Vancouver Island, contact the **Tourism Association of Vancouver Island,** Suite 203, 335 Wesley St., Nanaimo, B.C. V9R 2T5 (☎ **250/754-3500;** www.islands.bc.ca; e-mail: tavi@islands.bc.ca).

For details on the after-dark scene, pick up a copy of *Monday* magazine (☎ **250/ 382-6188;** www.monday.com), available free in cafes and record shops around the city. *Monday* not only is an excellent guide to Victoria's nightlife but also has driven at least one mayor from office with its award-winning muckraking journalism.

WEB SITES   See "Planning Your Trip: An Online Directory" following chapter 2.

CITY LAYOUT

Victoria was born at the edge of the Inner Harbour in the 1840s and grew outward from there. The areas of most interest to visitors, including the **downtown** and **Old Town,** lie along the eastern edge of the **Inner Harbour.** (North of the Johnson Street Bridge is the **Upper Harbour,** which is almost entirely industrial.) A little farther east, the **Ross Bay** and **Oak Bay** residential areas around Dallas Road and Beach Drive reach the beaches along the open waters of the Strait of Juan de Fuca.

Victoria's central landmark is **The Empress hotel** on Government Street, right across from the Inner Harbour wharf. If you turn your back to the hotel, the downtown and Old Town are on your right, while the provincial **Legislative Buildings** and the **Royal BC Museum** are on your immediate left. Next to them is the dock for the **Seattle–Port Angeles ferries** and beyond that the residential community of **James Bay.**

MAIN ARTERIES & STREETS   Three main **north-south arteries** intersect just about every destination you may want to reach in Victoria.

Government Street goes through Victoria's main downtown shopping-and-dining district. Wharf Street, edging the harbor, merges with Government Street at The Empress hotel. **Douglas Street,** running parallel to Government Street, is the main business thoroughfare as well as the road to Nanaimo and the rest of the island. It's also Trans-Canada Highway 1. The "Mile 0" marker sits at the corner of Douglas and Dallas Road. Also running parallel to Government and Douglas Streets is **Blanshard Street** (Hwy. 17), the route to the Saanich Peninsula, including the Sidney-Vancouver ferry terminal, and Butchart Gardens.

Important **east-west streets** include the following: **Johnson Street** lies at the northern end of downtown and the Old Town, where the small E&N Station sits opposite Swans Hotel at the corner of Wharf Street. The Johnson Street Bridge is the demarcation line between the Upper Harbour and the Inner Harbour. **Belleville Street** is the Inner Harbour's southern edge. The Legislative Buildings and the ferry terminal are here. Belleville Street loops around westward toward Victoria Harbour before heading south, becoming Dallas Road. **Dallas Road** follows the water's edge past residential areas and beaches before it winds northward up to Oak Bay.

FINDING AN ADDRESS   Victoria addresses are written like those in Vancouver: The suite or room number precedes the building number. For instance, 100-1250 Government St. refers to suite 100 at 1250 Government St.

Victoria's streets are numbered from the city's southwest corner and increase in increments of 100 per block as you go north and east. (1000 Douglas St., for example, is 2 blocks north of 800 Douglas St.). Fort Street starts its 500 block at Wharf Street.

STREET MAPS   Detailed street maps are available free at the **Tourism Victoria Visitor Info Centre** (see "Visitor Information" above). The best map of the surrounding area is the **B.C. Provincial Parks** map of Vancouver Island, also available at the Info Centre.

Neighborhoods in Brief

Downtown & Old Town   These areas have been the city's social and commercial focal points since the mid-1800s, when settlers first arrived by ship. This is also the area of the city most popular with visitors, filled with shops, museums, heritage buildings, and lots of restaurants. The area reflects its fascinating Barbary Coast–style history, which includes rum smuggling, opium manufacturing, gold prospecting, whaling, fur trading, and shipping.

The two neighborhoods are usually listed together because it's difficult to say where one leaves off and the other begins. The Old Town consists of the pre-1900 commercial sections of the city that grew up around the original Fort Victoria at View and Government Streets. Roughly speaking, it extends from Fort Street north to Pandora and from Wharf Street east to Douglas. Downtown is everything outside of that, from the Inner Harbour to Quadra Street in the east and from Belleville Street in the south up to Herald Street at the northern edge of downtown.

Chinatown   Victoria's Chinatown is tiny—2 square blocks—but venerable. In fact, it's the oldest Chinese community in North America. Its many interesting historic sites include Fan Tan Alley, Canada's narrowest commercial street, where legal opium manufacturing took place in the hidden courtyard buildings flanking the 1.2-meter-wide (4 ft.) way. (If you saw the movie *Bird on a Wire,* you may remember Mel Gibson riding through Fan Tan Alley in a great motorcycle chase scene.)

James Bay, Ross Bay & Oak Bay   When Victoria was a busy port and trading post, the local aristocracy—merchant princes and their merchant princess daughters, for the most part—would retire to homes in these neighborhoods to escape the hustle-bustle in the city center below. Today they remain beautiful residential communities. Houses perch on hills overlooking the straits or nestle amid lushly landscaped gardens. Golf courses, marinas, and a few cozy inns edge the waters, where you can stroll the beaches or go for a dip if you don't mind a slight chill.

2 Getting Around

Strolling along the Inner Harbour's pedestrian walkways and streets is very pleasant. The terrain is predominantly flat, and with few exceptions, Victoria's points of interest are accessible in less than 30 minutes on foot.

BY PUBLIC TRANSPORTATION

BY BUS The **Victoria Regional Transit System (BC Transit),** 520 Gorge Rd. (☎ 250/382-6161; www.bctransit.com), operates 40 bus routes through greater Victoria as well as the nearby towns of Sooke and Sidney. You can take the bus to Butchart Gardens and the Vancouver ferry terminal at Sidney. Regular service on the main routes runs daily from 6am to just past midnight.

Schedules and routes are available at the Tourism Victoria Visitor Info Centre (see "Visitor Information," above), where you can pick up a copy of the *Victoria Rider's Guide* or *Discover Vancouver on Transit: Including Victoria*. These publications provide transit routes for many of the city's neighborhoods, landmarks, and attractions.

Popular Victoria bus routes include **no. 2** (Oak Bay), **no. 5** (downtown, James Bay, Beacon Hill Park), **no. 14** (Victoria Art Gallery, Craigdarroch Castle, University of Victoria), **no. 61** (Sooke), **no. 70** (Sidney, Swartz Bay), and **no. 75** (Butchart Gardens).

Fares are calculated on a per-zone basis. One-way single-zone fares are C$1.75 (US$1.15) for adults and C$1.10 (US75¢) for seniors and children 5 to 13; two zones cost C$2.50 (US$1.65) and C$1.75 (US$1.15), respectively. Transfers are good for travel in one direction only, with no stopovers.

A **DayPass,** C$5.50 (US$3.70) for adults and C$4 (US$2.70) for seniors and children 5 to 13, covers unlimited travel throughout the day. You can buy passes at the Tourism Victoria Visitor Info Centre (see "Visitor Information" above), convenience stores, and ticket outlets throughout Victoria displaying the "FareDealer" symbol.

BY FERRY Crossing the Inner, Upper, and Victoria Harbours by one of the blue 12-passenger **Victoria Harbour Ferries** (☎ 250/708-0201) is cheap and fun. Identical to Vancouver's False Creek Ferries, these boats have big windows all the way around and look like they're straight out of a cartoon. Fortunately, the harbor is smooth sailing. May through September, the ferries to The Empress hotel, Coast Harbourside Hotel, and Ocean Pointe Resort hotel run about every 15 minutes daily from 9am to 9pm. In March, April, and October, ferry service runs daily from 11am to 5pm. November through February, the ferries run only on sunny weekends from 11am to 5pm. The cost per hop is C$3 (US$2) for adults and C$1.50 (US$1) for children.

Instead of just taking the ferry for a short hop across, try the 45-minute **Harbour tour** for C$12 (US$8) adults and C$6 (US$4) children, or the 50-minute **Gorge tour** for C$14 (US$9) adults, C$7 (US$4.70) children, and C$12 (US$8) seniors.

Finally, starting at 9:45am every Sunday during summer, the ferries gather in front of the Empress to perform a **ferry "ballet"**—it looks much like the hippo dance in Disney's *Fantasia*.

BY CAR

If you're planning out-of-town activities, you can rent a car in town or bring your own. If you have a city-bound agenda, make sure your hotel has parking. Keep a few things in mind: Traffic is heavy and parking is scarce. Gas is sold by the liter, averaging around C70¢ (US45¢). That may seem inexpensive until you consider that a gallon of gas costs about C$2.80 (US$1.85). In addition, speeds and distances are posted in kilometers. The downtown area is easily explored by foot.

RENTALS   Car-rental agencies in Victoria include the following: **Avis,** 1001 Douglas St., bus 5 to Broughton Street, (☎ **800/879-2847** or 250/386-8468); **Budget,** 757 Douglas St. (☎ **800/268-8900** or 250/953-5300); **Hertz,** 655 Douglas St., in the Queen Victoria Inn (☎ **800/263-0600** or 250/360-2822); and **National,** 767 Douglas St. (☎ **800/227-7368** or 250/386-1213). These three can be reached on the no. 5 bus to the Convention Centre. Rates run about C$32 to C$48 (US$21 to US$32) per day for a compact to midsize vehicle.

PARKING   Metered **street parking** is hard to come by in the downtown area, and rules are strictly enforced. Unmetered parking on side streets is rare. All major downtown hotels have guest parking; with rates from free to C$20 (US$13) per day. There are parking lots at **View Street** between Douglas and Blanshard Streets; **Johnson Street** off Blanshard Street; **Yates Street** north of Bastion Square; and **the Bay** on Fisgard at Blanshard Street.

DRIVING RULES   Canadian driving rules are similar to regulations in the United States. Seat belts and daytime headlights are mandatory. Children under 5 must be in child restraints. Motorcyclists must wear helmets. It's legal to turn right on a red light after you've come to a full stop. Some of the best places on Vancouver Island can be reached only via gravel logging roads, on which logging trucks have absolute right-of-way. If you're on a logging road and see a logging truck coming from either direction, pull over to the side of the road and stop to let it pass.

AUTO CLUB   Members of the **American Automobile Association (AAA)** can get emergency assistance from the **British Columbia Automobile Association (BCAA)** (☎ **800/222-4357**).

BY BIKE

Biking is the easiest way to get around the downtown and beach areas. There are bike lanes throughout the city and paved paths along parks and beaches. Helmets are mandatory, and riding on sidewalks is illegal, except where bike paths are indicated. You can rent bikes for C$6 (US$4) per hour and C$20 (US$13) per day (lock and helmet included) from **Budget,** 757 Douglas St., bus 5 to the Convention Centre (☎ **250/953-5300**).

BY TAXI

Within the downtown area, you can expect to travel for less than C$6 (US$4), plus tip. It's best to call for a cab; drivers don't always stop on city streets for flag-downs, especially when it's raining. Call for a pickup from **Empress Cabs** (☎ **250/ 381-2222**) or **Blue Bird Cabs** (☎ **250/382-4235**).

Fast Facts: Victoria

American Express   The office is at 1203 Douglas St. (☎ **250/385-8731**) and is open Monday to Friday from 8:30am to 5:30pm and Saturday from 10am to 4pm. Get there on bus 5 to Yates Street.

Area Code   The telephone area code for all of Vancouver Island, including Victoria and most of British Columbia, is **250.** For the greater Vancouver area, including Squamish and Whistler, it's **604.**

Baby-Sitters   Most major hotels can arrange baby-sitting services; check the guest services directory for the phone number or hotel extension.

Business Hours   Victoria **banks** are open Monday to Thursday from 10am to 3pm and Friday from 10am to 6pm. **Stores** are generally open Monday to Saturday from 10am to 6pm. Some establishments are open later in summer. Many stores are also open on Sundays during summer. Last call at the city's **bars** and **cocktail lounges** is 2am.

Consulates   See "Fast Facts: Vancouver" in chapter 3.

Currency Exchange   The best exchange rates in town can be found at banks and by using ATMs. **Royal Bank,** 1079 Douglas St. at Fort Street, is in the heart of downtown. Take bus 5 to Fort Street.

Dentist   Most major hotels have a dentist on call. **Cresta Dental Centre,** 3170 Tillicum Rd. at Burnside Street (☎ **250/384-7711**), in the Tillicum Mall (bus 10), is open Monday from 8am to 5pm, Tuesday to Friday from 8am to 9pm, Saturday from 9am to 5pm, and Sunday from noon to 5pm.

Doctor   Hotels usually have doctors on call. The **Tillicum Mall Medical Clinic,** 3170 Tillicum at Burnside Street, (☎ **250/381-8112**), accepts walk-in patients daily from 9am to 9pm. Take bus 10 to Tillicum Mall.

Electricity   The same 110 volts AC (60 cycles) as in the United States.

Emergencies   Dial ☎ **911** for fire, police, ambulance, and poison control.

Hospitals   Local hospitals include the **Royal Jubilee Hospital,** 1900 Fort St. (☎ **250/370-8000;** emergency 250/370-8212), and the **Victoria General Hospital,** 1 Hospital Way (☎ **250/727-4212;** emergency 250/727-4181). You can get to both hospitals on bus 14.

Hot Lines   Emergency numbers include: **Royal Canadian Mounted Police** (☎ 250/380-6261); **Emotional Crisis Centre** (☎ 250/386-6323); **Sexual Assault Centre** (☎ 250/383-3232); **Poison Control Centre** (☎ 800/567-8911); **Help Line for Children** (dial ☎ 0 and ask for Zenith 1234).

Internet Access   To check on your messages or send e-mails, head to the **Victoria Cyber Cafe,** 1414B Douglas St. (☎ **250/995-0175**). Bus 5 to Johnson Street will get you there.

Library   The **Greater Victoria Public Library** is at 735 Broughton St., near the corner of Fort and Douglas Streets, (☎ **250/382-7241**). Get on bus no. 5 to Broughton Street.

Luggage Storage/Lockers   Most hotels will store bags for guests who are about to check in or who have just checked out. Otherwise, coin lockers for C$1 (US65¢) are available outside the bus station (behind The Empress hotel). Take bus 5 to the Convention Centre.

Newspapers   The morning *Times Colonist* comes out daily. The weekly entertainment paper *Monday* magazine comes out, strangely enough, on Thursday.

Pharmacies   **Shopper's Drug Mart,** 1222 Douglas St. (☎ **250/381-4321**), is open Monday to Friday from 7am to 8pm, Saturday from 9am to 7pm, and Sunday from 9am to 6pm, bus 5 to View Street. **McGill and Orme,** 649 Fort St., at the corner of Broad Street (☎ **250/384-1195**), is open Monday to Friday from 9am to 6pm, Saturday from 9am to 6pm, and Sunday from noon to 4pm, bus 5 to Fort Street.

Police   Dial ☎ **911.** The **Victoria City Police** can also be reached by calling ☎ **250/995-7654.**

Post Office   The **main post office** is at 714 Yates St. (☎ **250/953-1352**), bus 5 to Yates Street. There are also postal outlets in **Shopper's Drug Mart** (see "Pharmacies," above) and in other stores displaying the CANADA POST postal outlet sign.

Safety   Crime rates are quite low in Victoria, but transients panhandle throughout the downtown and Old Town areas. The most common crimes are property crimes, which are usually preventable with a few extra common-sense precautions like not leaving items in plain sight when you park your car.

Weather   Call ☎ **250/656-3978** for weather updates.

11

Where to Stay in Victoria

Victoria has been welcoming visitors for well-nigh 100 years, so it knows how to do it with style. You'll find a wide choice of fine accommodations in all price ranges, most in the Old Town or around the Inner Harbour. All are in or within easy walking distance of the downtown core. A half-hour drive east or west takes you to Sooke and Malahat—wonderful hideaways offering more peace and solitude.

1 The Inner Harbour & Nearby

VERY EXPENSIVE

✪ **The Empress.** 721 Government St., Victoria, B.C. V8W 1W5. ☎ **800/ 866-5577** or 250/384-8111. Fax 250/381-4334. www.fairmont.com. 460 units. MINIBAR TV TEL. May–Oct C$295–C$490 (US$198–US$328) double; Nov–Apr C$200–C$395 (US$134–US$265) double. Year-round C$425–C$1,500 (US$285–US$1,005) suite. Wheelchair-accessible units available. AE, DC, DISC, JCB, MC, V. Underground valet parking C$17 (US$11). Bus: 5. Small pets allowed for C$50 (US$34).

Francis Rattenbury's 1908 harborside creation is such a joy to look at, The Empress should probably charge for the view. When you see it, you'll know immediately that you absolutely *have* to stay there. However, here's one thing you should know before throwing down the credit card: With 90 different configurations, not all rooms are created equal. Some of the deluxe rooms and all the Entree Gold rooms are a dream (or a Merchant/Ivory film), with large beds, wide windows, high ceilings, and abundant natural light. The Entree Gold rooms also include private check-in, a concierge, breakfast in the private lounge, and extras like CD players and TVs in the bathrooms. Many of the other rooms—despite a $4-million renovation (US$2.7-million) in 1996—are built to the "cozy" standards of 1908. And the fact that they come with down duvets, ceiling fans, and minibars doesn't make them any bigger. If you can afford an Entree Gold or a deluxe room— go for it. If you can't, it may be better to admire The Empress from afar or confine your relationship to afternoon visits.

Dining: The Bengal Lounge serves curry buffets and an à la carte menu; The Empress Room serves Pacific Northwest cuisine in an elegant formal setting; the more affordable Kipling's serves regional cuisine in a casual setting. The famous afternoon tea is served under the stained-glass dome of the Palm Court and in the Tea Lobby. Cost is C$42 (US$28) per person in summer and C$32 (US$21) in winter.

Accommodations Advice

Quality is generally very high in Victoria's hotels, but there are still some tricks of the trade to keep in mind when looking for a place to lay your head.

• Quoted prices don't include the 10% provincial accommodations tax or the 7% goods-and-services tax (GST). Non-Canadians can get a GST rebate on short-stay accommodations by filling out the Tax Refund Application (see "Taxes" under "Fast Facts: Vancouver" in chapter 3).

• The prices I supply are the "rack rates"—the ones listed on the door and given out to the public. Always ask about discounts (AAA, corporate, whatever) or vacation packages, particularly in the October-to-April low season when hotels are half-empty. A simple inquiry could save C$50 to C$75 (US$34 to US$50). In the summer high season, the prices, like the desk clerks' faces, are set in stone. Which brings up the following point:

• Reservations are absolutely essential in Victoria from May through September.

• If you do arrive without a reservation and have trouble finding a room, **Tourism Victoria** (☎ **800/663-3883** or 250/382-1131) can make reservations for you at hotels, inns, and B&Bs. It deals only with establishments that pay a fee to list with them, but fortunately most do.

• Beware of the incidentals. A C$5- to C$10-per-night (US$3.35-US$7) parking charge has become commonplace. Fair enough, perhaps, when you consider the parking situation, but the same can't be said for the penny-ante $1 surcharge many hotels still tack on each time you make a local call. To avoid unpleasant surprises, ask beforehand what kind of surcharges exist. If presented with a sizable surcharge bill on checkout, complain—loudly. Local telephone fees have a way of magically evaporating.

Amenities: Concierge, room service, valet, dry cleaning/laundry, express checkout, massage, indoor 40-foot lap pool, children's wading pool, health club, sauna, whirlpool, shopping arcade, meeting and banquet space for up to 1,500, car-rental desk.

✪ **Ocean Pointe Resort.** 45 Songhees Rd., Victoria, B.C. V9A 6T3. ☎ **800/667-4677** or 250/360-2999. Fax 250/360-1041. www.oprhotel.com. E-mail: ocean_pointe@pinc.com. 280 units. A/C MINIBAR TV TEL. Apr 16–May 31 C$322–C$574 (US$216–US$385) double; June 1–Oct 11 C$448–C$736 (US$300–US$493) double; Oct 12–Dec 31 C$340–C$448 (US$228–US$300) double; Jan 1–Apr 15 C$295–C$403 (US$198–US$270) double. Promotional rates available all seasons. Children under 17 stay free in parents' room. Wheelchair-accessible units available. AE, DC, ER, MC, V. Underground valet parking C$9 (US$6). Bus: 24 to Colville. Pets under 30 lb. allowed.

On the Inner Harbour's north shore, the luxurious modern "OPR" (as the staff call it) offers commanding views of downtown, the legislature, and The Empress. Other great pluses are the things you expect in a top property—fancy giveaway stuff in the bathrooms, fluffy robes, hair dryers, coffeemakers with quality coffee, and large beds with fine linen. In a city with a fetish for floral prints, the OPR's decor is refreshingly modern—polished woods and solid muted colors and not a lot of bric-a-brac. The Inner Harbour rooms offer the best views, many with floor-to-ceiling windows; rooms facing the Outer Harbour top that with floor-to-ceiling bay windows. In the grand lobby, that floor-to-ceiling theme is repeated with windows two stories tall, facing toward downtown.

A Little Hotel Trivia

The Empress's fantasy of being a little bit of England was given a rather rude jolt of B.C. reality in February 1992, when a 60-kilogram (132-lb.) female cougar stopped in for a visit. Fully grown but still immature, the cat had lost its bearings and wandered into The Empress's parking garage during the night. Conservation officers took her captive after injecting her with a sedative slightly stronger than afternoon tea and later released her into a less refined setting, somewhere up island.

Dining/Diversions: All three restaurants have fabulous views. The Victorian Restaurant has lately been winning awards from the likes of *Wine Spectator* magazine for its elegant West Coast cuisine; the Boardwalk Restaurant is more casual. Rick's Lounge & Piano Bar is a warm and friendly spot. In season, there's seating on the large waterfront patio as well.

Amenities: Concierge, 24-hour room service, dry cleaning/laundry, newspaper delivery, in-room massage, baby-sitting, secretarial services, express checkout, tennis and squash courts, pool, sauna, sundeck, spa generally acknowledged to be the best in town.

EXPENSIVE

✪ **Andersen House Bed & Breakfast.** 301 Kingston St., Victoria, B.C. V8V 1V5. ☎ **250/ 388-4565.** Fax 250/388-4563. www.andersenhouse.com. E-mail: andersen@islandnet.com. 4 units, 1 yacht, 2 manor units. TV TEL. June–Sept C$195–C$250 (US$131–US$168) double, C$250 (US$168) yacht. Oct–May up to 40% discount. High season C$250 (US$168) manor unit, off-season C$115–C$195 (US$77–US$131) manor unit. Rates include breakfast. MC, V. Free parking on street. Bus: 30 to Superior and Oswego Sts.

The art and furnishings in Andersen House are drawn from the whole of the old British Empire and a good section of the modern world beyond. The 1891 house has the high ceilings, stained-glass windows, and ornate fireplaces typical of the Queen Anne style, but the art and decorations are far more eclectic: hand-knotted Persian rugs, raku sculptures, large cubist-inspired oils, and carved-wood African masks. Each room has a unique style: The sun-drenched Casablanca room on the top floor, for example, boasts Persian rugs, a four-poster queen bed, and a lovely boxed window seat. All rooms have private entrances and come with books and CD players and CDs; some feature soaker tubs. If you're looking for something even more unconventional, how about a 50-foot yacht moored in the Inner Harbour? The 1927 *Mamita* provides double bed accommodations in the teak wheelhouse. Sit on the deck watching the floatplanes go by or lounge in the art-deco salon beneath the skylights. *Mamita* guests get the same gourmet breakfast as those staying in the house. The same couple who runs Andersen House has recently opened Baybreeze Manor, a restored 1885 farmhouse a 15-minute drive from downtown. The two farmhouse units feature hardwood floors, fireplaces, queen beds, and Jacuzzi tubs, as well as free bicycle, canoe, and kayak usage and easy access to Cadboro Beach.

✪ **Clarion Hotel Grand Pacific.** 450 Quebec St., Victoria, B.C. V8V 1W5. ☎ **800/ 228-5151** or 250/386-0450. Fax 250/386-8779. www.hotelgrandpacific.com. 324 units. A/C MINIBAR TV TEL. July 1–Sept 15 C$229–C$299 (US$153–US$200) double, C$349– C$439 (US$234–US$294) suite; Sept 16–May 15 C$179–C$249 (US$120–US$167) double, C$249–C$369 (US$167–US$247) suite; May 16–June 30 C$179–C$249 (US$120–US$167) double, C$299–C$369 (US$200–US$247) suite. Off-season and weekend discounts available. AE, DC, DISC, MC, V. Free parking. Bus: 30 to Superior and Oswego Sts.

Victoria Accommodations

Abigail's Hotel **27**
Admiral Motel **9**
Andersen House B&B **14**
The Beaconsfield Inn **28**
The Bedford Regency **5**
Chateau Victoria Hotel **24**
Clarion Hotel Grand Pacific **16**
Coast Harbourside Hotel
& Marina **8**
Dashwood Manor **29**
Days Inn on the Harbour **15**
The Dominion Hotel **6**
The Empress **21**
Executive House Hotel **25**
The Gatsby Mansion **10**
Harbour Towers **13**
A Haterleigh Heritage Inn **11**
Holland House Inn **18**
The James Bay Inn **20**
Laurel Point Inn **7**
The Magnolia **22**
Medana Grove Bed
& Breakfast **19**
Ocean Pointe Resort **1**
Ramada Huntington Manor **12**
Royal Scot Suite Hotel **17**
Swan's Suite Hotel **2**
The Strathcona Hotel **23**
Victoria International
Youth Hostel **3**
The Victoria Regent Hotel **4**
YM-YWCA of Victoria **26**

The Best Bed & Breakfast Registries

If you prefer to stay at a B&B other than those listed in this chapter, the following agencies specialize in matching guests to the B&B that best suits their needs (see chapter 4 for more information):

- **Beachside Bed & Breakfast Registry,** 4208 Evergreen Ave., West Vancouver, B.C. V7V 1H1 (☎ **800/563-3311** or 604/922-7773; www.beach.bc.ca; e-mail: info@beach.bc.ca).
- **Born Free Bed & Breakfast of BC,** 4390 Frances St., Burnaby, B.C. V5C 2R3 (☎ **800/488-1941** in the U.S. or 604/298-8815; www.vancouverbandb. bc.ca; e-mail: vancouverbandb@direct.ca).
- **Canada-West Accommodations Bed & Breakfast Registry,** P.O. Box 86607, North Vancouver, B.C. V7L 4L2 (☎ **800/561-3223** or 604/990-6730; www.b-b.com; e-mail: ellison@b-b.com).
- **Town and Country Bed & Breakfast,** P.O. Box 74542, 2803 W. Fourth Ave., Vancouver, B.C. V6K IK2 (☎/fax **604/731-5942;** www. townandcountrybedandbreakfast.com).

Overlooking the Inner Harbour, steps from the Legislative building, the Clarion gives off an indefinable sense of luxury. The standard rooms are elegant and comfortable, with either two doubles or a king bed. All rooms have balconies, with the best views overlooking the water. It's great for business travelers as the desks come equipped with phones, data ports, and good lighting. The spacious one-bedroom suites include extras like cordless phones, bathrobes, and makeup mirrors. Executive suites feature double Jacuzzis, fireplaces, three balconies, and wet bars. So successful has this eight-story property been since it opened in 1989, it's now cannibalizing its neighbors. The adjoining Quality Inn has been demolished so the Clarion can add another 160 rooms, with the completion set for the spring of 2001.

Dining/Diversions: The dining room serves breakfast and dinner daily, including a breakfast buffet in summer, Trophies Lounge offers light dining.

Amenities: Concierge, 24-hour room service, valet cleaning, courtesy transportation; impressive fitness facility with 25-meter lap pool, hot tub, aerobics classes, squash courts, exercise equipment.

Coast Harbourside Hotel and Marina. 146 Kingston St., Victoria, B.C. V8V 1V4. ☎ **800/663-1144** or 250/360-1211. Fax 250/360-1418. www.coasthotels.com. 132 units. A/C MINIBAR TV TEL. May–Sept C$240–C$260 (US$161–US$174) double, C$375 (US$251) suite; Oct–Apr C$119–C$129 (US$80–US$86) double, C$220 (US$147) suite. Children under 18 stay free in parents' room. Wheelchair-accessible units available. AE, DC, JCB, MC, V. Free underground parking. Bus: 30 to Erie and St. Lawrence Sts. Pets accepted for C$20 (US$13).

The Blue Crab Bar and Grill here is truly top-notch, among Victoria's best seafood spots. The hotel itself, however, comes in several places lower on the totem pole. Not that it's a dive, it's just that all the touches you expect of a hotel in its price range and location (on the Inner Harbour's southwest shore) are absent or present in name only. Take the "view balconies"—with a width of perhaps 8 inches. The same token approach to quality is taken throughout. The rooms are standard boxes, with one king or two queen beds. Top-quality bedding is reserved for those who've paid tip-top price. The same stingy policy applies to terry robes and giveaway bathroom products. The corridors are heavily scuffed, as if the cleaning staff play a daily game of smash-up derby. All in all, staying at the Coast is like scrunching your feet out onto an 8-inch balcony for a view. You could do it, but why bother?

Dining: The Blue Crab Bar and Grill offers fresh and adventurous West Coast cuisine with a fabulous view of the harbor.

Amenities: 24-hour room service, complimentary downtown shuttle, laundry, valet, heated indoor/outdoor pool, small fitness center, sauna, whirlpool, private marina, conference facilities for up to 150.

Harbour Towers. 345 Quebec St., Victoria, B.C. V8V 1W4. ☎ **800/663-5896** or 250/385-2405. Fax 250/385-4453. 185 units. A/C MINIBAR TV TEL. Apr 16–May 31 C$220 (US$147) double, C$278–C$520 (US$186–US$348) suite; June 1–Oct 11 C$260 (US$174) double, C$358–C$620 (US$240–US$415) suite; Oct 12–Dec 31 C$120 (US$80) double, C$218–C$520 (US$146–US$348) suite; Jan 1–Apr 15 C$180 (US$121) double, C$248–C$500 (US$166–US$335) suite. Promotional rates available. Children under 16 stay free in parents' room. Extra adult C$15 (US$10). AE, CB, DC, ER, MC, V. Underground parking C$2 (US$1.35). Bus: 30 to Superior and Oswego Sts.

Though there are a few standard rooms in this 12-story tower by the Inner Harbour, the one- and two-bedroom suites are a much better value, with fully equipped kitchens containing two-burner stoves, microwaves, and small refrigerators. Thanks to a recent renovation, the last of the 1970s decor is gone, replaced by contemporary furnishings with teal and burgundy accents. All units feature floor-to-ceiling windows opening onto private balconies. You can guarantee a harbor view by paying an extra C$15 (US$10). For C$40 (US$27) extra, the 11th-floor "Royal Treatment" suites add a continental breakfast, a newspaper, upgraded amenities, free local calls, robes, and unobstructed views. The 12th-floor deluxe penthouse suites have fireplaces and stereo systems.

Dining: Impressions Café covers the culinary bases with a slight emphasis on West Coast cuisine.

Amenities: Room service, business center, shuttle service, fitness center, spa, indoor pool, sauna, whirlpool, gift shop, meeting space for up to 300.

✪ **A Haterleigh Heritage Inn.** 243 Kingston St., Victoria, B.C. V8V 1V5. ☎ **250/384-9995.** Fax 250/384-1935. www.haterleigh.com. 6 units. TEL. C$195–C$338 (US$131–US$226) double. Rates include full breakfast. MC, V. Free parking. Bus: 30 to Superior and Montreal Sts.

Why "A Haterleigh" and not "The Haterleigh"? I've no idea. Had I gotten around to asking, I'm sure innkeeper Paul Kelly would've had an answer, for he's a font of information, on Victoria in general and on this lovingly restored 1901 home in particular. With his wife, Elizabeth, he runs this exceptional B&B that captures the essence of Victoria's romance with a combination of antique furniture, stunning stained-glass windows, and attentive personal service. The spacious rooms boast high arched ceilings, large windows, sitting areas, and enormous bathrooms with hand-painted tiles and Jacuzzi tubs. The second-floor Secret Garden room has a small balcony with stunning views of the Olympic mountain range. The Day Dreams room downstairs is the dedicated honeymoon suite, but if truth be told, all the suites make for wonderful romantic weekends. The bathrooms come with terry robes, candles, and plastic champagne flutes.

Dining: A full gourmet breakfast is served family style at 8:30am sharp. Paul likes it that way because it gives guests a chance to meet and chat. There's complimentary sherry in the drawing room each evening.

Holland House Inn. 595 Michigan St., Victoria, B.C. V8V 1S7. ☎ **250/384-6644.** Fax 250/384-6117. www.hollandhouse.victoria.bc.ca. E-mail: stay@hollandhouse.victoria.bc.ca. 17 units. TV TEL. May–Sept C$145–C$295 (US$97–US$198) double; Oct–Apr

C$100–C$250 (US$67–US$168) double. Extra person C$35 (US$23). Rates include full breakfast. Wheelchair-accessible unit available. AE, MC, V. Free parking. Bus: 5 to Superior and Government Sts.

This elegant inn provides all the amenities and comfort of a modern B&B in a classy and romantic setting. The rooms (14 in the original building, three in a new coach house connected to the inn via an atrium) are tastefully decorated, each done in a unique style. Some have wood-burning fireplaces, others balconies, large tubs, or Jacuzzis; a number have canopied beds and vaulted ceilings. The color schemes and decorations range from English country to bright and bold. Attention to detail is obvious in the lovely antique furnishings, an ongoing passion of the owners. TV and phones are available for those who can't do without. After a scrumptious breakfast served in the conservatory, step outside and you're a block behind the Legislature and Royal BC Museum and just a 5-minute walk to the Inner Harbour.

✪ **Laurel Point Inn.** 680 Montreal St., Victoria, B.C. V8V 1Z8. ☎ **800/663-7667** or 250/386-8721. Fax 250/386-9547. www.laurelpoint.com. E-mail: andersen@islandnet.com. 200 units. A/C TV TEL. June 16–Oct 15 C$195 (US$131) double, C$255 (US$171) junior suite, C$380 (US$255) bedroom suite, C$455 (US$305) full suite; Oct 16–May 15 C$130 (US$87) double, C$190 (US$127) junior suite, C$260 (US$174) bedroom suite, C$330 (US$221) full suite; May 16–June 15 C$160 (US$107) double, C$220 (US$147) junior suite, C$355 (US$238) bedroom suite, C$430 (US$288) full suite. Seasonal discounts available. Children under 12 stay free in parents' room. Wheelchair-accessible units available. AE, DC, DISC, ER, JCB, MC, V. Free parking. Bus: 30 to Montreal and Superior Sts. Pets accepted for C$25 (US$17).

Strolling through the lobby of the Laurel Point Inn is like entering an early James Bond movie. The original owners were deeply enamored of Japan, so the lobby and hotel design reflect Japanese artistic principals: elegant simplicity, blond wood surfaces, and the subtle integration of light, water, and stone. As for the James Bond part, that comes from the aura of 1970s cool. That sense of Eastern suave is heightened as you pass the little gurgling fountains on your way to the elevator; in your room you'll find a crisp cotton kimono laid out—something to slip into before stepping out onto the private terrace, with a panoramic view of the harbor and the hills. The hotel, occupying most of a promontory jutting out into the Inner Harbour, consists of a new south wing and the original north wing. Rooms in the north wing are better than many in town, but as Moneypenny might say, "Not really up to your standard, are they, James?" The south wing is where you want to be: All the rooms here are suites, featuring blond wood with black marble accents, shoji-style sliding doors, Asian artworks, and deep tubs and floor-to-ceiling glassed-in showers in the bathrooms.

Dining/Diversions: The Terrace Room serves full meals in a glassed-in atrium by a formal Japanese garden. Cafe Laurel serves casual fare. Cooke's Landing is a lounge with a view of the Inner Harbour.

Amenities: Concierge, 24-hour room service, valet, laundry, heated indoor pool, Jacuzzi, sauna, exercise bikes, gift shop, business center, meeting and banquet space for up to 250.

MODERATE

✪ **Admiral Motel.** 257 Belleville St., Victoria, B.C. V8V 1X3. ☎ **888/823-6472** or fax 250/388-6267. www.admiral.bc.ca. E-mail: resvns@admiral.bc.ca. 29 units. A/C TV TEL. May–Sept C$125–C$175 (US$84–US$117) double, C$135–C$185 (US$90–US$124) suite; Oct–Apr C$79–C$99 (US$53–US$66) double, C$89–C$109 (US$60–US$73) suite. Extra person C$10 (US$7). Children under 12 stay free in parents' room. Rates include continental breakfast. Senior, weekly, and off-season discounts available. AE, DISC, MC, V. Free parking. Bus: 5 to Belleville and Government Sts.

The family-operated Admiral is in an attractive three-story building on the Inner Harbour, near the Washington-bound ferry terminal and close to restaurants and shopping. The combination of comfortable rooms and reasonable rates attracts young couples, families, seniors, and other travelers in search of a harbor view at a price that doesn't break the bank. The rooms are pleasant and comfortably furnished, with balconies or terraces, coffeemakers, and small refrigerators. The suites come with full kitchens. Some units can sleep up to six (on two double beds and a double sofa bed). The very friendly owners provide sightseeing advice as well as extras like free bicycles, an Internet terminal in the lobby, and a self-service laundry.

Days Inn on the Harbour. 427 Belleville St., Victoria, B.C. V8V 1X3. ☎ and fax **250/ 386-3451.** www.daysinnvictoria.com. E-mail: welcome2@daysinn-vic.com. 71 units. TV TEL. May–June C$125–C$165 (US$84–US$111) double; July–Sept C$173–C$203 (US$116– US$136) double; Oct–Apr C$95–C$125 (US$64–US$84) double. Units with kitchenette C$10 (US$7) extra. Children under 12 stay free in parents' room. Off-season discounts available. AE, CB, DC, MC, V. Free parking. Bus: 5 to Belleville and Government Sts.

This newly refurbished hotel is across from the MV *Coho* ferry terminal on the edge of the Inner Harbour. It has subtle nautical decor: In the lobby is a scale model of the HMS *Royal Sovereign,* a 17th-century English vessel. The restaurant and lounge are named for the HMS *Swiftsure,* one of the last of the tall ships that served in the Pacific. Half the rooms face the Inner Harbour; the other half have views of the nearby residential area. View rooms cost a little more, but the vista's worth it. The rooms come with queen, king, or two double beds (the most expensive) and are decorated in forest-green and floral prints with comfortable modern furnishings and step-up bathtubs. Eighteen rooms are also equipped with kitchenettes. The heated outdoor pool is open only in summer, but the hot tub is open year-round. The Swiftsure Restaurant offers all meals daily, and the handsome Swiftsure Lounge serves light meals and features late-night fondues. In summer, there's an outdoor barbecue.

The Gatsby Mansion. 309 Belleville St., Victoria, B.C. V8V 1X2. ☎ **250/388-9191.** Fax 250/920-5651. www.bctravel.com/gatsby. E-mail: huntingdon@bctravel.com. 20 units. TV TEL. C$155–C$299 (US$104–US$200) double. Rates include full breakfast. Off-season discounts available. AE, JCB, MC, V. Free parking. Bus: 5 to Belleville and Government Sts.

Built in 1897, this white clapboard Victorian across from the Seattle–Port Angeles ferry has been faithfully restored to resemble a period museum, from the foyer, with its hand-painted ceramic-tiled fireplace and rich wood paneling, to the stained-glass windows and velvet tapestries. The atmosphere is that of a slightly dashing 1920s seaside resort, with frescoed ceilings supporting crystal chandeliers. The rooms feature down duvets, fine linen, and lots of Victorian antiques. Some rooms have views of the Inner Harbour, while others have private parlors.

Medana Grove Bed & Breakfast. 162 Medana St., Victoria, B.C. V8V 2H5. ☎ **800/269-1188** or 250/389-0437. Fax 250/389-0425. http://victoriabnb.com. E-mail: medanagrove@home.com. 3 units. TV. Mid-May to mid-Sept C$110–C$135 (US$74–US$90) double. Rates include gourmet breakfast. Off-season discounts available; call for rates. MC, V. Street parking. Bus: 11 to Simcoe at Menzies.

This charming 1908 James Bay district home is a short walk from downtown and the Inner Harbour. Tucked away on a tree-lined street, the Medana Grove is readily identified by the red English call box (telephone booth) on the front lawn. Friendly hosts Garry and Noreen Hunt (who once managed an orphanage in Ireland) opened the B&B in 1993. The decor reflects the early 1900s; the antique-filled living room has a welcoming fireplace and a small library. The dining room is comfortable and cheery, with just a hint of formality. The rooms are decorated in subtle floral patterns. Smoking and pets aren't permitted.

Ramada Huntingdon Manor. 330 Quebec St., Victoria, B.C. V8V 1W3. ☎ **800/663-7557** or 250/381-3456. Fax 250/382-7666. www.bctravel.com/huntingdon. E-mail: huntingdon@bctravel.com. 116 units. TV TEL. May 11–June 14 C$143–C$223 (US$96–US$149) double, June 15–Sept 26 C$163–C$243 (US$109–US$163) double, Sept 27–Oct 14 C$135–C$210 (US$90–US$141) double, Oct 15–May 10 C$87–C$177 (US$58–US$119) double. AE, JCB, MC, V. Free parking. Bus: 5 to Belleville and Government Sts.

"Dynasty" meets "Fawlty Towers." I arrived at the Huntingdon—a four-story hotel on Victoria's Inner Harbour—to find senior managers bawling out the check-in clerks. While they sorted things out, I went to grab a coffee in the restaurant, only to discover the espresso girl in emotional meltdown and yet another suited managerial type stomping angrily away. The girl looked at me with tears streaming down her cheeks and managed to marshal some shreds of professional pride. "Espresso?" she asked. A while later, a bellhop was detailed to show me the rooms. These were nice enough, if nothing special—singles, one- and two-bedroom suites, some with lofts and kitchenettes, all with dated colonial furniture. The real eye grabber was the corridors—painted a deep red, with bright-red Tartan carpeting. It was like a Stephen King version of an Englishman's club. Price-wise, the Huntingdon is quite reasonable. Should you stay there? Depends if you like melodrama. And red walls.

◆ Royal Scot Suite Hotel. 425 Quebec St., Victoria, B.C. V8V 1W7. ☎ **800/663-7515** or 250/388-5463. Fax 250/388-5452. www.royalscot.com. E-mail: royalscot@royalscot.com. 176 units. TV TEL. June–Sept C$139 (US$93) double, C$149–C$329 (US$100–US$220) suite; Oct–May C$119 (US$80) double, C$119–C$259 (US$80–US$174) suite. Weekly, monthly, and off-season rates available. AE, DC, MC, V. Free parking. Bus: 5 to Belleville and Government Sts.

A block from the Inner Harbour, the Royal Scot provides excellent value, particularly if you opt for a studio or bedroom. It was constructed as an apartment building, so the rooms are spacious (okay, huge). Each studio suite has a divider separating the bedroom from the living room, dining area, and kitchen. One-bedroom suites have separate bedrooms with king, queen, or twin beds. All suites have lots of closet space, fully equipped kitchens, complimentary refreshments, and sofa beds in the living rooms. The decor runs to pastels, pinks, and florals (this is Victoria after all). In summer, the Royal Scot fills up with families. Kids make heavy use of the game room and video arcade, which thankfully is tucked away out of earshot of other guests. In winter, the hotel is favored by retirees from the prairie provinces escaping subzero weather. The fully licensed Jonathan's restaurant offers outdoor seating in summer and serves all meals daily. Room service is available, along with valet and guest laundry. Local phone calls are free. There's also an indoor pool, a sauna, a Jacuzzi, a just-revamped fitness area, and a gift shop.

INEXPENSIVE

The James Bay Inn. 270 Government St., Victoria, B.C. V8V 2V2. ☎ **800/836-2649** or 250/384-7151. Fax 250/385-2311. www.jamesbayinn.bc.ca. E-mail: info@jamesbayinn.bc.ca. 45 units. TV TEL. May–June C$80–C$119 (US$54–US$80) double, July–Sept C$107–C$189 (US$72–US$127) double, Jan–Apr C$57–C$89 (US$38–US$60) double. AE, MC, V. Free limited parking. Bus: 5 or 30 to Niagara St.

The Inner Harbour/James Bay area isn't especially blessed with cheap digs, but this Edwardian manor on the edge of Beacon Hill Park is one of the few. Built in 1907, it was the last home of famed Victoria-born painter Emily Carr. Old-fashioned dark-wood furnishings predominate, creating an overall impression of a clean but aging fussiness. In the past year, however, the management has begun serious renovations, including new beds and TVs in the rooms, some new decor in the pub (including an

ⓘ Family-Friendly Hotels

B&Bs are typically not good places to take children. Other guests are often intent on romance, and owners are justifiably concerned about their precious antiques. The kids, on the other hand, are wondering what the big fuss about this old junk is and why can't everyone stop smooching so we can run around and have some fun. It's a clash of cultures best avoided. Most hotels welcome kids, and many let them stay for free. The ones listed below go the extra step to make kids feel welcome.

Admiral Motel *(see p. 204)*   Friendly prices, friendly management, a central location, refrigerators, and harbor views attract families year-round.

Executive House Hotel *(see p. 209)*   Lots of space, full kitchens, intelligent suite arrangements, and affordable prices make this a good bet for families.

Royal Scot Suite Hotel *(see p. 206)*   Apartment-style suites come with fully equipped kitchens, dining rooms, and living rooms.

Swan's Suite Hotel *(see p. 210)*   Duplex suites filled with homey furnishings (and full kitchens) make this small hotel a home away from home.

outdoor patio), and the creation of several luxurious rooms in an adjacent heritage home. Despite the upgrades, prices have remained relatively low, which means the inn is somewhat of a bargain. The restaurant serves all meals daily, and the adjacent neighborhood pub is popular with locals. Guests of the inn receive a 15% discount in both places.

2 Downtown & Old Town
EXPENSIVE

✪ **Abigail's Hotel.** 906 McClure St., Victoria, B.C. V8V 3E7. ☎ **800/561-6565** or 250/388-5363. Fax 250/388-7787. www.abigailshotel.com. E-mail: innkeeper@abigailshotel.com. 22 units. TEL. C$199–C$329 (US$133–US$220) double. Rates include full breakfast. Winter discounts up to 40%. AE, MC, V. Free parking. Bus: 1 to Cook and McClure Sts.

The most serious existential problem you'll face here is determining at exactly what point you slipped from semi-sensuous luxury into full decadent indulgence. It could be when you first entered your room and saw the fresh flowers in crystal vases or came across the marble fireplace with wood in place. More likely, it's when you slipped into the double Jacuzzi in your marble bathroom or nestled into your four-poster canopied bed. In a Tudor mansion just east of downtown, Abigail's began life in the 1920s as a luxury apartment house before being converted to a boutique hotel and then being taken over in the mid-1990s by Daniel Behune and his German-born wife, Frauke. Not all rooms come with all the frills, but pampering is always an objective. In the original building, some of the 16 rooms are bright and sunny and beautifully furnished, with pedestal sinks and goose-down comforters. Others boast soaker tubs and double-sided fireplaces, so you can relax in the tub by the light of the fire. The six Celebration Suites in the new Coach House addition are the apogee of indulgence.

Dining: In the main building's sunny breakfast room, the chef prepares a multi-course gourmet breakfast that may include lemon-pecan muffins, French toast with chocolate and raspberries, and eggs with champagne-and-chive sauce.

Amenities: Concierge, dry cleaning, free coffee or refreshments, gift shop, location near YMCA health club.

The Beaconsfield Inn. 998 Humboldt St., Victoria, B.C. V8V 2Z8. ☎ **888/884-4044** or 250/384-4044. Fax 250/384-4052. www.islandnet.com/beaconsfield. 9 units. TEL. May 15–June 14 C$150–C$295 (US$101–US$198) double; June 15–Sept 15 C$200–C$350 (US$134–US$235) double; Sept 16–Oct 15 C$150–C$295 (US$101–US$198) double; Oct 16–May 14 C$125–C$225 (US$84–US$151) double. Full breakfast, afternoon tea, and sherry hour included. No-smoking facility. MC, V. Free parking. Bus: 1 or 2 to Humboldt and Quadra St. Children not permitted.

Built in 1905 by Victoria's leading domestic architect, Samuel McClure, this elegantly restored Edwardian mansion now serves as a charming retreat favored by newlyweds and other incurable romantics. Just 4 blocks from downtown, the inn boasts rich mahogany paneling, antique English furnishings, hardwood floors, and delicate stained-glass window trim. The cozy library has wall-to-wall books and a welcoming fireplace. A half split of champagne, fresh flowers, and delicate chocolate truffles await you in your room upon arrival. Each lavishly decorated room and suite is unique; some have fireplaces or skylights and French doors that open onto the garden. The spacious Emily Carr Suite features a massive polished bedstead, a Jacuzzi tub within sight of the fireplace, and a chandelier above the two-person shower. Children, pets, and smoking aren't permitted.

Dining: A gourmet breakfast is served in the sunroom or the dining room, and afternoon tea (featuring self-service tea, port, sherry, scones, crème fraîche, fruit, and cheese) is served in the library.

Amenities: Concierge, complimentary umbrellas.

✪ **The Magnolia.** 623 Courtney St., Victoria, B.C. V8W 1B8. ☎ **877/624-6654** or 250/381-0999. Fax 250/381-0988. www.magnoliahotel.com. E-mail: sales@magnoliahotel. com. 66 units. A/C MINIBAR TV TEL. June 1–Oct 15 C$239–C$279 (US$160–US$187) double, C$399–C$419 (US$267–US$281) suite; Oct 16–Apr 15 C$169–C$209 (US$113–US$140) double, C$249–C$269 (US$167–US$180) suite; Apr 16–May 31 C$209–C$229 (US$140–US$153) double, C$289–C$309 (US$194–US$207) suite. Rates include continental breakfast. AE, DC, ER, JCB, MC, V. Valet parking C$10 (US$7). Bus: 5 to Courtney St.

A new boutique hotel in the center of Victoria, the Magnolia offers luxury at a reasonable price. The tiny lobby, with a fireplace, a chandelier, and overstuffed chairs, immediately conveys a sense of quality. The room decor manages to be classic without feeling frumpy, from the two-poster beds with high-quality linen and down duvets to the bathrooms with walk-in showers and deep tubs. The windows extend floor to ceiling, providing excellent harbor views from some rooms. The needs of business travelers have also been kept in mind: The work desks are well lit and large enough to spread your work out on. Two phone lines run to every room, and the phone itself is cordless. The top-floor Diamond Suite features a sitting room with a fireplace.

Dining/Diversions: The ground-floor restaurant (run by a separate company) opened first as the Capitol Steakhouse, then closed, then reopened as Hugo's Grill. It's still probably best avoided. However, the next-door Hugo's Lounge offers good beer and above-average pub food in a hip space.

Amenities: Concierge, room service, full-service Aveda spa, in-room ironing boards, secretarial service, express checkout, boardroom for up to 30.

The Victoria Regent Hotel. 1234 Wharf St., Victoria, B.C. V8W 3H9. ☎ **800/663-7472** or 250/386-2211. Fax 250/386-2622. www.victoria-regent-hotel.com. E-mail: regent@ victoria-regent-hotel.com. 48 units. MINIBAR TV TEL. May–June C$149–C$179 (US$100–US$120) double; July–Oct 17 C$179 (US$120) double, C$239–C$409 (US$160–US$274) suite; Oct 18–Apr 30 C$119–C$149 (US$80–US$100) double, C$120–C$359 (US$80–US$240) suite. Rates include continental breakfast. Wheelchair-accessible units available. AE, DC, DISC, JCB, MC, V. Free underground parking. Bus: 6, 24, or 25 at the Johnson St. Bridge to the hotel on Wharf St.

There's something vaguely seedy about the Regent's exterior. It could be the wedding-cake architecture. Or it could be that the hotel's foundation, jutting out onto the Inner Harbour, has the air of a deserted underground parking garage, late at night. Anyway, the impression doesn't carry over to the rooms and suites, which are large and comfortable, if a little dated when it comes to furnishings. The views on the harbor side are good. The beds in the suites are either king or queen, and all come with fold-out couches in the sitting room (children under 16 stay free). All the suites have full kitchens, which makes the Regent popular with visiting snowbirds in winter.

Amenities: Guest laundry, morning newspaper, baby-sitting referrals, secretarial service, meeting space for 30.

MODERATE

The Bedford Regency. 1140 Government St., Victoria, B.C. V8W 1Y2. ☎ **800/665-6500** or 250/384-6835. Fax 250/386-8930. www.victoria.bc.com/accom/bedford.html. E-mail: bedford@victoriabc.com. 40 units. TV TEL. C$165–C$250 (US$111–US$168) double. Off-season discounts available. AE, MC, V. Parking C$10 (US$7). Bus: 5 to Douglas and Johnson Sts.

One of Victoria's oldest hotels, the Bedford has undergone a tasteful renovation, bringing it up to modern standards. However, the rooms have the quirky features and intriguing layout you expect in a place with such a venerable past—all are long and thin like railway carriages. Some are pleasantly spacious, with a queen bed in a room at one end joined by a small corridor to a sitting room with a fireplace at the other; some tend toward the compact, such as the one with a bed in an alcove and pedestal sink in the room. The 12 Superior rooms have Jacuzzi tubs and fireplaces. In summer, guests in rooms facing the outdoor patios on View Street may find that a little of the noise seeps in. The Red Currant serves all meals daily in summer (breakfast and lunch only in winter) and a reasonably priced afternoon tea year-round. The Garrick's Head Pub is a friendly spot for a drink or a casual meal.

Chateau Victoria Hotel. 740 Burdett Ave., Victoria, B.C. V8W 1B3. ☎ **800/663-5891** or 250/382-4221. Fax 250/380-1950. www.chateauvictoria.com. E-mail: reservations@chateauvictoria.com. 177 units. TV TEL. May–June C$117–C$250 (US$78–US$168) double, C$275–C$300 (US$184–US$201) suite; July–Oct C$147–C$315 (US$98–US$211) double, C$295–C$315 (US$198–US$211) suite. Off-season discounts available. Children under 18 stay free in parents' room. 2 no-smoking floors available. AE, CB, DC, ER, MC, V. Free parking. Bus: 2 to Burdett Ave.

This 18-story hotel was built in 1975 on the site of the "parrot lady's" house: Victoria Jane Wilson lived in a big white manor on the hill behind The Empress. When she died in 1949, she left her house and fortune to Louis, her talking parrot, with explicit instructions that the bird remain in the house for as long as he lived. His caretaker passed on in 1966, and the estate's lawyers talked Louis into moving to a retirement home so the house could be demolished to make way for an apartment tower (Louis lasted until 1985). Because this was the original idea, the hotel's rooms and one-bedroom suites are extremely spacious; many suites have kitchenettes and all have private balconies. The decor is a bit dowdy—1970s colonial furniture, washed-out pink walls, and floral patterns everywhere—and the bathrooms were clearly built with nothing more than function in mind. Don't think luxury, but value for your money. The Parrot House, Victoria's only rooftop restaurant, offers magnificent views and is open daily for breakfast and dinner. There's a skylit indoor pool, business center, and meeting space for up to 50.

Executive House Hotel. 777 Douglas St., Victoria, B.C. V8W 2B5. ☎ **800/663-7001** or 250/388-5111. Fax 250/385-1323. http://executivehouse.com. E-mail: executivehouse@executivehouse.com. 179 units. TV TEL. C$99–C$195 (US$66–US$131) double, C$195–C$275 (US$131–US$184) suite, C$295–C$795 (US$198–US$533) penthouse rooms and suites. Extra person C$15 (US$10). 10%–50% seasonal discount, depending on availability. Children under 18 stay free in parents' room. AE, DC, JCB, MC, V. Parking C$2.15 (US$1.45) per night. Bus: 2 to the Convention Centre. Pets accepted for C$15 (US$10) per night.

You can't miss the Executive House, a concrete high-rise looming above The Empress on Old Town's east side; the 1960s-style architecture is unmistakably New World. Step inside, however, and you'll find an ambiance evoking 1880s London. If the transition—or the thought of staying in a 13-story British club—isn't too much for you, this place is really rather nice. A lot of thought went into designing the rooms, which are of better-than-average size. Some suites come with a queen bed in the bedroom and a fold-out sofa, so parents can put the kids to bed and relax on the sofa bed. Other suites have a double bed in the living room and bedroom, so business associates traveling together can economize. The furnishings are a bit fussy, but hey, it is 1880. Each penthouse-level suite has a Jacuzzi in its own little atrium, a fireplace, a garden terrace with a panoramic view, a dining table, and a fully equipped kitchen. Bartholomew's pub offers beer and light jazz, the elegant Barkley's serves steak and seafood, and the informal Caffe d'Amore offers Italian/Californian cuisine. Doubles is the singles oyster bar. There's also a full health spa with a steam room, a tanning bed, massage, and herbal wraps; plus meeting space for up to 70.

✪ **Swan's Suite Hotel.** 506 Pandora Ave., Victoria, B.C. V8W 1N6. ☎ **800/668-7926** or 250/361-3310. Fax 250/361-3491. www.swanshotel.com. 30 suites. TV TEL. C$159–C$249 (US$107–US$167) suite. Off-season discounts available. AE, DC, MC, V. Parking C$8 (US$5). Bus: 23 or 24 to Pandora Ave.

This heritage building was abandoned for years until 1988, when Victoria renaissance man (entrepreneur, art collector, and eccentric bon vivant) Michael Williams turned it into a hotel, restaurant, brew pub, and nightclub all in one. Just by the Johnson Street Bridge, it's one of Old Town's best-loved buildings. Like any great inn, Swan's is small, friendly, and charming. The suites are large, with the quirky layouts you'd expect in a heritage renovation. Many are split-level, featuring open lofts and huge exposed beams. All come with fully equipped kitchens, dining areas, living rooms, and queen-size beds. The two-bedroom suites have the space and "Upstairs, Downstairs" feel of little town houses—they're great for families, accommodating up to six comfortably. Swan's also works for business travelers—it's one of the few hotels in town with dual data ports. The original Pacific Northwest artwork is a little disappointing—high-quality stuff, but not nearly up to the avant-garde level Williams sets for himself with the pieces hung in the bar and restaurant. The fine-dining Fowl Fish Café is open daily for dinner. Swan's Pub has excellent pub grub, and the on-site Buckerfield's Brewery produces a half-dozen truly inspired lagers, ales, stouts, and bitters. In the basement, the Neptune Sound Bar features DJs and occasional live entertainment (see chapter 16).

INEXPENSIVE

The Dominion Hotel. 759 Yates St., Victoria, B.C. V8W 1L6. ☎ **800/663-6101** or 250/384-4136. Fax 250/382-6416. www.dominion-hotel.com. 101 units. TV TEL. May 1–Oct 15 C$129–C$149 (US$86–US$100) double, Oct 16–Apr 30 $65–C$85 (US$44–US$57) double. Children under 16 stay free in parents' room. AE, MC, V. Parking C$5–C$10 (US$3.35–US$7) Bus: 10, 11, or 14 to Yates St.

Victoria's oldest hotel, the Dominion opened in 1876 and recently underwent a C$7-million restoration. It's a lovely family-oriented heritage property decorated throughout the public areas with rich woods, marble floors, brass trim, and red velvet upholstery on antique chairs. The rooms have more modern appointments but maintain the flavor of times past, with ceiling fans and brass lamps. There are dozens of types of rooms. The deluxe rooms, occupying the four corners of each floor, are spacious and very comfortable. The Lettuce Patch family-style restaurant serves all meals daily. Hunters, a mesquite-grill steak house, is open for lunch and dinner daily. Room service and valet laundry are offered, and guests have the use of a health club and steam rooms.

✪ **The Strathcona Hotel.** 919 Douglas St., Victoria, B.C. V8W 2C2. ☎ **800/663-7476** or 250/383-7137. Fax 250/383-6893. www.strathconahotel.com. E-mail: reservations@ strathconahotel.com. 82 units. TV TEL. Oct–Apr C$54 (US$36) budget, C$64 (US$43) standard; May–June C$71 (US$48) budget, C$87 (US$58) standard; July–Sept C$89 (US$60) budget, C$99 (US$66) standard. AE, DC, DISC, MC, V. Free limited parking. Bus: All city routes stop within 1 block.

It's fair to say that most people come to the Strathcona for the booze. In operation since 1876, the Strath got its liquor license back when the government was freer with such things. Now the five-story entertainment complex is home to no fewer than four pubs. Pool tables, a big rooftop patio with two sand-filled beach volleyball courts, horse racing via satellite with on-site wagering, and a host of other diversions keep visitors amused. On top and to the side of all this is actually a hotel, and it's neither a dive nor the sort of place that rents by the hour. Instead, the Strathcona aims for the single independent traveler—backpackers mostly. The rooms come in a variety of configurations. Basic rooms have two twin beds, and the price is the same whether one person sleeps there or two. All rooms are well kept and secure, all that backpackers ever ask for. The Strathcona's location is superb.

✪ **Victoria International Youth Hostel.** 516 Yates St., Victoria, B.C. V8W 1K8. ☎ **250/ 385-4511.** Fax 250/385-3232. www.hihostels.bc.ca. 104 beds. International Youth Hostel members C$17 (US$11), nonmembers C$20 (US$13). Wheelchair-accessible unit available. MC, V. Parking on street. Bus: 70 from Swartz Bay ferry terminal.

The location is perfect—right in the heart of Old Town. In addition, this hostel has all the usual accoutrements, including two kitchens (stocked with utensils), a dining room, a TV lounge with VCR, a game room, a common room, a library, laundry facilities, an indoor bicycle lockup, 24-hour security, and hot showers. The dorms are on the large side (16 to a room) and segregated by gender, and a couple of family rooms are available. There's an extensive ride board, and the collection of outfitter and tour information rivals that of the tourism office. The front door is locked at 2:30am, but you can make arrangements to get in later.

YM-YWCA of Victoria. 880 Courtney St., Victoria, B.C. V8W 1C4. ☎ **250/386-7511.** Fax 250/380-1933. 17 units, 1 dorm (with 5 beds). A/C. C$20 (US$13) dorm, C$50 (US$34) double, C$35 single (US$23). MC, V. Bus: 1 to Humboldt and Blanshard Sts.

Though exercise facilities for men and women are located in this big brown-brick building, the residence is for women only. The entrance, which has a new lobby overlooking the workout area, is on the Broughton Street side. The Y has a diner (open weekdays 7:30am to 2:30pm), a pool, and a cozy TV lounge. The rooms are small and simply furnished but very well maintained. There are shared bathrooms and pay phones on each floor.

3 Outside the Central Area

EXPENSIVE

✪ **The Aerie.** 600 Ebedora Lane, P.O. Box 108, Malahat, B.C. V0R 2L0. ☎ **250/743-7115.** Fax 250/743-4766. www.aerie.bc.ca. E-mail: aerie@relaischateaux.fr. 24 units. A/C TV TEL. Apr 6–May 17 C$235–C$295 (US$157–US$198) double, C$345–C$455 (US$231–US$305) suite; May 18–Oct 31 C$285–C$325 (US$191–US$218) double, C$375–C$495 (US$251–US$332) suite; Nov 1–Apr 5 C$185–C$230 (US$124–US$154) double, C$285–C$350 (US$191–US$235) suite. Rates include 7am breakfast hamper at your door and full breakfast later. Accommodation and dinner packages available. AE, DC, MC, V. Free parking. Take Hwy. 1 to the Spectacle Lake turnoff; take the first right and follow the winding driveway up.

On a forested mountain slope by a fjord about half an hour from town, this Mediterranean-inspired villa was designed, built, and decorated by Marie Schuster, an Austrian hotelier with gobs of money and unlimited self-confidence. For some, it's the very picture of paradise. For others, the result is a tad over the top. The setting is certainly spectacular and the view over Finlayson Inlet unsurpassed. Inside, no expense has been spared: Dior bedcovers and duvets on gargantuan four-poster beds, overstuffed white leather couches in front of gas or wood fireplaces, carved gilt mirrors on the walls, and Persian carpets on the floors. The Aerie offers six room configurations; all but the standard rooms include a soaker tub for two, and as you move up into the master and residence suites you get private decks and fireplaces.

Dining: An excellent French-inspired West Coast cuisine is served in the dining room, which offers 180° views of the ocean and mountain (see chapter 12). It's open to the public only for dinner.

Amenities: Helipad, heated indoor pool, outdoor hot tub, tennis courts (rackets and balls available), full spa treatments, outdoor wedding chapel, conference facilities for 20, room service available upon request.

Oak Bay Beach Hotel. 1175 Beach Dr., Victoria, B.C. V8S 2N2. ☎ **800/668-7758** or 250/598-4556. Fax 250/598-6180. www.oakbaybeachhotel.com. E-mail: reservations@oakbaybeachhotel.bc.ca. 50 units. TV TEL. C$225–C$340 (US$151–US$228) double, C$340–C$450 (US$228–US$302) suite. Off-season discounts. Individual packages available through "Build your own package" system. AE, DC, MC, V. Free parking. Bus: 2 to Newport and Margate Sts.

This Tudor-style mansion, set in an extensive garden, is perched on the edge of Haro Strait overlooking the San Juan Islands. The furnishings and decor recall 1930s beach resorts in Brighton. For that reason, perhaps, the hotel is extremely popular with retirees and other elderly travelers. The lobby is a huge living room that features a century-old baby grand piano, Edwardian and Victorian antiques, and a big fireplace. Priced according to size and view, the large rooms are decorated with antique British furnishings and offer bay windows and private balconies overlooking the waterfront. The second-floor fireplace suites are the best choice.

Dining: The Snug is a British pub popular with professors and students from nearby U. Vic.

Amenities: Room service, valet, laundry, morning coffee and newspaper, evening hot chocolate and cookies, complimentary shuttle service.

✪ **Sooke Harbour House.** 1528 Whiffen Spit Rd., Sooke, B.C. V0S 1N0. ☎ **250/642-3421.** Fax 250/628-6988. www.sookeharbourhouse.com. E-mail: shh@islandnet.com. 28 units. TEL. May–June and Oct C$200–C$329 (US$134–US$220) midweek double, C$280–C$460 (US$188–US$308) weekend double; July–Sept C$212–C$365 (US$142–US$245) midweek double, C$297–C$512 (US$199–US$343) weekend double; Nov–Apr C$125–C$211 (US$84–US$141) midweek double, C$175–C$395 (US$117–US$265) weekend double. Rates include full breakfast and picnic lunch. AE, ER, JCB, MC, V. Free parking. Take the Island Hwy. (Hwy. 1) to the Sooke/Colwood turnoff (Junction Hwy. 14). Follow Hwy. 14 to Sooke. About 1.6km (1 mile) past the town's only traffic light, turn left onto Whiffen Spit Rd.

This little inn/restaurant, at the end of a sand spit about 30 kilometers (19 miles) west of Victoria, has earned an international reputation thanks to the care lavished on the guests and rooms by owners Frederique and Phillip Sinclair. Frederique looks after the rooms, sumptuously furnishing and decorating each according to a particular Northwest theme. The Herb Garden room, looking out over a garden of fragrant herbs and edible flowers, is done in pale shades of mint and parsley. The large split-level Thunderbird room is a veritable celebration of First Nations culture, with books, carvings, totems, and masks, including one of a huge Thunderbird. Thanks to some clever architecture, all the rooms are awash in natural light and have fabulous ocean views. In addition, all boast wood-burning fireplaces and sitting areas, all but one have sundecks, and most have Jacuzzis or soaker tubs. The other half of the Harbour House's reputation comes from the outstanding cooking of Sinclair Philip.

Dining: Sooke Harbour House has one of the best restaurants in the area, perhaps in all of Canada (see chapter 12).

Amenities: Massage therapist by appointment, in-room breakfast, optional in-room dinner, baby-sitting referrals, newspaper.

MODERATE

✪ **The Boathouse.** 746 Sea Dr., RR 1, Victoria, B.C. VM8 1B1. ☎ **250/652-9370.** www. members.home.net/boathouse. E-mail: boathouse@home.com. 1 unit. TEL. C$175 (US$117) double. Rate includes continental breakfast. MC, V. Free parking. Bus: 75 to Wallace St. and Benvenuto Ave.

It's a short row (or a 25-min. walk) to Butchart Gardens from this secluded red cottage in Brentwood Bay, a converted boathouse on pilings over the Saanich Inlet. The only passersby you're likely to encounter are seals, bald eagles, otters, herons, and raccoons. The cottage is at the end of a very long flight of stairs behind the owner's home. Inside are a new queen bed, a dining table, a kitchen area with a small refrigerator and toaster oven, an electric heater, and a reading alcove overlooking the floating dock. Toilet and shower facilities are in a separate bathhouse, 17 steps back uphill. All the makings for a delicious continental breakfast are provided in the evening, plus free coffee and newspaper delivery. You have use of a private dinghy, a sundeck, a beach, and nature trails.

Dashwood Manor. 1 Cook St., Victoria, B.C. V8V 3W6. ☎ **800/667-5517** or 250/385-5517. Fax 250/383-1760. www.dashwoodmanor.com. E-mail: reservations@dashwoodmanor.com. 14 suites. TV. June–Sept C$175–C$385 (US$117–US$258) suite, Nov–Mar C$70–C$215 (US$47–US$144) suite, Apr–May and Oct C$80–C$285 (US$54–US$191) suite. Extra person C$45 (US$30). AE, DC, MC, V. Free parking. Bus: 5 to Dallas Rd and Cook St.

This cozy Tudor manor, built in 1912 and renovated in 1994, looks south over the Strait of Juan de Fuca toward the Olympic Mountains. The beach is just across Dallas Street, one of the most scenic drives in Victoria, and Beacon Hill Park borders the manor on the west. Downtown is a 20-minute stroll away, but the walk through the park is worth it. The lobby is an Edwardian showcase, with deep-stained oak paneling and burgundy carpeting. Each unique suite has a queen-size bed and a well-stocked kitchen (breakfast foods and coffee service are self-catered). Selected suites have fireplaces, Jacuzzis, balconies, or perhaps chandeliers. The basement suites are the least expensive but should be avoided. Stay upstairs to enjoy the view. Complimentary sherry, port, and wine are laid out in the lobby in the evenings.

INEXPENSIVE

Point-No-Point Resort. 1505 West Coast Hwy. (Hwy. 14), Sooke, B.C. V0S 1N0. ☎ **250/ 646-2020.** Fax 250/646-2294. www.pointnopointresort.com. 25 units. C$95–C$190 (US$64–US$127) cabin. AE, MC, V. Free parking. No public transit.

Away from it all in your own little cabin, you'll have 40 acres of wilderness around you and a wide rugged beach in front of you, with nothing to do but laze away the day in your hot tub. Or walk the beach. Or the forest. Or look at an eagle. Or three. That's Point-No-Point. Since 1950 this oceanfront resort has been welcoming guests, first to a pair of tiny cabins, now to 24 units. Cabins vary depending on when they were built. All have fireplaces, full kitchens, and bathrooms; newer ones have hot tubs on their private decks. Food isn't included in the price, so come prepared. Lunch and high tea are available daily at the small but sunny central dining room. Dinner is served Wednesday to Sunday. The dining-room tables are conveniently equipped with binoculars, so you won't miss a bald eagle as you eat.

University of Victoria. Housing, Food, and Conference Services. P.O. Box 1700, Sinclair at Finerty Rd., Victoria, B.C. V8W 2Y2. ☎ **250/721-8395.** Fax 250/721-8930. www. hfcs.uvic.ca/uvichfcs.htm. 898 units. May–Aug C$38 (US$25) single, C$50 (US$34) twin, C$146 (US$98) suite. Discounts available for longer stays. Room rates include full breakfast and taxes; suite rates include taxes. Closed Sept–Apr. Parking C$5 (US$3.35). Bus: 4 or 14 to University of Victoria.

One of the best deals going is when Victoria's major university opens its dorms to summer visitors when classes aren't in session. All rooms have single or twin beds and basic furnishings, and there are bathrooms, pay phones, and TV lounges on every floor. Linens, towels, and soap are provided. The suites are an extremely good value—each has four bedrooms, a kitchen, a living room, and 1½ bathrooms. The disadvantage, of course, is that the U. Vic. campus is a painfully long way from everywhere—the city center is about a half-hour drive away. For C$5 (US$3.35) extra per day, however, you can make use of the many on-campus athletic facilities. Each of the 28 buildings has a coin laundry.

Where to Dine in Victoria

12

Though early Victoria settlers were intent on re-creating a little patch of the Old Country on their wild western island, the one thing they were never tempted to import was British cooking. Thankfully. Instead, following the traditional Canadian norm, each little immigrant group imported its own cuisine, so that now Victoria is a cornucopia of culinary styles from around the world. With over 700 restaurants in the area, there's something for every taste and wallet. (The one aspect of English cuisine Victoria did import was the quaint but delicious custom of afternoon tea. American visitors in particular should give it a try—you'll never go back to lukewarm water with a tea bag on the side.)

In Victoria, keep one good rule of thumb in mind: You can have good food or you can have a view, but (with few exceptions) you can't have both. The touristy restaurants along Wharf Street serve up mediocre food for folks they know they'll never have to see again. The canny visitor knows to head inland (even a block's enough) where the proportion of tourists to locals drops precipitously and the quality jumps by leaps and bounds.

Another thing to keep in mind is that Victorians time their dinner to the setting of the sun. Try for a seat at 7pm and the restaurant will be packed. Try at 9pm and it'll be empty. Try at 10pm and it'll be closed, especially on weekdays. Reservations are strongly recommended for prime sunset seating during summer.

There's no provincial tax on restaurant meals in British Columbia, just the 7% federal goods and services tax (GST). Tipping is the standard North American 15% to 20%, calculated on the pretax bill.

1 Restaurants by Cuisine

BAKERY
Q V Bakery & Café (p. 224)

BISTRO
Cassis Bistro (p. 220)
Süze Lounge and Restaurant (p. 222)

CHINESE
Don Mee Restaurant (p. 223)
J&J Wonton Noodle House (p. 224)

CONTINENTAL
The Marina Restaurant (p. 226)
Pablo's Dining Lounge (p. 218)

DELI
Sam's Deli (p. 224)

ENGLISH

James Bay Tea Room & Restaurant
(p. 218)

FISH & CHIPS

Barb's Place (p. 219)

FRENCH

The Aerie (p. 225)
Deep Cove Chalet (p. 226)

GREEK

Millos (p. 222)

INDIAN

Da Tandoor (p. 220)

ITALIAN

Cafe Brio (p. 219)
Il Terrazzo Ristorante (p. 220)
Med Grill (p. 222)
Pagliacci's (p. 222)

MEXICAN

Café Mexico (p. 223)

PASTA

Herald Street Caffe (p. 221)

PUB GRUB

Harbour Canoe Club (p. 225)
Hugo's Brewpub (p. 225)

SEAFOOD

The Blue Crab Bar and Grill (p. 216)
Chandler's Seafood Restaurant
(p. 218)
Pescatore's Fish House and Piano Bar
(p. 218)

TEA

Butchart Gardens Dining Room
Restaurant (p. 221)
The Empress Tea Lobby (p. 221)
Point Ellice House (p. 221)

THAI

Siam Thai Restaurant (p. 225)

VEGETARIAN

Green Cuisine (p. 224)
Re-bar (p. 224)

WEST COAST (PACIFIC NORTHWEST)

Cafe Brio (p. 219)
Camille's (p. 219)
Herald Street Caffe (p. 221)
Sooke Harbour House (p. 226)
The Victorian Restaurant (p. 218)

Six Mile Pub (p. 227)
Spinnaker's Brew Pub (p. 225)
Swan's Pub (p. 225)

2 The Inner Harbour

EXPENSIVE

✪ **The Blue Crab Bar and Grill.** 146 Kingston St., in the Coast Hotel. ☎ **250/480-1999.** Reservations recommended. Main courses C$19–C$30 (US$13–US$20). AE, DC, ER, MC, V. Daily 6:30am–10pm (open for dinner at 5pm). Bus 30 to Erie St. SEAFOOD.

Victoria's best seafood spot, the Blue Crab combines fresh ingredients, inventive recipes, and beautiful presentation. It also has a killer view—floatplanes slip in and out while you're dining, little ferries chug across the harbor, and the sun sets slowly over the Sooke Hills. After you've had a chance to check out the understated elegance of the room and perhaps chose from the extensive selection of excellent B.C. wines (by the bottle and glass), peruse the chalkboard of daily seafood specials. What's on the board is entirely dependent on what came in on the boats or floatplanes that day— salmon, spotted prawns, and crab in season are strong possibilities. Occasionally, little Salt Spring Island lambs are on offer. The chef is particularly fond of unusual combinations: sea bass with taro root, grapefruit, and blood orange or foie gras with raspberries. And how about house-smoked chicken sausage in portobello-mushroom broth or tenderloin with Indonesian *pindasaus* (peanut sauce)? The service is deft, smart, and obliging.

LEGEND

i Information

0 — 1/2 Mi
0 — .5 Km

Barb's Place **25**
The Blue Crab Bar & Grill **24**
Cafe Brio **15**
Café Mexico **5**
Camille's **11**
Cassis Bistro **18**
Chandler's Seafood Restaurant **7**
Da Tandoor **17**
Don Mee Restaurant **2**
Green Cuisine **4**
Herald Street Caffe **1**
Il Terrazo Ristorante **6**
James Bay Tea Room & Restaurant **22**
J&J Wonton Noodle House **16**
Med Grill **14**
Millos **19**
Pablo's Dining Lounge **23**
Pagliacci's **13**
Pescatore's Fish House & Piano Bar **20**
Q V Bakery & Café **3**
Re-bar **10**
Sam's Deli **21**
Siam Thai Restaurant **12**
Süze Lounge & Restaurant **9**
The Victorian Restaurant **8**

Pablo's Dining Lounge. 25 Quebec St. ☎ **250/388-4255.** Reservations recommended. Main courses C$14–C$29 (US$9–US$19). AE, MC, V. Daily 5pm to around 11pm. Bus: 30. CONTINENTAL.

Pablo Hernandez's paella Valenciana—saffron rice baked with a medley of meats, seafood, and vegetables—has been a favorite for nearly 20 years. This intimate restaurant is in an Edwardian house near Laurel Point. Special dinners for two include rack of Salt Spring Island lamb and chateaubriand *forestière* (with mushrooms). Or try a classic French seafood dish (the border between French and Spanish cuisines becomes a little fuzzy at Pablo's, but the fusion produces excellent results). Wednesday to Saturday, a guitar player does a muted version of the Gypsy Kings while you sip Spanish coffee and nibble flambéed crepes and ice cream.

The Victorian Restaurant. 45 Songhees Rd., in the Ocean Pointe Resort. ☎ **250/ 360-2999.** www.oprhotel.com. Reservations recommended. Main courses C$14–C$29 (US$9–US$19). AE, MC, V. Daily 11am–10:30pm. Bus: 24 to Colville. WEST COAST.

One of the only good bets when it comes to waterfront dining in Victoria is this elegant restaurant in the Ocean Pointe Resort. The views are tremendous, and in recent years the food has begun to win some recognition, including awards from *Wine Spectator* and *Western Living* magazines. In culinary terms, the chef takes few risks, sticking to fresh ingredients with a slight emphasis on seafood but enough lamb, steak, and veggie dishes to cover all the bases. The service is polished and the wine list one of the better ones in town.

MODERATE

Chandler's Seafood Restaurant. 1250 Wharf St. ☎ **250/385-3474.** Reservations recommended. Main courses C$15–C$24 (US$10–US$16). AE, DC, MC, V. Daily noon–10pm. Bus: 23 or 24. SEAFOOD.

If you're absolutely set on dining on the Wharf Street waterfront, Chandler's is the best bet. In an 1896 warehouse next door to the Victoria Regent Hotel, Chandler's interior is pleasantly nautical, with big windows looking over the seaplane docks and Inner Harbour. The seafood cuisine is workmanlike—a step and a half up from good pub grub. (Chandler's claims as Victoria's "best seafood restaurant" should be taken with a large grain of sea salt.) Dishes include salmon in teriyaki glaze; pasta with lobster; seafood brochettes with halibut, salmon, and prawns; Dungeness crab; and herb-crusted rack of lamb.

James Bay Tea Room & Restaurant. 332 Menzies St. ☎ **250/382-8282.** Reservations recommended. Main courses C$13–C$16 (US$9–US$11); tea C$7 (US$4.70). AE, MC, V. Mon–Sat 7am–8pm, Sun 8am–8pm. Tea service offered all day. Bus: 5 or 30. ENGLISH.

This cozy spot wouldn't win awards for best afternoon tea, but for most authentic, you've got a case. Like the mother country herself, this teahouse is slowly going to seed. Still, must keep a stiff upper lip and all that. The countless knickknacks and portraits of English monarchs give a real taste of the old country. So, too, does the food. Tarts and scones with cream and jam are edible, the piping-hot tea potable. The sandwiches are best avoided. A better bet are the breakfasts, with omelets or eggs and kippers, hash browns, muffins, and lots of weak brown coffee. For dinner there are Cornish pasties, mixed grill (lamb chop, liver, sausage, bacon, onions, and tomato), and roast prime rib of beef with Yorkshire pudding. The service is deft and friendly.

Pescatore's Fish House and Piano Bar. 614 Humboldt St., across from The Empress. ☎ **250/920-4846.** www.pescatores.com. Reservations recommended. Main courses C$11–C$24 (US$7–US$16). AE, DC, JCB, MC, V. Daily 11am to around 11pm. SEAFOOD.

ⓘ Family-Friendly Restaurants

Barb's Place *(see p. 219)*   Old-style fish-and-chips, complete with the newspaper wrapper. The food is fun, can be eaten with fingers or fed surreptitiously to the seagulls, and the wharf is a great place for kids to run around and make noise.

Millos *(see p. 222)*   Victoria's best Greek restaurant offers a children's menu, lively and friendly waiters who love kids, and new tastes.

Re-bar *(see p. 224)*   Healthy finger-friendly food, a fun and funky downstairs room decorated with a collection of cake tins that just seems to keep growing, and an affordable list of goodies make Re-bar a great bet for a pick-me-up snack or supper.

For a town surrounded by an ocean literally teeming with fish, Victoria is surprisingly lacking in good seafood restaurants—as if residents were somehow wary of provoking Neptune's wrath. Fortunately there's Pescatore's for those with no such hang-ups. The food in this Italian-influenced restaurant floats somewhere between good and very good. The grand ceilings and striking wall paintings by local artist Luis Merino set the ambiance, and the well-stocked oyster bar will grab your attention. Get past that and you're in danger of getting caught by the lunch specials, including items like prawns, crab cakes, and lushly creamy seafood bisques. Come supper time, the menu expands to include scallops, trout, and salmon. There are also burgers and New York strip loin.

INEXPENSIVE

✪ **Barb's Place.** 310 St. Lawrence St. ☎ **250/384-6515.** Reservations not accepted. Menu items C$2.25–C$9 (US$1.50–US$6). No credit cards. Daily 7am–sunset. FISH-&-CHIPS.

The best "chippie" in town, Barb serves lightly breaded halibut and hand-hewn chips served in folded-newspaper pouches from a floating restaurant at Fisherman's Wharf. There are picnic tables to sit on and boats and seagulls and lots of other eye candy to amuse the kids. Barb's is a favorite among locals.

3 Downtown & Old Town

EXPENSIVE

✪ **Cafe Brio.** 944 Fort St. ☎ **250/383-0009.** www.cafe-brio.com. Reservations recommended. Main courses C$13–C$25 (US$9–US$17). AE, MC, V. Tues–Sat 11:30am–2pm; daily 5:30pm–closing. WEST COAST/ITALIAN.

Still Victoria's most exciting restaurant after 5 years, Cafe Brio is a collaboration between restaurateurs Sylvia Marcolini and Greg Hays (who together created the Herald Street Caffe and the revamped Marina) and noted West Coast chef Sean Brennan. The result is a Tuscan-influenced cuisine strongly reflecting the seasons, the availability of fresh local produce, and Brio's location on the edge of the Pacific. Appetizers may include potato-crusted Alaskan scallops with heirloom tomatoes, purple basil, and crème fraîche, while entrees may feature seared ahi tuna with mushroom pave and pinot-noir sauce, venison, duck, and free-range chicken. The wine list is excellent, with an impressive selection of B.C. and international reds and whites. The service is deft and knowledgeable. Brennan will keep the kitchen open as long as guests keep ordering.

✪ **Camille's.** 45 Bastion Sq. ☎ **250/381-3433.** www.camillesrestaurant.com. E-mail: camilles@pacificcoast.net. Reservations recommended. Main courses C$19–C$29 (US$13–US$19). AE, MC, V. Daily 5:30–10pm. WEST COAST.

The most romantic of Victoria's restaurants, Camille's is seductively tucked away in a two-room enclave beneath the old Law Chambers. The decor contrasts blinding white linen with century-old exposed brick, stained-glass lamps, antique books, and old wine bottles. The ever-changing menu is Mediterranean meets West Coast—European dishes made with the freshest and finest local ingredients. Seasonal dishes include smoked salmon pinwheels with avocado and horseradish cream and Salt Spring pork tenderloin with clams baked with sherry, paprika, and caramelized apples. Fillet of salmon and delicate roasted rack of lamb are perennial specialties. The reasonable and extensive wine list comes with liner notes that are amusing and informative. On Sundays, wine tastings introduce you to the best cellar selections.

Cassis Bistro. 253 Cook St. ☎ **250/384-1932.** Reservations recommended. Main courses C$13–C$23 (US$9–US$15). MC, V. Daily 5:30–9:30pm; Sun brunch 10am–2pm. BISTRO/ITALIAN.

In Cook Village, just off Beacon Hill Park, this neighborhood bistro has been making quite a name for itself. If you have time, the neighborhood is worth a stroll, but if you have come straight for the food, you're in the right place: The cozy candlelit room is the perfect place to end your day of sightseeing. The owner describes the menu as eclectic Italian, but there are also some French and Moroccan influences, notably in the Harissa sauce served with the halibut. The menu changes frequently; the restaurant is still young and experimenting with different flavors. Considering how well they're doing now, time will only improve things. The emphasis is on fresh ingredients and lots of seafood. The tapas are a great way to mix and match various dishes. Leave some room for dessert—who can resist a chocolate brownie with roasted banana ice cream?

✪ **Il Terrazzo Ristorante.** 555 Johnson St., off Waddington Alley. ☎ **250/361-0028.** www.ilterrazzo.com. Reservations recommended. Main courses C$15–C$31 (US$10–US$21). AE, MC, V. Mon–Sat 11:30am–3:30pm; daily 5–10:30pm. Bus: 5. ITALIAN.

This quirky, charming spot in a converted heritage building off Waddington Alley is always a top contender for Victoria's best Italian restaurant. The food hails from northern Italy—think wood-oven–roasted meats and pizzas as well as homemade pastas—but there's also an emphasis on fresh produce and local seafood. Thus do we have appetizers like thinly sliced smoked tuna over fresh arugula with horseradish dressing and potato pancakes and entrees like linguine with prawns, mussels, clams, calamari, and tomatoes in a white wine/saffron broth. The atmosphere is bustling and upbeat, with the exposed brick walls, wood beams, and intriguing nooks and crannies offering extra spice. And not surprisingly, given the name, Il Terrazzo indulges those who love patio dining—the courtyard not only is romantically furnished with flowers, marble tables, and wrought-iron chairs, but also has warming heaters for when nights grow colder. That and a good Chianti and a piping hot pizzetta are enough to keep even the fiercest chill at bay.

MODERATE

Da Tandoor. 1010 Fort St. ☎ **250/384-6333.** Reservations recommended. Main courses C$9–C$17 (US$6–US$11); combination dinners C$14–C$21 (US$9–US$14). MC, V. Mon–Fri 5–10pm, Sat–Sun 5–10:30pm. INDIAN.

The best of Victoria's several Indian restaurants, Da Tandoor hides itself behind an unprepossessing facade on the outer edge of Fort Street's antiques row. The cuisine, however, is well worth the 10-minute walk from downtown. Tandoori chicken, seafood, and lamb are the house specialties, but the extensive menu also includes masalas, vindaloos, goshts, and vegetarian dishes, as well as classic appetizers like

Taking Afternoon Tea

Okay, so it's expensive and touristy. Go anyway. Far from a simple beverage, afternoon tea is both a meal and a ritual. The pot is warmed, the water poured over the tea leaves is boiling hot. The sweet and subtle flavor will almost certainly put you off the warm-water-and-tea-bag thing for life. While you sip, trays of cucumber, smoked salmon, or watercress sandwiches come by, plus scones with butter and the freshest berry preserves. Pick up a cup and adopt a posture of unshakable confidence.

Any number of places in Victoria serve afternoon tea (some also refer to high tea—both come with sandwiches and berries and tarts, but high tea usually includes some more substantial savory fare such as a pasty). All serve up something better than the pale liquid Americans call tea. Still, though the caloric intake at a top-quality tea can be substantial, it's really about the ritual of it all. For that reason you don't want to go to any old teahouse, but a place where you could be sipping with the Marquess of Pomp and the Lord of Circumstance. Note that in summer, afternoon tea becomes highly popular. Consider booking at least a week ahead, if not longer.

If you want the experience, you may as well do it right and go for the best. **The Empress hotel,** 721 Government St. (☎ **250/384-8111**), bus 5 to the Convention Centre, serves tea in the Palm Court or in the main lounge—both are beautifully ornate and luxurious. For C$42 (US$28) (C$32/US$21 Nov through Mar), the Empress will pamper and spoil you shamelessly: fresh berries and cream; sandwiches of smoked salmon, cucumber, and carrot and ginger; scones, strawberry preserves, and thick Jersey cream. Even the tea is a special house blend. When you leave you receive a package to brew at home. There are four seatings a day: 12:30pm, 2pm, 2:30pm, and 5pm.

More affordable and just as historic is tea on the lawn of **Point Ellice House,** 2616 Pleasant St. (☎ **250/380-6506**), where the creme of Victoria society used to gather on pleasant afternoons in the early 1900s. On the Gorge waterway, Point Ellice is just a 5-minute trip by harbor ferry from the Inner Harbour, or take bus 14 to Pleasant St. Afternoon tea costs C$17 (US$11) and includes a half-hour tour of the mansion and gardens, plus the opportunity to play a game (or two) of croquet. Open daily 10am to 4:30pm April 1 through Labour Day (first Mon of Sept.); phone ahead for Christmas hours.

With impeccably maintained and groomed gardens as a backdrop, "Afternoon Tea at the Gardens," at the **Butchart Gardens Dining Room Restaurant,** 800 Benvenuto Ave. (☎ **250/652-4422**), bus 75, is a memorable experience. Looking out over the flowers, you can sit back and savor this fine tradition at C$25 (US$17) per person. Tea is served daily from noon to 4pm April 1 through Labour Day (first Mon of Sept.). The rest of the year open for group bookings only (min. of 20 people), with reservations only.

vegetable and meat samosas, pakoras, and papadums. If you get inspired to try it at home, the restaurant sells a wide variety of spices and chutneys.

✪ **Herald Street Caffe.** 546 Herald St. ☎ **250/381-1441.** Reservations required. Main courses C$11–C$20 (US$7–US$13). AE, ER, MC, V. Wed–Sat 11:30am–2:30pm, Sun brunch 10am–3pm; Sun–Thurs 5:30–11pm, Fri–Sat 5:30pm–2am. Bus: 5. PASTA/WEST COAST.

An old warehouse on the far side of Chinatown, this cafe sizzles from midweek onward with the sound of diners young and old. The room is large, its walls painted a warm red and covered with an ever-changing display of local art. This is a fun place to dine and drink, so perhaps the first order of business is a martini—the menu comes with a list of more than 20. For oenophiles, the wine list is divided about evenly between bottles from France and Canada, with quite a good selection of B.C. reds and whites, many available by the glass. The cuisine is sophisticated without going too far over the top. Appetizers may include barbecued duck in phyllo pastry with apple-current chutney or oysters in cornmeal crust on a nest of new potatoes. The entrees are equally inventive, including many clever seafood dishes; for those averse to the ocean, there's also delicious free-range chicken, duck and lamb dishes, and a whole page of pastas. Portions are generous and the service is knowledgeable and helpful, particularly when it comes to wine pairings. Don't miss the Boca Negra (a chocolate cake with rich chocolate bourbon sauce and fresh raspberries) for dessert.

Med Grill. 1010 Yates St. ☎ **250/360-1660.** www.medgrillfood.com. Reservations recommended. Main courses C$8–C$18 (US$5–US$12). AE, MC, V. Sun–Wed 11am–10pm, Thurs–Sat 11am–11pm. ITALIAN.

The dining room is done up with wrought iron, an open fire, and little indoor trees, and there's a great patio. The food is casual and above average, featuring West Coast ingredients cooked up in a kind of fusion-y Italian style. Think wraps with ginger- and garlic-infused chicken with wasabi, aioli, and hoisin dipping sauce, cedar-roasted salmon, or tiger prawns with mushrooms, red peppers, Pernod-scented cream sauce, and fresh Parmesan. The servings are substantial, making the Med a good value. And the juice bar is both fun and healthy. Talk about West Coast.

✪ **Millos.** 716 Burdett Ave. ☎ **250/382-4422.** Reservations recommended. Main courses C$10–C$30 (US$7–US$20). AE, DC, MC, V. Mon–Sat 11:30am–11pm, Sun 4:30–11pm. Bus: 5. GREEK.

Millos isn't hard to find—look for the blue-and-white windmill behind The Empress or listen for the hand clapping and plate breaking as diners get into the swing of things. Flaming *saganaki* (a sharp cheese sautéed in olive oil and flambéed with Greek brandy), grilled halibut souvlaki, baby back ribs, and succulent grilled salmon are a few of the menu items at this lively five-level restaurant. Kids get their own menu. Folk dancers and belly dancers highlight the entertainment on Friday and Saturday nights, and the wait staff is remarkably warm and entertaining at all times.

✪ **Pagliacci's.** 1011 Broad St. ☎ **250/386-1662.** Reservations not accepted. Main courses C$11–C$19 (US$7–US$13). AE, MC, V. Sun–Thurs 11:30am–11pm, Fri–Sat 11:30am–midnight, light menu 3–6pm. ITALIAN.

Victoria's night owls come here. Opened in 1979 by expatriate New Yorker Howie Siegal, Pagliacci's has an un-Victorian kind of big city buzz and energy. Tables jostle up against one another as guests ogle one another's food and eavesdrop on one another's conversations while Howie works the room, dispensing a word or two to long-lost friends, many of whom he's only just met. The menu is southern Italian—veal parmigiana, tortellini, and 19 or 20 other à la carte pastas, all fresh and made by hand, many quite inventive. The service isn't blindingly fast, but when you're having this much fun, who cares? Grab some wine, munch some steaming focaccia, and enjoy the atmosphere. Sunday to Wednesday there's live jazz, swing, blues, or Celtic starting at 8:30pm. On Sunday, Howie hosts a very good brunch.

✪ **Süze Lounge and Restaurant.** 515 Yates St. ☎ **250/383-2829.** Main courses C$9–C$17 (US$6–US$11). AE, DC, MC, V. Daily 11:30am–2am. BISTRO.

Finding High-Octane Coffee

Good coffee is one of the necessities of life—it should be one of the four basic food groups. Fortunately, Victoria's Englishness hasn't stopped it from gleefully throwing itself into the same coffee-craze that's engulfing the rest of the Pacific Northwest.

Starbucks has any number of outposts here. The one at the corner of Fort and Blanshard Streets (☎ **250/383-6208**) is fairly central, open 6am to 11pm Sunday through Thursday and 6am to midnight Friday and Saturday, bus 5 to Fort St. Better for taste and with interesting hand-painted mugs is **Torrefazione,** 1234 Government St. (☎ **250/920-7203**), open Monday through Saturday 6:30am to 10pm, Sunday 6:30am to 7pm, bus 5 to View St. Out in Cook Street Village, the **Moka House,** 345 Cook St. (☎ **250/388-7377**), open daily 6am to midnight, offers a good brew, great desserts, and deli-style snacks, as well as a pleasant sunlit place to sit. Bus 5 to Cook and Mary St. For a more bohemian crowd, go to the **Demitasse Coffee Bar,** 1320 Blanshard St. (☎ **250/386-4422**). Lattes, mochas, dark rich java, and more elaborate concoctions all come in big mugs, allowing plenty of sipping time to peruse the avant-garde art on the walls. Open Monday to Friday 7am to 7pm, Saturday to Sunday 9am to 5pm. Bus 5 to Douglas Rd and Johnson St.

This fun and happening little lounge is in the heart of the Old Town. The owner's intent was to create the perfect spot for a first date—little tables on their own but not so isolated that escape is impossible, and lots of background noise and eye candy in case you get bored with the one what brung ya. The crowd is young, moneyed, and generally good-looking. The menu—covering a huge swath of territory, from dim sum and sushi bento boxes to herb-crusted salmon and pizza and pasta and fusion-y Thai noodle dishes—has made great strides since Süze fired its last chef and brought in Toronto-trained Gordon O'Neil. The quality is now consistently high. Süze is also one of the few—and possibly the most fun—spots for late-night dining in Victoria.

INEXPENSIVE

Café Mexico. 1425 Store St. ☎ **250/386-1425.** www.coastnet.com/~cafemexico. Main courses C$7–C$15 (US$4.70–US$10). AE, MC, V. Mon–Sat 11am–11pm, Sun 11am–10pm. MEXICAN.

Bullfighting and Dos Equis posters decorate the walls of this Market Square cantina, where you can get all the usuals—enchiladas, tacos, burritos, chimichangas, and fajitas—served with verve and big pitchers of sangria. The Vista del Mar (a grilled flour tortilla topped with prawns and scallops in wine-cream sauce and covered with melted cheese, avocado, and sour cream) is a favorite special. If you're looking for just a light bite, nibble on some nachos as Latin music plays in the background.

✪ Don Mee Restaurant. 538 Fisgard St. ☎ **250/383-1032.** Reservations accepted. Main courses C$9–C$14 (US$6–US$9); 4-course dinner from C$14 (US$9). AE, DC, MC, V. Daily 11am–10pm. Bus: 5. CANTONESE/SZECHUAN.

Since the 1920s, elegant Don Mee's has been serving Victoria's best dim sum, chop suey, and chow mein, along with piquant Szechuan seafood dishes and delectable Cantonese sizzling platters. You can't miss this second-story restaurant, for a huge neon Chinese lantern looms above the small doorway. A 4-foot-tall gold-leaf laughing Buddha greets you at the foot of the stairs leading up to the huge dining room, where, if it's lunchtime, you'll find many Chinese-Canadian businesspeople munching away. The dinner specials are particularly good deals if you want to sample lots of everything on the menu.

Green Cuisine. 560 Johnson St., in Market Sq. ☎ **250/385-1809.** www.greencuisine.com. Main courses C$3.95–C$10 (US$2.65–US$7). AE, MC, V. Daily 9:30am–8pm. VEGETARIAN/ VEGAN.

In addition to being undeniably healthy, Victoria's only fully vegan enclave is remarkably tasty, with a self-serve salad bar, hot buffet, dessert bar, and full bakery. Available dishes range from Moroccan chickpea and vegetable soup to pasta primavera salad to pumpkin tofu cheesecake, not to mention a wide selection of freshly baked breads (made with natural sweeteners and fresh-ground organic flour). Green cuisine also has a large selection of freshly squeezed organic juices, smoothies and shakes, and organic coffees and teas. And for the sake of the truly discriminating diner, the ingredients for every dish are carefully listed. The atmosphere is casual—bordering on cafeteria—but comfortable. And for healthy-dessert hounds, order the wheat-free chocolate raspberry cake.

⭐ **J&J Wonton Noodle House.** 1012 Fort St. ☎ **250/383-0680.** Main courses C$7–C$17 (US$4.70–US$11); lunch specials C$6–C$7 (US$4–US$4.70). MC, V. Tues–Sat 11am–2pm and 4:30–8:45pm. Bus: 5. CANTONESE.

Real Chinese noodle houses are rare in North America, which is a shame, because they're so much fun. The kitchen here is glassed in so you can watch the chefs spinning out noodles and expertly whisking soups through woks into bowls. Lunch specials—which feature different fresh seafood every day—are good and cheap, so expect a line of locals at the door. If you miss the specials, noodle soups, chow mein, chow fun (wide noodles), and other dishes are also quick, delicious, and inexpensive.

Q V Bakery & Café. 1701 Government St. ☎ **250/384-8831.** Main courses C$3.95–C$10 (US$2.65–US$7). MC, V. Daily 24 hours. BAKERY.

The main attraction of the cuisine on offer at this spot on the edge of downtown isn't so much its quality—though the coffee, muffins, cookies, and light meals like lasagnas, quiches, and salads are all quite good—but its availability. Q V is open 24 hours, which in Victoria is enough to make it very special indeed.

Re-bar. 50 Bastion Sq. ☎ **250/361-9223.** Main courses C$7–C$14 (US$4.70–US$9). AE, MC, V. Mon–Thurs 8:30am–9pm, Fri–Sat 8:30am–10pm, Sun 8:30am–3:30pm. Bus: 5. VEGETARIAN.

Even if you're not hungry, it's worth dropping in for a juice blend—say grapefruit, banana, melon, and pear with bee pollen or blue-green algae for added oomph. If you're hungry, then rejoice: Re-bar is the city's premier dispenser of vegetarian comfort food. Disturbingly wholesome as that may sound, Re-bar is not only tasty but fun and a great spot to take the kids for brunch or breakfast. The room—in the basement of an 1890s heritage building—is pastel-tinted funky, with loads of cake tins glued to the walls. The service is friendly and casual. The food tends to the simple and wholesome, including a vegetable-and-almond patty with red onions, sprouts, and fresh tomato salsa on a multigrain kaiser roll as well as quesadillas, omelets, and crisp salads with toasted pine nuts, feta cheese, fresh vegetables, and sun-dried tomato vinaigrette. Juices are still the crown jewels, with over 80 blends on the menu. And if the one you want's not there, they'll make it anyway.

⭐ **Sam's Deli.** 805 Government St. ☎ **250/382-8424.** www.samsdeli.com. Main courses C$3.95–C$10 (US$2.65–US$7). MC, V. Daily 9am–7pm. DELI.

Pub Grub

When brew pubs arrived in the late 1980s, Victorians took to them instinctively—part of the British heritage perhaps. Now there are four on the scene, with rumors of another two to come. For those in the mood for more solid nourishment, they're an extremely attractive option—the atmosphere is fun and casual, and the food is often excellent. (For a more detailed description of these establishments, see "Bars & Pubs" in chapter 16.)

First and oldest is ✪ **Spinnaker's Brew Pub,** 308 Catherine St. (☎ **250/386-2739**), bus 24 to Songhees Rd, just over the Johnson Bridge, on the far side of the Inner Harbour. Both the food and views here are impressive. **The Harbour Canoe Club,** 450 Swift St. (☎ **250/361-1940**), bus 24 to the Johnson St. Bridge, overlooking the water just north of the Johnson Street Bridge, is a sunlit cathedral of a room, with good food and live music. ✪ **Swan's Pub,** 506 Pandora Ave. (☎ **250/361-3310**), offers probably the best food, plus a warm windproof glass patio on which to bask and, inside, better art than you're likely to see in a museum or gallery. Bus 5 to Pandora St. The newest, **Hugo's Brewpub,** 625 Courtney St. (☎ **250/920-4844**), has gotten good reviews food-wise, though most are more impressed with the crowd and the room's bullet-riddled brick walls. Bus 5 to Courtney St.

If you don't like lines, avoid the lunch hour, for Sam's is *the* lunchtime Victoria soup-and-sandwich spot. Sandwiches come in all tastes and sizes (mostly large), but the shrimp and avocado is the one to get. Sam's homemade soups are excellent, as is his chili. And Sam's is but a hop, skip, and sandwich-laden lurch from the harbor—so unless it's raining, there's no excuse not to order to go.

Siam Thai Restaurant. 512 Fort St. ☎ **250/383-9911.** Main courses C$9–C$14 (US$6–US$9). MC, V. Daily 11:30am–10pm. THAI.

There aren't many opportunities to satisfy your craving for Thai food in Victoria, but tucked away in a vintage building just half a block or so from the waterfront, this little local favorite offers good-quality Thai cooking done with varying levels of spiciness to suit every palate. Menu items are starred from mild to spicy (one to four stars), so there's no risk of having your tongue inadvertently scorched. The menu includes many Thai signature dishes such as coconut/lemon grass chicken or shrimp soup, Pad Thai noodles, garlic and pepper pork, as well as a variety of curries (red, yellow, and green). The lunch specials, C$7.95 (US$5.25) are a great deal, including soup, a spring roll and a choice of a main course, served with steamed rice.

4 Outside the Central Area

VERY EXPENSIVE

✪ **The Aerie.** 600 Ebedora Lane, Malahat. ☎ **250/743-7115.** www.aerie.bc.ca Reservations required. Main courses C$27–C$35 (US$18–US$23); 7-course set menu C$75 (US$50), C$105 (US$70) with wine pairings. AE, DC, MC, V. Daily noon–1:30pm and 6–8:30pm. Free parking. Take Hwy. 1 to the Spectacle Lake turnoff; take the first right and follow the winding driveway. FRENCH.

Elaborate. Ornate. Overwhelming? Depends on your tastes. The dining room of this red-tile villa boasts panoramic windows overlooking Finlayson Inlet, a 14-carat gold-leaf ceiling, crystal chandeliers, intricately carved high-backed gilt chairs, faux-marble columns, and a large open-hearth fireplace. When it comes to French cooking, over-the-top is a good thing. Consider, for example, an appetizer of venison-and-pistachio pâté with dried-fruit compote, juniper-and-port glaze, and herbed sunflower croutons. Or a mille-feuille of B.C. salmon pastrami, honey-and-thyme mascarpone, and crisp misch toasts. Entrees include beef tenderloin with caramelized shallot crust in red wine/rosemary reduction; roasted lamb chop and loin with currant/cracked pepper glaze; and free-range chicken breast with mushroom-and-nut mousse and savory tarragon/onion bread-and-butter pudding. The Aerie wine list leans toward France, including vintage Margaux and Bordeaux. Topping off the evening, there's white coffee crème brûlée, gingered mascarpone mousse, or a Belgian chocolate-and-hazelnut nougat pyramid with Frangelico ganache. An excellent selection of brandies and Kona coffee will take you over the peak and down the far side.

✪ **Deep Cove Chalet.** 11190 Chalet Rd., near Sidney. ☎ **250/656-3541.** Reservations required. Main courses C$28–C$40 (US$19–US$27). AE, MC, V. Wed–Sun 11am–2pm; Tues–Sun 5–10pm. Free parking. FRENCH.

Life is to be lived, so why not spend a little (or a lot) and live life well? Such could be the philosophy of Deep Cove chef/proprietor Pierre Koffel. To be sure, he delivers his end of the bargain with a truly fine dining experience. A good half hour north of Victoria, the Chalet sits on carefully manicured lawns on the very edge of its eponymous inlet. The menu is French, but Koffel is a constant innovator, so expect some cheeky surprises. The seafood is always fresh—the lobster bisque is a perennial favorite, but then so is the C$38-a-bowl truffle soup. Dishes include such delicacies as escargots in puffed pastries and caviar-and-lobster spread. Presentation of the meat and fish entrees is superb and, despite his traditional French training, Koffel's sauces are light yet very flavorful. The service can be a bit off-hand—particularly on busy weekend evenings—but there, too, Koffel shows his French side. Sip what's left of your wine and wait for the cheese tray to make it around.

✪ **Sooke Harbour House.** 1528 Whiffen Spit Rd., Sooke. ☎ **250/642-3421.** www.sookeharbourhouse.com. Reservations required. Main courses C$29–C$36 (US$19–US$24). AE, ER, MC, V. Daily 5–9pm. Take the Island Hwy. to the Sooke/Colwood turnoff (Junction Hwy. 14). Continue on Hwy. 14 to Sooke. About a mile past the town's only traffic light, turn left onto Whiffen Spit Rd. WEST COAST.

In a rambling white house on a bluff on the edge of the Pacific, this small restaurant/hotel (see chapter 11) offers spectacular waterfront views, a relaxed atmosphere, and what could be the best food in all Canada. Chef/proprietor Sinclair Philip is both a talented innovator and a stickler for details. The result is an ever-changing menu in which each of the dishes is prepared with care, imagination, and flair. The ingredients are resolutely local (many come from the inn's own organic herb garden or from the ocean at the Harbour House's doorstep). On any given night, dishes might include seared scallops with sea asparagus (harvested from the sand spit below the inn), nori rolls with goose-neck barnacles in mustard broth, or chinook salmon with red wine/gooseberry sauce. The presentation is always interesting—often with edible flowers—while the service is knowledgeable and professional. The wine cellar is extensive, and the pairings for Philips' culinary creations are particularly well chosen.

EXPENSIVE

✪ **The Marina Restaurant.** 1327 Beach Dr., Oak Bay. ☎ **250/598-8555.** Reservations recommended. Main courses C$8–C$17 (US$5–US$11) at lunch, C$17–C$27 (US$11–US$18) at dinner; Sun brunch C$23 (US$15). AE, DC, ER, JCB, MC, V. Mon–Sat 11:30am–2:30pm, Sun brunch 10am–2:30pm, Sun–Thurs 5–10pm, Fri–Sat 5–11pm. Bus: 2. CONTINENTAL.

Did I mention the view at the Marina restaurant? Most people do. Set above the yachts of the fashionable Oak Bay marina, the semicircular dark-wood dining room has two levels of seating and panoramic floor-to-ceiling windows. Ask about the food, however, and people quickly steer the conversation back to the view. Or they tell you that between the food and the view, it's the latter you pay for. When this restaurant opened, the cuisine was top quality. But after the initial buzz, the downtown foodies stopped making the trek out, and the management discovered that conservative Oak Bay residents weren't quite up to their flights of culinary fancy. So they pulled back and aimed for something a little more down to earth (most say they overshot). It's been coming back since, however, as the Oak Bay burghers warm to the concept of something else for supper besides a patty and two buns. The Marina is perhaps best known for its Sunday brunch—the all-you-can-eat buffet overflows with oysters, clams, prawns, prime rib, poached salmon, fresh salads, marinated vegetables, fruit salads, breakfast foods, and an array of handmade Belgian chocolate truffles, tall cakes, and puddings. The service is quick and friendly, and on a sunny day, the view does really seem to make it all worthwhile.

INEXPENSIVE

✪ **Six Mile Pub.** 494 Island Hwy., View Royal. ☎ **250/478-3121.** www.sixmile.com. Main courses C$7–C$10 (US$4.70–US$7). MC, V. Mon–Sat 11am–1am, Sun 11am–midnight. PUB GRUB.

In an 1855 building, this pub has a rich history. Originally named the Parson's Bridge Hotel (after the man who built Parson's Bridge, which opened the Sooke area to vehicle traffic), it was filled with sailors when the Esquimalt Naval Base opened nearby in 1864. When Victoria elected to continue Prohibition until 1952, the Six Mile Pub became the hub for provincial bootleggers. With a big lively bar, a huge banquet room, and a few intimate dining rooms, it has broad appeal. Loyal locals come for the atmosphere and the dinner specials. You can enjoy the warm ambiance of the fireside room, which has an oak bar with stained glass and other classic British touches, or the beautiful scenery from the outdoor patio. The food is seasoned with fresh herbs from the pub's own garden. Start with one of the 10 house brews on tap, then enjoy a hearty Cornish pasty (stringy mystery meat, peas, potatoes, and carrots in a pastry envelope), steak-and-mushroom pie, or juicy prime rib. If meat isn't part of your diet, try a tasty veggie burger.

13 Exploring Victoria

Victoria's top draws are its waterfront—the beautiful viewscape created by The Empress and the Parliament Buildings on the edge of the Inner Harbour—and its historic Old Town. So attractive are these, in fact, that folks sometimes forget to notice what a beautiful and wild part of the world the city is set in. If you have time, step out of town a little and see some nature: Sail out to see killer whales, beachcomb for crabs and anemones, go kayaking, or hike into the hills for some fabulous views and scenery.

Sightseeing Suggestions

If You Have 1 Day

Have breakfast on the water at the **Blackfish Cafe,** 950 Wharf St. (☎ **250/385-9996**), open 8am to 4pm daily, or grab some croissants and coffee for a wharfside picnic. Stroll along the **Inner Harbour** past The Empress hotel to **Thunderbird Park** and watch a totem pole being made. Then head to the **Royal BC Museum,** one of the world's best small museums. Afterward, refresh your brain with a stroll through **The Empress Rose Garden** on your way in to have **afternoon tea.** Later, walk around the **Old Town.** Duck through **Trounce Alley** into **Market Square** and see if there's a band playing on the outdoor stage. Stop in at the **Starfish Glassworks** (630 Yates St.) and watch some glass-art being blown or browse for antiques on Fort Street. Then head off for some seafood, preferably at a restaurant overlooking the water like the Coast Hotel's **Blue Crab Bar and Grill** or the Ocean Pointe's **Victorian Restaurant.** After sundown, see if there's any jazz playing downtown.

If You Have 2 Days

Take a boat out to **see the orcas**—they gather here like almost nowhere else, and seeing them up close is something special. Back in town, lunch at one of the dockside **brew pubs** like Spinnaker's or the Harbour Canoe Club. Then take a walk through **Chinatown.** In the late afternoon, drive out to **Butchart Gardens.** If you have kids (or even if you don't), stop in at the **Victoria Butterfly Gardens** on the way. Watch as the sun goes down and subtle illumination gives the gardens a whole new character. Back in town, have a late-night supper somewhere like **Pagliacci's.** For a nightcap, go for drinks in The Empress's **Bengal Lounge.**

If You Have 3 Days

Rent a bike and cycle along the oceanside Dallas Road to **Clover Point** and **Ross Bay** cemetery, then head up to **Craigdarroch Castle.** In the afternoon, do some **kayaking** in the sheltered waters around Victoria. Or **cycle (or drive) the Galloping Goose trail** to East Sooke Park and do some beachcombing. In the evening, treat yourself to supper somewhere out of town like the **Deep Cove Chalet** (near Sidney) or the **Sooke Harbour House.**

If You Have 4 or 5 Days

Explore farther afield. Drive out and poke (*gently!*) the anemones and sea stars at **Botanical Beach** park near Port Renfrew. On the way back, stop in at the **Sooke Harbour House** for a meal you won't soon forget. Alternatively, hike up **Mount Work** and see the whole peninsula spread out beneath you. Walk back down and have a picnic on the **Finlayson Arm fjord.** Then drive the lonely Finlayson Arm road to **Goldstream Provincial Park** and—with luck—see **bald eagles** or **salmon.** Or take a road trip up to **Cowichan Valley.** Tour the wineries and have dinner on the docks at Cowichan Bay. Then go out for an evening sail. For an overnight trip, consider driving out to **Bamfield** on the wild west coast to see bald eagles by the bucketful or to **Tofino** where you can walk Long Beach and kayak Clayoquot Sound.

1 Seeing the Sights

THE TOP ATTRACTIONS

Maritime Museum of British Columbia. 28 Bastion Sq. ☎ **250/385-4222.** www. mmbc.bc.ca. E-mail:info@mmbc.bc.ca. Admission C$5 (US$3.35) adults, C$4 (US$2.70) seniors, C$3 (US$2) students, C$2 (US$1.35) children 6–11, C$13 (US$9) families; children under 6 free. Daily 9am–4:30pm. Closed Dec 25. Bus: 5 to View St.

Housed in the former provincial courthouse, this museum is dedicated to recalling the province's rich maritime heritage. The displays do a good job of illustrating maritime history, from the early explorers to the fur trading and whaling era to the days of grand ocean liners and military conflict. There's also an impressive collection of ship models and paraphernalia—uniforms, weapons, gear—along with photographs and journals. Thanks to a recent renovation, the museum also shows films in its Vice Admiralty Theatre. The gift shop offers an excellent selection of nautical books.

Miniature World. 649 Humboldt St. ☎ **250/385-9731.** www.miniatureworld.com. E-mail: info@miniatureworld.com. Admission C$8 (US$5) adults, C$7 (US$4.70) youths, C$6 (US$4) children; children under 4 free. AE, MC, V. Summer daily 8:30am–9pm, winter daily 9am–5pm. Bus: 5, 27, 28, or 30.

It sounds cheesy—hundreds of dolls and miniatures and scenes from old fairy tales. And Miniature World's case isn't helped by its brochure, which features photos of "Brady Bunch" clones in 1950s fashions grinning like idiots as they loom over yet another diorama. And yet Miniature World—inside The Empress hotel (the entrance is around the corner)—is actually kinda cool. You walk in and you're plunged into darkness, except for a moon, some planets, and a tiny spaceship flying up to rendezvous with an orbiting mother ship. This is the most up-to-date display. Farther in are re-creations of battle scenes, fancy 18th-century dress balls, a miniature CPR railway running all the way across a miniature Canada, a three-ring circus and midway, and scenes from Mother Goose and Charles Dickens stories. Better yet, most of these displays do something. The train moves at the punch of a button; the circus rides whirl around and light up as simulated darkness falls.

Parliament Buildings (Provincial Legislature). 501 Belleville St. ☎ **250/387-3046.** www.parl-bldgs.gov.bc.ca. Admission free. Daily 9am–5pm. Tours offered every 20 min. in summer, hourly in winter.

Designed by 25-year-old Francis Rattenbury and built between 1893 and 1898 at a cost of nearly C$1,000,000, the Parliament Buildings (also called the Legislature) are an architectural gem. The half-hour tour comes across at times like an eighth-grade civics lesson, but it's worth it just to see the fine mosaics, marble, woodwork, and stained glass. And if you see a harried-looking man surrounded by a pack of mini-cam crews, don't be alarmed. It's likely just another BC premier getting hounded out of office by the aggressive and hostile media. Politics is a blood sport in BC.

British Columbia Aviation Museum. 1910 Norseman Rd., Sidney. ☎ **250/655-3300.** www.bcam.net. Admission C$4 (US$2.70) adults, C$3 (US$2) seniors; children under 12 free. Summer daily 10am–4pm, winter daily 11am–3pm. Closed Dec 25. Bus: Airport.

This is a working museum inside a hangar at Victoria International Airport. Volunteers keep busy restoring vintage aircraft to add to the collection, which already includes World War II fighters and bombers, a 1929 Eastman Flying Boat, a Gibson Twin (built in Victoria in 1911), and much more. Currently underway is the restoration of a vintage Anson aircraft. Thursday (work day at the museum) is a particularly opportune time to stop by if you want to see the restorers in action.

Fort Rodd Hill & Fisgard Lighthouse National Historic Site. 603 Fort Rodd Hill Rd. ☎ **250/478-5849.** www.parkscanada.pch.gc.ca. Admission C$3 (US$2) adults, C$2.25 (US$1.50) seniors, C$1.50 (US$1) children 6–16, C$8 (US$5) families; children under 6 free. Mar–Oct daily 10am–5:30pm, Nov–Feb daily 9am–4:30pm.

Perched on an outcrop of volcanic rock, the **Fisgard Lighthouse** has guided ships toward Victoria's sheltered harbor since 1873. The light no longer has a keeper (the beacon has long been automated), but the site itself has been restored to its 1873 appearance. Two floors worth of exhibits in the light keepers' house narrate stories of the lighthouse, its keepers, and the terrible shipwrecks that gave this coastline its ominous moniker "the graveyard of the Pacific."

Adjoining the lighthouse, **Fort Rodd Hill** is a perfectly preserved 1890s coastal artillery fort that—though in more than half a century it never fired a shot in anger—still sports camouflaged searchlights, underground magazines, and its original guns. Audiovisual exhibits bring the fort to life with the voices and faces of the men who served at this key outpost. Displays of artifacts, room re-creations, and historic film footage add to the experience. It's so close to the lighthouse that concussion from the guns once blew out all the lighthouse's windows.

✪ **Butchart Gardens.** 800 Benvenuto Ave., Brentwood Bay. ☎ **250/652-4422;** dining reservations 250/652-8222. www.butchartgardens.bc.ca. E-mail: email@butchartgardens. com. Admission C$18 (US$12) adults, C$9 (US$6) youths 13–17, C$2 (US$1.35) children 5–12, free for children under 5. Spring, fall, and winter discounts. Daily from 9am. Gate closes around sundown (call for seasonal closing time). Visitors can remain in gardens for 1 hour after gate closes. AE, MC, V. Take Blanshard St. (Hwy. 17) north toward the ferry terminal in Saanich, then turn left on Keating Crossroads, which leads directly to the gardens—about 20 min. from downtown Victoria. It's impossible to miss if you follow the trail of billboards. Bus: 75.

These internationally acclaimed gardens were born after Robert Butchart exhausted the limestone quarry near his Tod Inlet home. His wife, Jenny, gradually landscaped the deserted eyesore into the resplendent **Sunken Garden,** opening it for public display in 1904. A **Rose Garden, Italian Garden,** and **Japanese Garden** were added. As the fame of the 50-acre gardens grew, the Butcharts also transformed their house into an attraction. The gardens—still in the family—now display more than a million plants throughout the year. As impressive as the numbers is the sheer perfection of

Victoria Attractions

Emily Carr House **14**
Craigdarroch Castle **11**
Crystal Garden **10**
The Empress **6**
Helmcken House **9**
Maritime Museum of
  British Columbia **2**
Market Square **1**
Miniature World **5**
Pacific Undersea
  Gardens **4**
Parliament Buildings
  (Provincial Legislature) **7**
Ross Bay Cemetery **12**
Royal British Columbia
  Museum **8**
Royal London Wax
  Museum **3**
Trans-Canada Highway
  Mile 0 **13**

each garden—not a blade out of place, each flower the same height, all blooming at the same time. Gardeners will be amazed. Evenings in summer, the gardens are beautifully illuminated with a variety of softly colored lights. June through September, musical entertainment is provided free on Monday to Saturday evenings. You can even watch fireworks displays on Saturdays in July and August. A very good lunch, dinner, and afternoon tea are offered in the Dining Room Restaurant in the historic residence; afternoon and high teas are also served in the Italian Garden (reservations strongly recommended). Casual family fare is served in the Blue Poppy Restaurant. At the Seed and Gift Store on the grounds, you can buy some of the seeds of the plants you've seen, gardening books, cards, calendars, and other items.

✪ **Royal British Columbia Museum.** 675 Belleville St. ☎ **888/447-7977** or 250/387-3701. www.royalbcmuseum.bc.ca. E-mail: tcoyle@royalbcmuseum.bc.ca. Admission C$8 (US$5) adults, C$5 (US$3.35) seniors/students/youths, C$21 (US$14) families; children under 6 free. Higher rates sometimes in effect for traveling exhibits. Daily 9am–5pm. Closed Dec 25 and Jan 1. Bus: 5, 28, or 30.

One of the world's best regional museums, the Royal BC features natural history dioramas indistinguishable from the real thing (except the grizzly bear won't rip your face off), full-size re-creations of frontier towns and Native longhouses, and a collection of Native art and artifacts that'll leave you gasping. The museum's mandate is to present the land and the people of coastal British Columbia. The second-floor **Natural History Gallery** shows the coastal flora, fauna, and geography, from the Ice Age to the present; it includes dioramas of a temperate rain forest, a seacoast, an underground ecology of giant bugs, and (particularly appealing to kids) a live tidal pool with sea stars and anemones. The third-floor **Modern History Gallery** presents the recent past, including historically faithful re-creations of Victoria's downtown and Chinatown. On the same floor, the **First Peoples Gallery** is an incredible showpiece of Native art that also houses many artifacts showing day-to-day Native life, a full-size re-creation of a longhouse, and many smaller village scenes. The museum also has an **IMAX theater** showing an ever-changing variety of large-screen movies. On the way out (or in), be sure to stop by **Thunderbird Park,** beside the museum, where a cedar longhouse (Mungo Martin House, named after a famous Kwakiutl artist) houses a workshop where Native carvers work on new totem poles.

✪ **Victoria Butterfly Gardens.** 1461 Benvenuto Ave. (P.O. Box 190), Brentwood Bay. ☎ **877/722-0272** or 250/652-3822. www.butterflygardens.com. E-mail: butterfly@victoriabc.com. Admission C$8 (US$5) adults, C$7 (US$4.70) students/seniors, C$4.50 (US$3) children 5–12; children under 5 free. DC, MC, V. Mar 1–May 13 and Oct daily 9:30am–4:30pm, May 14–Sept 30 daily 9am–5:30pm. Closed in winter. Bus: 75.

This is a great spot for kids, nature buffs, or anyone who just likes butterflies. Hundreds of exotic colorful butterflies flutter freely through this lush tropical greenhouse. You're provided with an ID chart and set free to roam around. Species present range from the tiny Central American Julia (a brilliant orange butterfly about 3 inches across) to the Southeast Asian Giant Atlas Moth (mottled brown and red, with a wingspan approaching a foot). Other butterflies are brilliant blue, yellow, or a mix of colors and patterns. Naturalists are on-hand to explain butterfly biology, and there's even a display where you can see the beautiful creatures emerge from their cocoons.

Pacific Undersea Gardens. 490 Belleville St. ☎ **250/382-5717.** Admission C$7 (US$4.70) adults, C$6 (US$4) seniors, C$5 (US$3.35) youths 12–17, C$3.50 (US$2.35) children 5–11; children under 5 free. Sept–June daily 10am–5pm, July–Aug daily 10am–7pm. Bus: 5, 27, 28, or 30.

A gently sloping stairway leads down to this unique marine observatory's glass-enclosed viewing area, where you can observe the Inner Harbour's marine life up close. Some 5,000 creatures feed, play, hunt, and court in these protected waters. Sharks,

On the Lookout: Victoria's Best Views

In town, the best view of The Empress and the Parliament Buildings (the Legislature) comes from walking along the pedestrian path in front of the **Ocean Pointe Resort** off the Johnson Street Bridge. In summer, there's a nice patio where you can grab a coffee. The sunlight's good early in the day.

When the fishing fleets come in, head over to **Fisherman's Wharf** at St. Lawrence and Erie Streets, where you can watch the activity as the fishermen unload their catches. Later on, take in the sunset from the wharf along the eastern edge of the Inner Harbour or from the **Parrot House Restaurant,** 740 Burdett Ave. (☎ **250/382-9258**).

Just south of downtown, you can see across the Strait of Juan de Fuca and the San Juan Islands to the mountains of the Olympic Peninsula from the **Ogden Point** breakwater, from the top of the hill in **Beacon Hill Park,** or from the walking path above the beach along **Dallas Road.** Farther afield, **Fort Rodd Hill** and **Fisgard Lighthouse** offer equally good views of the mountains, as well as a view of the warships in Esquimalt Harbour.

✪ **Mount Douglas,** a 15-minute drive north of the city on Shelbourne Street, offers a panoramic view of the entire Saanich Peninsula, with a parking lot just a 2-minute walk from the summit. To the east, **Mount Work** offers an equally good view, but you have to walk up. It takes about 45 minutes. At the top of Little Saanich Mountain (about 16km/10 miles north of Victoria) stands the **Dominion Astrophysical Observatory,** 5071 W. Saanich Rd. (☎ **250/363-0001**), where you can survey all that's around you during the day; April through October, resident astronomers and volunteers are on-hand Saturday from 7 to 11pm to give you a view of the starlit skies with the aid of various-sized telescopes.

wolf eels, poisonous stonefish, sea anemones, starfish, sturgeon, and salmon are just a few of the organisms that make their homes here. One of the harbor's star attractions is a remarkably photogenic huge octopus (reputedly the largest in captivity). Injured seals and orphaned seal pups are cared for in holding pens alongside the observatory as part of a provincial marine-mammal rescue program. The gardens are a great spot for kids or any budding marine biologist.

Royal London Wax Museum. 470 Belleville St. ☎ **250/388-4461.** www.waxworld.com. E-mail: khl@pinc.com. Admission C$8 (US$5) adults, C$7 (US$4.70) seniors, C$3.50 (US$2.35) children. Daily 9am–7pm. Bus: 5, 27, 28, or 30.

See the same royal family you already get too much of on television. See other, older royals of even less significance. See their family pets. All courtesy of Madame Tussaud's 200-year-old wax technology. There's also the chamber of horrors, which rates, well, below a "Buffy the Vampire Slayer" episode on the scariness scale. Still not thrilled? The management of the wax museum seems to suspect as much; they've started taking liberties with their wax figures' figures. Look especially for the Princess Diana dummy with the Pamela Anderson implants.

✪ **Craigdarroch Castle.** 1050 Joan Crescent. ☎ **250/592-5323.** www.craigdarrochcastle. com. E-mail: ccastle@islandnet.com. Admission C$8 (US$5) adults, C$6 (US$4) students, C$2.50 (US$1.65) children 6–12; children under 6 free. June 15–Sept 3 daily 9am–7pm, Sept 4–June 14 daily 10am–4:30pm. Take Fort St. out of downtown, just past Pandora, and turn right on Joan Crescent. Bus: 11.

What do you do when you're the richest man in British Columbia, when you've clawed, scraped, and bullied your way up from indentured servant to coal baron and merchant prince? You build a castle, of course, to show the other buggers what you're worth. Located in the highlands above Oak Bay, Robert Dunsmuir's home is a stunner. The four-story, 39-room Highland-style castle is topped with stone turrets and chimneys and filled with the opulent Victorian splendor you'd expect to read about in a romance novel—detailed woodwork, Persian carpets, stained-glass windows, paintings, and sculptures. The nonprofit society that runs Craigdarroch does an excellent job showcasing the castle. You're provided with a self-tour booklet; on every floor are volunteer docents who are happy to provide further information.

ARCHITECTURAL HIGHLIGHTS & HISTORIC HOMES

First a fortified trading post, then a gold-rush town, naval base, and sleepy provincial capital, Victoria bears architectural witness to all these eras. The best of its buildings date to the years before World War I, when gold poured in from the Fraser and Klondike Rivers, fueling a building boom responsible for most of the downtown.

For an excellent guide to many of Victoria's buildings, as well as short biographies of its most significant architects, pick up *Exploring Victoria's Architecture,* by Martin Segger and Douglas Franklin. There are copies in **Munro's Books,** 1108 Government St. (☎ **250/382-2464**).

Perhaps the most intriguing downtown edifice isn't a building at all but a work of art. The walls of **Fort Victoria,** which once covered much of downtown, have been demarcated in the sidewalk with bricks bearing the names of original settlers and fur traders. Look on the sidewalk on Government Street at the corner of Fort Street.

Most of the retail establishments in Victoria's Old Town area are housed in 19th-century shipping warehouses that've been carefully restored as part of a heritage-reclamation program. You can take a **self-guided tour** of the buildings, most of which were erected between the 1870s and 1890s; their history is recounted on easy-to-read outdoor plaques. The majority of the restored buildings are between Douglas and Johnson Streets from Wharf Street to Government Street. The most impressive structure once housed a number of shipping offices and warehouses and is now the home of a 45-shop complex known as **Market Square,** 560 Johnson St./255 Market Sq. (☎ **250/386-2441**).

Some of the British immigrants who settled Vancouver Island during the 19th century built magnificent estates and mansions. In addition to architect Francis Rattenbury's crowning turn-of-the-20th-century achievements—the provincial **Parliament Buildings,** 501 Belleville St. (completed in 1898), and the opulent **Empress** hotel, 721 Government St. (completed in 1908)—you'll find a number of other magnificent historic architectural sites.

Emily Carr House, 207 Government St. (☎ **250/383-5843**), is the birthplace of one of Victoria's most distinguished early residents, painter/writer Emily Carr. Though trained in the classical European tradition, Carr developed her own style in response to the powerful landscapes of the Canadian west coast. Eschewing both marriage and stability, she spent her life traveling the coast, capturing the landscapes and Native peoples in vivid and striking works. The house has been restored to the condition it would've been in when Carr lived there. In addition, many of the rooms have been hung with samples of Carr's work or quotations from her writings. (A talented writer as well as painter, Carr's tales of travel on the coast, *Klee Wyck,* is still in print and available in the Carr House gift shop.) Mid-May to mid-October, the house is open daily 10am to 5pm (occasionally for special exhibits the rest of the year; off-season call ahead). Admission is C$5 (US$3.35) for adults, C$4 (US$2.70) for students/seniors, and C$3 (US$2) for children 6 to 12; children under 6 are free.

Helmcken House, 610 Elliot St. Square (☎ **250/386-0021**), was the residence of a pioneer doctor who settled in the area during the 1850s. The doctor's house still contains the original imported British furnishings and his medicine chest. Admission is the same as for Carr House. May through October, the house is open daily from 10am to 5pm; November through April, hours are Thursday to Monday from 11am to 4pm.

On a promontory above the Gorge Waterway, the completely restored **Point Ellice House,** 2616 Pleasant St. (☎ **250/380-6506**), was the summer gathering place for much of Victoria's Victorian elite. Mid-May to mid-September, it's open for 30-minute guided tours daily from noon to 5pm; admission is the same as for Carr House. Point Ellice is also one of the better spots for afternoon tea (see chapter 12). The easiest way to reach the house is by harbor ferry from in front of The Empress, costing C$4 (US$2.70) one-way.

✪ **Craigdarroch Castle,** 1050 Joan Crescent (☎ **250/592-5323**), was built during the 1880s to serve as Scottish coal-mining magnate Robert Dunsmuir's home (see "The Top Attractions," above). Dunsmuir's son James built his own palatial home, **Hatley Castle.** The younger Dunsmuir reportedly commissioned architect Samuel Maclure with the words "Money doesn't matter, just build what I want." The bill, in 1908, came to over C$1 million. The grounds of the castle, now home to **Royal Roads University** (☎ **250/391-2511**), feature extensive floral gardens and are open to the public free of charge. There's also a volunteer-run **Hatley Park Castle and Museum,** 2005 Sooke Rd. (☎ **250/391-2600,** ext. 4456), which offers tours of the grounds and the castle Monday to Friday from 1 to 4pm. Admission is C$3 (US$2) for adults and C$2 (US$1.35) for children. Call ahead because if no volunteers show up, the museum doesn't open. Hatley Castle is off Highway 14 in Colwood.

CEMETERIES

There can be no better place to die than Victoria. **Ross Bay Cemetery,** 1495 Fairfield St. at Dallas Rd., has to be one of the finest locations in all creation to spend eternity. Luminaries interred here include the first governor of the island, James Douglas; frontier judge Matthew Begbie; and West Coast painter Emily Carr. *An Historic Guide to Ross Bay Cemetery,* available in Munro's Books as well as other bookstores, gives details on people and directions to grave sites.

Pioneer Square, on the corner of Meares and Quadra Streets beside Christ Church, is one of British Columbia's oldest cemeteries. Hudson's Bay Company fur traders, ship captains, sailors, fishermen, and crew members from British Royal Navy vessels lie beneath the worn sandstone markers.

Contact the **Old Cemeteries Society** (☎ **250/598-8870;** www.oldcem.bc.ca; e-mail: oldcem@pinc.com) for more information on tours of both of these graveyards.

NEIGHBORHOODS OF NOTE

From the time the Hudson's Bay Company settled here in the mid-1800s, the historic **Old Town** was the center of the city's bustling business in shipping, fur trading, and legal opium manufacturing. Market Square and the surrounding warehouses once brimmed with exports like tinned salmon, furs, and timber bound for England and the United States. Now part of the downtown core, this is still a terrific place to find British, Scottish, and Irish imports (a surprising number of these shops date back to the early 1900s), souvenirs of all sorts, and even outdoor equipment for modern-day adventurers.

Just a block north on Fisgard Street is **Chinatown.** Founded in 1863, it's the oldest Chinatown in North America. One of the more interesting structures is a three-story school built by the Chinese Benevolent Society in the early 1900s, when non-Canadian

Heading North to a Provincial Park, a Native Village & Some Wineries

North of Victoria along the Island Highway are three sites worth visiting: Goldstream Provincial Park, the Cowichan Native Village, and the Cowichan Valley wineries. The drive along the east coast is pleasant, with mountain and ocean views, and the three sites are close enough together to do in 1 day.

GOLDSTREAM PROVINCIAL PARK This tranquil arboreal setting overflowed with prospectors during the 1860s gold-rush days. Trails take you past abandoned mine shafts and tunnels as well as 600-year-old stands of towering Douglas fir, lodgepole pine, red cedar, indigenous yew, and arbutus trees. The **Gold Mine Trail** leads to Niagara Creek and the abandoned mine that was operated by Lt. Peter Leech, a Royal Engineer who discovered gold in the creek in 1858. **The Goldstream Trail** leads to the salmon spawning areas. (You might also catch sight of mink and river otters racing along this path.)

For general information on Goldstream Provincial Park and all other provincial parks on the South Island, contact **BC Parks** at ☎ **250/391-2300.** Throughout the year, Goldstream Park's **Freeman King Visitor Centre** (☎ **250/478-9414**) offers guided walks, talks, displays, and programs geared toward kids but interesting for adults, too. July and August, it's open daily from 9:30am to 6pm (to 4:30pm the rest of the year). Take Highway 1 about 30 minutes north of Victoria.

Three species of salmon (chum, chinook, and steelhead) make **annual salmon runs** up the Goldstream River during October, November, December, and February. You can easily observe this natural wonder along the riverbanks. Contact the park's **Visitor Centre** for details.

DUNCAN The main reason for visiting Duncan is to see the **Cowichan Native Village.** Created by the Cowichan Indian Band itself, the center, 200 Cowichan Way, Duncan (☎ **250/746-8119**), brings Native culture to visitors in a way that's commercially successful yet still respectful of native traditions.

The longhouses built along the Cowichan River contain an impressive collection of cultural artifacts and presentations of life among the aboriginal tribes who have lived in the area for thousands of years. There are regular tours at 11am, 1pm, 3pm, and 4:30pm, as well as ceremonial dances and daily afternoon salmon barbecues. Master and apprentice carvers create poles and masks and feasting bowls in workshops open to the public. Two large gift shops in the complex sell some of those works as well as Native-made jewelry, clothing, silk-screened prints, and other items. May through September, the village and gift shops are open daily from 9am to 6pm (10am to 4pm the rest of the year); admission is C$10 (US$7) for adults, C$6 (US$4) for seniors, C$4 (US$2.70) for children under 12, and C$20 (US$13) for families.

As for the city of **Duncan,** don't be misled by its new "City of Totems" tag line. Duncan is a strip mall of a town, and the hundreds of totem poles plunked

Chinese children were banned from public schools. Lined with Chinese restaurants, bakeries, and specialty shops, Chinatown is a wonderful spot to stop for dim sum or for a full Hong Kong–style seafood dinner.

The **James Bay** area on the southern shores of the Inner Harbour is a quiet middle-class residential community. As you walk through its tree-lined streets, you'll find many pristine older private residences that have maintained their original Victorian flavor.

down in the parking lots of every third 7-Eleven do nothing to redeem it. Fortunately, the City of Strip Malls is very close to Cowichan Bay (see below), so you can first visit the Native Village, then immediately take off for somewhere pleasant.

The **Duncan-Cowichan Visitor Info Centre** is at 381A Trans-Canada Hwy., Duncan, B.C. V9L 3R5 (☎ **250/746-4636;** www.duncancc.island.com; e-mail: duncancc@island.com). July and August, it's open daily from 9am to 6pm; September through June, hours are Tuesday to Saturday from 9:30am to 5pm.

THE COWICHAN VALLEY   A gorgeous agricultural valley a couple hours' drive from Victoria, the Cowichan Valley is a little like the south of England, except for the mountain, of course. Both the wineries and the seaside town of Cowichan Bay are worth a stop.

The vintners of the Cowichan Valley have gained a solid reputation for producing fine wines. Several of the wineries have opened their doors and offer 1-hour tours that are a great introduction for novices. They usually include a tasting of the vintner's art as well as a chance to purchase bottles or cases of your favorites.

Cherry Point Vineyards, 840 Cherry Point Rd., Cowichan (☎ **250/743-1272**), looks like a slice of California's Napa Valley. The wine-tasting room and gift shop is open daily from 11:30am to 6pm. **Blue Grouse Vineyards,** 4365 Blue Grouse Rd., Mill Bay (☎ **250/743-3834**), is a smaller winery that began as a hobby. April through September, it's open for tastings and on-site purchases Wednesday to Sunday from 11am to 5pm (closed Sun the rest of the year). **Merridale Cider,** another small winery, located just south of Cowichan Bay at 1230 Merridale Rd., is worth a stop to taste their ciders. Phone ahead to confirm opening hours. You may also want to stop at Cobble Hill (☎ **800/998-9908**), open daily from 10:30am to 4:30pm in July and August, and Monday to Saturday the rest of the year.

Just southeast of Duncan, **Cowichan Bay** is a pretty little seaside town with a few attractions that make it a worthwhile stop, in addition to the view of the ocean. The **Cowichan Bay Maritime Centre,** 1761 Cowichan Bay Rd., Cowichan Bay (☎ **250/746-4955**), is a unique museum where the displays sit atop a pier that stretches out into the bay. If you have kids along, go see and touch the sea creatures at the **Cowichan Marine Ecology Station,** Pier 66, 1751 Cowichan Bay Rd., Cowichan Bay (☎ **250/748-4522**). Or go for a sail on the bay on the sailing ketch *Meriah* (☎ **250/748-7374;** www.great-northwestern.com).

Cowichan Bay (off Hwy. 1, south of Duncan) is a pleasant half-hour drive from the wine country, so you can take a tour, do some sampling, and be back in Victoria before nightfall.

Beautiful residential communities such as **Ross Bay** and **Oak Bay** have a more modern West Coast appearance. Houses perch on hills overlooking the beaches amid luscious landscaped gardens. Private marinas are filled with perfectly maintained sailing craft.

Fernwood, northeast of downtown and Old Town, attracts Victoria's youth. Originally a 120-hectare (300-acre) estate with a Tudor-style house (Fernwood Manor) at its center, it was filled in with urban sprawl over the past century. Fernwood, like New York's SoHo, now has a run-down and rebuilt character that accounts for its charm.

PARKS & GARDENS

In addition to **Butchart Gardens** (see "The Top Attractions" above), several city parks attract strollers and picnickers whenever the weather is pleasant. The 154-acre **Beacon Hill Park** stretches from Southgate Street to Dallas Road between Douglas and Cook Streets. In 1882, the Hudson's Bay Company gave this property to the city. Stands of indigenous Garry oaks (found only on Vancouver Island, Hornby Island, and Salt Spring Island) and manicured lawns are interspersed with floral gardens and ponds. Hike up Beacon Hill to get a clear view of the Strait of Georgia, Haro Strait, and Washington's Olympic Mountains. The children's farm (see below), aviary, tennis courts, lawn-bowling green, putting green, cricket pitch, wading pool, playground, and picnic area make this a wonderful place to spend a few hours with the family. The Trans-Canada Highway's "Mile 0" marker stands at the edge of the park on Dallas Road.

Government House, the official residence of the lieutenant governor, is at **1401 Rockland Ave.,** in the Fairfield residential district. The house itself is closed to the public (and not worth touring anyway), but the formal gardens are open and well worth a wander. Round back, the hillside of Garry oaks is one of the last places to see what the area's natural fauna looked like before European settlers arrived. At the front, the rose garden is sumptuous.

Victoria has an indoor garden that first opened as a huge saltwater pool in 1925 (Olympic swimmer and original *Tarzan* star Johnny Weissmuller competed here) and was converted into a big-band dance hall during World War II. The **Crystal Garden,** 731 Douglas St. (☎ **250/953-8800**), is filled with rare and exotic tropical flora and fauna. The garden is open daily from 10am to 5:30pm (later during summer). Admission is C$9 (US$6) for adults, C$7 (US$4.70) for seniors, C$4 (US$2.70) for children 5 to 16, and C$25 (US$17) for families; children under 5 are free.

Just outside downtown, **Mount Douglas Park** offers great views of the area, several hiking trails, and—down at the waterline—a picnic/play area with a trail leading to a good walking beach.

About 45 minutes southwest of town, **East Sooke Park** is a 1,400-hectare (3,458-acre) microcosm of the West Coast wilderness: jagged seacoasts, Native petroglyphs, and hiking trails up to a 270-meter (886-foot) mountaintop. Access is via the Old Island Highway and East Sooke Road.

2 Especially for Kids

Nature's the thing for kids in Victoria. The city offers unique opportunities for kids to pet, prod, and point out creatures from whales to goats to giant butterflies and flying insects to sea anemones to hermit crabs. The oldest of petting zoos is the **Beacon Hill Children's Farm,** Circle Drive, Beacon Hill Park (☎ 250/381-2532), where kids can ride ponies; pet goats, rabbits, and other barnyard animals; and even cool off in the wading pool. Mid-March to mid-October, the farm is open daily from 10am to 5pm. Admission is by donation; most visitors are asked to give C$1 (US65¢) toward the park's upkeep.

For a new take on this old concept, visit the **Victoria Butterfly Gardens** (see "The Top Attractions" above). The **Crystal Gardens** (☎ 250/953-8800), behind The Empress hotel, also has butterflies, as well as macaws and pelicans, though the tawdry monkey cages give the place something of the aura of a run-down zoo. Closer to town and two shades creepier than the Butterfly Gardens is the **Victoria Bug Zoo,** 1107 Wharf St. (☎ 250/384-BUGS; www.bugzoo.bc.ca; e-mail: cmaier@bugzoo.bc.ca), home to praying mantises, stick insects, and giant African cockroaches; knowledgeable guides bring the bugs out and let you or your kids handle and touch them. Admission is C$6 (US$4) for adults and C$4 (US$2.70) for children 3 to 16; children under 3 are free.

Taking the Sightseeing Train

Daily at 8:15am, VIA Rail (☎ **800/561-8630** in Canada) offers a **sightseeing train** departing Victoria's E&N Station, 450 Pandora Ave. (near the Johnson Street Bridge), for the up-island city of Courtenay. Once in Courtenay, the train turns around, departs at 1:30pm, and arrives back in Victoria at 6pm. Round-trip adult fare (including tax) is C$51 (US$34) with 7-day advance purchase or C$81 (US$54) otherwise. Children under 12 travel free provided you book 5 days in advance, otherwise, the cost is C$41 (US$27).

Leaving from Victoria, the train climbs up the Malahat, providing spectacular views of Finlayson Arm and Goldstream Provincial Park. It then crosses the Niagara and Arbutus Canyons on trestles over 400-feet-long, and rises to approximately 300 feet up from the canyon floors. Descending once again towards sea level, the train follows the coast of the Straight of Georgia, offering unobstructed views of the Gulf Islands and the Coast Mountains, while the train winds through the wine region of the Cowichan Valley and the communities of Duncan, Chemainus, and Nanaimo, and the ocean resorts of Qualicum Beach and Parksville, before arriving in Courtenay. Many passengers simply stretch their legs then climb back aboard for the return journey. However, Courtenay also makes a great jumping off point for skiing at Mt. Washington, exploring Strathcona Park, visiting the Northern Gulf Islands, or continuing up to Northern Vancouver Island for some whale watching or kayaking.

The **Pacific Undersea Gardens** (see "The Top Attractions," above) is a face-to-face introduction to the sea creatures of the Pacific coast. In the underwater observatory, kids can meet a wolf eel eye-to-eye, view a giant octopus up close, and watch harbor seals cavort underwater with their pups. Better still, take the kids out to explore any of the tide pools on the coast. **Botanical Beach Provincial Park,** near Port Renfrew, is excellent, though the 60-kilometer (37-mile) drive west along Highway 14 may make it a bit far for some. Closer to town, try **French Beach** or **China Beach** (also along Hwy. 14), or even the beach in **Mount Douglas Park.** The trick is to find a good spot, bend down over a tide pool, and look—or else pick up a rock to see crabs scuttle away. Remember to put the rocks back where you found them.

In **Goldstream Provincial Park,** the Visitor Centre (☎ **250/478-9414**) has nature programs and activities geared especially for children. The **Swan Lake Christmas Hill Nature Sanctuary,** 3873 Swan Lake Rd. (☎ **250/479-0211;** www.swanlake.bc.ca), offers a number of nature-themed drop-in programs over the summer, including Insectmania and Reptile Day.

Back in the city, the **Royal British Columbia Museum** (see "The Top Attractions," above) has many displays geared toward kids, including one simulating a dive to the bottom of the Pacific. Others illustrate the intriguing life and culture of the West Coast Native tribes, who've inhabited the province for more than 10,000 years, and show the majestic beauty of the province's temperate rain forests and coastlines.

Miniature World (see "The Top Attractions" above), with its huge collection of dolls and dollhouses, model trains, and diminutive circus and battlefield displays, is a favorite with kids of all ages.

Located in Elk and Beaver Lake Regional Park (see "Outdoor Activities," below), **Beaver Lake** is a great freshwater spot where kids can enjoy a day of water sports and swimming in safe, lifeguard-attended waters.

On truly hot days, head for the mile-long water slide at the **All Fun Recreation Park,** 227 Millstream Rd. (☎ **250/474-3184;** www.allfun.bc.ca). June 14 to September 3, it's open daily from 11am to 7pm. The cost is C$18 (US$12) for sliders 11 years and older and C$14 (US$9) for those 4 to 10 years old; children under 4 are free. Cost for observers (which includes use of the hot tub, mini-golf, and beach volleyball courts) is C$6 (US$4). The park also has go-carts and batting cages.

3 Organized Tours

BUS TOURS

Gray Line of Victoria, 700 Douglas St. (☎ 250/388-5248), conducts tours of Victoria and Butchart Gardens. The 1½-hour "Grand City Tour" costs C$18 (US$12) for adults and C$9 (US$6) for children. In summer, tours depart every 30 minutes daily from 9:30am to 4:30pm; December to mid-March, there are daily departures at 10am, noon, and 2pm.

SPECIALTY TOURS

Victoria Harbour Ferries, 922 Old Esquimalt Rd. (☎ 250/708-0201), offers a terrific 45-minute tour of the Inner and Outer harbors for C$12 (US$8) for adults and C$6 (US$4) for children. Tours depart from any of the harbor ferry docks. A 50-minute tour of the gorge opposite the Johnson Street Bridge, where tidal falls reverse with each change of the tide, costs C$14 (US$9) for adults, C$12 (US$8) for seniors, and C$7 (US$4.70) for children. The ferries are adorably cartoonish, 12-person, fully enclosed blue boats, and every seat is a window seat. Harbor tours depart from seven stops around the Inner Harbour every 15 minutes daily from 10am to 10pm. If you wish to stop for food or a stroll, you can get a token good for reboarding at any time during the same day. June through September, gorge tours depart from the dock in front of The Empress every half hour from 10am to 8pm; at other times, the tours operate less frequently, depending on the weather.

    Heritage Tours and Daimler Limousine Service, 713 Bexhill Rd. (☎ 250/474-4332), guides you through the city, Butchart Gardens, and Craigdarroch Castle in a six-passenger British Daimler limousine. Rates start at C$65 (US$44) per hour per vehicle (not per person).

    The bicycle-rickshaws operated by **Kabuki Kabs,** 15-950 Government St. (☎ 250/385-4243), can usually be found on the causeway in front of The Empress. Prices for a tour are C$1 (US65¢) per minute for a two-person cab and C$1.50 (US$1) per minute for a four-person cab.

    Tallyho Horse-Drawn Tours, 2044 Milton St. (☎ 250/383-5067), has conducted tours of Victoria in horse-drawn carriages since 1903. Excursions start at the corner of Belleville and Menzies Streets; fares are C$14 (US$9) for adults, C$12 (US$8) for seniors, C$9 (US$6) for students, C$6 (US$4) for children 17 and under, and C$35 (US$23) for families (two adults and two children). Tours operate daily every 30 minutes from 9am to 10pm during summer (10am to 5:30pm in late Mar, Apr, May, and Sept). Tallyho also offers private tours (maximum six people) costing C$35 (US$23) for 15 minutes, C$60 (US$40) for 30 minutes, or C$105 (US$70) for an hour.

    To get a bird's-eye view of Victoria, take a 30-minute tour with **Harbour Air Seaplanes,** 1234 Wharf St. (☎ 250/385-9131). Rates are C$76 (US$51) per person; flights depart whenever there are four or more people ready (usually about every 30 to 45 min.).

    For a pleasant and informative stroll, join a guided walking tour through the downtown and Old Town neighborhoods. **First Island Destination and Travel** (☎ 250/658-8169; www.firstislandtours.com; e-mail: firstisland@islandnet.com) offers guided 3-hour tours of the Inner Harbour, Old Town, and Chinatown. Tours depart at 9am and 1pm Wednesday and Sunday. The cost is C$50 (US$34). The **Victoria Heritage**

Foundation, #1 Centennial Square (☎ **250/383-4546;** e-mail: vhf@ pinc.com), offers the excellent free pamphlet *James Bay Heritage Walking Tour.* The well-researched pamphlet (available at the Visitor Info Centre or from the Victoria Heritage office) describes a self-guided walking tour through the historic James Bay neighborhood.

The **Old Cemetery Society of Victoria** (☎ **250/598-8870;** www.oldcem.bc.ca; e-mail: oldcem@pinc.com) runs regular cemetery tours throughout the year. Particularly popular are the slightly eerie **Lantern Tours of the Old Burying Ground,** which begin at the Cherry Bank Hotel, 845 Burdett St., at 9pm nightly in July and August. The tour lasts about 1 hour. On Sundays throughout the year the Society offers historically focused tours of Ross Bay Cemetery. Tours depart at 2pm from Bagga Pasta, in the Fairfield Plaza, 1516 Fairfield Rd., across from the cemetery gate. Both tours are C$8 (US$5) per person or C$2 (US$1.35) for society members.

The **Haunted Walk of Victoria** (☎ **250/361-2619;** www.hauntedwalk.com) runs a regular lantern-light tour of Victoria's creepier spots. Call the info line for up-to-date rates and schedules.

4 Outdoor Activities

Mountain biking, kayaking, ecotouring, and in-line skating are popular in Victoria year-round, but that's just a smattering of what you can do. Alpine and Nordic skiing, parasailing, sea kayaking, canoeing, tidal-water fishing, fly-fishing, diving, and hiking are a few more options.

You don't have to lug all your equipment with you. In the sections below, specialized rental outfitters are listed with each activity. **Sports Rent,** 611 Discovery St. (☎ **250/385-7368**), is a general-equipment and water-sport rental outlet to keep in mind. Its entire inventory, including rental rates, is online at **www.sportsrentbc.com.**

BEACHES

Because you're on the sunny side of western Canada, you can take advantage of the beaches in and around the area. The most popular is Oak Bay's **Willows Beach,** at Beach and Dalhousie Roads along the esplanade. The park, playground, and snack bar make it a great place to spend the day building a sand castle. **Gyro Beach Park,** Beach Road on Cadboro Bay, is another good spot for winding down. At the **Ross Bay Beaches,** below Beacon Hill Park, you can stroll or bike along the promenade at the water's edge.

For a taste of the wild and rocky west coast, hike the oceanside trails in beautiful **East Sooke Regional Park.** (Take Hwy. 14 west, turn south on Gillespie Road, and then take East Sooke Road.)

Two inland lakes give you the option of swimming in freshwater. **Elk and Beaver Lake Regional Park,** on Patricia Bay Road, is 11 kilometers (7 miles) north of downtown Victoria; **Thetis Lake,** about 10 kilometers (6 miles) west, is where locals shed all their clothes but none of their civility.

BIKING

This is one of the best ways to get around Victoria. You can rent a bike for a few hours or a few days in the downtown area (see "Getting Around" in chapter 10). The 13-kilometer (8-mile) **Scenic Marine Drive** bike path begins at Dallas Road and Douglas Street, at the base of Beacon Hill Park. The paved path follows the walkway along the beaches before winding up through the residential district on Beach Drive. It eventually turns left and heads south toward downtown Victoria on Oak Bay Avenue. The **Inner Harbour pedestrian path** has a bike lane for cyclists who want to take a leisurely ride around the entire city seawall. The new **Galloping Goose Trail** (part of the Trans-Canada Trail) runs from Victoria west through Colwood and Sooke all the way up to Leechtown. If you don't want to bike the whole thing, there are numerous places to park along the way, as well as several places where the trail intersects with public transit. Call **BC Transit** at ☎ **250/382-6161** to find out which bus routes take bikes.

Bikes, helmets, locks, and child trailers are available by the hour or day at **Budget Car Rentals,** 727 Courtenay St., behind The Empress (☎ **250/953-5300**). Rentals run C$6 (US$4) per hour and C$20 (US$13) per day.

BIRDING

For those wanting to hook up with the local birding subculture, the **Victoria Natural History Society** runs regular weekend birding excursions. Their **event line** at ☎ 250/479-2054 lists upcoming outings and gives current contact numbers. For the self-propelled, **Goldstream Provincial Park** (see "Parks & Gardens" above) and the village of **Malahat**—both off Highway 1 about 40 minutes north of Victoria—are filled with dozens of varieties of migratory and local birds. Ninety-seven eagles were spotted at Goldstream Provincial Park one January day in 1995. **Elk and Beaver Lake Regional Park,** off Highway 17, has some rare species such as the rose-breasted grosbeak and Hutton's vireo. Ospreys also nest there. **Cowichan Bay,** off Highway 1, is the perfect place to observe ospreys, bald eagles, a few great egrets, and purple martins.

BOATING

Kayaks, canoes, and powerboats are available from **Island Boat Rentals,** 811 Wharf St., (☎ **250/995-1661;** www.greatpacificadventures.com). At the Oak Bay Marina, **Newport Yacht Sales** (☎ **250/595-2628;** www.newportyachtsales.bc.ca) offers single and multiday powerboat charters, while **Pacifica Sailing Charters** (☎ 250/ 744-7305; www.pacificacharters.com) offers skippered sailboat charters by the hour, as well as longer-term rentals. **BC Yacht Charters,** 1406-450 Simcoe St. (☎ 800/ 708-SAIL; www.sailbc.com), also offers sail trips and sailboat charters. The **Marine Adventure Centre,** 950 Wharf St. (☎ **250/995-2211;** www.marine-adventures. com), on the floatplane docks in the Inner Harbour, can arrange powerboat rentals and almost anything else marine related. Skippered sailing charters cost about C$90 (US$60) per hour. Unskippered (bareboat) powerboat rentals start around C$45 (US$30) per hour, usually with a 3- or 4-hour minimum. If you're taking the wheel yourself, don't forget to check the **marine forecast** by calling ☎ 250/ 656-7515 before casting off.

BUNGEE JUMPING

Did you ever want to jump off a bridge? Well, you can fulfill your dreams from a 42-meter (140-ft.) trestle at the **Bungy Zone** (☎ 250/753-5867; www. bungyzone. com) near Nanaimo. North America's only legally sanctioned bridge jump, it has given a wedding party a flying start and sponsored more than one nude-jumping weekend to benefit charity. To leap high over the Nanaimo River from a specially constructed steel-trestle bridge, you'll pay C$95 (US$64) for your first leap and C$25 (US$17) for all subsequent jumps for the remainder of your jumping life. You can even choose how far into the icy mountain waters you want to go. The Bungy Zone is open daily from 11:30am to 7pm in summer, with reduced hours in fall and winter. There's a C$2 (US$1.35) admission fee for those who just want to watch. The Bungy Zone is 66 kilometers (41 miles) north of Victoria and 13 kilometers (8 miles) south of Nanaimo, off Highway 1. There's free shuttle service from Nanaimo.

CANOEING & KAYAKING

✪ **Ocean River Sports,** 1437 Store St., Victoria, B.C. V8W 3J6 (☎ **250/381-4233;** www.oceanriver.com), can equip you with everything from single-kayak, double-kayak, and canoe rentals to life jackets, tents, and dry-storage camping gear. Rental costs for a single kayak range from C$14 (US$9) per hour to C$42 (US$28) per day. Multiday and weekly rates are also available. In addition, the company offers numerous guided tours of the Gulf Islands and the B.C. west coast. For beginners, there's the guided 3-hour Explore Tour of the coast around Victoria or Sooke, costing C$75 (US$50). There's also a guided 2-day/1-night Coastal Expedition trip to a nearby coastal island and back costing C$199 (US$133).

DIVING

The coastline of **Pacific Rim National Park** is known as "the graveyard of the Pacific." Submerged in the water are dozens of 19th- and 20th-century shipwrecks and the marine life that has taken up residence in them. According to the Cousteau Society, the dive site is second in the world only to the Red Sea. Underwater interpretive trails help you identify what you see in the artificial reefs. If you want to take a look for yourself, contact **Ocean Sports,** 800 Cloverdale St. (☎ **250/475-2202;** www. oceansports.com), or **The Ogden Point Dive Centre,** 199 Dallas Rd. (☎ **250/ 479-0244;** www. divevictoria.com). Through Ocean Sports, head-to-toe equipment rental is C$50 (US$34) for 2 days, and dive trips start at C$50 (US$34) for two dives plus lunch.

FISHING

Saltwater fishing's the thing out here, and unless you know the area, it's probably best to take a guide. **Adam's Fishing Charters** (☎ **250/370-2326;** www.adamsfishingcharters. com) and the **Marine Adventure Centre,** 950 Wharf St. (☎ **250/ 995-2211;** www.marine-adventure.com), are good places to start. Both are on the Inner Harbour down below the Visitor Info Centre. (See also "Boating," above.) Chartering a boat and guide starts around C$75 (US$50) per hour, with a minimum of three or four hours.

To fish, you need a nonresident saltwater fishing license. Licenses for saltwater fishing (including the salmon surcharge) cost C$14 (US$9) for 1 day for nonresidents and C$12 (US$8) for BC residents. Tackle shops sell licenses, have details on current restrictions, and often carry copies of the current publications *BC Tidal Waters Sport Fishing Guide* and *BC Sport Fishing Regulations Synopsis for Non-Tidal Waters.* Independent anglers should also pick up a copy of the *BC Fishing Directory and Atlas.* **Robinson's Sporting Goods Ltd.,** 1307 Broad St. (☎ **250/385-3429**), is a reliable source for information, recommendations, lures, licenses, and gear.

GOLFING

Fortunately for golfers, Victoria's Scottish heritage didn't stop at the tartan shops. The greens here are as beautiful as those at St. Andrew's, yet the fees are reasonable. The **Cedar Hill Municipal Golf Course,** 1400 Derby Rd. (☎ **250/595-3103**), is an 18-hole public course 3.3 kilometers (2 miles) from downtown Victoria; day-time greens fees are C$32 (US$21) and twilight fees (after 3pm) are C$28 (US$19). The **Cordova Bay Golf Course,** 5333 Cordova Bay Rd. (☎ **250/658-4075;** www. cordovabaygolf. com), is northeast of the downtown area. Designed by Bill Robinson, the 18-hole course features 66 sand traps and some tight fairways. Greens fees are C$47 (US$31) Monday to Thursday and C$50 (US$34) on Friday, Saturday, Sunday, and holidays. The **Olympic View Golf Club,** 643 Latoria Rd. (☎ **250/474-3673;** www. olympicview.bc.ca), is one of the top 35 golf courses in Canada. Amid 12 lakes and a pair of waterfalls, this 18-hole, 6,414-yard course is open daily year-round. Greens fees are C$49 (US$33) Monday to Thursday and C$55 (US$37) on Friday, Saturday, Sunday, and holidays. You can also call the **Last Minute Golf Hotline** at ☎ 800/684-6344 or 604/878-1833 for substantial discounts and short-notice tee times at courses around the area.

HIKING

Goldstream Provincial Park (30 min. west of downtown along Hwy. 1) is a tranquil site for a short hike through towering cedars and clear, rushing waters. The hour-long hike up **Mount Work** provides excellent views of the Saanich Peninsula and a good view of Finlayson Arm. The trailhead is a 30- to 45-minute drive. Take Highway 17 north to Saanich, then take Highway 17a (the West Saanich Road) to Wallace Drive, turn right on Willis Point Drive and right again on the Ross-Durrance Road, looking for the parking lot on the right. There are signs along the way. Equally good, though more of a scramble, is the hour-plus climb up **Mount Finlayson** in Gowland-Tod Provincial Park (take Hwy. 1 west, get off at the Millstream Road exit, and follow Millstream Road north to the very end). The very popular **Sooke Potholes** trail wanders up beside a river to an abandoned mountain lodge. Take Highway 1a west to Colwood, then Highway 14 (the Sooke Road). When you reach Sooke, turn north on the Sooke River Road and follow it to the park.

For a taste of the wild and rocky west coast, hike the oceanside trails in beautiful **East Sooke Regional Park.** (Take Hwy. 14 west, turn south on Gillespie Road, and then take East Sooke Road.)

For a serious backpacking run, go 104 kilometers (65 miles) west of Victoria on Highway 14 to Port Renfrew and **Pacific Rim National Park.** The challenging **West Coast Trail,** extending 77 kilometers (48 miles) from Port Renfrew to Bamfield, was originally established as a lifesaving trail for shipwrecked sailors (see chapter 17). Plan a 7-day trek if you want to cover the entire route; reservations are required, so call ☎ 604/663-6000. The trail is rugged and often wet, but the scenery changes from old-growth forest to magnificent secluded sand beaches, making it worth every step. You may even spot a few whales along the way. **Robinson's Sporting Goods Ltd.,** 1307 Broad St. (☎ 250/385-3429), is a good place to gear up before you go. Ask at Robinson's about the newer, less challenging Juan de Fuca Marine Trail, connecting Port Renfrew and the Jordan River, about 48 kilometers (30 miles).

For groups of 10 or more who want to learn more about the surrounding flora and fauna, book a naturalist-guided tour of the island's rain forests and seashore with **Coastal Connections Interpretive Nature Hikes,** 1027 Roslyn Rd. (☎ 250/480-9560; www.islandnet.com/~coastcon/). A 6-hour rainforest hike, including a gourmet picnic lunch, provides a wonderful introduction to this unique ecosystem. C$79 (US$53) per person. Another company offering guided nature hikes is **Nature Calls,** 12 Falstaff Place (☎ 877/361-HIKE; http://members.home.net/ecotours/). Tours cost from C$60 to C$110 (US$40 to US$74) and go to **Botanical Beach, East Sooke Park,** or the **Carmanah Valley.** The same company also offers a 4-day trip on the **Juan de Fuca trail** for C$595 (US$399), meals, tents, and guide included.

For something less strenuous but still scenic, try the **Swan Lake Christmas Hill Nature Sanctuary,** 3873 Swan Lake Rd. (☎ 250/479-0211; www.swanlake.bc.ca). A floating boardwalk wends its way through this 40-hectare (100-acre) wetland past resident swans that love to be fed; the adjacent Nature House supplies feeding grain on request.

SKIING

Mount Washington Ski Resort, P.O. Box 3069, Courtenay, B.C. V9N 5N3 (☎ 604/619-0550; 250/338-1515 snow report; www.mtwashington.bc.ca), in the

Comox Valley, is British Columbia's third-largest ski area, a 5-hour drive from Victoria and open year-round (for hiking or skiing, depending on the season). A 480-meter (1,600-ft.) vertical drop and 50 groomed runs are serviced by four chairlifts and a beginners' tow. Nineteen miles of track-set Nordic trails connect to Strathcona Provincial Park. Full-day rates are C$43 (US$29) for adults, C$35 (US$23) for seniors and students, and C$22 (US$15) for kids 7 to 12; kids under 7 are free. Equipment rentals are available at the resort. Take Highway 19 to Courtenay and then the Strathcona Parkway. It's 37 kilometers (23 miles) to Mount Washington.

WATER SPORTS

The **Crystal Pool & Fitness Centre,** 2275 Quadra St. (☎ 250/361-0732), is Victoria's main aquatic facility. The 50-meter lap pool, children's pool, diving pool, sauna, whirlpool, and steam, weight, and aerobics rooms are open daily from 6am to midnight. Drop-in admission is C$4.20 (US$2.80) for adults, C$3.15 (US$2.10) for seniors and students, and C$2.10 (US$1.40) for children 6 to 12; free for children under 6. **Beaver Lake** in Elk and Beaver Lake Regional Park (see "Birding" above) has lifeguards on duty as well as picnicking facilities along the shore.

Surfing has recently taken off on the island. The best surf is along the west coast at **China, French,** and **Mystic** beaches. You can rent boards and wet suits–along with almost any kind of water-sport gear–at **Ocean Sports,** 800 Cloverdale St. (☎ 250/475-2202; www.oceansports.com).

Windsurfers skim along outside the Inner Harbour and on Elk Lake when the breezes are right. Though there are no specific facilities, French Beach, off Sooke Road on the way to Sooke Harbour, is a popular local windsurfing spot.

WHALE WATCHING

The waters surrounding the southern tip of Vancouver Island teem with orcas (killer whales), as well as harbor seals, sea lions, bald eagles, and harbor and Dall porpoises. With the boom in ecotourism, Victoria teems with whale-watching outfitters. They aren't hard to find, and prices are very competitive. The main difference is between the 12-person Zodiac, where the jolting ride is almost as exciting as seeing the whales, and tours that take larger, more leisurely craft. Both offer excellent platforms for seeing whales.

The **Victoria Marine Adventure Centre,** 950 Wharf St. (☎ 250/995-2211; www.marine-adventures.com), is just one of many outfits offering whale-watching tours in Zodiacs and/or covered boats. Adults and kids will learn a lot from the naturalist guides, who explain the behavior and nature of the orcas, gray whales, sea lions, porpoises, cormorants, eagles, and harbor seals encountered along the way. Fares are C$75 (US$50) for adults and C$49 (US$33) for children.

Pride of Victoria Cruises, Oak Bay Beach Hotel, 1175 Beach Dr. (☎ 250/592-3474; www.oakbaybeachhotel.com), offers 3½-hour whale-watching charters daily from March through October (on Sat only during the rest of the year) on either a 45-foot catamaran or a 28-foot converted pleasure cruiser. Both have washroom facilities and bar service. A picnic-style lunch is served on the cruise. Fares are C$79 (US$53) for adults and C$39 (US$26) for children 4 to 12; free for children under 4; lunch is C$8 (US$5) per person. There's a complimentary shuttle from downtown.

Other reputable whale-watching companies are **Prince of Whales,** 812 Wharf St. (☎ 250/383-4884; www.princeofwhales.com), just below the Visitor Info Centre, and **Orca Spirit Adventures** (☎ 250/383-8411; www.orcaspirit.com), which departs from the Coast Harbourside Hotel dock.

14 Victoria Strolls

Victoria has always been a transient's town, from miners and mariners to loggers and lounge-lizards, from hard-core hippies to retired but involved investment counselors. On three occasions I've packed up and moved from Victoria myself.

—folk singer Valdy

Victoria's ambiance is made for the wanderer, its pavements picture-perfect for perambulation—Victoria, in short, is a great place to walk. In-line skating's good, too. Scooters and skateboards are also gaining ground. The tours below work whatever your favored form of transportation.

Walking Tour 1—The Inner Harbour

Start: The Tourist Info Centre (812 Wharf St.) on the Inner Harbour.
Finish: The Tourist Info Centre.
Time: 2 hours, not including shopping, museum, and pub breaks.
Best Times: Late afternoon, when the golden summer sunlight shines on The Empress.
Worst Times: Late in the evening, when the shops close and the streets empty.

Victoria was born on the Inner Harbour. When the Hudson's Bay Company's West Coast head of operations, James Douglas, happened across this sheltered inlet in 1843 while searching for a new corporate HQ, it was love at first site. "The place appears a perfect Eden," he wrote to a friend. High praise indeed, although as Douglas was pretty deep into local real estate, his words should be taken with a wee bit of salt. His confidence in the location certainly paid off, however, for less than 20 years after Douglas set foot onshore, the native stands of Garry oak had been supplanted by small farms, the town was choked with miners and mariners, and the harbor was full of ships, many of which had circumnavigated the globe. This trip doesn't go nearly as far, but it does circumnavigate the Inner Harbour, showing some of its lesser-known nooks and crannies while providing an opportunity to enjoy the view as a Victorian sailor would have, quaffing a locally brewed pint from the deck of a stout Victoria pub.

We begin our tour at the:

1. **Victoria Tourist Info Centre,** 812 Wharf St., without a doubt the finest-looking tourist center in the world—a masterful art

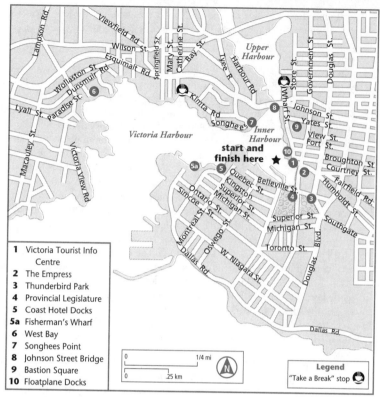

Legend

"Take a Break" stop

1 Victoria Tourist Info
  Centre
2 The Empress
3 Thunderbird Park
4 Provincial Legislature
5 Coast Hotel Docks
5a Fisherman's Wharf
6 West Bay
7 Songhees Point
8 Johnson Street Bridge
9 Bastion Square
10 Floatplane Docks

deco pavilion topped with a shining white obelisk rising high above the Inner Harbour. It would be a tribute to the taste and vision of city tourism officials, except that it started out life as a gas station.

From the Info Centre, thread your way south through the jugglers and musicians on the causeway until you're opposite:

2. The Empress, 721 Government St. "There is a view, when the morning mists peel off the harbor, where the steamers tie up, of the Houses of Parliament on one hand, and a huge hotel on the other, which is an example of cunningly fitted-in waterfronts and facades worth a very long journey." Thus spoke Rudyard Kipling during a visit to the city in 1908. If he'd come only 5 years earlier he would've been looking at a swamp, and a nasty garbage-choked one at that. The causeway was then a narrow bridge over the tidal inlet, and as Victorians made a habit of pitching their refuse over the rail, the bay was, not surprisingly, a stinking cesspit of garbage and slime. In 1900, the ever-shrewd Canadian Pacific Railway made an offer to the city—we'll build a causeway and fill in the stinky bay if you let us keep the land. The city jumped at the offer. Little was expected—the land was swamp after all. But taking their cue from the good folk in Amsterdam, the CPR drove long pilings down through the muck to provide a solid foundation. And on top of that, they built The Empress. The architect was Francis Rattenbury, and his design was masterful, complementing his own Legislature Buildings to create the viewscape that has defined the city ever since.

Round the south side of The Empress is a formal rose garden—well worth poking your nose in for a sniff. Cut through the garden and cross over Belleville Street and continue another half-block west to the corner of Douglas Street, where you'll find:

3. **Thunderbird Park**, instantly recognizable by its forest of totem poles. Even if you've overdosed on the ubiquitous 6-inch souvenir totem, take a second look at these. The original poles on this site had been collected in the early 1900s from various villages up and down the coast. Some decades later, when officials decided the severely weathered poles needed restoring, they discovered the art of native carving had eroded even more than their collection of poles. From all the thousands of carvers on the coast, only one man still carried on the craft. In 1952, Kwakiutl artist Mungo Martin set up a carving shed on the park grounds and began the work of restoration. Martin replaced or repaired all the existing poles. At the same time, he taught his son and step-grandson-in-law to carve. Seeing them at work renewed public interest in the form. Other young artists came to learn and train. Eventually, this modest training ground led to a revival of totem carving and native artistry among coastal natives.

All poles have a purpose; most tell a story. The stories associated with the poles in Thunderbird Park have unfortunately been lost, but many of the figures are easily recognized, including Thunderbird (look for the outstretched wings and curly horns on the head), Raven, Bear, and Killer Whale.

On the edge of the park is the shed where Martin carved many of the poles. Feel free to poke your head in to take a look and ask the carvers what they're up to. The Native artists generally welcome questions and enjoy sharing their stories.

Walk west along Belleville past the modern-looking **Carillon Tower** (a gift from the Dutch people who settled in B.C.) and the not-to-be-missed-in-a-million-years-or-you're-wasting-your-time-in-Victoria **Royal BC Museum** (see "The Top Attractions" in chapter 13) and cross Government Street. You're now standing in front of the:

4. **Provincial Legislature**, 501 Belleville St. In 1892, a 25-year-old Yorkshireman arrived on the West Coast just as an architectural competition for a new Legislature Building in Victoria was announced. Francis Mawson Rattenbury had no professional credentials but was blessed with both talent and vaulting ambition. He submitted a set of drawings and, to the surprise of all, beat out 65 other entries from around the continent. It made his career. For the next 30 years, nearly all official buildings in Victoria, and many around the province, would be Rattenbury creations.

The Provincial Legislature is open for tours from 9am to 5pm. In summer, the 40-minute tours start every 20 minutes (see "The Top Attractions" in chapter 13).

Across the street, the Greek temple–style **Royal Wax Museum** (see "The Top Attractions" in chapter 13) is another Rattenbury creation, built originally as the CPR's Steamship ticket office. From here, ocean liners once departed for San Francisco, Sydney, and Canton.

From the Legislature lawn, dodge past the horse-drawn calèches parked on Menzies Street and walk west on Belleville Street for 2 blocks to Pendray Street. The road takes a sharp right, but follow the path leading down to a waterfront walkway as it curves around Laurel Point. This headland was long the site of a stinking, fuming paint factory, so Victorians were delighted when it finally shut down and the luxurious **Laurel Point Inn** was erected in its place. Round the back of the Laurel is a pleasant Japanese garden if you're in a restrained and contemplative mood, and a patio restaurant if you're not. Continuing around the pathway past the first few jetties takes you to the:

5. Coast Hotel Docks, one of several ports of call of the Victoria Harbour Ferry Company (☎ **250/708-0201**). From here, the official Frommer's route is to take the ferry all the way across the harbor to West Bay (Point 6). Along the way there'll be views of the Olympic Mountains to the south and possibly a seal or bald eagle for company. Alternatively, you can take a short hop out to Fisherman's Wharf, where there are fresh-fish sales in season. Or you can go directly across to Spinnaker's Brew Pub on the far shore. Or you can go across to Songhees Point (Point 7) or even directly to the Harbour Canoe Club docks (Point 8). You can even give up on your feet entirely and take the full Harbour Ferries tour. Presuming you stick with the program, however, the next stop is:

6. West Bay. A pleasant little residential neighborhood with a picturesque marina, West Bay isn't anything much to write home about. What is worthwhile is the waterfront walkway that wends its way from here back east toward the city. The trail twists and curves through several parks, and there are views south through the harbor out to the Strait of Juan de Fuca and the Olympic Mountains beyond. After about 20 minutes of walking, if you feel yourself tiring, it may be time to:

☕ **TAKE A BREAK**   Excellent beer brewed on the premises, combined with an above-average patio, make **Spinnaker's Brew Pub,** 308 Catherine St. (☎ **250/386-BREW**), open daily 11am to 11pm, a dangerously time-consuming port of call. For those looking for more substantial fare, the pub grub's very good and the entrees are above average. The on-site bakery makes inspired beer bread, as well as a range of more delicate goods.

From the pub, continue along the shoreline until you see the totem pole that stands at:

7. Songhees Point. The point is named after the Native band that once lived on the site. The Songhees had originally set up their village close to Fort Victoria, near the current site of Bastion Square, but relations with the Hudson's Bay Company were always a bit awkward. In 1844, a dispute over a pair of company oxen slaughtered by the Songhees was settled only after Commander Roderick Finlayson blew up the chief's house. A few years later, after a fire started in the Native village spread and nearly burned down the fort, Finlayson told the Songhees to relocate across the Inner Harbour. They refused at first, pointing out quite rightly that as it was their land, they could live wherever they liked. They assented to the move only after Finlayson agreed to help dismantle and transport the Songhees' longhouses.

The totem pole here is called the **Spirit of Lakwammen,** presented to the city to commemorate the 1994 Commonwealth Games. Continue on the pathway around the corner. The patio of the **Ocean Point Resort,** on your right, provides a great view of The Empress. In summer, they show silent movies after sunset. A little farther on is the:

8. Johnson Street Bridge. Trivia question: Who designed San Francisco's Golden Gate Bridge? Answer: The same guy who designed Victoria's Johnson Street Bridge. Alas, while the soaring Golden Gate span is justly famous for its elegance, this misshapen lump of steel and concrete is something designer Joseph Strauss would likely wish forgotten. Fortunately for him, word of this effort seems not to have reached San Fran.

Cross the bridge and walk past the Esquimalt and Nanaimo (E&N) Railway station (the daily sightseeing train to/from Nanaimo leaves and departs from here—see chapter 10) and turn left onto Store Street. Walk 1 block north to Swift Street, turn left, walk downhill to the end of the street, and:

☕ **TAKE A BREAK**   Having a drink at the **Harbour Canoe Club,** 450 Swift St. (☎ **250/361-1940**), it's hard to know who to admire more: the 19th-century engineers who built everything with brick and beam and always twice as thick as it had to be; the restorers who took this old building (once the site of the City Light Company) and turned it into a sunlit cathedral of a room; the owner, who had the vision to pay the restorers; the chef, who made the delicious plate of appetizers now quickly disappearing from the huge wooden bench; or the brewmaster, whose copper cauldrons produce such a superior brew. Try the taster option—six small glasses of different brews for about the price of a pint—and toast them all. The Club is open Sunday through Tuesday 11:30am to 11pm, Wednesday through Thursday 11:30am to midnight, and Friday through Saturday 11:30am to 1am.

Salutations complete, wander back up Swift Street, turn right, and continue south down Store Street for 2 blocks, where Store Street becomes Wharf Street. Walk another 3 blocks until you reach:

9. **Bastion Square.** As the name implies, this pleasant public space stands on the site of the Hudson's Bay Company's original Fort Victoria. The fort was demolished in 1863 and the land sold off for development. When the B.C. government bought and renovated the Rithet Building on the southwest corner of the square, workers uncovered Fort Victoria's original water well, complete with mechanical pump. It's now in the building's lobby.

Continue south on Wharf Street another 2 blocks until you come to the pinkish **Dominion Customs House.** Built in 1876, it was one of the first tangible signs of British Columbia's new status as a Canadian province. The Second Empire style was meant to impart a touch of Eastern civilization in the midst of this raw Western town.

Take the walkway by the Customs house down to the waterline and walk out on the:

10. **Floatplane Docks** for a totally different view of the harbor. Early in the morning these docks buzz with activity as floatplanes fly in and out on their way to/from Seattle, Vancouver, and points north. The **Blackfish Cafe,** 950 Wharf St. (☎ **250/385-9996**), open 8am to 4pm, is a good spot to tuck into a big greasy-spoon breakfast and eavesdrop on some pilot gossip. The docks are also the place to come to arrange for diving and whale-watching tours. Back up on Wharf Street you're just a hop, skip, and a jump from the Visitor Info tower, where the tour began.

Walking Tour 2—The Old Town & Chinatown

Start: The Empress hotel, 321 Government St.
Finish: The Empress.
Time: 2 hours, not including shopping, sightseeing, and eating stops.
Best Times: Any day before 6pm.
Worst Times: Any day after 6pm, when the shops close.

Walking Tour 2 —The Old Town & Chinatown

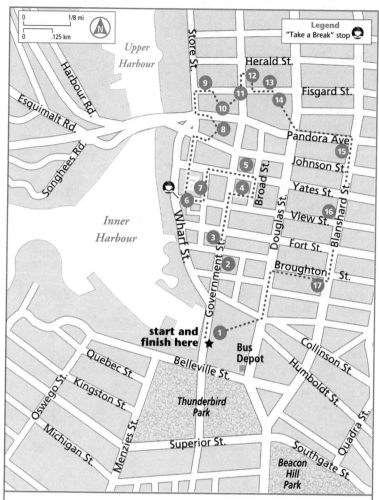

1 The Empress
2 Windsor Hotel building
3 Fort Victoria
4 Trounce Alley
5 Starfish Glassworks
6 Bastion Square
7 Maritime Museum
8 Market Square
9 Chinatown
10 Fan Tan Alley
11 Gate of Harmonious Interest
12 Chinese Settlement House
13 Chinese Imperial School
14 McPherson Playhouse
15 Congregation Emanu-El Synagogue
16 St. Andrew's Roman Catholic Cathedral
17 Greater Victoria Public Library

The Hanging Judge

Though Victorians were never quite as prim and proper as they liked to let on, they were still by and large a law-abiding bunch. Thus, it must have come as quite a shock to the sleepy outpost of 250 semi-English souls when, in 1858, the side-wheeler *Commodore* pulled into port, and 450 loud, smelly, drunken, and aggressive California miners swarmed into town. Gold had been discovered in the Fraser Canyon on the mainland, and Victoria was the first port of call.

By the end of that summer, more than 10,000 Yankee roughnecks had passed through town. Victorians weren't sure how to cope. The man who eventually brought order and the Queen's law to this roiling mob was a 39-year-old lawyer with a thick black beard and the piercing gaze of a gunfighter. Sent from England as Chief Judge, **Matthew Baillie Begbie** rode from town to town—bedroll in one saddlebag, judge's wig and bright red robes in the other—often quelling disturbances through sheer bravado. When a riot broke out in the town of Yale, Begbie rode in without escort. "Easy, boys," he told the restless crowd of miners. "There must be no killing. For if there is killing there will be hanging." And this was no mere bluff: Before he retired in 1894, Begbie sentenced 27 men to hang, 12 of them right outside the Victoria courthouse. When, as sometimes happened, the clannish miners refused to convict one of their own, Begbie didn't hesitate to let his true feelings be known. "It seems to me, sir," Begbie said to the accused on one of these occasions, "that you are plainly guilty, and this jury just as plainly a pack of fools. But as they have set you free I am powerless to keep you. I hope only that the next man you kill be a member of the jury."

This tour also begins at one of Victoria's most impressive landmarks. In front of you is:

1. **The Empress,** 321 Government St. (see "Architectural Highlights & Historic Homes" in chapter 13), designed by Francis Rattenbury.

   Walking north up Government Street, you'll find a number of historic buildings. British Columbia's oldest brick structure is the:

2. **Windsor Hotel building,** 901 Government St. Built in 1858 as the Victoria Hotel, the building's actually a perfect metaphor for the city. The original structure was a robust yet stylish piece of frontier architecture, with heavy red bricks formed into graceful Romanesque arches. Then, in the 1930s, when the city began pushing the "little bit of England" shtick, the original brick was covered over with stucco and fake Tudor half-timbering. Somewhere under the phony gentility, however, the robust frontier structure survives. (It's been through worse. In 1876, the hotel underwent major unexpected remodeling after the owner searched for a gas leak with a lit candle.)

   On the next block, you'll find a brass sidewalk plaque indicating the former site of:

3. **Fort Victoria,** 1022 Government St., constructed in 1843 by the Hudson's Bay Company as the western headquarters of its fur-trading empire. Bounded by Broughton and View Streets, between Government and Wharf Streets, the fort had two octagonal bastions on either side of its tall cedar picket walls. It was torn down during the 1860s gold boom to make room for more businesses. You can get an idea of its size and shape from the line of light-colored bricks—inscribed with the names of early settlers—in the sidewalk that delineates the boundaries

of the original walls. The first school in British Columbia was built on this site in 1849. The spot now houses **The Spirit of Christmas** shop.

Continue north 2 more blocks, just past View Street, where a little byway cuts off on the right, running 1 block to Broad Street. It's known as:

4. Trounce Alley. This is where miners and mariners spent their extra cash on the ladies. The alley is still lit by gas lamps, hung with heraldic crests, and ablaze with flower baskets and potted shrubs. You can stroll through shops selling jewelry, fashions, and crafts, or stop for a bite to eat. Trounce Alley ends abruptly at Broad Street.

Turn left on Broad Street, walk north 1 block, turn left on Yates Street, and walk east 1 block until you come to the:

5. Starfish Glassworks, 630 Yates St. Closed Tuesday, open Monday and Wednesday through Saturday 10am to 6pm, also Sunday noon to 6pm. This ex-bank building is one of the city's finest examples of the Moderne style, but what makes it worth a visit are the gallery and workshop inside. Set up by a couple of glassblowing artists who couldn't get kiln time in Vancouver, the interior has been cleverly designed with the workshop on the ground floor and the gallery space on an open catwalk above. Step inside and watch the glassblowing, or wander around the gallery and admire the finished products.

From here, go 1 more block west on Yates, turn left on Langley Street, and go 1 block south. Turn right on View Street and you're in:

6. Bastion Square, which was a bustling area with waterfront hotels, saloons, and warehouses during the late 19th century. Earlier it had been the site of one of Fort Victoria's octagonal gun bastions. In 1963, the area was restored as a heritage square. This is a good place to:

☕ **TAKE A BREAK**   Even if you're not hungry, it's worth stopping at **Re-Bar,** 64 Bastion Sq. (☎ **250/361-9223**), for a juice—say a combination of grapefruit, banana, melon, and pear, with bee pollen to keep your energy up. If you're hungry then rejoice: Re-bar has the city's best vegetarian comfort food. Disturbingly wholesome as that may sound, it's not only tasty, it's also fun, and a great spot to go with kids. It's open Monday to Thursday from 8:30am to 9pm, Friday and Saturday from 8:30am to 10pm, and Sunday from 8:30am to 3:30pm.

The provincial courthouse and hangman's square were once located on this restored pedestrian mall, but the courthouse is now occupied by the:

7. Maritime Museum, 28 Bastion Sq., where you can get a glimpse into Victoria's naval and shipping history (see "The Top Attractions" in chapter 13). It's housed in Victoria's original courthouse and jail.

More than a century ago, Victoria's business was transacted in this area of winding alleys and walkways. Warehouses, mariner's hotels, and shipping offices have been carefully restored into shops, restaurants, and galleries. You'll occasionally find historic plaques explaining the function of each building before it was renovated.

Turn north up Commercial Alley. Cross Yates Street, and a few steps farther west, turn north again up Waddington Alley. On the other side of Johnson Street is:

8. Market Square. This restored historic site was once a two-story complex of shipping offices and supply stores. It now contains more than 40 shops that sell everything from sports equipment and crafts to books and toys. There are also seven restaurants in the square; some have outdoor seating in the large open-air court where musicians often perform in summer.

Go north 1 block on Store Street and turn right (away from the harbor) onto Fisgard Street. You're now in North America's oldest:

9. **Chinatown.** Established in 1858 when the first Chinese arrived as gold seekers and railroad workers, this 6-block district fell into decline after World War I (as did many West Coast Asian communities when the U.S. and Canadian governments restricted Asian immigration). What remains is a fascinating peek into a well-hidden and exotic heritage.

On your right, halfway up the block, you'll find:

10. **Fan Tan Alley,** the world's narrowest street. It's no more than 4 feet wide at either end and expands to a little over 6 feet in the center. Through the maze of doorways (which still have their old Chinese signage), there are entries to small courtyards leading to more doorways.

During the late 1800s, this was the main entrance to "Little Canton," where the scent of legally manufactured opium wafted from the courtyards. Opium dens, gambling parlors, and brothels sprang up between the factories and bachelor rooms where male immigrants shared cramped quarters to save money.

Today you won't find any sin for sale here—just a few little shops dealing in crafts and souvenirs. You can enter the **Chinatown Trading Company,** 551 Fisgard St., from Fisgard Street or via a back door facing onto Fan Tan Alley. Hidden in its back room are a couple of mini-museums cleverly displaying artifacts from old Chinatown, including the original equipment from a 19th-century Chinese gambling house. When you're finished exploring the alley, return to Fisgard Street and continue heading east.

At the corner of Government and Fisgard Streets is the:

11. **Gate of Harmonious Interest.** This lavishly detailed dragon-headed red-and-gold archway was built in 1981 to commemorate the completion—after years of deterioration—of Chinatown's revitalization by the city and the Chinese Consolidated Benevolent Association. The gate is guarded by a pair of hand-carved stone lions imported from Suzhou, China.

One-half block up Government Street is the former location of the:

12. **Chinese Settlement House,** 1715 Government St. Newly arrived Chinese families once lived upstairs in this balconied building and made use of social services here until they were able to secure work and living quarters. The original Chinese Buddhist temple has been moved from the storefront to the second floor, but it's still open to visitors. Although admission is free, hours vary. You will have to check with temple staff to see if you may enter.

A half block up from the Gate of Harmonious Interest on Fisgard Street is the:

13. **Chinese Imperial School** (Zhonghua Xuetang), 36 Fisgard St. This red-and-gold pagoda-style building with a baked-tile roof and recessed balconies was built by the Chinese Benevolent Society. In 1907, the Victoria School Board banned non-Canadian Chinese children from attending public school, and in response, the society started its own community elementary school the following year. The school is open to the public during the week and still provides children and adults with instruction in Chinese reading and writing on weekends.

Just east of the school is the:

14. **McPherson Playhouse,** 3 Centennial Sq. (☎ **250/386-6121**). Formerly a vaudeville theater, it was the first of the vast Pantages Theatres chain (Alex Pantages went into showbiz after striking it rich in the Klondike goldfields). The

building was restored in the 1960s and is now Victoria's main performing arts center. The baroque interior is stunning—well worth a peek. City Hall and the police department are located in the office plaza surrounding the playhouse.

When you get to the southeast corner of Centennial Square, walk up 1 more block on Pandora Avenue to Blanshard Street. Here you'll find:

15. **Congregation Emanu-El Synagogue,** 1461 Blanshard St. (at Pandora Avenue), the oldest surviving Jewish temple on North America's west coast. Built in 1863, it has been proclaimed a national heritage site.

Turn south on Blanshard Street and walk 3 blocks to the corner of View Street, where you'll see the impressive:

16. **St. Andrew's Roman Catholic Cathedral,** 740 View St. Built during the 1890s, this is glorious Victorian High Gothic at its bodice-ripping best. The facade is 23 meters (75 ft.) across, the spire 53 meters (175 ft.) tall, and no frill or flounce or architectural embellishment was forgone in the design. Renovations in the 1980s incorporated the works of First Nations artists into the interior. The altar is by Coast Salish carver Charles Elliot.

One block south at Fort Street is the beginning of **Antique Row,** which stretches 3 blocks east to Cook Street. Ignore that for the moment (or go explore and then come back) and continue 1 more block south on Blanshard. Walk across the plaza into the:

17. **Greater Victoria Public Library,** 735 Broughton St. The attraction here is the huge skylit atrium, complete with George Norris's massive hanging artwork, *Dynamic Mobile Steel Sculpture.* Built in 1979, the library complex takes up most of the block. Library hours are Monday, Wednesday, Friday, and Saturday 9am to 6pm and Tuesday and Thursday 9am to 9pm. The Library is closed on Sunday.

Duck out through the portal on Broughton Street and walk west to Douglas Street, then turn left and walk a block and a half south on Douglas until you see the entrance to the Victoria Convention Centre. Walk in and admire the indoor fountain and aviary. The Centre connects to The Empress, which was our starting place.

Biking Tour—Dallas Road

Start: The Empress, 321 Government St.
Finish: The Empress.
Time: 2 hours, not including picnic stops, sightseeing, shopping, or food breaks.
Best Times: Clear days with the sun shining, when the Olympic Mountains are out in all their glory.
Worst Times: Gray, rainy days.

Victoria cries out to be biked. The hills are modest, the traffic light and very polite, and the views incredible. When touring around by bike, you rarely have time to stop and pull out a point-by-point guide, so the descriptions offered here are shorter than for walking tours. The route is designed to take you a bit beyond what would be possible on foot, without getting into an expedition-length tour.

Start at **Budget Bike Rental,** 757 Douglas St. (☎ **250/953-5300**), behind **The Empress** hotel. Ride south down Douglas Street to **Thunderbird Park** and have a look at the totem poles. Continue east along Belleville Street past the **Legislature** and the **Coho ferry terminal,** then go round the corner onto Kingston Street, and go left through the small park to **Fisherman's Wharf.** From here, go south along **Dallas**

Road, past the helijet pad and the car-ferry docks, and stop at the entrance to the breakwater at **Ogden Point.** By this time, you should have a fabulous view of the Olympic Mountains. Park your bike and wander out along the breakwater or stop in at the **Ogden Point Cafe,** 204 Dallas Rd., for the same view without wind.

Continue east along the seaside bike path or on Dallas Road. Stop here and there as the urge strikes and do some beachcombing. A little ways on, past Douglas Street, cross Dallas and cut north into **Beacon Hill Park.** Stop at the petting zoo, look at the 127-foot-tall totem pole, or just enjoy Victoria's favorite park. Exit the park by the northeast corner on Cook Street and cycle a few blocks north into **Cook Street Village.** This is a good spot to grab a coffee and dessert or to shop for picnic supplies at the local deli or supermarket. Head back south on Cook Street to Dallas Road; turn left and continue east a kilometer or so to **Clover Point,** a short peninsula sticking out into the Strait of Juan de Fuca. It makes a fine picnic spot. From here, head east to **Ross Bay Cemetery,** Victoria's second oldest, where many local notables are buried, including former governor James Douglas and painter Emily Carr. From the north side of the cemetery, ride up the hill on **Stannard Street,** skirting the eastern edge of **Government House,** the official residence of the lieutenant governor.

When you reach **Rockland Avenue,** turn right and ride a few hundred meters past the many fine homes of this elite enclave to the main entrance to Government House. Though the residence itself is closed to the public, the formal gardens are open and well worth a wander. Round back, the hillside of Garry oaks is one of the last places to see what the area's natural fauna looked like before European settlers arrived. At the front, the rose garden is sumptuous. Just west of the gate on Rockland Avenue, turn right onto **Joan Crescent** and ride up the small hill to opulent **Craigdarroch Castle,** built by coal magnate Robert Dunsmuir for his wife, Joan. The castle is open for self-guided tours. From here, continue up Joan Crescent to Fort Street, turn right and go a very short way east to Yates Street, turn left and go 1 block to Fernwood Street, turn right and go 1 block north to **Pandora Street,** then turn left again and ride west down the hill. Keep an eye out for the **Christian Science church** at 1205 Pandora (where the street widens to include a boulevard in its center). Another 6 blocks west and you're at **Pandora and Government Streets,** with **Chinatown** to your right and **Market Square** to your left, and The Empress and the bike rental spot just a few blocks south.

Victoria Shopping

Victoria has dozens of little specialty shops that appeal to every taste and whim, and because the city is built on such a pedestrian scale, you can wander from place to place seeking out whatever treasure it is you're after. Nearly all of the areas listed below are within a short walk of The Empress, and given Victoria's parking "situation," it's probably best to hoof it. For those shops located more than six blocks from the Empress Hotel, bus information is provided. Stores are generally open Monday to Saturday from 10am to 6pm; some, but not many, are open on Sunday during summer.

1 The Shopping Scene

Explorers beware: The brick-paved **Government Street promenade,** from the Inner Harbour 5 blocks north to Yates Street, is a jungle of cheap souvenir shops. There are gems in here, certainly—Irish linen, fine bone china, quality Native art, and Cowichan Indian sweaters thick enough to bivouac in—but to find these riches you'll have to hack your way through tangled creepers of Taiwanese-made knick-knacks and forbidding groves of maple-syrup bottles. Even the good shops stock a few of these at the door to lure the unwary.

Farther north, the **Old Town district and Market Square** feature a fascinating blend of heritage buildings and up-to-date shops. Victoria's **Chinatown** is tiny, and, since most of the city's Chinese population has moved elsewhere, it lacks some of the thrumming authenticity of Chinatowns in Vancouver or San Francisco. The area has been charmingly preserved, however, and there are a number of gallery-quality art and ceramic shops, quirky back alleys (including Canada's thinnest commercial street), and at least one tacky tourist trap that knows enough not to take itself seriously.

On the eastern edge of downtown, **Antique Row** is justifiably renowned for its high-quality British collectibles. And if you're at all interested in the Native art of the Pacific Northwest, Victoria is a great place to add to your collection. If you're unacquainted with its bold and stylized figures drawn from a mythology as rich as that of ancient Greece, Victoria's a great place to buy a piece or two and begin an education.

2 Shopping A to Z

ANTIQUES

Victoria has long had a deserved reputation for antiques—particularly those of British origin. That so much Georgian pewter should end up on the Canadian west coast is largely due to the city's reputation as a retirement home for aging Brits. It's slightly morbid, but so long as they keep coming and time keeps marching forward, estate sales will keep "new" antique stock rolling in. Many of the best stores are in **Antique Row,** a 3-block stretch on Fort Street between Blanshard and Cook Streets. In addition to those listed below, check out **Jeffries and Co. Silversmiths,** 1026 Fort St. (☎ 250/383-8315); **Romanoff & Company Antiques,** 837 Fort St. (☎ 250/480-1543); and for furniture fans, **Charles Baird Antiques,** 1044A Fort St. (☎ 250/384-8809).

David Robinson Antiques. 1023 Fort St. ☎ **250/384-6425,** bus 10 to Blanshard or Cook St.

Here you'll find oriental rugs, silver, brass, porcelain, and period furniture. Though it's not as large as Faith Grant's shop, Robinson's pieces—especially his furniture—are particularly well chosen.

✪ **Faith Grant's Connoisseur Shop Ltd.** 1156 Fort St. ☎ **250/383-0121,** bus 10 to Blanshard or Cook St.

The farthest from downtown, this shop is also the best. The 14 rooms of this 1862 heritage building contain everything from Georgian writing desks to English flatware, not to mention fine ceramics, prints, and paintings. Furniture is an especially strong suit.

Vanity Fair Antique Mall. 1044 Fort St. ☎ **250/380-7274,** bus 10 to Blanshard or Cook St.

This large shop is fun to browse through, with crystal, glassware, furniture, and lots more. If you're feeling flush, it's certainly possible to spend here, but there are also many items you can easily pick up without taking out a bank loan.

ART
CONTEMPORARY

Fran Willis Gallery. 1619 Store St. ☎ **250/381-3422,** bus 5 to Douglas and Fisgard.

Soaring white walls and huge arched windows make this one of Victoria's most beautiful display spaces. The collection is strong on contemporary oils, mixed media, and bronzes, almost all by B.C. and Alberta artists.

Open Space. 510 Fort St. ☎ **250/383-8833.**

When does a healthy dollop of self-confidence start edging into pure pretension? This artist-run gallery and self-declared flag-bearer of the avant-garde has trod one side or the other of that line since 1971. Mostly, they get it right, so the gallery's usually worth a visit.

Winchester Galleries. 1010 Broad St. ☎ **250/386-2773.**

This slightly daring gallery features mostly contemporary oil paintings. Unlike elsewhere in town, very few wildlife paintings ever make it onto the walls.

NATIVE

Alcheringa Gallery. 665 Fort St. ☎ **250/383-8224.**

What began as a shop handling imports from the Antipodes has evolved into one of Victoria's truly great stores for aboriginal art connoisseurs. All the coastal tribes are represented in Alcheringa's collection, along with a significant collection of pieces from Papua, New Guinea. The presentation is museum quality, with prices to match.

Hill's Native Art. 1008 Government St. ☎ **250/385-3911.**

Exquisite traditional Native art includes wooden masks and carvings, Haida argillite and silver jewelry, bentwood boxes, button blankets, drums and talking sticks, and carved wooden paddles. Hill's is the store for established artists from up and down the B.C. coast, which means the quality is high, and so are the prices. Of course, you don't stay in business for 50 years without pleasing all comers, so Hill's has its share of dream catchers and other knickknacks.

Sa Nuu Kwa Gallery. 606 Johnson St. ☎ **250/480-5515.**

Here you'll find Native art freed from the knickknack shop and placed in the gallery where it belongs—beautiful masks, carvings, prints, and jewelry.

BOOKS

Avalon Metaphysical Centre. 62–560 Johnson St. (in Market Square). ☎ **250/ 380-1721.**

It's not the West Coast unless you've had a spiritual experience or brushed auras with someone who has. Avalon specializes in New Age books, crystals, rune stones, body oils, and videotapes of gurus who've already trodden the path to enlightenment. Sales are timed to coincide with the vernal equinox and summer solstice.

Crown Publications Inc. 521 Fort St. ☎ **250/386-4636.**

In addition to dry but informative government publications, this store stocks an excellent selection of books covering the history, nature, and culture of the Victoria area.

✪ **Munro's Books.** 1108 Government St. ☎ **250/382-2464.**

All bookstores should look so good: a mile-high ceiling in a 1909 heritage building, complete with heavy brass lamps and murals on the walls. (Never mind that the building was originally a bank.) All bookstores should also stock so many well-chosen books—over 35,000 titles, including an excellent selection of books about Victoria and books by local authors. The staff is friendly and helpful and very good at digging out obscure titles. The remainder tables in the middle aisle have some incredible deals.

Russell Books. 734 Fort St. ☎ **250/361-4447.**

This shop offers two floors of used (and some new) books for browsing.

CAMERAS

Lens and Shutter. 615 Fort St. ☎ **250/383-7443.**

Come here for all your camera needs—film, filters, lenses, cameras, or just advice.

CHINA, CRYSTAL & LINENS

Irish Linen Stores. 1019 Government St. ☎ **250/383-6812.**

The store sells everything Irish since 1910. You'll find handkerchiefs, scarves, place mats, doilies, napkins, lace, and more.

Sidney Reynolds. 801 Government St. ☎ **250/383-3931.**

This building opened as a saloon in 1908, became a bank in 1909, was converted into a shop in 1929, and now houses a wide array of fine porcelains, including tea sets and Victorian dolls.

CHINESE ARTS & CRAFTS

✪ **Chinatown Trading Company.** 551 Fisgard St. ☎ **250/381-5503,** bus 5 to Douglas and Fisgard St.

This unobtrusive storefront on Fisgard opens onto a veritable bazaar—three connected shops stocked with Chinese goods either useful or endearingly corny or both. Who wouldn't want kung fu shoes or a tin pecking chicken? There are also bamboo flutes, origami kits, useful and inexpensive Chinese kitchenware, and a few small museum displays of artifacts from Chinatown's past. Look for the sneaky back entrance off Fan Tan Alley.

Magpie Gift Studio. 556 Fisgard St. ☎ **250/383-1880,** bus 5 to Douglas and Fisgard St.

Small, intricate Chinese decorative items like jade- and brass-inlay rosewood boxes are the stock-in-trade here. There are also larger Asian antiques and elegant jade and amber jewelry.

CHRISTMAS ORNAMENTS

✪ **The Spirit of Christmas.** 1022 Government St. ☎ **250/385-2501.**

The thought of a shop selling Christmas ornaments year-round may send you reaching for lost bits of Dickensian invective, but before you start hurling "Bah humbugs," step inside and have a look. The store has everything from $300 woven vine wreaths to cotton nightshirts with caroling cows.

CIGARS & TOBACCO

E.A. Morris Tobacconist Ltd. 1116 Government St. ☎ **250/382-4811.**

A century-old tradition of custom-blended pipe tobacco is maintained in this small shop. You'll also find an impressive selection of cigars, including Cubans. Cuban cigars can't be brought into the United States, but a few brands like Horvath Bances duck the blockade by importing the tobacco into Canada and rolling the cigars here. You miss out on the special flavor imparted by child labor, but you also miss the year or so in a federal pen.

A DEPARTMENT STORE & A SHOPPING MALL

The Bay (Hudson's Bay Company). 1701 Douglas St. ☎ **250/385-1311.**

Here you'll find camping and sports equipment, Hudson's Bay woolen point blankets, and fashions by Tommy Hilfiger, Polo, DKNY, and Liz Claiborne, all under one roof.

Victoria Eaton Centre. Between Government and Douglas Sts. off Fort and View Sts. ☎ **250/389-2228.**

The Eaton Centre is actually a full modern shopping mall disguised as a block of heritage buildings. Inside, there are three floors of shops and boutiques centered around a glass atrium with a pleasant fountain. The stores offer both classic and outrageous fashions, china and crystal, kitchenware, gourmet foods, and books.

FASHIONS
FOR WOMEN

Breeze. 1150 Government St. ☎ **250/383-8871.**

This high-energy fashion outlet specializes in Esprit, for which they're exclusive distributors.

Hughes Ltd. 564 Yates St. ☎ **250/381-4405.**

This local favorite features designer fashions and trendy casual wear.

The Plum Clothing Co. 1298 Broad St. ☎ **250/381-5005.**

This local chain features quality dressy casuals designed with the baby-boomer figure in mind.

FOR WOMEN & MEN

A Wear. 1205 Government St. ☎ **250/382-9327.**

This large airy space in a converted heritage building houses large collections of fashionable threads for men and women.

The Edinburgh Tartan Shop. 921 Government St. ☎ **250/953-7790.**

Women love a man who wears a kilt. Go figure. If there's even a drop of Celtic blood in ye, this shop can set you up in a kilt made from your family tartan. It also stocks sweaters, motoring blankets, tartan by the yard, and kilt pins with authentic clan crests.

W.& J. Wilson's Clothiers. 1221 Government St. ☎ **250/383-7177.**

Canada's oldest family-run clothing store, this shop has been owned/managed by the Wilsons and their descendants since 1862. When you're in it for the long haul, of course, you try not to get too far ahead of the pack. Look for sensible casuals from British and European designers.

FOR MEN

British Importers. 1125 Government St. ☎ **250/386-1496.**

Victoria may be laid-back, but a man still needs a power suit, and this is the place to get it. Designer labels include Calvin Klein and Hugo Boss. Ties and leather jackets are also on display in this award-winning retail space.

SPECIALTY

Carnaby Street. 538 Yates St. ☎ **250/382-3747.**

If there's a do-gooder lurking somewhere inside your inner consumer, this is the place to come. Owners Robert Usatch and Rosina Izzard parlayed their years traveling the globe into a phenomenal set of contacts with third-world co-ops and cottage industries. The result is a store packed with extravagant folk art, intricate jewelry, and hand-crafted caftans, djellabas, and other ethnic textiles by the yard. It's a fun place, even if you're totally amoral. The clothes, in fact, are every bit as impractical as high-end designer fashions, just a lot cheaper.

Still Life. 551 Johnson St. ☎ **250/386-5655.**

Come here for quality retro. Zoot suits. Flowered prints. Hip-hugging gowns. Box dresses with padded shoulders. Two-tone wingtips and Mary Janes. Bowling shirts à la Ralph Kramden. Hawaiian shirts you can wear to the Don Ho hum-alongs. In short, everything of quality from the 1930s, 1940s, and 1950s, plus a lot that should probably have been forgotten but wasn't.

FOOD

Murchie's. 1110 Government St. ☎ **250/383-3112.**

It's worth stepping in here just to suck up the coffee smell or sniff the many specialty tea flavors. While you're imbibing the air, browse the extensive collection of fine china, silver, and crystal.

Roger's Chocolates. 913 Government St. ☎ **800/663-2220** or 250/384-7021.

"Quite possibly the best chocolates in the world" is how Roger's bills itself. How daring. For a more accurate (but lawyer- and litigation-proof) description, how about "quite possibly the best 98-year-old shrine to all things dark and sweet, still with original Tiffany glass and old-fashioned counters, well stocked with a variety of delectable creams, almond clusters, chews, and hard candy, all attractively presented in a range of plain or fancy boxes. Oh, and free samples, too." Roger's has other shops in Oak Bay and Whistler, and they're quite possibly just as good.

Silk Road Aromatherapy and Tea Company. 1624 Government St. ☎ **250/382-0006,** bus 5 to Douglas and Fisgard St.

A wide selection of tea blends and aromatherapy products are gracefully presented in this pretty shop on the edge of Chinatown.

GLASS

✪ **Starfish Glass Works.** 630 Yates St. ☎ **250/388-7827.**

Who says artists don't have a head for business? The principals of this gallery-cum-workshop moved to Victoria when they couldn't get kiln time in Vancouver. They took over and renovated an ex-bank building, installing the kiln on the ground floor and the gallery on an open catwalk above, so potential customers could watch works in progress while browsing among the finished products. The glasswork is incredible, the view enjoyable, the gallery highly successful. Anyone at the Harvard Business School looking for a case study?

JEWELRY

Jade Tree. 606 Humboldt St. ☎ **250/388-4326.**

You'll find jewelry made from British Columbia jade, which is mined in northern Vancouver Island, then crafted in Victoria and in China into necklaces, bracelets, and other items.

MacDonald Jewelry. 618 View St. ☎ **250/382-4113.**

Ian MacDonald designs and makes all his own jewelry, which are some interesting creations: diamonds cut in squares and triangles and styles from the traditional to cutting edge. It's a great place to hunt for rings and pearls as well as precious gems like sapphires, rubies, and emeralds.

MUSIC

Endangered Species Music. 575 Johnson St. ☎ **250/995-0099.**

This is the place in Victoria to browse for obscure and esoteric music, with many works still on vinyl.

NATIVE CRAFTS

Natives from the nearby Cowichan band are famous for their warm, durable sweaters, knitted with bold motifs from hand-spun raw wool. In addition to these beautiful knits, craftspeople create soft leather moccasins, moosehide boots, ceremonial masks, sculptures carved from argillite or soapstone, intricate baskets, bearskin rugs, and jewelry.

Cowichan Native Village. 200 Cowichan Way, Duncan. ☎ **250/746-8119,** no public transit.

Though a bit of a drive out of town, this store, owned/operated by the Cowichan, sells beautiful crafts and stocks an excellent selection of books and publications on First Nations history and lore. You can also watch artisans at work.

Cowichan Trading Ltd. 1328 Government St. ☎ **250/383-0321.**

A downtown fixture for almost 50 years, Cowichan Trading follows the standard layout for its displays: junky T-shirts and gewgaws in front, Cowichan sweaters, masks, and fine silver jewelry farther in.

OUTDOOR CLOTHES & EQUIPMENT

Ocean River Sports. 1437 Store St. ☎ **250/381-4233.**

A kayak shop near Bastion Square, this is the place to go to arrange a sea kayak tour—they'll also be happy to sell you a boat and all the gear. This is also a good spot for outdoor clothing and camping knickknacks, like that solar-heated shower.

Pacific Trekking. 1305 Government St. ☎ **250/388-7088.**

This is an excellent source of rain and hiking gear, plus a good place to pick up information on local hiking trails.

A PAWNSHOP

Universal Trading. 584 Johnson St. ☎ **250/383-9512.**

So it's not where you normally shop. This isn't your usual down-at-heel pawnbroker, either, but rather a quirky little curio shop with a few pieces that wouldn't be out of place in Antique Row. Case in point, the 1940s-era Harley parked out front.

A PUBLIC MARKET

Market Square. 560 Johnson St. ☎ **250/386-2441.**

Constructed from the original warehouses and shipping offices built here in the 1800s, this pleasant and innovative heritage reconstruction features small shops and restaurants surrounding a central courtyard, often the site of live performances in summer.

WINE

The Wine Barrel. 644 Broughton St. ☎ **250/388-0606.**

This shop sells B.C. wine and so much more: everything to do with wine, from wineglasses and corkscrews to books on snacks to serve with wine. A must-see for any wine lover.

The Wine Shoppe at Ocean Pointe Resort. 45 Songhees Rd. ☎ **250/360-5804,** bus 24 to Colville.

Here you'll find a great selection of Vancouver Island, Okanagan, French, and Australian wines. The staff is knowledgeable and very helpful.

16 Victoria After Dark

"Victoria is God's waiting room. It's the only cemetery in the entire world with street lighting"
> —a visitor from Gotham, as quoted in *Monday* magazine.

Ouch. That's a little harsh. More important, it's not exactly accurate. True, with retirees and civil servants making up a sizable segment of the population, Victoria is never going to set the world on fire, but taken together, the U. Vic. students, tourists, and a small but dedicated cadre of Victoria revelers form a party-going critical mass large enough to keep a small but steady scene alive. You just have to know where to look.

Monday magazine, a weekly tabloid published on Thursdays, is the place to start. Its listings section provides near-comprehensive coverage of what's happening in town and is particularly good for the club scene. Thanks to a spate of ownership changes, license swaps, and mysterious 4am fires, Victoria's club scene has gone through a major restructuring, and as of press time there was no sign of its settling down. If you can't find *Monday* in cafes or record shops, visit it on the Web at www.monday.com.

For information on theater, concerts, and arts events, contact the **Tourism Victoria Visitor Info Centre,** 812 Wharf St. (☎ **250/ 53-2033;** www.tourismvictoria.com). You can also buy tickets for all of Victoria's venues from the Info Centre, but only in person. Another source of theater and event info is the **CHEK-by-phone line** at ☎ **250/389-6460.**

Whatever you decide to do with your evening, chances are your destination's close at hand. One of the great virtues of Victoria's compact, walkable downtown is that nearly all of its attractions—concert halls, pubs, dance clubs, and theatres—are no more than a 10 minute walk from the Empress Hotel, easily reached by taking bus 5 to the Empress Hotel/Convention Centre. For those few nightlife spots a little farther out, bus route information is provided.

1 The Performing Arts

The **Royal Theatre,** 805 Broughton St., and the **McPherson Playhouse,** 3 Centennial Sq., share a common box office (☎ **888/ 717-6121** or 250/386-6121; www.rmts.bc.ca). The **Royal**—built in the early 1900s and renovated in the 1970s—hosts concerts by the

Victoria Symphony and performances by the Pacific Opera Victoria, as well as touring dance and theater companies. The **McPherson**—built in 1914 as the first Pantages Vaudeville Theatre—is home to smaller stage plays and performances by the
Victoria Operatic Society. The shared box office is open Monday to Saturday from
9:30am to 5:30pm and on performance days for the two hours before showtime. Bus
6 to Pandora and Government.

THEATER

Performing in an intimate playhouse that was once a church, the **Belfry Theatre Society,** 1291 Gladstone St. (☎ **250/385-6815;** www.belfry.bc.ca), is a nationally
acclaimed theatrical group that stages four productions from October through April
and a summer show in August. Bus 22 to Fernwood Street. Expect dramatic works by
contemporary Canadian playwrights. Tickets are C$15 to C$25 (US$10 to US$17)
for adults; senior and student discounts are available. The box office is open Monday
to Friday from 9:30am to 5pm, with hours extended to an hour before showtime on
performance days.

The **Intrepid Theatre Company,** 301-1205 Broad St. (☎ **888/FRINGE2** or
250/383-2663), runs two yearly theater festivals. In spring, it's the **Uno Festival of
Solo Performance,** a unique event of strictly one-person performances. Normally
there are 10 to 15 acts, with tickets at C$12 (US$8). Come summer, Intrepid puts on
the **Victoria Fringe Festival.** Even if you're not a theater fan—*especially* if you're
not—don't miss the Fringe. Unlike mainstream theater, fringe festivals are cheap
(about C$8/US$5) and short (an hour or so), so you're not gambling much by stepping inside one of the six venues—and the rewards are often spectacular. More than
50 performers or small companies come from around the world, and the plays they
put on are often amazingly inventive: one-man comedy, sped-up Shakespeare, multimedia dance, comic film noir, anything's possible. The festival runs from late August
to mid-September, and performances go on at six downtown venues daily noon to
midnight.

The **Theatre Inconnu** (☎ **250/360-0234;** www.islandnet.com~tinconnu) is
mostly known for its annual production of Victoria's **Shakespeare Festival,** held in a
restored theater in the historic St. Ann's Academy, 835 Humboldt St. The festival puts
on two or three of the Bard's best for several weeks in July and August. Though the
actors are local and often semi-professional, the quality is excellent and the tickets are
an eminently affordable C$5 to C$14 (US$3.35 to US$9). The Theatre Inconnu also
stages a two-man adaptation of Charles Dickens's *A Christmas Carol* every year in
December.

The **Langham Court Theatre,** 805 Langham Court (☎ **250/384-2142**), performs works produced by the Victoria Theatre Guild, a local amateur society dedicated to presenting a wide range of dramatic and comedic works. From downtown
take bus 14 or 11 to Fort and Moss Street.

OPERA

The **Pacific Opera Victoria,** 1316B Government St. (☎ **250/385-0222;** box office
250/386-6121; www.pov.bc.ca), presents three productions annually during the
October-to-April season. Performances are normally at the McPherson Playhouse and
Royal Theatre. The repertoire covers the classical bases, from Mozart and Rossini to
Verdi and even Wagner. Tickets cost C$20 to C$72 (US$13 to US$48) and are available at the McPherson Playhouse box office or at the Opera box office during office
hours.

The **Victoria Operatic Society,** 10-744 Fairview Rd. (☎ **250/381-1021;** www. vos.bc.ca), presents old-time Broadway musicals and other popular fare done up with impressive production values at the McPherson Playhouse. In 2001, the company plans a spring performance of *On Broadway* and a fall showing of *The Secret Garden,* followed by a spring 2002 performance of the Tony-winning *Sweeney Todd.* Tickets cost C$18 to C$28 (US$12 to US$19).

ORCHESTRAL & CHORAL MUSIC

The well-respected **Victoria Symphony Orchestra,** 846 Broughton St. (☎ **250/ 385-9771;** www.victoriasymphony.bc.ca), a smaller orchestra, kicks off its season on the first Sunday of August with Symphony Splash, a free concert performed on a barge in the Inner Harbour. Regular performances begin in September and last through May, always under the guidance of musical director Kees Bakels. The Symphony Orchestra normally performs at the Royal Theatre or the University Farquhar Auditorium. Repertoire leans to German masters such as Haydn, Mozart, and Beethoven, but the symphony also performs concertos and brings in internationally known guest performers. Tickets are C$15 to C$28 (US$10 to US$19) for most concerts; senior, student, and group discounts are available.

DANCE

Dance recitals and full-scale performances by local and international dance troupes such as **Danceworks** and the **Scottish Dance Society** are scheduled throughout the year. Call the **Visitor Info Centre** at ☎ 250/953-2033 to find out who's performing when you're in town.

COMEDY & SPOKEN WORD

Mocambo, 1028 Blanshard (☎ **250/384-4468**), a coffeehouse near the public library, hosts a range of semi-intellectual spoken-word events through the week (multimedia fusion demos, philosopher's cafes, argument for the joy of it, slam poetry), then lets loose on Saturdays with improv comedy. No cover.

2 Music & Dance Clubs

MUSIC FESTIVALS

Folkfest. ☎ **250/388-4728.** www.icavictoria.org/folkfest.

A multicultural celebration of song, performances, food, and crafts, Folkfest is sponsored by the International Cultural Association of greater Victoria. It takes place in June on Ship Point (the parking space below Wharf Street on the edge of the Inner Harbour).

Summer in the Square, Centennial Square. ☎ **250/361-0388.**

Early July to late August, this festival in downtown's Centennial Square is popular because it offers free music outside every day. Each day features a different band and musical style: The Monday noon-hour concerts feature mostly jazz. Tuesdays offer a noon-hour selection of big-band golden oldies. Wednesday to Saturday is potluck (show up at noon and take your chances). The festival's showstoppers are the Concerts Under the Stars held each Sunday from 7 to 9:30pm; the series features some 15 local bands over the 6-week length of the festival. And if you can't make it down to the square, the concerts are also broadcast live over local radio station, the Q (FM 100.3).

The TerrifVic Jazz Party. ☎ **250/953-2011.** www.islandnet.com/~bbs.jazz.html.

What was for many years known as the Dixieland Jazz festival, recently changed names and expanded formats after authorities discovered extended exposure to the bright, relentlessly happy tunes of Dixieland was causing large numbers of locals to throw themselves in front of the red double-decker buses. The new lineup for the 5-day late-April festival features swing, honky-tonk, fusion, some blues, and even Dixieland.

Victoria Jazz Society / Jazz Fest International. ☎ **888/671-2112.** www.vicjazz.bc.ca.

The Jazz Society's a good place to call any time of year to find out what's happening; it runs a hot line listing jazz events throughout the year. It's raison d'être, however, is the **Jazz Fest International,** held late June to early July. The more progressive of Victoria's two summer jazz fests, this one offers a range of styles from Cuban and salsa and world beat to fusion and acid jazz. Many free concerts are given in the Market Square courtyard. Other concerts are in live-music venues around the city.

LIVE MUSIC

The Blues House. 1417 Government St. ☎ **250/386-1717,** bus 5 to Douglas and Fisgard St.

Don't let the name fool you. The Blues House, just on the edge of downtown, is now an all-DJ dance spot, featuring everything from house to trip funk to retro-1970s and 1980s nights. Cover hovers around C$5 (US$3.35).

D'Arcy McGee's. 1127 Wharf St. ☎ **250/380-1322.**

This Bastion Square Irish pub is named for an Irish-Canadian politician assassinated by Irish Canadians. What's that mean to you and me? Music. Celtic, to be sure, Friday and Saturday nights, and almost always free with the price of a pint, which is enough to delight the Irish in anyone. There's no cover.

Hermann's Jazz Club. 753 View St. ☎ **250/388-9166.**

For two-plus decades Hermann's has offered straight-ahead jazz in a low-lit room with nice acoustics and bright red walls. The musicians are normally local, and adventure isn't what people pay to hear. Hermann's, instead, is all about good food, decent beer, and a slightly jazzed-up atmosphere. Dixieland and Big Band are the house specialties, though fusion, Celtic, and blues put in an appearance. There's no cover. A recent fire in the next-door nightclub did enough collateral damage to force Hermann's to close, and as of press time it was still unclear whether this Victoria institution would reopen. Let's hope.

The Ice House. 1961 Douglas, in the Horizon West Hotel. ☎ **250/382-2111,** bus 5 to Douglas and Fisgard St.

House and trance and techno DJs spin their stuff Monday to Wednesday; Thursday to Saturday, the Ice House warms up and goes live. Which band is playing depends mostly on who's touring: it could be anything from aging rockers like Trooper to Bob Marley's old backup band to new electronica to blues. Cover ranges from C$6 to C$16 (US$4 to US$11) depending on the band. There's no cover on DJ nights.

✪ **Legends.** 919 Douglas St. ☎ **250/383-7137.** www.strathconahotel.com.

This live-music venue is in the city within a city that's the Strathcona Hotel. Below street level, Legends had degenerated into a veritable black pit when the owners pumped in a major cash injection, transforming it into a pop-music palace. Even better, they began booking some hopping international bands, covering the gamut from afro-pop to blues to R&B and zydeco. Legends is now one of the best places to see live

Gambling

At the **Great Canadian Casino,** 3075 Douglas St. (☎ **250/389-1136;** www.gcgaming.com), there are no floor shows, no alcohol, no dancing girls in glittering bikinis—just a casual and slightly genteel casino. Games include blackjack, roulette, sic bo, red dog (diamond dog), and Caribbean stud poker. It's open daily from noon to 3am. Bus 30 or 31 to Douglas and Finlayson Streets.

music in the city. Thursday to Saturday, the cover is C$4 (US$2.70) or more depending on the band.

The Neptune Soundbar. 506 Pandora St., in the basement of Swan's Hotel. ☎ **250/388-5758.**

DJs spin records Tuesday to Friday in this dance-oriented spot; on Saturdays there's a band. Cover hovers around C$5 (US$3.35) on dance nights, more depending on the band or DJs fame. Music is decidedly un–Top 40. Beyond that though, it's hard to nail down. The Soundbar's sound covers several stylistic octaves, from funk and rare groove to house, trance, techno, and garage, remaining all the while firmly in the dance-oriented DJ world.

Steamers. 570 Yates St. ☎ **250/381-4340.**

Once a very grubby peeler parlor, Steamers got a totally new interior and was reborn as the city's premium blues bar. "Blues" here isn't taken too literally, of course. Acts often stray into the far-off musical realms of zydeco, Celtic, and world beat. Cover ranges from nothing to a maximum of C$5 (US$3.35). On Mondays there's an open-stage acoustic jam.

DANCE CLUBS

Most places are open Monday to Saturday until 2am and Sunday until midnight. Drinks run from C$3 to C$4.50 (US$2 to US$3).

The Boom Boom Room. 1208 Wharf St. ☎ **250/381-2331.**

This waterfront club plays popular Top 40 dance tracks for an early 20-something crowd. There's a C$5 (US$3.35) cover after 8pm on weekends.

Hush. 1325 Government St. ☎ **250/385-0566.**

This new gay-yet-straight-friendly space (crowd is about 50-50) features top-end touring DJs, hosted by Brent Carmichael, the 40-something granddaddy of Victoria DJs. There's a C$5 (US$3.35) cover on weekends.

The Lucky Bar. 517 Yates St. ☎ **250/382-5825.**

Currently the hottest spot in Victoria, this long, low cavernous space has a pleasantly grungy feel to it, like something in Seattle's Pioneer Square. Owned and operated by the team in charge of next-door Süze, the Lucky Bar features DJs ("Stir Fry") on Wednesdays, rockabilly on Thursdays, and a mix of bands and DJs on weekends. Cover hovers around C$5 (US$3.35). Unlike in Seattle, there's no smoking inside.

The One Lounge. 1318 Broad St. ☎ **250/384-3557.**

This Top 40 club spins dance tracks for a late twenties to early thirties crowd. The format (1970s retro, 1980s retro) depends on the night of the week. There's a C$5 (US$3.35) cover on weekends.

Sweetwaters Niteclub. 27–570 Store St. ☎ **250/383-7844.**

This elegant singles spot for a late-twenties-to-early-forties demographic features classic tracks and Top 40 tunes. Cover is C$3 (US$2) on Friday and Saturday.

3 Lounges, Bars & Pubs

LOUNGES

✪ **Bengal Lounge.** 721 Government St., in The Empress hotel. ☎ **250/384-8111.**

A truly unique experience. The Bengal is one of the last outposts of the old empire—a Raffles or a Harry's Bar—except the martinis are ice cold and jazz plays in the background (and on weekends, live in the foreground). The couches are huge and covered in leather thick enough to stop an elephant gun, while the cocktail list is extensive. The combination has lately attracted the young and elegant lounge lizard crowd who blithely amuse themselves beneath the baleful glare of a huge Bengal tiger—a gift from a visiting maharaja—hung above the fireplace.

Hugo's Brew Club & Lounge. 625 Courtney St. ☎ **250/920-4844.**

Decorated in the faux-industrial style popular with dot-com geeks (timber rafters and acres of exposed brick, in this case with authentic imitation bullet holes), this 2-year-old brew pub/lounge has become one of Victoria's most popular spots for late-night drinking, dining, and all-round schmoozing. On Fridays and Saturdays, the tables get pushed back and the crowd gets dancing.

Rick's Lounge. 45 Songhees Rd., in the Ocean Pointe Resort. ☎ **250/360-2999,** bus: 24 to Colville.

This is, without a doubt, the best place to watch as the last light of day fades from the Inner Harbour and the lights on the fairy-tale Legislature Building switch on. And besides the commanding view, Rick's offers casual elegance, low-volume live music, and a vast selection of single-malt whiskies.

BARS & PUBS

Big Bad John's. 919 Douglas St., in the Strathcona Hotel. ☎ **250/383-7137.**

You have to go to John's. Victoria's first, favorite, and only hillbilly bar is a low, dark warren of a place, with wall gak by the gross ton, inches of discarded peanut shells on the plank floor, and a crowd of drunk and happy rowdies. Tradition dictates that the bartender waits until you aren't looking and then…ha, like I'm tellin'. (It involves latex and something long and squirmy.)

✪ **The Harbour Canoe Club.** 450 Swift St. ☎ **250/361-1940.**

Having a drink at the Harbour Canoe Club, it's hard to know who to admire more: the 19th-century engineers who built everything with brick and beam and always twice as thick as it had to be; the restorers who took this old building—once the site of the City Light Company—and turned it into such a sunlit cathedral of a room; the owner, who had the vision to pay the restorers; the chef, who made the delicious plate of appetizers now quickly disappearing from the huge wood bench; or the brewmaster, whose copper cauldrons produce such a superior brew. Try the taster option—six small glasses of different brews for more or less the price of a pint—and toast them all. Particularly on weekend nights when the house blues band sets up just beside the bar, the Canoe Club is an excellent spot to let "just one" stretch into an entire evening's sojourn.

Spinnaker's Brew Pub. 308 Catherine St. ☎ **250/386-2739,** bus 24 to Songhees Rd.

Without doubt one of the best brew pubs in town, Spinnaker's did it first and did it well, setting standards other pubs had to match. Overlooking Victoria Harbour on the west side of the Songhees Point Development, Spinnaker's view of the harbor and Legislature is fabulous. On sunny days it's worth it for the view alone. At other times (all times in fact) the brewed-on-the-premises ales, lagers, and stouts are uniformly excellent. For those looking for more substantial fare, the pub grub's good and the entrees are above average. An on-site bakery sells various beer breads. On the weekends there's often a band, or, if that doesn't suit you, there are dart-boards and pool tables. Taken together with the friendly and casual crowd of professionals and visitors, it all makes Spinnaker's a dangerously time-consuming port of call.

The Sticky Wicket. 919 Douglas St., in the Strathcona Hotel. ☎ **250/383-7137.**

This is yet another pub in the Strathcona Hotel—but the Wicket is a standout. Originally installed on an ocean-liner, the beautiful wood interior—including dividers, glass, and a long teak bar—was later taken to a new home in Dublin. Only very recently—as part of a C$4-million renovation—was the whole package packed up and shipped here to Victoria, making it about as original an Irish bar as you're likely to find. Elevators can whip you from deepest Dublin up three floors to the mini-Malibu on the outdoor patio balcony. Faster than you can say Sein Fein, that Guinness in your paw has been replaced with a fuzzy navel and you're spiking and diving on the beach volleyball courts. Rad.

Süze Lounge and Restaurant. 515 Yates St. ☎ **250/383-2829.**

This great little lounge is in the heart of the Old Town. It's the perfect spot, in fact, for a first date: little tables on their own but not so isolated the escape is impossible, and lots of background noise and eye candy if you get bored. The crowd is young and moneyed, and the beer selection's good.

Swan's Pub. 506 Pandora Ave., in Swans Hotel. ☎ **250/361-3310.**

There are few drinking spots anywhere more intriguing—or more enjoyable—than Swans. The enjoyment comes from the room itself, on the ground floor of a beautifully converted 1913 feed warehouse across from the Johnson Street Bridge. A massive raftered ceiling gives Swans the feel of a great warm cavern on colder evenings, while the wraparound sidewalk-level greenhouse lets you strip off layers and pretend it's L.A. when the sun is shining. The intrigue comes from the owner's vast art collection, portions of which he rotates through the pub on a regular basis. Almost every piece is exquisite; most of it is challenging, from intricate Heiltsuk transformation masks to cedar carvings 4.5 meters (15 ft.) high to a graphic charcoal rendering of an S&M dungeon. Appreciation for both art and the room is nourished by the beer, which is brewed on-site and utterly delicious.

4 Gay & Lesbian Bars

BJ's Lounge. 642 Johnson St. (entrance on Broad St.). ☎ **250/388-0505.**

With a full menu, a lounge decor, and regular drag shows, BJ's makes for a pleasant enough place to spend the evening. On non-show nights the tunes follow the conventional gay canned music format: a little bit of techno and lots of Gloria Gaynor. Heteros take note: BJ's is militant about preserving its homo-only ambiance. Straights are often refused admission. There's no cover.

Friends of Dorothy's Café. 615 Johnson St. ☎ **250/381-2277.**

Dorothy's gone but not forgotten. The *Wizard of Oz* used to play continuously at this pleasant kitschy cafe, but the new owners found it was driving them over the rainbow. Now they make do with the voluminous Dorothy memorabilia. Dorothy's staff is friendly and just slightly outré, and the crowd is definitely fun-loving. Try the cocktails, or if you're looking for sustenance in solid form, the enchiladas, burgers, pastas, and salads.

The G-Spot. 1910 Store St. ☎ **250/382-SPOT.**

Afternoon Delight at this lesbian locus features herbal teas and well-centered, stimulating conversation from 3 to 6pm. For women only.

Side Trips: The Best of British Columbia

Set on the very edge of a great wilderness, British Columbia offers some experiences that are truly world-class—like the skiing in Whistler—and some that are like nothing else on earth.

1 Squamish, Brackendale & Britannia Beach

ESSENTIALS

GETTING THERE   By Train   BC Rail's **Royal Hudson Steam Train** (☎ **604/984-5246**) is a 1930s steam locomotive that chugs up Howe Sound to the town of Squamish on a route that winds through forests and glacier-topped mountains in about 2 hours. Bring your camera to the glass-domed observation car. Mid-May to mid-September, you can take this spectacular nostalgic ride Wednesday to Sunday, leaving North Vancouver at 10am and returning to the North Vancouver station at 4pm. Round-trip fares, which include lunch on the way up and tea on the return in the parlor car, are C$80 (US$54) for adults, C$75 (US$50) for seniors and students, and C$58 (US$39) for children.

By Car   The drive up the scenic **Sea-to-Sky Highway** (Hwy. 99) from downtown Vancouver to Squamish and Brackendale takes about 60 minutes. The 83.3-kilometer (50-mile) route winds along the craggy tree-lined coast of Howe Sound through the town of Britannia Beach and past two beautiful natural monuments: Shannon Falls and the continent's tallest monolithic rock face, the Stawamus Chief. Parts may look familiar because many of the areas along the route have been the backdrop for movies and television shows—it's that beautiful.

By Bus   Greyhound, Pacific Central Station, 1150 Station St., Vancouver (☎ **604/482-8747**), operates bus service from the Vancouver Bus Depot to the Garibaldi Bus Depot, 40446 Government Rd., just outside the Squamish city limits at 8 and 11am and 1, 5, and 7pm daily. The trip takes about 1¼ hours. The driver makes stops in downtown Squamish only by passenger request. The one-way fare is C$8 (US$5) for adults, C$7 (US$4.70) for seniors, and C$4.15 (US$2.80) for children; children under 4 are free.

VISITOR INFORMATION   Contact the **Squamish & Howe Sound Visitor Info Centre,** 37950 Cleveland Ave., Squamish, B.C. V0N 3G0 (☎ **604/892-9244;** fax 604/892-2034; www. squamishchamberofcommerce.bc.ca). June through September, it's

Southwestern British Columbia

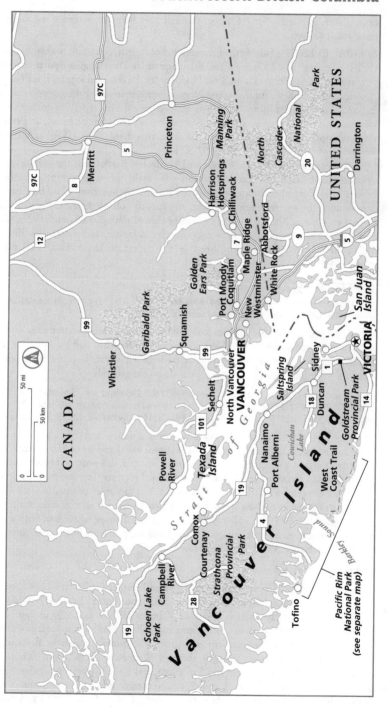

open daily from 9am to 5pm; October through May, hours are Saturday and Sunday from 10am to 2pm.

SPECIAL EVENTS   During the first weekend of August, Squamish townsfolk show their lumberjack roots by hosting the 3-day **Squamish Days Logger Sports** celebration at the Loggers Sports Ground off Highway 99. Professional loggers from North America, New Zealand, Australia, and Norway compete in such events as pole climbing and free falling, birling, ax throwing, springboard chopping, log rolling, and women's team hand sawing, plus there's food, music, children's activities, and crafts displays. Most events are free; a few of the top events charge C$9 (US$6) admission. For more information, call ☎ **604/892-9244.**

The ✪ **Annual Bald Eagle Count and Festival** in Brackendale draws thousands of spectators to view the beautiful raptors who make the neighboring fjords their homes from November through January. In 1994, a world-record 3,700 bald eagles were counted by rafters, hikers, canoeists, and kayakers observing the eagles gathered to feed on salmon. Although the eagles can be viewed throughout winter, the official count generally takes place on the second Sunday in January and starts at the Brackendale Art Gallery, Government Road at the corner of Depot Road (☎ **604/898-3333**).

WHERE TO STAY

Alice Lake Provincial Park. ☎ **604/898-3678.** C$19 (US$13) per night for walk-in or drive-in site. Off Hwy. 99 10km (6 miles) north of Squamish.

The 108 campsites at this park are consistently among those Vancouverites rate as their favorite weekend getaway. Free hot showers, flush toilets, and a sani-station are just the beginning of a long list of available facilities. Hiking trails, picnic areas, sandy beaches, swimming areas, and fishing spots are on the grounds.

The Howe Sound Inn & Brewing Company. 37801 Cleveland Ave., Squamish, B.C. V0N 3G0. ☎ **604/892-2603.** Fax 604/892-2631. www.howesound.com. 20 units. TV TEL. May–Sept C$105 (US$70) double; Oct–Apr C$95 (US$64) double. AE, MC, V. Free parking.

Here you'll find excellent accommodations, informal dining, and great ales under one roof. The brewery's 20 guest rooms—in a beautiful wood-and-stone lodge—are comfortably furnished with queen-size beds, cozy comforters, day beds, and bathrooms. A reading lounge and sauna are also available. The Red Heather Grill and the inn's Brewpub and Patio feature Pacific Northwest menus. You can order steamed mussels with shallots and garlic in pale-ale cream broth, grilled lime-cured salmon steak with seasonal vegetables and Asian-style noodles, medallions of peppered venison with wild-mushroom/herb glaze, or a hand-stretched pizza topped with lime-cured chicken, Monterey Jack cheese, chilies, and tomatoes.

WHERE TO DINE

Squamish isn't blessed with fine cuisine. The **Red Heather Grill** at the Howe Sound Inn (above) offers good West Coast cuisine, main courses C$12 to C$17 (US$8 to US$11), open Monday through Friday 11:30am to 2:30pm and 5:30 to 9pm, and Saturday through Sunday 10am to 2:30pm and 5:30 to 9pm. At the same place, the more casual Brewpub has excellent pub grub. The **Sunrise Japanese Restaurant** (☎ **604/898-2533**), open Tuesday through Wednesday 5 to 10pm, Thursday through Friday 11:30am to 2pm and 5 to 10pm, and Saturday through Sunday 12:30 to 10pm, a little off the highway at 40022 Government Rd., looks unpromising but actually has quite good Japanese fare, main courses C$6 to C$12 (US$4 to US$8).

Closed on Mondays. Down the road in Britannia (near the Mining Museum), the **Britannia House Restaurant & Tea Room,** Highway 99 (☎ 604/896-2335), has freshly baked scones, an all-day breakfast, homemade soups, and burgers. The room also has a spectacular view of the surrounding sound, the mountains, and the Murchison Glacier. Main courses run from C$3.95 to C$9 (US$2.65 to US$6). Open Thursday through Monday 9am to 5pm. Closed Tuesday and Wednesday.

EXPLORING THE AREA

Long a grubby mill town, **Squamish** has been slowly converting over to ecotourism as the supply of wood has dried up and residents and newcomers have begun to realize just how spectacular Squamish really is. Numerous outdoor activities are offered. The most famous is the annual eagle watch.

Although the bald eagle is only just recovering in the States, the Canadian population is thriving. On weekends from November 15 to February 15, you can take **a day-long guided rafting trip** to the prime viewing areas for C$119 (US$80) per person. The tours, conducted by **Canadian Outback Adventure Company,** 100-657 Marine Dr., West Vancouver (☎ **604/921-7250;** www.canadianoutback.com), include a late lunch at the Brackendale Art Gallery's teahouse and a lecture about bald eagles by the founder of the Annual Bald Eagle Count. Reserve at least a week in advance. For the same price, the company offers **white-water rafting trips** down the Squamish and Elaho rivers that include a riverside barbecue lunch.

Whether you're a rock climber or just a curious observer, I highly recommend stopping at the **Stawamus Chief.** It's a stark monolithic rock wall looming above Squamish at the head of Howe Sound. Each day you can see dozens of mountaineers from around the country and the continent scaling its face. Spectators and climbers will find plenty of parking off Highway 99. Look for the designated parking lots for climbers, just past Shannon Falls. For the fit and active, there's also a 3-hour hiking route (no climbing gear required) running round the back to the top of the Chief, beginning from the Shannon Falls parking lot.

During the 1920s, the largest copper mine in the British Empire was located at Britannia Beach—then called Britannia Mines. Built into the mountainside, the mill mined and processed more than 7,000 tons of raw copper ore daily until demand waned in the 1960s. Converted into the **B.C. Museum of Mining,** Highway 99 at the head of Howe Sound (☎ **604/688-8735**), this landmark is as alluring to kids and grown-ups today as it was in its heyday. (Vintage photos in the museum show children being given tours even then.) A 235-ton truck is parked in front. The museum offers 1½-hour guided tours into the old copper mine, an underground ride on the old mine train, live demonstrations of mining techniques, a gift shop, and even a gold-panning area where you can try your hand. Summer hours are daily from 10am to 4:30pm, but call ahead for a tour schedule (closed from early October until early May). Admission is C$10 (US$7) for adults and C$8 (US$5) for students/seniors; children under 5 are free. You can also just stop in for gold panning for C$3.50 (US$2.35) per person.

Salmon are another major attraction in this area. Throughout the year, the **Tenderfoot Hatchery** near Brackendale breeds and releases chinook, coho, and steelhead salmon into the streams feeding the Cheakamus River. You can observe the cycle of a salmon's life year-round through the observation tanks and viewing platforms. To get there, drive north from Squamish on Highway 99 about 2 kilometers (1.2 miles). Turn left at Chekeye Road and drive 5 kilometers (3 miles). Cross the bridge and immediately turn right onto Paradise Road, then right onto Midway Road. Follow this road for 3 kilometers (1.8 miles) to the hatchery.

2   Whistler: One of North America's Premier Ski Resorts

The premier ski resort in North America, according to *Ski* and *Snow Country* magazines, the **Whistler/Blackcomb complex** boasts more vertical, more lifts, and more and varied ski terrain than any other ski resort in North America. And it isn't all just downhill skiing. There's also backcountry, cross-country, snowboarding, snowmobiling, heli-skiing, and sleigh riding. In summer, there's rafting, hiking, golfing, and horseback riding as well.

And then there's **Whistler Village.** Back in the 1970s, the city fathers, having made a conscious decision to build a resort town, looked to their minions in the planning department and ordered them to make it so. The results are impressive—a resort town of 40,000 beds, arranged around a central village street in a compact enough fashion that you can park your car and remain a pedestrian for the duration of your stay.

What was sacrificed in this drive to become the perfectly planned community was space for the odd, the funky, the quaint, and the nonconforming. Whistler has none of the strip malls, cheap motels, and filling stations that mar some resort towns; however, you won't find that quaint little restaurant run by an old Tyrolean couple, tucked away on an out-of-the-way hillside. So it goes.

The towns north of Whistler, **Pemberton** and **Mount Currie,** are refreshment stops for touring cyclists and hikers and the gateway to the icy alpine waters of **Birkenhead Lake Provincial Park** (see "Fishing" below) and the majestic **Cayoosh Valley,** which winds through the glacier-topped mountains to the Cariboo town of Lillooet.

ESSENTIALS

GETTING THERE   By Car   Whistler is about a 2-hour drive from Vancouver along Highway 99, also called the **Sea-to-Sky Highway.** The drive is spectacular, winding first along the edge of Howe Sound before climbing through the mountains. Parking at the mountain is free for day skiers. For overnight visitors, most hotels charge about C$7 (US$4.70).

By Bus   The **Whistler Express,** 8695 Barnard St., Vancouver (☎ **604/266-5386** in Vancouver or 604/905-0041 in Whistler), operates bus service from Vancouver International Airport to the Whistler Bus Loop, as well as drop-off service at many of the hotels. In summer, there are five daily departures between 8:30am and 7:30pm. In winter, there are eight departures daily between 9:30am and 11:30pm, with extra buses on weekends. The trip takes about 2½ to 3 hours; round-trip fares are C$92 (US$62) for adults in summer and C$106 (US$71) in winter and C$58 (US$39) for children in summer and C$60 (US$40) in winter; children under 5 are free. Reservations are required year-round.

Greyhound, Pacific Central Station, 1150 Station St., Vancouver (☎ **604/ 662-8051** in Vancouver or 604/932-5031 in Whistler), operates bus service from the Vancouver Bus Depot to the Whistler Bus Loop at 8 and 11am and 1, 3, 5, and 7pm daily. Return trips to Vancouver leave at 5, 8:30, and 10:30am and 1:30, 4:45, and 7:15pm. The trip takes about 2½ hours; one-way fares are C$18 (US$12) for adults and C$9 (US$6) for children 5 to 12; children under 5 are free.

By Train   BC Rail (☎ **604/984-5246**) operates the *Cariboo Prospector* throughout the year. It leaves the North Vancouver train terminal daily at 7am and chugs up the Howe Sound coastline through the scenic Cheakamus River Canyon and Garibaldi

Provincial Park until it reaches the Whistler train station on Lake Placid Road, arriving at 9:35am. The same train leaves Whistler at 6:20pm and returns to the North Vancouver train terminal at 9pm. The 2½-hour trip includes breakfast or dinner. A one-way ticket is C$31 (US$21) for adults, C$28 (US$19) for seniors, C$19 (US$13) for children 2 to 12, and C$6 (US$4) for children under 2.

VISITOR INFORMATION   The **Whistler Visitor Info Centre,** 2097 Lake Placid Rd., Whistler, B.C. V0N 1B0 (☎ **604/932-5528**), is open daily from 9am to 5pm. **Information kiosks** on Village Gate Boulevard at the entry to Whistler Village, the main bus stop, and a number of other locations are open from mid-May to early September during the same hours. **Tourism Whistler** is at the Whistler Conference Centre at 4010 Whistler Way, Whistler, B.C. V0N 1B0, open 9am to 5pm daily (☎ **604/932-3928;** www.tourismwhistler.com). This office can assist you with event tickets and last-minute accommodations bookings, as well as provide general information.

GETTING AROUND   Compact and pedestrian-oriented, Whistler Village has signed trails and pathways linking together all shops and restaurants. If you're staying in the Village, you can park your car and leave it for the duration of your stay. The walk between the Whistler Mountain (Whistler Village) and Blackcomb Mountain (Upper Village) resorts takes about 5 minutes.

By Bus   A year-round **public transit service** (☎ 604/932-4020) operates frequently from the Tamarisk district and the BC Rail Station to the neighboring districts of Nester's Village, Alpine Meadows, and Emerald Estates. Bus service from the Village to Village North and Upper Village accommodations is free. For other routes, one-way fares are C$1.50 (US$1) for adults and C$1.25 (US85¢) for seniors/students; children under 5 are free.

By Cab   The Village's taxis operate around the clock. Taxi tours, golf course transfers, and airport transport are also offered by **Airport Limousine Service** (☎ 800/278-8742 or 604/273-1331), **Whistler Taxi** (☎ 604/938-3333), and **Sea-to-Sky Taxi** (☎ 604/932-3333).

By Car   Rental cars are available from **Budget,** at the Holiday Inn Sunspree, 4295 Blackcomb Way (☎ 604/932-1236); and **Thrifty,** in the Listel Whistler Hotel, 4121 Village Green (☎ 604/938-0302).

SPECIAL EVENTS   Dozens of downhill **ski competitions** are held December through May. They include the Owens-Corning World Freestyle Competition (Jan), Power Bar Peak to Valley Race (Feb), Kokanee Fantastic Downhill Race (Mar), Air Canada Whistler Cup and World Ski & Snowboard Festival (Apr), and Whistler Snowboard World Cup and World Cup Freestyle (Dec).

Mountain bikers compete in the Power Bar Garibaldi Gruel (Sept) and the Cheakamus Challenge Fall Classic Mountain Bike Race (Sept).

During the third week in July, the Villages host **Whistler's Roots Weekend** (☎ 604/932-2394). Down in the Villages and up on the mountains, you'll hear the sounds of Celtic, zydeco, bluegrass, Delta blues, Latin, folk, and world-beat music at free and ticketed events.

The **Whistler Summit Concert Series** (☎ 604/932-3434) is held during August weekends, with the mountains providing a stunning backdrop for the on-mountain concerts. In the past, concert performers have included the Barenaked Ladies, Amanda Marshall, Great Big Sea, the Matthew Good Band, and Blue Rodeo. Call for dates and details.

The **Alpine Wine Festival** (☎ 604/932-3434) takes place on the mountaintop during the first weekend in September. Featuring wine tastings, a winemaker's dinner, a Sunday brunch, and other events highlighting North America's finest vintages, the festival has become a classic.

And the second weekend in September ushers in the **Whistler Jazz & Blues Festival** (☎ 604/932-2394), featuring live performances in the village squares and the surrounding clubs. It's a great opportunity to see some Pacific Northwest jazz, gospel, R&B, and blues.

Cornucopia (☎ 604/932-3434) is Whistler's premier wine-and-food festival. The opening gala showcases 50 top wineries from the Pacific region. Other events include a celebrity chef competition, food and wine seminars, and wine tastings.

WHERE TO STAY

There are over 40,000 guest beds in Whistler Valley, but the biggest decision you'll make is whether to stay in or out of Whistler Village. Staying in the Village, you can forget your car for the duration of your visit and walk along cobblestone pathways from hotel to ski lift to restaurant to pub. Visitors from around the world stroll from shop to shop or sit sipping something in an outdoor cafe. The Village is thus a lively place; however, with all those voices talking, the Village is never completely quiet. Staying outside the Village, you'll have a short drive to the lifts or restaurants (though many places offer shuttle service), but you'll also have a touch more of that mountain tranquillity.

All the studios and one- and two-bedroom condos or hotel suites in the Village are top-quality. By the same token, there's little to choose from in terms of room quality between a midrange hotel like the Holiday Inn and the higher-end hotel like the Pan Pacific. In both you can expect a gas fireplace, a kitchenette and dining table, a small balcony, a pull-out couch and Murphy bed, and one or two bedrooms. (The price difference normally pays for extra amenities. The Pan has a heated pool and set of Jacuzzis on a deck overlooking Whistler Mountain.)

Outside the Village, there is a bit more variety, including a fine Austrian-style inn reviewed below. Whether you decide to stay in or out of town, the best thing to do is simply decide on your price point and call one of the central booking agencies. The studios, condos, townhouses, and chalets are available year-round. Prices run from C$90 to C$1,400 (US$60 to US$938) per night. **Whistler Central Reservations** (☎ **800/944-7853** or 604/664-5625; fax 604/938-5758; www.whistler-resort.com) has over 2,000 rental units and can book a wide range of accommodations in the Whistler area, from B&Bs to hotel rooms or condos. Furthermore, they can provide a customized package with lift tickets and air or ground transportation to and from Vancouver.

Other booking agencies, including **Whistler Chalets and Accommodations Ltd.,** 4360 Lorimer Rd. (☎ **800/663-7711** in Canada or 604/932-6699; www.whistlerchalets. com), and **Rainbow Retreats Accommodations Ltd.,** 2129 Lake Placid Rd. (☎ **604/ 932-2343;** www.whistler.net/rainbow), have many properties to suit every budget and group size.

Reservations for peak winter periods should be made by September at the latest.

IN THE VILLAGE

Canadian Pacific Chateau Whistler Resort. 4599 Chateau Blvd., Whistler, B.C. V0N 1B4. ☎ **800/441-1414** in the U.S., 800/606-8244 in Canada, or 604/938-8000. Fax 604/ 938-2099. 558 units. MINIBAR TV TEL. Winter C$385–C$435 (US$258–US$291) double, C$570–C$1,200 (US$382–US$804) suite; summer C$299–C$335 (US$200–US$224) double, C$425–C$1,000 (US$285–US$670) suite. Wheelchair-accessible units available. AE, ER, MC, V. Underground valet parking C$22 (US$15).

The one exception to the everything's-the-same-in-Whistler rule, the Chateau Whistler is outstanding. The Canadian Pacific hotel chain spared little expense in re-creating the look and feel of an old-time country retreat at the foot of Blackcomb Mountain. Massive wooden beams support an airy peaked roof in the lobby, while in the hillside Mallard Bar, double-sided stone fireplaces cast a cozy glow on the couches and leather armchairs. The rooms and suites feature double queen- and king-size beds, duvets, robes, and soaker tubs. Gold service guests can have breakfast or relax après-ski in a private lounge with the feel of a Victorian library. All guests can use the heated indoor/outdoor pool and Jacuzzis, which look out over the base of the ski hill.

Dining/Diversions: The Wildflower Restaurant offers perhaps the Village's best buffet-style brunch daily from 7 to 11am for C$17 (US$11) per person or C$9 (US$6) per child 6 to 12; free for children under 6. It's also an excellent spot for fine dining, featuring mostly West Coast cuisine. The Mallard Bar has a great view of the Blackcomb lifts. With cocktails, coffee, light meals, good beer, plus a relaxed atmosphere, it's easily the most sophisticated spot to après-ski in Whistler.

Amenities: Room service, concierge, ski and bike storage, full-service spa, massage therapy, sauna, whirlpool, steam room, weight room, terrace barbecue, tennis courts, 18-hole golf course.

The Pan Pacific Lodge Whistler. 4320 Sundial Crescent, Whistler, B.C. V0N 1B4. ☎ **888/ 905-9955** or 604/905-2999. Fax 604/905-2995. www.panpac.com. 121 units. Nov 23– Dec 21 C$349–C$399 (US$234–US$267) studio, C$449–C$499 (US$301–US$334) 1-bedroom suite, C$679 (US$455) 2-bedroom suite; Dec 22–Jan 1 C$569–C$619 (US$381–US$415) studio,C$719–C$769 (US$482–US$515) 1-bedroom suite, C$919 (US$615) 2-bedroom suite; Jan 2–Apr 15 C$409–C$459 (US$274–US$308) studio, C$559–C$609 (US$375–US$408) 1-bedroom suite, C$759 (US$509) 2-bedroom suite; Apr 15–Nov 22 C$239–C$269 (US$160–US$180) studio, C$289–C$319 (US$194–US$214) 1-bedroom suite, C$339–C$389 (US$227–US$261) 2-bedroom suite. Wheelchair-accessible units available. AE, ER, MC, V. Underground valet parking C$15 (US$10).

The Pan-Pacific's furnishings and appointments are top-notch, and the kitchenettes (in all suites) contain the cutlery and equipment required to cook up a gourmet meal. With sofa beds and fold-down Murphy beds, the studio suites are fine for couples, while the one- and two-bedroom suites allow a bit more space for larger groups or families with kids. Comfortable as the rooms are, however, the true advantage to the Pan Pacific is its location at the foot of the Whistler Mountain gondola. Not only can you ski right to your hotel, but thanks to a large heated outdoor pool and Jacuzzi deck, you can sit at the end of the day sipping a glass of wine, gazing up at the snowy slopes, and marvel at the ameliorative effects of warm water on aching muscles.

Dining/Diversions: There's fine dining at Arthur's Restaurant; more fun and a better value is the Dubh Linn Gate Irish Lounge/Pub, a convincing re-creation of a Dublin pub, with good-quality pub food, excellent beer, and, more often than not, a balladeer singing a song or two about the auld sod.

Amenities: Room service; concierge; laundry; heated outdoor pool and Jacuzzis; fitness center and steamroom; ski, bike, and golf bag storage.

OUTSIDE THE VILLAGE

Cedar Springs Bed & Breakfast Lodge. 8106 Cedar Springs Rd., Whistler, B.C. V0N 1B8. ☎ **800/727-7547** or 604/938-8007. Fax 604/938-8023. www.whistlerbb.com. 8 units, 6 with bathroom. C$85–C$239 (US$57–US$160) double, C$130–C$279 (US$87–US$187) suite. Rates include full breakfast. MC, V. Take Hwy. 99 north toward Pemberton 4km (2.4 miles) past Whistler Village. Turn left onto Alpine Way, go a block to Rainbow Dr. and turn left, go a block to Camino St. and turn left. The lodge is a block down at the corner of Camino and Cedar Springs Rd.

Guests at this charming modern lodge have a choice of king-, queen-, or twin-size beds in comfortably modern yet understated surroundings. The honeymoon suite boasts a fireplace and balcony. The guest sitting room has a TV, VCR, and video library. A sauna and hot tub on the sundeck overlooking the gardens add to the pampering after a day of play. The gourmet breakfast is served by the fireplace in the dining room, and guests are welcome to enjoy an afternoon tea. Owners Joann and Jackie Rhode can provide box lunches and special-occasion dinners at this cozy hideaway. A complimentary Alpine Meadows bus provides transportation to and from the Village.

✪ **Durlacher Hof Pension Inn.** 7055 Nesters Rd. (P.O. Box 1125), Whistler, B.C. V0N 1B0. ☎ **604/932-1924.** Fax 604/938-1980. www.durlacherhof.com. E-mail: peterika@direct.ca. 8 units. Dec 18–Mar 31 C$179–C$259 (US$120–US$174) double; June 19–Sept 30 C$120–C$199 (US$80–US$133) double. Extra person C$30 (US$20). Discounts for spring and fall available. Rates include full breakfast and afternoon tea. 1 wheelchair-accessible unit available. MC, V. Free parking. Take Hwy. 99 about 0.83km (0.5 mile) north of Whistler Village to Nester's Rd. Turn left and the inn is immediately on the right.

This lovely inn boasts both an authentic Austrian feel and a sociable atmosphere. Both are the result of the exceptional care and service shown by owners Peter and Erika Durlacher. Guests are greeted by name at the entranceway, provided with slippers, and then given a tour of the two-story chalet-style property. The rooms (on the second floor) vary in size from comfortable to quite spacious and come with goose-down duvets on extra long twin- or queen-size beds, fluffy robes, private bathrooms (some with jetted tubs) with deluxe toiletries, and incredible mountain views from private balconies. Better still is the downstairs lounge, with a welcoming fireplace and complementary après-ski appetizers baked by Erika (these are delectable enough that guests are drawn from all over the inn to snack, share stories, and strategize on ways to obtain Erika's recipes). For much the same reason, many guests seem to linger over the complimentary (and substantial) hot breakfast. Add to all this a whirlpool, sauna, and well-chosen little library, and its easy to see why so many guests return year after year.

Hostelling International Whistler. 5678 Alta Lake Rd., Whistler, B.C. V0N 1B0. ☎ **604/932-5492.** Fax 604/932-4687. www.hihostels.bc.ca. 33 beds in 4- to 6-bed dorms. C$20 (US$13) IYHA members, C$24 (US$16) nonmembers; annual adult membership C$27 (US$18). Family and group memberships available. MC, V. Free parking.

One of the few inexpensive spots in Whistler, the hostel also happens to have one of the nicest locations: on the south edge of Alta Lake, with a dining room, deck, and lawn looking over the lake to Whistler Mountain. Inside, the hostel is extremely pleasant; there's a lounge with a wood-burning stove, a common kitchen, a piano, Ping-Pong tables, and a sauna, as well as a drying room for ski gear and storage for bikes, boards, and skis. In the summer, guests have use of a barbecue, canoe, and rowboat. As with all hostels, most rooms and facilities are shared. Beds at the hostel book up very early. Book by September at the latest for the winter ski season.

CAMPGROUNDS

South of Whistler on the Sea-to-Sky corridor is the very popular **Alice Lake Provincial Park** (see "Squamish, Brackendale & Britannia Beach" above). You can reserve spots for Alice Lake at **Discover Camping** (☎ 800/689-9025). Twenty-seven kilometers (16 miles) north of Whistler, the well-maintained campground at **Nairn Falls** on Highway 99 (☎ 604/898-3678) is more adult-oriented, with pit toilets, pumped well water, fire pits and firewood, but no showers. Its proximity to the roaring Green River and the town of Pemberton makes it appealing to many hikers, and the sound of the river is sweeter than any lullaby. Prices for the 88 campsites are C$15 (US$10) per night, on a first-come, first-served basis. The 85 campsites at **Birkenhead Lake**

Provincial Park, off Portage Road, Birken (☎ **604/898-3678**), fill up very quickly in summer. To reserve a spot, call **Discover Camping** (see above). Boat launches, great fishing, and well-maintained tent and RV sites make this an angler's paradise and one of the province's top 10 camping destinations. Facilities include fire pits, firewood, pumped well water, and pit toilets. Campsites are C$12 (US$8) per night.

WHERE TO DINE

Whistler literally overflows with dining choices. A stroll through the village will take you past 25 or 30 restaurants.

A good meal for gourmets on the go can be found at **Chef Bernard's,** 4573 Chateau Blvd., Whistler Village (☎ **604/932-7051**), open daily from 7am to 9pm. It serves full breakfasts, soups, salads, and sandwiches, as well as hot entrees—quiche, chicken with penne, cannelloni, and an incredible fried meat-loaf sandwich with mushroom/red-wine sauce, cambozola cheese, and a side of roasted garlic mashed potatoes—for C$4.95 to C$8 (US$3.30 to US$5).

Ingrid's Village Cafe (☎ **604/932-7000**), open daily 8am to 5pm, is another local favorite, for quality and price. A large bowl of Ingrid's clam chowder costs just C$4.50 (US$3), while a veggie burger comes in at C$5 (US$3.35). **Citta Bistro,** in Whistler Village Square (☎ **604/932-4177**), is a favorite dining and night spot, open daily 11am to 1am. It serves thin-crust pizzas, gourmet burgers, and delicious finger foods like bruschetta, spring rolls, and nachos. Besides having great food and good prices (main courses are C$7 to C$11/US$4.70 to US$7), it has umbrella-covered tables on the terrace, the best people-watching corner in town.

Equally fun indoor dining can be had at the **Dubh Linn Gate Irish Lounge/Pub** (see the Pan Pacific Whistler listing) in the Pan Pacific hotel. The Gate offers solid pub grub and the atmosphere of the Emerald Isle. Open Monday through Saturday from 7am to 1am, Sundays 7am to midnight. Main courses C$11 to C$17 (US$7 to US$11). New to Whistler but long known in Vancouver for its quality beef is **Hy's Steakhouse,** 4308 Main St. (☎ **604/905-5555**), daily 5:30 to 10pm (last reservation at 9pm). Main courses range from C$27 to C$44 (US$18 to US$30). Over Blackcomb way, the **Wildflower** in the Chateau Whistler (see the Chateau Whistler listing) does innovative West Coast cuisine in a quiet, civilized room. Open for dinner daily 6 to 10pm, main courses C$18 to C$40 (US$12 to US$27).

Araxi Restaurant & Bar. 4222 Village Sq. ☎ **604/932-4540.** Main courses C$11–C$27 (US$7–US$18). AE, MC, V. Daily 11am–10:30pm. ITALIAN/WEST COAST.

Consistently winning awards for its wine list, as well as voted "Best Restaurant in Whistler" in 1998 and 1999 by readers of *Vancouver* magazine, this is one of the top places to dine. And thanks to a C$250,000 renovation in the spring of 1999, Araxi now has storage enough for its 12,000-bottle inventory of fine B.C. and foreign wines. Outside, the heated patio seats 80 people amid barrels of flowers, while inside, the artwork, antiques, and terra-cotta tiles give it a subtle Italian ambiance. The menu, however, is less Italian and more West Coast, with the emphasis on fresh regional products. The locally caught trout is smoked in the Araxi kitchen. Appetizers include sweet chili-marinated prawns and grilled Fraser Valley quail. Various soups and salads are made from scratch with fresh ingredients like Pemberton sheep cheese and Okanagan tomatoes. Main courses include seafood like ahi tuna, salmon fillet, and scallops. For meat lovers, the menu offers rack of lamb, tenderloin, and alder-smoked pork loin. And considering the near encyclopedic length of Araxi's famous wine list, don't hesitate to ask sommelier Chris Van Nus for suggestions.

Caramba! Restaurant. 12-4314 Main St., Town Plaza. ☎ **604/938-1879.** Main courses C$11–C$17 (US$7–US$11). AE, MC, V. Daily 11:30am–10:30pm. MEDITERRANEAN.

The room is bright and filled with the pleasant buzz of nattering diners. The kitchen is open, and the smells wafting out hint tantalizingly of fennel, artichoke, and pasta. These are good signs. However, the waitresses all bear the 300-watt smiles of Amway reps and greet every guest with an overly enthusiastic call of "Hi! How are you doing tonight!" That, and the menu notes indicating that Caramba! is part of a chain with kitchens in Calgary and suburban Port Moody, might have you wondering whether you've wandered into a glorified burger bar. Blissfully, your first instincts were correct. Caramba! may be casual dining, but its Mediterranean-influenced menu offers fresh ingredients, prepared with a great deal of pizzazz. Try the pasta, free-range chicken, or roasted pork loin. Better still, if you're feeling especially good about your dining companions, order a pizza or two, a plate of grilled calamari, some hot spinach, cheese, artichoke-and-shallot dip, and a plate of sliced prosciutto and bullfighters toast (savory toasted Spanish bread with herbs).

✪ **Rimrock Cafe and Oyster Bar.** 2117 Whistler Rd. ☎ **604/932-5565.** www.rimrockwhistler.com. E-mail: rimrock@direct.ca. Main courses C$13–C$30 (US$9–US$20). AE, MC, V. Daily 11:30am–11:30pm. SEAFOOD.

Upstairs in a long narrow room with a high ceiling and a great stone fireplace at one end, Rimrock is very much like a Viking mead hall of old. It's not the atmosphere, however, that causes people to hop in a cab and make the C$5 (US$3.35) journey out from Whistler Village. What draws folks in is the food. The first order of business should be a plate of oysters. Chef Rolf Gunther serves them up half a dozen ways, from raw with champagne to cooked in hell (broiled with fresh chilies). For my money, though, the signature Rimrock oyster is still the best: broiled with béchamel sauce and smoked salmon. Other appetizers are lightly seared ahi tuna or Québec foie gras with portobello mushrooms. Mains are equally seafood oriented and inventive. Look for lobster and scallops in light tarragon sauce on a bed of Capellini pasta or swordfish broiled with pecans, almonds, pistachios, and a mild red Thai curry. A few nonseafood dishes are also included, like rack of lamb marinated in Dijon mustard in shallot/wine jus. The accompanying wine list has a number of fine vintages from B.C., California, New Zealand, and Australia. Quite a few are available by the glass.

Uli's Flipside. 4433 Sundial Place (upstairs). ☎ **604/935-1107.** Main courses C$11–C$17 (US$7–US$11). AE, DC, MC, V. Mon–Sat 3pm–1am, Sun 3pm–midnight. PASTA/ITALIAN.

At least one longtime Whistler resident threatened dire, if unspecified, consequences if I told Frommer's readers about this local favorite. It's not that Uli's is the best restaurant in town or even the best pasta place (though for this title it's certainly in the running); it's just that few other spots offer the same combination of excellent pasta, a good wine list, and a pleasant room with vaulted ceiling and intimate window-side booths, all at a very moderate price. Given that Whistler shares the West Coast affliction of early dining (few kitchens are open as late as 10pm), Uli's is also the best bet for late-night dining. Try for yourself and see, just don't say you heard it from me.

Val d'Isère. 4314 Main St., Whistler Town Plaza. ☎ **604/932-4666.** www.valdisere-restaurant.com. Main courses C$22–C$34 (US$15–US$25). AE, MC, V. Daily 5–10pm except June–Oct 11:30am–11pm. FRENCH.

For a different kind of French cuisine, the elegant Val d'Isère offers a taste of Alsace, a hearty regional cuisine that'll warm you even on the coldest days. Try the goat-cheese soufflé to begin, followed by braised duck on a bed of figs, red cabbage, and polenta with port-wine reduction. For lighter fare—perhaps on a summer day on Val d'Isère's

Après Ski

"Après ski" refers to that delicious hour after a hard day on the slopes, when you sit back with a cold drink, nurse the sore spots in your muscles, and savor the glow that comes from a day well skied. On the Blackcomb side, **Merlin's Bar** (☎ 604/ 938-7735), at the base of Blackcomb, is the most obvious après-ski spot, but hidden away inside the Chateau Whistler is something better: the **Mallard Bar** (☎ 604/938-8000), one of the most civilized après-ski bars on earth.

---

great patio—try the seared scallops with candied lemon/ginger sauce. The wine list has a good number of bottles, many hailing from Alsace, but is unfortunately deficient in wines by the glass. The staff is friendly and knowledgeable enough to point out good wine pairings: a glass of Alsatian Riesling went particularly well with the candied scallops. As in proper French tradition, the desserts are luscious: profiteroles with vanilla ice cream and hot chocolate sauce, a warm chocolate orange gâteau, or a lemon soufflé with chocolate.

THE OUTDOORS: WHISTLER'S RAISON D'ETRE
DIFFERENT SLOPES FOR DIFFERENT FOLKS

✪ **Whistler/Blackcomb Mountain.** 4545 Blackcomb Way, Whistler, B.C. V0N 1B4. ☎ **604/932-3434;** snow report 604/687-7507 in Vancouver, 604/932-4211 in Whistler. www.whistler-blackcomb.com. Winter lift tickets C$59–C$61 (US$40–US$41) adults, C$50–C$52 (US$34–US$35) youths and seniors, C$30–C$31 (US$20–US$21) children, per day for both mountains. A variety of multiday passes are also available, but rates for the 2001 season weren't available at press time. Lifts open daily 8:30am–3:30pm (4:30pm mid-Mar until closing, depending on weather and conditions).

Now that both mountain resorts are jointly operated by Intrawest, your pass gives you access to both ski areas. Locals have their preferences, but the truth is that both offer great skiing.

Whistler Mountain has 1,502 meters (5,006 ft.) of vertical and over 100 marked runs that are serviced by a high-speed gondola and eight high-speed chairlifts, plus four other lifts and tows. Helicopter service from the top of the mountain makes another 100-plus runs on nearby glaciers accessible. There are cafeterias and gift shops on the peak as well as a fully licensed restaurant. **Blackcomb Mountain** has 1,584 meters (5,280 ft./1 mile) of vertical and over 100 marked runs that are serviced by nine high-speed chairlifts, plus three other lifts and tows. The cafeteria and gift shop aren't far from the peak, and the fully licensed restaurant is worth the gondola trip even if you're not skiing. The view is spectacular, the food decent. Both mountains also have bowls and glade skiing, with Blackcomb Mountain offering glacier skiing well into August.

Whistler/Blackcomb mountain offers **ski lessons and ski guides** for all levels and interests. (For skiers looking to try snowboarding, a rental package and a half-day lesson are particularly attractive options.) Phone **Guest Relations** at ☎ **604/932-3434** for details.

You can **rent ski and snowboard gear** at the base of both Whistler and Blackcomb Villages, just prior to purchasing your lift pass. No appointment is necessary (or accepted) but the system is first-come, first-served. Arrive at 8am and you'll be on the gondola by 8:15am. Arrive at 8:30am, and you won't be up until 9:15 at the earliest.

Summit Ski (☎ **604/938-6225** or 604/932-6225), at various locations, including the Delta Whistler Resort and Market Pavilion, rents high performance and regular skis, snowboards, telemark and cross-country skis, and snowshoes.

The *Whistler Explorer*

If you have only a day to explore the backcountry of Southern B.C., don't miss the ***Whistler Explorer.*** For centuries, the arid canyons, alpine meadows, and crystal-clear lakes of the area between Whistler and Kelly Lake were inaccessible to all but the most experienced hikers. However, **BC Rail's** (☎ 800/339-8752 or 604/984-5246) *Whistler Explorer* offers you a leisurely way to see the remote landscape. Departing from the Whistler train station on Lake Placid Road at 8am, the *Explorer* takes an 8½-hour round-trip ramble through the spectacular Pemberton Valley and past Seton Lake and Anderson Lake. After leaving the historic town of Lillooet, the train follows the Fraser River, climbing high above the canyon and offering breathtaking views before arriving at Kelly Lake, which is adjacent to the historic Cariboo Gold Rush Trail.

After a 1-hour stretching-and-strolling break, passengers reboard the train, returning to Whistler at 5:30pm. It's the ideal way to discover the backcountry without braving an overnight camping-and-hiking expedition into this stretch of pristine wilderness. The round-trip fare is C$114 (US$76) for adults/seniors/children over 12 and C$78 (US$52) for children 2 to 12.

BACKCOUNTRY SKIING   The **Spearhead Traverse,** which starts at Whistler and finishes at Blackcomb, is a well-marked backcountry route that has become extremely popular in the past few years.

Garibaldi Provincial Park (☎ 604/898-3678) maintains marked backcountry trails at **Diamond Head, Singing Pass,** and **Cheakamus Lake.** These are ungroomed and unpatrolled rugged trails, and you have to be self-reliant—you should be at least an intermediate skier, bring appropriate clothing and avalanche gear, and know how to use it. There are several access points along Highway 99 between Squamish and Whistler.

HELI-SKIING   For intermediate and advanced skiers who can't get enough fresh powder or vertical on the regular slopes, there's always heli-skiing. A helicopter whisks you and fellow skiers and boarders up to the pristine powder. **Whistler Heli-Skiing** (☎ 888/HELISKI or 604/932-4105; www.heliskiwhistler.com) is one of the more established operators. A three-run day, with 2,400 to 3,000 meters (8,000 to 10,000 ft.) of vertical helicopter lift, costs C$495 to C$515 (US$332 to US$345) per person. A four-run day for expert skiers and riders only, with 3,000 to 3,600 meters (10,000 to 12,000 ft.) of vertical helicopter lift, costs C$560 to C$580 (US$375 to US$389) per person, including a guide and lunch.

CROSS-COUNTRY SKIING   Well-marked, fully groomed cross-country trails run throughout the area. The 30 kilometers (18 miles) of easy-to-very-difficult marked trails at **Lost Lake** start a block away from the Blackcomb Mountain parking lot. They're groomed for track skiing and ski-skating. They're also patrolled. Passes are C$8 (US$5); a 1-hour cross-country lesson runs about C$35 (US$23) and can be booked at the same station where you buy your trail pass. The **Valley Trail System** in the village becomes a well-marked cross-country ski trail during winter.

OTHER WINTER PURSUITS

SNOWMOBILING & ATVing   The year-round combination ATV and snowmobile tours offered by **Canadian Snowmobile Adventures Ltd.,** Carleton Lodge, 4290

Mountain Sq., Whistler Village (☎ 604/938-1616; www.canadiansnowmobile. com), are a unique way to take to the Whistler Mountain trails. All tours are weather and snow conditions permitting. In summer 1999 there was so much snow on top of Whistler Mountain that by early August, the company was still offering full snowmobile tours. After a gondola ride up the mountain, a 1-hour tour costs C$59 (US$38) for a driver and C$39 (US$26) for a passenger. Drivers on both the snowmobile and ATV must have a valid driver's license. On Blackcomb Mountain, Snowmobile Adventures offers a popular ATV trip, the 2-hour Mountain Explorer, costing C$109 (US$73) for a driver and C$59 (US$38) for a passenger. Conditions permitting, inquire about the combined ATV/snowmobile trip where you ride up to the snowline on the ATV and then switch to a snowmobile for a summertime snow ride.

Blackcomb Snowmobile (☎ 604/905-7002; www.snowmobiling.bc.ca) offers 4- to 8-hour guided snowmobile tours on Blackcomb Mountain. The Fresh Tracks tour, including breakfast, costs C$169 (US$113) per person, with two people for a 4-hour tour, or C$259 (US$174) per person with two people for an all-day Braelorne Back Country tour, lunch included.

SNOWSHOEING   Snowshoeing is the world's easiest form of snow locomotion; it requires none of the training and motor skills of skiing or boarding. You can wear your own shoes or boots, provided they're warm and waterproof, strap on your snowshoes, and off you go! Rentals are available at a number of the ski-and-board rental companies. See above.

Outdoor Adventures@Whistler (☎ 604/932-0647; www.adventureswhistler. com; e-mail: outdoors@whistler.net) has guided snowshoe tours for novices at C$39 (US$26) for 1½ hours. A 4-hour tour to a ghost town costs C$69 (US$46), including lunch. If you want to just rent the snowshoes and find your own way around, rentals are C$15 (US$10) per day. **Cougar Mountain at Whistler,** 36-4314 Main St. (☎ 888/297-2222 or 604/932-4086; www.whistlerbackcountry.com), has guided tours to the Cougar Mountain area at C$49 (US$33) for 2 hours.

SLEIGHING & DOGSLEDDING   Whistler Backcountry Adventures (see below under "Fishing") offers dogsled rides. A musher and his team of Inuit sled dogs will take you for a backcountry ride at C$249 (US$167) per sled, with a maximum of two people or 400 pounds.

For a different kind of sleigh ride—with horses—contact **Blackcomb Horsedrawn Sleigh Rides,** 103-4338 Main St. (☎ 604/932-7631; www.whistlerweb.net/resort/ sleighrides). In winter, tours go out every evening and cost C$45 (US$30) for adults and C$25 (US$17) for children under 12. The tour will take you up past the ski trails and into a wooded trail with a magnificent view of the lights at Whistler Village. A stop at a cabin for a mug of hot chocolate will warm you up for your ride home.

SUMMER PURSUITS

BIKING   Some of the best mountain bike trails in the village are on **Whistler and Blackcomb mountains.** It's not unusual to see bikers loading into the gondolas at both lifts during summer. Some of the backcountry trails at **Lost Lake** are also marked for mountain biking. Lift tickets at both mountains are C$19 to C$30 (US$13 to US$20) per day, and discounted season mountain bike passes are available.

You can rent a mountain bike from **Trax & Trails,** Chateau Whistler Hotel, 4599 Chateau Blvd., Upper Village (☎ 604/938-2017), and the **Whistler Bike Company,** Delta Whistler Resort, 4050 Whistler Way, Whistler Village (☎ 604/938-9511). Prices run C$10 (US$7) per hour to C$30 (US$20) per day.

M.X. Mountain Bike Vacations (☎ 604/905-4914; www.mx.whistler.bc.ca) offers affordable 6- and 8-day mountain bike camps for C$900 to C$1,200 (US$603 to US$804). Packages include accommodation, meals, and daily mountain bike coaching, as well as extracurricular activities such as white-water rafting and rock climbing. Ages 15 and up.

CANOEING & KAYAKING   The 3-hour River of Golden Dreams Kayak & Canoe Tour offered by **Whistler Sailing & Water Sports Center Ltd.** (☎ 604/932-7245) is a great way for novices, intermediates, and experts to get acquainted with an exhilarating stretch of racing glacial water running between Green Lake and Alta Lake behind the village of Whistler. Packages begin at C$29 (US$19) per person unguided and include all gear and return transportation to the village center. The same company offers lessons and clinics as well as sailboat and windsurfing rentals.

FISHING   Spring runs of steelhead, rainbow trout, and Dolly Varden char; summer runs of cutthroat and salmon; and fall runs of coho salmon attract anglers from around the world to the area's many glacier-fed lakes and rivers and to **Birkenhead Lake Provincial Park,** 66.6 kilometers (40 miles) north of Pemberton. Bring your favorite fly rod and don't forget to buy a fishing license when you arrive at **Whistler Backcountry Adventures,** 36-4314 Main St. (☎ 604/932-3474).

Whistler River Adventures (see "Jet Boating" below), **Sea-to-Sky Reel Adventures** (☎ 604/894-6928), and **Off the Beaten Track Wilderness Expeditions** (☎ 604/938-9282; www.otbt.bc.ca) offer half-day and full-day catch-and-release fishing trips in the surrounding glacier rivers. Rates are C$125 to C$185 (US$84 to US$124) per person, based on two people, which includes all fishing gear, round-trip transport to/from the Whistler Village Bus Loop, and a snack or lunch.

GOLFING   Robert Trent Jones's **Chateau Whistler Golf Club,** at the base of Blackcomb Mountain (☎ 604/938-2092; pro shop 604/938-2095), is an 18-hole, par-72 course. With an elevation gain of more than 120 meters (400 ft.), this course traverses mountain ledges and crosses cascading creeks. Midcourse, there's a panoramic view of the Coast Mountains. Greens fees are C$135 to C$185 (US$90 to US$124), which includes golf-cart rental.

A multiple-award-winning golf course, **Nicklaus North at Whistler** (☎ 604/938-9898) is a 5-minute drive north of the village on the shores of Green Lake. The par-71 course's mountain views are spectacular. It's only the second Canadian course designed by Nicklaus and, of all the courses he's designed worldwide, the only one to bear his name. Greens fees are C$100 to C$185 (US$67 to US$124).

Whistler Golf Club (☎ 800/376-1777 or 604/932-4544), designed by Arnold Palmer, features nine lakes, two creeks, and magnificent vistas. Recently having undergone a C$2-million renovation, this 18-hole, par-72 course offers a driving range, putting green, sand bunker, and pitching area. Greens fees are C$150 (US$101).

A-1 Last Minute Golf Hotline (☎ 800/684-6344 or 604/878-1833) can arrange a next-day tee time at Whistler golf courses and elsewhere in B.C. at over 30 courses. Savings can be as much as 40% on next-day, last-minute tee times. No membership is necessary. Call between 3 and 9pm for the next day or before noon for the same day. The hot line also arranges advanced bookings, as much as a year ahead, as well as group bookings.

HIKING   There are numerous easy hiking trails in and around Whistler. Besides taking a lift up to Whistler and Blackcomb Mountains' high mountain trails during summer, you have a number of choices.

Lost Lake Trail starts at the northern end of the Day Skier Parking Lot at Black-comb Mountain. The lake is less than a mile from the entry. The 30 kilometers (18 miles) of marked trails that wind around creeks, beaver dams, blueberry patches, and lush cedar groves are ideal for biking, cross-country skiing, or just strolling and picnicking. The **Valley Trail System** is a well-marked paved trail that connects parts of Whistler. The trail starts on the west side of Highway 99 adjacent to the Whistler Golf Course and winds through quiet residential areas as well as golf courses and parks.

Garibaldi Provincial Park's **Singing Pass Trail** is a 4-hour hike of moderate diffi-culty. The fun way is to take the Whistler Mountain gondola to the top and walk down the well-marked path that ends in the village on an access road. Winding down from above the tree line, the trail takes you through stunted alpine forest into Fitzsim-mons Valley. There are several access points into the park along Highway 99 between Squamish and Whistler.

Nairn Falls Provincial Park is about 33.3 kilometers (20 miles) north of Whistler on Highway 99. This provincial park features a mile-long trail that leads you to a stu-pendous view of the icy-cold Green River as it plunges 59 meters (196 ft.) over a rocky cliff into a narrow gorge on its way downstream. There's also an incredible view of Mount Currie peeking over the treetops.

On Highway 99 north of Mount Currie, **Joffre Lakes Provincial Park** is an inter-mediate-level hike that leads past several brilliant blue glacial lakes up to the very foot of a glacier. The **Ancient Cedars** area of Cougar Mountain is an awe-inspiring grove of towering cedars and Douglas firs. (Some of the trees are over 1,000 years old and measure 3m/9 ft. in diameter.) This 4-kilometer (2½-mile) hike can be made even more exciting by taking a Land Rover 4-by-4 up the backcountry route. **Off the Beaten Track Wilderness Expeditions** (☎ **604/938-9282**) (see "Fishing" above) offers this unique off-road experience and provides a knowledgeable guide and snacks. Three- and 6-hour tours depart from the Whistler Village Bus Loop for C$59 to C$89 (US$40 to US$60) per person.

HORSEBACK RIDING   **Whistler River Adventures** (see "Jet Boating" below) offers 2-hour trail rides along the Green River, through the forest, and across the Pem-berton Valley from its 4-hectare (10-acre) riverside facility in nearby Pemberton. You will need your own transportation to get out to Pemberton, a 35-minute drive north of Whistler. The 2-hour ride costs C$49 (US$33); longer rides available on request.

JET BOATING   **Whistler River Adventures,** Whistler Mountain Village Gondola Base (☎ **888/932-3532** or 604/932-3532; fax 604/932-3559; www.whistlerriver. com), takes guests up the Green River just below Nairn Falls, where moose, deer, and bear sightings are common in the sheer-granite canyon. The Lillooet River tour goes past ancient petroglyphs, fishing sites, and the tiny native village of Skookumchuk. **Whistler Jet Boating Company Ltd.** (☎ **604/894-5200**) runs sightseers down the icy rapids of the Green River or takes them speed cruising through the Lillooet River valley throughout the summer, water levels permitting.

Tours by both companies range from 1-hour-long trips for C$75 (US$50) to 6-hour cruises for C$135 (US$90).

RAFTING   **Whistler River Adventures** (☎ **604/932-3532**) (see "Jet Boating" above) offers 2-hour and full-day round-trip rafting runs down the Green, Elaho, and Squamish rivers. They include equipment and ground transportation for C$59 to C$129 (US$40 to US$86). Children and youths are welcome as long as they're able to hold on by themselves and weigh a minimum of 90 pounds. Novices are taken to the Green River, where small rapids and snowcapped mountain views highlight a half-day trip. Experts are transported to the Elaho River or Squamish River for full-day,

Class IV excitement on runs with names like Aitons Alley and Steamroller. May through August, trips depart daily. The full-day trip includes a salmon barbecue lunch. The company also conducts 3-hour round-trip jet-boat tours of the river for C$75 (US$50) per person, including ground transport and wet suit.

For first-timers, **Wedge Rafting,** Carleton Lodge, Whistler Village (☎ 604/932-7171; www.whistler.net\wedgerafting), offers a Green River or a Birkenhead River tour. For the Green River trip, about 2½ hours, the shuttle picks up rafters in Whistler and takes them to the wilderness launch area for briefing and equipping. It's an exciting hour or more on the icy, bubbling rapids. After the run, rafters can relax at the outfitter's log lodge with a snack and soda before being shuttled back into town. Tours cost C$59 (US$40), with up to three daily departures. The Birkenhead River tour takes about 4 hours and costs C$76 (US$51). Discounts are available for youths 10 to 16, however, they must weigh at least 90 pounds.

TENNIS   The **Whistler Racquet & Golf Resort,** 4500 Northland Blvd. (☎ 604/932-1991; www.whistlertennis.com), has three covered courts, seven outdoor courts, and a practice cage, all open to drop-in visitors. Indoor courts are C$24 (US$16) per hour and outdoor courts C$12 (US$8) per hour. Adult and junior tennis camps are offered in summer. Camp prices run C$250 to C$350 (US$168 to US$235) for a 3-day camp. Kids' camps cost C$36 (US$24) per day drop-in, or C$150 (US$101) for a 5-day camp. Book early, as these camps fill up very quickly.

The **Mountain Spa & Tennis Club,** Delta Whistler Resort, Whistler Village (☎ 604/938-2044), and the **Chateau Whistler Resort,** Chateau Whistler Hotel, Upper Village (☎ 604/938-8000), also offer courts to drop-in players. Prices run about C$10 (US$7) per hour per court; racquet rentals are available for C$5 (US$3.35) per hour.

There are **free public courts** (☎ 604/938-PARK) at Myrtle Public School, Alpha Lake Park, Meadow Park, Millar's Pond, Brio, Blackcomb Benchlands, White Gold, and Emerald Park.

URBAN PURSUITS

A MUSEUM   To learn more about Whistler's heritage, flora, and fauna, visit the **Whistler Museum & Archives Society,** 4329 Main St., off Northlands Boulevard (☎ 604/932-2019). The museum exhibits reveal the life and culture of the native Indian tribes that have lived in the lush Whistler and Pemberton valleys for thousands of years. There are also re-creations of the village's early settlement by British immigrants during the late 1800s and early 1900s. The museum is open daily from 10am to 4pm in summer, until Labor Day (call ahead for winter hours). Admission is by donation.

SHOPPING   The **Whistler Marketplace** (in the center of Whistler Village) and the area surrounding the **Blackcomb Mountain lift** brim with clothing, jewelry, crafts, specialty, gift, and equipment shops that are generally open daily from 10am to 6pm. **Horstman Trading Company** (☎ 604/938-7725), beside the Chateau Whistler at the base of Blackcomb, carries men's and women's casual wear, from swimwear and footwear to polar-fleece vests and nylon jacket shells. **Escape Route** (☎ 604/938-3228), at Whistler Marketplace and Crystal Lodge, has a great line of outdoor clothing and equipment. **Whistler Backcountry Adventures,** 4314 Main St. (☎ 604/932-3474), sells fishing licenses and carries a great selection of fishing rods, tackle, sports gear, and outdoor clothing.

The **Whistler Inuit Gallery,** 4599 Chateau Blvd. (☎ 604/938-3366), on the lower concourse of the Chateau Whistler Resort, specializes in Inuit, West Coast, and contemporary artists. Gallery Row in the Delta Whistler Resort consists of three galleries: the **Whistler Village Art Gallery** (☎ 604/938-3001), **Northern Lights Gallery** (☎ 604/932-2890), and **Adele Campbell Gallery** (☎ 604/938-0887). Their collections include fine art, sculpture, and glass. **Keir Fine Jewelry,** Village Gate House (☎ 604/932-2944), sells Italian gold, Swiss watches, and Canadian handmade jewelry.

SPAS That resort lifestyle can be hard on the body, so why not try some relaxation at one of the outstanding spas offered by Whistler? The **Spa at Chateau Whistler Resort** (☎ 604/938-2086) is the best in town. Open daily from 8am to 9pm, the spa offers massage therapy, aromatherapy, skin care, body wraps, steam baths, and makeup, and can put together a package of your choice.

Whistler Body Wrap, 210 St. Andrews House (☎ 604/932-4710), next to the Keg in the Village, can nurture you with an array of services, such as shiatsu massage, facials, pedicures or manicures, waxings, sunbeds, and aromatherapy. If something didn't quite go right on the slopes or on the trails, **Whistler Physiotherapy** specializes in sports therapy. The therapists at this clinic treat many professional athletes and have a lot of experience with the typical ski, board, and hiking injuries. There are two locations: 339-4370 Lorimer Rd., at Marketplace (☎ 604/932-4001), and 202-2011 Innsbruck Dr., next to Boston Pizza in Creekside (☎ 604/938-9001).

ESPECIALLY FOR KIDS

Near the base of the mountains, Whistler Village and the Upper Village sponsor daily activities tailor-made for active kids of all ages. There are mountain bike races; an inline skating park; trapeze, trampoline, and wall-climbing lessons; summer skiing; snowboarding; and snowshoeing. There's even a first-run multiplex movie theater.

Based at Blackcomb Mountain, the **Dave Murray Summer Ski and Snowboard Camp** (☎ 604/932-5765; www.skiandsnowboard.com) is North America's longest-running summer ski camp. Junior programs cost about C$1,475 (US$988) per week from mid-June to mid-July. The packages include food, lodging, and lift passes, as well as tennis, trapeze, and mountain-biking options. Mornings and early afternoons are spent skiing, boarding, or free-riding on the excellent terrain parks and half-pipes. This ski-and-board camp isn't for beginners; the age group is 10 to 18 years. In the afternoons, youths have a choice from a wide range of other outdoor activities. The comprehensive instruction and adult supervision at this activity-oriented camp are excellent.

WHISTLER AFTER DARK

For a town of just 8,000, Whistler has a more-than-respectable nightlife scene. Bands touring through Vancouver regularly make the trip up the Sea-to-Sky; some even make Whistler their Canadian debut. Concert listings can be found in the *Pique,* a free local paper available at cafes and food stores. Fittingly for such a cosmopolitan place, the night scene divides up not by language or ethnicity but by age.

Tommy Africa's (☎ 604/932-6090), beneath the Pharmasave at the entrance to the Main Village, and the dark and cavernous **Maxx Fish** (☎ 604/932-1904), in the Village Square below the Amsterdam Cafe, cater to the 18-to-22-year-old crowd: lots of beat and not much light. The crowd at **Garfinkel's** (☎ 604/932-2323), at the entrance to Village North, is similar, though the cut-off age can reach as high as 27. The **Boot Pub** (☎ 604/932-3338), Nancy Green Drive, just off Highway 99, advertises itself as Whistler's living room and more than lives up to its billing: Throngs of young Australian ski-lift operators cram the room, bouncing to the band or DJ and spilling draft beer over the floor and their mostly unwashed clothes. **Buffalo Bills** (☎ **604/932-6613**), across from the Whistler Gondola, and the **Savage Beagle** (☎ **604/938-3337**), in the Village, cater to the 30-something crowd. Bills is bigger, with a pool table and video ski machine, a smallish dance floor, and music straight from the 1980s. The Beagle has a fabulous selection of beer and bar drinks, with a pleasant little pub upstairs and house-oriented dance floor below.

3 Bamfield

You're alone on the shoreline, where the beach goes on forever. Waves crash in on the rocky outcrops. A seal pops out of the water, stares you in the face for a moment, then drops back beneath the surface. A gull cries. You turn and see the outstretched wings of a bald eagle gliding along the shoreline, passing 6 meters (20 ft.) over your head. Another follows. And a third. That's **Bamfield.**

There can be few if any towns on earth quite like it. Nestled in a tiny bay between the mountains and a raging ocean, Bamfield's wooden houses are linked by an elevated wooden boardwalk running from house to shop to inn along the rocky shoreline. It gives the place a unique charm. Add to that a beach with sea caves and blowholes, seabird and mammal life galore, and a native site up for Unesco World Heritage designation, and you're in a memorable location indeed. Curiously, though thousands hike the **West Coast Trail** every year (see the box below), few make it the extra few kilometers into town.

ESSENTIALS

GETTING THERE   By Car   Bamfield is a 3-hour drive from Victoria. Take Highway 1 to just north of Duncan, then Highway 18 west to Cowichan Lake. When you get to the lake, take the road around the north shore of the lake (through Youbou) and follow the signs to Bamfield. The last 100 kilometers (62 miles) are along gravel logging roads. The road surface is kept smooth enough even for a subcompact two-wheel drive, but signage is poor, and the logging trucks can be a little intimidating. (It's best to pull over completely when you see one coming.) Tough it out, wait for weekends or evenings when the trucks aren't running, or—best of all—take the boat.

By Bus   May through September, the daily **West Coast Trail Express** (☎ **888/ 999-2288** or 250/477-8700) provides Victoria-Bamfield service for C$53 (US$36). Because it partially travels along an unpaved logging road, the ride is usually about 5 hours. This company will also pick you up at the other end of the trail in Port Renfrew and transport you back to Victoria for C$32 (US$21).

By Boat   A 4½-hour ride aboard the **Alberni Marine Transportation** (☎ **250/ 723-8313**) passenger ferry MV *Lady Rose* takes you from Port Alberni through the Alberni Inlet fjord to the boardwalk fishing village of Bamfield. It makes brief stops along the way to deliver mail and packages to solitary cabin dwellers along the coast and to let off or pick up kayakers bound for the Broken Islands Group. The *Lady Rose*, built in Scotland in 1937, departs three times a week (more sailings in summer) to

A Weather Warning

They don't call this the rain coast for nothing. Winter storms with lashings of rain and wind gusts up to 100 kilometers per hour (62 m.p.h.) have their appeal, but it's still an esoteric pleasure. Go between May and September.

Vancouver Island

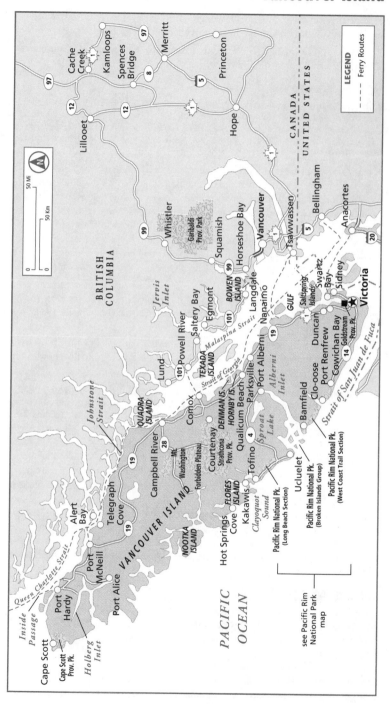

each destination from Alberni Harbour Quay's Angle Street. The one-way fare to Bamfield is C$20 (US$13); the round-trip fare is C$40 (US$27).

VISITOR INFORMATION　Call the **Bamfield Chamber of Commerce** at ☎ 250/728-3006 or visit online at www.alberni.net/bamcham.

WHERE TO STAY

Bamfield Lodge. 275 Boardwalk, P.O. Box 23, Bamfield, B.C. V0R 1B0. ☎ **250/728-3419.** Fax 250/728-3417. www.alberni.net/bamfieldlodge. E-mail: barry@bamfieldlodge.com. 2 units, 2 cottages, 1 1-bedroom house. C$75 (US$50) double, C$100 (US$67) cottage, C$250 (US$168) house. Off-season discounts. No refunds July–Aug. V. There are no access roads. The owners pick up guests and transport them by boat, just a short ride across the inlet.

A pair of rustic cottages, a lodge, and a two-bedroom house are the waterfront offerings at this retreat. The twin-bed and double-bed cabins and the guest house have fully equipped kitchens, and all are simply decorated in earth-tone fabrics. Bring your own food (freezer space is available) or partake of the lodge's gourmet meals. The restaurant is open to the public at dinner, with main dishes from C$7 to C$18 (US$4.70 to US$12). Sip an espresso in the resort's cappuccino bar while watching the birds, whales, and boats pass by. Moorage is available if you boat to the lodge. The staff can also arrange hiking, kayaking, fishing, diving, whale watching, and intertidal field trips.

Pacheena Bay Campground. Box 70, Bamfield, B.C. V0R 1B0. ☎ **250/728-1287.** 80 sites. C$19 (US$13) site, summer only. No credit cards. Entrance is on the road to Bamfield, about 5km (3 miles) out of town.

On the Pacheena River estuary and the beach beyond, this is one of the most beautiful campsites in the province. The campground has flush toilets and hot showers. Each site also has a fire pit.

✪ Woods End Landing Cottages. Box 108, Bamfield, B.C. V0R 1B0. ☎ **250/728-3383.** Fax 250/728-3383. www.woodsend.travel.bc.ca. E-mail: woodsend@island.net. 6 cottages. C$95–C$185 (US$64–US$124) per cottage for up to 4 people. Off-season discounts. MC, V. There are no access roads. The owners pick up guests and transport them by boat, just a short ride across the inlet. Pets accepted.

The picturesque timbered cottages on this secluded waterfront wilderness property offer fully-equipped kitchens, propane barbecues, and private porches overlooking the 0.8-hectare (2-acre) perennial gardens, with an herb garden available for guest use. The decor features Canadian antiques and collectibles as well as double-size hand-hewn log beds, duvets, large farmhouse tables, exposed timber beams, and skylights. Hiking, fishing, whale watching, diving, and eagle and sea-lion watching; Keeha Beach; part of the West Coast Trail; and the Cape Beale Lighthouse are within walking distance. A private dock, moorage, freezer space, canoe, and fishing tackle are available. Smoking isn't permitted, but pets are accepted.

WHERE TO DINE

Haute cuisine, alas, hasn't yet reached these far-flung shores. Bamfield, in fact, has only two restaurants. At the **Hawk's Nest Pub,** 48 Grappler Rd. (☎ 250/728-3422), there's a bar, a pool table, a fireplace, daily specials on the chalkboard, and pub food on the menu. The cuisine is fresh and well prepared and goes great with beer. A sandwich, burger or dinner special ranges from C$7 to C$11 (US$4.65 to US$7). May through September open 11am to midnight, October through April open 11:30am to 2:30pm and 4:30 to 11pm, closed Monday and Tuesday. With a reservation, the **McKay Bay Lodge** (☎ 250/728-3323) will let you sit in on the seafood supper

The West Coast Trail

After the SS *Valencia* ran aground in 1906 and most of the survivors died of exposure on the beach, the Canadian government built a rescue trail between Bamfield and Port Renfrew. For years, the lifesaving trail was maintained by solitary watchmen who groomed it and checked the telephone line strung along the path.

Upgraded by Parks Canada in the 1970s, the ✪ **West Coast Trail** has gained a reputation as one of the world's greatest extreme hiking/camping adventures. Each year, about 9,000 people hike the entire challenging 72.5-kilometer (43½-mile) route, and thousands more hike the very accessible 11-kilometer (7 mile) oceanfront stretch at the northern trailhead near Bamfield.

Planning (get a topographic map and tidal table), stamina (besides hiking, you should train for rock climbing), and experience (advanced wilderness survival and minimum-impact camping knowledge) are imperative for the full hike. Veterans recommend you go with at least two companions, pack lightweight weatherproof gear, and bring about 15 meters (50 ft.) of climbing rope per person. To reduce the impact on the environment, only 52 people per day are allowed to enter the main trail (26 from Port Renfrew, 26 from Bamfield), and registration with the park office is mandatory.

Call **Discover BC** (☎ **800/663-6000** or 604/435-5622) after February 1 to schedule your entry for the coming season (May 1 to Sept 30). Make your reservations as early as possible and be prepared for busy signals and long waiting times; you can book only a maximum of 3 months ahead of your travel date. Limited access and increased popularity mean you may not gain admission if you call too late in the season. The C$25 (US$17) per person advance booking fee includes the price of a waterproof trail map, plus there are C$70 (US$47) trail-use fees and C$25 (US$17) ferry fees for various crossings. During summer, you can also contact the parks service at ☎ **250/728-3234** or 250/647-5434.

created by their trained chef, for C$20 (US$13) per person. The **Tyee Resort** (☎ **888/493-8933** or 250/728-3296) also accepts nonguests at its supper table, with a previous reservation. Both McKay Lodge and Tyee Resort are accessible by water only. Call ahead for availability, transportation, and hours of operation.

The other option, of course, is to cook your own. Officially, for the usual meddling bureaucratic reasons beloved of interfering governments everywhere, fishers down at the docks aren't allowed to sell their wares directly to the public. On the other hand, were one to inquire of, say, a prawn or shrimp captain whether he had any extra catch on hand, there's a strong possibility fresh spotted prawns might be available.

After dinner, wander down to the boardwalk, where **Judy's Cappuccino** (☎ **250/728-3419**) serves up a potent brew.

ACTIVITIES

BEACH WALKING   **Brady's Beach,** a 10-minute walk from the village of Bamfield, is alive with eagles, seals, mink, and other creatures. **Keeha Beach,** a 20-minute drive from town, is one of the most impressive beaches on the West Coast. For those wanting a taste of the West Coast Trail, the trailhead is also just a short drive out of town.

DIVING   The waters off the **West Coast Trail** are known as "the graveyard of the Pacific." Hundreds of 19th- and 20th-century shipwrecks silently attest to the hazards of sailing without an experienced guide in these unforgiving waters. The Cousteau Society rates this dive area as one of the world's best, second only to the Red Sea. There are even underwater interpretive trails that narrate the area's unique history. **Broken Island Adventures** (☎ **888/728-6200** or 250/728-3500) leads guided diving tours to various locations.

The **Bamfield Marine Station** (☎ **250/728-3301**), a research facility associated with four western Canadian universities, offers free guided tours of its research labs Saturday and Sunday during July and August.

FISHING   The waters off Bamfield teem with fish of all kinds. **Ka-ka-Win Charters** (☎ **250/728-1267**) can show you where. Run by Ed and Pearl Johnson of the nearby Huu-ay-aht native band, the company has years of experience fishing in Barkley Sound and the open ocean.

KAYAKING   For C$50 (US$34), the **Bamfield Kayak Centre** (☎ **877/728-3535; www.bamfieldkayak.com**) offers a 3-hour marine-biology paddle, exploring the rich intertidal zones, inlets, and surge channels with a local marine biologist. Rentals, instruction, and full-day tours are also available. **Broken Island Adventures** (☎ **888/728-6200** or 250/728-3500) runs kayak and wildlife adventures to the Broken Islands and the Deer Group. The 6-hour Broken Islands tour is C$90 (US$60) per person.

4 Ucluelet, Tofino & Pacific Rim National Park (Long Beach Section)

The west coast of Vancouver Island is a magnificent area of old-growth forests, stunning fjords (called "sounds" in local parlance), rocky coasts, and long sandy beaches. And though **Pacific Rim National Park** was established in 1971 as Canada's first marine park, it wasn't until 1993 that it really exploded into the consciousness of people outside the area. That was when thousands of environmentalists from across the province and around the world gathered to protest the clear-cutting of old-growth forests in Clayoquot Sound. Wherever you stand in that debate, one result of the protest was incontrovertible. When news footage of the protests ran on the evening news, people at home who saw the landscape for the first time were moved to come experience it first-hand. Tourism in the area has never looked back.

The three main areas belonging to this section of the West Coast are **Ucluelet, Tofino,** and the **Long Beach section** of Pacific Rim National Park. They lie along the outer edge of a peninsula about halfway up the western shore of Vancouver Island.

The town of Ucluelet (pronounced you-*clue*-let, meaning "safe harbor" in the local Nuu-chah-nulth dialect), sits on the southern end of this peninsula, on the edge of Barkley Sound. Though it has a winter population of only 1,900, thousands of visitors arrive between March and May to see as many as 20,000 Pacific gray whales pass close to the shore as they migrate north to their summer feeding grounds in the Arctic Circle.

About a 15-minute drive north is Long Beach, part of the Pacific Rim National Park group. The beach is more than 30 kilometers (19 miles) long, broken here and there by rocky headlands and bordered by tremendous groves of cedar and Sitka spruce. The beach is popular with countless species of birds and marine life, and, lately, also with wet-suited surfers.

At the far northern tip of the peninsula, Tofino (pop. 1,300) borders on beautiful Clayoquot Sound. It's the center of the West Coast ecotourism business, though it's

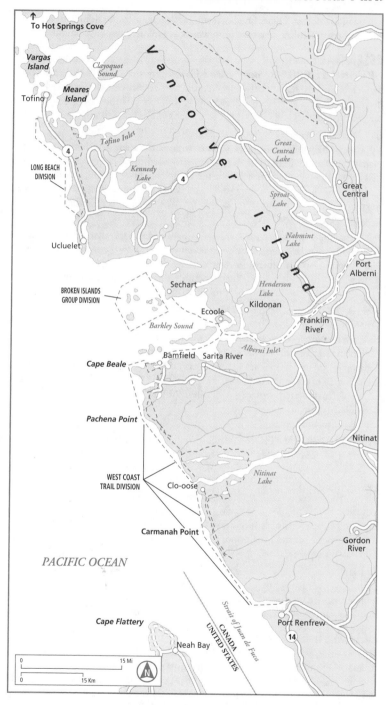

To Hot Springs Cove

Vargas Island

Tofino

Meares Island

Clayoquot Sound

Tofino Inlet

V a n c o u v e r   I s l a n d

4

LONG BEACH DIVISION

Kennedy Lake

4

Great Central Lake

Great Central

Sproat Lake

Nahmint Lake

Ucluelet

BROKEN ISLANDS GROUP DIVISION

Sechart

Ecoole

Barkley Sound

Henderson Lake

Kildonan

Port Alberni

Franklin River

Alberni Inlet

Cape Beale

Bamfield   Sarita River

Pachena Point

Nitinat

WEST COAST TRAIL DIVISION

Clo-oose

Nitinat Lake

Carmanah Point

PACIFIC OCEAN

Gordon River

Cape Flattery

Neah Bay

Strait of Juan de Fuca

CANADA
UNITED STATES

Port Renfrew

14

0   15 Mi

0   15 Km

N

still small for all that. Hikers and beachcombers come to Tofino simply for the scenery, while others use Tofino as a base from which to explore Clayoquot Sound.

ESSENTIALS

GETTING THERE   By Bus   Island Coach Lines (☎ 250/724-1266) operates regular daily bus service between Victoria and Tofino/Ucluelet. The 7-hour trip, departing Victoria at 7:30am and arriving in Tofino at 2:45pm, costs C$45 (US$30) one-way to Ucluelet and C$48 (US$32) to Tofino. The bus also stops in Nanaimo and can pick up passengers arriving from Vancouver on the ferry.

By Car   The same route takes you to Tofino, Ucluelet, and Long Beach. From Nanaimo, take the Island Highway (Hwy. 19) north for 51.6 kilometers (31 miles). Just before the town of Parksville is a turnoff for Highway 4, which leads first to the midisland town of Port Alberni (about 38.3km/23 miles west) and then the coastal towns of Tofino (135km/81 miles west of Port Alberni) and Ucluelet (103.3km/62 miles west). The road is well paved the whole way but gets windy after Port Alberni.

By Ferry   A 4½-hour ride aboard the **Alberni Marine Transportation** (☎ 250/723-8313; www.ladyrosemarine.com) passenger ferry MV *Lady Rose* takes you from Port Alberni through Alberni Inlet to Ucluelet. It makes brief stops along the way to deliver mail and packages to solitary cabin dwellers along the coast and to let off or pick up kayakers bound for the Broken Islands Group. In summer, the *Lady Rose* departs three times per week to each destination from Alberni Harbour Quay's Angle Street. The fare to Ucluelet is C$23 (US$15) one-way or C$45 (US$30) round-trip.

By Plane   North Vancouver Air (☎ 800/228-6608) operates twin-engine, turbo-prop plane service daily between Vancouver or Victoria and Tofino from May through September; it runs four times per week from October through April. One-way fare, including all taxes and airport fees, is C$175 (US$117); flying time is approximately an hour. **Northwest Seaplanes** (☎ 800/690-0086) and **Sound Flight** (☎ 800/825-0722) offer floatplane service between Seattle and Tofino during the summer (mid-June to late Sept).

VISITOR INFORMATION   March through September, the **Tofino Visitor Info Centre** (☎ 250/725-3414; www.island.net/~tofino), 380 Campbell St., Tofino (P.O. Box 476, Tofino, B.C. V0R 2Z0), is open Monday to Friday from 11am to 5pm. June through September, the **Ucluelet Visitor Info Centre** (☎ 250/726-4641; www. ucluelet.com/ucoc), at the Junction of Highway 4, Ucluelet (P.O. Box 428, Ucluelet, B.C. V0R 3A0), is open the same hours. Mid-March through September, the **Long Beach Visitor Information Centre** (☎ 250/726-4212), about a mile from the Highway 4 junction to Tofino, is open daily from 9:30am to 5pm.

SPECIAL EVENTS   About 20,000 whales migrate here annually. During the third and last week of March, the **Pacific Rim Whale Festival** (☎ 250/726-4641 or 250/726-7742) is held in Tofino and Ucluelet. Crab races, the Gumboot Golf Tournament, guided whale-watching hikes, and a native festival are just a few of the events that celebrate the annual Pacific gray whale migration.

UCLUELET

When fishing was the major industry on the coast, **Ucluelet** was the big town. Thanks to its harbor, it was here that most of the ships docked and where the processing and packing plants were located. With the recent boom in ecotourism, however, the roles have been reversed, and Ucluelet is scrambling to catch up. At the moment it has a beautiful location and a couple of fine B&Bs, but it has yet to develop the same range of restaurants and activities as Tofino. But things are changing fast. And at the moment, Ucluelet is cheaper and just as close to Long Beach. In the high summer when Tofino is packed, Ucluelet will likely still have spots.

WHERE TO STAY

Ocean's Edge B&B. 855 Barkley Crescent, Box 557, Ucluelet, B.C. V0R 3A0. ☎ **250/ 726-7099.** Fax 250/726-7099. www.oceansedge.bc.ca. E-mail: waves@oceansedge.bc.cam. 3 units. May–Sept C$120 (US$80) double; Oct–Apr C$105 (US$70) double. MC, V. 2-night minimum on long weekends, holidays, and high season. No children permitted.

This remarkable little B&B sits on its own tiny peninsula jutting out into the Pacific, with only a thicket of interwoven hemlocks sheltering it from the wind and the surf of the ocean, which roars up surge channels on either side. The rooms are pleasant and spotless, without being opulent. The real attractions are the scenery and the wildlife, which abound. Owners Bill and Susan McIntyre installed a skylight in the kitchen so breakfasting guests could keep an eye on the pair of bald eagles and their chicks nesting in a 200-year-old Sitka spruce in the driveway. The former chief naturalist of Pacific Rim National Parks, host Bill McIntyre is a font of information and also does nature tours (see "Guided Nature Hikes" under "Tofino" below).

A Snug Harbour Inn. 460 Marine Dr., Box 357, Ucluelet, B.C. V0R 3A0. ☎ **888/936-5222** or 250/726-2686. www.awesomeview.com. E-mail: asnughbr@island.net. 4 units. May–Sept C$200–C$280 (US$134–US$188) double; Oct–Apr C$180–C$200 (US$121–US$134) double. MC, V.

A beautiful clifftop B&B overlooking its own little bay, A Snug Harbour Inn makes the most of its location. There are several large viewing decks (one with a hot tub), and guests can make use of a monster-size telescope to watch the sea lions on the reef just offshore. The inn is luxurious—the rooms are spacious, with queen- or king-size beds, opulent bathrooms, and jetted tubs. The heart-shaped tub with a waterfall may be a bit over the top, but who's complaining? Owner Skip Rowland had the inn built by a shipwright, and the craftsmanship shows. The nautical theme is carried out in the decor. If you visit during the winter storm season and the wind blows full gale force, Skip will put either a C$50 bill under your pillow or provide a chilled bottle of champagne for your storm-viewing pleasure.

Tauca Lea By The Sea. 10 Harbour Rd. Ucluelet, B.C. V0R 3A0 ☎ **800/979-9303** or 250/ 726-4625. www.taucalearesort.com. 44 units. C$130–C$170 (US$87–US$114) 1-bedroom suite, C$190–C$230 (US$127–US$154) 2-bedroom suite. MC, V.

If there were ever a sure sign that Ucluelet is a town on the verge of a big tourism boom, it would be the opening of the Whistler-style condos of the Tauca Lea resort in the spring of 2000. The spacious one- and two-bedroom town houses are on a beautiful forested island on the edge of the harbor just off the main area of town. (A causeway connects the resort to the mainland.) All the suites are comfortably furnished and fully equipped with kitchens and all dining and living-room amenities. You have easy access to whale watching, kayaking, dining, and day hikes along the beaches and bays of the rugged West Coast. To ease away the winter blahs, Tauca Lea plans to have opened an Aveda Spa by the time you get there.

WHERE TO DINE

Fine dining's only just beginning in this seacoast town, as urban refugees with a flair for cooking arrive and try to make a go of it. Two that have done so are the wharf-side **Kingfisher Restaurant** (☎ **250/726-3463**), 168 Fraser Lane; and the pleasant outdoor **Matterson Teahouse and Garden,** 1682 Peninsula Rd. (☎ **250/726-2200**).

Rail & Ranch

To experience British Columbia's backcountry—its mountains, alpine lakes, gold-rush towns, and ranch land—combine a scenic rail trip with a stay at a Cariboo guest ranch. **BC Rail** (☎ **800/339-8752**) offers a number of rail-and-ranch packages for every budget and activity.

At an altitude of 1,050 meters (3,500 ft.), the **Echo Valley Ranch Resort** (☎ **800/253-8831** or 250/459-2386; www.evranch.com) is an oasis in the heart of B.C.'s hard-working ranch land. Norm and his wife, Naan, have built an exquisite ranch resort with all the luxury of a spa. Activities include horseback riding, hiking, gold panning, native studies, and a four-by-four excursion to the Fraser River Canyon. This section of the river is unbelievably beautiful: steep canyon walls, arid hills, and a rugged inaccessible landscape. Back at Echo Valley, chef Kim Madsen pampers guests with three gourmet meals a day. The Echo Valley Spa, meanwhile, provides the ultimate in relaxation; being a modern cowboy isn't exactly roughing it.

For a more authentic experience and to ride the range on your own, visit the **Flying U Ranch** (☎ **250/456-7717**; www.flyingu.com). The Cariboo Prospector will drop you off at the ranch's own Flying U Station. After you've checked into a cozy log cabin with a wood-burning stove, you'll be given riding gear and outfitted with a horse that suits your riding skill and style. And then you're on your own. The Flying U is one of the few ranches in North America that allows unsupervised riding: no guides, no trail rides. Guests are free to explore the ranch's 40,000 acres of lake, meadow, forest, and rangeland, with only each other and perhaps one of the frisky ranch dogs for company. At the end of the day, relax in the Longhorn Saloon or kick it up with the Flying U band. The meals—served at long tables in the main lodge—are hearty but unsophisticated. The showers and bathrooms are shared. The Flying U is affordable enough to bring along the kids; hay rides, camp fires, a dozen friendly dogs, canoeing, and swimming will keep them busy even after they tire of riding. Four-day Rail-and-Ranch packages, including all meals and activities, start at C$700 (US$469).

Overlooking the waters of Barkley Sound, you'll have a front-row view of barking sea lions, soaring bald eagles, and the comings and goings of fish boats and floatplanes. Seafood's the chief focus at the **Kingfisher.** Just let Soren the Danish chef know what you're interested in eating, and chances are he can make it. Whatever you order, make sure you try at least a few of Famous Oyster Jim's beach oysters, served with lime juice and tequila, saffron cream and chablis, or a variety of other flavors. Main courses C$14 to C$23 (US$9 to US$15), open daily May through September 11:30am to 2pm and 5 to 10pm. October through April 5 to 9pm Tuesday through Saturday.

The **Matterson Teahouse and Garden** is on the main street and a great spot for lunch; sandwiches, salads, and a great chowder in the cute dining room. On a nice summer day, you have the option of sitting on the shady porch or the sunny back deck, listening to the surfers plan their next ride. The teahouse also serves dinner, but check for seasonal hours.

Somewhat less ambitious but still good is the **Eagles Nest Marine Pub,** 140 Bay St. (☎ **250/726-7515**).

ACTIVITIES

Fishing, kayaking, and whale watching are the big attractions in Ucluelet. Of the three, fishing still predominates. Charter companies that can take you out after salmon, halibut, and other fish include **Quest Charters,** in the boat basin (☎ 250/726-7532), and the much larger **Canadian Princess Resort** (☎ 800/663-7090). **Sea Fin Charters,** 1295 Eber Rd. (☎ 250/726-2104), and **Subtidal Adventures,** 1950 Peninsula Rd. (☎ 250/726-7336), also do fishing charters as well as whale-watching trips and rides for kayakers out to the Broken Islands or other popular spots. **Jamie's Whaling Station,** 168 Fraser Lane, above the Kingfisher restaurant (☎ 800/667-9913; www.jamies.com), has been operating in the Clayoquot Sound area since 1982 and now organizes whale-watching or bear-watching trips out of Ucluelet. Looking for these wild critters is only half the fun—the Barkley Sound area offers spectacular scenery that's best explored from the water. **Majestic Ocean Kayaking,** 1932 Peninsula Rd. (☎ 250/726-2868), runs single- and multiday guided kayak trips. The **Long Beach Nature Tour Company** (☎ 250/726-7099), run by retired Pacific Rim Park chief naturalist Bill McIntyre, does guided beach, rain-forest, and storm walks that explain the ecology and wildlife of the area. His walks will take you to the most interesting trails, beaches, and wildlife-viewing spots.

TOFINO

The center of the environmental protest against industrial logging—and the center of the ecotourism business ever since—**Tofino** remains a schizophrenic kind of town. One half of the town is composed of ecotourism outfitters, nature lovers, activists, and serious granolas, while the other half is composed of loggers and fishermen. Conflict was common in the early years, but recently the two sides seem to have learned how to get along. For a hilarious take on the culture clash between incoming eco-freaks and long-term rednecks during the summer of discontent, pick up *The Green Shadow* by local eco-freak (and closet redneck) Andrew Stretchers.

WHERE TO STAY

The Clayoquot Wilderness Resort. P.O. Box 728, Tofino, B.C. V0R 2Z0. ☎ **888/333-5405** in North America or 250/725-2688. Fax 250/725-2689. www.wildretreat.com. 16 units, 4 camps. May–Oct C$369 (US$247) per person, per night; Nov–Apr C$269 (US$180) per person, per night. Rate includes 3 meals and transfer to and from Tofino. AE, MC, V. Parking provided in Tofino.

The latest in absolute luxury in the area, the Clayoquot Wilderness Resort (CWR) floats alone in splendid isolation on Quoit Bay, about a half-hour boat ride from Tofino. Guests are encouraged to use the lodge as base camp for exploring the natural beauty of the sound. The CWR has set up a number of forest trails nearby and also runs trips out to Hot Springs Cove, as well as horseback-riding excursions and mountain-biking trips. (Most of these activities are charged separately.) There are also spots to fly-fish or simply laze in the sun. Meals, prepared by noted West Coast chef Timothy May, are included and served up with a view of Clayoquot Sound.

The Inn at Tough City. 350 Main St., P.O. Box 8, Tofino, B.C. V0R 2Z0. ☎ **250/725-2021.** Fax 250/725-2088. www.alberni.net/toughcity. E-mail: cityinn@cedar.alberni.net. 6 units. Mar 1–May 15 C$90–C$120 (US$60–US$80) double; May 16–Oct 15 C$140–C$165 (US$94–US$111) double; Oct 16–Feb 28 C$75–C$100 (US$50–US$67) double. MC, V.

This is possibly Tofino's nicest small inn and certainly the quirkiest. Built in 1996 from salvaged and recycled material, it's filled with antiques, stained glass, and bric-a-brac. The rooms are spacious, and several feature soaker tubs, fireplaces, or both. Crazy Ron and Johana are the innkeepers.

Middle Beach Lodge. P.O. Box 100, Tofino, B.C. V0R 2Z0. ☎ **250/725-2900.** Fax 250/725-2901. www.middlebeach.com. E-mail: lodge@middlebeach.com. 7 units, 6 single cabins, 4 duplex cabins, 9 triplex cabins, 6 sixplex suites. C$110–C$165 (US$74–US$111) double, C$165–C$275 (US$111–US$184) suite, C$175–C$370 (US$117–US$248) single cabin, C$160–C$295 (US$107–US$198) duplex cabin, C$110–C$210 (US$74–US$141) triplex cabin, C$125–C$195 (US$84–US$131) sixplex suite. AE, MC, V. No smoking.

This beautiful lodge/resort complex is on a headland overlooking the ocean. The rustic look was accomplished by using largely recycled beams, and the result is very pleasant. Accommodations range from simple lodge rooms to cabins with waterside decks, soaker tubs, gas fireplaces, and kitchenettes. All guests have access to a lofty common room overlooking the ocean. It's a good place to pour a coffee or something stronger and look out over the waves crashing in.

Red Crow Guest House. Box 37, 1084 Pacific Rim Hwy., Tofino, B.C. V0R 2Z0. ☎ and fax **250/725-2275.** www.bbhost.com/redcrowtofino. E-mail: tofinoredcrow@_hotmail.com. 3 units. C$115–C$160 (US$77–US$107) double. Extra person C$20 (US$13). V.

Where the Wickaninnish and other coastal lodges show you the wild, stormy side of the coast, the Red Crow displays a kinder, subtler beauty. By the sheltered waters of Clayoquot Sound, this pleasant Cape Cod cottage looks like it could be set on a lake in Michigan or northern Ontario. That is, until you paddle 15 meters (50 ft.) out in a canoe or rowboat (free for guests) and see the glaciers. Oh, and twice a day the water disappears completely with the tide. Red Crow host and owner Cathy Whitcomb runs an extremely friendly and laid-back inn. Guests are welcomed to their rooms with tea and cookies, then given the run of the extensive grounds, usually with one of two large and friendly dogs for company. The rooms are large and pleasant, with queen beds and 1920s-style furnishings. On the lower level of the large house, they have their own porch and look out on a fabulous view of the sound. Substantial hot breakfasts are served downstairs in the sunshine or under cover of the veranda.

✪ **The Wickaninnish Inn.** Osprey Lane at Chesterman Beach, P.O. Box 250, Tofino, B.C. V0R 2Z0. ☎ **800/333-4604** in North America or 250/725-3300. Fax 250/725-3110. E-mail: wick@island.net. 46 units. Mar–May C$230–C$330 (US$154–US$221) double: June–Sept C$340–C$440 (US$228–US$295) double; Oct C$250–C$350 (US$168–US$235) double; Nov–Feb C$200–C$300 (US$134–US$201) double. Special packages available year-round. Wheelchair-accessible units available. AE, DC, MC, V. Drive 5km (3 miles) south of Tofino toward Chesterman Beach to Osprey Lane.

No matter which room you book in this beautiful new cedar, stone, and glass lodge, you'll wake to a magnificent view of the untamed Pacific. The inn is on a rocky promontory, surrounded by an old-growth spruce and cedar rain forest and the sprawling sands of Chesterman Beach. You do have to make some choices: select king- or queen-size beds and decide whether you want a room with an ocean view from the tub. Rustic driftwood, richly printed textiles, and local artwork highlight the rooms, each of which features a fireplace, down duvet, soaker tub, and private balcony. Winter storm-watching packages have become so popular that the inn is as busy in winter as it is in summer. The Pointe Restaurant (see "Where to Dine" below) and On-the-Rocks Bar serves three meals daily and features an oceanfront view. The staff can arrange whale-watching, golfing, fishing, and diving packages. No-Stress Express packages include air transport and accommodations.

Campgrounds

The 94 campsites on the bluff at **Green Point** are maintained by Pacific Rim National Park (☎ 250/726-7721). The grounds are full every day in July and August, and the average wait for a site is 1 to 2 days. Leave your name at the ranger station when you arrive to be placed on the list. In July and August, the cost is C$14 to C$20 (US$9 to US$13) per night, and in the shoulder season C$12 to C$18 (US$8 to US$12) per night. You're rewarded for your patience with a magnificent ocean view, pit toilets, fire pits, pumped well water, and free firewood, but no showers or hookups. The campground is closed October through March.

Bella Pacifica Resort & Campground (☎ 250/725-3400; www.bellapacifica. com), 3.3 kilometers (2 miles) south of Tofino on the Pacific Rim Highway (P.O. Box 413, Tofino, B.C. V0R 2Z0), is privately owned. March through November, it has 165 campsites from which you can walk to Mackenzie Beach or take the resort's private nature trails to Templar Beach. Flush toilets, hot showers, water, laundry, ice, fire pits, firewood, and full and partial hookups are available. Rates are C$18 to C$36 (US$12 to US$24) per two-person campsite. Reserve at least a month in advance for a spot on a summer weekend.

WHERE TO DINE

If you're just looking for a cup of java and a snack, it's hard to beat the **Coffee Pod,** 151 Fourth St. (☎ 250/725-4246), a laid-back, semi-granola kind of place at the entrance to town. The Pod, open 7am to 6pm, check for seasonal hours, also does an excellent breakfast. Main courses C$7 to C$10 (US$4.65 to US$7). The **Common Loaf Bakeshop,** 180 First St. (☎ 250/725-3915), open 8am to 9pm, is locally famous as the gathering place for granola lovers, hippies, and other reprobates back when such things mattered in Tofino. At the "far" end of town, the Loaf does baked goods really well and a healthy lunch or dinner can be had for C$6 to C$9 (US$4 to US$6). Liquids include herbal teas, coffee, juices, and wine and beer.

The Pointe Restaurant. The Wickaninnish Inn, Osprey Lane at Chesterman Beach. ☎ **250/725-3100.** Reservations recommended. Main courses C$18–C$30 (US$12–US$20). MC, V. Daily 8am–2:30pm, 2–5pm (snacks), 5–9:30pm. PACIFIC NORTHWEST.

Perched on the water's edge at Chesterman Beach is the Pointe, where a 280° view of the roaring Pacific is the backdrop to a dining experience that can only be described as pure Pacific Northwest. Top chef Rodney Butters applies his talents to an array of local ingredients, including Dungeness crab, spotted prawns, halibut, salmon, quail, lamb, and rabbit. His signature version of bouillabaisse, Wickaninnish Potlatch, is a chunky, fragrant blend of soft and firm fish, shellfish, and vegetables simmered in a thick seafood broth. Other offerings include delectable appetizers like goat-cheese tarts and shaved fennel salad and entrees like grilled lamb chops with new potatoes, fresh artichokes, and sea asparagus. Butters's top dessert—a double-chocolate mashed-potato brioche—is superb when accompanied by a glass of raspberry wine.

The Rain Coast Cafe. 120 Fourth St. ☎ **250/725-2215.** Main courses C$11–C$20 (US$7–US$13). AE, MC, V. Daily 11:30am–3pm and 5–10pm. WEST COAST.

This cozy restaurant, just off the main street, has developed a deserved reputation for some of the best—and best value—seafood and vegetarian dishes in town. To start off, try the popular Rain Coast salad—smoked salmon, sautéed mushrooms, and chèvre cheese on a bed of greens, with maple balsamic vinaigrette. Fresh fish is a big part of the cuisine, and the menu is supplemented by a catch-of-the-day special. Mainstays include seafood and pasta dishes, such as the linguini with prawns and fresh herbs.

WHAT TO SEE & DO

FIRST NATIONS TOURISM   Clayoquot Sound is the traditional home of the Nuu-chah-nulth peoples. Accessed via water taxi, the **Walk the Wild Side Trail** (☎ 888/670-9586) runs along the south side of Flores Island to the village of

Ahousat. The cost is C$20 (US$13) on your own or C$30 (US$20) with a guide, plus the water taxi to Flores. The above-referenced booking line is supposed to arrange both. Some who've done the trail have reported having incredible experiences: Afterward, they were invited by elders to come to the village to celebrate a potlatch. Others have paid their money only to be foisted off on 12- and 13-year-old native boys more interested in playing with their two-way radios than looking at nature. So it's a toss-up. If you're interested in native ecotourism, however, it's probably worth giving it a try. Keep an open mind and spirit of adventure and you may be rewarded.

FISHING   Sportfishing for salmon, steelhead, rainbow trout, Dolly Varden char, halibut, cod, and snapper is excellent off the west coast of Vancouver Island. Long Beach is also great for bottom fishing. To fish here, you need a nonresident saltwater or freshwater license. Tackle shops sell licenses, have information on current restrictions, and often carry copies of the current publications *BC Tidal Waters Sport Fishing Guide* and *BC Sport Fishing Regulations Synopsis for Non-tidal Waters.* Independent anglers should also pick up a copy of the *BC Fishing Directory and Atlas.*

   Chinook Charters, 450 Campbell St., Tofino (☎ **800/665-3646** or 250/725-3431; www.chinookcharters.com), organizes fishing charters throughout the Clayoquot Sound area. Fishing starts in March and goes until December. The company supplies all the gear, a guide, and a boat. Prices start at C$85 (U$57) per hour, with a minimum of 4 hours. A full-day, 10-hour fishing trip for four people, on a 25-foot boat, is C$750 (U$503).

GUIDED NATURE HIKES   Owned and operated by **Bill McIntyre,** former chief naturalist of Pacific Rim National Park, the ✪ **Long Beach Nature Tour Co.** (☎ **250/726-7099;** fax 250/726-4282) offers guided beach walks, storm watching, land-based whale watching, and rain-forest tours, customized to suit your needs. Also excellent are the tours offered by wildlife author Adrienne Mason of **Raincoast Communications** (☎ **250/725-2878;** e-mail: amason@port.island.net). A local naturalist and science writer, she can accommodate various group sizes and will greatly enhance your knowledge of the local flora and fauna and the ecology of this unique rain forest.

HIKING   The 11-kilometer (7-mile) stretch of rocky headlands, sand, and surf along the **Long Beach Headlands Trail** is the most accessible section of the park system, which incorporates Long Beach, the West Coast Trail, and the Broken Islands Group. No matter where you go in this area, you're bound to meet whale watchers in spring, surfers and anglers in summer, hearty hikers during the colder months, and kayakers year-round.

   In and around **Long Beach,** numerous marked trails 0.83 to 3.3 kilometers (0.5 mile to 2 miles) long take you through the thick, temperate rain forest edging the shore. The 3.3-kilometer (2-mile) **Gold Mine Trail** near Florencia Bay still has a few artifacts from the days when a gold-mining operation flourished amid the trees. And the partially boardwalked **South Beach Trail** (less than a mile long) leads through the moss-draped rain forest onto small quiet coves like Lismer Beach and South Beach, where you can see abundant life in the rocky tidal pools.

   If you're canoeing or kayaking in Clayoquot Sound, there's another trail to discover. The **Big Cedar Trail** on Meares Island is a 3.3-kilometer (2-mile) boardwalked path that was built in 1993 to protect the old-growth temperate rain forest. Maintained by the Tla-o-qui-aht native Indian band, it has a long staircase leading up to the Hanging Garden Tree, the province's fourth-largest western red cedar. If you aren't paddling yourself, the water taxi (☎ **250/725-3793**) can drop you off and pick you up.

In town, the **Tofino Botanical Garden,** 1084 Pacific Rim Hwy. (☎ **250/ 725-1237**), is still very much a work in progress, now in year 3 of a 10-year plan. A number of projects have been completed, such as the frog pond, the old-growth boardwalk, the native plant collection, the iris garden, bird blinds, and the children's garden. This lovely landscaped walking garden with native and exotic plants and gazebos for sitting and contemplating the surroundings is worth a visit. The visitor center and part of the garden are wheelchair accessible.

HOT SPRINGS COVE   A natural hot spring about 66.6 kilometers (40 miles) north of Tofino, the cove is accessible only by water. Take a water taxi, sail, canoe, or kayak up to Clayoquot Sound to enjoy swimming in the steaming pools and bracing waterfalls. A number of kayak outfitters and boat charters offer trips to the springs (see "Whale Watching & Birding," below).

KAYAKING   Perhaps the quintessential Clayoquot experience, and certainly one of the most fun, is to slip into a kayak and paddle out into the waters of the sound. For beginners, half-day tours to Meares Island (usually with the chance to do a little hiking) are an especially good bet. For rentals, lessons, and tours, try **Pacific Kayak,** 606 Campbell St., at Jamie's Whaling Station (☎ **250/725-3232;** www.tofino-bc. com/pacifickayak); the **Tofino Sea Kayaking Company,** 320 Main St. (☎ **800/ 863-4664** or 250/725-4222; www.tofino-kayaking.com); or **Remote Passages Sea Kayaking,** 71 Wharf St. (☎ **800/666-9833** or 250/725-3330; www.remotepassages. com), which offers kayaking packages ranging from 4-hour paddles around Meares Island (from C$52/US$35 per person) to weeklong paddling and camping expeditions. Instruction by experienced guides makes even your first kayaking experience a comfortable, safe, and enjoyable one.

STORM WATCHING   Watching the winter storms behind big glass windows has become very popular in Tofino over the past year or so. For a slight twist on this, try the outdoor storm-watching tours offered by the **Long Beach Nature Tour Co.** (☎ **250/726-7099;** fax 250/726-4282). Owner Bill McIntyre used to be chief naturalist of Pacific Rim National Park. He can explain how storms work and where to stand so you can get close without getting swept away.

SURFING   More and more people make the trip out to Tofino for one reason only: the surfing. The wild Pacific coast is known as one of the best surfing destinations in Canada, and most surfers work in the tourism industry around Tofino, spending all their free time in the water. To try this exciting and exhilarating sport, call **Live to Surf,** 1180 Pacific Rim Hwy. (☎ **250/725-4464;** www.livetosurf.com). Lessons start at C$45 (US$30) for 1½ hours. Live to Surf also rents boards at C$25 (US$17) and wet suits (don't even think about going without one) at C$20 (US$13).

WHALE WATCHING & BIRDING   A number of outfitters conduct tours through this region, which is inhabited by gray whales, bald eagles, porpoises, orcas, seals, and sea lions. **Chinook Charters,** 450 Campbell St. (☎ **800/665-3646** or 250/725-3431), offers whale-watching trips in Clayoquot Sound on 25-foot Zodiac boats. The company also conducts trips to Hot Springs Cove on its 32-foot *Chinook Key.* **Jamie's Whaling Station,** 606 Campbell St. (☎ **800/667-9913** or 250/ 725-3919), uses a glass-bottomed 65-foot power cruiser as well as a fleet of Zodiacs for tours to watch the gray whales from March through October. A combined Hot Springs Cove and whale-watching trip aboard a 32-foot cruiser is offered year-round. Fares for both companies' expeditions generally start at C$75 (US$50) per person for a 3-hour tour; customized trips can run as high as C$200 (US$134) per person for a

Two Trips of a Lifetime

These two trips are within striking distance of Vancouver or Victoria and can be done no place else on earth.

✪ **SAILING THE GREAT BEAR RAIN FOREST**   If you look at a map of British Columbia, about halfway up the West Coast you'll see an incredibly convoluted region of mountains, fjords, bays, channels, rivers, and inlets. There are next to no roads in this area—the geography's too intense. Thanks to that isolation, this is also one of the last places in the world where grizzly bears are still found in large numbers, not to mention salmon, large trees, killer whales, otters, and porpoises. But to get there you'll need a boat. And if you're going to take a boat, why not take a 100-year-old, 92-foot-long, fully rigged sailing schooner?

Run by an ex-pilot turned naturalist and sailor, **Maple Leaf Adventure,** 2087 Indian Crescent, Duncan (☎ **888/599-5323** or 250/715-0906; fax 250/715-0912; www/gorp.com/mapleleaf), runs a number of trips to this magic part of the world. Owner Brian Falconer is extremely knowledgeable and normally brings along a trained naturalist to explain the fauna, especially the whales, dolphins, and grizzlies. Covering territory from the midcoast to the Queen Charlotte Islands (Haida Gwaii) to the coasts of Alaska, the trips vary in duration from 4 days to 2 weeks and in price from C$2,000 to C$4,100 (US$1,350 to US$2,750). All include gourmet meals (more than you could ever eat) and comfortable but not luxurious accommodations aboard Brian's beautiful schooner.

✪ **HORSE TREKKING THE CHILCOTIN PLATEAU**   The high plateau country of the B.C. interior has some of the most impressive scenery around. Soaring peaks rise above deep valleys, and mountain meadows are alive with flowers that bloom for just a few weeks in high summer. The advantages to taking in this territory on horseback are that the horse's feet get sore, not yours; if you come across grizzlies, you've got some height on them; and horses can carry far more and far better food.

In British Columbia, one guide company is granted exclusive rights to run tours through that section of wilderness. The territories are typically 5,000 square kilometers (1,930 sq. miles)—5,000 square kilometers of high-country wilderness, where you won't meet another horse team except your own. One of the guide-outfitters closest to Vancouver is **Chilcotin Holidays Guest Ranch,** Gun Creek Road, Gold Bridge (☎ 250/238-2274; www.chilcotinholidays.com), in the Chilcotin Mountains north of Whistler. Their trips, running from 4 to 7 days and costing C$600 to C$900 (US$402 to US$603), involve encounters with wildflowers, bighorn sheep, grizzly bears, and wolves.

full day. For an interesting combination, try the Sea-to-Sky tour, a 5-hour trip with a boat ride, a hike through the rain forest, and a return to Tofino by floatplane, at the cost of C$109 (US$73) adults.

Remote Passages, Meares Landing, 71 Wharf St. (☎ **800/666-9833** or 250/725-3330), runs 2½-hour-long whale-watching tours in Clayoquot Sound on Zodiac boats, daily from March through November. Fares are C$50 (US$34) for adults and C$35 (US$23) for children under 12. The company also conducts a 7-hour combination whale-watching and hot-springs trip at C$75 (US$50) for adults and C$50 (US$34) for children under 12. Reservations are recommended.

For land-based bird watching, contact local naturalist/science writer Adrienne Mason of **Rainforest Communications** (☎ 250/725-2878). Adrienne knows the area and can customize a tour depending on your needs.

5 The Gulf Islands

The several dozen mountainous **Gulf Islands** sprawl across the Strait of Georgia between the B.C. mainland and Vancouver Island. Though only a handful of the islands are served by regular ferry service, this entire area is popular with holidaymakers—and with good reason. In the rain shadow of Washington State's Olympic Mountains, the Gulf Islands have the most temperate climate in all of Canada. Indeed, the climate here is officially listed as semi-Mediterranean.

There have been radical changes in the traditional agricultural quality. Starting in the 1960s, the Gulf Islands developed a reputation as countercultural hippie enclaves, a reputation the islands still maintain—and still somewhat deserve, for the immigration of artists and back-to-the-landers continues apace. The 1990s witnessed a parallel but different land rush. High-tech moguls, Hollywood stars, and other wealthy refugees from urban centers have been moving here in droves. Land prices have skyrocketed, and so has the quality of island facilities: The islands now boast fine restaurants, elegant small inns, and a multitude of art galleries.

If you're traveling with kids, you'll find the Gulf Islands a fairly inhospitable place to find accommodations. Nearly all B&Bs have minimum ages for guests (usually 12 or 16), and there are only a few standard motels or cottage resorts where families are welcome. It's mandatory to make reservations well in advance, as the ferry system doesn't make it exactly easy to just drive on to the next town to find a place to stay.

ESSENTIALS

GETTING THERE   Getting to the Gulf Islands is half the fun of visiting, but it can be a tad confusing. **BC Ferries** (☎ 888/223-3779 or 604/444-2890; www.bcferries. bc.ca) operates three ferry runs to the Gulf Islands: from Tsawwassen on the B.C. mainland and from Swartz Bay and Crofton on Vancouver Island. Be certain to pick up one of the "Southern Gulf Islands" schedules and give yourself plenty of time to analyze it. You can get to any of the major Gulf Islands from Swartz Bay or Tsawwassen, except Saturna Island, which is accessible only from Swartz Bay.

To insure that you actually make the ferry you want, arrive at least 30 minutes early; on a summer weekend, allow 45 minutes or more lead time. You can make reservations on the service from Tsawwassen, and these are recommended on summer weekends; however, you can't reserve space on the runs from Swartz Bay.

Here are sample peak-season fares: A car and two passengers from Tsawwassen to Mayne Island costs C$54 (US$36); the same service as a foot passenger is C$9 (US$6). From Swartz Bay to Salt Spring Island for a car and two passengers is C$31 (US$21); a single foot passenger is C$6 (US$4). Interisland fares are C$13 (US$9) for a car plus two passengers or C$3 (US$2) for a walk-on. For payment, all Gulf Island ferry terminals take Visa and MasterCard in addition to cash and traveler's checks.

A number of small commuter airlines offer regularly scheduled floatplane service to the Gulf Islands from Vancouver Harbour and Vancouver International Airport's Coal Harbour Terminal. One-way tickets to the islands usually run C$60 to C$70 (US$40 to US$47), not a bad fare when you consider the time and hassle of the ferries. For schedules and reservations, contact **Harbour Air** (☎ 800/665-0212 or 604/688-1277; harbour-air.com), **Seair** (☎ 800/447-3247 or 250/273-8900), or **Pacific Spirit Air** (☎ 800/665-2359 or 250/537-9359).

A Gulf Islands B&B Reservation Service

Reserve B&Bs, lodges, resorts, and country inns in all price ranges free through a centralized booking agency: The **Canadian Gulf Islands B&B Reservation Service** (☎ **888/539-2930** or 250/539-2930; www.gulfislandreservations.com; e-mail: reservations@gulfislands.com) is operated by Galiano Island natives who've inspected all the participating lodgings. They're able to connect you up with exactly what you're looking for, whether it's a farm vacation, a honeymoon suite, a cozy B&B, or a cottage on the beach.

VISITOR INFORMATION   For general information on the Gulf Islands, contact **Tourism Vancouver Island,** 302-45 Bastion Sq., Victoria, B.C. V8W 1J1 (☎ **250/ 382-3551;** fax 250/382-3523; www.islands.bc.ca; e-mail: tavi@islands.bc.ca). A comprehensive Web site is www.gulfislands.com.

GETTING AROUND   Most innkeepers are happy to pick up registered guests at either the ferry or the floatplane terminal, if given sufficient notice. There are also taxis on most islands.

Bicycling   Winding country roads and bucolic landscapes make the Gulf Islands a favorite destination of cyclists. Although the islands' road networks aren't exactly large, it's great fun to cycle the back roads, jump a ferry, and peddle to an outlying inn for lunch. Several island parks have designated mountain bike trails. Bicycles can be taken onboard BC Ferries for a small surcharge, usually less than C$1.50 (US$1), depending on the route. Bicycle rentals are available on most islands, and it's not unusual for inns and B&Bs to have bikes available for loan for guests.

Kayaking   The Gulf Islands' lengthy and rugged coastline, plus their proximity to other more remote island groups, make them a great base for kayaking trips. Low-drawing kayaks are perfect for exploring shallow bays and rocky inlets, centers of marine life. Most of the islands have kayak outfitters; however—depending on their insurance coverage—not all outfitters will offer rentals apart from guided kayak tours. If you're an experienced kayaker and just want to rent a kayak and get out on the water, be sure to call ahead to make sure rentals are available at your destination.

SALT SPRING ISLAND

The largest of the Gulf Islands, **Salt Spring** is a bucolic island getaway filled with artisans, sheep pastures, and cozy B&Bs. It's also a busy cultural crossroads: The super-rich, movie stars, economy-minded retirees, high-tech telecommuters, and hippie farmers all rub shoulders here. The island's hilly terrain and deep forests afford equal privacy for all lifestyles, and that's the way the residents like it.

ESSENTIALS

GETTING THERE   By Plane   Regularly scheduled floatplane service operates between Vancouver International Airport and Vancouver's Inner Harbour seaplane terminal and Ganges Harbour. See above for contact information.

By Ferry   Salt Spring Island is served by three **BC Ferries** routes (☎ **888/724-5223** in B.C.). From Tsawwassen on the B.C. mainland, ferries depart twice daily for Long Harbour, on the island's northeast coast. If you're on Vancouver Island, you have a choice of the roughly once-per-hour Vesuvius Bay–Crofton run or the approximately every-90-minutes crossing from Swartz Bay to Fulford Harbour.

VISITOR INFORMATION   The Salt Spring Chamber of Commerce operates a **visitor center** at 121 Lower Ganges Rd., Salt Spring Island, B.C. V8K 2T1 (☎ 250/537-5252; www.saltspringisland.bc.ca; e-mail: chamber@saltspring.com).

GETTING AROUND   There's no public transport on Salt Spring, so if you don't have a car, you'll need to rely on a bicycle or call **Silver Shadow Taxi** (☎ 250/537-3030). Another option for interisland transport is **Gulf Islands Water Taxi** (☎ 250/537-2510; www.saltspring.com/watertaxi), offering speed-boat service among Salt Spring, Mayne, and Galiano islands on Wednesdays and Saturdays. The taxi leaves from Government Dock in Ganges Harbour.

WHERE TO STAY

Beddis House B&B. 131 Miles Ave., Salt Spring Island, B.C. V8K 2E1. ☎ **250/537-1028.** Fax 250/537-9888. www.saltspring.com/beddishouse. E-mail: beddis@saltspring.com. 3 units. C$150–C$180 (US$101–US$121) double. Rates include breakfast and tea. MC, V. Closed Dec 15–Feb 1.

Perched above a strand of pebble beach, white clapboard Beddis House was built as a farmhouse in 1900. When the property was purchased for development as a B&B, the owners retained the old farmhouse as the dining room and parlor area and built a new beachfront guesthouse—the Coach House—in the style of the original home. The spacious rooms have wonderful ocean views, with private patios or balconies, wood-burning stoves, private entrances, and access to multilevel decks, beautifully land-scaped gardens, and manicured lawns. Three-course breakfasts are served in the farmhouse dining room.

Hastings House. 160 Upper Ganges Rd., Salt Spring Island, B.C. V8K 2S2. ☎ **800/661-9255** or 250/537-2362. Fax 250/537-5333. www.hastingshouse.com. E-mail: hasthouse@saltspring.com. 17 units. C$400–C$500 (US$268–US$335) suite. Rates include breakfast and tea. Off-season rates available. AE, DC, MC, V. Open Mar–Dec. Children must be 16 or older.

One of British Columbia's most noted lodgings, the utterly charming Hastings House is just east of Ganges, in a steep-sided forested valley that drops directly onto Ganges Harbour. The half-timbered, rose-draped Manor House serves as the inn's restaurant and library, with two suites on the second floor. The original 19th-century farmhouse has been converted into two two-story suites, while the old Hudson's Bay trading post is now a two-room cottage suite. All rooms—including five suites in the converted barn—are beautifully furnished with original art, antiques, and fine furniture and have fireplaces and eiderdown comforters. A member of the exclusive French Relais et Châteaux network, Hastings House has a tremendous international reputation, and getting a room can be difficult. Make reservations at least 6 months in advance.

✪ The Old Farmhouse B&B. 1077 North End Rd., Salt Spring Island, B.C. V8K 1L9. ☎ **250/537-4113.** Fax 250/537-4969. www.islandnet.com/~pixsell.bcbbd/1/1000182.html. E-mail: Farmhouse@saltspring.com. 4 units. C$170 (US$114) double. Rates include breakfast. No smoking. MC, V.

The Old Farmhouse is a Victorian-era homestead built in 1894 at the center of 1.2 hectares (3 acres) of grassy meadows, orchards, and specimen trees—the massive red-barked arbutus tree in the front meadow is one of the largest and oldest in British Columbia. The B&B's rooms are in a new stylistically harmonious guest house adjoin-ing the restored original farmhouse, which means you get the charm of the old home (breakfast is served in the dining room, and there's a comfortable sitting room) and the comforts of a modern, spacious room with new plumbing and nonsqueaky floor-boards, plus a balcony or patio. The extensive meadows are perfect for lolling with a book and lawn chair or for a game of croquet.

Seabreeze Inn. 101 Bittancourt Rd., Salt Spring Island, B.C. V8K 2K2. ☎ **800/434-4112** or 250/537-4145. Fax 250/537-4323. www.ferrytravel.com/seabreeze. E-mail: seabreeze@ saltspring.com. 28 units. TV TEL. C$79–C$89 (US$53–US$60) double. Extra person C$10 (US$7). Kitchens C$10 (US$7). Rates include breakfast. Senior discounts and off-season rates available. Weekly and monthly rates. AE, DC, DISC, MC, V.

An excellent alternative to Salt Spring's expensive B&Bs, the Seabreeze is a well-maintained, attractive motel just south of Ganges. All rooms are very clean and nicely furnished, with extras like refrigerators and coffeemakers. The 16 kitchen units come with electric cooktops, full-size refrigerators, and microwaves. Just below the motel is a large deck and garden area, with grapevine-covered arbors, picnic tables, and a gas barbecue for use by guests. The Seabreeze is perfect for families, cyclists, or anyone who doesn't feel the need to be fussed over in a B&B.

WHERE TO DINE

If you're heading off on a picnic or traveling on your bicycle or kayak, pick up a pack lunch at the **Tree House Café,** 106 Purvis Lane, (no phone), an aptly named little outdoor cafe under an old octopus-limbed plum tree near the waterfront behind Mouat's Hardware Store, 106 Fulford-Ganges Rd. in Ganges. Also a great place to spend a summer evening. Open daily May through September 7am to 10pm, October through April 9am to 3pm. Main courses C$8 to C$13 (US$5 to US$9).The deck and glass-fronted dining room at **Vesuvius Inn Neighborhood Pub** (☎ **250/537-2312**), perched above the ferry dock at the tiny village of Vesuvius Bay, is a great place for a drink or a meal. Main courses C$9 to C$15 (US$6 to US$10). Open daily 11am to 11pm. Check for hours in the winter.

✪ **Hastings House.** 160 Upper Ganges Rd. ☎ **250/537-2362.** Reservations required. Prix-fixe 5-course dinner C$70 (US$47). Summer sitting at 7:30pm, spring and fall sitting at 7pm. AE, MC, V. PACIFIC NORTHWEST.

The dining room at Hastings House combines old-world sophistication (jackets are required for men) with the freshest of West Coast ingredients and up-to-the-moment kitchen savvy. The menus change daily and are designed to incorporate local produce and fish. Dinner begins with cocktail hour, drinks served before the fireplace an hour before dinner seating. Dinner includes an appetizer (perhaps eggplant-and-goat-cheese roulade or ahi sashimi with black sesame seeds), a bowl of excellent soup rich with seasonal ingredients, and a small fish course (gingered scallops with citrus cream and saffron-and-tomato-poached black cod with honeyed eggplant confit were two recent selections). You have a choice of four main dishes. Salt Spring lamb is nearly always featured, as are local salmon or other seasonal fish. Island venison is grilled and served with braised fennel; also featured was halibut and red shrimp with caper risotto. An inventive dessert is the chocolate crepes with cappuccino cream and berry compote.

House Piccolo. 108 Hereford Ave., Ganges. ☎ **250/537-1844.** Reservations required. Main courses C$18–C$29 (US$12–US$19). AE, DC, MC, V. CONTINENTAL.

In a heritage home in Ganges, House Piccolo offers excellent à la carte dining and a good wine list in casually formal surroundings. The northern European accents in the unusual menu reflect the Finnish origins of the chef/owner, particularly the fresh-fish specials that feature the best of the local catch. Sole in sorrel sauce was one night's special, while the seasonal menu features baked chicken breast in persillade crust and local Camembert and grilled lamb chops with aioli.

EXPLORING SALT SPRING ISLAND

With a year-round population of 10,000, Salt Spring is served by three ferries, making it by far the easiest Gulf Island to visit. The center of island life is **Ganges,** a little village with gas, grocery stores, banks, and galleries, all overlooking a busy pleasure-boat harbor. You could easily spend most of a day poking around art galleries and boutiques and drinking coffee.

CHECKING OUT THE STUDIOS, GALLERIES & MARKET In fact, many people head to Salt Spring expressly to visit the galleries; the island is famed across Canada as an artists' colony. At the tourist office, pick up a copy of the *Studio Tour Map,* which locates 35 artists—glassblowers, painters, ceramists, weavers, carvers, and sculptors—around the island. As you're driving, just watch for the STUDIO sign with the blue sheep on it, and if the sign says open, stop in.

Ganges has a number of galleries offering local crafts. **Coastal Currents,** 133 Hereford Ave. (☎ 250/537-0070), is an old home converted to a housewares-and-decor gallery. The **Pegasus Gallery,** in Mouat's Mall at 1-104 Fulford Ganges Rd. (☎ 250/537-2421), displays contemporary Canadian painting and sculpture as well as a good selection of Northwest native carving and basketry. Just south of Ganges, the **Ewart Gallery,** 175 Saltspring Way (☎ 250/537-2313), offers paintings and sculpture from blue-chip Canadian artists.

April through October, a not-to-be-missed Salt Spring event is **Market in the Park,** held every Saturday from 8am to 4pm on the waterfront's Centennial Park; it brings together an infectious mix of craftspeople, farmers, musicians, bakers, and just about everyone else on the island who might plausibly be able to sell or buy something. It's great fun and a good chance to shop for local products at fair prices. As you might guess, the people-watching possibilities are matchless.

HIKING On the southeast corner of Salt Spring Island, **Truckle Provincial Park** is the largest park in the Gulf Islands. Eight kilometers (5 miles) of trails wind through forests to rocky headlands where tide-pool exploration is excellent; some trails are designated for mountain bikes. Truckle Park is also the only public campground on Salt Spring.

BIKING Although Salt Spring is the largest of the Gulf Islands and has the best network of paved roads, it's not the best island for cycling. Few roads have shoulders, and with 10,000 inhabitants and three ferries unleashing cars throughout the day, there's a lot more traffic here than you'd think. However, these same ferries—plus the summer bikes-and-passengers–only **Gulf Islands Water Taxi** (☎ 250/537-2510) from Ganges to Mayne and Galiano islands—make Salt Spring a convenient base for cyclists. For bike rentals, contact **Salt Spring Kayaking** (☎ 250/537-4664) on the Ganges Harbour docks.

KAYAKING **Island Escapades,** 118 Natalie Lane (☎ 888/529-2567), offers guided introductory lake trips starting at C$30 (US$20), with guided 3-hour ocean tours at C$50 (US$34). It also offers paddle and mountaineering holidays. **Salt Spring Kayaking** (☎ 250/537-4664) on Ganges Harbour, also rents kayaks. **Sea Otter Kayaking,** 1168 North End Rd. (☎ 250/537-5678; www.saltspring.com/kayaking), rents both kayaks and canoes, starting at C$20 (US$13) per hour. Guided tours begin at C$35 (US$23) for a 2-hour harbor exploration; overnight packages are also available.

GALIANO ISLAND

Galiano is a long yet mountainous stringbean of an island stretching along the Gulf Islands' eastern flank. It's the closest Gulf Island to Vancouver, and many of the properties are the second homes of the city's elite. The rural yet genteel feel of the island is perfect for a romantic getaway or a relaxing weeklong break from the urban hassle.

ESSENTIALS

GETTING THERE   BC Ferries (☎ **888/724-5223** in B.C.) reach Sturdies Bay on Galiano Island from Tsawwassen and Swartz Bay. Floatplanes serve Galiano Island from the docks at Montague Harbour. For contact information, see "Getting There" at the beginning of the Gulf Islands section.

VISITOR INFORMATION   Contact Galiano Island Tourist/Visitor Info, 2590 Sturdies Bay Rd., Box 73 Galiano Island, B.C. V0N 1P0 (☎ **250/539-2233;** www. galianoisland.com; e-mail: infor@galianoisland.com).

GETTING AROUND   For ferry pickup and other taxi service, contact Go Galiano (☎ **250/539-0202**).

WHERE TO STAY

The only public campground on Galiano Island is **Montague Harbour Provincial Marine Park,** with 40 sites for C$10 (US$7) per site. The park offers beach access but no showers or flush toilets. Call ☎ **800/689-9025** for reservations or 250/391-2300 for information.

Driftwood Village. 205 Bluff Rd. E., Galiano Island, B.C. V0N 1P0. ☎ **888/240-1466** or 250/539-5457. www.driftwoodcottages.com. 11 cottages. TV. Studio cottages C$98 (US$66) double, 1-bedroom C$115 (US$77), 2-bedroom C$135 (US$90). Extra person C$5–C$15 (US$3.35–US$10). Complimentary ferry pickup. MC, V.

This venerable cottage resort is perfect for a laid-back family vacation with the kids and the family pets in tow. Indeed, like a little hamlet, Driftwood Village is a collection of 11 fully-equipped cottages of differing vintages and styles scattered around a shady 0.8-hectare (2-acre) garden with ponds, flowers, and fruit trees. Each cottage has a full kitchen, private bathroom, and TV, and most have fireplaces and private decks with views of Sturdies Bay. The one- and two-bedroom cottages are effectively small furnished houses, suitable for two to four people. All are decorated with a sense of artful thrift that will instantly bring back youthful memories of idealized lakeside cabins. The cottages share a large central deck area with a hot tub and a badminton court; barbecues are available to guests. Unlike most places in the Gulf Islands, kids and pets are welcome.

✪ **Woodstone Country Inn.** 743 Georgeson Bay Rd., RR 1, Galiano Island, B.C. V0N 1P0. ☎ **888/339-2022** or 250/539-2022. Fax 250/539-5198. www.gulfislands.com/woodstone. E-mail: woodstone@gulfislands.com. 12 units. C$99–C$185 (US$66–US$124) double. Rates include full breakfast and afternoon tea. No smoking. Packages available. AE, ER, MC, V.

The quintessential small country inn, Woodstone sits amid fir trees overlooking a series of meadows serving as a de facto bird sanctuary (in fact, the inn was built as a retreat for birders). The entire two-story inn is beautifully decorated with the owners' personal collection of folk art and sculpture from their world travels, including marvelous carvings from Arctic Canada and southern Africa. The 12 units (a mix of king, queen, and three twin rooms) are large and beautifully furnished with writing tables, upholstered chairs, and intriguing art. Gleaming white-tiled bathrooms are fitted with hair dryers, soaker or Jacuzzi tubs, and luxury soaps and lotions. All rooms have fireplaces, some have soaker tubs and sofa beds, and one is fitted for the guests with disabilities. All main-floor rooms have small private patios. The inn's restaurant, in a high-ceilinged tiered room off the library, serves Galiano Island's finest cuisine, a mix of classic French savoir faire and Pacific Northwest vitality.

WHERE TO DINE

Galiano has a limited number of fine-dining establishments, though there are a number of informal places to eat. The **Daystar Market Café** (☎ **250/539-2800**), just north of Sturdies Bay at the intersection of Georgeson Bay Road and Porlier Pass Road, serves mostly vegetarian light meals and baked goods for lunch and dinner daily. Main courses C$6 to C$12 (US$4 to US$8). Summer hours Monday through Saturday 11:30am to 3pm and 6 to 9pm, Sunday 10:30am to 2:30pm. The **Montague Café** (☎ 250/539-5733), at the Montague Harbour Marina, has sandwiches and light dining right on the water; it's open daily from 8am to 9pm daily in summer, check for winter hours. Main coursed C$7 to C$12 (US$4.65 to US$8). For a pub meal, go to the pleasant, woodsy **Hummingbird Pub,** 47 Sturdies Bay Rd. (☎ 250/ 539-5472). Main courses C$10 to C$14 (US$7 to US$9). Open year round 11am to midnight, kitchen closes at 9pm.

La Berengerie Restaurant. Montague Rd. ☎ 250/539-5392. Reservations advised. Prix-fixe 4-course menu C$25 (US$16). MC, V. Daily 5–9pm. FRENCH.

La Berengerie has a truly country-French atmosphere. The menu offers a choice of entrees (perhaps duck breast with kumquat sauce or seafood-stuffed sole), plus soup, salad, and dessert. The dining room is simply decorated—wooden floors, pots of flowers, and colorful Provençal linens—yet warm and inviting. The food can be somewhat inconsistent, though on a good day your meal can be memorable.

✪ **Woodstone Country Inn.** 743 Georgeson Bay Rd. ☎ 250/539-2022. Reservations required. 4-course dinner C$22–C$27 (US$15–US$18); minimum menu charge C$22 (US$15) per person. AE, DC, MC, V. Sun–Thurs 5–9pm, Fri–Sat 5–10pm. INTERNATIONAL.

The dining room at Woodhouse Country Inn is easily the best place to eat on Galiano Island and one of the best restaurants in all the Gulf Islands. The daily changing menu is a compelling blend of classic French cuisine enlivened with vivid international flavors. Each day's menu includes three entree choices—meat, fish, or vegetarian—and comes with homemade breads, soup, and a delightful salad course. The Woodstone's specialty dressing (a tart/sweet mix of honey and citrus oils) is wonderful over arugula and slices of pear, and another standout is the pungent salad of grilled tuna, sweet red onion, and balsamica. Desserts like warm bread pudding, white-chocolate/raspberry ice-cream cake, and fresh fruit and berry sorbets end the meal. The wine list is an interesting mix of Okanagan, Californian, and French vintages.

EXPLORING GALIANO ISLAND

Galiano is also a center for artists and craftspeople. The **Studio One Gallery,** in the Galiano Lodge in Sturdies Bay (☎ 250/539-2216), displays the work of over 30 Gulf Island painters and sculptors. Check a selection of local and international crafts at **Ixchel,** with locations at both Montague Marina (☎ 250/539-9819) and at 61 Georgeson Bay Road (☎ 250/539-3038).

Galiano is perhaps the most physically striking of the Gulf Islands, particularly the mountainous southern shores. **Mount Sutil, Mount Galiano,** and the exposed cliffs above Georgeson Bay simply called **The Bluffs,** rise above sheep-filled meadows, shadowy forests, and steep fern-lined ravines. **Active Pass,** the narrow strait separating Galiano from Mayne Island, is another scenic high spot: All the pleasure-boat and ferry traffic between Vancouver and Victoria negotiates this turbulent cliff-lined passage (tides churn through this cleft at speeds of 9 knots).

BICYCLING The farther north you go on Galiano, the more remote the island becomes, making this a favorite of cyclists. While you won't have to worry overly about traffic on the 30-kilometer-long (19 miles) paved road running up the island's west side, there are enough steep ascents to keep your attention focused. Mountain bikers can follow unmaintained logging roads that skirt the eastern shores. Contact

Galiano Bicycle Rental, 36 Burrill Rd. (☎ 250/539-9906), for a full range of rental options, including mountain, touring, and tandem bikes.

HIKING   Several short hikes lead to Active Pass overlooks, including the trail to the top of 330-meter (1,082-ft.) **Mount Galiano** and the cliff-edge path in **Bluffs Park.** Another good hiking destination is **Bodega Ridge,** a park about two-thirds of the way up the island with old-growth forest, wildflower meadows, and extensive views onto the distant Olympic and Cascade mountains.

KAYAKING & BOATING   Home to otters, seals, and bald eagles, the gentle island-shielded waters of Montague Harbour are a perfect kayaking destination. If you haven't kayaked before, **Galiano Island Sea Kayaking** (☎ 888/539-2930) at Sutil Lodge, 637 Southwind Rd., offers guided 2- and 4-hour trips out onto the bay; a 2-hour wildlife-viewing paddle is C$19 (US$13). If you have more time and want to really get away, consider one of the daylong (C$68/US$46) or multiday kayak camping trips from **Gulf Island Kayaking** (☎ 250/539-2442). Both of the above also offer rental kayaks.

MAYNE ISLAND

Bucolic **Mayne Island** is a beautiful medley of rock-lined bays, forested hills, farm fields, and pastureland. Seemingly distant from the pressures of modern life, Mayne feels like a real island community where most people know and care about one another.

ESSENTIALS

GETTING THERE   **BC Ferries** serves Mayne Island with regularly scheduled runs from Tsawwassen and Swartz Bay. Three commuter airlines offer floatplane service to and from Vancouver. For more information, see "Getting There" above.

VISITOR INFORMATION   Contact the **Mayne Island Community Chamber of Commerce,** Box 2, Mayne Island, B.C. V0N 2J0, or visit the Web site **www. gulfislands.com/mayne_chamber.**

GETTING AROUND   Midas Taxi (☎ 250/539-3132) provides ground transportation.

WHERE TO STAY

Fernhill Lodge B&B. 610 Fernhill Rd., Mayne Island, B.C. V0N 2J0. ☎ **250/539-5244.** Fax 250/539-2544. 3 units. C$99–C$199 (US$66–US$133) double. Extra person C$20 (US$13). Rates include breakfast. No smoking. MC, V.

Drive up a winding road through dense forest to find Fernhill Lodge B&B, a secluded country inn with a noted restaurant and comfortable rooms. With a private entrance and private bathroom, each room is fancifully designed around a theme: The oak-beamed Jacobean Room is dominated by a huge antique bed from England, the India Room is swathed with colorful Indian fabric, and the Oriental Room has hand-cut wood filigreework on the bed and walls. Two have hot tubs. All the rooms look out onto a dense canopy of forest, making this rural hideaway seem even more private. The gracious innkeepers are serious cooks and gardeners, so expect a delicious breakfast made from homegrown organic produce. Facilities also include a hot tub and sauna.

✪ **Oceanwood Country Inn.** 630 Dinner Bay Rd., Mayne Island, B.C. V0N 2J0. ☎ **250/539-5074.** Fax 250/539-3002. www.oceanwood.com. E-mail: oceanwood@gulfislands.com. 12 units. C$149–C$299 (US$100–US$200) double. Extra person C$25 (US$17). Rates include breakfast and afternoon tea. MC, V. Open Mar–Nov.

This large inn has grown from a home-style B&B in a beautiful location to a luxury lodging with an excellent restaurant, a knowledgeable and attentive staff, and extremely spacious rooms with sumptuous furnishings. Each room and suite is decorated according to an understated floral and wildlife theme, and all but one have magnificent views over formal gardens to boat-flecked Navy Channel. The less-expensive rooms, in the original inn, are charming and beautifully fitted with fine furniture and large bathrooms; two have balconies. However, the multitiered rooms in the New Wing are truly large and wonderfully well appointed, all with private water-view decks, large sitting areas with comfy couches and chairs, queen beds, and two-person jetted or soaker tubs facing wood-burning fireplaces.

WHERE TO DINE

In Miner's Bay's tiny strip mall, the **Manna Bakery Café** (☎ 250/539-2323) is the place to go for a cappuccino and freshly baked cinnamon rolls. A soup and sandwich may set you back C$6 (US$4), open daily 9am to 5pm. **Miner's Bay Café** (☎ 250/539-9888), open for lunch and dinner, features light home-cooked meals and sandwiches (some vegetarian choices) and fresh-baked pies and pastries. Prices C$4.95 to C$8 (US$3.30 to US$5), open Monday through Saturday 7am to 4pm, Sundays 8am to 4pm. Just above the marina and floatplane dock in Miner's Bay, the **Springwater Lodge** (☎ 250/539-5521) is a comfortably ramshackle pub/restaurant with great views. Open for lunch and dinner from 9am to 9pm, reduced hours in the summer. Main courses C$14 to C$20 (US$9 to US$13).

Fernhill Lodge. 610 Fernhill Rd. ☎ **250/539-2544.** Reservations required before 1pm the day of dining. Prix-fixe 4-course dinner C$28 (US$19). MC, V. Daily 6–9pm. INTERNATIONAL/HISTORICAL.

The darkly Gothic atmosphere of the Fernhill Lodge dining room is the perfect backdrop to the delightful and unusual food created by chef/owner Brian Crumblehulme. He has researched the role of food in society throughout history and has become an expert in historical menus and food preparation. A four-course traditional Roman meal might begin with gingered pork ribs and dates fried in olive oil and honey, then move on to squab with mustard-and-nut sauce. For a medieval meal, the entree might be venison in spicy Carmeline sauce, with chicken blancmange and creamy rose-petal pudding for dessert. Crumblehulme also excels at "normal" cooking, though his flair for unusual ingredients and flavors make his International Northwest style anything but pedestrian. He enjoys incorporating guests' personal tastes and preferences into his cooking, and the first couple reserving for dinner gets to help select the menu for that evening.

✪ **Oceanwood Country Inn.** 630 Dinner Bay Rd. ☎ **250/539-5074.** Reservations required. Prix-fixe 4-course menu C$39 (US$26). AE, DC, MC, V. Sun–Thurs 5:30–9pm, Fri–Sat 5:30–10pm. PACIFIC NORTHWEST.

At the Oceanwood, chef Paul McKinnon brings together the rich bounty of Pacific Northwest fish, meat, game, fruit, and vegetables in a daily-changing tableau of vivid tastes and textures. Dinners include a soup and appetizer course (perhaps roast eggplant soup with chive flowers, followed by rabbit strudel with carrot-and-beet confit) plus a choice of two entrees. The fish selection might be local paupiettes of sole with herb gnocchi and blackberry vinaigrette. Meat selections have included grilled duck breast with cranberry demiglace served on ravioli stuffed with foie gras. Dinners also include the special dessert, which can be a compote of seasonal fruit or a confection of chocolate, cream, and genoise. To end the evening, dally over coffee or after-dinner drinks (Oceanwood has a good selection of single-malts and ports) in the fireplace-dominated library.

EXPLORING MAYNE ISLAND

Miner's Bay is by default the island's commercial center, though in most locales this somewhat aimless collection of shops, homes, and businesses lolligagging along the Active Pass bayfront wouldn't really qualify as a village. However, it's this understated and soft-focus approach to life that provides Mayne Island its substantial charm. Don't let the rural patina fool you: Some of the lodging and dining is absolutely world-class, and even though organized activities are few, few people will be bored on such a lovely island.

There are two beach access paths at **Bennett Bay,** on the island's northeast coast; this is considered the best swimming beach on Mayne. **Campbell Bay,** just northwest, is another favorite pebble beach. Closer to the Village Bay ferry terminal, **Dinner Bay Park** is a lovely site for a picnic. On a sunny day, the grounds of the **Georgina Point Lighthouse** provide dramatic viewpoints; the grounds are now preserved as a national heritage park, with picnic tables and access to the rocky headland.

BIKING   Mayne is one of the best islands for cyclists. The rolling hills provide plenty of uphill challenges, but the terrain is considerably less mountainous than on other islands.

HIKING   The roads on Mayne are usually quiet enough that they can also serve as walkways for hikers and jogging paths for runners. Hikers looking for more solitary forest walks should consider **Mounte Parke Regional Park,** off Fernhill Road in the center of the island. The park's most spectacular views reward hikers who take the hour-long hike to Halliday Viewpoint on the crest of the island.

KAYAKING & BOATING   At Seal Beach in Miner's Bay, **Mayne Island Kayak & Canoe Rentals** (☎ **250/539-2667**) rents kayaks and canoes for C$20 (US$13) for 2 hours or C$42 (US$28) for a day. The company will drop off kayaks at any of six launching points on the island and, if you get stranded, will even pick up kayaks (and too-weary kayakers) from other island destinations.

If you'd rather let the wind do the work, see the island on an **Island Charters sailboat** (☎ **250/539-5040**). A half-day excursion at C$135 (US$90) for two explores the coast of Mayne, Saturna, and the Pender Islands; or you can arrange for the sailboat to pick up or deliver you to other island destinations (this is the really classy way to get to your country inn). Full-day excursions are C$160 (US$107) per couple, including lunch.

THE PENDER ISLANDS

The Penders consist of **North Pender Island** and **South Pender Island,** separated by a very narrow channel spanned by a one-lane bridge. North Pender is much more developed than South Pender, which is a very relative thing out in the Gulf Islands. The Penders have some lovely sand beaches and several public parks with good hiking trails. Toss in a handful of local artists and craftspeople, and you have the recipe for a tranquil island retreat.

Mount Norman Regional Park encompasses the northwest corner of South Pender Island and features hiking trails through old-growth forest to wilderness beaches and ridge-top vistas. Access to trails is just across the Pender Island bridge. The extensive and somewhat confusing network of roads on the Penders makes these islands good destinations for cyclists. **Bicycle rentals** are available from Otter Bay Marina (☎ **250/629-3579**). Also at Otter Bay Marina, **Mount Point Kayaks** (☎ **250/629-6767**) rents kayaks.

If beachcombing or sunning on the sand is more your style, try **Hamilton Beach** on the east side of North Pender or **Medicine Beach** and the beaches along Beaumont Marine Park, both of which flank Bedwell Harbour.

ESSENTIALS

GETTING THERE   **BC Ferries** serves Pender Island with regularly scheduled runs from Tsawwassen and Swartz Bay. Three commuter airlines offer floatplane service to and from Vancouver. For more information, see "Getting There" above.

VISITOR INFORMATION   Contact the **Pender Island Visitor Info Centre** at 2332 Otter Bay Rd., Pender Island, B.C. V0N 2M1 (☎ **250/629-6541;** fax 250/ 629-6541), open May 15 to September 2.

WHERE TO STAY

Cliffside Inn. 4230 Armadale Rd, N. Pender Island, B.C. V0N 2M3. ☎ **250/629-6691.** www.penderisland.com. E-mail: cliffside@penderisland.com. 4 units. C$129–C$229 (US$86–US$153) suite. 2-day escape and honeymoon packages available. Off-season rates available. V.

The Cliffside Inn is cantilevered above a rocky cliff overlooking Navy Channel and—just hundreds of yards away—Mayne Island. The ancient arbutus trees lining the shore are home to families of bald eagles and rookeries of turkey buzzards; wild mink streak along the shoreline. This dramatic setting itself strongly commends the Cliffside Inn; the fact that it has been redecorated and renovated and is now operated by a charming host make the inn even more of a find. Three of the four suites face Navy Channel and have private decks and patios; two have fireplaces. All rooms have private bathrooms and private entrances, plus small refrigerators, hair dryers, and robes. The glass-roofed and -fronted dining room is open to guests only; weekend packages include one dinner for two (from C$299/US$200).

Inn on Pender Island. 4709 Canal Rd., N. Pender Island, B.C. V0N 2M0. ☎ **800/ 550-0172** or 250/629-3353. Fax 250/629-3167. www.penderisland.com or www. travel.bc.ca/i/innonpender. 9 units, 3 cabins. TV. Motel rooms C$79 (US$53) double, cabins C$110–C$130 (US$74–US$87) double. Extra person C$10 (US$7). MC, V. Small pets C$2 (US$1.35).

This is an enterprising lodging/dining complex at the center of North Pender. Nine of the rooms are in a modern wood-sided two-story motel unit. The large unfussy rooms have small refrigerators, six have two queen beds, and one has a sofa bed and will sleep up to six. Pets and children are welcome, and rooms come with a breakfast tray delivered to your door. These basic motel rooms are a real deal on the otherwise expensive Gulf Islands. Also part of the inn's lodging selection are three new log cabins in the forest above the motel/restaurant. Each cabin has a kitchenette, full bathroom, deck, and queen bed; two also have private outdoor hot tubs. Memories is a slightly upmarket family restaurant with good pizza and Northwest-cuisine specials.

WHERE TO DINE

One of the Pender's basic design flaws is its lack of dining options. The best bet is the **Bedwell Harbour Island Resort** (☎ **250/629-3212**), with a pub and a fine-dining room. Open daily March through October from noon to 9pm (later in July and August). Main courses C$7 to C$17 (US$4.65 to US$11). **Memories,** at the Inn on Pender Island (☎ **250/629-3353**), is the only other real dining choice. Don't let the rather plain exterior of the restaurant put you off. The food—ranging from pizza to ribs to fresh fish—C$11 to C$19 (US$7 to US$13)—is quite tasty. Open for dinner only; May through September daily 5:30 to 8pm, October through April closed Monday through Tuesday. Open for dinner only.

Appendix: History 101

Your visits to Vancouver and Victoria will be so much more rewarding if you know a little about their history and culture. With that in mind, here's a short introduction to these vast subject areas.

THE FIRST NATIONS

British Columbia's first residents arrived from northern Asia, most likely via a land bridge that stretched across the Bering Sea. By about 10,000 years ago, ancestors of today's tribes, including the Haida, Tsimshian, Nisga'a, and Kwakiutl, were already settled along the temperate rain forest of the B.C. coast. Steeped in tales of the world and its animals, these coastal Natives evolved a sophisticated culture that used the potlatch ceremony as the centerpiece of social order.

A village chief would invite an entire neighboring village for a feast, sometimes lasting a full cycle of the moon. Daily banquets, storytelling dances, and generous gift giving were planned years before the guests' arrival. Potlatches could be used to settle disputes or to mark the accession of a new chief or the coming of age of a chief's son or daughter. Gift giving was considered a kind of payment to the guest for having served as a witness to the event. No guest left hungry or empty-handed. As the prestige of a potlatch giver was directly measured by the number and the quality of the gifts given, hosting chiefs sometimes gave away all their worldly possessions during these lavish events.

Thanks to the bounty provided by the sea, West Coast Natives had one of the few hunter-gatherer cultures in which permanent settlements were possible. As a result, they developed a rich and sophisticated body of stories and artwork.

TERRITORIALITY

Around 1790, Spanish explorers searching for gold and new trade routes arrived to claim the region in the name of the king of Spain. But their explorations ceased 2 years later. After encountering Spanish explorer Dionisio Alcala Galiano, Capt. George Vancouver charted the Burrard Inlet and claimed the same land as British territory during his search for the Northwest Passage in 1792.

With the arrival of European traders in the 1780s, the artwork of the resident Coast Salish tribes blossomed. The new wealth brought by the fur trade allowed time for leisure; the new iron tools made the work of fashioning wood into masks, poles, and intricately carved cedar boxes much less physically demanding. Coastal native art reached heights it had never before attained.

And then it crashed. European diseases like smallpox and influenza spread among the Native peoples, who had no natural immunity, and wiped out perhaps 80% of the population. The survivors were often forbidden to speak their Native tongues or to practice Native religion. The potlatch was outlawed for close to 50 years.

Drawn by stories about the abundance of whales, seals, otters, beavers, salmon, and lumber, trading firms like the North West Company and the Hudson's Bay Company established themselves in the area about a decade later. They erected trading posts along the Fraser River and on Vancouver Island with the blessing of the British crown. Towns such as Victoria emerged from these centers of commerce as more settlers arrived in the area. When the United States and Canada signed the Oregon Treaty in 1846, the nations agreed to set the 49th Parallel as their boundary. Victoria became a major port of entry to the western Canadian wilderness.

Soon after the 1849 California gold rush fizzled out, gold was discovered in British Columbia, east of Vancouver in the Fraser River valley and then in the mountainous Cariboo region northeast of Vancouver. Thousands of California miners poured in. To prevent these southern invaders from claiming possession of the territory, England officially created the mainland colony of British Columbia, with its capital at New Westminster.

By 1865, the gold rush was over. Though a few of the gold hunters remained and built homes, most went back to San Francisco or dispersed to the four winds. By this time, Britain had grown weary of empire building and was looking for a respectable way to shed its North America colonies. In 1866, the separate colonies of British Columbia and Vancouver Island were merged under the name British Columbia. Victoria became the capital. And in 1871, in return for the promise of a railway, the merged colonies joined the budding Dominion of Canada.

Dateline

- **Prehistory** Archaeologists estimate that the first Coast Salish tribal villages were established on the Burrard Inlet and Fraser River delta's shores around 3000 B.C.
- **1774** Capt. Juan Perez Hernandez drops anchor off Vancouver Island and trades for furs with natives.
- **1790** The Songhees Coast Salish people find explorer Manuel Quimper claiming their land as Spanish territory.
- **1791** Navigator José María Narváez sails into the Burrard Inlet but doesn't explore the inner harbor.
- **1792** Capt. George Vancouver charts the Burrard Inlet on his search for the Northwest Passage. He claims the land as British territory.
- **1808** North West Company fur trader Simon Fraser survives the Hell's Gate rapids and lands at the mouth of the Fraser River, only to be chased back upstream by Musqueam warriors.
- **1827** The Hudson's Bay Company establishes Fort Langley as a fur-trading post.
- **1831** Trade between Fort Langley and Hawaii begins.
- **1842** Hudson's Bay Company chief factor James Douglas selects a site called Camosack as the company's new depot site. He builds Fort Victoria there.
- **1846** The Oregon Treaty sets the 49th Parallel as the U.S.–Canadian boundary.
- **1849** The British crown grants the Hudson's Bay Company rights to Vancouver Island.
- **1858** Some 30,000 prospectors flood in from the United States to search for gold in the Fraser River valley and on Vancouver Island. The British crown claims British Columbia as a colony.

continues

- **1859** Coal is discovered on Coal Harbour's shores by a British survey ship. New Westminster becomes the colonial capital.
- **1861** The first West Coast hockey game is played, on the frozen Fraser River.
- **1862** Three early B.C. settlers ("The Three Green-horns") acquire 500 acres of land for $1 an acre to start a brickworks, which fails. They later attempt to develop it for housing, which also fails. This area is now Vancouver's West End. Victoria is incorporated.
- **1865** The first telegraph line reaches from San Francisco to British Columbia en route to Alaska.
- **1866** The colonies of British Columbia and Vancouver Island are united; New West-minster remains the capital.
- **1868** Victoria becomes the provincial capital.
- **1869** The town that grew up around Gassy Jack's Globe Saloon is incorporated as the town of Granville.
- **1871** British Columbia enters the confederation and becomes a Canadian province.
- **1885** The Canadian-Pacific Railway decides to build its transcontinental terminus at Granville. Railway executives suggest that the town change its name to Vancouver.
- **1886** On April 6, the town of Granville is incorporated and becomes the city of Vancouver. On July 13, Vancouver is consumed by fire in less than an hour.
- **1887** A Canadian-Pacific Railway steam train com-pletes its maiden coast-to-coast voyage when it arrives in Vancouver.
- **1893** The Hudson's Bay Company replaces its fur-trading post with its first department store.

continues

VANCOUVER IS BORN

The father of Vancouver was a loud-mouthed Yorkshire steamboat pilot named "Gassy" Jack Deighton. In 1867, Gassy Jack—the nickname referred to his habit of going on at length about almost everything, that is, "gassing"—offered the men at nearby Hastings Mill all the whiskey they could drink if they'd give him a hand with a business venture he had in mind, a saloon. Legend has it the Globe Saloon got built in a day. Two years later, the lumber-and-coal town that grew up around Gassy Jack's saloon (affec-tionately called Gastown) was incorporated as the town of Granville.

An inventory of businesses at the time showed six saloons, three hotels, and a hard-ware store. No one expected Granville/ Gastown to amount to anything much. But the young town became a center of attention in 1885, when—in return for 2,400 hectares (6,000 acres) of prime real estate—the Cana-dian Pacific Railway (CPR) agreed to choose it as the western terminus of its transcontinental railway, instead of the more established settle-ment of Port Moody, 26 kilometers (16 miles) east. The boom was on.

CPR officials "suggested" the new city change its name to Vancouver—an appellation they felt would be more marketable to eastern and English businessmen and tourists. Houses, hotels, and businesses began springing up like mushrooms. But in a single hour in 1886, a year before the railway was completed, almost every building in town was consumed by a fire. Undaunted, the town's hopeful citizens met the next day in a tent erected in present-day Gas-town and planned the rebuilding of their com-munity, this time in brick.

The Canadian-Pacific Railway continued to play a key role in the development of the city. It built hotels, rail yards, and housing devel-opments, and convinced other investors to install telephone and ferry services, linking British Columbia to the rest of the world. As interior logging and prairie agriculture devel-oped, the city grew into the continent's lead-ing port for grain and lumber exports. Immigrants arrived from England, India, and China, first to build the railways, then to work in the port, the mills, and the logging camps. The False Creek waterfront was soon covered with lumber mills and beehive burn-ers, and the smoke of industry filled the sky.

Native Indians, who still sailed canoes and small fishing boats into the harbor from time to time, began calling Vancouver a new name—The Big Smoke.

VICTORIA IS BORN

Though he's never mentioned, the true father of Victoria is a Scottish explorer by the name of David Thompson. In 1809, while exploring the headwaters of the Columbia River, Thompson received direct orders from his employer, the vast fur-trading enterprise known as the Hudson's Bay Company (HBC), to proceed down to the mouth of the Columbia and establish a fort and fur-trading post. HBC officials had heard rumors that American John Jacob Astor was planning to send out an expedition by sea, and they wanted to make sure Thompson got there first. But by the time he arrived on the coast, the Americans had set up Fort Astoria.

Astor's business soon failed and the HBC bought him out, renamed the stronghold Fort Vancouver (now Vancouver, WA), and made it their western headquarters. But by the logic of exploration, the Americans had first claim to the territory, and in the 1840s it had become clear that the HBC's hopes of maintaining British North America's border on the north bank of the Columbia River would prove fruitless. A new HQ was needed, one firmly in British territory. Chief Factor James Douglas was sent north to seek one out. And the site he chose was on the southern tip of Vancouver Island, a place the natives called Camosack.

A sleepy little outpost of British officers and their wives for its first 10 years, Victoria was transformed by the discovery of gold, first on the Fraser River in 1858, then later in B.C.'s Cariboo region and on the Klondike in the Canadian north. As one of the closest settlements and supply deports to the goldfields, Victoria boomed. Hotels, warehouses, saloons, and whorehouses went up overnight. Real-estate speculation became the favored way to make a killing.

Alas, the fundamentals just weren't there. Located on an island, Victoria made no sense as a railway terminus, and it was just too far from everywhere to make it as an industrial center. A census in the late 1800s showed Victoria's population had dropped below that of upstart Vancouver's. The bottom fell out of the property market and Victoria was left with

- **1895** For the first time, Vancouver's population surpasses that of Victoria.
- **1903** The Victoria Terminal Railway and Ferry Company begins ferry service between Sidney and Tsawwassen.
- **1905** The Canadian-Pacific Railway begins constructing Victoria's Empress hotel.
- **1908** The University of British Columbia is founded.
- **1912** Vancouver's first reinforced-concrete structure, the fireproof Hotel Europe, opens as a luxury lodging.
- **1929** The Marine Building, a masterpiece of art deco design, opens just in time for the Great Depression. The owners offer to sell it to Vancouver as a new city hall for C$1 million, but the city declines.
- **1936** Vancouver's permanent City Hall is completed.
- **1938** The Guinness Brewing Company builds the Lions Gate Bridge, linking its extensive North Shore property holdings to the city of Vancouver.
- **1939** A decade after construction was suspended during the Great Depression, the Canadian-Pacific's third Hotel Vancouver opens its doors.
- **1957** BC Hydro builds its new corporate headquarters on Burrard Street; it's the first skyscraper built since the 1929 Marine Building.
- **1963** Victoria College becomes the University of Victoria.
- **1965** Designed by Arthur Erickson, Simon Fraser University opens its doors.
- **1967** The first issue of the weekly independent paper, the *Georgia Straight,* appears.
- **1969** Hippies hold their first love-in at Stanley Park.
- **1970** The Vancouver Canucks play their first National Hockey League game.

continues

- **1977** The SeaBus commuter catamaran ferry service begins regular runs between North Vancouver's Lonsdale Quay and downtown Vancouver.
- **1986** Vancouver celebrates its centennial by hosting Expo '86.
- **1990** After Chinese tanks crush demonstrations in Tianaman Square, many Hong Kong residents begin applying for Canadian visas and start arriving in Vancouver in large numbers. Property prices soar.
- **1992** Vancouver celebrates the bicentennial of Captain Vancouver's arrival.
- **1994** Victoria hosts the 15th Commonwealth Games.
- **1995** Vancouver adds the new Vancouver Grizzlies of the National Basketball Association to its roster of professional sports teams.
- **1996** Statistics Canada announces that fewer than half of Vancouver's residents speak English at home.
- **1997** Environment Canada reports the highest rainfall in Vancouver's recorded weather history.
- **1997** Hong Kong is peacefully reincorporated into China. Hong Kong immigration declines greatly.
- **1999** Treaty-in-Principal signed with the Nisga'a First Nation of the Nass River valley, the first such treaty to be signed in the modern era.
- **2000** Vancouver submits its bid to host the 2010 Olympic Winter Games.

more commercial buildings than it knew what to do with.

Shortly after that, Victoria came up with the idea of selling itself as a destination for the new class of rail and steamship tourists then just beginning to make their way round the globe. Tourism and government—Victoria is the provincial capital—have been the mainstays of the city ever since.

HEADING TOWARD THE MILLENNIUM & BEYOND

In the lull between the two world wars, both cities succumbed to the ravages of the Great Depression. New building construction ceased, and industry fell into a severe decline. But development moved forward again when the need for raw materials to support the war effort brought the area back to life with industrial centers and critical military operations bases.

The demand for wood-pulp products kept the region going for decades after World War II. But despite its natural beauty, relatively few travelers made their way to Vancouver and Victoria.

That changed when Vancouver celebrated its 100th birthday in 1986 by hosting the 5-month Expo '86 (a world's fair whose main theme was transportation). In honor of the event, the SkyTrain light-rail rapid-transit system and the Canada Place cruise-ship terminal were constructed to welcome the millions of visitors. In the decade or so since, Vancouver has evolved into the quintessential postmodern city. Factories closed and sawmills disappeared, but the city continued to thrive.

Vancouverites now seem to make their money from tourism, film production, multimedia, and software. Or maybe they sustain themselves just by looking at the scenery— that alone would keep you going for quite a while.

Index

See also Accommodations and Restaurant indexes below.

General Index

General Index

ACCOMMODATIONS

Accommodations Index

RESTAURANTS

Restaurant Index

NOTES

FROMMER'S® COMPLETE TRAVEL GUIDES

Alaska
Amsterdam
Arizona
Atlanta
Australia
Austria
Bahamas
Barcelona, Madrid & Seville
Beijing
Belgium, Holland & Luxembourg
Bermuda
Boston
British Columbia & the Canadian Rockies
Budapest & the Best of Hungary
California
Canada
Cancún, Cozumel & the Yucatán
Cape Cod, Nantucket & Martha's Vineyard
Caribbean
Caribbean Cruises & Ports of Call
Caribbean Ports of Call
Carolinas & Georgia
Chicago
China
Colorado
Costa Rica
Denmark
Denver, Boulder & Colorado Springs
England
Europe

European Cruises & Ports of Call
Florida
France
Germany
Greece
Greek Islands
Hawaii
Hong Kong
Honolulu, Waikiki & Oahu
Ireland
Israel
Italy
Jamaica
Japan
Las Vegas
London
Los Angeles
Maryland & Delaware
Maui
Mexico
Montana & Wyoming
Montréal & Québec City
Munich & the Bavarian Alps
Nashville & Memphis
Nepal
New England
New Mexico
New Orleans
New York City
New Zealand
Nova Scotia, New Brunswick & Prince Edward Island
Oregon
Paris
Philadelphia & the Amish Country

Portugal
Prague & the Best of the Czech Republic
Provence & the Riviera
Puerto Rico
Rome
San Antonio & Austin
San Diego
San Francisco
Santa Fe, Taos & Albuquerque
Scandinavia
Scotland
Seattle & Portland
Shanghai
Singapore & Malaysia
South Africa
Southeast Asia
South Florida
South Pacific
Spain
Sweden
Switzerland
Thailand
Tokyo
Toronto
Tuscany & Umbria
USA
Utah
Vancouver & Victoria
Vermont, New Hampshire & Maine
Vienna & the Danube Valley
Virgin Islands
Virginia
Walt Disney World & Orlando
Washington, D.C.
Washington State

FROMMER'S® DOLLAR-A-DAY GUIDES

Australia from $50 a Day
California from $60 a Day
Caribbean from $70 a Day
England from $70 a Day
Europe from $70 a Day

Florida from $70 a Day
Hawaii from $70 a Day
Ireland from $60 a Day
Italy from $70 a Day
London from $85 a Day

New York from $80 a Day
Paris from $80 a Day
San Francisco from $60 a Day
Washington, D.C., from $70 a Day

FROMMER'S® PORTABLE GUIDES

Acapulco, Ixtapa & Zihuatanejo
Alaska Cruises & Ports of Call
Bahamas
Baja & Los Cabos
Berlin
California Wine Country
Charleston & Savannah
Chicago
Dublin

Hawaii: The Big Island
Las Vegas
London
Los Angeles
Maine Coast
Maui
Miami
New Orleans
New York City
Paris

Puerto Vallarta, Manzanillo & Guadalajara
San Diego
San Francisco
Sydney
Tampa & St. Petersburg
Venice
Washington, D.C.

FROMMER'S® NATIONAL PARK GUIDES

Family Vacations in the
  National Parks
Grand Canyon

National Parks of the
  American West
Rocky Mountain

Yellowstone & Grand Teton
Yosemite & Sequoia/
  Kings Canyon
Zion & Bryce Canyon

FROMMER'S® MEMORABLE WALKS

Chicago
London

New York
Paris

San Francisco
Washington, D.C.

FROMMER'S® GREAT OUTDOOR GUIDES

New England
Northern California

Southern California & Baja
Southern New England

Washington & Oregon

FROMMER'S® BORN TO SHOP GUIDES

Born to Shop: France
Born to Shop: Italy

Born to Shop: London
Born to Shop: New York

Born to Shop: Paris

FROMMER'S® IRREVERENT GUIDES

Amsterdam
Boston
Chicago
Las Vegas

London
Los Angeles
Manhattan
New Orleans

Paris
San Francisco
Seattle & Portland
Vancouver

Walt Disney World
Washington, D.C.

FROMMER'S® BEST-LOVED DRIVING TOURS

America
Britain
California

Florida
France
Germany

Ireland
Italy
New England

Scotland
Spain
Western Europe

THE UNOFFICIAL GUIDES®

Bed & Breakfasts in
  California
Bed & Breakfasts in
  New England
Bed & Breakfasts in
  the Northwest
Bed & Breakfasts in
  Southeast
Beyond Disney
Branson, Missouri

California with Kids
Chicago
Cruises
Disneyland
Florida with Kids
Golf Vacations in the
  Eastern U.S.
The Great Smoky &
  Blue Ridge
  Mountains

Inside Disney
Hawaii
Las Vegas
London
Miami & the Keys
Mini Las Vegas
Mini-Mickey
New Orleans
New York City
Paris

San Francisco
Skiing in the West
Southeast with Kids
Walt Disney World
Walt Disney World
  for Grown-ups
Walt Disney World
  for Kids
Washington, D.C.

SPECIAL-INTEREST TITLES

Frommer's Britain's Best Bed & Breakfasts and
  Country Inns
Frommer's Britain's Best Bike Rides
The Civil War Trust's Official Guide
  to the Civil War Discovery Trail
Frommer's Caribbean Hideaways
Frommer's Adventure Guide to Central America
Frommer's Adventure Guide to South America
Frommer's Adventure Guide to Southeast Asia
Frommer's Food Lover's Companion to France
Frommer's Gay & Lesbian Europe
Frommer's Exploring America by RV
Hanging Out in Europe

Israel Past & Present
Mad Monks' Guide to California
Mad Monks' Guide to New York City
Frommer's The Moon
Frommer's New York City with Kids
The New York Times' Unforgettable
  Weekends
Places Rated Almanac
Retirement Places Rated
Frommer's Road Atlas Britain
Frommer's Road Atlas Europe
Frommer's Washington, D.C., with Kids
Frommer's What the Airlines Never Tell You